Marketing for Tourism

FOURTH EDITION

J Christopher Holloway

FT Prentice Hall
FINANCIAL TIMES

An imprint of **Pearson Education**
Harlow, England • London • New York • Boston • San Francisco • Toronto • Sydney • Singapore • Hong Kong
Tokyo • Seoul • Taipei • New Delhi • Cape Town • Madrid • Mexico City • Amsterdam • Munich • Paris • Milan

Pearson Education Limited
Edinburgh Gate
Harlow
Essex CM20 2JE
England

and Associated Companies throughout the world

Visit us on the World Wide Web at:
www.pearsoned.co.uk

Second edition published by Pitman Publishing 1992
Third edition published by Longman Group Limited 1995
Fourth edition 2004

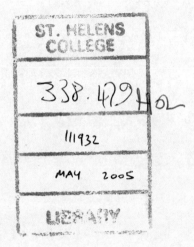

ISBN 0 273 68229 6

British Library Cataloguing-in-Publication Data
A catalogue record for this book is available from the British Library

Library of Congress Cataloging-in-Publication Data
A catalog record for this book is available from the Library of Congress

10 9 8 7 6 5 4 3 2 1
08 07 06 05 04

Typeset in 9/12pt Stone Serif by 35
Printed by Ashford Colour Press Ltd, Gosport

The publisher's policy is to use paper manufactured from sustainable forests.

Marketing for Tourism

Contents

Part II   Reaching the customer

Part III Case studies

Website Resources

For Lecturers:
■ PowerPoint slides that can be downloaded and used as OHTS

Preface

Since the last edition of this text appeared, the world of marketing has altered out of all recognition. The impact of new applications in computer technology is changing the nature of marketing almost on a daily basis, with new directions in distribution threatening more traditional forms of retailing, new opportunities in website advertising revising long-standing media strategy, and the ability to target the individual through better customer relationship management placing more power and choice into the hands of the customer. Marketing within the sectors is also changing radically: the phenomenal growth of the budget airlines offering rock-bottom prices challenges the established carriers, with their former reliance on quality products and premium prices designed to reflect perceived value for money.

Fluctuations in demand for tourism products are now commonly so extreme that survival has become the driving concern of travel companies throughout the world, and price has come to dominate the marketing mix. A succession of international disasters – terrorism, SARS and other pandemics, the collapse of world stock markets, economic recession, political tension and wars in the Middle East – has severely affected generating and destination countries alike. It is scarcely surprising, then, that marketing, and tourism marketing in particular, faces the greatest challenge of its short history. Some observers have gone as far as to suggest that the discipline has finally lost the plot – external factors have now become so invasive that companies can no longer compensate, however efficient their marketing practice.

This is, perhaps, too extreme a view, and already as this preface is prepared there are signs of a return to stability, although whether this is merely short term remains to be seen. Nonetheless, the global changes that have taken place in society, and the sheer pace of those changes, will inevitably mean that the way marketing has to respond to challenge in the future will be different; that businesses and destinations must be ever more flexible in managing tourism – and perhaps become less reliant on this single source of income in order to achieve greater flexibility.

In a much more minor way, these issues have also affected the completion of this text. The speed of change is such that any marketing text is likely to be dated before it gets into the hands of its readers, unless written in such generalised terms as to substantially reduce its value. It was the original intention to have the same two co-authors collaborating in this edition as had worked together so successfully in the previous, third, edition, with Chris Robinson contributing to the underlying theory by drawing on his valuable up-to-date experience to provide current industry examples and cases, particularly from North America, where he is now based as marketing director of a major tour operating business. In the event, circumstances overtook this plan, work pressures making it impossible for him to contribute in the months leading up to the completion of the text. I am nevertheless very grateful to him for the contributions he made to the previous edition, some of which are unaffected by the passage of time and have been retained, and I trust that he will be back as co-author for future editions.

This has led on my part to a very substantial rewrite of the material, with major new areas of focus. A chapter has been added, the order of presentation altered to produce a more cohesive and understandable text, and in particular a great deal of new material is included, especially in the area of technological innovation which is so profoundly affecting the marketing of travel and tourism products. While primarily destined for British and European readership, the international perspective has been retained and supplemented, particularly in the case studies appearing at the end of the text. My thanks go to all those who have helped to produce these, often under very difficult circumstances.

Beyond these issues, many essentials of tourism marketing fortunately remain unchanged, underpinned by the philosophy that the principles involved are common to all goods and services. The aim of the text remains one of bridging the gap between general principles and their application to travel and tourism products, and guidance is provided for further reading in the various elements of marketing appropriate to the businesses addressed.

No manager who plans to engage in marketing any products within this fascinating and complex industry should be without a sound understanding of general marketing theory and its applications, whether the product concerned be an aircraft seat, a holiday resort, a guided tour or a bed and breakfast establishment. This is borne out by the criteria that are listed in advertisements for senior marketing posts in tourism today; where experience in tourism is often described as 'useful, but not essential', while evidence is frequently sought of substantial experience in other businesses, especially the fast moving consumer goods (FMCG) sector. Many leading entrepreneurs in marketing have cut their teeth in the FMCG sector, before moving on to practise their skills in travel or other service industries.

By and large, small firms within the travel sector – and these continue to make up the bulk of organisations in the industry – still have only a hazy idea of what constitutes marketing, and how to apply it professionally. The new edition therefore places more emphasis on marketing within small and medium-sized enterprises (SMEs), impressing on readers that these businesses also need to adopt a professional approach when managing their operations. In many ways, these have the advantage over their competitors, in that they have greater inbuilt flexibility and can retarget their markets or reposition their products more readily. However, many show less willingness to adapt, failing to update their technology as quickly as larger organisations, thus placing themselves at a disadvantage.

Some things do not change. Tourism is as much a people industry today as it has always been; the product is inseparable from the staff who deliver it, be they waiters, tour guides, travel agents or coach drivers. Each member of the industry has a marketing function to perform in their dealings with the public, and it is therefore vital that they acquire and put into use the practical skills of marketing.

The concept of corporate social responsibility has also become important in the management of all businesses, and this is acknowledged in the new edition. Sustainability, largely a buzzword when the previous edition appeared, has now taken on a life of its own, and travel firms recognise that they can no longer merely pay lip-service to the concept. Social responsibility to all a firm's publics will be increasingly addressed in annual reports (there are pressures to make this a legal requirement in Britain), and issues such as the widening gap in pay between senior staff and those at the chalk face are receiving increasing attention in the world's press. Bad publicity can undermine much good marketing, by projecting a negative image of the organisation which is difficult to reverse.

The book is designed to be read by students and others starting out in their careers in the travel and tourism business. It is ideally suited to those studying for General National Vocational Qualifications (GNVQs) in Leisure and Tourism at levels 3 and 4, as well as those on Higher National Diploma (HND) courses, or as an introductory text for first degree courses, in which tourism marketing is studied either as a core or as an option. It will also prove a useful introduction to theory and practice for those taking professional courses such as those of the HCIMA, the Chartered Institute of Transport (CIT) or the Institute of Leisure and Amenity Management (ILAM). Others presently employed in the tourism industry, who either hope to move into a marketing post or seek to gain a better understanding of marketing in order to carry out their tasks more effectively, can also benefit from reading this text.

Chris Holloway

Website Resources

Downloadable Powerpoint slides can be found at www.booksites.net/holloway

Acknowledgements

We are grateful to the following for permission to reproduce copyright material:

Punch Cartoon Library for 'You booked us a holiday . . .' cartoon on page xviii © Punch, Ltd; The National Trust for Figure 3.2; Tourism Ireland for Figures 4.3 aqnd 4.4; Grupo Osborne, S.A. for the Black Bull logo on page 135; Spanish Tourist Office for Figures 7.2 and 10.1 (a–e); Tourism New Zealand for Figure 7.3; MyTravelLite for Figure 7.4; Thomas Cook UK Ltd/TBWA London for Figure 7.5 (a–c); HDM Agency for Figure 7.6; Eurocamp for Figures 10.2 and 14.1 (a and b); Condor Ferries Ltd for Figure 10.3; Maison de la France/DDB & Co, Paris for Figure 10.4; ABLE for Figure 8.3; Jersey Tourism for Figure 12.1; The Walker Agency for Figure 13.1; Wales Tourist Board for Figures 13.4 and 13.5; The Wigan Pier Experience for Figure 14.2; The Caravan Club for Figure 14.3 (a and b); Travelocity UK Ltd for Figures CS1.1, CS1.2, CS1.3, CS1.4, CS1.5, CS1.6, CS1.7, CS1.8 and CS1.9, and Tables CS1.1, CS1.2, CS1.3, CS1.4, CS1.5, CS1.6 and CS1.7; Trips Worldwide for Figures CS2.1 and CS2.2; Adria Airways for Figures CS4.1, CS4.2, CS4.3 and CS4.4; Leeds Castle for Figures CS5.1, CS5.2, CS5.3, CS5.4, CS5.5 (a and b), CS5.6, CS5.7 and CS5.8; Wessex Tourism Association for Figures CS6.1 and CS6.2; Senior King for Figures CS7.1 and CS7.2; David Young, The Cross at Kingussie for Figure CS9.1; NBGW for Figures CS10.1 and CS10.2; Kuressaare Town Government, Tourist Information Centre for Figures CS11.1, CS11.2 and CS11.3; Museum of Bath at Work for Figures CS12.1, CS12.2 and CS12.3. Museum of Bath at Work is operated by The Bath Industrial Heritage Trust Ltd.

List of abbreviations and glossary

3G	Third generation. Refers to mobile phones with access to broadband communications
AA	Automobile Association
ABLE	Association of Bath and District Leisure Attractions
ABTA	Association of British Travel Agents
ACD	automatic call distribution
ADSL	Asynchronous/asymmetric digital subscriber line. The most popular version of permanent broadband Internet connection, using existing telephone cable
AGB	Audits of Great Britain
AIDA	Attention, Interest, Desire, Action
AITO	Association of Independent Tour Operators
APEX	advance purchase excursion fare
ASTA	American Society of Travel Agents
ATOL	Air Travel Organiser's Licence
AUC	Air Transport Users' Council
B2B	business to business relationships
B2C	business to consumer relationships
B&B	bed and breakfast
BA	British Airways
BCG	Boston Consultancy Group
BMI	British Midland International Airways
BMRB	British Market Research Bureau
BRAD	*British Rate and Data*
Broadband	fast, permanently connected Internet access
BTA	British Tourist Authority, now VisitBritain
C2C	commercial relationships between consumers
CAA	Civil Aviation Authority
CBI	Confederation of British Industry
CIM	Chartered Institute of Marketing
CIMTIG	Chartered Institute of Marketing Travel Industry Group
CIT	computer integrated telephoning, also Chartered Institute of Transport
CSQ	customer service questionnaire

CTB	Cumbria Tourist Board
DATA	Devon Area Tourist Association
DCMS	Department for Culture, Media and Sport
DMO	Destination Marketing Organisation
DRTV	direct response television
e-	Suffix for all electronically controlled business operations, thus e-marketing, e-tailing (retailing), e-commerce, e-business, etc.
EETB	East of England Tourist Board
EFTPOS	electronic funds transfer at point of sale
EFTS	electronic funds transfer system
EIU	Economist Intelligence Unit
ETC	English Tourism Council, now VisitEngland
Extranet	private consumer network linking trading partners
FAA	Federal Aviation Authority
FMCG	fast moving consumer goods
FTO	Federation of Tour Operators
FTTC	fibre to the curb. Using optical fibres between computers and the Internet to speed up communications. Under test in the USA at the time of writing
GIT	group inclusive tour
HCIMA	Hotel and Catering International Management Association
HETB	Heart of England Tourist Board
IATA	International Air Transport Association
IBA	Independent Broadcasting Authority
ICT	information and communications technology (replacing the more familiar IT)
iDTV	interactive digital television
IIT	independent inclusive tour
ILAM	Institute of Leisure and Amenity Management
Intranet	private computer network for use of an organisation's staff
IPC	International Publishing Corporation
ISDN	integrated services digital network. Digital dial-up telephone line for voice and/or data. Operates faster than modems, but slower than ADSL
ISO	International Standards Organization
ISP	Internet service provider
ITB	Irish Tourist Board
iTV	Interactive television
ITX	inclusive tour-basing fare
JND	just noticeable difference
MIS	Marketing Information System
MORI	Market and Opinion Research Institute
NETB	North East Tourist Board
NITB	Northern Ireland Tourist Board
NWTB	North West Tourist Board
OFT	Office of Fair Trading
OHP	overhead projector
PEX	passenger excursion (discounted airline fare)

PLC	product life cycle
POP	point of purchase
POS	point of sale
PR	public relations
PRO	public relations officer
RAC	Royal Automobile Club
ROI	return on investment
RTW	round the world
SDSL	symmetric digital subscriber line. Similar to ADSL, but allows convergence of voice, data and Internet communications along a single line
SIA	Singapore Airlines
SME	Small and medium-sized enterprises
SSEETB	Southern and South East England Tourist Board
STB	Scottish Tourist Board, now VisitScotland
SWT	South West Tourism (formerly West Country Tourist Board)
TATR	Travel and Tourism Research
TIA	Travel Industry Association of America
TGI	Target Group Index
TIC	tourist information centre
TIP	tourism information point
TQM	total quality management
TTG	*Travel Trade Gazette*
TVR	television viewing rating
UKTS	United Kingdom Tourism Survey
USP	unique selling proposition, unique selling point
VDU	visual display unit
VFR	visiting friends and relatives
WiFi	wireless networks connected to broadband without a socket via radio, for laptop computer use
WTB	Wales Tourist Board/Bwrdd Croeso Cymru
WTM	World Travel Market
YTB	Yorkshire Tourist Board

'You booked us a holiday abroad
during the summer. Could you tell us,
please, where we went?'

Part I Laying the groundwork

1 The marketing perspective

Learning outcomes

After studying this chapter, you should be able to:

- understand the concept of marketing, and ways in which this has been interpreted by marketing theorists and practitioners
- distinguish between product and marketing orientation
- understand how the marketing concept is applied to the travel and tourism business, and its importance to that business
- recognise the ethical dimension in marketing, and be aware of the constraints under which marketing is conducted.

Introduction

A business school professor in the United States reported hearing the following exchange between an Eastern Airlines passenger and the air stewardess:

'These scrambled eggs – they're the worst I've ever eaten.'
'I know. We keep telling them, but they won't listen.'

Reported in the *Observer* 29 April 2001

It does not take a great leap of imagination on the part of readers, even without any foreknowledge of marketing, to recognise that the above exchange demonstrates a significant weakness on the part of the company concerned, which goes to the very heart of what we will be discussing in this text. Instinctively, all of us know that a product about which many customers are complaining needs to be examined and replaced. Perhaps we should not be too surprised that the airline concerned ceased to exist shortly after this event!

Although marketing as a concept is now much better and more widely understood than was the case when the first edition of this text appeared back in 1988, it is true to say that the travel and tourism industry's understanding of the concept and its willingness to apply it in its everyday business still varies significantly from company to company, and from sector to sector. While some elements of the industry have adopted the principles wholeheartedly, and as a result can be counted among the most effective marketing organisations in their field, good marketing is still the exception rather than the rule, particularly in the case of small to medium-sized enterprises (SMEs) whose businesses represent 90 per cent of the industry and whose resources are often too limited to consider the appointment of specialist marketing personnel. Let us look at a recent example of marketing failure, as experienced by the author.

Examples ### Are British hotels meeting their customers' needs?

(a) The mid-price seaside resort hotel
The setting is a hotel in a popular seaside resort in south-west England. The building, dating, like so many English seaside resort hotels, from the Victorian era, has been inadequately updated; in the bedroom the curtains are too small, leaving a gap in the centre when pulled, the toilet fails to flush properly, and the TV remote control is missing. A noticeboard in the room provides a long list of dos and don'ts. Facilities for tea-making in the room are strictly limited: one teabag and one coffee bag per person, with an invitation to 'purchase extra bags from Reception'. Meals require prompt attendance: 0830 for breakfast, 1830 for dinner.

One couple arrives ten minutes late for dinner. Their soup plates are put out promptly at 1830 and left to cool, with a muttered 'They know what time they're supposed to be here' from the waitress. Although Reception advertises the provision of newspapers, a request solicited the reply, 'Well, I have to pick them up so I can't say when they'll arrive.'

(b) The London budget business hotel
Guest checks in at 7.20 pm and is informed that last orders for dinner are at 8 pm ('Sorry, there are only two of us on tonight'). Shown to the room, 'The lock's a bit tricky till you get used to it – but it usually works after a time.' Furniture is neo-Georgian melamine in cream colour with gold trim – the ubiquitous cheap decor with pretensions of elegance for the underclass. A quite pleasant watercolour print hangs on the wall, for some reason, just four inches from the ceiling, and well above eye height. Wallpaper is lifting at the seams. The bath-room door is stuck and has to be forced open. Wire hangers are provided in the wardrobe, with one flimsy plastic hanger, too thin to take the weight of a jacket. The bathroom shower provides a pathetic dribble in lieu of a spray; the toilet flush is weak, and the handle could not be operated with the lid raised.

In the restaurant:

'Can I have a steak?'
'Sorry, that's off tonight. There's just chicken chasseur, steak and kidney or seafood platter.'
'Is the steak and kidney commercial?'
'I'm afraid so.'

Perhaps we should not be surprised that the seaside hotel closed less than a month later! In this example we find a combination of both product failure and service failure – sadly a picture still not untypical of hotels at many British seaside resorts, even in a time of extreme competition and difficult trading conditions. British hotels also labour under the disadvantage of a lack of new-build properties – unlike so many countries on the Continent of Europe, where popular coastal resorts have developed only since the 1960s and which can therefore offer better and more modern facilities to their current, more demanding markets. This, however, is not to excuse other failures of service identified in this example. In example (b), this hotel – in a central capital city where demand frequently outstrips supply – shares the complacency common in urban budget hotels, where occupancy rates will remain high even in the absence of basic decoration and maintenance. The concern of management here is to maximise revenue rather than to satisfy the customer.

Hotels are perhaps an easy target, but their failings are by no means uncommon in other spheres of business. There are a number of reasons for the failure to come to terms with good marketing practice. One is the inherent conservatism of British society, our suspicion of new ideas and reluctance to change old, well-tried ways of doing things. Another is a very real ignorance, on the part of small businesses, of what marketing is all about – one result of a tendency to believe that the best way of learning the business is to recruit staff straight from school and 'train them up' in the ways of the company. Under this system, methods of business operation tend to perpetuate themselves, and innovation, where it exists, depends upon the 'gut feel' of the proprietor rather than skilled analysis of the market. Smaller companies tend to believe that marketing is something that can be undertaken only by large corporations. The tourism industry is a relatively young one, consisting predominantly of small businesses still getting to grips with modern business practice. This plays a large part in inhibiting the application of modern marketing techniques.

This text will attempt to show that marketing is not just a 'flavour of the month' jargon term, but a total business philosophy that should underpin our whole approach to running any organisation. Marketing is a practice that can be employed by any business, no matter how small, and is not even necessarily dependent upon increasing the budget – in fact, it will be argued that without its application no business, whatever its size, can succeed in the long term.

Marketing is not 'something done by the marketing department' alone. Its philosophy should permeate every element of a business. All too often, a travel company which declares itself to be marketing orientated is in fact product orientated; for example, it may be concerned principally with finding ways to utilise surplus capacity rather than tackling the question of what the customer really wants. The belief, widely held in the travel industry, that low price is the key to success has resulted in inconvenience, discomfort and dissatisfaction among the travelling public. An interesting example of recent product orientation in travel is the case of a major city bus company which used its buses for sightseeing on Sundays only, because that was the only day on which the company had spare capacity. Unfortunately, passenger demand was for midweek and Saturday excursions, and the product was a failure.

So let us start by defining marketing in some detail, and considering its role in the wider context of business practice before going on to examine its relevance within the travel and tourism industry.

What is marketing?

Perhaps the best way of describing what marketing is, is to show what it is not. The author accompanied his daughter while she was shopping for a new bikini. After a fruitless search through countless shops for a top and bottom that would fit her, she tried the branch of a well-known department store. The saleswoman was polite and helpful, but after the umpteenth costume had been tried on unsuccessfully, she cried in exasperation, 'I just don't know what's happening these days; people don't seem to fit our clothes any longer!'

As a postscript to that story, for years in the United States it has been possible to buy the tops and bottoms of bikinis separately, a marketing-orientated solution which is gradually (but by no means rapidly) being adopted in Britain. Could the clothing manufacturers have discovered that changing social habits were leading to new body shapes? On the one hand, many individuals are spurred to undertake exercise, to diet and to show more concern for what they eat to maintain their healthy, slender figures, while on the other hand there is global concern about the trend to more sedentary occupations (watching computer and television screens), unhealthy fast foods and overeating. All of these factors are likely to have lasting implications for the average shape and weight of our bodies, which will in turn affect the demand for clothes.

In fact, there is a postscript to this story also. Research reveals that waist sizes alone have increased in Britain from the typical 32 for men and 27 for women in 1953 to 36 for men and 30 for women in 2003. In France, after widespread complaints from consumers that clothes were difficult to fit, research involving the measurement of 12 000 citizens revealed that the French had become both taller and more angular than formerly, leading the Union of Clothing Industries to plan new standard garment sizes for the nation.

A more serious consequence of ignoring changes in consumer needs is evidenced in the USA. The average American airline passenger is now 20 pounds heavier than in 1995, while estimated passenger weights remained unchanged. The crash on take-off of an overloaded small aircraft in January 2003 led the FAA (Federal Aviation Authority) to add 10 pounds to estimated airline passenger weights to compensate.

Example   Are transport companies meeting customer needs?

Size 12 dresses are now an inch and a half bigger than they were 20 years ago – a deft example of marketing in the clothing business! Yet minimum airline seat pitch, last determined at the beginning of the 1990s, is still 26 inches, in spite of a steady increase in height and weight of European and American populations. Some rail networks' seats on new trains [including the brand-new Pendolino tilting train] are up to six inches narrower than on older trains, and are also closer together.

Source: The Times, 15 February 2001

Too many people equate marketing with selling, as if the two terms were synonymous, but this is far from accurate as a definition, although selling certainly has a role to play as a function of marketing. Rather, marketing should be seen as an all-embracing term to indicate the direction and thrust of a firm's policies and strategies.

Marketing is about anticipating demand, recognising it, stimulating it and finally satisfying it; in short, understanding consumers' wants and needs, as to what can be sold, to whom, when, where and in what quantities. There are literally dozens of acceptable definitions of marketing, and this is not the book to discuss the semantics of these definitions. Instead, let us look at just two well-considered definitions. First, that of the Chartered Institute of Marketing:

> Marketing is the management function which organises and directs all those business activities involved in assessing customer needs and converting customer purchasing power into effective demand for a specific product or service, and in moving that product or service to the final consumer or user so as to achieve the profit target or other objective set by the company or other organisation.

This definition has three important implications. First, it is seen as a management function within the company. Second, it underlies, and provides the framework for, all the activities which a business undertakes. Finally, and herein lies the whole philosophy of marketing, it places the emphasis on customers' needs as the starting-point for the business's operations. As Theodore Levitt expressed it, while 'selling focuses on the needs of the seller, marketing focuses on the needs of the buyer'.[1] Marketing is about finding out what the customer wants first, and then producing the product to fit those needs (a marketing-orientated approach) as opposed to producing the product or service and then seeing to whom it can be sold (a product-orientated approach).

Our second definition is taken from a text by leading marketing theorists Philip Kotler *et al.*, who define it as:

> A social and managerial process by which individuals and groups obtain what they need and want by creating and exchanging products and value with others.[2]

In this definition, value is defined as the consumer's assessment of a product's overall ability to satisfy their needs. The definition also recognises the wider application of the term 'marketing' as both a social and managerial process, something which permeates every transaction in our lives.

Equally, a marketing-orientated company is one in which the philosophy of marketing pervades the entire organisation. If decisions at board level are production-orientated, or the chief executive is either unsympathetic to the marketing philosophy or views it as relevant only to the marketing department, the marketing manager's task becomes that much more difficult. Marketing cannot function effectively unless it has the support and cooperation of all departments of an organisation. If the company's costs are excessive, or inadequate control over product quality results in poor value for money, no amount of 'marketing' will make the company a success. The customer's needs will remain unsatisfied, however well advertised, or hard sold, the product is.

A historical overview

It took a long time for British companies to recognise the importance of marketing, largely due to historical circumstance. In earlier times, Britain did not need to market its products; Britain's colonies around the world created a ready demand for its manufactured goods. However, with independence, these countries turned to production of their own goods, or bought from Britain's competitors. For too long, Britain traded in the belief that what was British was best; meanwhile, quality deteriorated, British companies failed to match their competitors on delivery dates, and after-sales service weakened. Workers lost confidence in their companies' management, and lost pride in their own performance. In consequence, Britain's share of world markets in almost every commodity became smaller, and Britain grew less wealthy compared with its competitors. At the same time, the introduction of mass production methods meant that Britain needed to sell more goods, in order to take advantage of the benefits of economies of scale by reducing the unit cost of products. Britain's declining markets meant higher costs against those of other countries, making it still harder to sell British goods.

At first, the response of many companies was to sell harder. This failed, so they attempted to undercut their competitors on price, selling inferior products cheaply. This failed to take into account the customers' preference for quality and reliability, and again sales were lost.

While some major industries learned the lesson in the early post-war years, it was only in the late 1960s and 1970s that industry started to apply the marketing concept – some 50 years later than the USA. This process accelerated in the 1980s, with emphasis on design and quality coming to the fore. Firms discovered that it was better to tailor their products to the specific needs of one market, rather than trying to produce products that would meet everyone's needs. They learned to appreciate that people do not buy products, but the benefits which those products offered. This encouraged companies to research specific needs and how to satisfy them. Above all, companies have come to understand that marketing is a dynamic concept; people's needs change over time, requiring companies to identify and respond to change. Companies successful today can no longer guarantee that their products will remain in demand tomorrow. Hence marketing is coming to play an ever more important role in the management of organisations.

Some issues in travel and tourism marketing

There is some confusion about the terms 'travel' and 'tourism' which we need to clear up before discussing how marketing is applied in the industry. The confusion arises because the industry itself, for no very good reason, tends to see *travel* as embracing transport and tour operating companies and retail travel operations, while *tourism* is seen as concerning itself with the accommodation sector, public sector bodies such as national tourist offices and constructed tourist attractions such as heritage sites or theme parks. This division is largely artificial, and need not concern us unduly, although clearly travel can involve the movement of people for reasons other than tourism (such as emigration) and in that sense is a more widely applied concept. Since concern in this text is with the deliberate marketing of products serving both fields, use is made of both terms throughout the text, but since travel is a necessary element in all tourism activity, the word tourism will be used as an all-encompassing term.

The early post-Second World War years saw the birth of modern tourism as an industry. Initially, this industry's activities were sales-led and product orientated. The spectacular growth of package holidays in the 1960s was generated by the ideas of entrepreneurs who saw opportunities to create holidays utilising spare airline capacity that resulted from the ending of the Berlin Airlift and the introduction of new technology in aircraft. Linked with low-cost accommodation in newly emerging resorts on the Continent (particularly in Spain), they were able to offer exciting holidays in the sun for less than 'dreary' holidays in Britain. Little surprise, then, that modern marketing methods did not feature prominently in early tourism enterprises, where the product was infinitely more attractive than what had been available up to that point, and as long as prices could be kept down demand appeared to be unlimited.

However, excessive demand creates its own problems for marketing. The success of the new foreign package holidays led to pressures to increase available stocks rapidly. Hotels remained uncompleted or poorly finished in the popular destinations, and staff were inadequately trained to provide the levels of service expected. Unfamiliar food gave rise to complaints, and aircraft reliability and safety gave cause for considerable concern. It was time for underlying assumptions to be questioned.

Companies began to recognise that if they were to sell an increasing number of holidays abroad successfully it would be necessary for them to allay three public fears:

- fear of flying
- fear of foreign food
- fear of foreigners.

The early marketers of overseas holidays set about providing reassurance, and undertook research as a prerequisite for marketing action.

Fear of flying

Such importance is now attached to safety that it seems inconceivable that risks should have been taken with people's lives for commercial gain, yet effectively this was done. Elderly aircraft were being pressed into service to the limits of their capabilities. Due to restrictive pricing policies promoted by state airlines, and backed by bilateral agreements, unsuitable airports were being used (especially the notorious Perpignan in the French Pyrenees). Poor on-board layouts were uncomfortable and resulted in dangers from loose cabin baggage. Even the British government added to individuals' uncertainty by insisting that aircraft used for trooping flights should have seats facing rearward to increase survival probability in the event of a forced or bad landing. When holiday passengers enquired about the reasons for this bizarre configuration, the answer hardly added to their confidence! (But it is interesting to note that no modern aircraft is fitted with rear-facing seats, although it is widely accepted that this arrangement would offer the safest configuration. The public still prefer forward-facing seats – so aviation marketers oblige.)

From the original concept of cheap redundant aircraft availability, it soon became apparent that much greater gains could be achieved by purchasing leading edge equipment which would not only offer operational economies through better utilisation and higher load factors, but would also increase customer confidence.

Today, flying has become so much a part of public life that few are constrained by this particular fear. Nevertheless, periodically new products appear on the market, and new problems emerge, which require marketers to reassure the public on issues of safety. One thinks of the move from four engines to two on transatlantic routes (still a consideration to many flyers), the efforts to reassure passengers about modifications to Concorde (in the aftermath of the tragic crash of one of these aircraft near Paris) prior to the eventual withdrawal of the aircraft. By 2003, other new fears had also surfaced – the fear of DVT (deep vein thrombosis) resulting from long-distance flights, fear of terrorist attacks and the perceived vulnerability of aircraft and airports to such attacks, concern over SARS (severe acute respiratory syndrome) and the ease with which this could be caught through recycled air in an aircraft. In the case of other forms of transport, the safety of travel through the Channel Tunnel, especially at a time when threats of terrorism are rife, offers another challenge to the marketer.

Fear of foreign food

Foreign foods presented different problems. At a time when British eating habits were much less adventurous than they are today, many of the normal Mediterranean ingredients were reviled as 'greasy' or 'foreign rubbish'. Even the ways of presentation and service were misunderstood, with different traditions, such as serving meat and vegetables separately, and the time taken over mealtimes, much criticised. Hoteliers complained of doing their best under the constraint of tight budgets. They probably complained even louder than the holidaymakers about the awkwardness of customers and the levels of food waste. A little research into methods soon paid off. Catering experts were dispatched, who advised hoteliers how to spend less on ingredients and yet achieve greater satisfaction through changes in cooking methods, presentation and service. As labour became more expensive, many hotels introduced buffet-style meals where holidaymakers could make their own choices. Though ingredient costs rose as a result, the savings in service and in wasted food balanced the cost, and the overall result was improved satisfaction for the majority of travellers.

Fear or dislike of foreigners (xenophobia)

Fear of foreigners is really an insoluble problem if taken literally, for it would remove one of the main incentives for travel, which is to meet and understand others better. It arose in part from the unreliability in the provision of accommodation, together with a misunderstanding of local customs and habits. In the 1970s, the large British travel companies decided that the only way of overcoming this barrier was to control totally the overseas accommodation and services they supplied. They invested heavily in properties built to their own specification, managed by themselves or their nominees.

They introduced expertise that had not previously been available locally and raised standards substantially. Probably the most salutary changes in attitudes were created by the need of tour operators to comply with the Trade Descriptions Act (1968) in Britain, and later, the European Union's Package Holiday Regulations (1992). Tour operators were required to take more responsibility for the services they provided, careless overbooking was restrained, accuracy in brochure descriptions became legally enforceable. Positive moves were made by tour operators to create even greater consumer confidence by offering substantial cash compensation if failure to provide accommodation occurred. The follow-through was that the tour operators' contracts with hoteliers provided that in the event of such failures, the punitive compensation was deductible directly from the hotelier.

On a personal level, the role of the resort representative was changed from merely being an arrival/departure escort and seller of excursions to being a uniformed staff member dedicated to assisting customers to get the most out of their holidays. Now holidaymakers can expect the same quality of product in the package holidays they buy from leading European operators as they have come to expect of the major companies selling more tangible products in the high street.

Today, the market for overseas holidays is far more sophisticated – and demanding – than it was 20–30 years ago. Adventurous holidays, to more distant and exotic destinations, have become the norm. Familiarity with foreigners, through immigration and mass travel, has greatly lessened the former provincial attitudes of even the mass tourist market. The nature of travel fear has changed, to issues such as fear of terrorism, or concern about health risks such as malignant malaria now prevalent even in popular tourism destinations – and these are concerns over which the marketer has far less control. With new methods of distribution proliferating rapidly through information and communications technology (ICT), marketers will increasingly have to focus on reassuring travellers of the safety of booking through the Internet rather than dealing face to face with the traditional travel agent. There is also a growing recognition as mass tourism continues unabated that in future tourism must become more sustainable, and this is providing travel marketers with new challenges in designing and planning tourism products, as we shall see later in this text.

Marketing as a field of study

Marketing as a field of serious study originated in the United States early in the last century, and was adopted in the UK only in the second half of that century. However, it has now become an essential ingredient of any business course, at all levels up to postgraduate level. While the body of knowledge forming a marketing syllabus has been refined to nationally agreed standards in many countries, no one individual who has studied marketing can be expected to be an expert in all facets of the discipline. Marketing tasks are extremely diverse, requiring the application of both management and craft skills. The ability to sell effectively, to put together an effective advertisement, to create an eye-catching and attractive window display, to conduct research interviews successfully are skills which are as important in their own way as the assiduous research, planning, recording and analysis that we associate with the management function of marketing.

It will be apparent that the strengths of the larger organisation include the ability to employ several marketing staff, who can offer widely differing talents within the sphere of marketing. Certainly, good marketing will always call for an element of entrepreneurial flair, but if our view of marketing is limited to the extrovert, dynamic salesperson who catches the headlines, we are in danger of overlooking the less visible qualities of good marketing: the ability to interpret statistical data and draw rational conclusions, to demonstrate understanding of tourist needs and behaviour patterns. 'Flair' alone is no longer enough. This will be readily apparent to those who are familiar with the great figures within the British tourism industry in its early stages. Names such as Freddie Laker of Laker Airways and Harold Bamberg of Eagle Airlines, who did so much to expand travel abroad in the early post-Second World War period, were noted for their marketing flair and enterprise. While these skills are still valuable, the large travel corporations today are more sober, their marketers 'lower-profile'. Even the occasional exception to the rule (think Sir Richard Branson) is backed by a team of little-known faces with specialist expertise to provide evolution, rather than revolution, in managing and marketing the tourism product.

Constraints in marketing

Good marketing forms the basis of the so-called 'growth economy', to which the industrialised world is committed. However, it is not without its critics, both on economic and social grounds. Economically, it is criticised for its wasteful use of resources. Huge amounts of money are spent in advertising products which are almost identical to other products, in an attempt to persuade consumers that they are unique, or better in some way than their competitors. Products are designed to date before their normal lifespan, in order to increase sales of more recent models, while consumer goods are designed with parts that will wear out within a given time so that the entire product will require to be replaced. Social critics point to the emphasis that marketers place on material values by playing on consumer emotions in order to build an acquisitive society where wants, rather than needs, are manipulated, with the consumer led to believe that the possession of more and more goods and services is the key to a happy and successful life. As one critic puts it, marketers first persuade you that you have a problem, and then tell you they can help you to solve it!

Defending their role, marketers argue that in creating growth they are helping to create employment and wealth; that Britain's failure to compete against foreign products will lead to its becoming an impoverished country without political power or influence, with the British way of life dominated by its more successful neighbours. This book is not the place for a full discussion of these issues, but some understanding of the arguments and counter-arguments is important, because marketers will need to be aware of the pressures they face in their work. It is also important for those who intend to work in the marketing field that they believe in their work, and in the products they are selling. This is both a moral issue and a practical one; salespeople are not likely to perform to maximum efficiency if they do not believe in the product they are selling. If we are obliged to sell products about which we are cynical, we denigrate both ourselves and our society.

In this respect, we are fortunate that the product under consideration is tourism. Most of those involved in the tourism business can genuinely believe in the product they are selling, as one that is beneficial to their clients, whether holidays are being sold to relieve stress, to aid health or to provide clients with a novel or cultural experience. But those with the responsibility of selling tourism must take care to sell the products which will satisfy their clients' needs. It is not enough for travel agents to sell whatever holidays will generate the most profits. Agents have a moral responsibility towards their clients – and incidentally, by satisfying them, agents will ensure that they will return to book with their company another year. And that is what marketing is all about.

This is not to say that tourism marketers will not face from time to time some serious soul-searching. A destination which is popular will achieve a level of demand which threatens the very attractiveness it offers. This is the paradox of mass tourism – that it can be a victim of its own success. Anyone who has visited a popular destination in the height of the season will be aware of the problems of congestion and pollution caused by the influx of huge numbers of tourists. The seaside resorts of Clovelly or Polperro in Britain are examples close to home, but there are many examples of similar sites along the Mediterranean shores, or one can look further afield to see the recent impact of long-haul travel on destinations such as Pattaya Beach in Thailand, or even the famed Angkor Wat Temples in Cambodia (Siem Reap, the gateway to this World Heritage site, had 30 recently built tourist hotels with a further 12 under construction in 2002). Should the industry continue to promote such destinations with impunity? What should the marketing role of a local tourism officer be in such a situation?

In fact, contrary to popular opinion, marketing is not just concerned with selling more. It is also about regulating demand, and this applies particularly where the supply of a product is finite. In this example, the tourism officer's role may be to counter-market the destination in the summer, and to try to switch demand to the shoulder season or off-season; to attempt to select market segments to increase the average spend (by focusing on staying visitors, rather than day trippers, for example); to maintain the quality of the product at present levels of consumption. The management of marketing is about the management of demand, and a marketing manager's role can be to demarket, to stabilise demand levels. Marketing plans by VisitBritain (formerly the British Tourist Authority [BTA]) in recent years have included the aims of spreading tourist traffic geographically and seasonally as a means of relieving the pressure of high demand for popular British tourist destinations. Just as a popular theatre show will be packed to capacity throughout its run and unable to expand to satisfy the total level of demand it is experiencing, so a destination, or a facility such as an airport, has a finite capacity which calls for demand management. In such a situation, marketing may be restricted to attempts to improve levels of existing service, rather than trying to accommodate all those wishing to use the service.

Above all, recognition has finally dawned that tourism, to be truly ethical, must be sustainable, and this is rapidly becoming a major issue in tourism marketing. Briefly, sustainable tourism is defined[3] as tourism which:

- uses resources sustainably
- reduces over-consumption and waste
- maintains diversity
- integrates tourism into planning
- supports local economies
- involves local economies
- consults stakeholders and the public
- trains staff
- markets tourism responsibly
- undertakes research in furtherance of these aims.

These are all issues with which marketing can be directly involved. To be sustainable, tourism must protect the environment and ensure that the local populations at the destination derive direct benefit, in terms of income and employment, from visiting tourists. While lip-service is paid by many companies to these needs, too often it is treated as an exercise in public relations. The kind of 'slash and burn' tourism which despoliates a destination by overdevelopment and then moves on to other, less tarnished, resorts is still all too familiar, and is a subject to which we shall return in Chapter 14.

Since tourism is a product which must be purchased in advance of its consumption, and since it must be described rather than demonstrated to consumers, many opportunities arise for unethical practice in the industry. The product may be oversold, or services promised that are not fulfilled. However, the days when companies and their brochures deliberately set out to mislead are now largely gone, killed by a combination of statutory legislation and internal 'policing' in the industry. The Association of British Travel Agents (ABTA) has Codes of Conduct for travel agencies and tour operators and also guidelines for booking conditions, which have substantially reduced the possibility for misleading the public. The European Union Directive on Package Travel (1992), mentioned earlier, has further tightened regulations requiring that tour operators be more accurate in their brochure descriptions. Constraints are also exercised by the media, always anxious to exploit any evidence of malpractice in the industry, and by organisations such as the Consumers' Association, publishers of *Holiday Which?* Carriers, too, have their own watchdogs – the Air Transport Users' Committee in Britain, and on a global scale the International Airline Passengers' Association. Such organisations have been set up to monitor and safeguard the interests of the travelling public.

However, as companies grow, they generally seek for themselves a more professional standard of conduct, and therefore are more sensitive about their public image. A company seeking long-term survival cannot afford to ignore its critics, nor can it tolerate too high a level of complaints from its customers. As we shall see later, 'branding', which seeks to impart certain qualities and values to a company and its named products, is crucial to success for the larger companies. Newer and smaller companies may be less reliant on branding and image, but should the industry itself not take effective action to police their activities, even without further legislation the consumer movement will identify and publicise weaknesses and thus deter future bookings.

Categories of marketing

If you look back at the definition of marketing given earlier in the chapter, you will see that the aim of an organisation's marketing is to achieve a profit *or other objective*. This distinction is important, since it clarifies the fact that marketing embraces the activities of all kinds of other organisations besides businesses.

Social marketing

Even within the commercial sphere, not all organisations will have profit as their objective. VisitBritain, for example, has no direct profit objective, its goal being to generate tourism to Britain, hence stimulating the economy, employment and the profits of private tourist enterprises. In the same way, other organisations providing non-commercial services, such as educational institutions, have to communicate their 'product' to their 'customers', their students. Ideas, too, will require communicating. The churches, charity organisations, political lobbies, all aim to satisfy certain needs, and the employment of effective communications techniques will help them to do so (has your eye ever been caught by one of those punchy slogans on the noticeboards outside your local church?). Present concern about the pollution of our environment has led to the formation of a strong ecology movement, whose aim is to market an idea to opinion leaders such as Members of Parliament and journalists, as well as to the general public. This concept of 'social marketing' is a relatively recent one, and brings home the point that organisations of all types can apply good marketing practice to their activities.

Increasingly, tourism enterprises are formed by a combination of public–private partnerships, in which one of the partners will have a profit motive while the other's concern will be to achieve a given target. Both aims will be achieved only through successful collaboration, and will need to be in harmony with one another. For example, a regional tourist board may have the ambition to increase the number of visitors to a given destination mainly out of season; any commercial partner must be willing to establish its own aims and target profits within these parameters.

Consumer and industrial marketing

At this point, it will be helpful to clarify what we mean by the term *product*. In marketing terms, the word encompasses not only tangible goods, but also anything that can be offered to people to satisfy their needs or wants, including services.

Products are sold to two kinds of buyers; those who buy for their own consumption, and those who buy on behalf of others. The term *consumer marketing* is used to describe the practice of marketing to the former category, and *industrial marketing* to the latter. Just as manufacturing industries buy raw materials to convert into finished products

Figure 1.1
Categories
of product
marketing

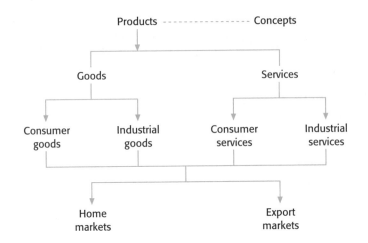

for their customers, and retail shops buy stock to sell to their customers, so in the travel world there are many forms of industrial buyers. Many large companies whose staff are engaged in frequent business travel will employ travel managers, whose task it is to arrange all the business travel of the company employees. Business conferences are often organised by professional firms of conference organisers, rather than by firms whose employees actually attend the conference. Hotels, airlines, and other travel companies will be eager to solicit business from these industrial buyers.

Home and export marketing

Finally, we need to draw a distinction between marketing products in the home (or domestic) market, and marketing them abroad to foreign markets. Export marketing, or international marketing, is a specialised field of marketing which will have to take into account different legal systems and business climates, different cultures affecting buyer behaviour, and the problems associated with transporting products abroad. Tourism, again, is substantially concerned with export marketing. British Airways has to sell the concept of flying with a British airline to Americans in competition with American carriers, and VisitBritain must market Britain as a destination to travellers in dozens of countries around the world, in competition with other tourist destinations. Incoming tour operators must understand the needs of visitors from different countries and learn how to cater for them.

We can now bring all these forms of marketing together in a diagram (see Figure 1.1).

The nature of tourism services

Since we are dealing throughout this book with a service industry, we shall look at the nature of services to understand how their marketing needs, and those of tourism services in particular, differ from those of goods. There are four main factors to be considered:

- intangibility
- heterogeneity
- perishability
- inseparability.

First, services are *intangible*. They cannot be inspected or sampled in advance of their purchase, therefore an element of risk is involved on the part of the purchaser. This is a critically important aspect of the transaction. From one perspective, this makes marketing services much easier; none of the usual problems of physical distribution is encountered, and there is no question of storing the product in warehouses prior to its delivery to the customer. However, intangible products have many drawbacks. The fact that travel agents, for example, do not have to purchase their products before they sell them to their clients reduces their commitment to the sale and their loyalty to particular brands. In place of a distribution system, the travel industry must deal with a *reservations system*, which is simply a method of matching demand with supply. The problems inherent in this form of distribution will be discussed in Chapter 8.

Tourism marketers must attempt to overcome the drawbacks posed by an intangible product, and there are a number of imaginative ways in which this has been achieved in practice. First, the development of video cassettes, which produced a more faithful (and more favourable) image of the holiday product than could be obtained from a holiday brochure, allowed tourists to take a moving picture of their destination home with them to play back on their screens. Advances in technology have meant that this is being rapidly overtaken by the use of DVDs (digital versatile disks) which allow better quality pictures to be screened on home computers, and interactive television will take us one step further in imparting an in-depth picture of a destination to the holidaymakers of the future. Another idea, introduced briefly during the rapid growth era of the 1960s before oil price rises sent air fares rocketing, was low-price 'trial flights' to a destination, whereby unsold charter air seats were made available to the public at a very low fare to enable prospective purchasers of package holidays to 'sample' the destinations and the experience of flying. Sometimes the fare charged (as low as £1) would be refunded against the later purchase of a holiday. In the 1990s, the British company Airtours experimented with low-price short flights to help prospective passengers overcome their fear of flying.

The second problem with services is *heterogeneity*. If one buys a tangible product – say, a dining-room table or a television set – mass production methods can go a long way to ensuring that each article produced is homogeneous, that is, standardised, with each unit sharing identical characteristics. With good quality control, 'lemons' occur very infrequently, and the customer can be assured of a product of a certain uniformity and quality. This is not the case with a service. Although the package tour, and the concept of the 'identikit' destination, have gone a long way to help the standardisation of the travel product, with its combination of flight, transfer and hotel room, there are elements of the product over which the 'manufacturer', that is, the tour operator, can have no control. A holiday taken in a week of continuous rainfall is a very different product from one taken in glorious sunshine. Although operators might offer the consolation of an insurance against bad weather, they cannot guarantee good weather. At the same time, a consumer buying a service such as tourism is buying a range of services provided by individuals, and these too are difficult to control. Hotel waiters who have had a tiff with their partners the previous evening will not render the same friendly service at breakfast that they had offered at dinner the day before. Resort representatives facing redundancy due to a takeover of their company by a rival are unlikely to treat their clients with the same consideration as they would have done in normal circumstances. While good quality control procedures can help to reduce extreme variations in performance, they cannot overcome the human problems inherent in the performance of tourism services.

Third, the tourism product is a highly *perishable* one. If the television set in the showroom is not sold today, it can be sold tomorrow, if necessary, at a reduced price. Or it can be stored and offered at a later date. But an airline seat or hotel room not sold today is lost for ever. This fact is of great importance for marketing, particularly when determining pricing. The heavy discounts on rooms sold after 6 pm and the 'standby' fares offered by airlines to fill empty seats reflect this need to offload products before their sale potential is lost. The problem is compounded by the fact that the travel industry suffers from *time-variable demand*. Often, holiday demand is concentrated in peak summer months such as July and August, and short trips are more likely to be taken at weekends than weekdays. Business travellers wish to fly from Heathrow at a convenient time to them, say between 10 am and noon, whereas airports and airlines prefer to offer a balanced service around the clock to maximise the use of their resources. Once again, pricing strategies can help spread demand by offering substantial reductions during periods of low demand, but this does not totally solve the problem.

Finally, there is the question of *inseparability*. Services are highly personalised, the product being the outcome of the performance of the seller. The simplest way to demonstrate this is again to take the television set as an example. If we see an advertisement for a particular brand of set that we want to buy, at a price which is highly competitive against those of other stores, we are likely to visit the shop. If we find that the salesperson selling the television is unkempt and lacking interest, this alone is unlikely to dissuade us from making the purchase; price and brand reputation have already predetermined our actions. However, transpose the same scenario to a restaurant or hotel, and our reaction will be very different. Whatever the quality of the food, however attractive the decor, service is so much an integral part of the product that it would be unlikely that we should be prepared to purchase from such a poor representative. The travel agent who sells us our holiday, the airline cabin staff who cater to our needs en route, the resort representative who greets us on arrival, the hotel's front office receptionist – all are elements in the product we are purchasing, and their social skills in dealing with us are an essential part of the product. It is for this reason that training becomes so vital for the successful marketing of travel and tourism.

Figure 1.2
A military
historian guides
a Holt's tour of
Holocaust sites,
Warsaw, Poland

(Photographed by the author)

Example   Holt's Tours

Holt's Tours is a company which niche markets special interest escorted tours to sites famous in martial history: World War I and II sites, US civil war sites, Gallipoli and the Crimea, etc. They are leaders in their field within the UK, and ensure they stay ahead of their potential rivals through exceptional service. Examples of this service include the employment of ex-British Army officers and military historians as lecturer/tour managers (with good language skills), and provision of access to places not normally open to visitors (see Figure 1.2). Appropriate tapes (dramas, speeches, etc.) are played on board coaches approaching sites visited.

The very fact that the product is a composite of several services leads to further problems associated with product development. In a package holiday, customers will normally expect to receive broadly comparable levels of quality in all the components of their travel arrangements, regardless of whether they have bought a high-priced or budget holiday. The tourist booked at a premium-priced hotel who purchases an optional excursion associated with that holiday will justifiably feel cheated if the coach providing the service is dirty or in poor mechanical condition. This 'law of tourism harmony' has been an important element in quality assurance in the holiday industry. However, there is now some evidence emerging that patterns of tourist demand are becoming more complex, with better-travelled tourists opting for a mix of variable-quality products to meet their needs – for example, a luxury hotel coupled with budget activities by day, or cheap accommodation with meals taken nearby at a first-class restaurant. Marketing managers will need to be aware of such trends and become flexible enough to cater for them.

These issues will have helped to demonstrate that, while basic principles of marketing apply to all products, in practice there are special considerations to take into account when marketing tourism. It is the very peculiarity of tourism that makes it such a problematic, and at the same time fascinating, product to create and sell.

Questions, tasks and issues for discussion

1   In the above chapter, it was revealed that our body shapes are changing. This is particularly true of body weight; due partly to our dietary changes and reduced exercise, we are all getting heavier. In 2002, Southwest Airlines introduced a policy of charging overweight passengers for two seats (it is left to check-in staff to determine who is 'overweight'), while elsewhere a passenger sued the airline with which she travelled for medical conditions arising from sitting next to an overweight passenger who crushed her. Examine the alternative solutions to resolving this problem, taking into account all the factors that will influence your decision. What policy would you advocate an airline to adopt on this issue?

2   'Marketing a country is not like promoting a chocolate bar or a car. Rather than creating a product and monitoring its quality, you are presented with a highly complex product and required to elucidate its best features. But that's not to say there is no control over the product. The Government, the principal funder of VisitBritain, needs to take a longer view of tourism. No one wants to rebrand Britain again, but there's nothing wrong with taking a look at where the product could be improved for the sake of tourists . . . to begin with a 21st-century transport system, grown-up licensing hours and a warm welcome for families in pubs and restaurants . . .'
      (Danny Rogers, associate editor of *Marketing*, writing in *Travel Weekly*, 7 April 2003)

Discuss the above view, and compare with the view expressed by an earlier director of marketing for the former British Tourist Authority:

'In a way, a tourist organisation is not involved in marketing, because marketing *per se* supposes you've got control of the product, and that you can change it.'
      (Frank Kelly, former director of marketing, BTA)

How can a public sector tourist board 'control its product'?

3   It is debatable to what extent holidaymakers are still afflicted with any of the three fears outlined in this chapter. Perhaps today we should include the 'new fears' of disease, crime and terrorism as issues with which tourists must contend. Identify areas of the world which suffer from one or more of these concerns but remain popular tourism destinations. What steps need to be taken (i) to overcome the problems within the destinations, and (ii) to reassure potential visitors of their safety? Who would be responsible for taking these steps? What role might marketing have in support?

4   Identify one company in the travel and tourism industry which clearly demonstrates a marketing-orientated philosophy. What are the factors which support this view?

5   Tourism Concern reported in its spring 2003 edition of *Tourism in Focus* that visitors to the Middle East were being offered four-day 'terror tours' of Gaza and the West Bank, organised by an Israeli settler, during which the tourists could fire weapons, sit in the cockpit of a fighter plane

and have paintball fights in rooms of deserted buildings to 'clear out' Arab terrorists. Each client paid $5500 for the privilege – a useful contribution in an economically depressed area.

However, a fellow tour operator described these offerings as 'disgusting'. 'The tours do a disservice to humanity by feeding into a racist stereotype of Arabs as terrorists … anything that alienates one group of people from another has to be wrong. For a country to allow such activities and even profit by it is unthinkable.'

In your view, should a tourism programme like this be considered unethical, or would the economic contribution ameliorate the ethical dilemmas raised by critics towards such a package? How might this programme be modified to make it both acceptable to an adventure-seeking visitor and to its critics?

6   What are the ethical implications of accepting a job in marketing in:

■   the tobacco industry
■   the fast food sector
■   a time-share company touting for customers in the streets of Mediterranean resorts
■   a low-profit, low-service budget airline
■   an in-bound operator in the UK promoting medieval banquets to US visitors
■   a specialist tour operator which organises tours to destinations where the availability of under-age sex is a recognised attraction to visitors (although not specifically promoted by the operator).

Can a case be made for accepting such employment?

Exercise

Museums are changing from their traditional role of providing exhibits for inspection at a distance and under glass, to centres of interpretation and experience for their visitors. Visit a local museum and undertake research which will indicate:

■   how far the museum appears to be taking this approach
■   what could further be achieved.

Your research should be based on talks to museum staff – curators, guards, guides, educational assistants – and to members of the general public visiting the attraction. Use semi-structured interviews, aided by tape recorders, to record the discussions. Also spend time observing the attraction and its exhibits, noting such features as signs, descriptive boards or literature, interactive opportunities for visitors, etc. Is there an education officer or department responsible for educational visits? How well does the museum meet the different needs for interpretation among its varied visitors – adults, children, foreign tourists, and so on?

Write a brief report indicating what has been achieved, how well this has been implemented, and what remains to be done to improve customer satisfaction.

References

1 Levitt, T, Marketing Myopia, *Harvard Business Review* July/August 1960, pp 45–56 (full text is also contained in Enis, B and Cox, K, *Marketing Classics: a Selection of Influential Articles*, Allyn & Bacon, 8th edn 1991, pp 3–21)
2 Kotler, P, Armstrong, G, Saunders, J and Wong, V, *Principles of Marketing*, Prentice Hall, 3rd edn 2001

3 Eber, S, *Beyond the Green Horizon: Principles of Sustainable Tourism*, Tourism Concern/ WWF, 1992

Further reading

Kotler, P, *Marketing Management*, Prentice Hall International, 11th edn 2003

McDonald, M, *Marketing Plans: How to Prepare them, How to Use them*, Butterworth Heinemann, 5th edn 2002, ch 1 pp 3–17

Zuboff, S and Maxmin, J, *The Support Economy: Why Corporations are Failing Individuals and the Next Episode of Capitalism*, Allen Lane Penguin Press, 2003

2 Marketing planning

Learning outcomes

After studying this chapter, you should be able to:

- explain the planning function and its role within marketing
- understand the elements of a marketing plan and how to construct one
- recognise how uncontrollable factors affect the planning process
- employ SWOT analysis as the foundation for a marketing plan
- describe simple forecasting methods and understand their role in the planning process
- list organisational systems for marketing, and evaluate their suitability for different marketing conditions
- list the elements of the marketing mix, and understand their role in the marketing plan.

What is marketing planning?

All tourism organisations, however small and whether consciously or not, engage in marketing activity. The local travel agent, for example, has to make decisions about which services to offer, which brochures to rack and how they will be displayed. The choice of brochures, level of service, type of decor and furnishings, all reflect the market segment(s) the agent has decided to cater for and the ways in which the needs of those markets will be met. Advertising the products, drawing attention to special opportunities, perhaps providing free coach travel to the local airport as an incentive for clients to book with that particular agent, checking past records to see who the regular clients are, and undertaking mailshots with details of holidays that may appeal to them are all examples of marketing activity. There is, however, an important distinction between so-called 'seat of the pants' marketing, where decisions are taken on the spur of the moment, and a carefully thought out and coordinated approach to marketing. This latter process is known as the marketing planning process, and it is this process which will be described in this chapter.

Expressed simply, planning is designed to link an organisation's goals and resources to its marketing opportunities, and in doing so to make the best uses of its resources. Clearly then, we have first to know what our goals and resources are, as well as what opportunities exist for us to exploit. If a market is growing quickly, as was the case with foreign holidays from the 1960s to the mid-1980s, opportunities may be comparatively simple to identify, and in these circumstances even relatively inefficient and poorly managed companies may be able to survive and prosper. But the marketing environment is subject to constant change, and if demand stabilises or falls (as happened quite frequently, in the case of package holidays, since the early 1990s), the failure to develop a strategic marketing plan which responds to that change may result in the collapse of less efficiently managed organisations. Planning is simply a means of survival in a competitive and quickly changing environment.

Planning for what?

In the case of companies that are presently trading, all planning starts from a base of knowing where the company is now; who are its competitors, who are its customers. Planning involves taking decisions based on this knowledge, and determining where the company wants to be; who will be its future customers, how it will reach them, what revenue and profit targets it seeks to achieve. In short, planning sets targets and determines how they will be achieved.

Planning is carried out by a combination of strategies and tactics. Although the distinctions between these two are not always clear-cut, strategies are generally more concerned with long-term plans, involving significant decisions about the direction of marketing action over a period of one to three years or longer. Tactics involve short-term decisions about what action should be taken over the next few weeks to six months. To make the distinction clear, a company's strategy may be to switch budget support from advertising to public relations over the coming three years in order to generate goodwill and a strong image within the community, while tactical measures may involve generating immediate sales within the community by increasing advertising expenditure in the local press over the coming few weeks.

Marketing plans require the organisation to establish both short-term and long-term objectives. At its most basic, short-term planning is required simply in order to identify where the company is now, and where it will be next week, or next month. Managers need to be able to judge their cash flow position, since without knowing how much money will be flowing into a company, it will not be possible to predict whether funds will be adequate to pay the organisation's running costs, such as salaries. The marketing plan determines what needs to be sold in a given period, at a given price, and how this is to be achieved, to meet operating costs.

Beyond this, the company must plan to achieve its longer-term objectives. This could mean finding additional sources of capital for future investment. No banker is likely to look favourably at a request for further funds unless the organisation's aims and strategies are clearly defined. The marketing plan is, of course, only one aspect of a company's overall planning, and as such must be coordinated with the financial plans, organisational plans, purchasing plans and other aspects of the organisation's total business activity. Marketing is simply a tool by which an organisation achieves its objectives, by identifying new product and market opportunities, evaluating them and taking action to develop them. In diagrammatic form, a company's marketing action plan will look like that shown in Figure 2.1.

Figure 2.1
A marketing action plan

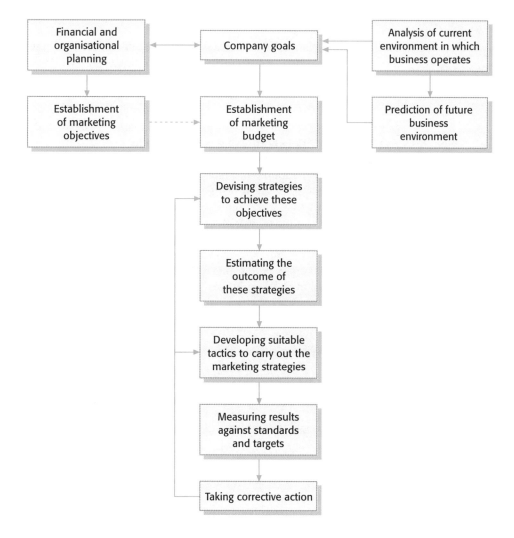

Setting objectives

Typical objectives likely to be sought by the company will include:

■ achieving a certain level of sales growth within a given period of time

■ increasing the profitability of the organisation by a given percentage within an agreed time scale

■ obtaining a given percentage share of the market within a given period of time (new product), or increasing current market share by x per cent within the period (existing product)

■ reducing business risk by diversifying the product range

■ obtaining a measured increase in the return on capital employed by the company.

The marketing plan will be designed to achieve one or more of these objectives by the use of a selected choice of strategies. There is a danger in trying to achieve too many objectives simultaneously within a marketing plan, since this can result in conflicting strategies. If asked, most managers would declare their aims would be to satisfy all of the objectives listed above; but, as tour operators and other travel firms have learned to their cost, the achievement of increases in market share or a policy of long-term growth may be at the expense of short-term profits.

A marketing manager is faced with many alternative strategies from which to choose when drawing up a marketing plan. To achieve an increase in the return on capital invested, for example, the tour operator might choose to raise prices, to find ways of reducing costs, to seek higher productivity from present resources, to push for increased sales to present markets served, or to introduce products to new markets. Which of these is adopted will depend upon the analysis of the current market situation in which the company is operating. A large tour operator like First Choice Holidays, for example, which has several brands aimed at different market sectors – Sovereign aimed at the luxury market, Freespirit for the more independent traveller without children and First Choice for mainstream family holidays – may set quite distinct objectives, involving different strategic plans, for each of these divisions.

The business environment

In drawing up a marketing plan, a balance must be struck between establishing rigid bureaucratic guidelines and a dependency upon entrepreneurial 'flair'. Any plan has to be flexible, to take into account changing circumstances. If a company sticks too rigidly to its pre-established plans, it stands in danger of missing new opportunities which arise in the course of the plan's implementation. The collapse of a specialist tour operator in mid-season, for instance, will allow another operator to move into a new market or a new geographical area which may have been considered and rejected earlier. At the same time, any company which chooses to ignore its plans will be in

Figure 2.2
The business
environment of
a tour operator

danger of heading off in a number of different directions, not only disrupting the organisation's overall planning but also possibly overstretching its resources.

A business has within its power the ability to change any aspect of its internal operations as it sees fit. However, it operates within an environment over which it has little, if any, control. This environment comprises the political, legal, economic, geographical and cultural framework in which all businesses operate. It is subject to continual change, and the business, if it is to survive, must learn to adapt to these changes. An understanding of the current business environment is an essential prerequisite for planning. We can demonstrate this by taking the example of a typical mass market tour operator. Figure 2.2 illustrates the range of influences on the operator. The operator needs to understand first the nature and scope of the *competition* which it faces from other tour operating companies. How easy is it for new companies to enter the market? Who are the company's main competitors, what share of the market do they possess, and what are their marketing strategies? The dog-eat-dog nature of the tour operating business should not be underestimated. The activity of competitor tour operators is probably *the* dominant factor in planning – spiced by the challenge of second guessing their likely strategy for 12 months ahead. With little consumer loyalty or perception of difference between operators, many holidays are booked after meticulous comparisons between the brochure offerings of the different companies.

In some countries, entry to the market may be controlled by government legislation, a *political* constraint, but in most countries a relatively free market exists, in which, subject to satisfying certain criteria, any company can enter and trade. There will, however, be *legal* considerations to take into account; licences may have to be obtained and restrictions on night flights may inhibit 24-hour operations.

One important factor in tourism, over which companies have no control, is that of *weather*. A poor early summer in Britain will lead to an increase in late demand for holidays, while a mild winter followed by a promisingly warm spring may lead British people to plan to take their holidays at home. Increasingly, a factor that must be integrated into tourism planning is terrorism or the perceived threat of terrorism. The attack on New York's World Trade Center on 11 September 2001 followed by the bombing a year later in Bali, both had a calamitous impact on world travel, and subsequently further organised terrorist attacks in Kenya and Morocco compounded the fear of travel to areas perceived as vulnerable to threats.

A *cultural* factor is changing fashion. While it is true that businesses can sometimes manipulate fashion (the great fashion houses in the clothes trade provide ample evidence of this), there are a great many complex factors at work which will make one country or resort more fashionable than another, and marketing planners have to be sensitive to such changes in consumer demand resulting from changing taste. By and large, the mainstream destinations for European tourists – Spain, Cyprus, Turkey, Greece, Portugal – remain dominant but enjoy cycles of popularity. Thus 2002 saw a switch away from Greece to Turkey and a decline for Cyprus and many Spanish resorts. Not every country or resort exploits its tourism opportunities effectively. A glance at any holiday brochure from the early 1980s will reveal many 'lost' destinations, for example the Italian Rivieras were then significant destinations, but are now hardly featured. Florida, on the other hand, has become almost as popular as short-haul destinations for Europeans (admittedly, strongly boosted by the development and promotion of Disneyworld and other attractions around Orlando). Status pressures, coupled with falling air fares, are encouraging long-haul holidays to increasingly exotic destinations.

The other side of the coin of fashion is the consumer's restless search for 'new' experiences and 'unspoilt' destinations. It is not sufficient for operators to offer a balanced programme of holidays across the established resorts. New hotels, new resorts, new countries and new types of holidays must all be part of a continuing programme of product development.

Above all, *economic* influences are at work which will affect demand for the company's products. The business must be aware of the extent to which its suppliers dictate the prices at which accommodation, air seats and other travel facilities are offered. A poor summer in Britain, leading to sudden late demand for foreign holidays, will have the effect of pushing up prices as many operators try to purchase extra arrangements at short notice. Operators negotiating for hotel rooms in Majorca, whatever share they may enjoy in the British market, will find themselves competing with German, Dutch, Swedish and other operators who may be prepared to pay higher prices, or have greater bargaining power, driving up prices for British operators.

Operators must be aware, too, of the *elasticity of demand* for their product; that is, the extent to which a change in price of the holidays leads to a change in demand from consumers. A product such as a package tour, which is not clearly differentiated from products of other tour operators, is highly price sensitive, and price reductions will lead to substantial expansion in the total demand for holidays, as well as attracting holiday-makers away from other operators; just as any price increase not also affecting competitors can lead to a dramatic fall in the company's market share.

Consumer demand for holidays is also determined by the *substitutability* of the package tour, not only against other forms of holidays, but also against other goods and services, such as a new television set or a three-piece suite for the living room. Economists use the term *cross-elasticity of demand* to describe this highly important factor (and one too readily overlooked by many in the travel industry). The annual holiday has now become a habit for millions of Britons, who have shown their willingness to sacrifice purchases of consumer goods in order to continue to take their annual holiday in the sun during periods of recession. However, if prices of these foreign holidays are driven up at a significantly faster rate than other goods and services (due, for example, to changes in exchange rates between, or inflation rates within, the two countries) then consumers may switch their spending patterns. Holidaymakers may decide to stay at home working in the garden, spending the money on shrubs, a greenhouse or garden tools (especially if the summer is good) rather than taking their traditional fortnight (or second holiday) in the sun. Finally, we must recognise that holiday demand can also be affected by the demand for goods 'in fashion' which compete for leisure money. Home computers, camcorders, DVD players and other technological equipment all represent a considerable outlay for the consumer, who may sacrifice holidays in order to 'join the crowd' in buying new products on the market.

In addition to the factors we have cited here, a host of other factors can affect the company's business objectives. Demographic changes – a rise or fall in population, a decline in a particular age group, changes in traditional marriage patterns – should be understood, and taken into account when planning for long-term objectives, while the need to take into account shareholders' demands to sustain satisfactory dividends must also figure in the company's short-term marketing plans. Requirements imposed by finance houses and banks, as conditions for loans, will have to be considered. In Britain the national trade body, ABTA, imposes its own standards on its members, while the Office of Fair Trading (OFT) will press for conditions which improve the consumers' interests, such as insisting on brochures showing all-inclusive prices, instead of listing airport taxes and other ancillary costs separately. Environmental lobbyists or Members of Parliament may be pressing for reductions in the number of night flights, or greater utilisation of less popular airports. Even the media exercise influence over the business practices of the travel trade (think of the influence of programmes such as the BBC's annual *Holiday* programme or ITV's *Wish You Were Here*, for example). In short, the business environment is made up of a huge complex of public and private institutions and individuals, each of which may pose constraints on the way in which marketing planners function.

Tour operators, in fact, are in a particularly vulnerable position, since they can be affected both by changes in the environment of their consumers and by changes in the countries in which they operate. They may be operating to a region suddenly beset by political unrest, where the safety of their clients can no longer be assured, or by industrial strife, such as an air traffic controllers' strike in Spain or France. A destination country may change the value of its currency, or impose a higher airport tax on departing passengers, or introduce a swingeing increase in value added tax (VAT), all of which will substantially affect the operators' prices and/or reduce demand to that destination. Even comparatively small increases in charges can affect demand for a destination; although other factors may have contributed, the drop in demand for travel to the Balearics in 2002 has been attributed in some measure to the introduction of a small bed tax to pay for environmental improvements. Marketing planners must be prepared to react quickly to amend their marketing plans as these factors become evident.

It will be helpful at this point to summarise the main features of the business environment in which tourism organisations operate. We see an environment in which competition is becoming increasingly global (most leading British operators and their associated travel agents are now owned by foreign firms), and where SMEs represent by far the largest proportion of the industry, perhaps as many as 90 per cent of all travel businesses being composed of less than 250 employees. At the same time, no industry has been so affected by the growth in ICT, and the large global corporations have been quicker to exploit the opportunities for new methods of distribution offered by the new technology. These large global organisations are faced with intense competition as the growth in world demand flattens, while economic and political uncertainty throughout the developed world makes forecasting future recovery, and the direction of future demand, difficult. Over-exploitation of popular short-haul destinations has led to concern about the effect of tourism on the environment, in common with global concern over pollution on the planet and the overuse of scarce resources (airline fuel burn is a major factor in world pollution but no action has yet been taken to control or reduce consumption or emissions of noxious gases – a situation unlikely to continue for long). As demand growth tapers off, principals are finding themselves faced with an increasingly sophisticated market of well-travelled and increasingly demanding consumers, with whom they are insufficiently trained and resourced to cope.

SWOT analysis

This broad analysis of the business environment which we have just described is a necessary first step in systematically appraising the present position of the company and identifying its problems, prior to determining objectives for the coming year. Whether the company is preparing a feasibility study for a new product launch, or merely assessing the current market situation in order to prepare a new marketing plan, it must be aware of:

- the economic, political, legal, socio-cultural and technological events which currently affect or could have a bearing on company operations and performance
- the current shape of the markets served by the company, including their size, growth and trends; product ranges on offer and prices charged in each market; channels through which the products are distributed; and ways in which product knowledge is communicated to the consumers and distributors
- the nature of the competition, including size of each competitor, share of the market they hold, their reputation, marketing methods, strengths and weaknesses
- full details of the company's own market share, sales, profitability, and patterns of trading.

This review is often undertaken using a technique known as SWOT analysis; that is, the identification of *strengths* and *weaknesses* in the business, the *opportunities* presented by the trading environment and any *threats* faced by the company. This information provides the basis for further action.

Let us look at the kinds of issues likely to be considered by travel companies in a typical SWOT.

Strengths

These have to be seen from the perspective of the customer, not the company. For example, with a travel agency, the fact that the internal size of the office will be large enough to accommodate a separate office for the manager is of little concern to the customers. On the other hand, if the company has an established reputation in the region, so that it will be already known in the area for its reliability or service, this will be a distinct advantage in early trading. Convenience of location is extremely important for customers, so a new agency opening in the heart of a new shopping precinct, perhaps adjacent to a popular chain store, will be a clear strength. The attraction of a new shop front and smart modern decor with comfortable seating will be another plus in the company's efforts to win customers from the competition.

A tour operator will be concerned with the image of the brand, as perceived by both travel agents and consumers. A strong brand and high levels of awareness within the target market are critical for the leading players in the field, while a strong and positive image is a key strength for any principal. A loyal body of past customers is a considerable asset to be exploited, as repeat business is easier and less costly to win than new sales. Product strengths, particularly those that differentiate the operator from its competition, are important. The operator may also benefit organisationally from unique contracts overseas or other organisational factors that facilitate the delivery of the holiday product and result in higher quality, lower costs, or both.

Weaknesses

One difficulty always facing an agent is that of finding sales staff of the right calibre. If in addition the agency is located in the London area, where employment is high and good staff at affordable salaries difficult to come by, the problem is compounded. At the same time, competitive agencies in the area may have well-established, competent staff, popular with their customers, which will make it difficult to attract business. Perhaps the shop fronts on to a street with a traffic barrier, requiring customers to use an unattractive underpass in order to reach the agency from across the road. This would be a serious weakness in attracting passing trade. So would inadequate or expensive parking facilities.

The tour operator will be highly conscious of its competitive position: is it disadvantaged in terms of price, scope of destinations, quality of accommodation, product features or service to the travel agents? And is it weak in promotional terms, with the competition advertising its sales messages more effectively?

Opportunities

Opportunities are naturally presented by the chance to exploit any particular strengths of the business. Both agent and principal should also be on the lookout for opportunities presented by changes in the market. For the agent this might be a new housing estate being built in the vicinity. A new industrial development may be planned, with potential for business travel; or a new department store may be opening in the near future. This kind of opportunity needs to be not only recognised but acted upon.

Marketing tactics should take advantage of the opportunity, such as directing a mail-shot to all residents on the new estate.

A tour operator might see an opportunity to specialise in a new destination following the introduction of a new air route by an independent carrier to the area. Perhaps a competitor is going out of business, thus opening up an opportunity to capture their share of the market. The market may have reacted positively to particular promotional tactics in the past, presenting the opportunity to repeat or enhance their effect. The enhancement of tourist infrastructure within an existing resort presents further opportunities to an enterprising operator.

Threats

Both travel agent and tour operator will be subject to national economic and political events, such as the imposition of a departure tax in the UK, affecting the price of all flights out of UK airports. World politics and terrorist threats can pose major problems for the travel industry, as demonstrated by the debacle of the global travel market following the September 11th disaster. The local economy will affect the travel agent, as it will any regionally based tour operator. The agent will be concerned with such factors as major companies in the area laying off staff or planning to close; the agency manager or one of the sales staff planning to quit in order to open up an agency in competition. Perhaps present traffic patterns are to change as a result of road improvements in the area.

The operator will be alert for threats posed by currency fluctuations and fuel cost increases – both major contributors to fixed costs. Any competitive activity that is affecting sales will also represent a major threat – for example, a price reduction or a significant advertising campaign.

There are always threats in any business; but if they are recognised and tackled early enough, they can be overcome and perhaps even turned into opportunities.

At this point it might be helpful to introduce a case study of a fictitious SWOT analysis undertaken by an upmarket city break tour operator which is part of a larger travel organisation. Let us call the operator 'Worldaway Holidays'.

Worldaway Holidays: a SWOT analysis

Strengths

- brand name heritage, providing exclusive cachet and upmarket image within the target market
- loyal customer base with high repeat purchase, held on database and thus available for direct contact
- economies of scale linked to parent operation
- uniquely strong coverage of Eastern European capitals
- price guarantee and no-discount policy now well understood and liked by agents and consumers.

Weaknesses

- fewer destinations by comparison with the competition – a weakness perceived by agents to be greater than it actually is
- less attractive flight departure times to several destinations than the competition
- lack of knowledge of reservations staff compared to specialist operators
- limited information on website pages, and no ability to book directly through Internet
- profits unduly impacted by unsold holidays and ineffective 'late sales' tactics
- customer satisfaction questionnaire process not comprehensive – customer names gathered are only 50 per cent of the total customers carried
- existing advertising campaign now 'tired' and response rates are dropping.

Opportunities

- market research shows strong growth in the upmarket sector of the holiday business, with social group A/B consumers increasingly taking more than one holiday per year
- direct mail trials have shown that this technique is extremely effective when targeted at customers in order to generate brochure requests and 'push' sales into agents. A good database provides ample material to target these customers effectively
- overseas staff report good opportunities to increase the programme to Eastern Europe, with good facilities being provided through investment in tourism in cities such as Tallinn (where tourism is increasing dramatically), Riga and St Petersburg; there is an opportunity to increase the programme into unspoilt, historic and novel city destinations.

Threats

- relatively 'naive' tourist industry in Eastern Europe, increasing demands upon overseas staff and with a greater risk of a lapse in quality resulting in bad publicity
- specialist operators are offering better, more knowledgeable service to travel agents, and hence are preferred for the more 'undiscovered destinations'
- the major tour operating competitor to Worldaway Holidays is owned by a major airline, from whom 55 per cent of flights are negotiated; a satisfactory contract has still not been agreed
- the same competitor is running a significantly larger promotional campaign than Worldaway budgets would allow.

Worldaway Holidays: resultant marketing plan

Product

To exploit the anticipated increase in the size of the overall market, the programme should be increased to offer a further 10 000 holidays next season. These should be made up as follows:

1   4000 increased capacity to existing destinations. This represents a modest increase in market share of 0.5 per cent, which we hope to achieve through better management of the travel agent channel. The intention is to maximise the profit opportunities available from existing destinations.
2   1000 to 'established' city break destinations which are new to Worldaway, but fill perceived gaps in product portfolio, for example Istanbul. This modest capacity will still mean that we are seen to provide a wider choice of destinations, and it can be highlighted in our promotional activities.
3   5000 to new Eastern European destinations, with emphasis on Tallinn. We are becoming known for Eastern European breaks, and have good contacts through our parent company. This is the logical area for expansion, if sufficient safeguards can be put in place with respect to quality. This will be achieved through a policy of 'quality before rates' – and we should be strongly placed here with little competition and less price sensitivity for these destinations. Quality guidelines will be issued to staff which must be adhered to when contracting beds for next season.

The price advantage that we obtain through economies of scale with our parent company should not be used, as last season, to undercut the competition. The objective is to match the competition for price but use the extra margin we make to add in some 'product pluses' that will differentiate the product. Ideas on this include Worldaway leather luggage tags, taxi transfers from the airport and a free bottle of wine in the room on arrival.

The contracts for all flying should be reviewed. Again, quality standards must be higher – flight departure times should be more attractive. It should also be included in this year's hotel contracts that customer satisfaction questionnaires must be distributed to our customers on departure from the hotel. This will increase the capture of names and addresses for the marketing database.

The knowledge of the reservations staff must be improved to increase our credibility with agents as a specialist operator, and to enable us to sell the new destinations that we have planned with confidence. The reservations staff will be involved with our planned travel agent promotions through a programme of outbound calls to agents. Not only will this be motivating for them, but also it will improve their product knowledge.

Though this will offset to some extent the limitations of our website pages, a budget should be allocated to cover essential systems enhancements, boosting the number of pages and information available, ensuring regular updates and including an interactive booking system in preparation for sales next season.

Price

Prices will be set to match the competition, rather than undercut them.

Our guarantee not to raise surcharges has been well received and should be continued. Equally, our policy of no discounting has done much to build our upmarket image. Both of these pricing policies can be capitalised upon in promotion.

A feasibility study should be undertaken to investigate the implications of a 'never knowingly undersold' policy of matching the price of an identical holiday if it occurs in a competitor's programme. Hopefully, with the introduction of product pluses such as taxi transfers, the identical holiday will not exist elsewhere anyway. This claim could work well in promotional terms as it builds upon our existing well-received policies.

Promotion

Direct mail campaigns targeted at customers worked well last season and should be expanded. A test group of 'profiled' prospects should also be evaluated next season, and if cost-effective, planned in future years' programmes. The promotion needs a fresh creative treatment to revitalise response figures, but as last year the promotion should generate brochure requests.

Sales messages should include:

- the price promise of no surcharges and possibly 'never knowingly undersold'
- new destinations: a fresher, more varied programme than ever before
- special strengths in Eastern Europe
- emphasise even more the quality heritage of the brand coupled with the value for money from our parent operation.

We shall run a sales promotion to travel agents with the objective of raising awareness of Worldaway as a specialist operator. This should use the device of, for instance, a competition to draw to agents' attention to the specific cities we cover. Outbound calls from our reservation teams to key outlets can support the promotion. Prizes of free trips to unusual Eastern European destinations should be backed up by a carefully controlled programme of selective educational visits.

A separate programme of visits for journalists and travel writers should again focus on the new destinations and the growing tourist trade in Eastern Europe.

The value of our customer database is now so great that it is worth incentivising the completion of customer satisfaction questionnaires. A modest donation to a Romanian orphanage project would position us well as an Eastern European specialist.

Further fund-raising activities for this good cause could be undertaken if the incentive proves successful.

Tactical advertisements to generate late sales should be planned in conjunction with a specialist advertising agency. Last year's activity suffered from a lack of skills and resources. In particular, we should benefit from quicker placement of advertisements and better choice of media. This should include some limited pop-up advertisements on the web pages to test the effectiveness of this form of promotion.

Place

Travel agency distribution remains our key channel. This is to be supported by the activities already mentioned. Nevertheless, the opportunity exists to improve profits through direct sales for late availability. As well as brochure requests, we should trial advertisements quoting our reservations number direct. This will again impact on the training of reservations staff, who will need to be comfortable in dealing with the public as well as travel agents.

A select group of key travel agents will be offered increased commission subject to sales targets. We can further improve our service to these agents through:

■ increased calls from sales staff at the expense of less productive outlets
■ a joint promotion fund and support for travel agents prepared to mount evening events on holidays in Eastern Europe.

The marketing plan devised above will introduce readers to many of the issues discussed later in this book, dealing as it does with proposals for product policy, pricing decisions and communications with customers and trade buyers. Above all, it introduces the idea that formal marketing planning is essential in any travel organisation, in lieu of ad hoc decision-making. It also leads us to consider issues of strategic planning in travel, which will now be examined.

Strategic planning

Once a company has evaluated its marketing position, it has, broadly speaking, three directions in which it can move, strategically:

■ low price leadership
■ product differentiation
■ market focus.

Low price leadership

If a company is big and powerful enough to undercut its rivals on price, it may choose this strategy as the basis for its consumer appeal. Price reductions are achieved through cost reductions. Large companies can benefit from economies of scale. A company the size of TUI, with international markets spread across Europe, can negotiate very low prices with hotels at its proposed destinations because of the sheer number of beds for which it is contracting. However, it is worth bearing in mind that while large companies can more effectively compete on price than SMEs, they frequently suffer from diseconomies of scale, in the sense that as organisations become larger, they become more difficult to manage. This can result in problems of impersonality for their customers and difficulties in communicating effectively with staff in the organisation.

Because large tour operators carry large numbers of clients, this can preclude them from dealing with the many small family-run hotels and guesthouses at the destinations they serve, whereas a small tour operator may be able to negotiate to fill such small hotels at even lower prices than those offered by the major operators.

Product differentiation

As an alternative to price leadership, a company may choose to specialise in certain kinds of products which are not provided by its competitors. It may also opt to focus on quality, justifying a higher price than the large competitors by adding value. This will require a heavy emphasis in the marketing plan on quality control to ensure that standards are maintained. One tour operator chose to differentiate its products by emphasising the comprehensive nature of the package, in which entertainments, excursions and child-minding services were all included in the basic price of the holidays.

In cases where prices are broadly similar, as on certain airline routes, it becomes vital to differentiate products in other ways to compete, since one airline's Boeing 747 is very like any other's. One airline might stress on-time reliability, another its safety record ('our multi-million-mile pilots . . .'), while yet another will seek to create an atmosphere of relaxed informality on board. Singapore Airlines have been widely recognised for the marketing success they have achieved with a campaign aimed at stressing the beauty of their cabin crew and the level of service rendered to their customers. Another airline chose to stress safety in its advertisements aimed at the US market.

Example   LOT Polish Airlines

'The average passenger airplane is 15 years old.
The average LOT airplane, just 3.'

LOT advertisement in the *New Yorker* magazine

Market focus

In this strategy, the decision is taken to concentrate on one or more specific markets (this market segmentation approach will be discussed in greater depth in Chapter 4). By catering for individual markets in this way, and adapting products to meet the precise needs of those markets, the company reduces the competition it faces and becomes, in effect, a 'big fish in a small pond'. Within these markets, the company can develop a policy of either cost leadership or product differentiation. A notable benefit in reducing the levels of competition in this way is that markets are less price-sensitive, and therefore profits can be boosted. Examples in the tour operating field include niche marketers such as Solo Holidays, Holt's Battlefield Tours and One Parent Family Holidays, where the choice is to market either to a limited segment within the population or to offer a specialist product which is likely to appeal to only a small number of people even if drawn from a wider population.

In choosing to focus on particular markets, a company can avoid the danger of trying to do all things well but excelling in none. Marketing managers must always ask themselves, 'Why should my customers buy my products rather than those of my competitors?' Unless they can provide a sound answer to that question, the success of their products will remain in doubt.

As the larger operators have moved more and more to mass market, low-price strategies, so SME operators have turned to specialisation, whether by geographical region, type of activity or market served.

Travel agencies, too, can develop their marketing strategies along similar lines. Indeed, many smaller agencies will need to do so in order to survive, as the marketplace for mass package tours becomes increasingly dominated by a handful of large travel chains which can discount to a point where independent agencies can no longer compete. The smaller agency may opt to provide old-fashioned, high quality service, or offer specific kinds of product knowledge, such as an in-depth knowledge of cruising and different cruise lines. Alternatively, the agency may choose to deal only with customers from one sector of the market for holidays, or specialise in business house travel.

A popular exercise for marketing managers, now being adopted by travel companies, is to produce a product-positioning map, revealing the customers' image of existing companies competing in certain fields. This can be very helpful both to a company already operating in the market, or one contemplating launching a new product. A survey is conducted among a random sample of holidaymakers, who are asked a series of questions designed to provide an image of the various companies. This image can then be plotted on a matrix. One specialist operator undertook such a study, in which the image of nine competitive operators was mapped along a two-dimensional matrix, as illustrated in Figure 2.3.

This exercise clearly reveals a gap in the market for mass market, culture-orientated long-haul holidays, which a new programme might be designed to fill. However, a word of warning is necessary in this exercise; it is possible that the product gap exists precisely because there is no demand for the product. Further research is needed to find

Figure 2.3
Product-
positioning
map, showing
perceived image
of long-haul
holidays offered
by nine
companies

Figure 2.4
BCG Growth-Share Matrix applied to a major tour operator's package tour programme

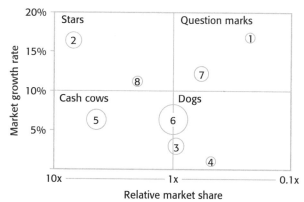

Key: 1 Long-haul holidays
2 Young people's holidays
3 Lakes and mountains holidays
4 Coaching holidays

5 Holidays for the elderly
6 Summer sun holidays
7 Winter sports holidays
8 Winter sun holidays

out if this is the case, or whether it is simply the case that the competition has not yet seen the marketing opportunities.

Where a larger company offers a range of products, each with its own market strengths, it is helpful to analyse this portfolio of products using a tool developed by the Boston Consultancy Group (BCG). The BCG Growth-Share Matrix enables the company to compare the performance of each of its products, allowing the company to identify what planning decisions must be made for each.

A typical BCG Matrix is shown in Figure 2.4. The eight circles represent the current sizes and market positions of each product marketed by a hypothetical tour operator. The size of each circle is proportional to the amount of revenue that the product range generates, while location in the matrix indicates the growth rate and share of the market compared to its leading competitor.

The vertical axis shows the rate of growth of the market in which the product is sold, while the horizontal axis represents the market share of the product compared with its major competitor. A market share of 0.1 would indicate that the company has only one-tenth of the market share of its leading rival, while a figure of 10 would reveal it has ten times its rival's share.

The matrix is divided into four cells. If the company had a product which is both a leader in the market and that market is expanding rapidly, the product is termed a *star*, since it offers the prospect of stable profitability (although not necessarily high profitability, since the company may be forced to defend itself against intense competition for such a lucrative market). *Question marks* offer the promise of success, since they are trading in high growth markets, and here the company's objective will be to seek a greater share of the market for such products. *Cash cows* identify products which have a large market share, but in a declining or low growth market. Their benefit is that they can often prove highly profitable in terms of cash flow to cover the company's operating expenses, since competition will be less fierce, and hence marketing costs less. Finally, *dogs* are weak both in market share and growth rate, and unless the company has some expectation of gaining greater market share or of seeing an expansion in the market growth, it will gain little from pumping additional resources into marketing the product. Planning for each of these products will therefore entail policies of either building up the product to increase market share or sales, fighting to hold the present market share, milking the product for its immediate cash returns, or retreating from the market altogether. If, in the situation explored here, the tour operator sees itself in danger of losing market share to its rivals, it can choose to increase its sales effort, to improve the product in some way, or to find ways of reducing its prices to make it more competitive. These are vital marketing decisions which will form the linchpin of the marketing plan.

Each sector of the tourism industry must make its own decision on which strategy to adopt, as there are common factors affecting the sector, as well as each individual company. While we have looked at travel agencies and operators in these examples, transport companies, resort destinations and tourist attractions each have other factors to take into consideration. If one looks at the airline industry, for example, one sees decisions being taken principally on price and, as an outcome of that decision, targeted markets. The most notable phenomenon in airline marketing in the early twenty-first century has been the success of the low-cost airlines and the decline of the prestigious carriers. Budget airlines have reduced their costs to a minimum by reducing their levels of service and fringe benefits, concentrating on low-cost airports, and have therefore been able to reduce prices to a fraction of those of the well-established carriers. British Airways, on the other hand, decided first to reduce its dependency on the economy market and aim at the premium (essentially business) passenger, at a time when this market was itself looking for ways of cutting costs. It had to backtrack rapidly in the face of the continuing success of the budget airlines (according to the CAA, over 60 per cent of passengers flying between Luton and Glasgow on the easyJet service in 2001 were business passengers).

Destinations which have adopted an 'Identikit' image, such as many of the Mediterranean resorts, are closely tied to pricing for their success. If their costs rise, forcing price increases, the market simply moves on. Only those destinations where the product is clearly differentiated can hope to continue to attract markets in line with rising costs – although even here there are dangers of losing significant market share if costs spiral. This is evident in London, which in spite of its unique attractions was beginning to price itself out of international markets in the early years of the twenty-first century. Lack of budget hotels, high food and shop prices and an inadequate but expensive transport system encouraged many tourists from abroad to seek other major European capitals for their short city breaks.

Collaborative marketing

Yet another feature of contemporary marketing in the tourism industry is the trend to collaboration between organisations in order to cut marketing costs while reaching wider audiences more effectively. This cooperation extends to public–private partnerships, a notable feature in North American, British and Continental European tourism marketing in recent years. This can involve a public, or quasi-autonomous public, body such as a regional or local tourist board forming a partnership with a private concern such as a hotel chain. Theoretically, this offers the public body the opportunity to attract marketing expertise and capital from the private sector, although the different interests and ambitions of the partners often result in a less than harmonious relationship. A good example of collaborative marketing is shown below.

Example   The Mekong World Heritage Tour

In 2002 Bangkok Airways introduced a new World Heritage Network tour to encourage visitors to UNESCO World Heritage sites in Thailand, Laos, Vietnam and Cambodia. The eight-day, seven-night package included visits to Sukhothai (700-year-old former Thai state capital), Luang Prabang (capital of the Lan Xang kingdom around the same period), Hué (via Danang, and early seat of the Nguyen dynasty) and Siem Reap, gateway to the Angkor Wat temples. The programme was compiled and promoted with the cooperation of three private operators, Diethelm Travel, Indochina Services and Pink Rose Holidays, and was launched through an educational press trip for travel journalists, supported by the Tourism Authority of Thailand, Bangkok Airways and Siem Reap Airways International.

Cities which are geographically close and can offer compatible attractions have also learnt to cooperate to reach a wider audience, through so-called 'cluster marketing'. Examples include Williamsburg–Jamestown–Yorktown which share a common heritage in the United States, and Liège–Aachen–Maastricht, an international triangle of cities close to the borders of Belgium, Germany and the Netherlands.

Affinity marketing can also include joint promotions between two companies whose markets share common characteristics but whose products are unconnected and uncompetitive. This can also reduce marketing costs while increasing awareness of both companies' products. Sometimes, however, such promotion can backfire spectacularly.

Example   The Hoover promotion

A joint travel promotion between Hoover and Your Leisure in 1992 offered two air tickets to the USA for those purchasing a vacuum cleaner for a minimum of £100. Unfortunately, the offer was so successful that Hoover could not keep up with demand, and both companies received very bad publicity.

Forecasting

'Monkeys are often more accurate than me' – Jamie Rollo, Vice-President, Morgan Stanley, on forecasting performance of his business.

As well as measuring where it is at the moment, a company must also determine where it is going, and where it will be at any given point in the future, following the execution of the marketing plan. A forecast is prepared to reflect the anticipated results, with projected sales, profitability and cash flow. In turn, the forecast will influence future marketing plans. If sales are forecast to fall by 10 per cent in the following year, due for example to a fall in visitors to the UK, it will be the marketing department's task to consider ways in which the shortfall can be made up through new product development, increased promotional activity or whatever other means the department can devise.

Unfortunately, forecasting is a notoriously unreliable science. The sheer number of different factors which influence the flow of international tourism makes it difficult to create an economic model that will permit accurate forecasts to be made. The volatile nature of tourism means that unforeseen events can overtake projected forecasts (particularly those longer than one year into the future).

Marketing plans will usually include short-term forecasts (between three and six months) and medium-term to longer-term forecasts of expected performance. The former can make use of simple statistical principles to project sales, and will be useful in making day-to-day tactical marketing decisions (reduction of prices for late bookings of package holidays is a typical example). Longer forecasts will tend to be more subjective, drawing on a wider selection of forecasting techniques, and will be used as an aid in strategic marketing decisions, such as new product development. The long-term forecast will help to pinpoint changing trends in travel, enabling a company to take advance action if one particular destination appears to be in decline, so that a new product can be developed to fill the gap. Public sector bodies in tourism tend to take forecasting more seriously than the private sector, and forecasts are used to underpin government or local authority development policies in order to aid regional development and employment opportunities. In the private sector, demand for overseas holidays has been consistently overestimated in recent years, leading to massive overcapacity and subsequent heavy discounting to offload surplus stock (although to some extent this was accounted for by the desire of the largest companies to achieve greater market share). Forecasting for the most part remains a process of 'educated guesswork' among travel companies, few of which employ methods that go beyond simple statistical extrapolation of existing trends.

If forecasting is to be of any value, it must be undertaken systematically, and be made subject to continual revision in the light of changing circumstances. Even allowing for typical margins of error that occur with most forecasts, the process is deemed an improvement over the 'gut feel' method of operation employed by most travel firms. Not all the methods discussed here will be appropriate for SMEs, since they can be expensive and time-consuming to introduce; but the simpler ones are easy to incorporate into marketing plans of any sized company.

Demand

Obviously, the basis of any forecast will be the measurement of existing market demand – anticipated sales of holidays, visits, or whatever the organisation presently offers. This can be relatively easily refined by breaking the figures down by geographical region or market sector. Estimates then must be made of the total market for the product sold (including that share sold by competitors), and the proportion of the total market the company expects to attract.

Let us take the example of a tour operator who deals exclusively in medium-priced holidays from one particular regional airport. In order to forecast demand, the operator must know or estimate:

- the number of people living in the catchment area of the airport, i.e. within a reasonable travel time compared with other airports that could be used
- the proportion of these likely to take package holidays abroad
- how many of these are likely to take a holiday at the price, and to the destinations, provided for in the company's programme.

There is of course a trade-off to be estimated here, as to the willingness of consumers to pay more for the convenience of flying from a regional airport compared with the lower-priced package tours available from airports centred around the country's major hubs. This figure will represent the served market. The company must finally determine:

- the proportion of those willing to buy the company's packages compared with those of competitors offering flights to the same destinations from the same airport.

This final figure will represent the sales potential for holidays.

Sales

Forecasting should be taken at three levels:

1   Environmental forecasts, which take into account the uncontrollable factors – economic, political, etc. – which affect travel generally. This will integrate economic growth forecasts, expectations of changes in exchange rates, growth in leisure time and discretionary incomes, the propensity to spend discretionary income on holidays, and comparative studies of inflation rates in different countries. We can refer to such forecasts as macro-studies.

2   Industry forecasts, which take into account levels of competition and profitability in the travel industry, legislation affecting the industry, and other factors within the business but outside the control of the company.

3   Company forecasts, in which the firm projects its own expectations of sales based on controllable and uncontrollable factors operating within the company.

Figure 2.5
Forecast of future performance based on the marketing plan

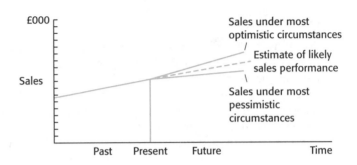

All forecasts will be prepared on the basis of an assumed set of circumstances. However, it is also helpful to include forecasts which examine performance based on the most pessimistic view of future events and the most optimistic view. This will allow for a mid-range of the 'most likely' result, as demonstrated in Figure 2.5.

Trends in sales

Most short- to medium-term forecasts are based on the use of statistical methods to extrapolate trends from sales occurring in the past. *Time series analysis*, which smooths out the effects of seasonal or cyclical variation in sales, will be commonly used to project travel sales. Sales may be projected either as a *linear* trend (as in Figure 2.5) or as an *exponential* trend, in which sales are expected to multiply at a constant rate, giving a steady upward curve.

More complicated forecasting methods will take into account a variety of variables to build economic models which are beyond the means of most travel firms, who tend to fall back on *assumptive forecasting*, that is, forecasts developed through a process of making assumptions of what people think will happen. If these assumptions are based on one person's expectations, they are unlikely to provide much degree of accuracy, but if they are refined through a process of integrating many individual views within and outside the company, this will improve their accuracy. Interviews with a cross-section of senior staff within the firm, coupled with trade opinions, the views of sales staff closest to the market, and views of the travel 'pontiffs' can all help to refine forecasts. It should be remembered, though, that sales staff will be inclined to conservatism in their projections if their sales targets are to be tied to forecasts.

Refinements on assumptive forecasting include the *Delphi forecast*, which asks for independent assessments to be made by senior staff, with justifications for their figures. Staff are then shown the forecasts of their colleagues, and asked to refine their own forecasts on the basis of this new knowledge. In this way a more considered view is obtained.

Intention-to-buy surveys, such as those which have in the past been undertaken by the English Tourist Board (a forerunner of VisitEngland, the national tourism organisation), are helpful as indicators for short-term trends. Random surveys ask such questions as:

How likely are you to take a holiday abroad this year?

definitely	very likely	quite likely	quite unlikely	very unlikely	definitely not
☐	☐	☐	☐	☐	☐

Earlier in the chapter, reference was made to the greater use of forecasting within the public sector. Many of these forecasts can also be helpful to private sector companies undertaking feasibility studies for the introduction of new products. Let us take a hypothetical example of how a forecast of future tourism flows can assist the planning for new hotels in a region.

Let us say the region currently welcomes some 1.5 million staying visitors a year, and forecasts suggest that this will increase to about 3 million over the next five years. What hotel provision is needed to cater to this influx? The planners will need to know:

■ average length of stay of tourists

■ the proportion of visitors staying in hotels

■ the distribution of visitors over the months of the year

■ average hotel occupancy anticipated.

These figures may have to be refined to take into account different rates of increase between business and holiday visitors, different average lengths of stay between these two markets, etc., but for simplicity's sake, let us use the following figures:

average length of stay: 14 nights
60% of visitors stay in the four months of summer
50% of visitors stay in hotels
50% of visitors require double rooms, 50% single rooms
planned high season occupancy rate will be 90%

The increase in visitors of 1.5 million will require 1.5 million × 14 nights = 21 million bed nights. Assuming that accommodation will be planned to satisfy average demand over the peak period, that is, 15 per cent over each of the four summer months, this would require 3 150 000 bed nights if everyone stayed at hotels (15 per cent × 21 million). But only 50 per cent stay in hotels, therefore we need 1 575 000 bed nights. At an average of 30.5 days in the month, the daily bed night increase required will be

$$\frac{1\,575\,000}{30.5} = \text{approx. } 51\,640$$

If occupancy of these rooms is to be planned at 90 per cent, we shall require 10 per cent more rooms, i.e. 56 804 rooms. Assuming room demand is for 50 per cent doubles, every 100 visitors will require 75 rooms. The region will therefore require another 42 603 rooms within the next five years.

It must be recognised that forecasts are dynamic in nature. If an organisation merely extrapolates its existing sales, rather than planning to achieve a certain level of sales, the result may be a decline in sales growth due to the greater marketing activity of its competitors. Forecasts must be based on what the organisation expects to happen as a result of its marketing plan, as well as what is expected to happen as a result of changes in the environment within which the company operates.

New product development

Based on the overall strategic direction planned by the company and assisted by forecasts of future demand, the marketer can begin to evaluate new product development necessary to meet the overall marketing objectives.

A case study will illustrate the planning process whereby a major tour operator identified the opportunity to introduce a new destination. This operator had already identified a marketing objective: to improve its position in the summer long-haul market.

A tour operator's new destination development

Initially, office-based analysis was carried out on information available from research and forecasts, travel agent feedback and competitor brochures. This analysis identified the following:

- the operator had fallen behind in market share in long haul, compared with competitors' performance
- the operator's current long-haul offering concentrated on Florida, whose market share had shrunk from 55 to 38 per cent
- all-inclusive holidays had grown rapidly in the long-haul marketplace, albeit most destinations of this type were located in the Caribbean; recorded volumes had increased by up to 44 per cent
- Central/South America was one of the operator's fastest growing destinations and an area where it scored over the competition
- all-inclusive prices in Central/South America were highly competitive when compared with the Caribbean
- opportunities existed for the operator to build upon the experience and buying power of its North American outlet, which already featured resorts in Mexico, many of which were unknown to the UK marketplace
- new free trade agreements between Mexico and the United States promised large future investment in the Mexican tourist infrastructure.

Based upon this initial analysis, the operator decided to carry out further detailed planning to determine the feasibility of introducing such a new resort. This plan was compiled following resort visits to Mexico and further discussion with travel agent contacts, the North American operation, hoteliers and airlines. This resulted in a much more detailed feasibility document recommending the specific resort of Puerto Vallarta. The report contained detailed information on:

- the resort and bed stock available
- quality, service levels and facilities available (star rating, beachfront positions, etc.)
- cost, route, flight times and departure dates that could be negotiated with carriers
- potential for the tour operator's different brands to exploit the resort in different ways (children's facilities for the family brand, five-star hotel accommodation for the premium brand, etc.)
- promotional opportunities, including joint advertising with the Mexican Tourist Board
- recommended pricing and margin structure
- projected sales volume and profit forecast.

It is interesting to see how the planning process never ceases. After the successful introduction of Puerto Vallarta, the new product development team went on to assess the viability of a separate 'all inclusive' programme of holidays to be launched in a new brochure for the summer season 12 months ahead.

Setting the marketing budget

The establishment of an overall budget for marketing will be part of the corporate financial planning process, but should represent the outcome of negotiation between the head of the marketing department and other planning executives. These budgets are generally based on estimates of sales revenue and cash flow for the coming year, and introduce a measure of control over cash flow expenditure during the year. The budget determines both the resourcing of the department (including staff) and promotional expenditure.

How this figure is to be calculated is one of the most difficult decisions in corporate planning. Often budgets are determined, particularly in the case of smaller companies, by no more sophisticated methods than some arbitrary decision on 'what the company can afford'. Alternatively, a rule of thumb is applied, such as the allocation of some percentage of the previous year's revenue, or a percentage of next year's expected revenue. However, in both these cases, what the company is suggesting in effect is that the marketing budget should be the outcome of sales, rather than determining what those sales should be. In other instances, companies attempt to estimate what their main competitors are spending on promotion, and match this sum. It is by no means clear why a competitor should be judged better at determining what should be spent on promotion, but in any case, a rival firm is likely to have very different resources and objectives, which will require different budgetary considerations. A more logical approach to budget setting is an attempt to relate that budget to the objectives that the company intends to achieve. If, for example, the objective is to increase the company's market share by, say, 2 per cent, it is the marketing manager's responsibility to estimate what needs to be spent, and how, in order to achieve this. While it is never easy to forecast revenue based on a given expenditure, this approach is certainly more scientific than the kind of guesswork which more usually takes place in travel companies, and it has the advantage of forcing the marketing manager to consider the relationship between expenditure and sales, through the appraisal of alternative promotional strategies.

One other important consideration is the need to recognise the relationship between profits, as opposed to sales, and the promotional budget. An airline could be expecting to sell 65 per cent of its capacity in the coming year with its present marketing strategies. Assuming its prices are set to enable the airline to break even with a load factor of 60 per cent, this will enable it to make an operating profit on the other 5 per cent sold. However, airlines have very high fixed costs, so that the cost of carrying another 10 or 20 per cent is very small – a few extra meals, a little extra fuel. If an extra market can be attracted, this would represent almost pure profit, and the company would be justified in spending a very considerable proportion of the profit on marketing to attract those other customers, provided it could be reassured that it would not dilute sales to present customers as a result.

Organising for effective marketing

No marketing plan will be effective unless the organisation is equipped to achieve its objectives. In marketing terms, this means that the company as a whole develops a marketing-orientated approach, with staff sharing common aims and the will to achieve those aims.

Marketing is not just 'something which the marketing department does'. Its philosophy should permeate the whole organisation. Many companies pay lip-service to marketing, but remain production orientated, concerned principally with finding ways to utilise surplus capacity rather than tackling the question of what the customer really wants.

At board level in large companies, it is common for marketing to be thought of in terms of sales and promotion activities, rather than the guiding philosophy of the company. Clashes occur between the marketing department and its operations staff, or financial controllers (how often does a company, faced with a decline in sales, take measures to cut back marketing expenditure instead of expanding it?) Chief executives who are sympathetic to the marketing concept can play a major role in coordinating a common set of marketing goals for their company. However, according to the Chartered Institute of Marketing, only 20 per cent of UK companies have a marketer at board level. This compares with over 25 per cent who have a background in finance. Moreover, fewer than 15 per cent of FTSE 100 companies in Britain have a chief executive with some background in marketing. Cynicism towards marketing appears to be based largely on the fact that so little of what marketers actually do can be quantified and measured. Everyone recognises, for instance, the importance of the brand name and the public perception of its image, but *measuring* the value of this – or the extent to which the marketing team have contributed to it – is another matter.

Within the marketing department itself, staff must be equipped to function effectively. This means effective organisation of staff. Many small travel companies, of course, must function with very few staff, and marketing, such as it is, will be undertaken by the proprietor or managing director, as a part of the general duties of management. While this has the advantage of reducing problems of communications, it does not in itself guarantee more effective marketing. Larger organisations, however, will be likely to employ specialist staff with marketing responsibility, and will have to decide how to organise this staff best for the achievement of their aims.

Should the company be sufficiently large to afford a marketing department, this can be organised in one of four ways:

■ by marketing function

■ by the geography of the marketplace

■ according to the range of products and brands

■ according to markets served.

We shall look at each of these in turn.

Functional organisation

Perhaps the most traditional way of organising a department is to give staff individual responsibility for one or more of the marketing functions. Marketing entails a great many functions, and in an organisation such as a major tour operator, we may find the marketing organisation chart looking like Figure 2.6.

This form of organisation has the advantage that each functional manager can concentrate on one specific area of marketing expertise, under the overall control of a single marketing manager or director who coordinates and controls their activities.

Some functionally organised departments are split, with sales and marketing each having independent executives. This arrangement does seem to run counter to the concept of sales as a function of marketing, but it has worked successfully in some major travel companies, and can function well enough if there are good communications, cooperation and goodwill between the respective managers.

When Owners Abroad restructured to become First Choice Holidays, the sales and marketing functions were brought together under the commercial director. The commercial director also controls the research and new product development department

Figure 2.6
Possible organisation of a tour operator's marketing department

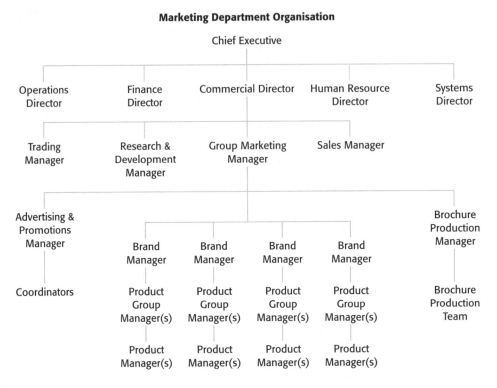

Figure 2.7
The organisation
of a major
overseas holiday
company

and the day-to-day trading function of flights, beds and inventory management. Thus the senior management team provide a focused, all-round commercial view with marketing playing a significant and integrated role.

The marketing department itself separates brand management and brochure production more clearly than many tour operators. This reflects a determination to allow a focus on true brand and marketing issues removed from the actual production of the product. Brand managers are responsible for both summer and winter seasons to ensure that brand values are upheld consistently year round. Marketing also includes the specialist advertising and promotions function, ensuring a close liaison with brand managers, yet a coherent advertising strategy for the whole company (see Figure 2.7).

Geographic organisation

Companies with very large national or international markets may prefer to organise their marketing functions by geographic area. This is particularly useful where the nature of those markets differs greatly, as for example is the case with many travel firms selling to both home (domestic) and overseas (export) markets. A company such as TUI, which sells its holidays in a number of European countries, will necessarily undertake some, if not all, of its marketing functions separately, with different marketing staff in each country.

Hotel chains take a number of different approaches to the problem, in some cases directing most of their marketing effort from a corporate marketing headquarters in the parent company's head office, with only local sales functions in the hands of marketing staff in each individual hotel, while in other cases chains have decentralised their marketing responsibilities by country or region. The latter arrangement allows a greater measure of response to local market conditions, although naturally it loses some of the benefits of economies of scale and requires larger numbers of staff. According to market conditions, objectives are also likely to vary considerably from one country to another, requiring distinct marketing plans to be developed in each region, although these may be coordinated through head office. Regional organisation of this kind can, of course, be further subdivided along functional lines as described earlier.

Product and brand organisation

Where a company produces a variety of different products or brands, it can prove advantageous to provide separate marketing expertise for each. This is apparent in the organisation chart of a major holiday company, in which separate marketing staff are responsible for distinct package holiday programmes. In a large hotel, the banqueting manager is often made responsible for the marketing of catering functions which exclude accommodation services, while the sales manager is responsible for convention and tour sales, and the front office manager for individual transient sales (mail, telephone and personal) and all reservations.

Where companies market their products under quite distinct brand names, the marketing may be organised quite separately for each brand. A company such as Bourne Leisure, with diverse travel interests which include Butlin's, Haven Holidays and Warner Holidays, may find it beneficial to appoint separate marketing staff for each, as long as it is intended to retain distinct identities for the brands. Again, the functional breakdown within the marketing departments is possible.

In practice, product managers often have less autonomy than do marketing managers, but they can control strategies for the marketing of their own product lines, and therefore can react quickly to changes in demand or other circumstances affecting their markets.

Market organisation

Finally, instead of brand or product divisions, it is possible to organise marketing according to the markets served. Hotels, for instance, may separate marketing by business and leisure guests, since the nature of demand is clearly different in each case, and the strategies designed to attract guests will differ in each case as well. This can be further organised according to functional or geographical divisions of responsibility.

It is important to recognise that there are no right or wrong ways to structure marketing departments. Each firm must develop the structure that meets its needs best, and this can often only be assessed in the long term after experimentation. Needs will change over time, too, so that what works best for a company today will not necessarily suffice as the company grows, or diversifies its product range.

The marketing mix

The concept of the marketing mix is one of the most important in marketing – indeed, it can be called the core of all marketing planning. It determines how the marketing budget is allocated, forms the foundation of the marketing plan's strategy, and provides the marketing manager with the techniques to optimise budgetary expenditure.

The marketing mix is defined by Kotler *et al.*[1] as:

> The set of controllable tactical marketing tools that the firm blends to produce the response it wants in the target market.

These so-called 'tools' are numerous, but are traditionally grouped together into four groups of variables, popularly referred to as the four Ps – product, price, place and promotion. Figure 2.8 lists these in more detail.

In the case of tourism, each of these tools is quite complex to describe. The product is what is actually delivered to the consumer, and will be composed of both tangible and intangible elements. For example, the consumer will be buying the use of a room in a hotel as part of their package, and this will include various facilities including a bed (whose comfort is all-important), a bathroom, perhaps a balcony or terrace, coffee-making equipment, etc. The guest may also choose to eat in the hotel's restaurant, so food is another key tangible component of this experience. However, there are intangible elements in each hotel which add to the satisfaction of the experience – the hotel

Figure 2.8
The traditional four Ps of the marketing mix

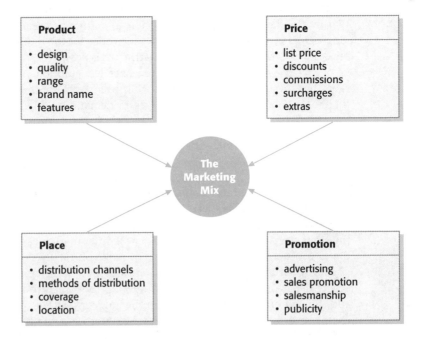

room may include a sea view (an intangible asset that is seen as such a bonus that a higher price is usually charged for this), the ambience of the public rooms may meet a guest's individual needs for status-building or relaxation, or the room may be decorated in a way which enhances their satisfaction. The professional manner in which the front of house staff deal with the incoming guest, and the service received from waiters in the restaurant, are intangible benefits which are every bit as important as the rooms and food.

Price refers to the amount of money eventually paid for the product or service by the consumer. In the case of tourism, price is often variable, and negotiable, as we shall see, with the consumer seeking to obtain best value for money between a range of competitive products on offer. Product and price are inextricably interconnected, together representing the 'bundle of benefits' which the consumer purchases. From the standpoint of the producers, or principals, price is the figure at which they are prepared to make the product available to the consumer, taking into account cost, market conditions and other factors such as sales targets.

Place is a controversial variable in considering the tourism product. In general marketing theory it represents the point of sale, i.e. the place where the product can be inspected and purchased, and the means by which it is delivered to the consumer. Some tourism marketing theorists argue that place also refers to the destination of the tourist, but this is to confuse the concept, since in that sense place is clearly the *product* purchased by the consumer. It seems logical for the sake of clarity to retain these distinctions, and in this text place will be defined only in terms of the channels of distribution of the product. Traditionally, tourism products would be purchased through travel agents or through the outlets of travel principals, but in recent years the advent of new forms of delivery system, particularly in the use of computer technology, has vastly expanded the choice in delivery systems for tourists, as we shall see.

Finally, promotion is concerned with the techniques by which products and their prices are communicated to the marketplace. This includes advertising, sales promotion techniques, public relations activities, direct selling and the use of more recent forms of reaching the customer through ICT (information and communications technology). It will be readily apparent to the reader that there are overlaps in these concepts, given that both place and promotion involve communicating and delivering messages about products to the consumer, but perhaps if we accept that the former refers to the process by which the product is presented, and the latter to the techniques of persuasion to buy the product, the distinction between these concepts will be clearer.

In common with the view taken today that all marketing should be approached from the perspective of the consumer's interests, we can see that these four Ps relate to the consumer's demand to know what benefits can be expected from purchasing the product or service, how much must be paid for it, how information can be obtained about it and where and when it can be bought.

While the marketing of goods is still based on these four variables, in the case of services (and particularly tourism), some marketers[2] have argued that a further three, or even four, Ps should be added to the original list: those of **people**, of **process**, of **physical evidence** and of **productivity and quality**. It is debatable whether the theory is enhanced by these additions, given that each can be subsumed under one of the four traditional Ps. However, the additions do give emphasis to the importance of these elements, and for this reason will merit inclusion in this chapter.

The inclusion of people adds emphasis to the fact that these are a vital component of the product benefits. First, tourism is a service product, and employees are therefore an integral part of that service – whether we speak of the travel agent selling the package behind the counter, the resort representative aiding customers in their chosen resort, the air cabin crew caring for their passengers en route to the destination, front of house staff in the hotel where the customers are staying, or the local guide interpreting sites on excursions at the destination. Arguably, no other service depends as much for its satisfaction on the quality of personal service provided by so many different human participants in the package. There are also others who form a critical component of the package. Fellow travellers are critical to the experience of travel, and if one considers, say, a small long-haul tour group comprising around a dozen people travelling together for two weeks or longer, the interrelationships between these are crucial for the success of the experience. Similarly, tourists come into contact, to a greater or lesser extent, with members of the host community, and these local interrelations form another key element of the experience. These interrelations may be limited to commercial contacts with shopkeepers, guides, restaurant and bar staff, etc., as is often the case with mass-market package tours (especially of the all-inclusive variety), but independent travellers may enjoy more personal contacts with locals, through discussions on public transport, in bars, cafés and the like. While arguably all of these people form part of the product within the marketing mix, it helps to emphasise their importance by treating them as a distinct element in the mix.

Process as a distinct element in marketing is more controversial. Middleton[3] focuses on the *service delivery* process in defining this, and in particular considers *service recovery* as the critical issue in the marketing process. By these two terms, he means the various encounters between the tourist and representatives of the principal, and in particular the 'critical incidents' in such encounters which ensure satisfaction. The ability of employees to turn round a negative experience by appropriate handling, and to deal with complaints as they arise, is crucial in such encounters. Tourists find themselves in unfamiliar situations where they will need help more frequently than is likely to be the case on their home grounds, and the ability of staff to step in and ease this process is immensely important for overall satisfaction. To illustrate this, one might consider the uncertainty about whether or not to tip in foreign settings, the problems facing the confused tourist at a congested airport or what is the required protocol for purchasing a ticket on a foreign bus or underground railway (often a surprisingly complex process for foreigners, involving cancelling the ticket in a machine when boarding the vehicle, within a given period of time, etc.). The clarity with which this information is imparted and the help given to resolve this complexity by locals will be a significant factor in the overall satisfaction levels of the tourist.

Example[4]

The guide stations himself at the foot of the steps [of the bus] to say goodbye . . . meanwhile, ***** [a passenger] holds back with his wife, clearly distressed about whether to tip or not. He leans over the seat to look out of the window and observe the guide. 'I don't think they are . . . yes, they ARE!' He walks confidently to the front of the coach to say farewell to the guide.

Physical evidence involves all of the cues received by the tourist experiencing their flight, package or other service, based on sight, sound, smell, touch and taste. One might cite elements of the package embracing the design of buildings, the taste of a meal, the sound of taped music in a hotel lift – all without doubt elements of the product but ones which it is difficult to quantify to customers in advance. All are nevertheless features subtly designed by the marketing team to enhance the experience of their customers. Once again, one could argue that these are all components which should rightly be incorporated into the product element of the mix, but because in many cases they are almost indefinable (and for the most part would not in any case be communicated by the seller in advance of the experience itself) there is an argument favouring this as yet another unique component of the marketing mix for tourism products.

Finally, the inclusion of productivity and quality as separate elements of the mix by some marketing theorists emphasises the manner in which inputs are transformed into outputs that are valued by customers, and successfully meet their needs, wants and expectations. Identifying this as a separate issue reinforces the importance of monitoring costs to find ways in which products can be delivered to customers more cheaply, without reducing the quality which customers rightly expect from the product.

The variety of ways in which a marketing manager can decide to distribute the budget between these multiple tools is almost infinite. Furthermore, expenditure on some tools can be changed at very short notice (promotion, price), while others (new product development, channels of distribution) are likely to take much longer to alter.

A tour operator's marketing plan

Once again, using our hypothetical tour operator as an example, let us think through a set of possible strategies which the marketing manager may adopt as the basis for the new marketing plan. Within the *product* category, the manager may choose to focus on two new destinations to be added to the summer sun programme, and to change some of the hotels used currently in the programme in order to provide a better overall standard of product and push the programme

▶

upmarket slightly. For the winter programme, two hotels owned by the company in Fuengirola are to be marketed in holiday packages for elderly people, and all holiday packages henceforth are to include a cocktail welcome party on the first night. Under *pricing*, the operator will offer a 'no surcharge' guarantee for all holidays booked and paid for prior to 30 April, agrees new extended payment terms for holidays in a new credit scheme, and introduces for the first time reductions of 30 per cent for children on all holidays booked for the first week of September onwards. Under the category of *place*, the operator decides to encourage more direct sell through a newly established Internet website, setting a target of 20 per cent direct bookings for next summer's packages, while simultaneously still providing extra support for key agents. Agency sales calls are to be reduced, and the company's representatives will no longer call on agents providing fewer than 10 bookings in any one year. Finally, under *promotion*, the operator allocates $1.5 million from the budget to be spent on selective television and national press advertising campaigns, and introduces a cooperative advertising scheme with travel agents, whereby it is agreed to pay 50 per cent towards the cost of joint advertising in local papers. Two hundred selected agents are to be taken on educational study trips to the company's recently launched destinations, and 20 travel writers and journalists will be invited on another educational visit to the company's resorts in southern Spain.

These ideas are designed only to indicate the diversity of decisions facing an operator when drawing up a marketing plan for the year. In practice, a much wider range of decisions will have to be made, outlining both the strategy to be adopted and the tactics that will be employed to help achieve the plan's objectives. These issues will be examined at greater length in subsequent chapters.

Controlling the marketing plan

Any plan which a company introduces must be subject to control. In order to do so, the marketing plan must be clear in its objectives, with each objective quantified and measurable. Control will be required over budget expenditure, and the performance of each element in the plan should be continually monitored to ensure the plan is on target. Any deviations from the plan will require action to improve performance, or to consider alternative means of reaching objectives.

Ways in which control is exercised over a firm's marketing activities will be detailed in Chapter 15, and therefore will not need to be further examined in this chapter. However, it should be stressed above all that a marketing plan is dynamic by nature; it is not a set of bureaucratic rules to be followed faithfully for the duration of the plan, but rather a fluid set of guidelines for action that will require constant updating in the light of changing circumstances.

Questions, tasks and issues for discussion

1　The Belgian National Tourism Office recently split into two bodies, Tourism Flanders-Brussels and Brussels-Ardennes. It was claimed that this enabled the two bodies to focus more easily on different aspects of their country. Flanders offers historic cities (Bruges, Antwerp, Ghent) and the coast, while southern Belgium includes the Ardennes countryside. One of the BNTO directors claimed that it had become increasingly difficult to adopt a single marketing approach for such diversity, while the Ardennes region felt it was insufficiently known and promoted as a tourism destination abroad. The importance of Brussels as the capital city necessitated this city being represented by both bodies. An industry marketing manager criticised the move. 'I don't think the split will help consumers' understanding of the country. Belgium is too small to be chopped up into bits and pieces.'

　　Is this no more than a political decision enforced by the Flemish–Walloon cultural and language split within the country, or does it offer genuine opportunities for effective marketing?

2　A mini case study in this chapter referred to the obvious embarrassment and uncertainty experienced by an excursion passenger regarding the need to tip the guide. Taking into account the concept of service delivery and recovery, how would you, in the role of a guide, pre-empt this embarrassment, without personally embarrassing yourself (and your company) by making clear the expectation of a tip? Discuss the issue of tipping, and whether tips should be more usefully integrated into the cost structures of travel experiences to avoid such uncertainties.

3　The case of Ryanair:

Generally speaking, we won't take any phone calls . . . because they [the passengers] keep you on the bloody phone all day.

Michael O'Leary, CEO Ryanair, discussing complaints handling, quoted in *The Times*, 5 January 2002

Ryanair presents an example of a company apparently ignoring all the recognised theories about good marketing. What elements of the marketing mix discussed in this chapter are clearly being overlooked here?

　　Ryanair has often been hailed in the national press as an example of bad service in the travel industry. The press has accused the company of infringing safety regulations, and the company attacked a whistle-blowing report on their services by CHIRP (Confidential Human Factors Incident Reporting Programme) which had claimed the airline's pilots were cutting corners due to pressure to meet schedules. The airline had a history of lost bags, delays and weak customer service, and on one occasion referred to the AUC (Air Transport Users' Council, whose role is to protect air passengers' interests) as 'a bunch of halfwits'.

　　Yet for all these apparent weaknesses, Ryanair appeared stronger than ever in 2003, based on a total focus on low prices to attract passengers away from premium brand airlines. To what extent can such single-minded commitment to one factor in the marketing mix ensure long-term success? (Compare with comments made in Chapter 4 on the role of CRM.)

　　(Footnote: Ryanair appear to be learning the lesson, as this text goes to print. Early in 2003 the company expanded its staff, creating more check-in counters to reduce queueing and employing more staff to handle compaints in its Customer Care Department.)

4　Suggest some of the ways in which a new budget airline might 'differentiate' its product, or corporate identity, from those of its competitors.

5　Draft another two-dimensional matrix similar to that in Figure 2.3, using different variables of your own choice, which another tourism sector (e.g. a hotel) might use to discover marketing gaps.

Exercise

You have been employed as research assistant for a local tourist attraction (you may choose an appropriate attraction near you). Your manager has asked you to carry out a SWOT analysis of the attraction as a prelude to the new marketing plan she is developing. Undertake the research (using both primary and secondary research methods – see Chapter 3), and write a memorandum to your manager containing your SWOT analysis, and any suggestions you feel to be relevant and which will help your manager in her plans for the coming year.

References

1 Kotler, P, Armstrong, G, Saunders, J and Wong, V, *Principles of Marketing*, Prentice Hall, 3rd European edn 2001
2 See, for example, Lovelock, C, Vandermerwe, S and Lewis, B, *Services Marketing: a European Perspective*, Prentice Hall, 1999, pp 20–2
3 Middleton, VTC with Clarke, J, *Marketing in Travel and Tourism*, Butterworth Heinemann, 3rd edn 2001
4 Holloway, J C, The Guided Tour: a Sociological Approach, *Annals of Tourism Research*, vol viii no 3 1981, pp 377–402

Further reading

Adcock, D, Halborg, A and Ross, C, *Marketing Principles and Practice*, Prentice Hall, 4th edn 2001, ch 21 pp 401–24
Brassington, F and Pettitt, S, *Principles of Marketing*, Pitman, 2nd edn 2000, ch 21 pp 886–936
Frechtling, D, *Forecasting Tourist Demand: Methods and Strategies*, Butterworth Heinemann, 2001
Gunn, C and Var, T, *Tourism Planning: Basics, Concepts and Cases*, Routledge, 4th edn 2002
Heath, E and Wall, G, *Marketing Tourism Destinations: a Strategic Planning Approach*, Wiley, 1992
Horner, S and Swarbrooke, J, *Marketing Tourism Hospitality and Leisure in Europe*, International Thomson Business Press, 1996, part 4 pp 231–68
Vellas, F and Bécherel, L (eds), *The International Marketing of Travel and Tourism: a Strategic Approach*, Macmillan, 1999

3 Marketing research and its applications in tourism

Learning outcomes

After studying this chapter, you should be able to:

- understand the need for systematic, scientific research in an organisation
- describe a Marketing Information System and its elements
- plan a simple research programme, construct questionnaires and carry out surveys
- explain and evaluate different methods of gathering research information
- appreciate the ethical dimensions in carrying out research.

What is marketing research?

Marketing research can be defined as the planned, systematic collection, collation and analysis of data designed to help the management of an organisation to reach decisions, and to monitor the results of those decisions once taken. It embraces all forms of research undertaken to help the marketing of products, including product research, price research, distribution research, publicity research and consumer research. However, research into consumers and their patterns of behaviour is more commonly referred to as *market research* to distinguish it from the more all-embracing term of marketing research.

Research is closely linked to planning, in the sense that all companies need to know where they are now, before deciding where they want to be within a given period of time. Without knowing their present position, who their competitors are, how much share of the markets they have achieved, and what threats and opportunities they face in the coming months and years, no organisation can plan its future. To get this information requires research, some of which will be available from commercial or other sources, while much will not be readily available and may require the organisation to undertake its own research. Gathering research data is time consuming and expensive, but it should not be thought of only as the task of the largest businesses; SMEs, even the smallest companies, should still plan and act on the basis of reliable data rather than guesswork.

Research is designed to help an organisation to understand the nature of the marketplace in which it operates, to gain as comprehensive knowledge as is possible about its suppliers, wholesalers, retailers, competitors and customers.

We can start by categorising research into two forms: *descriptive research*, which can help us to gather factual data about what is happening in the marketplace, when it is happening, where it is happening, how it is happening and to whom; while *analytical research* attempts to explain the relationship between variables – in other words, to raise 'why?' questions, such as why some of these things are happening. However, we have to start by recognising that there is a real dearth of information readily available to those working in travel and tourism, and such information as is available is frequently imprecise or misleading. However, both forms of information have their place in helping to determine management strategy and tactics. It is still the case that most of the data available to the travel and tourism industry have focused on the descriptive – who goes where, when; market shares of the major companies; total sales in each category of travel – although there has been a growing awareness of the gaps in market knowledge concerning, for example, the nature and behaviour of the tourist.

In discussing research methods it is important to distinguish between quantitative and qualitative approaches. *Quantitative research* methods are those in which data are collected and subsequently analysed through a process sometimes mockingly referred to as 'bean-counting'. This normally involves the use of surveys with attendant questionnaires, although more rarely some forms of experimentation may be incorporated, using two groupings, one an experimental group where certain variables are manipulated to produce and measure change, the other a control group against which the results of the first group may be compared. The criterion for quantitative research is that all findings can be verified for accuracy through tests involving statistical probability. In general, such techniques are employed when what is required is a simple headcount or number count; for example, a firm may wish to know the numbers of people entering a particular attraction, the average spend in the shop or restaurant, or the percentage of people choosing to travel abroad independently rather than on inclusive tour arrangements. Hence we can say that most quantitative research is descriptive in nature, rather than analytical. More elaborate quantitative research may be undertaken to verify or refute a predetermined hypothesis, but in all cases the results should be both valid and reliable; that is, they should represent what they claim to represent, and if the research is replicated it should produce similar results.

Qualitative research, on the other hand, is designed to interpret data, rather than taking it as read. There are many points of distinction between the approaches of quantitative and qualitative research (see, for example, Daymon and Holloway[1] for a fuller treatment of these distinctions), but two critical distinctions are that this form of research tends to focus on the collection and interpretation of words rather than numbers, and that the researcher becomes personally engaged with the people being studied, rather than being deliberately remote from their informants. This engagement has much to do with the methods employed, which often involve in-depth interviewing or interpretative observation rather than surveys or structured interviews. The aim of such research is often to explore patterns of individual touristic behaviour, or the experiences or feelings tourists hold about an issue. Data collection and analysis proceed in parallel and interact, and because of the nature of the material gathered, results cannot be subjected to tests of statistical probability. For this reason, organisations have been less inclined in the past to sponsor such research, even though the evidence produced may well reveal much richer data than that obtained through a simple quantitative questionnaire. However, the results of in-depth research will often lead to opportunities to develop hypotheses which may be later subjected to testing through the use of more quantitative techniques.

Next, we must distinguish between primary and secondary research. Primary research involves commissioning or undertaking new research, while secondary research calls for a search of existing material to gather the data one requires. For examples of both, consider the case of a new tourist attraction planning to open in, say, south-eastern Spain. Secondary sources are likely to exist for information about the number and nature of tourists visiting the region, but to know something about demand for the particular attraction planned one would probably have to commission research, perhaps interviewing present tourists to the region to discover their attitudes to construction of a new attraction and the probability of their visiting it in the course of their holiday.

Research may also be categorised as either *ad hoc* (specific) or *ongoing* (continuous). Ad hoc research can be seen as a 'snapshot' taken at a particular moment in time, usually in the form of a survey commissioned to find answers to a specific question or set of questions. For example, an attraction may be trying to determine whether additional investment would best be spent on an extension to the catering facilities or an upgrading in the quality of the catering provided to reach a better market. As this involves a one-time decision, it would be appropriate to commission research at that point to aid decision-making. Ongoing research is designed to measure and monitor variables over time on a regular basis: for example, daily, weekly or monthly sales figures, patterns of demand for particular holidays and destinations, hotel bed-occupancy, etc. In this case, many data are already available within a company's computer systems and can easily be downloaded on a regular basis to assist monitoring. National tourism statistics are gathered on a regular basis through surveys carried out at airports and seaports.

Finally, one can make the distinction between omnibus and syndicated research. Many market research firms carry out omnibus national surveys on a regular basis, comprising an extensive set of questions commissioned from a wide variety of firms. A company which is interested in regularly monitoring its sales, or attitudes to its products, can append its own set of questions, paying fees for this service proportionate to the number of questions posed. This will, of course, be a far cheaper option than undertaking a similar wide-scale survey on its own. The results of these surveys are also made widely available to other non-participating organisations on subscription, and this can be a useful means for SMEs to gain knowledge about an industry or competitors without undertaking primary research at their own expense. Among those omnibus surveys which include travel-related questions the TGI (Target Group Index) Holidays and Travel surveys conducted periodically by BMRB (British Market Research Bureau) is among the best known in Britain, while Keynote Market Reports on the travel and tourism sectors and Mintel's Market Intelligence Reports which occasionally focus on these sectors can also provide valuable information. Syndicated research, on the other hand, describes research commissioned by a group of organisations who share the cost involved, and the full results of such research are not usually made known to outsiders.

Why marketing research?

One potential danger of focusing on the four Ps in marketing is that these omit a key element of the marketing role, on which every other marketing activity depends; the function of research. Unless we know what our customers want, we cannot be certain that the products we produce will appeal to them. If our sales are falling off, we have to know whether this is the result of a general economic malaise affecting all products, a problem specifically affecting the travel and tourism industry, or the result of clients switching their purchases to other travel products. In each case, we should have to devise a different marketing plan to respond to the challenge. Intelligence gathering is therefore a crucial precedent to planning.

Research has a place in the management of any company, however small. The belief, held by many independent travel agents and other small companies, that marketing research is a luxury affordable only by the larger travel corporations, is a dangerous fallacy. True, only the larger companies are likely to be able to buy in the expertise provided by research consultants, to commission, for instance, a survey of trends in travel purchasing. Summaries of such research are, however, often published in a variety of media available at the local library, a specialist travel library, or even from time to time in the travel trade press. Keeping up with these reports should be a part of the responsibilities of all travel managers who call themselves professional.

In the larger companies, formal intelligence-gathering techniques become essential, for two reasons. First, by its very nature the larger company has less opportunity for face-to-face contact with its customers; its feedback on changing consumer tastes and preferences has to be planned. Second, large businesses involve greater financial investment, which in turn means greater risk. Think of the investment an airline must make today to re-equip its fleet, with aircraft costing in excess of $100 million each. Consider the investment a hotel chain is making, when purchasing a new property in a large city.

The major tour operators are large spenders and sophisticated practitioners in marketing research. Their thirst for research information, both quantitative and qualitative, is driven by a number of factors:

1   All operators are watching their competitors very carefully indeed. They continually track the opposition's market share, advertising spend, product developments and image in the marketplace. The marketer is looking not just for chinks in the armour of competitors that can be exploited but also for a benchmark against which to measure their own company performance.

2   Consumer attitudes are continually changing and woe betide the marketer who misses out on these trends. For instance, recent research from a number of sources suggests that while sustainability in tourism was an issue of relatively little importance until late in the twentieth century, it has become of increasing concern for

the more sophisticated travellers of the twenty-first century. Travellers are asking more questions about sustainability and their tour operators' attitudes to the issue, and are apparently willing to pay more to ensure that this is taken into account by the operator of their choice.

3 Tour operators need to understand the process by which their product is selected and bought – and the role and impact of the travel agent intermediary. The retail outlets are having to adjust rapidly in the face of changing distribution patterns and the growing threat to traditional outlets posed by innovative ICT.

4 The dynamic nature of the market means that tour operators are continually investing in the 'new': new television advertising, new brochure design, new brands, new aircraft, new destinations and new forms of holidaymaking. These may reflect not only substantial investments in time and money but also a 'make or break' strategic decision for the company. Research is obviously essential to minimise risk.

What information do we need?

All organisations, regardless of size, need to know where they stand within the business environment. In the case of existing products, they need to know how many of each product they are selling; how sales are performing over time, and the forecast for future sales; how their products compare with those of the competitors, and the respective shares of the market held by their own company and their competitors. If a principal or tour operator is involved, they must monitor their distribution strategy, to determine what quantities of their products are being sold by each retailer and which of their retailing outlets are performing best. All companies need to know the effectiveness of their advertising and promotion campaigns. They should also know the profitability and contribution to overheads which each product makes. They must fully understand the customer: who buys what, when, where and why.

Where new products are planned, the company must research the market opportunities, test new product concepts on these markets, find the right appeals to attract attention, test market the product wherever possible, forecast sales and monitor sales performance against forecasts, as will be described in the following chapter dealing with new product development.

Commissioning research

Large companies will invariably have a marketing research team, possibly an entire department, and will therefore have the necessary expertise to carry out their own research should they choose to do so. In practice, however, very little ad hoc research is likely to be carried out within the company, and continuous research is likely to be limited to the collation and analysis of regular flows of data from secondary sources within the firm. Most ad hoc and continuous research is likely to be farmed out to one of the major market research agencies specialising in this kind of work. Commissioning an agency has its advantages and disadvantages. There may be higher cost implications, the work will have to be scheduled at a time convenient to both parties, possibly delaying results, and this may also mean opening up the department's – and company's – innermost thoughts and plans to an outside body, so discretion and trust are vital. On the other hand, the agency is likely to have a far greater pool of specialised talent than could be mustered within a company's marketing department, and what is more, they will bring an objective eye to the work, with no axe to grind and no preconceived ideas about what results should be expected. This may mean that the results they present will not always be what the company was hoping or looking for, and in consequence it may be less willing to accept the findings, or act on them. Sometimes, research is commissioned from an outside agency in order to postpone or avoid making difficult decisions, and expensively commissioned research may then wind up 'received and filed' without action.

The Marketing Information System

Research should form the basis of an ongoing system for gathering intelligence about the company, its products and its markets. Often, such intelligence is gathered informally and subconsciously by managers in the course of their everyday duties, by observing, listening to discussions, talking to colleagues in the industry and reading trade or other journals and papers. Valuable as this process is, it should be supported by more formal procedures carried out in a systematic and scientific way. Establishing a Marketing Information System (MIS) ensures that the company has a system for the regular planned collection, analysis and presentation of data. Designing an MIS requires the organisation to undertake two tasks:

■ to consider the decisions that its management has to take

■ to determine what information is needed to make these decisions.

Obviously, the availability of finance influences the kinds of information that can be obtained. Here, the company must realistically judge what proportion of its profits, or reserves, it should set aside for research, separating the costs of its annual research from any special ad hoc research needs which may arise from time to time (such as a feasibility study to judge the merits of taking over another company).

Since the MIS is designed to ensure that the company has a regular flow of information to monitor its markets and marketing effectiveness, a proportion of the annual budget should be allocated for this purpose, while exceptional research needs, such as those dictated by a decision to expand, will require a topping up of funds, either from reserves or even by way of a loan. A budget for research should be allocated regardless of the size of the company; even the smallest SME has need for regular information about its operations and will need to allocate resources to gather these data.

Let us take the case of a small regional chain of travel agents, which is considering setting up or purchasing a new branch in the region. The location of the branch will be critical for its chances of success, and a feasibility study will have to be undertaken to decide whether expansion in the region is the correct decision, and which of the available sites will stand the best chance of success. While a full-scale survey will be beyond the means of all but the largest chains, some research data can be bought in at moderate cost while substantial fieldwork can be undertaken by a branch manager at the expense only of time and effort.

Figure 3.1 details the setting up of an MIS, and it shows that there are several distinct ways in which information can be obtained in an MIS:

■ through the use of *internal records*, that is, the use of recorded data already available within the firm

■ by identifying and selecting suitable data available in *external records*

■ by undertaking or commissioning *primary research*

■ by carrying out *surveys*

■ by *observation*

■ by *experimentation*.

We shall go on to look at each of these methods of research in the sections that follow.

Internal records

The gathering of information from existing records, whether within or from outside the firm, is known as desk research, and falls under the general heading of *secondary research*, a term with which we are already familiar. In some ways this is the simplest means of gathering data, since many of the data are already available to the firm and need only to be collated and analysed. It is also relatively inexpensive to set up internal information systems to collect material as needed. Today, practically all businesses will have their data stored in computer files, and the task of retrieving this is straightforward, with minimal time and cost involved.

To take one example, travel agents have a huge range of data on tap. Computerised sales records will reveal which products they are selling, in what quantities and to whom. This information, and that provided by their principals, will enable them to break down their sales by company, brand, destination or other criteria. Some judgement about future sales can be made by comparing forward sales with bookings achieved during the comparable period in the previous year, or with any earlier period of trading, to give a picture of trends in sales over time. Travel agents can compute their average revenue per booking, average commission received for each type of travel product sold, and average sales achieved by each member of the counter staff (important information when considering rewarding staff for productivity). Agents can build up a complete profile of their customers: total numbers, breakdown by week of booking or week of departure (giving them the ability to judge whether and to what extent bookings are being made later in the year than formerly), by area of residence and type

Figure 3.1
Procedures for
setting up a
Marketing
Information
System

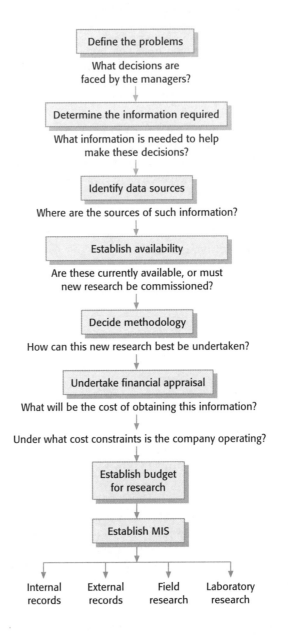

of holiday preferred. How such data can be used in the marketing of the agency is shown in Table 3.1.

Principals will be continually gathering information of this type both formally and through informal feedback through their personal contacts. For example, sales representatives will continually monitor data on clients and distributors and provide regular reports to their sales managers, which will be integrated into the information system.

Computerised records now being the norm in the travel industry, it is also a simple matter today to produce data for management decision-making at regular intervals,

Table 3.1   Travel agency data and their marketing applications

Data	Marketing application
Sales and revenue records	Develop promotional campaigns to achieve targets set by selected principals for bonus commissions Negotiate with principals for joint promotions Decide which brochures to rack and where
Average commission achieved	Decide to drop a product range or give it extra promotion
Bookings/revenue per member of staff	Set revenue targets for each member of staff Determine bonus payments for performance Ascertain sales training needs
Customer profiles	Establish mailing lists for special offers Devise direct mail campaigns to previous customers, or to catchment areas from which high numbers of bookings are being achieved

whether daily, weekly or monthly according to need. The danger of overload must be recognised, however; a manager's time has not expanded to keep pace with the increased flow of information, and therefore data must be selected and presented in a form which is easily assimilated, if they are to be useful.

External records

An enormous amount of data is available to the travel company from existing public records and archives, and simple desk research through these records can prove invaluable. Not all of it will automatically be seen as relevant to the needs of the tourism industry, but a selective search through public records can produce a mine of relevant information.

Public records

Within public archives we can distinguish between information specifically relating to travel and tourism, and information which is more general in nature but nevertheless provides a useful insight into patterns of travel and tourism. For example, statistics produced on a regular basis by the British government will indicate such factors as the growth of paid holiday entitlement, or the growth in single parent families, which will have significance for patterns of holiday-taking in Britain.

Sources of data are constantly changing, and of course will vary from country to country, but the public library (or the British Museum Library) is always a good starting point, as are other libraries accessible to the public, such as those of colleges and universities where leisure and tourism is taught. In some cases, specialist libraries may yield valuable sectoral data; the CAA library in Aviation House, Gatwick Airport, for example, has a wide range of statistical and other data on air transport. Some libraries make a small charge for access.

For those planning a more serious study of tourism, there are bibliographies of tourism to consult. Several of these have been published and should be available in good tourism libraries. However, bibliographies tend to date quickly, and any search of public records must include a study of the most recent data published, which may not yet appear in the listing of any bibliography. Increasingly, these data are available online, and are therefore regularly updated. Databases such as CAB International's TourCD which includes their Leisure, Recreation and Tourism abstracts in CD-ROM form, are invaluable for those embarking on more academic research. General information on tourism is often accessible through recognised online search engines such as www.askjeeves.com or www.google.com.

Publications of ABTA, VisitBritain, the BAA, the CAA, the Confederation of Passenger Transport UK and annual reports of major travel enterprises such as airlines, hotel chains and tour operators, all contain valuable statistical information. Perhaps the best known continuous public survey of tourism within the UK is the *United Kingdom Tourism Survey (UKTS)* commissioned on behalf of the country's tourist boards. Another equally valuable source is the *International Passenger Survey*, which includes information on UK residents travelling abroad and the purpose of their visits defined by destination area. Further material can be discovered in the travel trade press, and academic journals such as *Tourism Management*, *Annals of Tourism Research*, and the EIU's (Economist Intelligence Unit) *International Tourism Quarterly*.

Travel statistics are sometimes brought together in a very useful compendium, such as will be found in the *Keynote Reports* and *Market Assessment Reports*, the *Travel and Tourism Analyst*, and VisitEngland's (formerly the ETB) *Insights*. The VisitBritain (former BTA) research library is probably the best place to start one's search, particularly for data dealing with domestic and incoming tourists to Britain.

Subscription research

A company with adequate financial resources can choose between commissioning its own specific research, or subscribing to an ongoing 'syndicated' survey of consumers which includes information about the pattern of holidays or travel taken.

General surveys of consumer habits of purchasing are conducted by a variety of companies, and use different methods related to scale, speed of reporting and other criteria.

Retail and consumer audits represent another form of continuous market research. These deal with the demand for consumer goods and services generally, and are available to subscribers. The BMRB's TGI is perhaps the best known of these, in terms of travel and tourism data.

Because of the comprehensive and extensive nature of these surveys, the subscriptions are expensive, and only the largest companies are likely to be able to subscribe regularly. Advertising agents often subscribe to aid their own campaign planning in a variety of fields, and the travel companies using the larger advertising agencies can obtain the benefits of this knowledge through this source.

More specific services are offered by Travel and Tourism Research (TATR), who report regularly upon travel agencies and their attitudes to travel products, as well as their readership of the travel media. Other marketing research bodies provide services such as newspaper cuttings. Information about the advertising spend of major companies in the industry can be found by consulting MMS (Media Monitoring Service) reports, available on subscription and through advertising agencies.

One word of warning about the use of published statistics: one must avoid applying general findings to specific situations. Figures which indicate a growth of overseas package holidays may conceal the fact that there is a marked decline to one country at the expense of a growth to another. In the same way, a rise in visitors to the UK will not necessarily mean that there has been an increase of tourism to Northumbria, nor will statistics on the West Country in Britain necessarily throw light on levels of demand for tourism to Plymouth, St Ives, Bristol or Bath. Each of these destinations has its own niche markets of tourists, and an aggregate figure for tourism to the region will be of little help in estimating tourism flows to specific towns or districts. These will need to commission their own studies to have an accurate picture of tourism demand. There is, in fact, an acute shortage of data dealing with specific locations, and sadly the same must now be said of the broader collection of tourism data, as resource constraints have led to cost cutting in data collection by the national boards.

Primary research

If the knowledge required by the organisation is not available through a search of secondary material, it is necessary to undertake primary research (often referred to as *field research*), that is, information obtained directly from the market. There are two principal ways by which this is carried out: by asking people questions, and by observing their behaviour systematically.

Such research can be undertaken by research organisations on commission, but can be extremely costly. However, for the smaller company, simple quantitative research can be undertaken 'in-house', providing it is scientifically and systematically carried out. It is better to leave more qualitative methods to the experts.

Full-scale national surveys of the market will cost tens of thousands of pounds, well beyond the means of all but the largest travel firms, but some of these data may be already obtainable through commercial research organisations, and it is as well to shop around to find out what is the lowest cost at which one can acquire the information. At the other end of the scale, a local survey of a travel agent's market is unlikely to be available through secondary research, but could be undertaken by the firm itself. Questionnaires designed to find out, for example, whether existing customers would continue to use the agency if it were to move location, or whether clients would purchase charter flights to Greece if these were available from the local airport, but at a higher cost than from London, are relatively straightforward 'number-crunching' exercises which, if carefully planned and executed, can yield useful information. Researchers do need to be conscious of the fact that what people say they will do and what they actually do are not always the same thing, though! Quite a lot of research has been carried out now to test people's willingness to pay higher prices for sustainable tourism packages, but there is little evidence that the willingness expressed in surveys is converted into sales when prices rise.

Let us take a slightly more sophisticated example of primary research which an agent might undertake. A travel agent currently offers free transport to the local airport for all local package tour bookings, as an inducement to book. The agent wants to know how far this incentive is responsible for:

- keeping existing clients from going to competitors
- attracting clients away from other agencies.

The agent may also want to know whether some other incentive might give greater market satisfaction, without adding to costs, or how much business they stand to lose if they withdraw the present offer. While a questionnaire could be sent out to present customers, this will be no help in reaching competitors' clients, so some form of random survey of people in the *catchment area* will need to be undertaken. This could be done by talking to people in the streets or interviewing them in their homes. Both methods have advantages and drawbacks. Home interviews are more difficult to arrange and more costly in time to conduct, but are likely to result in fewer refusals (if carefully managed) and as more time is taken to consider the questions, responses are likely to be more accurate. Home interviews also allow the interviewer more time to draw out respondents on their opinions and attitudes towards travel generally, leading to more rewarding data; this does call for more skills as an interviewer, however. At the same time, the collation and analysis of information gained in this way are more complex than responses to simple questions in the street survey. Street surveys can be carried out quite quickly, whereas a home survey will take time to organise and conduct, delaying action, which may be crucial. Surveys are sometimes conducted by random telephone sampling to overcome this problem, but many respondents still resent this type of intrusion by market researchers. There is also a growth in approaching respondents through Internet surveys, and this form of research is likely to feature more prominently in the future.

Clearly, there are a great many factors which have to be taken into account in deciding which is the most appropriate method of research to adopt. We shall go on to look at the design of a piece of research, and then consider the different ways in which research can be conducted.

The elements of a research project

The following steps are necessary in planning a research programme.

1 Definition of the problem and the objectives

The organisation must be quite clear about its intentions – clear about what it hopes to achieve as a result of its research. This may seem an obvious point, but a surprising amount of questionnaires carry questions which do not actually throw light on the problem under investigation, but have been incorporated because 'it would be nice to know what the market feels about the issue'. Responses therefore may end up being unused.

Knowledge acquired through this step leads to the formation of the market research brief, as a basis for action.

2 Identification of sources of information

At this point the aim is to find out what, if anything, is known about the problem already. There is little point in paying good money for research which has already been undertaken by someone else, if one can get hold of this. However, a great deal of research which might be relevant will have been carried out by rival commercial organisations, and would not be accessible. How much will the organisation's existing records help in solving the problem? Where else might the information be found?

3 Develop the research plan

Depending upon the information available in step 2, the main stage of research may now be planned, or it may be thought necessary to conduct some exploratory research first, as a guide in developing a more detailed plan.

For instance, let us assume that a company is interested in developing a low-price multi-centre programme of package tours to the United States, using Greyhound buses for overland travel between the centres. While statistics on the use of Greyhound by British travellers will be available, attitudes towards travel by coach over long distances may be less well understood. As a prelude to knowing what questions to ask in a full-scale survey, it may be helpful first to conduct a panel interview (sometimes referred to as a focus group interview) to explore attitudes towards coach travel and to holidays in the USA. The use of this technique will be explained more fully later in the chapter.

4 Research design and methodology

The detailed plan for research can now be prepared. If this is to incorporate a survey, which is the customary means by which facts will be collected, the plan will include:

- selection of respondents – who is to be interviewed, the total size of the sample and how they will be chosen
- the form in which the survey will be conducted (personal interviews, mailed questionnaires, etc.)
- the design of the questionnaire to be used
- the organisation of the fieldwork, including recruitment, training and briefing interviewers
- establishment of the time schedule, and overall budget for the research.

Once these matters have been agreed, it is imperative to 'pilot test' the questionnaire, by trying it out on a handful of respondents selected at random. There will invariably be changes that must be made to the questions, and the pilot will pick these up, as well as giving an idea of the average time taken to carry out one interview. This will help in planning the schedule of interviews.

Once the questionnaire has been refined to a point where the research supervisor is satisfied that the questions and structure are right, the research can be implemented.

Survey data are collected and collated. Normally this is done by computer, rather than by hand, making it comparatively easy to *cross-tabulate*, that is, compare responses to any two or more variables in the questionnaire. We could, for example, discover how many women over 18 years of age went overseas for their holiday last year, and spent over £600 per person for their holiday. Here we are examining four variables: female, adult, those who went abroad, and those spending more than £600. This process is known as *analysis*, and calls for skills to select what is relevant, and interpret correctly what the data reveal, so that the correct conclusions can be drawn, and recommendations for action can be taken.

The results of the survey are presented in the form of a report, which will incorporate the following elements:

■ the title, date, company name, and name of organisation contracted to undertake the research

■ the brief: terms of reference, acknowledgements, and statement of objectives

■ a detailed statement of the methodology: methods used, reasons for their selection, and details of how the sample of respondents was drawn, number of interviews conducted, how the fieldwork was undertaken, etc.

■ the findings of the survey

■ conclusions and recommendations for action

■ appendices: these should contain the bulk of the statistical information gathered (full tables of results, etc.) and a copy of any questionnaire used.

Ethics in research

Up to now, no mention has been made of the ethical issues in carrying out research, but this is not to underestimate their importance. As Daymon and Holloway make clear,[2] there are a number of ethical principles to bear in mind when carrying out research, the most important being:

■ the right to free and informed choice

■ protection from harm to individuals and equipment

■ privacy: anonymity and confidentiality

■ autonomy: voluntary informed consent

■ honesty: omission, interpretation and plagiarism.

Professional researchers pay close attention to these requirements, because at the very least research methods and results could cause deep offence, and in extreme cases researchers could lay themselves open to legal action, if ethical considerations are ignored. Consider the following example.

Example

It was reported that a prominent University Business School in the United States had conducted spurious research by getting their researchers to write letters of complaint to 240 restaurants, purporting to be from clients who claimed to have experienced cases of food poisoning. The aim was to determine how the restaurants responded to complaints. When this became public, the Dean of the Business School was obliged to write a personal letter of apology to all the restaurants concerned. It was recognised that had a complaint against one of these restaurants (all of high repute) found its way into the press, this could have forced the restaurant's closure.

Reported in the *Observer*, 9 September 2001

The right to informed choice means that respondents have the right to give or withhold information, either initially or at any point in the research. With sensitive questions, such as asking a respondent their exact age or income, the researcher always faces the prospect of a refusal, and such questions are best left to the end of the questionnaire.

Protection from harm requires the researcher to ensure that no emotional or physical harm comes to respondents, either in the course of the research or in its outcome. Particular care has to be taken in cases where interviews are conducted with children under 18. For example, research into levels of satisfaction with play facilities and children's reps at a tourist destination will be very important for a tour operator, but care must be taken to ensure that parents are fully conversant with the details of the research and have given consent. Online research carries the additional danger of unwitting public exposure of participants, so particular care must also be taken where Internet or e-mail information is collected. In-depth interviews can be stressful and emotionally taxing, and must be handled with extreme tact. Where tape recorders are used, respondents must be reassured that the tape will be wiped after use, so that the material could not fall into others' hands and be misused.

There are similar issues with anonymity. Most research will end up in the public domain in one form or another, so it is imperative to ensure that respondents cannot be identified personally, and if companies or organisations are to be mentioned by name, permission must be obtained for the use of their names. Confidentiality is distinct from anonymity, and means that issues and ideas that have been revealed by respondents are not disclosed without express permission of the respondent. Often, respondents in an in-depth interview will reveal views about their bosses, colleagues or customers, which could do irreparable harm to their careers if released into the public domain.

Autonomy is based on informed consent of the respondents, who give their permission to participate based on an understanding of what the research is about and how it will benefit them. This means an obligation on the part of the researcher to reveal the overall aims of the research. Occasionally, research objectives will require the limited withholding of information for a period of time, but respondents should be made fully conversant with the nature of the research as soon as convenient, and their consent should be obtained.

Example

A study of tour guides on day excursions required the researcher to observe guides in action on board excursion coaches. The guides were made aware in advance only that the researcher was studying the nature of day excursions, and what took place on these. Following the completion of the tour, the guides were informed of the detailed nature of the study as focusing on the interaction between guides, drivers and passengers, and were asked if they would be prepared to engage in in-depth interviews. There were no refusals.

Finally, the honesty of the researcher is all-important. This of course extends to the collection and interpretation of data, which should be undertaken objectively. Material inconveniently compromising the results should not be omitted, and obviously fabrication of interviews, questionnaire responses or other results is a corruption of the professional integrity of the researcher. Plagiarism of ideas or material from earlier research is equally abhorrent. All research needs a system of checks and balances to ensure that the work is being conducted fairly and honestly. Professional agencies employ staff to oversee this aspect by carrying out appropriate inspections, and it is equally important that individuals and firms undertaking their own research ensure similar controls are in place.

We will now look in a little more detail at the ways in which surveys can be conducted.

The survey

Surveys are generally the best means of collecting descriptive information, and will invariably make use of a questionnaire, that is, a series of questions which will be put to respondents designed to help provide answers to the problems the organisation is investigating. The survey can be conducted in many different ways, as we shall see, but regardless of survey method, the procedure must be scientific. This requires that every possible effort is made to avoid or reduce bias in the response. It will usually be impossible to interview all the possible respondents in whom the company is interested, therefore those that are interviewed, the *sample*, must accurately reflect the general views of the total population, or *universe* (the total number of people in the category in which we are interested). Thus, if we are proposing to solicit the views of British tourists to Spain on some issue, we need first to have some idea of the total size of the universe, and must then choose a representative sample of that universe having regard to demographics.

Our first task is then to determine who is to be interviewed. Are we interested in the views only of British holidaymakers, or all British visitors to Spain, including business and VFR (visiting friends and relatives) visitors? Are we interested only in the opinions of those who take package holidays, or also of those on independent holiday arrangements, or staying in second homes? Is it only the views of adults that we seek, and if so do we interview only those over 16, over 18 or over 21? If we intend to include business travellers in the survey, are we interested only in the views of those who use the service, or of those who buy the service (many secretaries make the arrangements for their bosses)? If our interest is in those who travel regularly, how will we define regularity for the purposes of the survey?

Our next problem is the size of the sample we shall select. Large samples provide more accurate results than small ones, but the increase in accuracy becomes less and less significant as the sampling size is increased. As long as scientific methods of selection have been employed to get the views of 56 million people in Britain, we need no more than 2000 respondents to obtain views accurately reflecting the population's views on general matters to within 95 per cent probability; that is, we have only a 5 per cent chance of being wrong in our findings. This is sufficiently accurate for most purposes, where the question is one of a general nature. The additional cost of interviewing enough people to raise the level of accuracy is generally not justified, since we would have to increase the number of respondents fourfold to improve the level of accuracy from a 5 per cent chance of being wrong to only 2.5 per cent.

Scientific procedures are crucial, if this level of accuracy is to be retained. A *probability sample* of the universe must be selected. In the case of a simple random sample, this means selecting respondents in a scientifically random way so that each has one chance only, and an equal chance, of being selected. Other acceptable systems of scientific selection include *stratified random sampling*, in which the universe is divided into mutually exclusive groups (such as age ranges), in which the proportion of the total in each group is known, with random samples then drawn from each group in the same ratio as exists in the universe. A third method is known as *cluster sampling*, in which, for example, samples are taken by area of residence, again in the same proportion as the ratio of residents in the universe, and again with each respondent having an equal opportunity to be selected once only.

Major research companies employ sophisticated techniques to ensure that the samples are truly representative. In a national survey they will define how many respondents are to be chosen, and will ensure that the numbers in each category, that is age, sex, socio-economic status, domicile, correspond with the standards they have defined from previous work.

In order to correct any imbalances, a process known as *weighting* is employed, whereby a computer automatically adjusts the results to equate to the standards already set down; thus if the sample was correct in all aspects except the breakdown of respondents by social class, the views of the under-represented sectors may be given additional weight in the final analysis by increasing the relevant answers in proportion to the under-representation detected.

Having said that a 2000-person sample is enough for general questions, it must be emphasised that many questions are much more specific and require different techniques. It is very expensive indeed to establish the views of a minority group. This can be demonstrated by a simple example.

Example

A specialist tour operator decides that it needs to establish whether apartment holidays to Spain marketed by major package holiday companies are seen by customers to be satisfactory. Determining whether this is the case will require examination of the data in four stages.

Stage 1: 2000 respondents
Have you booked a holiday in the past year?
NO 65%   YES 35%

Stage 2: 700 respondents
Was it an independent or a package holiday?
INDEPENDENT 40%   PACKAGE 60%

Stage 3: 420 respondents
Did you go to Spain?
NO 70%   YES 30%

Stage 4: 126 respondents
Did you stay in an apartment?
NO 80%   YES 20%

Result: 25 relevant respondents

Whether the contribution of 25 respondents will generate sufficiently useful information will depend upon the nature of the questions to be asked. If the market research firm charges £2 per interviewee, the costing would be as follows:

$2000 \times £2 = £4000$
25 useful respondents
$= £160$ per usable respondent

It obviously involves going to a great deal of trouble to ensure scientific accuracy, and this is one of the factors in the high costs of such research. Because of this, firms sometimes undertake surveys using non-probability samples, such as stopping every tenth person in the street to ask their opinion. While this may help to throw light on the problem, the results cannot be subject to statistical tests and must always be in some doubt about degrees of accuracy achieved. It must be remembered that the test of any survey is that the results are both valid and reliable. *Validity* means that the survey proves what it sets out to prove; *reliability* means that if the survey were to be conducted with another sample of respondents, exactly the same results would be achieved (within the limits of probability established).

Let us take the example of a survey of visitors to a seaside resort by means of a *street interview*. An interviewer could be assigned to stand on a particular street corner and question every *n*th person who passed by. This *convenience sample* will have a number of inherent biases. Many visitors to the resort not passing these points will have no opportunity for selection, and the flow of visitors will be greater at certain times of the day and certain days of the week than at others (although this factor can be weighted to obtain more accurate results). It is also possible that other overt or covert biases will emerge. Passers-by with more time on their hands will be more likely to stop to answer questions than those who are busy, and there is a strong temptation for interviewers to approach those who look friendly, or are from the same age group, sex or social background. Ethnic minorities might be ignored, and people who cannot speak sufficient English to be interviewed will be rejected. By the use of good interviewer training, by weighting responses, and perhaps by supporting the survey with other forms of research such as hotel occupancy surveys and car park observation (licence plates reveal some very interesting statistics about visitor origins!) bias will be reduced, if never entirely eliminated. This is likely to be the most realistic approach to research for many small companies, such as the travel agent anxious for information about the local market. By instructing interviewers to deliberately choose a cross-section of respondents according to age, sex, group size, etc. (known as *quota sampling*) a wider range of opinions will be obtained, although not necessarily a more accurate one.

While the street interview is the most common form of interview, surveys can be carried out in a number of other ways. *Telephone interviews* are becoming more popular, and as the number of subscribers to telephones in Britain comes closer to 100 per cent, so this form of interview becomes more statistically significant. However, phones are increasingly being used by commercial firms to make *cold calls* (i.e. unsolicited efforts to sell) and there is a growing resistance among consumers to what is seen as an invasion of privacy, which will result in further biases as refusals grow. However, the telephone interview does reduce cost, especially if a national survey is being undertaken – a phone call is a lot cheaper than sending an interviewer to remote corners of the British Isles! Telephone interviews can, of course, also be carried out far more quickly.

Home interviews are best for longer questionnaires, for asking those questions which require some forethought or probing from the interviewer, and for open questions calling for opinions and attitudes. Once again, households must be selected scientifically, so that each has an equal opportunity for selection, and it may be necessary for interviewers to make several calls in order to find the householder at home. This delays the completion of the survey. Possible bias emerges through the closer relationship which is established between an interviewer and respondent in a longer, home interview, with respondents sometimes giving answers which it is thought the interviewer will want to hear, if the respondent finds the interviewer sympathetic.

The cheapest type of survey, dispensing entirely with the interviewer, is the *mailed questionnaire*. This means, however, that response rates are usually lower (although the inclusion of a stamped addressed envelope for the reply will boost responses) and replies are more likely to be attracted from those with an interest in the survey: the research may produce a higher level of people who have taken holidays abroad than those who have not, since they may be more interested in the questions. Respondents also have the opportunity to read the questionnaire through before answering the questions, and what they read later in the paper may prejudice the way they respond to the earlier questions. With this system, there can be no certainty that the person selected for the interview has filled out the questionnaire, or has given much thought to the questions.

Questionnaires may also be distributed to homeward-bound passengers on aircraft or on coaches, given to visitors leaving a tourist attraction with the request that they be mailed back, or left in hotel rooms to be handed in at the front desk on leaving.

Each of these approaches has its own advantages and drawbacks. However, where the opportunity is given to have passengers complete a questionnaire on the journey home, the method has significant benefits over others. To start with, one is dealing with a captive audience representing 100 per cent of the universe. Passengers have their experiences fresh in their minds, and they also have time on their hands during the journey, so seldom object to filling in a questionnaire. Response rates will therefore be unusually high, especially if the cabin staff or tour escort collect questionnaires. Staff can also clarify any uncertainties about the completion of the questionnaire. The major tour operators, such as TUI, MyTravel and First Choice (who also own the airlines carrying their customers), can make good use of this opportunity to monitor satisfaction, and thus to effect quality control.

When used to its full extent, this technique brings many benefits. Not only can the operators monitor the true level of any difficulties experienced with hotels or resorts, but also they can monitor satisfaction levels in respect of any aspect of the holiday, such as flights used. It is known that when airlines find that their 'ratings' relative to other competitors are slipping, they will take steps to improve service levels in order to impress the tour operator and to secure future business. This process has had a significant effect upon the quality of service given by the major independent charter airlines used for package tours. However, there are questions about the efficacy of this methodology, as will be seen in the question at the end of this chapter.

Questionnaire design

Good questionnaire design in itself is a well-developed skill, since even the way a question is phrased can bias the response. Questions must be expressed in as neutral a manner as possible, must be unambiguous and written in a language which is simple enough to be understood by respondents of all levels of intelligence. However, expressing a question neutrally is surprisingly difficult. Take the following two examples:

(a) *Do you think that the Spanish government should allow people to drink alcohol on the beach?*

(b) *Do you think that the Spanish government should forbid people to drink alcohol on the beach?*

Tests have shown that substituting the word 'forbid' for 'allow' suggests a greater level of control which results in respondents being less willing to answer in the affirmative to question (b).

A transport authority questioned respondents' attitudes towards special bus lanes during rush hours by asking:

Are you in favour of giving special priority to buses in the rush hour?

Of those responding, 62 per cent agreed that they were in favour. However, in a later questionnaire, the question was rephrased to read:

Are you in favour of giving special priority to buses in the rush hour, or should cars have just as much priority?

The number of those in favour now dropped to 40 per cent.

The designers of questionnaires must also avoid questions that are:

■ vague

■ ambiguous

■ contain double negatives (making them more difficult to understand)

■ set impossible tests of respondents' memory

■ lead respondents to reply in a particular way.

There follow some examples of questions that would need to be avoided, or rephrased, to make them acceptable.

1   *On your last trip abroad, how much did you spend on average per day in the bar of your hotel?*
    – this is a memory test, even if the respondent travelled abroad as recently as this year. A fair question to those returning from an overseas trip, or on the last day of their trip, but even here, at best the interviewer will get only an educated guess.

2   *Do you care enough about the family to ensure that they always carry enough insurance while on holiday?*
    – a loaded question. Who can reply no?

3   *How do the clothes you wear on holiday compare with those that you wear at home?*
    – vague. What is the question getting at? It will tend to encourage equally vague responses such as 'not at all', or 'very well', unless the interviewer has the opportunity to explain the question.

4   *What are your views about arbitrary surcharges for ITX packages?*
    – even if directed to members of the travel trade, the question makes a dangerous assumption about knowledge of technical expressions. Avoid all use of technical expressions, unless it is essential to include them, in which case an explanation of the term should be added (ITX stands for inclusive tour-basing fare). Respondents hate to admit their ignorance!

5   *How did you find the travel agent you booked with?*
    – ambiguous. You may get responses such as 'I looked him up in the Yellow Pages' coupled with other responses such as 'very friendly and helpful'!

6   *Would you prefer not to travel in a non-smoking flight?*
    – Help! What does it mean? The respondent will have to think too long to work it out.

7   *What do you think of the colour and taste of the ice-cream you have just bought?*
    – you are asking two questions in one. Respondents' views about colour may differ from their opinions about the taste.

As far as possible, for simplicity in collating and classifying information, *closed-end questions* should be used in questionnaires. These are questions in which the respondent is asked to pick from one of several responses possible, or the question is phrased so that the interviewer can check responses from a choice of possible replies. Closed-end questions vary from the simple dichotomous question calling for a 'yes/no' reply to checklists of responses such as the following:

How many times have you travelled abroad on a holiday of four nights or more in the past year?

once	1
twice	2
three or more times	3
none	4

Using this form of question, rating scales can be employed to obtain respondents' views about attributes:

What was your opinion of the food served in the hotel?

excellent	1
good	2
fair	3
poor	4
very poor	5

With questions of this nature, it is important that there is an equal balance between 'positive' rankings and 'negative' rankings, otherwise the overall result will indicate a skewing to one side or the other. It is not uncommon to find tour operator questionnaires which ask respondents to choose from the following categories:

excellent
good
fair
poor

This provides two positive responses, one 'neutral' and one negative. The result will make it appear that the product is slightly better than might be the case in a more objective set of choices. Usually, five choices are provided in scales such as these, but on occasion as many as seven or even nine have been used to provide 'fine tuning' of responses.

Views can also be solicited by the use of a simple scale from 1 to 10 to rate respondents' opinions of a product:

What was your opinion of the service you received while at the hotel?
(Give a mark from 1 to 10, with a maximum of 10 points if you thought it really outstanding, and a minimum of 1 point if you thought it very poor.)

In this way, an average grade for service can be more easily assessed. Similarly, the use of a *Likert scale* will solicit respondents' extent of agreement to a statement:

French hotels generally offer better food than do British hotels.

1	2	3	4	5
strongly disagree	disagree	neither disagree nor agree	agree	strongly agree

It is a useful tactic to vary the polarity of the scales where several questions of this type are used, so that sometimes 'strongly agree' appears on the left side of the scale, and sometimes 'strongly disagree' appears. This prevents the phenomenon of respondents checking automatically all one column if they generally have a favourable or unfavourable view of the product, causing them to think before responding. The statements should also reflect varying viewpoints, so that people will agree with some, and disagree with others, thus ensuring that thought is given to each reply.

Yet another technique is the *Guilford constant-sum scale* which requires the respondent to apportion 10 marks between two attributes or variables, as in the following question. Since the technique is quite complex, it will require careful explanation to make certain that every respondent understands it.

In the following question, you are asked to divide 10 marks between the two resorts shown, for each of the attributes shown in the left-hand column. For example, if you were asked about the quality of the food in each resort, and felt that the food in Corfu was much better than the food in Majorca, you might allocate 8 marks to Corfu and 2 to Majorca for this attribute. If you thought the food to be equally good in both resorts, you would allocate 5 marks to each.

attribute	Corfu	Majorca
sunny and warm	____	____
good beaches	____	____
good resorts for young children	____	____
inexpensive as a holiday destination	____	____

Questionnaires should always be constructed so that initial questions are broad in scope (*Did you have a holiday last year?*) and gradually become more specific as the interview progresses (*In what kind of accommodation did you stay while on holiday? . . . What were your views of the entertainment provided at the hotel?*). Questions of a personal nature, such as age range, occupation, salary, etc., are best left to the end of the questionnaire. Since it is seldom necessary to know respondents' exact ages, this question is best asked within a range, as follows:

15–24	1
25–34	2
35–44	3
45–54	4
55–64	5
65 or over	6
No response	7

In all such scales, make sure that each category is mutually exclusive. It is a common mistake to overlap categories (e.g. age range 25–35, 35–45).

Whether the questionnaire is to be filled in by the respondent or by the interviewer, clear instructions should be given on how to fill it in, and its completion should be designed to be as simple and rapid as possible. For example, instructions should be issued to circle the number corresponding to the respondents' choice:

Where did you buy your ticket? (circle your answer)

direct from the airline	1
from a travel agent	2
from a ticket machine	3
from some other source	4
don't know/can't remember	5

This will greatly simplify transposing the answers to the computer for processing.

In some cases, *open-ended questions* will be unavoidable, although the completely unstructured question should be rare in a questionnaire, since it becomes difficult to categorise answers in a form which will enable them to be processed. A question such as *What do you think of British Airways?*, for example, will result in answers in so many different categories that they become unmanageable. The question would be better rephrased to ask separately about respondents' opinions of the airline's service, food, reliability, etc.

The use of semi-structured questions such as the sentence completion question may make answers easier to classify:

When I enter a travel agency, the first thing that I look for is . . .

Figure 3.2 at the end of this chapter illustrates a well-devised and complete question-naire which will indicate how precoding simplifies the processing of information in order to enter this in the computer. With the growth of moderately priced personal computers and survey software, collation and cross-tabulation of survey material have become easier and within reach of the smaller company.

Observation

Whatever the strengths of scientific surveys, they have their limitations. Other techniques such as observation play a useful role in supporting evidence gained through the use of questionnaires. However, if observation is to be taken seriously as a research method, it must be conducted no less scientifically. This requires two things: the use of scientific procedure in conducting an orderly and sustained programme of investigation, and the ability of observers to 'distance' themselves from the event observed in order to record material in a dispassionate and professional manner. This second requirement is difficult for the untrained researcher, since attitudes and behaviour are moulded by our life experiences, and it is hard to step outside them. For this reason, most observation research is used at an exploratory stage in the research programme, and is carried out by professional researchers with psychological training. We should not fail to recognise, however, that much useful material can still be gathered by the non-expert through a process of careful observation, from the travel agents who observe patterns of behaviour of clients who enter the shop and select brochures from the racks, to airline managers who listen to the way check-ins are handled at airports and observe the behaviour of passengers waiting for their flights. The essential thing to remember is that one is doing more than 'gathering impressions'. Patterns of behaviour are being recorded in detail, through the use of field notes or a tape recorder, and over extended periods of time. A very high proportion of what is observed is likely to prove of little use, so that the process is both tedious and wasteful. The technique is none the less particularly valuable when researching competitors' products. The hotelier wishing to know more about competitors and how they handle conference enquiries might call the hotels in question, taking the role of a conference organiser, to see how the enquiry is handled, or may sit in the lobby of a hotel to listen to the comments of guests or observe how front office staff handle incoming guests. One American hotelier (evidently little recognised by his staff) made it a practice to stay as a guest in his hotels to check the levels of service provided. He would ask the lift operator or hotel porter to recommend a good place to eat (usually he was directed to somewhere other than the hotel's own restaurant) and in this way discover how the sales training of staff needed improvement.

On the whole, the technique is best used for generating hypotheses about situations, but it will improve the researchers' knowledge about what sort of questions need to be included in questionnaires.

The mystery shopper research

One of the most popular forms of research in observational research is the employment of a 'mystery shopper', a researcher posing as a normal shopper who provides feedback on employee and outlet performance based on a number of predefined criteria. The trade magazine *Travel Weekly*, for example, samples four retail travel agencies each week within the same town or district, taking in both independent and multiple outlets. A scoring system lists performance on five criteria: agency appearance (15 per cent), product knowledge (25 per cent), staff attitude (25 per cent), brochure racking (10 per cent) and sales techniques (25 per cent). Agents scoring a total under 30 per cent are identified as a 'shop of horrors', while the top-scoring agent receives a certificate of commendation. The press publicity accompanying this research heightens the pressure to perform well. Other research is undertaken by companies in-house, either by monitoring telephone sales calls – an important element of staff training in call centres – or by cold-calling their employees in the guise of a potential customer to judge how well sales are handled. In all these cases, for ethical reasons, staff must be made aware that this form of research is carried out as a normal part of the company's monitoring procedures.

Experimentation

Experiments usually conjure up an image of a laboratory, and indeed many tests are carried out under laboratory conditions which can be useful in travel and tourism research, such as testing the effectiveness of different advertisements on a cross-section of consumers. Many forms of experimentation can be carried out away from the laboratory, however. An agent who switches brochures around in the racks to see how this affects their selection is conducting a *controlled experiment*. Airlines test different seats on their aircraft to see which proves most comfortable for their passengers, and a tour operator might experiment with the use of different excursions on different departures to see whether these changes affect customer sales and satisfaction. The technique is useful in helping to establish whether there is a *causal relationship* between two variables, that is, a change in one variable produces a change in another. As well as demonstrating the cause and effect, the objective will be to offer an explanation for it as well.

Qualitative versus quantitative research methods

At the beginning of this chapter, mention was made of the distinction between qualitative and quantitative research. Much of what has been discussed up to this point can be described as quantitative in nature, and involves research which is concerned with gathering statistics to describe what is happening. In this, it is answering questions such as Who?, Where?, When? and How? Answers to these questions are usually sought through the use of questionnaires. However, there are serious weaknesses with the use of the questionnaire. Their statistical significance is dependent upon their being answered honestly and accurately, but we have no way of knowing whether this is the case. Nor is the survey useful in helping to answer questions dealing with the Why? of travel. Let us say, for example, that we are interested in knowing why people travel by ferry and road or rail rather than by air to the south of France. People may not actually know their real motives, or they may be reluctant to reveal them. Some will not want to admit to fear of flying, or being unable to afford the cost of a rail ticket (which now exceeds budget air fares for many routes), or they may be unaware of price comparisons with different forms of transport. Even if respondents aim to be totally honest, they may themselves have little understanding of their underlying motivation. Motives can be extremely complex, and result from a great many different factors, while the questionnaire may bring out only the more obvious ones.

Qualitative techniques such as in-depth motivation research come into use for this purpose, and involve less structured interviews in which the purpose is to get the respondent to talk freely about the issue. This may call for interviews lasting two or three hours at a time, and clearly these cannot be carried out on the same scale as a 10-minute street interview. They will need to be conducted by skilled researchers, and this will greatly add to the time and cost of the exercise. They are intensely valuable, though, in probing beneath the surface responses generated in structured surveys.

One such technique widely used in market research is the *panel interview*, sometimes termed the focus interview, in which around six to eight consumers are invited to meet in informal surroundings to discuss a product or topic under research, under the guidance and direction of a skilled interviewer. Through the process of group dynamics, people's deeper feelings about issues are explored, with answers from one participant triggering off comments from other members of the panel. The material is generally tape recorded for future analysis, and as a form of exploratory research this can be helpful in guiding the direction of future research.

Other forms of qualitative research include *projective tests*, where respondents are asked to project themselves into another person's role. Examples of projective tests include *picture completion* wherein respondents are shown a cartoon or illustration in which one character is making a statement; they are then asked to complete the illustration by stating what they think the second character might be replying. The *thematic apperception test* (*TAT*) employs a picture depicting a story, and respondents are asked to identify what they believe is going on in the picture. Respondents are able in this way to project what they themselves think as if these responses were a third person's views.

The beauty of research methodology is that there are so many ways in which research can be conducted, and researchers constantly seek new ways in which to secure evidence. One innovatory piece of research carried out some years ago by Thomson Holidays will illustrate this. Thomson were interested in finding out what image consumers had of the company, and how this image compared with that of other tour companies. To do this, they used a form of projective technique, in asking respondents to imagine that well-known tour companies had come alive as real people. In this way, Thomson discovered that the company projected an image of the solid, reliable family man, while Enterprise Holidays was personified as the rising young executive and Thomas Cook, the pernickety bossy squire. In this research, Thomson was judged to communicate 'parent to child'. The implications of 'looking after you' and being authoritative and protective are obvious: while such an image is appropriate for the mainstream, rather unadventurous package tour purchaser, it is certainly inappropriate for, say, the more experienced and adventurous traveller.

As an interesting extra insight into the relative positioning of the various tour operators, First Choice Holidays undertook qualitative discussion groups to establish the *emotional values* associated with different operators. They also undertook detailed desk research, analysing the 'tone of voice' and use of language in their advertising. This was interpreted in terms of the psychological technique of *transactional analysis*. Put simply, this determines the way First Choice Holidays' Freespirit brand targets just such holidaymakers. The 'emotional values' associated with the name and brand, and the 'adult to adult' tone of voice, were developed as a result of this research. Such knowledge can be enormously beneficial in planning a company's promotional strategy and knowing what strengths to build on.

Research today is characterised by a growing interest in such new techniques. A museum in the United States, planning to find out which exhibits were the most popular, chose to support surveys by measuring the patterns of wear on the carpets in the museum and the noseprints on the glass cases surrounding the exhibits. Both measures gave a good indication of the levels of popularity of different exhibits.

Although, as has been made clear, many such qualitative techniques do not lend themselves to tests of statistical probability, they will often throw light on issues which the more common forms of research technique cannot resolve, and should therefore play a part in the repertoire of any market research department.

Example British Airways

Before British Airways launched its Club World class in 1987, the company used qualitative research to generate ideas, and quantitative methods to prioritise its plans in line with the available budget. This resulted in the airline choosing the heaviest and dearest seats rather than the lightest and cheapest versions which had been favoured by their engineers. Return on investment was reduced from the anticipated two years to just nine months.

Econometric models

A model consists of a set of variables and their interrelationships, which are designed to reflect real-life experience. By identifying how variables move in sympathy with one another, models can be helpful in predicting the future. Their use in travel and tourism research and forecasting is still limited, although they are being developed at a macro level to predict tourism trends by research organisations such as the EIU. This organisation has shown how fluctuating exchange rates and rates of inflation affect flows of international tourism.[3] Research of this kind is essential for public sector planning, and can also be extremely useful in forecasting future sales in the travel business. Models can be constructed on a smaller scale to show the effect of advertising spend on sales, and how this relationship is affected by other factors such as competitors' spend and changes in discretionary income.

Since there are so many variables affecting travel behaviour, the construction of a model to predict changes in the market for tourism is a complex and expensive process, but it is one which is continually being refined and improved.

The effectiveness of research

While some firms in the travel industry, and virtually all organisations in public sector tourism, undertake some form of marketing research, there are still many smaller companies who make no allowance for research in their annual budget, seeing it as inaccurate and an expensive use of resources which can be better channelled into other forms of marketing expenditure. This is short-sighted at best, and at worst can be catastrophic, if managers continue to commit major expenditure to new product development with insufficient background knowledge. Even today, too many small hotels are being bought, and small travel agencies opened, based purely on the 'gut feel' of their proprietors.

Research is never an exact science, but it can reduce the margins of error to which hunches alone are subject. The feasibility study is an essential prerequisite to any new project, whether the launch of a new company, the introduction of a new logo or the development of a new product. Above all, the success of research will be based on three things:

1 Sufficient resources must be allocated to the project to do the job properly, both in terms of time and money. Good research does take time to do, and managers wanting research results 'yesterday', or allocating only a fraction of the necessary funds, will force the methodology to be skimped and the end result to be of questionable value.

2 Managers should be willing to believe the results of the research when they become available, even if they conflict with the management's own preconceived views.

3 The results should be used. All too frequently, research is commissioned in order to avoid taking an immediate decision. Expensively commissioned research is then left to gather dust in a drawer instead of being used to enable managers to make better decisions on the future direction of the company's strategy.

Figure 3.2
A survey of
visitors to
National Trust
properties in
the UK

National Trust Visitor Survey 2003

[Property Name]

Dear Visitor, Could you please help the National Trust by providing a few details of your visit today? We are constantly working to provide an enjoyable and informative experience at all of our properties. The information you provide will help us to do this well. Our questionnaire is completely confidential and will only take a few minutes to complete. We are attaching a stamped, addressed envelope so that you can take it away and complete at your leisure. Simply indicate your chosen answer by ticking the appropriate option or writing in the space provided. We ask that one person fill in the questionnaire only. Thank you for your help.

Q1 Date and time of visit?

Date _____

Time _____

Q2 What was the weather like?

Sunny	❑	Heavy rain	❑
Overcast	❑	Changeable	❑
Showers	❑	Other	❑

Q3 Are you a member of the National Trust?

Yes ❑ Please go to Q5   No ❑ Please go to Q4

Q4 If you are not a member of the National Trust how would you rate the admission charge in terms of value for money?

	Exceptional	Very good	Good	Not very good	Poor
Value for money	❑	❑	❑	❑	❑

If you ticked either 'Not very good' or 'Poor' please give some reasons for your decision.

_____

_____

Q5 Have you ever visited any other National Trust property?

Yes ❑   No ❑

Q6 Have you visited this property before today?

Yes ❑ Please go to Q7   No ❑ Please go to Q9

Q7 Approximately when did you last visit this property?

During the past 12 months	❑ Go to Q8	More than 3 years ago	❑ Go to Q9
Over 1 year ago	❑ Go to Q9	Don't know	❑ Go to Q9
2–3 years ago	❑ Go to Q9		

Q8 Approximately how many times have you visited this property in the past year, not including today?

Once	❑	More than twice	❑
Twice	❑	Don't know	❑

Q9 Where did you find the information you needed to make today's visit? Please tick all that apply.

Advertising on a Bus* (please specify below where seen)	❑	Brown road signs	❑
Advertising on Trains* (please specify below where seen)	❑	Article Newspaper/Magazine/TV/Radio	❑
Previous visits/local knowledge	❑	Advertising Newspaper/Magazine	❑
Recommended at holiday accommodation	❑	Posters	❑
Recommended by another National Trust property	❑	Historic Houses & Castles Guide	❑
National Trust Magazine	❑	Other Leaflet* (Please specify below)	❑
National Trust Newsletter	❑	Leaflet for this property alone	❑
National Trust Internet Website	❑	National Trust Local Leaflet	❑
Other Internet Website* (please specify below)	❑	National Trust Handbook	❑
Saw it on the map	❑	Organised tour	❑
Friends & relatives	❑	Other* (please specify)	❑
Tourist Information Centre* (Please write the location below)	❑		

*Location of Bus Stop _____

*Location of Train Station _____

*Name of Website _____

*Name of Tourist Info Centre _____

*Name of Leaflet _____

*Other _____

Figure 3.2
(cont'd)

Q10 What particularly attracted you to visit this property? Please tick the three most important.

To attend an event ❑	Peace and quiet ❑
To study an aspect of the site ❑	For a walk ❑
Shop ❑	Wildlife/birds ❑
Restaurant ❑	Gardens/Gardening ❑
In the area ❑	Guided tour ❑
A nice day out / for a change ❑	Introductory talk ❑
To show friends & relatives ❑	General interest in National Trust properties ❑
To entertain/educate children ❑	Organised tour ❑
Beautiful place ❑	Other ❑
Fresh air ❑	

If other, please specify _____

Q11 Overall how would you rate the time you have spent here today? If you are accompanied by children please rate their enjoyment.

	Very enjoyable	Enjoyable	Acceptable	Not enjoyable	Disappointing
You	❑	❑	❑	❑	❑
Children	❑	❑	❑	❑	❑

If you ticked 'Not enjoyable' or 'Disappointing' please give some reasons for your decision.

_____

Q12 Have you purchased a guidebook or other information for your visit today?

Yes ❑ Please specify below   No ❑

If 'yes', what did you buy? _____

Q13 Have you visited the National Trust shop on your visit today?

Yes ❑ Go to Q14   No ❑ Go to 16

Q14 How would you rate the following in connection with the National Trust shop. Please tick one box in each row.

	Exceptional	Very good	Good	Not very good	Poor	Don't know
Range of goods for sale in the shop	❑	❑	❑	❑	❑	❑
Service received in the shop today	❑	❑	❑	❑	❑	❑
Value for money of goods in the shop	❑	❑	❑	❑	❑	❑
Price of goods in the shop	❑	❑	❑	❑	❑	❑
Quality of goods in the shop	❑	❑	❑	❑	❑	❑

If you ticked 'Not very good' or 'Poor', please give some reasons for your decisions.

_____

Q15 If appropriate, is there anything else that you would like to see on sale in the National Trust shop?

Yes ❑ Please specify below   No ❑ Go to Q16

What else would you like to see on sale? _____

_____

Q16 Excluding the admission charge, approximately how much have you and the people in your personal group spent on your visit here today?

£ _____

_____

Q17 Have you attended any event, for instance concert, organised lecture/talk and so on at a National Trust property during the past 12 months?

Yes ❑   No ❑

Q18 Approximately how long has your visit lasted today?

Less than 1 hr ❑	Between 2–3 hrs ❑
1–2 hrs ❑	More than 3 hrs ❑

Q19 Where have you travelled from today?

Home ❑	Friends & relatives ❑
Hotel ❑	NT holiday cottage ❑
Guest house ❑	Other rented accommodation ❑
Camping/caravan site ❑	Other ❑

Travelled from _____

Q20 About how far away is this?

Under 5 miles ❑	25–49 miles ❑
5–14 miles ❑	50–74 miles ❑
15–24 miles ❑	75+ miles ❑

Q21 How did you travel to the property today? (Please tick one only)

Public transport ❑	Walked ❑
Coach (organised group) ❑	Car ❑
Taxi ❑	Parked car elsewhere and walked ❑
Bicycle ❑	Campervan ❑
Motorbike ❑	Other ❑
Given a lift ❑	

If other, please specify _____

Q22 What type of break are you on?

A day trip from home ❑	A weekend or short break ❑
A local business trip ❑	A morning/afternoon outing ❑
Other ❑	

If other, please specify _____

Figure 3.2
(*cont'd*)

Q23 Please rank the following aspects of the National Trust in terms of importance on a scale of 1 to 9, with 1 being the most important aspect and 9 being the least important aspect, using each number only once.

Peace and quiet	_____
Providing a good day out	_____
Showing how people lived	_____
Gardens	_____
Wildlife conservation	_____
Countryside Conservation	_____
The furniture collection	_____
The art collections	_____
Conservation of Houses	_____

Q24 How would you rate this property on each of the following points? Please tick one box in each row if appropriate to this visit.

	Exceptional	Very good	Good	Not very good	Poor	Don't know
Visitor reception area	❑	❑	❑	❑	❑	❑
Interesting things to see	❑	❑	❑	❑	❑	❑
Interesting presentation of life & times of the property	❑	❑	❑	❑	❑	❑
Facilities for children	❑	❑	❑	❑	❑	❑
Easy to find your way around	❑	❑	❑	❑	❑	❑
Information about the property	❑	❑	❑	❑	❑	❑
The service received at this property today	❑	❑	❑	❑	❑	❑
Service received in Restaurant	❑	❑	❑	❑	❑	❑
Service received in Tearoom	❑	❑	❑	❑	❑	❑
Range of food & drinks for sale	❑	❑	❑	❑	❑	❑
Value for money of food & drink on sale	❑	❑	❑	❑	❑	❑
Quality of food & drink available	❑	❑	❑	❑	❑	❑
Guidebook	❑	❑	❑	❑	❑	❑

If you ticked 'Not very good' or 'Poor', please give some reasons for your decisions.

Q25 Which daily newspaper do you read regularly if any? Please tick all that apply.

Daily Telegraph	❑	The Times	❑
Daily Mail	❑	Sun	❑
Daily Express	❑	Star	❑
Daily Mirror	❑	Local papers (please specify)	❑
Daily Post	❑	Sunday Papers	❑
Financial Times	❑	None	❑
Guardian	❑	Other (please specify)	❑
The Independent	❑		

Please specify _____

Q26 Please enter your full postcode in the box below. If you live outside the UK please state your home country instead.

Full Postcode or Home Country? _____

Q27 May we ask the approximate ages of people in your group? Please write the number of people in your group that fall into each age and gender category?

	Male	Female
Under 5's yrs	❑	❑
5–11 yrs	❑	❑
12–16 yrs	❑	❑
17–24 yrs	❑	❑
25–34 yrs	❑	❑
35–44 yrs	❑	❑
45–54 yrs	❑	❑
55–64 yrs	❑	❑
65+ yrs	❑	❑

Q28 To which of the following ethnic groups do you belong?

White	❑	Pakistani	❑
Black African	❑	Bangladeshi	❑
Black Caribbean	❑	Asian Other	❑
Indian	❑	Other	❑

Please specify _____

Q29 Please state the occupation (job title) of the main wage earner in your household. (If they are retired or currently not working for any reason please specify their last main job.)

_____

_____

More details about this property

Q30 Please include any other comments you may have below.

_____

_____

Thank You Very Much For Your Help

Figure 3.2
(cont'd)

SUPPLEMENTARY QUESTIONS 2003*

DECISION TO VISIT

Q1 If you used a National Trust leaflet, where did you pick it up?

Another National Trust property	❏
Another local tourist attraction	❏
Tourist Information Centre (TIC)	❏
Library	❏
At local accommodation	❏
Information delivered to my home	❏
Pub/restaurant	❏
Friends/relatives	❏
Other	❏

Please specify _____

_____

Q2 Did your knowledge of houses and gardens attract you to visit [Property] today?

Yes ❏ No ❏

Q3 How important were the following in your decision to visit [Property] today?

	Very important	Fairly important	Neither important nor unimportant	Fairly unimportant	Very unimportant
Garden	❏	❏	❏	❏	❏
House	❏	❏	❏	❏	❏

Q4 Which of the following two words or phrases best describes your reason for visiting today? (Please tick two only)

History/Architecture	❏
Furnishing/Art	❏
Horticulture professional	❏
Amateur gardener	❏
Literature	❏
Wildlife	❏
Day out	❏
Walk/Picnic (with or without dog)	❏
To use the shop/restaurant	❏
Accompanying friends/relatives	❏
Other	❏

Please specify _____

_____

TRAVEL TO THE PROPERTY

Q5 If you travelled by bus, did you find the bus stop you arrived at easily?

Yes ❏ No ❏

Q6 If you travelled by car, did you experience any of the following during your journey here?

Traffic congestion caused by roadworks	❏
Traffic congestion generally	❏
Excessive speeding by other road users	❏
Driving by other road users that caused you concern	❏

Q7 Did you find the property easily?

Yes ❏ No ❏

Q8 If you arrived by car, which route did you take?

A30 Eastwards	❏	M5 Southbound	❏
A30 Westwards	❏	B3181	❏
M5 Northbound	❏	Other	❏

Q9 If you arrived by car, where did you park?

National Trust Car Park at Castle View	❏
West Street Car Park	❏
Norden Park and Ride	❏
Street Parking	❏

Q10 If you used [area] park and ride . . .

	Yes	No
Did you walk to the Castle via Castle View Visitor Centre?	❏	❏
Did you take the steam train to Corfe Castle?	❏	❏
Were you offered a joint discount ticket for the railway and castle?	❏	❏

Q11 Have you used the train park and ride service before?

Yes ❏ No ❏

Q12 Did you use the park and ride service today?

Yes ❏ No ❏

RESTAURANT AND CAFE

Q13 Compared with similar restaurants or cafes that you have visited recently please rate the cost of your purchases, if applicable.

	Much more expensive	More expensive	Same	Less expensive	Much less expensive
Barn Restaurant	❏	❏	❏	❏	❏
Edgcumbe Arms	❏	❏	❏	❏	❏

Figure 3.2
(cont'd)

Q14 If you did not visit the restaurant, why was that?
(Please tick all the boxes that apply)

Not hungry or thirsty	❑	Restaurant too busy	❑
Brought our own	❑	Could not find it	❑
Not enough time	❑	Other	❑
Prices too expensive	❑		

If other, please specify _____

Q15 If appropriate, is there anything else you would like to see on sale in the restaurant?

Yes ❑   No ❑

If 'yes', what would you like to see on sale?

_____

Q16 Are you aware that we have a private function facility at [Property]?

Yes ❑   No ❑

MERCHANDISE

Q17 If you have visited any of the following, how would you rate the range of goods on sale? (Please tick one box in each row if appropriate to this visit)

	Very good	Fairly good	Neither good nor poor	Fairly poor	Very poor
Gift Shop	❑	❑	❑	❑	❑
Plant Sales	❑	❑	❑	❑	❑
Quay Gallery	❑	❑	❑	❑	❑

Q18 If you purchased a locally made item how was it labelled?

Labelled as locally made ❑   Not labelled ❑

Q19 If you purchased a locally made item was it . . .

Very good value for money	Fairly good value for money	Neither good nor poor VFM	Fairly poor value for money	Very poor value for money
❑	❑	❑	❑	❑

Q20 If you did purchase an item who was it for?

Yourself	❑	Neighbour	❑
Family	❑	Other	❑
Friend	❑		

Q21 If you were looking for something specific in the shop, how easy was it to find what you were looking for?

	Very easy	Fairly easy	Neither easy nor difficult	Fairly difficult	Very difficult
Shopping	❑	❑	❑	❑	❑

Please give reasons for the answer you have given.

_____

_____

Q22 Is there anything else you would like to see on sale in the Shop, Mill or Tearoom?

Yes ❑   No ❑

If 'yes', please specify _____

_____

Q23 Would you visit the property just to use the shop and/or restaurant . . .

During the normal open season?	❑
For Christmas shopping?	❑
For a celebration meal?	❑
Other	❑
Please specify _____	

_____

Q24 Would you come to [Property] just to visit the shop?

Yes	❑	Don't know	❑
No	❑	Not applicable	❑

Q25 Were you aware that we have a Tearoom and Shop at [Property]?

Yes ❑   No ❑

Q26 We are planning a speciality food shop selling produce exclusively from the local area at [Property], how important would it be in your decision to visit?

Very important	Fairly important	Neither important nor unimportant	Fairly unimportant	Very unimportant
❑	❑	❑	❑	❑

Q27 Would you visit the property just to visit the speciality food shop?

Yes	❑	Don't know	❑
No	❑	Not applicable	❑

Q28 If you are a paying visitor, would you use the speciality food shop only, and still pay the normal entry price?

Yes ❑   No ❑

Figure 3.2
(*cont'd*)

AREAS VISITED

Q29 Which of the following parts of the property have you used or visited today?

Garden	☐	Shop	☐
Restaurant	☐	Gallery	☐

Q30 Please indicate on the following list, the areas you did not visit and why?

	Been before	No time today	Could not find	Too far to walk
Reception	☐	☐	☐	☐
House	☐	☐	☐	☐
Lavatories	☐	☐	☐	☐
Gardens	☐	☐	☐	☐

Q31 Please indicate from the following list which areas you did NOT visit or use today and why?

	Visited before	No time	Not found	Hard to get to	Too expensive	Don't know
The House	☐	☐	☐	☐	☐	☐
Courtyard	☐	☐	☐	☐	☐	☐
Children's Playground	☐	☐	☐	☐	☐	☐
Estate walks	☐	☐	☐	☐	☐	☐
Tea-room	☐	☐	☐	☐	☐	☐
Shop	☐	☐	☐	☐	☐	☐

Q32 How important are the following for you to enjoy a day out at any attraction?

	Very important	Fairly important	Neither	Fairly unimportant	Very unimportant	Don't know
Brown road signs	☐	☐	☐	☐	☐	☐
Interesting things to see	☐	☐	☐	☐	☐	☐
Interesting presentation of life & times of the property	☐	☐	☐	☐	☐	☐
Facilities for children	☐	☐	☐	☐	☐	☐
Easy to find your way around	☐	☐	☐	☐	☐	☐
Information about the attraction	☐	☐	☐	☐	☐	☐
Service at the attraction	☐	☐	☐	☐	☐	☐
Range of food & drink on sale	☐	☐	☐	☐	☐	☐
Value for money of food & drink on sale	☐	☐	☐	☐	☐	☐
Quality of food & drink on sale	☐	☐	☐	☐	☐	☐
Range of goods for sale in the shop	☐	☐	☐	☐	☐	☐
Value for money of goods in shop	☐	☐	☐	☐	☐	☐
Guidebook	☐	☐	☐	☐	☐	☐
Guided tour	☐	☐	☐	☐	☐	☐
Walks	☐	☐	☐	☐	☐	☐
Safety information	☐	☐	☐	☐	☐	☐

Figure 3.2
(cont'd)

INFORMATION

Q33 If you have children in your group, what do you think of the information provided for them?

	Very good	Fairly good	Neither good or poor	Fairly poor	Very poor
Information	❏	❏	❏	❏	❏

If you ticked 'Fairly poor' or 'Very poor' please give some reasons for your decision.

_____

_____

Q34 Did you receive a welcome to [Property] leaflet when you arrived today?

Yes ❏   No ❏

Q35 When seeking information on a visit to an historic property, how do you like the information to be available?

Guidebook	❏	Exhibition	❏
Leaflets	❏	Free Leaflet	❏
Audio tape	❏	Questioning a room steward	❏
Video	❏	Other	❏
Guided tour	❏		

If other, please specify _____

_____

Q36 Did you purchase a guidebook or leaflet for your visit today? Please rate the publications you purchased.

	Very good	Fairly good	Neither good nor poor	Fairly poor	Very poor
Colour guide book	❏	❏	❏	❏	❏
Guide leaflet	❏	❏	❏	❏	❏
Children's guide book	❏	❏	❏	❏	❏
Estate map & walks guide	❏	❏	❏	❏	❏
Tree guide	❏	❏	❏	❏	❏

Q37 If you did not purchase a guidebook, why not?

Not offered one	❏	Not interesting enough	❏
Too expensive	❏	Other	❏

If other, please specify _____

_____

Q38 If you purchased a guidebook, how would you rate it on the following points?

	Very good	Fairly good	Neither good nor poor	Fairly poor	Very poor
Value for money	❏	❏	❏	❏	❏
Ease of reading	❏	❏	❏	❏	❏
Depth of information	❏	❏	❏	❏	❏
Interest of information	❏	❏	❏	❏	❏

Q39 How informative was the information contained within the guidebook?

Very informative	Fairly informative	Neither informative nor uninformative	Fairly uninformative	Very uninformative
❏	❏	❏	❏	❏

Q40 On your visit today, what information have you used to help you find out about [Property]? (Please tick all that apply)

Introductory video	❏	Colour guidebook	❏
Introductory talk	❏	Short guide	❏
Guided tour	❏	Children's guide	❏
Audio guide	❏	Other	❏
Free welcome leaflet	❏		

If other, please specify _____

_____

Q41 How could our provision of information be improved?

_____

_____

_____

_____

Q42 Please rank the type of information which will help you enjoy your future visits, where 1 is the most important and 9 is the least important.

Introductory video _____

Introductory talk _____

Guided tour _____

Audio guide _____

Free welcome leaflet _____

Colour guidebook _____

Short guide _____

Children's guide _____

Other _____

If other, please specify _____

_____

Q43 If you sought information on the garden, was it available?

Yes ❏   No ❏

Q44 If you visited the museum, what features did you particularly want information on during your visit?

History of the building	❏
Pictures and contents	❏
People who worked here	❏
Architecture	❏
Care and conservation	❏
The way of life	❏
Things to see and do	❏
Other	❏

If other, please specify _____

_____

Figure 3.2
(cont'd)

Q45 In your opinion is the amount of information on the [INSERT],

too little? ❑   too much? ❑

about right? ❑

Q46 On your visit today, what information have you used for directions to help you find your way about? (Please tick all that apply)

Free welcome ❑   Signs ❑
leaflet

Guidebook ❑   Information ❑
panels

Previous ❑   Information from ❑
knowledge   staff / volunteers

Q47 Were you aware that we have a guided tour at [Property]?

Yes ❑   No ❑

Q48 What aspects of [Property] would you like more information on?

_____
_____
_____
_____

Q49 If a short (5 minute) introductory talk were available at [Property], would you listen to it?

Yes ❑   No ❑

Q50 If you visited the centre and exhibition . . .

	Yes	No	N/A
Did it help your understanding of the Castle?	❑	❑	❑
Was it suitable for children?	❑	❑	❑
Did the children in your party enjoy it?	❑	❑	❑

How could the exhibition be improved? _____

_____
_____
_____

Q51 If you did not visit the exhibition at Castle View, was there a particular reason for this?

_____
_____

Q52 Did you take advantage of today's guided tours?

Yes ❑   No ❑

Q53 If 'yes', how would you rate the tour?

Very good	Fairly good	Neither good nor poor	Fairly poor	Very poor
❑	❑	❑	❑	❑

Q54 If 'no', was this because . . .

Starting time not ❑   Did not know ❑
convenient   there was a tour

No tour today ❑   Prefer to go ❑
around on my
own.

MEMBERSHIP

Q55 Were you a National Trust member before today?

Yes ❑   No ❑

Q56 If you were a National Trust member, were you asked to join here today?

Yes ❑   No ❑

ADVERTISING

Q57 Do you recall any of the following in connection with this property over the past three months?

Newspaper/ ❑   Radio ❑
magazine article   advertisement

Newspaper/ ❑   Television report ❑
magazine
advertisement

Radio report ❑

Q58 Have you seen any National Trust advertising recently on . . . (Please tick all that apply)

Radio ❑   Leaflets ❑

Newspapers / ❑   Other ❑
magazines

Posters ❑

Please specify _____

_____

Q59 How important was the advertising in your decision to visit here today?

Very important	Fairly important	Neither important nor unimportant	Fairly unimportant	Very unimportant
❑	❑	❑	❑	❑

Q60 If you live locally, what local newspapers do you read?

_____
_____

EVENTS & ACTIVITIES

Q61 Would you be interested in a programme of events at this property?

Yes ❑   No ❑

Figure 3.2
(cont'd)

Q62 Have you visited today because of a special event being held here?

Yes ☐   No ☐

Q63 Have you ever visited this property on an activity day (when an additional event/exhibition took place)?

Yes ☐

No ☐

Can't remember ☐

Q64 If you answered 'Yes' to the previous question, please tick the statement that most applied to you:

The particular event/exhibition prompted me to visit ☐

I was visiting on that day anyway ☐

Q65 How did you find out about the event/exhibition?

Local press advert	☐	'Events in REGION 2002' leaflet	☐
Radio	☐	Word of mouth	☐
TV	☐	Other	☐

If other, please specify _____

SERVICE & VALUE FOR MONEY

Q66 How would you describe the service and help received in the following areas

	Very good	Fairly good	Neither good nor poor	Fairly poor	Very poor
Reception	☐	☐	☐	☐	☐
Shop	☐	☐	☐	☐	☐
Tearooms	☐	☐	☐	☐	☐
House	☐	☐	☐	☐	☐

Q67 How would you rate the following areas in terms of value for money?

	Very good	Fairly good	Neither good nor poor	Fairly poor	Very poor
Shop	☐	☐	☐	☐	☐
Restaurant	☐	☐	☐	☐	☐

Q68 How would you rate the visit in terms of value for money?

Very good	Fairly good	Neither good nor poor	Fairly poor	Very poor
☐	☐	☐	☐	☐

FOR HIRE

Q69 Would you like to be able to hire any of the following at [Property]?

	Yes	No
An audio trail	☐	☐
Binoculars	☐	☐

OVERALL VISIT

Q70 What did you particularly enjoy about your visit?

_____

_____

_____

Q71 If there were children in your party, what did they enjoy most about their visit?

_____

_____

_____

Q72 How would you rate this property on each of the following points? (Please tick one box in each row if appropriate to this visit)

	Very good	Fairly good	Neither good nor poor	Fairly poor	Very poor
New Drake ceiling	☐	☐	☐	☐	☐
New Drake sundial window	☐	☐	☐	☐	☐
Any special event seen today	☐	☐	☐	☐	☐

If you ticked either 'very good' or 'very poor' please give some reasons for your decision.

_____

_____

_____

Q73 Is there anything about [Property] which makes it a particularly special place for you personally?

Yes ☐   No ☐

If yes, please can you tell us why? _____

_____

_____

Q74 Have you visited any of the following National Trust properties recently? (Please tick all that apply)

[List local properties] ☐

Figure 3.2
(*cont'd*)

Q75 How did you feel with regards to your safety during your visit to [Property] today?

Very safe ❑   Unsafe ❑
Safe ❑   Very Unsafe ❑

Please give details _____

_____

_____

Q76 Did you see the Dorset Police beach quad bike in operation during your visit?

Yes ❑   No ❑

DOGS & LITTER

Q77 Does your group include a dog owner?

Yes ❑   No ❑

Q78 If yes, was the dog with you today?

Yes ❑   No ❑

If no, please can you tell us why? _____

_____

_____

Q79 In your opinion, is there a problem with dogs at [Property]?

Yes ❑   No ❑

Q80 In your opinion, is there a litter problem at [Property]?

Yes ❑   No ❑

THE PROPERTY

Q81 During your visit did you spend time walking the footpaths on the Estate and/or will you walk on the Estate in the future?

	Yes	No
Walked on the Estate today?	❑	❑
Will walk in the future?	❑	❑

Q82 Do you have any comments about the way marking on the Estate?

_____

_____

_____

Q83 Prior to your visit, were you aware of the timed entry system which operates here?

Yes ❑   No ❑

Q84 Did you have to wait to enter the Garden and if so how long?

I did not have to ❑   90 minutes ❑
wait

30 minutes ❑   2 hours ❑
1 hour ❑

Q85 Will the wait deter you from re-visiting?

Yes ❑   Don't know ❑
No ❑

Q86 [Property] is currently closed to visitors throughout the winter months and on Thursdays and Fridays in the summer. Would you like the 'opening' times to be different?

Yes ❑   No ❑

If 'yes', please indicate your desired change and reasons _____

_____

Q87 If the property was open all year, please tick the months of the year in which you would be most likely to visit.

January	❑	July	❑
February	❑	August	❑
March	❑	September	❑
April	❑	October	❑
May	❑	November	❑
June	❑	December	❑

Q88 If the property was open every day, please tick the three days in which you would be most likely to visit. (Please tick only three)

Monday	❑	Friday	❑
Tuesday	❑	Saturday	❑
Wednesday	❑	Sunday	❑
Thursday	❑		

IMPROVING THE PROPERTY

Q89 Due to a major building programme during 2001 we regret that some facilities you used today were temporary. Did you feel fully informed\ about the following . . .?

	Yes	No
What building work was going on	❑	❑
Why the building work was being undertaken	❑	❑
How the building work was being done	❑	❑
Where the temporary facilities were	❑	❑

Q90 We are planning to change the displays and presentations of life at [Property] and would be grateful for your comments on the following:

	Yes	No
Adding life and colour to the displays	❑	❑
Reconstructions	❑	❑

Q91 We are planning to change the displays and presentations at [Property] and would be grateful for your comments.

_____

_____

_____

_____

Figure 3.2
(*cont'd*)

Q92 What facilities would you expect to see within the new [INSERT]?

_____

_____

_____

Q93 If we had a children's play area, would you be more or less likely to visit the property?

More likely ❑   Less likely ❑

Neither more or ❑
less likely

Q94 From 2003, we will be closing the [INSERT] one day a week for conservation work. Which day would you be least likely to visit? (Please tick one only)

Monday ❑   Friday ❑

Tuesday ❑   Saturday ❑

Wednesday ❑   Sunday ❑

Thursday ❑

FUTURE

Q95 If you could change one thing for future visitors, what would it be?

_____

_____

_____

Q96 Will you visit this property in the future? (Please tick one only)

Yes, this year ❑   Unlikely ❑

Probably ❑   Don't know ❑

Q97 If the choice was theirs, would the children in your party visit again?

Yes ❑   Don't know ❑

No ❑   Not applicable ❑

Q98 Would you visit the property just to use any of the following areas?

	Yes	No
Shop	❑	❑
Restaurant	❑	❑
Gallery	❑	❑
Toilets	❑	❑

Q99 What would make you want to visit [Property] again?

Another look inside the house ❑

The gardens ❑

An exhibition ❑

A family event ❑

A children's event ❑

New exhibition in gallery ❑

To eat in the tea-room/restaurant ❑

Q100 What would prompt you to return to this property?

_____

_____

_____

(Courtesy: The National Trust and Bournemouth University)

Note: the National Trust conduct surveys each year, sampling visitors to each of their sites. At each sampling point there is a general set of questions to be answered, and an additional list of questions specific to visitors to that site. Both are illustrated here.

*Each National Trust property can select six to eight questions from the supplementary list (shown in full here) and have these added to the general questionnaire to meet their specific needs.

Questions, tasks and issues for discussion

1   It is fairly routine for satisfaction questionnaires to be administered to clients by tour operators or airlines during homeward flights. In some cases satisfaction questionnaires are given out, and then collected, by resort representatives. Frequently, these questionnaires contain questions designed to ascertain the levels of satisfaction with the reps themselves.

   What might be the consequences of this strategy? Could this method compromise the validity and reliability of the results? What are the ethical issues involved? How could this information be better obtained, or the confidentiality of the research ensured? Would reassurance by the rep that the forms 'would be sealed and not seen by her' be sufficient to put clients' concerns about confidentiality at rest?

2   A student of tourism, while employed in a summer placement as a resort representative, undertook formal research among holidaymakers and resort representatives at a Mediterranean destination, as part of her dissertation, to discover to what extent patterns of sexual behaviour were changing as a result of the HIV and AIDS scare.

   What are the ethical dimensions of such research? Should the tutor have dissuaded the student from the project? How should the student have been advised?

   (Note: In fact, the end results of this particular research were excellent. The findings: That only the reps had chosen to exercise more caution in their behaviour, holidaymakers remaining largely unconcerned!)

3   Draw up a strategy for operationalising the above research, justifying your methodology and identifying what difficulties you would expect to encounter.

4   Taking the questionnaire in Figure 3.2 as an example, draw up a questionnaire which is designed to throw light on the market of visitors to an attraction of your choosing and their behaviour while on site. Pilot the questionnaire among your colleagues. How many amendments did this lead to? How many of the questions framed would have been better answered by the use of qualitative techniques?

5   Discuss how you would plan a survey to obtain a market profile of visitors to your nearest tourism resort. Using a plan of the resort, identify the points most suitable for conducting street interviews and explain the reasons for your choice. What biases might arise as a result of your sampling strategy?

6   Identify the sources of data which exist on the number and profile of visitors to your town or region. What gaps in knowledge about the market exist, and what weaknesses are there in the available data?

   Suggest a plan of action to help to fill these gaps, taking into account the budget limitations for research.

Exercise

Working in small groups, plan an observation exercise which might provide useful qualitative data about customers for a local travel agent. Carry out the research, and present a report to the agency on your findings.

References

1 Daymon, C and Holloway, I, *Qualitative Research Methods in Public Relations and Marketing Communications*, Routledge, 2002
2 Ibid, ch 5
3 Economist Intelligence Unit, *Choosing Holiday Destinations: the Impact of Exchange Rates and Inflation*, London, EIU, 1987

Further reading

Brassington, F and Pettitt, S, *Principles of Marketing*, Prentice Hall, 2nd edn 2000, ch 6
Churchill, G and Iacobucci, D, *Marketing Research: Methodological Foundations*, South Western, 8th edn 2002
Finn, M, Elliott-White, M and Walton, M, *Tourism and Leisure Research Methods: Data Collection, Analysis and Interpretation,* Longman, 2000
Goodson, L and Phillimore, J (eds), *Qualitative Research in Tourism*, Routledge, 2004
Ryan, C, *Researching Tourist Satisfaction: Issues, Concepts, Problems*, Routledge, 1995
Veal, A J, *Research Methods for Leisure and Tourism: a Practical Guide*, Longman, 2nd edn 1997

4 The tourist market

Learning outcomes

After studying this chapter, you should be able to:

- understand consumer needs and wants, and the distinction between these
- appreciate the factors affecting consumer motivation and demand
- understand basic principles of psychology and sociology, as they relate to consumer buying behaviour
- apply behavioural theory to the marketing of travel and tourism services
- understand market segmentation and its value in the marketing plan.

Introduction

[A] characteristic typical of tourists is their wish to find the confirmation of their image formed of the holiday area, of the dreams and pictures that are mainly shaped by tourist trade advertising. . . . The tourist industry takes this wish up on the spot and offers a picture-postcard world.

Krippendorf, J, *The Holidaymakers*, p 33

Marketing uses the term 'consumer' when making reference to individual customers, but when referring to consumers in aggregate, or groups of consumers, the term 'market' is commonly employed. A *market* can be described as *a defined group of consumers for a particular product or range of products*. By a defined group, we mean any group of consumers who can be identified by a variable or set of variables that distinguish one group of individuals from others. To take a simple example, people over the age of 50, or those between the ages of 18 and 30 are easily distinguished by age from any other consumers – and both have been targeted in Britain by specialist tour operators for this reason alone. Such groups are *measurable*, so that we can determine the overall number of our market, they are *reachable*, in that marketers can communicate with them through specialist magazines or similar techniques, and the market size is *viable* – there are sufficient of them to make it worthwhile for an organisation to adopt a strategy of niche marketing directed at them. Exactly how these markets are determined, and how they behave as consumers, is of critical importance for marketers, whose understanding of the markets will shape their strategy.

Tourists are consumers who purchase a number of diverse travel and tourism services. If those in the industry have a clear understanding of who buys their products and why, they will not only be able to tailor their products more closely to the needs and wants of their clients, but also be better able to select the advertising and sales messages used to inform and persuade those clients to buy the products.

Curiously, as we have noted earlier, most research expenditure in the travel industry has tended to be focused on what tourists buy, when they buy it, where they buy it and how they buy it. This is vital information, to be sure, but such bare facts tell us little about *why* the client purchases the product. Why, for instance, do certain tourists choose to holiday in Florida rather than Greece? What variables are at work here apart from cost? Why do they choose to travel with British Airways rather than, say, Virgin Airways? Why do they buy an independent inclusive tour rather than a group tour? Why have they booked direct with the airline, rather than going into their local travel agency? Answers to such questions as these can be enormously helpful in the preparation of marketing plans.

Understanding needs and wants

As elsewhere in this book, our aim will be to impart an understanding of basic principles, while relating these to the context of tourism. We shall start by looking at consumer needs and wants, and learning to understand how these arise.

As consumers, we often talk about our 'needing' a new television set, a new dress, or a holiday. Do we in fact really *need* these things, or are we merely expressing a desire for more goods and services? All developed economies today are orientated to increasing material consumption. We measure our success as a nation against other nations in terms of gross national product (GNP), a measure of material wealth; we are therefore encouraged to discover new wants, or 'needs', as soon as existing ones are satisfied. One result of this is that it becomes increasingly difficult to distinguish between wants and needs. Many people will search through a packed wardrobe of clothes and agonise that they do not have 'a thing to wear' for their forthcoming holidays. To what extent are the new clothes they intend to buy to take abroad actually fulfilling a need?

To answer that question, we have to determine what is meant by a need. People have certain physiological needs that are basic to survival; the need to eat, to drink, to sleep and to keep warm, and to reproduce, are all essential for the survival of the human race. However, for our psychological well-being, we also have other needs which require satisfaction; the need to give and receive affection, the need for self-esteem, for recognition of our abilities by others, for status and respect. There is also a fundamental human drive for competence, a desire to control the environment, and to gain understanding for its own sake. Abraham Maslow[1] has conveniently categorised these needs into a hierarchy (Figure 4.1), theorising that more basic needs have to be satisfied before our desires will be aroused for higher-level needs. Until we are

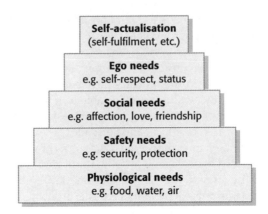

Figure 4.1
Maslow's
hierarchy of
needs

fed and sheltered satisfactorily (and 'satisfactorily' means according to the needs of our cultural group) we are unlikely to give much thought to self-esteem or 'mastering our environment'.

The way we perceive our needs is built up of a complex interrelationship of beliefs and attitudes which arise out of our knowledge and opinions. Let us take the purchase of a car, for instance. At its basic level, a car provides us with transportation, and our choice is based partly on economic considerations. It may be more convenient to use a car than public transport, and we look for a car that is cheap to run, reliable in operation, with easy access to maintenance and servicing, roomy enough for ourselves and our luggage. But we may also seek to satisfy certain psychological needs in the purchase of our car. The design of a particular model may appeal to us, either for aesthetic reasons or because its fast, sporty shape will be envied by others, gaining us status. Different colours appeal for similar reasons, and we may choose a bigger car to demonstrate our wealth to others. Our choice of car, as with our choice of so many other goods and services we buy, reflects the way we see ourselves – our perception of the kind of people we are.

It is not the role of this book to moralise about individual lifestyles. Our aim is only to bring the reader's attention to the impulses – not all of them healthy or desirable – that shape consumer motivation. It is sufficient at this point to emphasise that there is a very complex set of motives influencing most of the products we buy, and this is as true of holidays as of any other products.

Segmenting markets by needs and wants

All of us have the same basic physiological needs. But how is it that in various countries and regions, different needs arise, leading to different patterns of demand? Why are many Americans satisfied with 'convenience' food, but insist it be served quickly and accompanied by a glass of iced water, while many French people will still consider a meal to be the most important event of the day, to be lingered over and enjoyed, with a glass of wine an essential accompaniment? Why is the demand for personal computers and video recorders in Britain among the highest in the world? Why is the sale of toothpaste relatively small in France compared with other Western nations?

In this chapter we began by identifying variables which distinguish one market from another. The process of dividing markets by their variables is known as market segmentation, and as few companies produce products which are in equal demand among all segments of the population, similarly very few marketers will fail to break down the demand for their products by identifying those segments which purchase, or would be willing to purchase, their company's products. This process of market segmentation can be undertaken in four ways: by geographic variables, by demographic variables, by psychographic variables and by behavioural variables. We will examine each of these categories in turn.

Geographic segmentation

Perhaps the simplest way of dividing up our consumers is according to where they live. This can mean focusing marketing effort on global areas (such as Europe or North America), on individual countries (such as Canada and the United States), or on smaller elements of a country such as its regions, districts or towns. While there are cultural commonalities within a country or a group of countries, marketers need to be sensitive to the fact that cultural and other distinctions also exist both between contiguous countries and within countries. Climate, for example, can affect demand for products and services, as will be readily apparent in looking at the vast differences in climate between the northernmost and southernmost states in the USA. There are also sharp cultural differences between northern and southern European countries, and between southern and northern states in the USA, which are by no means restricted to the influence of climate alone. Even countries we might assume to share similar consumer traits, such as Denmark and Sweden, or Canada and the USA, demonstrate radically different patterns of consumer behaviour.

Demographic variables

In segmenting by demographic variables, marketers divide the population according to such characteristics as age, gender, family composition and size, life cycle, income, occupation, education or ethnic background. Marketers will be interested to know not only the present statistics of the population, but also any changing trends taking place in the population. Regular research by Mintel,[2] for example, reveals that household sizes are shrinking in the UK, with a fall in the number of births, and this is affecting the pattern of UK holiday-taking. However, the British Household Survey, regularly sampling the population of the UK, finds that by mid-point in the next decade there will be big rises in the numbers of 45–54-year-olds, 55–64-year-olds and the biggest rises in those between the ages of 65 and 74. Additionally, there will be a sharp increase in single-person households, to around 3.4 million, and some 30 per cent of those over 60 years of age will be living alone. Some tour operators such as Kuoni, First Choice and Saga Holidays, recognising this trend, have responded by scrapping their single supplements on standard packages and increasing allocations of single rooms in hotels, or single cabins on cruise ships (although pressure to maximise revenue during peak seasons often tends to restrict these offers to off-peak departures).

If the number of young people in a country is found to be stabilising or declining, to take another example, while the number of those of retirement age is increasing, this will have important implications both for tour operators specialising in holidays for the elderly and for the young adult market.

If, in addition, we know something about the disposable income of these segments (i.e. the amount of money with which they are left to buy goods and services after making their regular contributions to mortgages, insurance, taxes and other essential household expenses), this will further aid our marketing strategy. In Britain, for example, two groups with substantial discretionary income are young single people and 'empty nesters' – those aged about 45+ whose children have grown up and left home, and who may have two earners in the family with a good income potential for the next 15 years or so. It is also a characteristic of the developed world's changing patterns of population that with lower birth rates the numbers of young people will continue to decline, while the numbers of those in later middle age will increase. We are likely to see much more attention focus on marketing new goods and services to the middle-aged and elderly in the future – although there is some reluctance to focus on the latter segment due to their well-documented resistance to advertising!

A popular means of exploiting marketing opportunities to differing segments of the demographic population has been the development of pinpoint geodemographic marketing. Through analysis of census data and postal code areas it is possible to segment markets according to their geodemographic characteristics. In Britain, this is most evident in the development of CACI Information Services' ACORN (A Classification of Residential Neighbourhoods), which breaks down a country's population into six categories, further subdivided into some 17 groups and 54 types, based on such factors as age, family structure and lifestyle, and income. The six major categories define residents in terms of their behavioural characteristics, as it has been found that the majority of those living within defined regions tend to share common backgrounds and similar lifestyles. The six categories, which are valuable as niche markets, identify residents as:

A thriving
B expanding
C rising
D settling
E aspiring
F striving

Category A (Solihull near Birmingham being one example) comprises wealthy achievers in suburban areas, affluent elderly people in rural communities and prosperous pensioners, who would be good niche markets for lakes and mountains packages, while category C, which embraces the rising metropolitan areas, would include many residents favouring city breaks. Categories B and D tend to include many families whose main income earners are employed in less skilled occupations, and who favour beach holidays. CACI continuously refines its methodology, and with its recently introduced 'Monica' programme claims to be able to provide a significantly accurate profile of personality, social status and age of individuals based on no more than first names and postcodes.

Aided by computer mapping, marketers can develop databases selecting those elements of the population most likely to favour the company's products, and to target these by direct mail or other marketing activity. Travel agents, for instance, can identify the residents within their branch catchment areas and target them through direct mail with appropriate messages.

As subcultures, *ethnic groups*, with their differing racial or religious characteristics, are among the most prominent in splintering the marketers' convenient behavioural models for a given national or regional market. Recent high levels of immigration throughout Europe have led to concentrated populations of West Indians, Pakistanis, Bangladeshis, Chinese, Indians, and more recently refugees from Vietnam, Iraq, Afghanistan and the Balkan states, and these have tended to settle in major cities in Britain and the Continent, where they will find others of their cultural background. This has naturally given rise to demand for specialist foods as well as clothing and other products and services (including long-haul air travel to the maternal countries). In Germany, specialist travel agencies have sprung up to cater for the huge foreign travel demand created by the *Gastarbeiter* – foreign workers from countries such as Turkey and the former Yugoslavia – who return home periodically for holidays and to visit relatives. In the USA, New York counts among its population a high proportion of Jews, who have marked preferences for travel – weekend breaks in the Catskill mountains, and holidays in Miami Beach, for example. In turn, this has led to hotel proprietors learning to cater for the particular needs of these markets, by providing kosher food and traditional Jewish dishes, such as 'lox [smoked salmon] and bagels'.

Example   The guest house

The proprietor of a guest house in England recognised that there was a rapidly growing demand from independent Japanese tourists to visit England, but they were dissuaded by the different culture, language difficulties and the problem of adapting to Western food. She took the trouble to learn a modicum of Japanese, recruited (with some difficulty) a Japanese chef, provided green tea and Miso soup in the bedrooms and advertised her guesthouse (in Japanese) in the Japanese press. So successful was this ploy that it proved no longer necessary to advertise in other media – word of mouth brought other tourists from Japan to fill the accommodation.

Psychographic variables

Simply counting heads in the ways described unfortunately tells us little about the motivation of individuals within these demographic groups. How many will prefer coloured shirts to white ones? How important to young people is it to buy clothes made with natural fibres (cotton, linen, wool) rather than with synthetic materials? And of those pinpointed as sufficiently wealthy to choose between a cultural long-haul holiday and an expensive skiing holiday, what determines choice? To answer questions such as these, we need to know much more about the cultural climate of a country and the psychological needs of its population.

Countries (and regions) develop their own unique cultures and values, which are learned rather than instinctive. Thus the British tend to seek a greater measure of privacy in their lives than do Americans, leading to a greater demand for products such as garden fencing. VisitBritain (formerly the British Tourist Authority), as part of its marketing research undertaken abroad, has in the past monitored the differing holiday needs of consumers living in those countries which generate substantial numbers of tourists to Britain. They have found, for example, that many Germans love beauty and art, appreciate their environment, and are obsessed with physical well-being; their tourists demand accommodation with private facilities, accommodation that is clean and simple, which offers fresh food with large helpings in the restaurant. They enjoy family-run accommodation and a 'local atmosphere'. Knowledge such as this will be much more helpful in determining the basis for a hotel's marketing plan designed to attract German tourists.

Life would be relatively simple if we could so conveniently classify people according to their nationality and national cultures. Unfortunately, regional differences within countries are also often pronounced, leading to different patterns of behaviour, and of course the additional complexity of *subcultural* behavioural differences, such as those based on ethnic background discussed earlier, further muddy the picture. The demand for so-called health foods in Britain is far greater in the south than the north, while products such as mushy peas, popular in the north of England, are hard to sell in southern England; and centres of ethnic diversity, such as cities like Coventry, Bradford and Leicester with their high populations of Asian background, will impose their own requirements for ethnic food. Although North Americans share a common culture that is quite distinctive from the British, there are huge differences in culture and lifestyle between those residing in the north and south of the United States, and between those in the east and the Mid-West; US marketers have long been aware of the need to treat domestic markets as consisting of up to nine distinctive *market regions* when drawing up marketing plans (although curiously many US firms marketing their products in other parts of the world often appear to overlook these regional dissimilarities).

Within cultures, *social class* attempts to stratify societies according to criteria mainly based on the occupation of the 'head of household' (now usually defined as the major income earner in the family). Occupation is usually defined as a demographic variable, while class is generally seen as a psychographic variable,[3] even though closely linked to occupation. However, this form of stratification is no longer as useful as it was formerly. Not only are developing countries more egalitarian in taste and behaviour, but occupation no longer dictates product choice to the same extent. Many skilled manual jobs (such as plumbers) now provide incomes that exceed those of high-status white-collar jobs (such as university lecturers) – and many plumbers in these countries can afford to enjoy long-haul holidays in the sun. If one takes account of the added burdens of expenditure commonly found among middle-class consumers, such as private schooling for their children, it is highly likely that the discretionary purchasing powers of many manual workers will be substantially higher than those of the so-called 'middle class'.

The system of social grading in common use in Britain until 1998 divided occupations into six categories, known as socio-economic groupings:

Socio-economic groupings

A	Higher managerial, administrative or professional
B	Middle managerial, administrative or professional
C1	Supervisory or clerical, junior managerial
C2	Skilled manual workers
D	Semi-skilled and unskilled manual workers
E	Pensioners, unemployed, casual or lowest grade workers

In this categorisation, ABC1 are broadly defined as middle class, while C2 and D categories are working class. E groups, as a catch-all, are less easily defined in terms of social class, but represent those at the lowest level of subsistence in society. Other European countries use similar, although not identical, definitions, also based on occupation. In 1998, a much more complex 'official' system based on 17 categories of employment was introduced in Britain, which takes into account the size of the employee's organisation, contracts, fringe benefits and job security. Under the new categorisation, top groups are seven times as affluent as bottom groups – so while this helps to define societies in terms of spending power, it still leaves us uncertain about how spending power will be allocated within each individual group.

Of equal importance for those providing leisure services are the relative amounts of leisure time available for short breaks or holidays. Many managers and professionals are obliged to take work home and can give less time to relaxation than can the 'nine-to-five' manual worker, who today will enjoy as many as four to five weeks' holiday each year, and may take two or more foreign holidays.

Up to this point we have examined how consumers can be stratified into a number of cultural and subcultural groupings, according to nationality, racial origin or other form of common background. There are two further groups to be discussed here, of which marketers must be aware. These are *peer groups* and *reference groups* which, though sociological in nature, can be incorporated within our psychographic categorisation.

Peer groups

The first of these is the peer group. This is defined as the group with which an individual is most closely associated in his or her life. Such groups include fellow students, workmates, friends and relations or close neighbours, and there is a strong tendency for individuals to conform to the norms and values of their peer groups. The latter therefore exercise considerable influence on the buying decisions of individuals within their group. We have only to remember the pressures on us to conform in matters of dress or hairstyle in school to realise how great this pressure can sometimes be! The expression 'keeping up with the Jones's' reflects the desire to emulate the purchasing patterns of our neighbours.

Example   The specialist holiday company

Specialist holiday companies compete with larger operators by subtle manipulation of the product image. For example, operators selling Greek packages, such as Laskarina and Sunvil, launch thinly veiled appeals that their customers will find themselves with 'like-minded individuals' when they travel with their companies. This marketing approach provides a benefit which will ensure that customers will be less price-sensitive than would be the case for mass-market holidays.

Reference groups

In addition to the groups with which we as individuals are most closely associated, there are other groups with which we would choose to associate ourselves, either because we admire them or simply because we would like to emulate their lifestyle. These reference groups, as they are known, exercise strong influences on aggregate patterns of consumer demand. In particular, 'celebrities' such as film or TV personalities, pop stars, footballers and other sports stars, and some members of the Royal Family become trendsetters in introducing fashions in hairstyles or clothing. The so-called 'jet set' which surround prominent personalities are widely admired by impressionable people, who copy their way of life and purchase goods and services which are, or are thought to be, purchased by these 'innovators'. When products receive the personal endorsement of members of the reference group (film stars advertising soap or perfume, for example), this can lead to huge increases in sales. Many marketers for this reason are keen to see links established between their products and prominent people in society; Figure 7.4 (colour plate) illustrates a good example of marrying travel advertising with a popular figure from British television.

This desire to emulate those in an esteemed position in society gives rise to the phenomenon of the *trickle-down effect*, whereby products originally purchased by elite members of a society are adopted by those further down the hierarchy. Many products once thought of as 'upmarket' gradually trickle down the social scale, while those at the top of the social scale are continually seeking new products and services to distinguish themselves from the mass consumers. Articles such as filofaxes, duvets, cafetières or Austrian blinds spring to mind as examples of the trickle-down effect, which holds true equally for tourism. Consider, for example, the way in which resorts such as St Tropez or Antibes have over the years been transformed from exclusive holiday centres for rich and famous people to popular resorts for mass market tourism. Those at the top of the social spectrum are constantly seeking holiday destinations which remain undiscovered by the mass market, but as the price of long-haul travel drops, such destinations come increasingly within reach of all. Price is not the only factor, however; with advances in education, consumer tastes become more sophisticated, and a growing number of mass tourists will seek out destinations noted for high culture rather than mass culture.

Social class is, then, clearly not simply a factor of occupation or income. It is, rather, a compendium of norms and values to the extent that a marketer's real concern has less to do with social class than with *lifestyle*; the ways in which people within these social groups choose to live – and consume. Those following an unconventional lifestyle may be drawn from different social classes, but select the products and services they buy on the basis of their peer or reference groups. For example, people following an 'alternative lifestyle' may demand healthy wholefoods, natural fabrics for clothes (hand-woven rather than machine made), fashions in ethnic styles and designs, minimal use of cosmetics and simple 'folk' furniture. It is interesting to note that in spite of the growing influence of this group in buying behaviour, little is known of their habits in holidays and travel – although this group will clearly be more strongly committed to the concept of sustainable tourism than would many other travellers. However, some specialist operators have introduced new types of package tour arrangements to cater for the needs of this fast-growing sector of the market. One example is Cycling for Softies, a small specialist company which provides independent cycling holidays in France coupled with comfortable accommodation in traditional hotels: another small tour operator focuses on vegetarian holidays for the same market. The small independent tour operators who are members of AITO (the Association of Independent Tour Operators) are more likely to cater for the needs of these markets. Further applications of market segmentation will be examined later in this chapter.

Behavioural variables

Up to now we have dealt with patterns of consumer behaviour in aggregate. For a thorough understanding of consumers, however, we must also know how they act and react as individuals. Various models have been suggested by researchers of human behaviour, who are in general agreement that the number of, and interrelationship between, variables affecting product choice is extremely complex. In this chapter we can do no more than provide an introduction to consumer choice and outline some of the factors as a prelude to understanding how marketing can aid product choice.

Many models have been developed, of various levels of sophistication, to show how consumers react to stimuli. Howard and Sheth,[4] for example, have argued that consumers can be classified as being in one of three stages of behaviour: an initial extensive problem-solving stage, where they have little knowledge about products or brands, and are seeking information from a wide range of sources; a stage of more limited problem-solving, where decisions have narrowed and information seeking has become more directed; and routinised behaviour, where buying has become based largely on habit and previous satisfaction with the product.

Buyers choose products which they perceive as having the best potential to satisfy their needs; they will therefore be buying the *benefits* offered by the product. Buyers choosing a dietary product as an aid to slimming will be motivated by a product that offers some combination of low calories, nutrition, taste and value for money. Buyers learn about such products partly through experience with the same or similar products in the past, and partly by seeking information. Information is sometimes sought actively (as when the buyer has an immediate need), or passively (where the buyer may be responsive to information and stores it away for future use). Sources of information may be the commercial world, or the buyer's social environment. The commercial world produces messages about products which act as stimuli – for example, advertisements which describe a product's quality, price, availability, service, and its distinctive qualities against its competitors. Social sources of information include word of mouth recommendation from friends or family, or (presumed objective) articles about the product in newspapers, periodicals or other media. A number of variables which we have discussed earlier mediate the effect of these stimuli. Our social class, personality, culture and group influences, as well as economic influences such as our financial means, pressure of time and the importance of the purchase, all interact with our internal state of mind to affect our decision-making. Internally, individual decisions are based on the way we perceive and learn about new products. Research has shown that our perception of products is highly selective. We tend to 'screen out' information which is too simple or too familiar (hence boring), or too complex to take in, while we are more receptive to information to which we are predisposed. If, for example, we are thinking about a holiday, we become more aware of holiday advertisements. However, our perception of information is also biased: we tend to distort information to suit our own frame of reference. Many people who have never visited Britain quite genuinely believe that the country is veiled in permanent rain and fog. Such preconceptions form a formidable problem for VisitBritain's overseas marketing campaigns, but they can be modified by strong stimuli, such as the personal experience and recommendation of a member of the family or a friend.

Learning theory

One of the simplest models of the theory of how we learn is shown in Figure 4.2. The model suggests that our individual needs give rise to a drive which we take action to satisfy. If our action does indeed result in satisfying the need, we tend to repeat the experience, leading to the development of habit formation and customer loyalty to particular brands. In the same way, we tend to generalise from past experience of a product, so that the satisfaction we receive, for example, by taking a cruise will lead us to take another cruise, or another type of holiday with the same company. However, Howard and Sheth have shown that constant repeat purchase of the same product leads to monotony and a search for a new product or brand, with the consumer once again returning to intensive problem-solving activity. An awareness of this phenomenon is useful to marketers attempting to switch loyal users of rival products to their own company's products.

The interaction of *stimulus* and *exogenous variables* results in buyers responding in a number of ways. First, their attention may be drawn to new products. Second, they become conscious of the product and its benefits, at least superficially, and perhaps to an extent that they will recall and recognise again at a later date. Third, consumers become seriously interested in the product, with the possible intention of purchasing it at some time in the future. Finally, they will engage in overt purchasing behaviour, that is, they will purchase a particular quantity of the product at a particular time, through particular distributive outlets and at a particular price.

Figure 4.2
A model of
learning theory

This hierarchical pattern of response is known as AIDA – attention, interest, desire, action – representing four stages of response by consumers to a product. Marketing strategy is aimed at achieving one or more of these consumer responses. This will be discussed in greater depth in Chapter 10.

One other set of behavioural variables will be of interest to marketers, and that is the *patterns* of buying behaviour discerned from consumption. The extent to which one's customers are first-time buyers, regular buyers or occasional buyers of the product, whether they are light or heavy consumers, and their degree of loyalty to the product or the brand are all highly significant to the marketer in learning how to appeal to different market segments. These variables will, of course, in part be accounted for by psychographic or demographic factors discussed above, but there will inevitably be individual differences between consumers' attitudes to products and their benefits, their knowledge of the products and readiness to purchase, and these disparities represent a real challenge to marketers. One way in which tourism marketers are learning to meet their individual customers' needs is by tailor-making their packages, and even the largest operators today have established specialist departments or other means of serving the individual needs of their customers. Indeed, it is the growing recognition that the future lies with the individual rather than the mass consumer which offers a lifeline to the independent travel agents in their battle to survive in the face of competition from the large chains.

Organisational marketing

To this point we have been addressing the needs of individual or mass consumers. However, there is another important market which plays a role in travel and tourism marketing, and that is the organisational market. By this we mean those buyers within the commercial, governmental or institutional spheres. This process is also sometimes known as industrial marketing, or business to business (B2B) marketing, but many organisations are not profit-making, and therefore not businesses or industries as we understand the term. Brassington[5] defines organisational marketing as 'the management process responsible for the facilitation of exchange between producers of goods and services and their organisational customers'. Dealing with organisational customers calls for distinct approaches and strategies, and in many respects is far more complex than marketing to individual consumers, hence higher-level skills and, generally, higher salaries accompany these positions.

Key issues in organisational marketing, which distinguish this from consumer marketing, are:

■ The buyer is seldom the consumer. In fact, a variety of different employees may be involved in the buying decision. Together, these are sometimes known as the DMU, or decision-making unit. Apart from the end-user, they will include the influencer, who may have the power to influence which products are bought and from which companies; the decider, usually a senior member of the organisation who controls the budget for purchases; the gatekeeper (often the decider's or buyer's secretary), who as a go-between can hinder contact between buyer and seller; and the negoti-ator or buyer. Sometimes, decision-making is in the hands of a team or committee, rather than one individual. Marketers will have to understand how the DMU oper-ates within each organisation, and deal appropriately with staff at each level in the process.

■ Buying tends to be in much larger quantities (or involves much higher revenues) at less frequent intervals than would normally be the case with consumers. For this reason, the selling role becomes more high-key and personal; marketers will have much closer relationships with their customers. The DMU will expect more indi-vidual attention to their organisational needs.

■ Prices are negotiable. While in general it is true to say that prices are more inelastic than those paid by consumers, the belief that, simply because 'the company is pay-ing', premium prices can be charged, is a fallacy. Increasingly, cost pressures are encouraging businesses and other organisations to negotiate lower prices. There are fewer business travellers today willing to pay premium prices for first-class or business-class flights, and the budget airlines can boast that a significant proportion of their overall revenue is now business-related travel.

■ Organisational buyers make high demands in terms of quality consistency, supply reliability and personal service.

■ There are seldom intermediaries in the buying process – buyers and principals usually negotiate directly. However, there are exceptions to this rule with all prod-ucts, including travel and tourism. Conference organisers, for example, act as inter-mediaries between organisations wishing to arrange conferences for their staff and the hotels or other venues where such conferences are held.

■ Markets are far less diffused than are mass consumer markets. In many forms of organisational marketing, there are a relatively small number of easily identifiable customers. The number of companies within a given geographical area large enough to need a business house travel agent to deal with the travel arrangements of their staff, to take one example, is far fewer than the number of potential tourists resident in the same catchment area.

■ Branding is relatively unimportant in the purchase decision. Organisational buyers are more concerned with economic matters such as price, delivery, reliability, efficiency and service, than with emotional factors such as image.

However, this latter point is not to say that emotional factors play no part in decision-making. The prestige of dealing with a well-established firm of international repute may still enter the equation – and when one thinks of the importance of the com-pany car to the firm's employees, status still has a big part to play with some forms of organisational buying. Similarly, issues like friendship between business people still drives sales, and marketers go out of their way to cultivate personal contacts for this reason.

Example   Business travel agents

Business travel agents must be prepared to provide a much higher level of service to their customers than would normally be found in travel agents. Tickets are expected to be delivered by hand or by courier, and some members of staff may be required to be on call 24 hours a day to handle urgent business travel needs of employees, including the obtaining of visas, foreign currency, etc., often at short notice.

The variety of forms of B2B marketing can be also illustrated by taking two other examples. Institutional caterers (suppliers) supply the in-flight meals and drinks to airlines (buyers) on behalf of air passengers (end-users). In doing so, they have to balance the needs of their buyers (low cost, portion-controlled, easily handled, hygienic, reliable quality) with those of the end-users (taste, quantity, variety, appropriateness for the market served), bearing in mind that much food (and wines) served at altitude have reduced or altered taste, and that food served to premium fare-paying passengers must be significantly superior to that served in economy class. Food and service in-flight are significant means of differentiating what in most respects is a similar product experience (one aircraft is very like another) and buyers hence take on a very important marketing task for their companies when choosing which caterers and foodstuffs to purchase. A rather different challenge faces hotel chains which accommodate airline flight crews, where availability is crucial, sometimes at short notice due to flight delays, and rock-bottom prices are guaranteed for good rooms against the expectation of high and frequent demand patterns. Again, similarly ranked hotel chains offer a somewhat anodyne and impersonal product experience, so marketing must focus on other product benefits in a very competitive market.

Networking is immensely important in all businesses, as part of the process of maintaining personal contact with potential buyers and sellers. This is no less true of the tourism industry, and the World Travel Market, held annually in London (and similar large travel exhibitions held in other key European centres such as ITB Berlin and BIT International Tourism Exchange Milan) play a pivotal role in helping to establish and maintain such contacts. Networking is a key aspect of *relationship marketing* which will now be examined.

Relationship marketing

Relationship marketing can be defined as 'creating, maintaining and enhancing strong relationships with customers and other stakeholders',[6] and recognises the growing importance in marketing theory of establishing close, ongoing links with those individuals and businesses with which the organisation is most heavily involved. Although commonly identified with improving relationships with the organisation's customers, the concept embraces other stakeholders, such as key employees, who also play an important role in the success of any organisation. Better relations with employees, through regular communication, improved training, better facilities, more promotion opportunities and greater personal responsibility will lead to enhanced performance and in turn improved relations with customers. This employee relationship management is sometimes referred to as internal marketing, and its importance has only recently become a factor in tourism marketing, where many jobs are comparatively low skilled, low paid, poorly trained and seen as low status.

Example   Thistle Hotels

Thistle Hotels runs a 'More Than Just Accommodating' scheme designed to recognise and reward members of staff who offer a service beyond the 'call of duty'. Staff can be nominated either by their colleagues or by customers, and are rewarded with Marks & Spencer vouchers. The scheme has widespread approval and has led to increased staff satisfaction.

Customer relationship marketing (CRM) is a technique, or set of techniques, designed to help build up close and favourable contacts with an organisation's key customers, whether consumers or businesses, over a long time period. This will involve anything from maintaining a customer information service up to a close, long-term partnership involving financial and other forms of assistance – to take one example, a tour operator helping a travel agent by providing window displays and engaging in joint presentations to prospective customers, and helping to train staff through in-house 'academies' such as Kuoni's long-haul college.

Customer relationship management is already well established in travel and tourism. Regular customers of airlines, for instance, are entitled to the award of frequent flyer benefits, which might include selective upgrading or the accumulation of free air miles according to the number of paid-for miles travelled. Regular guests at hotels, and passengers on cruises, may qualify for upgrades based on the offer of one grade higher on booking, or the best rooms available when checking in.

Example   Cunard Line

Cunard, in common with many cruise companies, maintains contacts with former passengers through automatic membership of the Cunard World Club and regular distribution of a newsletter, the *Cunarder*. All members are notified of special offers, including heavy discounts on selected sailings, a Club Desk hotline, World Club representatives on board, and a members-only page on the Cunard website. A single voyage gives passengers Silver Cunarder membership of the Club, with additional benefits accruing to Gold and Platinum Cunarders, based on the number or lengths of voyages undertaken. These include the award of a Cunard pin, on-board World Club parties and, for the highest level of membership, priority check-in and embarkation at selected ports plus an invitation to the senior officers' party on board.

One should be aware that not all organisations would benefit from customer relationship marketing, and indeed, many deliberately avoid this approach within their marketing mix. As the managing director of one travel company declared,

Operators which market themselves strongly on price might be wasting their efforts on CRM[7]

and as we have seen earlier, companies like Ryanair, with its total focus on price, would have to compromise this approach if CRM were to be introduced. In fact, in-house research by Anite Travel Systems and Gensys found that CRM is more evident among smaller travel agents and tour operators than larger companies. It involves high initial investment, but also promises high returns in the long run. Typical techniques within the CRM fold include the guarantee to answer phone calls within a given number of rings. Readers who are becoming increasingly frustrated with the popularity of automated answerphones with their endless requirements to select appropriate buttons to press might feel that a human being on the end of the phone would be the best form of CRM possible (and, yes, some modest-sized operators like Bales and Journey Latin America still provide this service!).

ICT (information and communications technology) offers a number of particularly effective tools to aid the process of CRM. Databases containing full data on key customers are now the norm in business, and other forms of e-commerce such as website marketing, call centres and even interactive digital television are all playing a role in helping to generate closer ties between organisations and their customers.

Applying the theory in marketing tourism

It has been necessary to take a number of pages to explain the fundamentals of consumer and organisational marketing theory, with some selective examples. We now turn to examining ways in which this understanding can improve the organisation's ability to market travel and tourism.

Individual behaviour is complex, but we have shown that it is possible to identify patterns of generalised group behaviour among consumers sharing common characteristics. Marketers have long recognised that few organisations are powerful enough to aim their products at the consumer in general. The cost of such a strategy is huge, and, particularly if the organisation is also targeting international markets, such a 'shotgun' approach, which fails to identify which groups of customers are likely to be the best prospects for a purchase, also fails to make effective use of its resources.

In very few cases are the products of one organisation attractive to all consumers in the marketplace. It therefore makes good sense to target the products to specific types of consumers, for which the product offers specific benefits, thereby making it more distinctive from its competitors: adopting, as marketers refer to it, a 'rifle' approach instead of a 'shotgun' approach. This approach, the theory of which was explained earlier in this chapter, is known as *market segmentation*, the basis of which is that the company first determines the market or markets it will serve, and then develops its products to serve the needs of those markets. This *concentrated marketing* strategy reflects a marketing-orientated approach to business that is fundamental in planning.

As a prelude to this exercise, many companies find it useful to quantify their markets in terms of the numbers of consumers at various stages in the AIDA spectrum. Out of the total population – international, national, regional or however this is defined by the organisation – only a limited number of these will be *potential* consumers. To take a simple example, out of the total population in the United Kingdom, only those over 50 years of age are potential customers for Saga Holidays. Not all this market will necessarily be *available*; some may prove difficult to reach (and obviously those incarcerated in Her Majesty's prisons will be unlikely to qualify!). From the remaining pool, the organisation may wish to identify its *served* market – those with which it actually communicates or attempts to communicate, and who express interest. From this market the actual *penetrated* market is derived, this being the number of customers who have committed themselves to a purchase. This will obviously be only a small proportion of the original potential market, but the figures will enable the organisation to realistically assess its market penetration and potential for growth. Within the available market, a business can define the *segments* on which it will choose to focus.

A market segment can be defined as 'a subgroup of the total consumer market whose members share common characteristics relevant to the purchase or use of a product'. A criterion in market segmentation is that the selected market must be reachable through advertising messages or other forms of communication aimed exclusively at them. Let us now look at some of the ways in which markets can be segmented in the travel and tourism industry.

Segmentation in travel and tourism marketing

Markets can be segmented in many different ways. If we go back to our earlier description of the variables affecting the demand for goods and services, we can start by segmenting our customers according to these criteria.

We could, for instance, decide to cater for groups of holidaymakers according to their age, their social class, or their regional distribution. Let us assume that we have decided to become specialists in developing package holidays for customers living in a particular region of one country. We might feature, as benefits for this group, the convenience of local airport departures, free transport to the airport and/or free parking at the airport. While we would be carrying smaller numbers of clients than the large mass market operators, and would not therefore gain the same economies of scale, many consumers will be satisfied to pay slightly higher prices for the convenience of a local departure and the additional benefits offered. We could stress that we are a local company supporting the economy of the region, and be active in local community events, so that local residents tend to think of our company first when planning their holidays.

Example   Palmair

Palmair is exactly one such company in Britain. A division of Bath Travel and with aircraft based at Bournemouth International Airport, it focuses on the West Country within striking distance of Bournemouth, offering popular package holidays to the Mediterranean and day trips to European cities, often accompanied by a local tour manager, and flights are often seen off personally by the Managing Director (the company is customer relations oriented!)

Other tour companies have specialised by age. The popularity of companies like Club 18–30, which focuses on the provision of youth holidays, and Saga Holidays, which specialises in holidays for the over-50s, reflects the success of concentrated marketing strategies. Incoming tour operators have specialised in handling groups of tourists from specific countries, such as Japan, the USA or Israel. They make it their business to know, and cater for, the needs of nationals from these countries, and will frequently employ nationals of their customers' countries to greet and deal with incoming clients, in order to ease communication and put their clients at ease. In the USA, some tour operators have aimed to capture the black ethnic market (by, for example, establishing tours to West Africa for black Americans curious about their roots).

Just as with demographic segmentation, so can we segment by psychographic variables. Some companies have developed specialist villa holidays catering for young professional people, while other organisations have packaged tours for those with specific lifestyles. Research by the Irish Tourist Board (ITB) found that holidays in Ireland tend to meet the needs of those seeking to know and understand themselves better – a 'self-actualisation' need in Maslow's terms. This knowledge can be used by those promoting holidays to Ireland, by their emphasising Ireland as a destination for self-reflection and tranquillity. Figures 4.3 and 4.4 (colour plates) provide recent examples of advertising by Tourism Ireland (the body promoting Ireland and Northern Ireland jointly) which reinforce this emotive lure, coupled with price appeals and reassurance about repeat bookings from satisfied visitors.

Stanley Plog[8] in the United States has found that tourists can be categorised broadly as either psychocentrics or allocentrics. The former are self-inhibited, nervous and lack the desire for adventure, preferring well-packaged routine holidays in popular tourist destinations, mainly of the 'sun, sand, sea' variety, while the latter are more outgoing, have varied interests and are keen to explore new places and find new things to do. Such tourists are more likely to travel independently.

This model in itself is no doubt too simplistic. Most of us have some mix of these characteristics, and it is a noticeable fact that many mass tourists to popular destinations, who would fall into the psychocentric category, gain confidence after a number of trips abroad, and become more adventurous. They may hire a car, for instance, and drive to areas less frequented by tourists, during their routine package holiday. Nevertheless, the model is helpful in thinking about the facilities we should provide to meet these differing needs.

Yet another way of segmenting our markets is according to the benefits the product offers. In many cases, different benefits appeal to different markets, and this can be seen in the case of a hotel which attracts both business people and holidaymakers. Sometimes both markets are attracted at the same time (as with hotels in major cities, although weekend visitors are more likely to be leisure clients), while in other cases different markets are attracted at different times of the year. Seaside hotels may find that they are attracting a more upmarket clientele, and from an older age bracket, during the shoulder season than in the peak summer season.

Some hotels, particularly in country towns, will have to cater for different guests, based on whether their visitors are 'transient' (stopping only overnight while touring) or 'terminal' (using the hotel as a base for touring). Hotels in US cities (and certain other countries) have recognised the need among day trippers and shoppers for a base in the city to rest, leave their purchases or take a bath, and hoteliers have hired rooms by the hour for this market, thus finding a new way to use the product.

Major hotel chains have identified a steady rise in the number of businesswomen to whom they are catering, and have responded by providing facilities to meet their needs, including more feminine decor, cosmetic mirrors, hairdryers and other benefits. In some cases, floors in large hotels have been experimentally restricted for the use of women only, to enhance the security of females travelling alone – although not all businesswomen have welcomed this approach, viewing it as patronising. More welcome has been the decision not to announce openly the room numbers allocated to single females when handing out keys.

The development of motels in the USA was a direct marketing response to an identified need. Transient tourists required easy check-in and check-out facilities, minimal service or public rooms but convenient parking and low prices. The motel meets all these needs.

Example   **Las Vegas**

Las Vegas, long renowned as a gambling Mecca, primarily for the US market, has in recent years widened its attraction as a holiday destination by creating facilities for the family market. It has successfully overcome its earlier image and combined these two markets, thereby attracting many more long-haul travellers from Europe.

Major tour operators might be thought at first to be largely undifferentiated in their market segmentation. In fact, their products have in some cases become highly differentiated, even if less specialised than with small companies. To take advantage of the many different needs of their national market, they offer a huge range of different resorts, the convenience of local airports, holidays of different lengths, a wide range of hotels and prices, and catering arrangements varying from self-service to half board and full board.

Volume segmentation

There is one other form of market segmentation to which we must make reference, that of volume segmentation. This distinguishes between light and heavy users of the product (or loyal, repeat purchasers compared with occasional or infrequent purchasers). Hotel companies offer discounted rates, and other benefits, to regular purchasers such as companies booking employees regularly, or airlines who have contracts for crew accommodation. As we have seen, one technique within CRM is the benefit regular passengers gain from 'frequent flyer' programmes: once members exceed a certain annual mileage of travel with the airline, they are rewarded with a free trip for themselves, or their partners. While this strategy has proved highly successful in building brand loyalty, it rapidly became copied by all leading airlines, and has become so popular that there is, at the time of writing, an estimated 23-year backlog for the redemption of existing air miles: some 90 million people in the world holding air miles worth more than $500 billion.[9]

Other lessons from Maslow

It will by now be appreciated that an understanding of consumer needs is critical for successful marketing. It might be helpful at this point to summarise consumers' travel and tourism needs and relate these to the Maslow hierarchy discussed earlier.

Motivation for travel and tourism can be categorised as follows:

- holiday travel
- business travel
- health travel
- visiting friends and relatives (VFR)
- religious travel
- travel for economic benefit (e.g. shopping)
- travel for educational purposes (study tours, etc.)
- sports and activities travel (participation or observation).

In fact, we can summarise all of these activities under five basic needs: *physical*, *cultural*, *interpersonal*, *status and prestige* and *commercial*. Although there will be some overlap of motives between these categories, it will be useful to see how these needs are met by tourism facilities or destinations, and how they relate to levels of need in Maslow's hierarchy.

The demand for business travel is quite different from that for leisure travel, since it is by nature less 'discretionary', that is, less a matter of personal choice. We explored some of the issues which make business travel different from leisure travel when examining organisational marketing earlier in this chapter, but in considering the travel needs of the businessperson, the critical distinctions are, firstly, that such travel tends to be less price sensitive, since the company rather than the individual will be footing the bills (but note the caveat expressed earlier!) Additionally, businesspeople tend to make frequent short-duration trips, which are generally taken midweek rather than at weekends, and travel is not subject to seasonal fluctuations. Travel decisions often have to be taken at short notice, necessitating the availability of regular scheduled flights and a fast and convenient reservations service.

At a basic physiological level, travel can sometimes be essential for health as in the case of treatment overseas for complex surgery, or the need to travel to warm, dry climates to recover from illnesses such as asthma and tuberculosis. These are then survival-related needs. Many people in stressful occupations also need a break from the mental or physical strain of their work to avoid a breakdown in health, and this 'cathartic' travel is no less necessary for survival. Even business travel, usually only thought of in terms of economic need, may be required for the survival of the organisation in the face of overseas competition – but we must also recognise that quite a lot of business travel is in fact taken for prestige purposes – the requirement for first-class travel and top-price hotels, for instance – while conference travel may be ascribed to competence needs.

Many people fail to travel due to real or imagined fears – the fear of flying, or fear of being attacked. In these cases, the failure to travel is again related to basic safety needs of survival. In these cases, the marketer's responsibility is to overcome such fear, for example, by the national tourist office mounting a campaign to reassure visitors of the safety of their country, or bringing pressure on the government to provide protection for tourists, while airlines have to take steps to educate their clients about air safety. British Airways, for example, have run a series of flights designed for those with a psychological fear of flying.

Our social needs for loving and belonging are often met through package holiday programmes, since many tourists find group tours an excellent way to make new friends or seek romance. Cruises fulfil this function well, as well as providing a recognised outlet for those recently bereaved, who need a change of environment to escape their distress. A desire to appear attractive to others may be achieved by gaining a suntan, despite the health risks. Visiting little known and distant tourist destinations may give tourists prestige in the eyes of their friends who are less travelled. Cultural travel provides opportunities for self-actualisation, the process of achieving or fulfilling one's potential.

These examples will be sufficient to show that travel satisfies many physical, social and psychological needs. They will also have shown us that travel motivation can be both general and specific. We experience the general drive to get away from our present environment, to escape from routine and seek new and different experiences, while at the same time we demonstrate individual motivations to see specific destinations and undertake specific activities while on holiday.

Some of the ways in which tourist needs for physical and cultural experiences are met are shown in Table 4.1. It is important to appreciate, however, that tourists seek to satisfy not one single need but a number of quite distinct needs simultaneously. The most successful products are those which respond best to this 'bundle of needs' within a given market segment. As Pearce says,[10]

Table 4.1   Tourist needs and the marketing response

Need	Response
Physical	
Rest and relaxation	Beach holidays
	Lakes and mountains
Action and adventure	Trekking
	Ponytrekking, skiing
	Canoeing, sailing
	Safari parks
Health	Gentle walking trails
	Spas, mountain resorts
	Health farms
Cultural	
Educational	Lecture cruises
	Study tours
Historical/archaeological	Tours of war sites
	Birthplace museums
	Nile cruises
	Ironbridge Gorge
Political	Lenin's, Mao's, Ho Chi Minh's tombs
	Attending political rallies
	Tours of UN
	Houses of Parliament, Reichstag
Scientific/technical	NASA space centre
	Big Pit mining museum
	Car assembly plant
	Hollywood film studio
Arts	Music festivals
	Theatre visits
	Folk dance shows
	Craft or painting holidays
Religion	Mecca and the hajj
	Lourdes
	'Retreats'
	Oberammergau
Commercial	Shops/restaurants
	Conference facilities
	Freeports
	Craft centres
	Wine/beer fairs

It is not the specific qualities of a destination and its attractions which motivate, but the broad suitability of the destination to fulfil particular psychological needs.

Having now discussed consumer needs for travel, we can now examine one other important aspect of consumer behaviour, that of decision-making.

Decision-making for the travel purchase

Understanding how consumers reach decisions about their travel arrangements has advanced considerably in recent years. Interest centres not only on how decisions are taken, but also when they are taken, and why.

We earlier discussed the process by which consumers are first attracted to, and subsequently influenced to buy, products, in models such as AIDA. This process is also influenced by the degree of risk inherent in the purchase. Obviously, deciding whether to buy a new bar of chocolate involves minimal risk, whereas deciding where to take the annual holiday involves substantial expenditure and a high degree of uncertainty. The consumer often lacks sufficient experience on which to base a decision. Experience is a key element in the learning process, and gaining objective information about new destinations is not easy. For this reason, word of mouth recommendation plays a very significant role in reducing risk and helping to form decisions.

Risk can be reduced in a number of ways. First, *familiarity* with a product gives confidence and results in the regular repeat purchase of a product; hence the tendency among more conservative holidaymakers to return to their traditional seaside resort year after year (product loyalty), or to buy another holiday from the same tour operator (brand loyalty).

Second, risk can also be reduced by *lowering our expectation* of the product. However, consumers tend to idealise their major purchases, so this is rarely practical in the case of travel purchases. Nevertheless, there is great danger of overselling a travel experience, because of the frame of mind in which holiday purchasers are making their decision.

A third way of reducing risk is to *maximise knowledge*, seeking as much information about the product and selecting the 'best' choice from a wide selection of alternatives. An individual's personality plays a role here, as certain types of people tend to optimise their choice, while others, especially those with authoritarian personalities, consider fewer alternatives and are more easily satisfied. Advance booking is a characteristic of the search for security, reflecting not only the desire to make the booking of one's choice, but also the need to gather and consider information about the product well in advance. On the other hand, there is a trend to booking later in the UK, as the British travelling public become more sophisticated and willing to bear some risk in the expectation of a possible bargain.

Example Supplementary sales

Supplementary sales, such as shore excursions on cruises or optional excursions taken during package holidays, are an important source of revenue for principals, especially as payment is received up front sometimes months in advance. To encourage forward sales, many operators will stress the need to book ahead to be certain of getting on the excursion. Brochures may carry the message to the effect that 'these excursions are particularly popular, and fill quickly. It is advisable to book in advance if you wish to be certain of getting on the tour.' Customers sometimes complain when they find eventually that the tours when purchased locally are cheaper than those booked in advance, but are reassured that the premium avoids the risk of their being sold out.

The booking process is protracted, and there are a number of different influences at work here. The interplay between tour operator and travel agent is an interesting case in point. The tour operator works hard to be included in the initial selection of brochures through brand image and advertising. The clearer and more helpful the brochure, the more likely the operator is to survive the 'homework' stage. It follows that a little known operator whose brochure is poorly produced and 'me too' in style will stand little chance of winning the booking. Hence the chosen strategy of many small operators to specialise and excel in certain types of holidays. Hence also the price and advertising wars between large operators whose products offer very little real difference.

The travel agent is seen as the means to resolve the perceived lack of difference between operators, the easy and safe route to resolve the perceived complexities of price calculation and availability, and ideally as an information resource adding personal knowledge and expertise to back up the information in the brochure. It therefore follows that a travel agent who has not read the brochure and can add no information on a potential destination is not meeting consumer expectation and also stands little chance of winning the booking.

In consuming a product, risk is reduced by searching for familiarity. However, tourism by its nature involves some novelty. Hence the common tourist problem of how to balance the need for adventure and new experiences with the need for familiarity and reassurance. Studies of North American tourists show that this problem is resolved in a number of different ways. First-time US visitors abroad may venture into the border towns of Mexico, where they are close to the 'perceived safety' of their home country and culture. US visitors to Europe frequently make the UK their first stop, as the two countries share a common language and culture. Perceived security may also be increased by travelling to the foreign country in one's own national airline, and by staying in hotels operated or owned by a hotel chain from the generating country.

In the case of British tourists, Jersey has successfully promoted the island as a 'bit of France that is British', while Gibraltar has taken the approach 'so British, so

Mediterranean', effectively combining the appeal of security and familiarity with that of a warm climate in a foreign destination. French territories overseas, such as Guadaloupe, Martinique and Réunion Island, adopt a similar marketing approach in selling these destinations to the French market.

The package tour is the marketer's response to the need for familiarity. Tourists travel to mass tourism destinations where they will be in company with others from their own culture, where many locals will be conversant with their language, and where it may be possible to buy familiar food and drinks, but there is scope to sample new foods and different ways of life. The guided tour, particularly when led by a guide from the home country, gives psychological security, while the guide not only acts as 'culture-broker' but also caters to the tourists' social needs by acting as a catalyst in getting members of the group to know one another.

Family group decision-making

Where decisions have to be made together, rather than individually, it is important to understand who participates in the decision, and the degree of influence each member of the group exercises. In family travel, how far is the choice of where to go, and when to go, made by one member of the household, or is it a joint decision by all members of the household? Evidence suggests that women play a much more important role than was formerly thought in the process of deciding the family holidays. What has to be borne in mind when marketing travel is that, where joint decisions must be made, the parties involved may have different needs and objectives; consequently different messages may have to be directed to women and men. The typical travel brochure, with its pretty bikini-clad models on the cover, appears to be aimed at men, but may also appeal to a fantasy in some women which encourages them to believe that just possibly the holiday will make them become more like the model.

Market segmentation as a guide to marketing planning

It might be helpful to close our discussion of consumer behaviour by reviewing a segmentation exercise undertaken by one of the major UK tour operators. It has already been noted that the travel market is complex and can be segmented in various ways from destination to age of traveller. A very interesting exercise in segmentation started with the individual and identified different *archetypes* or *mood states* into which consumers could be grouped. These archetypes were by no means 'once and for all' categories. Individuals might well progress between them, with experience. They might also approach, for instance, a second holiday in a rather more cost-conscious mood within the same year.

The research went on to identify what the different groups were looking for from their tour operator – and the differences are very marked indeed, as shown in Table 4.2. This research clearly identifies to the operator opportunities for product differentiation to match the different types of consumers, and gives a strong indication of the advertising messages likely to be most effective in promoting the different products.

Table 4.2 Tour operator segmentation exercise

Archetype characteristics	Expectation of tour operator by customer
1 Once in a lifetime tripper One-off special trip, e.g. honeymoon, retirement, 25th anniversary. ■ high emotional investment ■ very high expectations ■ expects something memorable ■ would like 'perfection'	Tour operator should recognise importance and 'specialness'. Expectation to be pampered and provided with extras. Desire to be treated like a king/queen, not to be one of many.
2 Mainstream package taker Often families with diverse needs within group that includes children. Not confident in own self-sufficiency abroad. ■ enjoy sociability of package holidays ■ seeking UK on the Mediterranean	Tour operator must take care of everything and provide a buffer against the foreign location. Rep should be helpful but not intrusive, and the focus for a diverse range of facilities and excursions. Familiarity, especially food, is important.
3 Resort repeater Loyal to resort or even hotel, possibly also to operator. Often enjoys being 'old hand' and own expertise. ■ repeats a 'perfect' match for own needs ■ seeks the security of familiarity ■ knows exactly what to expect	Expectation of operator is lower. Wants certain level of comfort and a sense of security. Expects recognition of own knowledge and looks for some degree of sociability from a package. Basically looking for hassle-free organisation at the best price.
4 Upmarket package taker Prizes individuality and does not want to mix with hoi polloi. Frequently DINKYs or empty nesters (i.e. couples pre- or post-children). ■ may take only long-haul packages ■ often destination-driven ■ 'one-upmanship' a factor	Tour operator should provide something a little out of the ordinary, high quality and a 'tailored' product. There needs to be a sense of individuality and recognition of experience/confidence of the consumer. The fewer other Brits the better.
5 Aspiring individualist Takes fewer packages than upmarket package taker above. Often more experienced traveller. Not interested in mass sociability. ■ may seek package as not confident of location ■ likes sense of 'trail-blazing' ■ often picks less popular destinations	Tour operator is expected to provide efficient expertise and organisation, but no interference. Wants rarity from a package that is 'not a package'.
6 Deal seeker Out for a good deal. Limited desires, e.g. sun, sea, sand, cheap booze, can be satisfied by a number of locations.	Looking for a deal from the operator. Wants 'cheap and cheerful', not 'cheap and nasty'. No costs should be hidden. Still wants effective organisation and help if it is needed.
7 Upmarket deal seeker Looking for bargain, but among 'different', upmarket holidays. ■ often long haul or upmarket ■ unable or unprepared to pay more ■ often experienced in short haul and 'graduating' ■ confident via experience	Expects operator to provide a deal, yet still wants high level of looking after and cosseting. Wants guidance and expertise and a holiday that is different but not too different or unknown.
8 Confident individualist Anti-package and sees self as independent traveller. Very price conscious and seeks to achieve one-upmanship over operator. ■ wants to be in control ■ may do own independent research	Wants operator for cheap price, no interference, avenue for specific enquiries and help in a real emergency.

In-depth qualitative research of this kind can be invaluable in aiding a company to put together and deliver the kinds of holidays which different market segments are seeking, and then attract them with appropriate promotional themes.

Questions, tasks and issues for discussion

1   Where do the following destinations lie today on the social spectrum? What kind of markets are likely to be attracted to each? (Bear in mind that price/distance will be a factor in determining the appeal – a holiday destination in the Far East seen as exotic for a European tourist may be a comparatively cheap short-haul holiday for an Australian tourist.)

   Machu Picchu, Costa Rica, Galapagos, Phuket, Australian Gold Coast, Sardinia, Antibes, Florence, Marbella, Deia (Majorca), Las Vegas, Xian, Luang Prabang, Barcelona, Riga, Ostend, Antigua, the Dominican Republic, Hawai'i

2   It has been said that marketing is about giving customers what they want – yet this conflicts with the saying 'when in Rome, do as the Romans do'. Foreign hoteliers have successfuly tailored their products to meet the needs of their customers, thus – to take one example – traditional British food is available for British tourists in many popular Spanish resorts, and traditional German food for the German visitors. Does this, in your view, degrade local culture and customs, or is this merely common-sense marketing? If the latter, to what extent should products be tailored to meet the needs of overseas visitors? At one point a few years ago, a Thai tourism minister declared that sex tourism was welcomed, in that it contributed to the country's economy and many tourists visited Thailand to experience it. This (although exempting under-age sex) still represents an extreme point of view for many, and one which ministers today would be unlikely to share – but there are grey areas, such as the suggestion that Britain's changing of the guard should be programmed more frequently and at convenient times to meet the needs of visitors. What other examples of cultural degradation can you suggest, and what are the arguments for and against such developments?

   Note: It will be helpful to refer to the issue of sustainability (in Chapters 2 and 5 in this text), and to consider whether your suggestions are in any sense in conflict with the concept.

3   Examine and analyse:

   (a)   the factors which led to your own choice of a recent holiday, and
   (b)   your ambition to visit any destination in the world.

   What are the motivations behind these choices, and how were they influenced?

4   Can a better understanding of customers and their needs improve sales by travel agents? Ask a sample of people whether they prefer to arrange their holiday bookings direct or through a travel agent – and the reasons for their choices. How apparent is a lack of understanding of their needs a factor in their choice?

   For those replying 'direct', find out attitudes to booking through the Internet, by telephone or by calling at a principal's (e.g. airline) office. Do any clear-cut characteristics (e.g. age, sex, social background, travel experience) emerge from your research which place your sample in clearly defined categories?

5   What evidence is there that the 'trickle-down effect' operates in travel? Is the process desirable from a marketing point of view, and if not, can it be arrested? In the role of a tourist officer for a resort which is going downmarket, suggest how a reversal of this trend might be made possible in the marketing plan. (The well-travelled may be able to draw on personal experiences of

resorts which have attempted, sometimes successfully, to move upmarket again, e.g. certain resorts in Majorca, the Costa Blanca.)

6   Describe some of the ways by which tourists achieve a satisfactory compromise between their desire for novelty and adventure, and their need for security and familiarity.

Exercise

You have recently taken up a position in the research and development unit in the marketing department of a large tour operator. Research carried out by the unit has shown a significant market gap for holidays for the broadly defined 'middle-aged' – the 35–55-year-old group.

You are required to carry out further research on this market, to identify the types of holidays that this age band demands, following which you are to devise a programme of holidays aimed at this particular age group. You may further segment the market in any way you think fit.

Working in small groups, construct a questionnaire and carry out a survey of people in this age group. Use the results to plan an itinerary which will identify:

■   the destination (country, resort)
■   the type of accommodation to be used
■   the package arrangements (Independent or group? Escorted? What meal arrangements? What activities to be included? Any special considerations?).

Produce a mock-up of a brochure for the programme. Detailed copy and costings are not required.

Your team will be required to make a presentation to an audience of independent travel agents who specialise in unusual holidays, outlining the programme and the reasons why it has been selected.

References

1 Maslow, A, *Motivation and Personality*, London, Harper and Row, 1984
2 Mintel, *Family Holidays, the UK Market*, London, 2002
3 See for example Kotler, P *et al*, *Principles of Marketing*, ch 9
4 Howard, J A and Sheth, J N, *The Theory of Buyer Behaviour*, New York, John Wiley, 1969
5 Brassington, F and Pettitt, S, *Principles of Marketing*, Harlow, Prentice Hall, 2nd edn 2000, ch 4
6 Kotler *et al*, op cit, ch 11
7 Simon Beeching, MD Wexas International, quoted in *Travel Weekly*, 18 March 2002 (Wexas has invested heavily in CRM, and aims to answer its phones within three rings)
8 Plog, S, Why Destination Areas Rise and Fall in Popularity, paper presented to the Southern California Chapter of the Travel Research Association, 10 October 1972
9 Turbulence Threatens Currency of the Jet Set, *The Times*, 7 December 2002
10 Pearce, P, *The Social Psychology of Tourist Behaviour*, Oxford, Pergamon, 1982

Further reading

Engel, J, Blackwell, R and Miniard, P, *Consumer Behaviour*, Dryden Press, 8th edn 1995
Horner, S, *Consumer Behaviour in Tourism*, Butterworth Heinemann, 1999

Kotler, P, Bowen, J and Makens, J, *Marketing for Hospitality and Tourism*, Prentice Hall, 2nd edn 1999, ch 6 pp 177–209, ch 7 pp 211–35, ch 8 pp 237–69 and ch 11 pp 352–60

Krippendorf, J, *The Holidaymakers: Understanding the Impact of Leisure and Travel*, Butterworth Heinemann, 1987 (2nd edn 1999)

Peck, H, Payne, A, Christopher, M and Clark, M, *Relationship Marketing: Strategy and Implementation*, Butterworth Heinemann, 1999

Ross, G, *The Psychology of Tourism*, Hospitality Press, 1994

Ryan, C (ed), *The Tourist Experience: a New Introduction*, Cassell, 1997

Solomon, M, Bamossy, G and Askegaard, S, *Consumer Behaviour: a European Perspective*, Prentice Hall, 2nd edn 2002

Urry, J, *The Tourist Gaze: Leisure and Travel in Contemporary Societies*, Sage, 1990

Urry, J, *Consuming Places*, Routledge, 1995

Voase, R, *Tourism: the Human Perspective*, Hodder & Stoughton, 1995

5 Tourism product policy

Learning outcomes

After studying this chapter, you should be able to:

- define product policy and understand its place in the marketing mix
- explain how products are differentiated
- understand the role and significance of branding in product policy
- describe the product life cycle, and the actions necessary to launch a new product and revitalise a flagging one
- understand the concepts of product benefits and added value.

What is product policy?

Unfortunately, all too often, the tourism product and service delivered by the attractions and accommodation suppliers in this country [Britain] is woefully inadequate in service and quality.

Andrew Grieve, MD Discover Britain, writing in *Tourism*, Spring 2003

Getting the product right is the single most important activity of marketing. If the product is not what the market wants, no amount of price adjustment, dependable delivery or brilliant promotion will encourage consumers to buy it – or at least, not more than once, and very few companies produce products which are 'once-in-a-lifetime' buys. On the other hand, if the product does satisfy the consumer, the purchase is likely to be repeated, and the purchaser may go on to buy other products offered by the same company, and to recommend that company's products to other consumers: three very strong reasons why a company must make sure the product is right for the market at which it is aimed.

As we indicated in Chapter 1, a *product* is defined as anything that is offered to a market to satisfy a want or need. The term therefore includes tangible goods, services, people, places, organisations or ideas.

The tourism product is really quite a complex one, since it can comprise a place (the holiday destination), a service (a tour operator's package, incorporating the use of an airline seat, hotel room and sometimes other facilities) and on occasion certain tangible products such as free flight bags and other 'giveaways' such as a free bottle of wine or fresh fruit in the hotel room. When considering destination marketing, it soon becomes apparent that the destination is itself a composite, the terminology covering a region (such as the countryside, a national park or safari park, or a continent the size of Antarctica); a town, incorporating a number of individual attractions such as historical buildings, museums, shops; a seaside resort, offering beaches, sea bathing, sunshine. In each of these there will in turn be a range of tangible attractions, a less tangible 'experience' of the environment, and a range of facilities such as hotels and restaurants, local transport, etc., and the interface with locals, which will incorporate commercial services and casual exchanges. Even the accessibility of the destination must be incorporated as an element in the product.

When consumers buy products, they are buying features, of a perceived standard of quality and style which reflects the product's design. The product's image and value may be further enhanced through the use of a brand name, which acts as a cue, helping the consumer to identify a product as of a particular standard. Further enhancement may result from the product's packaging, which both protects the product and increases its attractiveness. The brand may also be indicative of reliable delivery and after-sales service. Such characteristics are features of any product. Let us now, by way of example, look at the features of a package holiday.

Let us say Mr and Mrs Jones are looking for a two-week beach holiday abroad. They have two young children aged 8 and 5 accompanying them. They are not too concerned where they go, as long as it is fairly hot, and the price fits their budget. But in fact they are looking for a complex bundle of features to fit their needs, some of which may not even be spelled out when they book the holiday, since they will presume they are included anyway (but if absent, this would constitute grounds for reasonable complaint). Table 5.1 provides a summary of what the Jones family may be expecting. The list is not necessarily exhaustive, and could be expanded into greater detail, but it is sufficient to demonstrate the complexity of the product being purchased, and the range of needs it is designed to satisfy. Almost inevitably, there will be some conflict between these needs, such as between cost and quality, or between the different needs of each member of the family (what Mrs Jones finds attractive hotel decor may not appeal to her husband, while the children's idea of entertainment will differ from their parents' ideas). Consumer decisions invariably require some compromise.

In fact, the needs listed in Table 5.1 are not *core needs* at all, but rather *second-level* needs. Core needs are those which give rise to the demand for a holiday in the first place, as discussed in the chapter on consumer behaviour. Mr Jones may be expressing his need to get away from the work environment, while Mrs Jones seeks a break from the responsibility of caring for her children 24 hours a day, from cooking and from housework, and may be looking to make new friends and widen her social contacts. Underlying needs of fitness, status, adventure and romance may all be implicit in the demand for this particular holiday.

Table 5.1 The composition of a package holiday product

Product segment	Features
1 Destination	Not too distant in flying time, clean, sandy beaches, reasonable certainty of sunshine, lively entertainment at night, good shops, reasonable prices, interesting excursions, friendly locals, safe to walk about, English widely spoken
2 Airport	Convenient local airport, car parking, not too congested, duty frees available
3 Airline	Flights at convenient time, reliable, good safety record, thoughtful, polite service. Type of aircraft
4 Coach transfers	Clean, modern coaches, reliable, competent and friendly driver and courier
5 Hotel	Location: accessible to beach, shops, etc. Staff: trustworthy, English speaking, competent, friendly; facilities: well-maintained, attractive decor, quiet at night, adequate public rooms, swimming pool, child care service. Bar with good range of drinks at moderate prices. Adequate size bedroom with balcony, sea view; comfortable beds, phone, colour TV, adequate cupboard space, wood (not wire) hangers, shower, toilet, shaver point, good lighting for make-up. Restaurant/meals: good food, well cooked, served hot, adequate portions, good variety and choice, pleasant atmosphere, comfortable seating, flexible meal hours, fast, polite and friendly service
6 Resort representatives	Knowledgeable, competent, friendly, reliable, accessible
7 Tour operator	Price reflects good value for money, secure, reliable, offers guarantees, extras
8 Travel agent	Convenient, competent, reliable, friendly, pleasant 'shopping atmosphere', extra services provided (e.g. free transfers to airport, free insurance)
9 Miscellaneous	Companionable fellow travellers with common interests, 'expectation', widening of general knowledge and interests, pleasant memories of experience

Differentiating the product

It is important to recognise at this point that what consumers are demanding are not products, or even features of products, but the benefits these products offer. What is sought is the satisfaction of needs; or, as Theodore Levitt once amusingly put it, 'purchasing agents don't buy quarter inch drills; they buy quarter inch holes'. Our needs are very diverse, and the greater number of needs that can be satisfied through the purchase of one product, the more attractive that product becomes to the consumer.

It is this essential role of marketing, to produce added or unique benefits, which enables the marketer to distinguish one product from another. The marketer must ask: 'If the product which I am supplying offers no appreciable benefits beyond those offered by my competitor, why shouldn't my customers buy my competitors' products?'

The need to invest distinctive benefits in a product gives rise to the concept of the *unique selling proposition* (USP). This is the feature or features of a product which are not to be found in those of its competitors. There are a number of holiday companies specialising in the organisation of package tours aimed at the young (18–30) travel market. While the product offered is similar in many respects, companies focusing on this market segment seek ways to differentiate their product from others. Thus for example, 2wenties emphasises that their hotels are used exclusively by their customers, while Club 18–30 places stress on the added adventure and, some might say, blatant sexual promise of their holidays. In 2002, MyTravel's youth brand, Escapes, was revamped to position the product clearly between Club 18–30 and 2wenties.

Example   JMC Group

JMC (Thomas Cook Group) rebranded JMC Essentials, its budget tour operation, Holiday Essentials in 2001. John Fair, Group Product Manager for JMC, declared, 'We want to establish a stand-alone budget programme with its own identity in the market rather than an economy version of JMC.' Low prices were secured by adding many items formerly included in the package as supplements, including transfers and pre-booked seats. However, JMC Essentials had itself replaced the well-known brand name Sunset – and the new name had failed to register; customers were still asking for the product by its original name. In 2002, the old Sunset name was reintroduced for the budget brand. At the end of that year, the tour operator's sales director admitted that while the brand had become recognised and was successful in the family market, it had made no impact on either the budget or mass markets.

Companies will differentiate products in a wide variety of ways. Some may provide added features at an inclusive price, others may choose to emphasise the reliability of the product on offer. Quality is an important attribute of many products, and not only premium-priced products. Japanese car manufacturers established an excellent international reputation for their products through the application of careful quality control in their manufacturing process, ensuring a finish and reliability which their rivals found hard to match. In the travel industry, certain airlines have chosen to identify their product with reliability ('multi-million-mile pilots', 'on-time arrivals'), and Thomson Holidays, in one advertising campaign, chose to stress their careful process of checking foreign resorts and hotels to reduce complaints and improve customer satisfaction.

At the opposite extreme, companies have also tried to distinguish their product by making it cheaper than their rivals, with their marketing emphasis on the reduction of production costs and/or low promotional expenditure. This will reduce unit profits, but the resultant increase in volume demand created by the attraction of low price can be sufficient inducement to adopt such a policy to establish a leading market share. The 'pile it high, sell it cheap' philosophy that was at one time the principle of Tesco Supermarkets has been taken up by a great many companies in the travel industry, particularly the budget airlines, but sometimes at the expense of quality control. The belief that low price is the key to success becomes a self-fulfilling prophecy, since if companies promote their products with low price as the only product benefit, their customers will soon expect and demand low price – but without forgoing the other attributes they expect, such as reliability and quality. This soon results in falling levels of satisfaction. Tour operators will concede that they receive a higher ratio of complaints on their cheapest holidays, especially late bookings for packages without a nominated hotel. It must be remembered that price is only one aspect of a product, and developed countries with relatively high labour costs have successfully focused on value for money, added benefits and high quality. Many travel companies formerly focusing on low price have adopted new marketing approaches to deliver higher profits and greater consumer satisfaction – indeed, Tesco itself amended its approach in the supermarket battle, no longer relying on the old 'pile it high, sell it cheap' concept, and increased its market share in so doing.

Good design, or 'style', can also form the basis of product differentiation. This is perhaps more readily appreciated in physical products, and the success of companies such as Gucci clothing and accessories, Bang and Olufsen hi-fi, Braun consumer durables or Olivetti office equipment spring readily to mind as examples of companies where style is closely associated with both distinctiveness and quality. Good design provides three important aids to the consumer: it represents the perceived value of the product, it enables the company to create a 'personality' for its products, and by judicious periodical alterations in styling, it creates demand through replacement with more fashionable new styles.

Style has a role to play in travel, too, both in terms of the physical features of the travel product and the image which certain companies have generated. The design and decor of hotels, ships and aircraft provide opportunities for companies to personalise their products, as well as periodically to update them, while some hotels and carriers have actually played on the nostalgia of travellers, with the Orient Express perhaps being one of the outstanding examples of 'style' in travel design. Major hotels around the world have made a point of being at the cutting edge of contemporary design; SAS Scandinavian Hotel in Copenhagen proudly promotes its stylish interior decor by the great Danish designer Arne Jacobsen, while the Schrager Hotels group employed top French designer Philippe Starck to create stylish minimalist decor in many of its hotels, including the St Martins Lane in London, the Royalton and Paramount in New York and the Mondrian in West Hollywood. Five-star cruise lines such as Crystal similarly make a feature of decor style in their vessels. However, a decision to focus on cutting-edge design has its dangers, in that high fashion moves on, and unless constant re-decoration can be afforded, a hotel's style can soon appear outdated – one of the contributing factors ascribed to Schrager's shaky financial position in 2003. Other hotels are renowned and eagerly sought out, due in part to their traditional decor and stylishness, but enriched by that indefinable quality which we can call 'atmosphere' – the Algonquin and Plaza Hotels in New York, Brown's and Claridges in London, the

George V in Paris, the Peninsula in Hong Kong and Raffles in Singapore spring to mind – which gives them a uniqueness unmatched by their competitors. A history or tradition is obviously helpful in creating this atmosphere.

Style can be a two-edged sword, however. Hotels are as subject as other products to the vagaries of fashion, and, unless their decor is to become a style icon (as some classic hotel interiors have become, such as the SAS Hotel referred to earlier or the art nouveau hotels of Prague), they must allow within their marketing plans for frequent refurbishing and new themes to attract their customers.

Sometimes these unique qualities arise over time through historical or other associations. At other times they can be deliberately *created*. The creation of a particular image or personality for a company or its products is a particularly astute form of marketing, and becomes invaluable where physical design forms no part of the product itself. The marketer aims to create an 'aura' or cluster of benefits for the product, which distinguish it from its competitors in often indefinable ways. Tour operators, for example, may try to differentiate their product from competitors, even those selling the same destination and accommodation, by focusing on intangibles such as personal service, or professionalism through product expertise. Airlines are a typical example of a product which is essentially homogeneous, yet many have succeeded in developing distinctive 'personalities'. This can sometimes be fostered by identifying the airline with its charismatic chief executive, as has been the case with Sir Richard Branson of Virgin Airways or Stelios Haji-Ioannou of easyJet (at the time of writing it remains to be seen how far this image will change, or be changed, as a result of the latter's stepping down in 2002). Smaller US airlines like Southwest and JetBlue have made much of their image as 'friendly' or 'easy-going', to distance themselves from their larger competitors. Managers marketing travel products must never forget that their customers are buying experiences, and the atmosphere of a hotel, cruise ship, airline or destination can make a major contribution to overall tourist satisfaction.

Branding

Giving a product a brand identity is not merely a useful way of helping to differentiate it from others, but is also a means of adding perceived value. A branded product is associated with specific attributes, and will determine the values that are to be associated with any newly launched product. This has implications for the price that can be charged for the product and the profit margins attainable on each unit sold.

A brand may be defined as a 'name, sign, symbol or design, or combination of these, intended to identify the products of an organisation and distinguish them from those of competitors'. This name, symbol or combination is referred to as a 'logotype' or *logo* when employed in the product's promotion, and the *brand mark* is the element of the brand identity consisting of the design or symbol only. The brand may also be registered as a trademark, legally protecting the company's right to use it exclusively in the home country and overseas. Registering the brand also makes it an offence for competitors to copy the design too closely; conversely, to be acceptable for registration, a brand must be sufficiently distinctive from others already registered.

Example   Osborne Bodega

The Osborne
Black Bull Logo

The Osborne Bodega (cellar), a well-established producer of brandy in El Puerto de Santa Maria, Spain, commissioned the design of a logotype from well-known local artist Manuel Prieto. The image was of a black bull, and after 1956, this was produced as a large metal two-dimensional cut-out. These structures were mounted in fields positioned randomly throughout Spain within full view of major trunk roads, where they were seen by countless Spanish domestic tourists and visitors. Sales burgeoned as the image of the black bull became instantly recognisable in its association with the company. Nearly 600 were eventually installed around the country.

The Spanish transport ministry planned to impose a blanket ban on roadside advertising as a safety measure, intending to include these structures. However, they overlooked the popularity of the signs among the Spanish, who had come to accept the symbol as an element of their national heritage in the Andalucian region, where bull-fighting remains a popular pastime. Following a widespread campaign to rescue the signs, in 1994 the Cortes (parliament) agreed to modify the ban, allowing the structures to remain, but retaining the ban on the use of the company's name or product. By this point, the symbol itself was already widely associated with the product, and the modification has had little impact on sales or brand awareness. Sadly, less than a quarter of the original structures survive, but those that remain retain their popularity with visitors, and feature prominently on postcards sold in the region. The ruling also benefited Gonzales Byass sherry, whose Tio Pepe brand was popularised in similar fashion by structures carrying the image of a stylised bottle-shaped man with guitar.

Note: The Black Bull device and the term Osborne are registered trademarks, and are reproduced with the consent of Grupo Osborne S.A.

Branding a product is one of the oldest techniques in product marketing, and it has become a potent tool in the modern marketing mix. Virtually anything can be branded, from matches (Swan Vestas) to petrol (Shell Oil) and turkeys (Bernard Matthews has been a notable success story). Often, in the case of tangible products, the package itself often becomes part of the brand – one has only to think of the bottle shape of Coca-Cola (a registered design) or that of certain perfume containers to realise how closely bound up with the product is the concept of the brand. Branding of services is equally popular today, since this helps to attribute benefits to an often intangible product, and many tourism brands have become household names. One has only to think of aircraft livery, the funnel colours of shipping companies, and such familiar logos as that of Holiday Inn to realise the extent to which branding has become important to the industry. However, more recent attempts to 'brand' destinations are open to criticism, given the lack of control exercised over the brand and the heterogeneous nature of a destination. This will be discussed a little further on in the chapter.

The benefits of branding

Ascribing a brand name or symbol to a product offers a marketer a number of advantages. First, it helps to identify a particular product, thus distinguishing it from competitors, as we have described. Second, it becomes associated with the benefits offered by the product, acting as a 'cue' to purchasers in their decision-making and enabling the company to target specific markets. In particular, it indicates to purchasers what level of quality they can expect, since a range of products marketed under the same brand name will carry similar expectations of quality standard (and for this reason it is essential that companies branding their products exercise very strong control over the quality of their production). Third, where the product is intangible, such as is the case with tourism products, since it cannot be seen or sampled in advance, the purchase of a branded product helps the consumer to avoid risk.

Consumers who are satisfied with the brand purchase are likely to repeat the purchase and, over time, to become regular purchasers of the brand. Repeat purchase becomes instinctive and finally habitual, at which point we can describe the customer as being 'brand loyal'. Some travel companies are already dependent upon brand loyalty. Cruise companies such as P & O, for example, claim as many as 60 per cent of their customers are regular repeat purchasers; it is also becoming a feature of the mass market tour operators, although the present emphasis on price tends to undermine efforts to build brand loyalty.

Branding becomes a key tool in market segmentation strategy. Associating a brand with a particular segment of the market can help to expand a company's market share at a time when the total market for a product is saturated. To take just one example from a fast moving consumer goods (FMCG) range, consider the variety of different washing powders (arguably one of the most homogeneous products available) offered by Procter & Gamble or Unilever in their attempt to widen their respective companies' market shares.

Finally, use of a brand name enables companies to employ a technique known as brand stretching – the introduction of new products into an existing range under the same brand name. In the FMCG market, this is a critical factor in the launch of new products by companies like Heinz or Campbell's. Well-established travel brands such as TUI or Cosmos can be stretched to include new ranges of holidays such as cruises or seat-only flight programmes, enabling them to gain immediate credibility in the market, as well as willingness on the part of travel agents to deal with the new products. 'Big name' brands become increasingly important as the competition intensifies to get brochures displayed on travel agency racks. Stelios Haji-Ioannou, founder of easyJet, recognises the power of the 'easy-' brand, with plans to diversify under the brand into other products such as cruises, hotels and cinemas; he is fiercely protective – if necessary, through the courts – against attempts by competitive businesses to usurp the 'easy' brand name.

With the growth of Internet marketing, brand recognition also becomes ever more important. Brand stretching offers the added advantage that, in the case of corporate branding such as TUI, any promotional spend on one individual product will boost recognition of the core name for all the brands.

Branding decisions

If a company decides to introduce a brand, it can do so in a number of ways. It can introduce a 'blanket', or family brand name, as is the case with Heinz; or, as with Procter & Gamble, it can introduce different brand names for each product it manufactures. There are examples of each of these approaches in travel. Accor Hotels offers a choice of some 17 accommodation brands (including such well-established names as Sofitel, Novotel, Mercure, Ibis and Formule 1) ranging from four-star to mid-market and budget categories, but recently relaunched its brand mark to include the Accor name on all hotel signage for the first time, reinforcing its corporate image along with the individual hotel brand. Holiday Inn, on the other hand, offers a single corporate brand which identifies a standard product for all its hotels. In the field of transport, scheduled airlines run charter offshoots under different brand names (Lufthansa: Thomas Cook, Iberia: Aviaco). Even some destinations have seen that their name is to all intents and purposes a brand, and have emphasised this in their marketing. The Balearic Islands of Majorca, Minorca, Ibiza and Formentera have incorporated their marketing into a single brand under a new logo and slogan 'A Family of Islands'. The Canary Islands are similarly marketed as a single 'branded' destination.

Inevitably, there will be examples of indecision about the value of a brand, and whether marketing's purpose is better served by retaining an old brand name or introducing a new one. A recent example of this confusion is that of Airtours, which rebranded under the corporate brand name of MyTravel, as described below.

Example   Airtours

Airtours was the leading travel company in the UK, operating tours and a charter airline under that brand name, as well as owning the large retail chain Going Places and two subsidiary chains, Travelworld and Holidayworld. In 2001, the company announced its intention to rebrand as MyTravel Group; all shops, aircraft, cruise ships and call centres were to be rebranded as MyTravel. Plans called for the rebranding of all 730 travel shops by the end of the following year. Many in the industry questioned the wisdom of jettisoning a well-established trading name, and, following a poor trading year in which serious deficiencies in accounting procedures were identified, only 146 branches had been rebranded. At this point the company announced its intention to retain the Going Places brand, immediately setting about to replace the facia boards of all converted branches. Managing Director Steve Endacott announced, 'it's not the moment to rebrand at a cost of £4–6 million'. The reversal was put forward as a cost-saving move in a difficult year, rather than a change in marketing strategy – the rebrand was being 'deferred until [the company could] afford to do it' – but the company confirmed that the MyTravel brand retained their confidence, with MyTravel Airways, new budget carrier MyTravelLite and website MyTravel.com remaining unchanged.

In 2002, the company, which had bought budget brand Aspro in the early 1990s, repositioned this range of holidays as Aspro Holidays for Less, a stand-alone budget brand to compete with First Choice's Sunstart and JMC's Sunset.

A similar confusion arises in the case of British Airways' livery, which has been redesigned a number of times in recent years. However, it is apparent that both public and trade are split over the merits of the changes (as detailed below).

Example British Airways

British Airways were criticised for changing their aircraft livery from a traditional crest emblem on the tail to a series of colourful ethnic designs aiming to reflect the airline's global role. As the company announced, 'Instead of being a British airline with global operations, BA has become a world airline whose headquarters happen to be in Britain.' The new designs attracted a great deal of criticism, most notably from Prime Minister Margaret Thatcher, who deplored the loss of national image implicit in the redesign. In 2001, following management changes, the airline had a rethink and ditched the ethnic tailfin designs in favour of a union flag design. Not everyone was satisfied with this move. Commented the trade paper *Travel Weekly*, 'BA's union flag design [is] outdated, stuffy and old-fashioned.' The ethnic tailfins, in this critic's view, had given the aircraft 'a modern, contemporary feel, shedding its slightly pompous, flag-waving image'.

There are arguments, too, against brand stretching where this would be counter to the appeal or goodwill of the brand. A company offering a premium-price product would be cautious about introducing a new budget range under the same brand name, and equally a brand which carries connotations of low price would be considered unsuitable as a choice when launching a more upmarket alternative. However, a slight modification in the brand might make brand stretching attractive (see the following example).

Example bmi British Midland

In 2001, medium-price airline British Midland was rebranded as bmiBritish Midland. Chief Operating Officer Paul Hogan declared, 'Being seen as British is key to us, and we couldn't throw that out. It's midground between BA and Virgin.' However, by 2002, the British Midland element had disappeared, suggesting a rethink – or the belief that the name bmi was by then sufficiently well understood to stand alone. Later, the airline introduced its new budget offshoot as bmibaby.

A new brand name should be chosen if an existing brand is too closely associated with a particular type of product, making it difficult to stretch and encompass new concepts. Companies carrying brand names such as Yugotours, Olympic, Austrotours or Paris Travel, whose original choice of name reflected the policy of specialisation in specific travel destinations, would find it difficult to introduce new destinations under the same brand name (although some tried to do so – and indeed, Yugotours, prior to its collapse, tried to generate, first, new destinations, and subsequently a new name, when the break-up of Yugoslavia in the 1990s decimated travel to the area). A company with a more universal brand name, such as Global or Cosmos, would be less restricted.

In first developing a brand, the objectives of the brand need to be carefully thought out. A brand is not just a means of drawing attention to the product: it should stand for something. It must act as a cue to the product characteristics, including the product's quality. Is it to be low, medium or premium quality? Is it to offer the economic appeal of 'value for money', or the more emotional appeal of high price for a status product? Think of the diverse messages associated with clothing labels such as Donna Karan, Calvin Klein and Marks & Spencer to realise the immense power of brands to communicate effective messages about product characteristics.

Branding provides the opportunity for a company to enhance its corporate image, because how consumers feel about a brand reflects their feeling about the company. Companies such as Shell use their brand names as a means of enhancing the corporate image, and this is reflected in travel companies like Singapore Airlines, Cunard and the Hilton Hotel chain.

Rebranding

Rebranding occurs when a company passes into another party's hands, or some other major event occurs that could unsettle the reputation of the brand. When the Thomson Organisation's travel interests were taken over by Preussag, owners of German tour operator TUI (Touristik Union International), the TUI logo and slogan 'world of TUI' were incorporated alongside the individual brand names of Thomson tour operations and the Lunn Poly retail outlets, and a number of measures were taken to enhance awareness of the new brand, including sponsorship of the football club Tottenham Hotspur (see Chapter 14 for further discussion on this).

Example Thomas Cook

In 1998, German companies Condor and Neckermann came together to form C&N, and subsequently this company took over British travel company Thomas Cook. The decision was taken to change the little-known C&N brand name in Germany to Thomas Cook, and at the same time to invest £200 million in the UK to integrate most of the well-known brand names into a single overarching brand, JMC (after the initials of John Mason Cook, son of the founder). Sunset, Flying Colours, Inspirations and Caledonian Airways were to be phased out, to be replaced by JMC Airlines and JMC Holidays, although the name Thomas Cook was retained for the retailing chain. At the time it was claimed that the change to JMC would 'create transparency of ownership across the company's different operations', but perhaps an equally important consideration was the fear that rival retailers would be reluctant to sell any product with the same name as a leading travel chain. However, the move to directional

▶

selling by the leading tour operator/retail agent linkages changed this perception. At the same time, the easily recognised pillar-box red used as the Thomas Cook background was amended to the yellow and blue background used in Germany by C&N, the company claiming this projected 'a more dynamic image'.

At the time of the launch the move was criticised, on the grounds that the new name offered no clear brand personality, brand values or positioning strategy. It was soon found that the new name failed to stretch adequately across all market sectors, and by early 2002 the lack of brand awareness and confusion among the travel market was apparent. The company decided to rebrand the airline as Thomas Cook Airlines, declaring, 'We have a well-established brand name in Thomas Cook and it would be crazy not to make the most of it.' The JMC name was retained for a limited number of programmes only, while Sunset was reintroduced as a budget brand.

Brand sponsorship

When a firm makes the decision to introduce a new brand, it may choose one of several strategies. First, it may choose to develop and use a brand exclusively for itself. Second, it can use another organisation's brand under licence. Its third option is to franchise the brand. In this situation, the company owning the brand allows others to sell the product, with certain preconditions attached, such as the obligation to purchase raw materials exclusively from the supplying company, or the obligation to pay a proportion of the earnings to the franchiser (royalty payments). Franchising offers the benefits of rapid expansion for a brand, and the security, on the part of consumers, of consistent and recognised standards of quality. To be effective, though, the brand must be well established in the market before it is launched as a franchised product. Fast food firms in particular have expanded rapidly with the use of franchises, so that companies such as Kentucky Fried Chicken, McDonald's and Burger King have become household names worldwide. In the travel industry, Holiday Inns and Hilton International are just two hotel chains which have expanded rapidly through franchising, and other sectors of the travel industry are just beginning to experiment with the technique. Franchising as a distributive technique is discussed in Chapter 8.

What makes a good brand name?

A number of guidelines have been drawn up by marketing theorists for the development of a good brand name. Since a critical function of the brand name is to obtain immediate recognition for both the product and its attributes, the name, symbol or design has to communicate these attributes with appropriate imagery. Names must be easy to pronounce and remember, as well as helping to convey the product's benefits. Symbols should be distinctive, their design and colour supporting the product concept.

Although corporate names, often associated with the founder (Thomson, Hilton) remain popular brand names, words conveying the nature of the product or with pleasant associations (Sunset, Blue Sky Holidays) help to reinforce the benefits in the purchaser's mind. 'Catchy' brand names (JMC) sometimes retain a connection with the parent organisation's original name but reduce it to a more easily communicated logo.

It is important, particularly in such an international field as travel, that brand names are registerable in all the countries in which the company can expect to operate, and that these names are both easy to pronounce and to remember by those speaking foreign languages. Words may need to be screened to ensure they do not project a different association in other languages: the French may be hard put if they were to try to market their popular soft drink 'Pschitt' in Britain. There are companies which will help international brand name choice by screening new product names in advance and singling out any judged unsuitable for any reason – a wise precaution.

The simplicity of a word or illustration will enhance recall and recognition. This is important in the travel industry, where the brand may have to be displayed on a fast-moving object such as an aircraft or coach.

Finally, one must remember that there are always examples of companies that have managed to break all the rules and nevertheless succeeded. Who would have imagined that Kawasaki or Mitsubishi could become household names in Britain? Yet these companies succeeded in establishing a reputation through the quality of their products. This is not to deny, however, that their marketing task might have been easier had they been marketing their products under a name like Honda or Mazda.

A brand will enhance the corporate identity of an organisation so that product and company become inseparable in the minds of the consumers. But to gain maximum impact, it must be used in all areas of the company's marketing. A travel company should exploit the brand on stationery, brochures, representatives' uniforms, shop-fronts, literature racks and in promotional aids such as flight bags, carrier bags or other 'giveaway' material. Brand marks will feature prominently on the first page of websites. This represents the 'total marketing' approach so essential in modern marketing.

Repositioning a brand

Periodically, it may prove necessary for a firm to reposition its brand; that is to say, to modify the brand in some way so as to widen its appeal or direct its appeal to another market segment. This becomes necessary when, for example, the original market associated with the brand experiences a decline or when fashions change. This usually, although not invariably, also requires a modification in the product itself. Since the early 1980s, the marketing strategy of several Japanese car companies provides us with a good example of periodic repositioning. Originally marketed as a cheap but reliable alternative to the domestic product in Britain, the companies have moved 'upmarket' by repositioning and refining the image of the cars sold, leading in some instances to products which are designed to appeal to a sophisticated market willing to spend for added refinement. In doing so, the companies have developed a high-status image for their range, adding product benefits and increasing profit margins. This is an exercise which must be undertaken with considerable care, however; images, once established, may be hard to adjust. Supermarket chain Tesco has not found it easy to rid itself of its original product concept and move upmarket.

Destination repositioning is common as regions or resorts lose their appeal, often as a result of becoming too popular. Two destinations that have recently undergone repositioning include Cyprus and Pattaya Beach in Thailand, and their cases will be examined later in this chapter under 'the product life cycle'.

What's in a name? The power of branding

We have already discussed the fact that there are many different segments of the travel market, each with very different requirements. While this can be very helpful for the smaller 'niche' operator to create a very precise image and positioning for a specialist product, it makes it difficult for the mass market holiday operator to create a brand image that is not 'bland'.

Research bears out how strongly the name in particular, but also the logo and design styles of different brands, can affect the perception of the holidays represented by those brands.

Example Virgin Airways

Brand consultancy Dragon asked a representative sample of the general public in 2001 whether they understood what a company was all about and where it was going. Three travel companies in a cross-section of industries sampled – Virgin, easyJet and British Airways – all scored highly, with over 80 per cent of those sampled having a clear picture of Virgin's brand identity. However, the consultancy warned that Virgin was in danger of brand stretching too far, and its identity was too closely associated with Sir Richard Branson himself. BA performed less well on trust, and poorly in its perceived ability to plan ahead for change.

Design conscious under-40s are influenced by good design as an indicator of a good operator. Familiar icons such as birds and sunsets have to be used with care, being seen as rather unimaginative and overused. Colour too can condition expectation; a lot of blue on a brochure cover reinforces an image of 'lakes and mountains' holidays.

While holidaymakers' requirements vary widely, research reveals a remarkable degree of consensus among consumers about what they do not like. In particular, consumers were found to dislike:

1   Regimentation, or any perceived suppression of individuality, whether it was mothers reacting against the standard issue T-shirts for the children's club, or single holidaymakers dreading attempts by reps to organise congas.

2   Crowds. Mothers feared they would lose children, young singles looked for peace on the beach to catch up on sleep and recover from the hangover before the next night of revelry. Older people saw crowded beaches as downmarket, and were willing to pay more for peace and quiet.

3   Children. All groups united in a loathing of too many children. Singles were unwilling to be woken early by other people's children, and feared families

complaining about the noise that they themselves made at night. Empty nesters whose own children had left home felt they were 'free at last' to enjoy a holiday without children. Even mothers recoiled from the idea of too many children and wanted just a few potential friends for their own children (with whom the latter could then go off and play, relieving mothers of the need to entertain).

These fears have a strong impact on the reaction of consumers to different brands, and affect the likelihood of selecting a particular operator's brochure for consideration.

Thus Thomson 'Small and Friendly' is very positive, in that it allays fears of crowds and large regimented resorts. First Choice 'Freespirit' again has strong connotations of individuality. Names such as 'Transun', 'The Sun Club' and 'Fanfare' all evoked images of crowds and regimentation.

As well as countering negative aspects, consumers are looking for a certain cachet and implication of quality in the name. Thus any name that sounds 'silly', or would be embarrassing to mention to 'the Joneses', puts an operator at a disadvantage. So, for instance, while a holiday booked with First Choice 'Sovereign' is considered upmarket and brings the consumer positive social status, the identical holiday branded 'Sunflower' was viewed much less positively.

This is even true of names that describe the nature of the holiday very accurately. Singles holidays have built up such a poor reputation that it is slightly embarrassing to admit to having gone on one, even among avid consumers of such holidays. It follows that even a hint of such an image is a large turn-off to non-singles. Thus names like 'Spree' invoke negative reactions among all consumers.

Bland and unimaginative names for the tour operator or brand conjure up the image of a rather unimaginative and 'ordinary' holiday. Asked what kind of company is the fictitious 'Sun Star', consumers read a tremendous amount into the name. Sun Star, they said, must be:

- a Mediterranean operator
- cheap and cheerful
- basic sun and sand holidays
- operating from a shabby 1960s office block in Oxford Street, London
- rather dodgy and disreputable.

Asked what kind of company is 'First Choice Holidays' (before Owners Abroad had adopted the name, and therefore at this point an equally fictitious name), consumers were united in declaring that it must be:

- operating to a wide choice of destinations
- providing quality but not dauntingly upmarket
- not just sun and sand, but promising more
- operating from a plate-glass high-rise office
- a very professional company with uniforms and BMW cars outside.

An interesting question is posed by asking whether it is equally appropriate to brand a destination, given that today there are strong attempts to identify destinations with brand names. Ritchie and Ritchie[1] claim that

A destination brand is a name, symbol, logo, word, mark or other graphic that both identifies and differentiates the destination; furthermore, it conveys the promise of a memorable travel experience that is uniquely associated with the destination; it also serves to consolidate and reinforce the recollection of pleasurable memories of the destination experience.

Mundt[2] argues that the term 'destination' is too broad and with too many meanings to be associated with a brand name in this manner. Destinations may be as small as a village or seaside resort, and as large as a country or continent, while some resorts offer radically different experiences at different times of the year, necessitating the creation of two distinct brands. However, he accepts that there may well be a case for branding the creation of an artificial destination, such as 'Heidiland' in Switzerland, the alpine region claimed as the fictional site of Johanna Spyri's book about Heidi, just as 'Doone Country' has become the fictional brand for the claimed West Country site of R D Blackmore's *Lorna Doone*. Case study 6 on the branding of Destination Wessex at the end of this text illustrates this conundrum neatly.

The difficulty of associating a brand with a destination is demonstrated by Table 5.2, which compares tangible goods with traditional destinations and other tourism services.

The product mix

Few companies produce a single product. Companies are therefore faced with making marketing decisions on the mix of products which they propose to offer to their customers. The product mix comprises the range of different product lines the company produces (the *product width*), together with the number of variants offered within each product line (the *product depth*). A white goods manufacturer such as Hoover, for example, will have to decide on the range of products it will manufacture (washing machines, dryers, dishwashers, vacuum cleaners, toasters, irons, etc.) as well as what options will be made available in each product – different motors, designs, capacity, colours and so on. Such decisions have implications for the whole marketing mix. Different products may be targeted at different market segments, for example, requiring different advertising and promotional strategies. Some products may be marketed in an intensely competitive environment, with consequent implications for pricing, and profit margins. Some, because of technical complexity or other factors, will need exceptional sales back-up, while others may be suitable for self-selection, affecting distribution strategies.

In the manufacturing process, a critical factor is to what extent existing resources such as machinery and skilled labour can be used in making diverse products. If a machine has spare capacity and can be used in the manufacture of a new product line, this may make all the difference as to whether it will prove profitable for the company

Table 5.2   Brand-relevant characteristics of goods, tourism services and destinations

Tangible goods	Services (hospitality, transport)	Traditional destinations
Producers		
■ identifiable producers	■ identifiable producers	■ non-identifiable producers
Products and services		
■ homogeneous	■ heterogeneous (external factors like weather, staff, other consumers, have significant impacts on service quality)	■ completely heterogeneous (due to number of different independent service providers)
■ complete product design is determined by the company	■ levels of service may be determined by the company	■ levels of service cannot be determined by the destination management organisation
Branding		
■ branding for products completely in the hands of the company	■ branding process for services in the hands of the company, but hampered by subjective factors of both staff and clients	■ 'branding' process with a destination management unit of very limited influence on the product
■ multipliable	■ mainly multipliable	■ non-multipliable – limited to a geographically confined region
■ strict quality control	■ direct quality control	■ only indirect quality control (i.e. through quality labelling of local hospitality sector)
Legal aspects		
■ no problems within legal framework	■ no problems within legal framework	■ names for geographically defined areas are exempted from branding by European Union legislation

Source: Mundt, J[2] p 343

to make the new line. For each product line, the manager must be knowledgeable about the market; who is buying the product and why, how competitive it is against those of rival organisations, what market share the product enjoys, the level of sales achieved, and the contribution it makes to overall revenue and profits. Such knowledge will enable further decisions to be made about new products: should existing products be strengthened or extended, should some options be withdrawn, should new product lines be introduced and should such products be consistent with the existing product range, or would it be better for the company to diversify into entirely new lines?

Just as with any other industry, most sectors of the travel and tourism business must also decide their product width and depth. A large mass market operator, to take one example, has to make a number of critical marketing decisions.

Although at first glance one might be inclined to think that a tour operating programme is a single product line, in fact the nature of package holidays makes each distinct in its appeal to different market segments, satisfying different needs. Large-scale operators have in the past tended to organise their products into separate divisions, under separate product managers, producing separate brochures, and often operating their range of holidays under different brand names – although the trend recently has been to reduce this diversification to bring products into line under a single brand, but as we have seen, this has not always been successful. At the time of writing, the Thomas Cook range includes Thomas Cook as the leading brand for principal products, with JMC brand restricted to families and young adults, Sunset as the budget brand and smaller-scale subdivisions such as Club 18–30, Nielsen and Style retaining their own brands. Within each of these programmes, decisions must be made on product depth: what holiday length to offer (3, 7, 10 or 14 days)? From which airports to operate? To which destinations and airports? How will the price of each product be determined in order to achieve the overall target profitability for the company?

Product lines may be 'stretched' to encompass new market segments. Such decisions might be taken if the current market is experiencing slow growth, or the company finds itself increasingly under attack from the competition. A company at the bottom end of the market may find profits squeezed, and attempt to reposition its products further up the market to allow a greater margin of profit; or a company which has focused on the upper end of the market may choose to widen its appeal by reaching a larger market, capitalising on its reputation for quality in the top-market field. Such policies carry the inherent danger that the public image of the company and its markets may become confused, causing it to lose its niche and original marketing strengths. Some shipping companies, for example, in their attempt to widen their appeal to reach new mass markets for cruising, downgraded the product, thereby losing the confidence of their loyal, original customers. It is interesting to note that this lesson has been learned and the experience acted upon – Carnival, now the world's biggest cruise operator, has been careful to retain the multiple brand names of the companies it has absorbed, which apart from the Carnival brand itself includes subsidiaries like Cunard, Holland America, Seabourn, Princess and Windstar, each with its own distinct target market.

The product life cycle

Although the exact duration of a product's life cycle can never be forecast, all products exhibit characteristic life cycles, which can be illustrated graphically, as in Figure 5.1. The 'bell curve' of this graph indicates that typically a product will experience slow

Figure 5.1
The product
life cycle

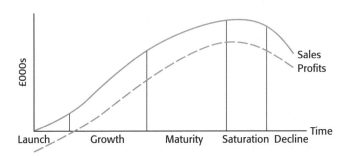

initial sales after launch, while it is still comparatively unknown, with accelerating sales as it becomes better known and its reputation established. Steady growth is then achieved until almost all the consumers likely to buy the product have done so, at which point sales even out. The product also faces increasing competition as its sales expand, so that at saturation point it may be fighting harder to retain its existing share of a stagnant market. If newer products are seen as better than the existing one, sales will decline. At this point the company must take action, with a decision either to restore the fortunes of the product or to kill it off.

This theoretical model holds true for all products, including tourism. A destination will gradually become known to tourists, who are initially attracted in small numbers. As it becomes more popular, and is exploited by other carriers and tour operators, sales will rise rapidly, perhaps attracting a different market. The uniqueness of the resort is lost, and it becomes another mass market destination, appealing to a more down-market holidaymaker. The expansion of hotels and other facilities at the resort may lead to a surplus of supply over demand, while the despoliation of the resort may make it less attractive to the holiday market, who will move on elsewhere. Eventually, the resort may decline to a point where tourism is no longer significant and other industries may be encouraged into the region, or the local authority decides to take action to improve the appeal of the destination again.

Examples   Cyprus and Pattaya Beach

Cyprus has suffered from the negative image linking its popularity to clubbing in key resorts like Ayia Napa, which had resulted in the media focusing on images of drunkenness, noise and occasional violence on the streets. In 2002 the Cyprus Tourist Organisation launched a new marketing campaign designed to move the image of the country upmarket. Director of Marketing Michael Metaxas claimed, 'we want to establish Cyprus as a high-quality island, not just another sun and sea destination' – although critics pointed to unsuccessful earlier efforts to move the island upmarket. However, the promotion was accompanied by a hotel building programme concentrating on five-star properties, leading to price rises which increased visitor spend.

Similarly, in 2001 the reputation of Pattaya Beach was suffering from its rapid over-development and image as a destination for sexual freedom. The tourist board sought to change this image by improving facilities and appealing to families and couples. A new water treatment plant was installed to reduce seawater pollution and improvements were made to the promenade and beach, attracting upmarket hotel investment. Recognising that the resort could never completely lose its reputation for sleaze, the authorities divided it into zones, with clear boundaries, to appeal discretely to those oriented towards the nightlife and entertainment and those seeking more leisurely beach-based holidays. Efforts were also made to attract conference and incentive markets.

Of course, each product life cycle is unique, however similar destinations, or indeed any other product, may appear. In some cases, this pattern of growth–maturity–decline may be quite rapid (think of Rubik's cube, or novelty items like pet rocks or hula hoops) while in others, the product can sell at saturation level for a very long period (Oxo, Marmite). It is also important to recognise that brands have their own life-cycle stages, although generally of a shorter duration. Clearly, the marketing manager must be aware of the stage in the life cycle both brand and product have reached. As competition increases, brand life cycles tend to shorten, requiring the introduction of new marketing strategies designed either to increase sales or to kill off one brand to make way for a new one.

Forecasting product life cycles, and when a product is about to move into a new stage, is clearly no easy matter, although the danger signals heralding a decline are clear enough – declining sales or market share, especially in relation to one particular brand or product in the product line. There is evidence to show that when life-cycle forecasting is attempted, it can prove surprisingly accurate. More generally, however, an understanding of the relationship between a product and its life cycle enables marketing managers to plan their campaigns more effectively and to be in a better position to judge product sales and profit potential.

As can be seen from Figure 5.1, as profits rise and fall at different stages of the life cycle, the extent to which a particular product will contribute to overall profit objectives of the firm can be anticipated, based on its position in the life cycle. At the launch stage, the marketing costs associated with a new product will be substantial, as the company tries to bring the new product to the attention of its market. Only as sales accelerate will these costs be recovered and the company start making a profit. Highest profitability is generally achieved at the maturity stage, with profits falling back thereafter as sales decline, although by careful manipulation it may be possible to maintain high profit levels at advanced stages, by reducing advertising expenditure and allowing the product to 'live on its reputation'. This is known as 'milking a cash cow', and as long as loyal purchasers continue to purchase the product, it may be worth the company's while to continue to produce it.

The value in understanding the nature of the product life cycle is in its relationship with marketing strategy. It will alert the company to the need for positive action at the *threshold point*, where some change to strategy will be essential if the product is to continue. But beyond this, the marketing mix will be different for every stage of the life cycle.

First of all, the type of consumer who purchases the product may be different when a new product is introduced, compared with those purchasing the product at a later stage in the cycle. This fact enables a company to use a market segmentation approach based on 'lifestyle'. Early buyers of a new product are frequently experimenters, willing to take chances for the novelty or status of being in possession of a little known product. This market segment will generally have more disposable income, and will be more 'value-conscious' than 'price-sensitive'. The product image will be based on its uniqueness, and its appeal to status or curiosity. Advertising and promotion will be aimed at communicating this message to a specific market, using the most suitable channels and giving potential consumers maximum information about the product's benefits. Price at this point may be relatively high. The system of distribution may be fairly selective, since it may be difficult for the company to support, or gain acceptability from, a wide selection of distributive outlets.

Once the product is well established, competitors will have introduced their own version of the product into the market. Faced with a growing choice of products, the consumer may become confused and uncertain about which to select. The marketer's role then becomes one of persuading and constantly reminding consumers about the product's benefits, ensuring convenience of purchase by maximising distributive outlets, manipulating price to keep the product competitive and reinforcing the brand image associated with the product.

Finally, as sales peak and falter, the company has to look at the merits either for revitalising the product, allowing it to decline slowly, or killing it off and planning a replacement.

Revitalising a product

There are many different ways in which a company can rejuvenate its product, and the method it will choose will depend on the reason or reasons for the product's initial decline. If this occurred through the introduction of a new competitive product with additional benefits, the company might choose to add similar benefits to its own product, to add new but different benefits, or to reduce the present price and emphasise its value for money perhaps trying to reach a new, more price-sensitive market in doing so. If on the other hand in the company's view the competitive product is not superior to its own, the decision may be taken merely to increase advertising spend, or introduce sales promotion to regain market share. Marketing is about selecting strategies which are either designed to counteract threats, or to take advantage of opportunities in the marketplace. If you remember the 'four Ps' of marketing, you will realise that the action a firm can take is limited to one of four areas: it can alter the *product*, the *price*, the *promotional* campaign or the *place* (where and how the product can be bought). Let us take a hypothetical example.

Maddington Hall: revitalising a product

Maddington Hall is an English stately home open to the public between Easter and the end of October each year. It is not a major visitor attraction, but has the appeal of a smaller home which has been in the hands of the present family for over 300 years. It has historical connections with the English Civil War, and prior to that was the home of a leading member of Queen Elizabeth I's court. There are also links with the USA through the settling of some members of the family at the beginning of the eighteenth century in New Jersey.

The house attracts over 20 000 visitors a year, but in recent years the pattern has shown a steady decline:

▶

Entrants to Maddington Hall, 1992–2002

1992	27 120
1993	26 580
1994	26 084
1995	25 312
1996	26 033
1997	25 441
1998	25 256
1999	24 802
2000	23 403
2001	20 857
2002	18 912

The sharp decline at the end of 2001 and throughout 2002 can be attributed to a combination of the BSE and foot and mouth scares and the after-effect of the attack on the twin towers in the United States in September 2001, which was followed by a huge fall-off of American visitors to Britain (a leading market for heritage properties), and especially visitors to the countryside. However, the major concern is not the temporary blip caused by external factors, but the steady decline in attendance over a decade, even at times when the economy has been performing relatively well.

Management faces the following choices. It can spend more money on advertising; but income from the house is barely enough to pay for upkeep and running costs, and the budget for promotion is very low. Because of the diversity of the market, it would be unrealistic to be able to advertise directly to overseas visitors, although it would pay to investigate opportunities for establishing a website which would attract enquiries. Much of the budget is spent on publishing a leaflet which is left in hotels and other places frequented by visitors to the immediate area. Attempts to interest coach and tour operators to include the house in packages have been unsuccessful, as the hall is not seen by the trade as sufficiently famous or interesting in itself to attract a market.

It could lower the entry price, but it is believed that this would result in a fall in revenue, as the increase in numbers attracted would be insufficient to make up for lost revenue. It could even increase the price, if it is believed that the added revenue will more than offset the fall in visitors.

It could also consider ways in which the product could be made more attractive to a wider market. For example, it could seek additional revenue by becoming more commercial – adding tea rooms, souvenir shops or other revenue-producing facilities, or staging events such as the re-creation of Civil War battles or jousting tournaments to attract larger crowds on specific days of the year. If willing, the owner could arrange to preside over candlelit dinners for exclusive groups of visitors who would be willing to pay handsomely for the privilege of meeting him and his family (particularly if titled). Some of these activities would need considerable capital expenditure, requiring a bank loan or other means of raising funds. Management would have to consider carefully whether this expense would result in a big enough jump in attendance to ensure profitability.

Finally, ways could be considered of improving distribution, for example, by identifying specialist tour operators abroad who could be interested in marketing the attraction, or by joining a consortium of other attractions in the region, or a group of stately homes who would produce a joint leaflet reaching a wider audience.

Whatever decision is made, it needs to be carefully thought through and researched. Each choice would need to be considered on its own merits, just as in the case of the launch of a new product.

The nature of demand for all products will shift over time, so that regular 'refreshing', or making minor modifications to the product in line with customer expectations, will help to keep sales up. To take just one example, demand for more flexible holidays has encouraged many tour operators to adjust their programmes. Thomson Holidays now allows variations in the length of stay of its short break holidays, while Thomas Cook has launched tailor-made holidays under its Cultura Trips banner. Attractions need to update their products regularly, and this can be difficult in the case of museums, where many curators still see their roles as custodial, preserving existing products rather than providing entertainment for visitors. Nevertheless, even existing products can be displayed more imaginatively to widen appeal.

Example   **Maidstone Museum**

Maidstone Museum is housed in a listed building and is therefore unable to expand through further building. It has nine times as many items in storage as can be exhibited at any one time.

To refresh its product, it invited 14 people, winners of a newspaper competition, each to choose two items from storage to be exhibited. These exhibits went on display in a special temporary exhibition under the strapline 'Surprises in Store'. Many of the items displayed had not been exhibited for many years, and the exhibition attracted considerable interest. Other museums have since followed suit.

Launching a new product

Launching a new product, be it aircraft, ferry route, hotel or tour package, is the riskiest undertaking in marketing. The statistical failure rate of new products is daunting, but the likelihood of product failure can be reduced (though never totally removed) by following a process of careful screening. But we should be quite clear about what is

Figure 5.2
New products

<table>
<tr><td></td><td></td><td colspan="2" align="center">**Market**</td></tr>
<tr><td></td><td></td><td align="center">existing</td><td align="center">new</td></tr>
<tr><td rowspan="2">**Product**</td><td>new</td><td>introduce new product to present market</td><td>launch of new product to new market</td></tr>
<tr><td>existing</td><td>modification to existing product for present market</td><td>reposition present product to attract new market</td></tr>
</table>

meant by a 'new product'. Improvements to an existing product can render that product so new as to make it seen by prospective purchasers as a genuinely new product. Similarly, if an existing product is launched to a new market unfamiliar with it, that product is also, to all intents and purposes, a new product. This can best be illustrated by Figure 5.2.

Clearly, the least risk is taken by the company which chooses to modify an existing product to make it more attractive to the present market – by adding additional benefits, for instance. If the product is losing its appeal to the present market, it may be feasible to *reposition* the product, that is, to direct its appeal to a different market segment – or to sell the product overseas instead of to domestic consumers. This may also call for changing the concept of the product to make it more appealing to a new type of consumer.

Example First Choice Holidays

In 2002, First Choice decided to reposition its tour operating brands. Its three key brands were to be more clearly identified with the markets they were to serve. The First Choice brand was aimed at the quality mass market, with an upgrade in the quality of hotels offered. Unijet would be aimed at experienced travellers, dropping the cheaper holidays included in the range. Sunstart was to be more clearly identified as the budget brand, absorbing the cheaper products formerly marketed under the other labels. Pricing panels in the First Choice brochure were simplified, and this brand and the Sunstart brand would carry the blue strip and 'starfish' design forming the livery used on Air 2000 tailfins, coaches and at airport check-in desks.

In the following year, the company took the decision to integrate its retail shops under the single brand of the parent, jettisoning the well-established brands Travel Choice, Holiday Hypermarket and Bakers Dolphin. As the company's MD declared, 'we have the smallest network of all the major players, yet we have three brands. It is inefficient on a number of fronts.'

Another alternative is to develop a genuinely new product (or new brand) to be sold to one's present consumers. The appeal of this is that if the company has an established reputation, the likelihood is that present satisfied customers will be prepared to give the new product a trial also. Finally, the company can choose to introduce a genuinely new product to a new market segment – a double risk, but one where research may show significant profit potential in the long run, hence a gamble worth taking.

It is difficult to determine exactly when a product can be termed genuinely 'new'. Most products we buy are advances on, and modifications of, existing products, but every now and again a concept is so original and different from any other product on the market that it can be defined as totally new. The ballpoint pen, although a modification of existing writing instruments, used technology so totally distinct from anything employed before that it must be accepted as unique, as must the photocopier or the folding bicycle. In travel and tourism, Concorde offered a totally new concept in air travel, while the catamaran has introduced a totally new, high-speed form of sea travel on short-sea routes. In the hospitality business the motel was distinctive enough when first introduced to be termed a new product. Billy Butlin, looking in the 1930s for a way of keeping seaside visitors entertained in all weathers, introduced the concept of the holiday camp, which was unlike any existing form of mass market holiday at the time.

Market gaps

The aim with any new product is to find the 'market gap' – a product opportunity with a ready market which has not yet been tapped. Again, this is derived from taking a market-orientated approach to new product development, in which the first step is to see what new products, or modifications of existing products, are wanted by con- sumers. The high cost of labour in Scandinavian hotels was resulting in prohibitively high prices for hotel food; the solution was to introduce self-service breakfasts which, although a break from the traditional service expected in hotels, proved to be very pop- ular with hotel guests because it both reduced prices and offered a comprehensive choice of quantity and menu selection. The *Sea Goddess* cruise ships incorporated an intriguing drop-down stern which converted the ship, when anchored, into a floating base from which passengers could swim or windsurf – a marketing breakthrough to reach a new type of clientele for the luxury cruise market, while at the other end of the scale new cheap markets have been tapped for cruising (see the following example).

Example   Tour operator and cruise line integrated marketing

Tour operator First Choice and cruise operator Royal Caribbean International came together in 2001 in a joint venture programme to launch a new cruising product, aimed at younger cruise passengers. Existing cruises were still predominantly targeting the older market and the new cruise line would attract those in their thirties and forties, especially newcomers to cruising. Focus group research revealed that prospective passengers disliked the perceived regimentation of cruise liners and were looking for greater informality, with the freedom to eat when they wished in a choice of catering facilities. The new line was marketed as a fresh, 'upbeat' concept with a relaxed and informal style of life on board.

Luxury coaches have been converted to appeal to business executives, by altering the layout of seats and making it possible to hold meetings round a table while travelling. Such concepts are based on modifying existing products, but in doing so, making them sufficiently distinctive to offer substantial advantages over existing products and filling wants, whether expressed or latent, of consumers. But the launch of each of these products should be more than a hit-or-miss gamble based on some executive's hunch. It should be the end product of a process of new product development which is carefully structured and well researched at each stage of its development.

The sustainable product

Sustainability has become a key issue in the development and operation of new holiday products, with growing concern about the effect of tourism on the environment. In the past, tourism developers tended towards a 'slash and burn' approach when developing new resorts, showing little consideration for the sensitivity of sites which, once ruined by excessive development and overpopulation, were abandoned in favour of more pristine destinations. Planning authorities with control over destination development, showing more concern for economic growth than the protection of their environments, did little to prevent the rape of their lands, as in turn the Mediterranean coastlines of France, Spain, Greece and Turkey fell to excessive building. Airlines, concerned only with high load factors and increased profits, marketed those destinations that proved easiest to sell, and as the popularity of the major seaside resort destinations moved downmarket, local culture became undermined, with the new breed of mass tourists demanding familiar food and drink, improved facilities and more popular entertainment. Inevitably, it was recognised – far too late in many cases – that mass tourism was killing the attractions tourists were coming to see, and the authorities began to exercise much-needed control. More general concern over the despoliation of the planet led to the wider demand for sustainable development advocated in the Bruntland Report of 1987, with tourism being seen as just one of many economic activities impacting upon the world's resources. It had become clear that the present needs and wants of the planet's existing citizens should not be satisfied at the expense of future generations.

It is now generally agreed that tourism development should not only take into account the protection of the landscape, but also ensure that locals in the host country benefited from the economic consequences. Tourism businesses were encouraged to hire and train local labour, to minimise any negative impacts on the environment caused by their developments, to reduce wastage in resources and to aid the economic growth of the area by involving locals in their overall plans.

In consequence, there are today a great many sustainable tourism initiatives in operation, and both businesses and tourists are far more aware of their impacts on the destinations they visit. There are far fewer new tourism products coming on to the market which have not taken into consideration their impacts on the environment, and the customers for these products are learning to demand their sustainability.

The countryside is particularly susceptible to tourism impact, and green tourism now encourages the growth of accommodation based on local B&Bs, farmhouses or forest lodges instead of hotel chains; meals purchased at local restaurants and pubs rather than popular chain eateries and hotel restaurants; and purchases made in local shops and craft centres instead of on-site resort shops.

Britain, in common with other developed nations, has not been slow to repair the ravages of earlier tourism by accepting that responsible tourism is an essential element in corporate social responsibility. Leading tour operators came together to create the Tour Operators' Initiative which, *inter alia*, runs projects in Cyprus and the Gambia to support local economies. The Foreign and Commonwealth Office established a Sustainable Tourism Initiative in 2002 supported by four leading operators, which ultimately led to the formation of the Travel Foundation in 2003 (see Chapter 14 on corporate responsibility for further details of this). Other operators have drawn up codes of conduct for the protection of children from sexual exploitation in Third World countries. Individual companies have made their own contributions to a greener environment. British Airways Holidays, for example, operates a hotel audit, checking on waste and energy conservation, and the sourcing of its supplies. Specialist operator Regent Holidays offers a programme of language assistance for local tourism providers who want to produce special tourism marketing materials. An outstanding example of green tourism is demonstrated by a new tourism attraction in Britain, as described below.

| **Example** | Restaurant at The Earth Centre, Doncaster |

The Earth Centre was funded by Millennium funding, and is an attraction designed to show man's impact on the environment and how this can be minimised. Its self-service restaurant serves 80 per cent of all visitors, and models itself on the core philosophy of sustainability; 10 per cent of all the food used is grown organically on site, and wherever possible local produce (within two hours' transport time) is used. All produce is sustainably packaged, and organic where possible. Fair Trade products from Third World countries such as tea and coffee are used exclusively, and coffee beans are bought in volume bags instead of wasteful foil packs, while fresh tea rather than tea bags are employed. Coffee freshness is maintained by grinding beans on site. Cruets are used for condiments to avoid waste. Recyclable paper cups are used for all take-aways. The refrigeration plant is ozone-friendly, and all furniture in the restaurant is from renewable oak sources. All cleaning materials used are biodegradable, and empty containers are returned for reuse. All waste is separated at source and recycled via eight separate bins; some material is composted, while waste water is purified via a reed bed water purification system and reused. The background music consists of recorded bird song instead of canned music.

Why do products fail?

Before looking at the process of new product development, we need to ask ourselves why so many products fail. It is not enough to say that this is simply the outcome of too much competition. Products have succeeded in exceptionally competitive markets, while others have failed despite having no serious competition. Again, explanation for the failure must lie within one of the four Ps.

If the product is not really new – if it is only an attempt to emulate existing products on the market, offering no appreciable advantages over what is currently available – it stands a poor chance of success. It may be that the competition in the marketplace is already too great to give the new product much scope for success; but over-supply in itself does not threaten a new product.

Example   Holiday Inns

When Holiday Inns announced plans to build a new hotel in Liverpool in the 1970s, hoteliers poured scorn on the idea; the city was already over-supplied with hotel rooms, and present hotels were achieving poor occupancy levels. But the hotel chain had correctly identified its market. The existing business clients of hotels in the city were dissatisfied with the facilities available, but their business required them to be in the city. When they were offered a more modern hotel, with the facilities they preferred, there was a rapid switch to the new hotel and away from the more traditional hotels, some of which were soon forced to close.

This is a simple illustration of the fact that there is more than one kind of demand. In fact, four distinct kinds of demands can be identified:

1   *Existing demand* – the demand which results from inadequate supply of the products the consumers want.

2   *Displacement demand* – the demand resulting from the dissatisfaction experienced by current consumers.

3   *Created demand* – the demand which marketers can develop, which results from wants that are latent and unrecognised by consumers, but can be awakened and promoted by effective marketing.

4   *Future demand* – the demand that will arise naturally in the future as a result of demographic or other changes in the population.

Projections on the future sales potential of the new product should take into account all four of these demands.

The product must also be sold at the right price. What is a 'right price' for a product must clearly depend on many different factors, which are discussed at length in Chapter 6. Suffice to say at this point that the price must be right in relation to other, competitive products, while ensuring an adequate level of profit for the company and remaining within the range of prices which the market can bear.

While no amount of promotion will sell a poor product, the promotion must be adequate to accomplish its task. Unless consumers are made aware of the product it will not be bought, no matter how good it is. That means that the choice of medium must be appropriate for the market segment at which the product is aimed; classical concert weekends at a hotel, or a classical cruise, would attract more attention in *The Gramophone* than in the *Golfer's Weekly*.

Lastly, it is no good creating demand for a product, if the consumer cannot buy the product easily. This means having the support of travel agents who are prepared to rack your brochure and sell the product, or else some equally effective form of distribution on which one can rely for sales. It also means effective briefing of agents. Many travel sales have been lost through inadequate briefing of retailers on new products and their benefits. Today, opportunities to sell direct have proliferated, with the introduction of call centres and websites, and less reliance on retailing intermediaries is necessary, as we shall see later.

Screening the new product

The process of screening new products is illustrated in Figure 5.3. Let us look at each of these steps in turn.

Ideas can be generated from many sources, both within and outside the company. Most typically, an idea for a new product is generated by a company executive, and may then be discussed between a group of executives responsible for new product development. However, other employees further down the ladder can also make significant contributions to new product development if encouraged, and this needs to go further than the usual suggestion box. The sales force in particular are in touch with dealers or customers, and can feed back to management many useful ideas for product improvements, based on either what competitors are offering or what customers and dealers are saying is needed. Regular reviews should be undertaken in retail outlets to ensure that the company's products are remaining competitive with others on the market. In larger companies, departmental heads can encourage individual staff to suggest improvements to products, or new product ideas, based on their separate spheres of knowledge.

In small to medium-sized enterprises – like many small tour operators, visitor attractions and independent travel agents – the resource pool for new ideas will of course be

Figure 5.3
Screening the
new product

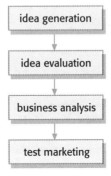

far smaller, but many proprietors or managers of small businesses are enterprising by nature, constantly thinking about how to innovate without draining limited resources. However, because these people are answerable to no one within the business, they sometimes become convinced of their own infallibility, failing to seek ideas from outside their organisations. The travel business today is highly dependent upon flexibility and capability to respond to rapid change, and SME managers cannot afford to ignore possibilities of advice from any sources, wherever found.

Ideas, whatever their source, should be carefully evaluated, so that those whose advantages seem less clear-cut are screened out from the alternatives put forward. This is most easily attained by drawing up a checklist of the strengths and weaknesses of each idea. The market at which the product is to be aimed must be identified, a listing of the benefits of the product over existing products made, and suggestions made on the price that could be charged for the product.

Once the most promising new ideas have been refined, they need to be tested for business viability. An estimate must be made of sales potential, based on the market expected to buy the product, the profit potential and the cash flow, so that management has a clear picture of how long it will take before the new product starts to realise a profit. Research will be undertaken at this stage to test public reaction to the concept. If this is positive, the programme can move on to the final stage, at which the product is made in limited quantities for test marketing.

In the case of tangible goods, test marketing has usually meant selling the product in one region of the UK to see if the potential sales are realised. If the projections on sales are met, then a full-scale launch is undertaken.

In the case of travel, test marketing is less easily undertaken. Aircraft cannot be produced for test marketing, and hotels cannot be built with the ability to be withdrawn if they are unsuccessful. Nevertheless, there are ways of reducing risk by testing product concepts, and some innovatory ideas have been used to overcome this problem in travel. Hotels, for example, have been able to test proposed new room decor by having a few rooms redecorated in existing properties and having guests pass comments on the appeal of the decor. Similar moves have been made by airlines, which will redecorate a single aircraft or part of an aircraft to test customer reaction before introducing a new theme throughout the fleet. There is also scope for introducing new package tours on a limited scale to test the market, before committing the full resources of a company to mass marketing a new destination. However, in general it has to be recognised that launching a travel product entails much greater risk than is the case for other products, and for this reason alone it is essential that much greater care is taken to follow the earlier screening processes outlined above.

Questions, tasks and issues for discussion

1 Bulgari is a well-established brand name in upmarket fashion accessories, and in 2002 announced its intention of establishing a new hotel brand, Bulgari Hotels. Is brand stretching in this fashion a good marketing policy, and can a good brand name like this be applied to any product, or other tourism products such as tour operating? Could Gucci, Prada, Dolce et Gabbana, Armani be equally successful as a hotel brand?

2 Butlins was for many years the leading holiday camp for the British mass market, but with the explosion of foreign holidays after the 1960s the popularity of holiday camps steadily declined. Revamping as 'holiday centres' in the 1980s and 1990s encouraged only marginal temporary improvement, with the overall decline of the product appearing inevitable. One holiday industry expert, quoted in the *Travel Weekly* of 5 May 2000, declared, 'Butlins seems on the one hand to be held back by its name because it is synonymous with holidays camps, but on the other hand it is a powerful brand and they need to keep it.'

   Is this a problem only with the brand, or with the product as a whole? Could brand or product be resurrected without throwing good money after bad? Where is the product on the BCG matrix? What actions would you recommend the company take to safeguard its future?

3 According to David Quarmby, former Chairman of the British Tourist Authority (now VisitBritain), the image of England as a destination is based on a patchwork of images, regional, subregional and local, rather than a single overarching image. In his view, the country's appeal centres on four distinct forms of attraction, all of which enhance the sense of place:

   ■ countryside and coast
   ■ history and heritage
   ■ culture and the arts
   ■ sports and outdoor activities (including walking).

   How far do you agree with this categorisation of England's attractions? How distinct are these categories from those of other regions of Britain – Wales, Scotland, Northern Ireland? And is it true that there is no single unifying image of the country on which to base England's overseas marketing campaigns?

   What image *does* England impart to foreign visitors? Attempts have been made to forgo the typical stereotypic image of Beefeaters, friendly bobbies, jolly pubs and cricket on the green so beloved of our image-makers in favour of a more modern approach to selling England by focusing on sites such as the Tate Modern, The Baltic in Gateshead and similar recent innovative buildings. Would a marketing campaign based on modern England be as successful in attracting overseas visitors?

4 In this chapter it was revealed that in 2003, First Choice Holidays took the decision to jettison the names of its three well-established retail chains – Travel Choice, Holiday Hypermarket and Bakers Dolphin – in favour of an overarching single retail brand: First Choice. Bakers Dolphin was acquired by the company in 1998, and had traded under this brand for more than 40 years. The brand was known and respected throughout the south-west of England, a point that was recognised by its new parent when it was first acquired.

   Examine the arguments for and against retaining the brand name and make your own recommendations, with a rationale for the decision.

5 Stelios Haji-Ioannou declared his intention in 2003 of introducing easyCruise budget cruises to tap an entirely new cruise market. Cruise fares would be reduced by 50 per cent or more by:

   ■ reducing the size of cabins to no more than 90 sq ft
   ■ contracting out all catering and activities on board, for which a charge would be made to passengers
   ■ charging extra for the provision of bed linen
   ■ introducing passenger/staff ratios of 8 : 1 in lieu of the more typical 2 : 1 or 3 : 1.

   The ships would be expected to cruise in the Mediterranean, where frequent ports of call would allow short-leg port-to-port bookings of one or two nights only.

   How successful do you feel this product will be? What markets will it attract? Will it be seen as competitive to any existing cruise operations or other forms of package tour?

Exercise

A great deal of attention has focused in this chapter on the branding of destinations. This exercise will give you experience of linking branding to destinations. Taking any resort, urban area or region known to you, you are asked to develop a new image for the destination to attract an increased number of tourists. This will require you to have knowledge of the existing and potential tourist markets (domestic and foreign, if appropriate), so a programme of research (primary and secondary) to discover these characteristics will be necessary. Once in possession of this information, develop a theme to sell the destination, creating a suitable slogan and, if thought to give added impetus, a logo or other 'brand' imagery to accompany this.

Consider how best to promote this destination and make your markets aware of the new image. What test marketing could be carried out to pilot the scheme?

References

1 Ritchie, J R B and Ritchie Robin, J B, The Branding of Tourism Destinations: Past Achievements and Future Challenges, pp 89–116 in Keller P (ed) *Destination Marketing: Scopes and Limitations*. Reports of the AIEST 48th Congress in Marrakesh, Morocco. St Gall, Edition AIEST, 1998
2 Mundt, J W, The Branding of Myths and the Myths of Branding: Some Critical Remarks on the 'Branding' of Destinations, *Tourism* vol 50 no 4, 2002, pp 339–48

Further reading

Honey, M, *Ecotourism and Sustainable Development: Who Owns Paradise?* Island Press, 1999

Kotler, P, Armstrong, G, Saunders, J and Wong, V, *Principles of Marketing*, Prentice Hall, 3rd European edn, 2001, pp 456–94

Kotler, P, Bowen, J and Makens, J, *Marketing for Hospitality and Tourism*, Prentice Hall, 2nd edn 1999, ch 9 pp 271–313

Laws, E, *Tourist Destination Management: Issues, Analysis and Policies*, Routledge, 1995 ch 4

Middleton, V T C with Clarke, J, *Marketing in Travel and Tourism*, Butterworth Heinemann, 3rd edn 2001, pp 121–37 and 327–47

Morgan, M, Pritchard, A and Pride, R (eds), *Destination Branding: Creating the Unique Destination Proposition*, Butterworth Heinemann, 2001

Seaton, A V and Bennett, M M, *Marketing Tourism Products: Concepts, Issues, Cases*, International Thomson Business Press, 1996

Vellas, F and Bécherel, L (eds), *The International Marketing of Travel and Tourism: a Strategic Approach*, Macmillan, 1999, ch 4 pp 121–40

6 Pricing the product

Learning outcomes

After studying this chapter, you should be able to:

- understand how pricing strategies affect the demand for products
- explain the economic relationship between price and demand
- understand how pricing can be used as a tool to achieve marketing objectives
- explain how costs affect price, and the significance of marginal costing in travel and tourism marketing
- recognise that price is only one factor influencing the demand for travel
- list key pricing policies
- know how to use strategic and tactical pricing as elemFents in a marketing plan.

Introduction

We have educated customers to expect five-star quality at one-star prices.

David Geddes, MD Geddes Travel, quoted in *Travel Weekly*, 7 May 2001

What determines the price of a product? Price is as much a tool of marketing as promotion, and plays a key – perhaps *the* critical – role in the marketing mix. The price of a product should be seen not only as the outcome of market forces. A marketing manager will be aware that price says something to the consumer about the nature of the product, and by manipulating price in combination with product quality and the promotional messages, sales can be orientated to a new market, or market share can be increased at the expense of competitors.

In order to understand how to use price as a tool, we need to have a clear picture of how customers interpret product prices. Here, the concept of the *fair price* is paramount. Buyers judge whether a product is fairly priced by asking themselves whether it represents value for money. Unfortunately, however, all consumers do not share the same view about what represents value for money, because, even assuming that we have the same disposable income, we establish different priorities for what we purchase, and attach different values to the benefits which products offer.

Many people are bemused by the willingness of avid collectors to pay huge sums of money for a work of art. Others will go heavily into debt in order to pay for a car or a house they covet, while still others treasure the ambition to experience a world cruise, and may well 'blow' an inheritance on such a luxury.

In a world where garages in Knightsbridge, London, can fetch more than £100 000 and a rare teddy bear can reach £32 000 at auction, the concept of the fair price becomes difficult to grasp. In the USA a baseball knocked into the crowd by the leading player of the day subsequently fetched $3 million, and possessions of the late Princess of Wales fetch fantastic sums since she became an icon for the masses. Twenty-five Cuban 'Trinidad' cigars were reported as having fetched £9980 in 1997, while a bottle of 1787 Château Lafite claret was sold at auction in 1985 for £105 000 – and the likelihood of its ever being opened is remote. The US financier Dennis Tito paid some £11 million to the Russian authorities for the privilege of being the first tourist in space. Were any of these items *worth* it?

The economics of price

Price and demand

From these examples, what will have become clear is that price has little to do with cost, and far more to do with what someone is willing to pay for a product. In a market where the product is unique, or without satisfactory substitute, or where the product is manufactured by a company which enjoys a monopoly or near monopoly, price will be set high. A luxury item, the purchase of which offers the owner prestige, will also command a high price. A flight on Concorde (before its withdrawal in 2003), or a round-the-world (RTW) cruise, are two examples from the world of tourism; and significantly, the top-price suites and deluxe cabins are often the first to be sold on RTW cruises, due to both their prestige and relative scarcity.

However, it is more customary for travel products to be sold in highly competitive environments, where price is constrained by the substitutability of the product by other, similar products. To understand the interplay between price and demand, we need to know something about how the individual responds to products at different prices, as well as how aggregate demand (the sum of all individual demand) is determined.

Individual demand

Individual consumers make judgements about products based, as we have seen, partly on price. Price acts as a guide to quality, and where consumers have the means to make comparisons with other products, price must be perceived as neither too expensive nor too cheap. If the price lies outside an acceptable range, customers will either reject the product outright, or will seek much more information before committing themselves to a purchase. This can be demonstrated in Figure 6.1. If the price of our holiday lies

Figure 6.1
Information
conveyed by
price

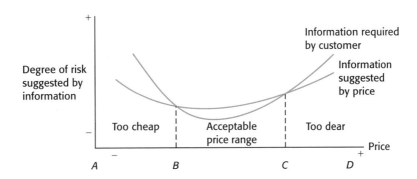

within the sectors *AB* or *CD*, customers will require much more information about the product to be convinced that it offers value for money.

If customers are unable to examine the product in advance of purchase, as is the case with most tourism services, judgements about value for money are similarly difficult to make. For example, overseas package campsite holidays, combining long-distance express coach transport with tent, mobile home or chalet accommodation, attract many buyers due to their low prices. Where the customers are first-time buyers of this type of product, having no prior knowledge of site, resort or nature of the pro-gramme, and with no clear way of establishing an acceptable price range, they may find their expectations are not met. Full information must be given in advance to cus-tomers, often through the medium of the brochure, or the advice given by the travel agent, but in the future this will become increasingly available through enhanced graphic information on websites. However, since many of these products are sold direct to the public, the information conveyed by the brochure alone may be inad-equate to gain an accurate and objective picture of the product.

Clarity is another important element of pricing, and nowhere is this more true than in the case of tourism pricing, often criticised for confusing presentation, concealed extras and add-ons. A good example of confused pricing is to be found in the hotel sector, as described below.

Example   Hotel pricing

Hotel pricing represents a good example of the confusion of prices facing customers. It is not only a question of the variety of prices for the same product – a room – which is almost infinitely variable, ranging from a hypothetical 'rack rate', through numerous 'special offers' dependent upon day of the week, date of the year, and the individual or institution booking the room, to even time of the day, when late bookings for the same night are left to front office managers to negotiate the best rate they can obtain, rather than leaving the room empty for the night. Customers are often also unclear, in the case of many hotel promotions, whether the price being quoted applies to the room (the hotel industry standard) or per per-son (the holiday industry standard). One study of leading hotel chains' websites found that over half did not make clear whether the per person or per room price was being quoted.[1]

Customer expectations play an important part in willingness to buy a product. One study into national park entry charges found that foreign tourists were unwilling to pay *any* charge if entry to the national parks in their own countries were free.[2]

Aggregate demand

The aggregate demand for a product is the demand resulting from the total of each individual consumer's demand patterns, and these will constantly change according to the price and market circumstances, such as availability, convenience of purchase, and competition level. The extent to which a change in price alone will affect a change in total demand is known as the price elasticity of demand, and is illustrated in diagrams (a) and (b) in Figure 6.2. In diagram (a), Q_1 represents the number of products (e.g. package holidays offered by a particular company to a specific destination) sold at the price of P_1. Now let us assume that the company finds itself able to reduce the price of these holidays to P_2, as a result of better negotiations with airlines and hotels. More holidaymakers now want to buy these packages, so the number of holidays sold rises to Q_2. If the revenue achieved by these extra sales exceeds the revenue lost by the reduction in price, we say that demand is relatively elastic. By the same token, an equivalent increase in price, from P_1 to P_3, will cause sales to drop off substantially to Q_3.

A different picture is presented by diagram (b). Here, Q_1 represents the number of units sold at a price of P_1, where price is not the major consideration in the purchase; say, club class seats in airlines operating on a major business route such as Frankfurt to London. In this case, if the price falls to P_2, sales will still increase only to Q_2, since business travellers for the most part have to travel to a particular destination, and are unlikely to be influenced to travel there more frequently, or to switch from other routes. If the gap between economy and club class fares narrows, it may cause a few holiday travellers to switch to the higher class, but such changes will be few and the increase in revenue achieved by the extra seats sold may be less than the revenue lost by reducing the seat prices. Equally, should the airlines on the route increase the fares to P_3, business travellers will be unlikely to cancel their journeys. Only a very substantial increase may cause the company to look at other means of travel such as rail, or to reduce the number of trips their staff makes, or cut back the staff sent to this destination. The quantity of seats sold drops therefore only to Q_3. We can say that demand is relatively inelastic for this product, and this will be reflected in the fairly steep demand curve shown in D_1D_2. However, demand patterns will be very different on deregulated routes, where each airline has the freedom to set its own price, or on routes where a

Figure 6.2
Price elasticity
of demand

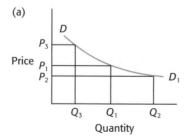

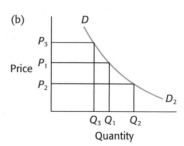

cheap budget airline has entered the competition. In such a competitive market, the business traveller may well switch to an alternative carrier, unless the airline charging the higher price can convince its customers that the extra expense is worth paying for – for example, by offering more convenient flight times, greater timetable reliability, superior service in-flight or on the ground or other improvements in conditions (such as an increase in free baggage allowance). Price decisions are always influenced by the extent to which customers are offered, and made aware of, acceptable substitutes for a product. In the example given, if lower air fares are available by flying to Maastricht in the Netherlands, or to Luxembourg, this will tempt some travellers to fly there instead, and continue their journey by road or rail to Frankfurt.

In setting prices, the company will want to know what levels of demand it is likely to experience at different prices. For a new product this is hard to gauge. The two most common methods of assessing demand are:

■ asking potential customers what they would be willing to pay for the service
■ test marketing the product at different prices in different regions.

The difficulty with the first method is that what people say they will do does not always translate into actual behaviour when the product is launched, while with the second method, it is difficult to control all the factors apart from price which will influence consumer decisions in different areas. With a major item of expenditure such as tourism, it is possible that consumers from other areas may take advantage of the low prices in other regions. If, for instance, it becomes cheaper for a British tourist to fly to Germany in order to benefit from a package tour to East Africa which is sold substantially cheaper in that country than it is in Britain, a number of British tourists will avail themselves of that opportunity, even if they have to suffer the cost and inconvenience of an extra flight.

Pricing and yield management

The aim of all pricing is to achieve a certain level of revenue overall for an organisation, and *managing the yield* is a critical aspect of marketing. This is particularly true of tourism and travel marketing, where the product itself is so volatile. Exchange rates are continually varying between countries, making certain destinations highly attractive – at the time of writing, the British pound was strong against certain currencies such as those of South Africa, Vietnam (at 15 000 dong to the pound) and above all Argentina, where the peso had collapsed, and operators could therefore offer bargain holidays to these destinations – although sometimes the advantages of cheap prices could be offset by other circumstances, such as the political decision to charge wealthy tourists from the developed countries high prices for visiting Vietnam, or the relatively high cost of flights to Argentina. However, by mid-2003 – and the start of the tourist high season – the pound had weakened considerably (by a factor of 15–20 per cent) against the euro, reducing demand from Britain to many European countries but making Britain more attractive as a destination to incomers from those countries as well as domestic tourists. As we have also seen, tourism is a highly seasonal occupation, and poor weather will restrict tourist visits for large parts of the year to many countries. The strength of competition varies continually, necessitating rapid price changes in response since unsold stock cannot be stored, and there is a finite capacity for tourists at peak periods of the year (and overcrowded destinations will discourage others from travelling). Thus marketers must juggle many balls in the air simultaneously to ensure they maximise their revenue, rather than simply maximising their customers.

Pricing is therefore a key tool to achieve the organisation's marketing objectives. If the target market has been clearly identified, and a decision taken about where the product is to be positioned, pricing bands will become easier to determine.

Looking back to our introduction to strategic marketing, you will recall that companies can adopt one of three broad marketing objectives. They can attempt to lead the field by keeping prices down (a policy vigorously pursued by the budget airlines); they can adopt a strategy of differentiating their product from the market leaders by product positioning; or they can select a particular market segment to which they will aim their appeal by *niche marketing*. A company with a substantial hold on a market may seek to maximise its profits by finding ways to reduce cost while maintaining or moderately increasing prices; or it may seek to increase still further its share of the market by cutting prices in line with its reduced costs. Companies with a more tenuous hold in the market will then either be forced to price low in order to survive, or to attempt still further to differentiate their product – for example, by using price as an indicator of quality.

As we have seen, below or above a certain price range there will be no demand for the product. But within the range, there will be some scope for flexibility to adjust prices, within three *concept bands*:

1 *Premium pricing*   Here the decision is taken to set prices above market price, either to reflect the image of quality or the unique status of the product. The product may be new, or it may have features not shared by its competitors, or the organisation itself may enjoy such a strong reputation that the 'brand image' alone is sufficient to merit a premium price. Within this bracket one can include upmarket tourism destinations such as the Costa Smeralda in Sardinia, or some of the more elite destinations in the Caribbean like the British Virgin Islands or the Turks and Caicos Islands, or Alpine skiing resorts such as Méribel. Five-star cruising companies like Crystal and Radisson, and hotels like the Ritz and Georges V in Paris also fall into this category.

2 *Value for money pricing*   Here the intention is to charge medium prices for the product, and emphasise that it represents excellent value for money at this price. Marks & Spencer have traded very successfully using this policy, which enables a company to achieve good levels of profit on the basis of an established reputation. Many of the leading tour operators in the Western world will aim to link their pricing to this appeal.

3 *'Cheap value' pricing*   The objective here is to undercut the competition, and price is used as a trigger to encourage immediate purchase. Unit profits are low, but satisfactory overall profits are achieved through high turnover. Low prices will often be

introduced by a company seeking to gain rapid expansion in the market, or a toe-hold in a new market. Budget airlines are the supreme example of this policy.

Example   The budget airlines

Budget airlines like easyJet and Ryanair aim to maximise their yields by attractive 'come-on' low prices – with limited availability – for those booking well in advance, with a gradual increase in pricing as the date of departure approaches. An example is given in the average fare structure for easyJet's London (Luton) to Barcelona route in 2002:

Cheapest seats	£45
Seats booked 20 weeks before departure	£69
Seats booked 16 weeks before departure	£80
Seats booked 10–12 weeks before departure	£66
Seats booked 7–8 weeks before departure	£98
Seats booked 5–6 weeks before departure	£78
Seats booked 3–4 weeks before departure	£89
Seats booked 2 weeks before departure	£110
Seats booked 1 week before departure	£137
Seats booked 5 days before departure	£132
Seats booked 2 days or less before departure	£160

It will be apparent that the changing prices given here do not represent a continual decline as departure date draws near. Rather, they represent the price sensitivity perceived by the company on the dates in question. These prices, available over the Internet, demonstrate the ability of the firm to change fares at very short notice when selling via websites, to reflect rapidly changing market conditions.

It must be stressed that any of these policies may be seen as 'fair pricing' policies, notwithstanding the criticism sometimes directed at companies achieving higher than average profits. Market orientation seeks to ensure that the customer is satisfied with the product at the price paid. A fair price can be defined as one which the customer is happy to pay while the company achieves a satisfactory level of profit. Thus a premium pricing policy is acceptable providing that the customer receives the benefits perceived as appropriate to the price. Only where companies are able to force up prices against the consumers' will, such as in the case of monopolies, can it be said that fair pricing is inoperative.

Pricing has become increasingly complex in marketing travel and tourism products, and although there are calls for simple more understandable price panels in printed literature, the reality is that, largely due to the nature of the product, better yield management has led to increasingly variable sets of prices depending upon changing circumstances within the various sectors of the industry. This has been heightened by the ability of organisations to effect rapid changes of price through booking sites on the World Wide Web and the simultaneous development of dot.com intermediaries negotiating flexible prices.

Example PriceLine

PriceLine operates an online auction in which prospective customers bid for the price they are willing to pay for an airline seat. PriceLine then approaches airlines to see if they can secure seats at the bid price. Once the customer has accepted the offer, they are locked into the price, with the exact time of the flight only revealed when the booking is effected.

Other examples include the growing number of auction websites in which airline tickets are sold to customers making the highest bids. Flexible pricing in the airline industry is a valuable tool in ensuring that load factors are as near as possible to 100 per cent, but airlines with seating in more than one class must take care to ensure that discounted seats do not attract those prepared to pay premium prices. This is often achieved by restrictive conditions, as the approximately 10 per cent of seats offered at premium prices can account for as much as 30–40 per cent of the revenue yield on key routes. Hotels are notable for their extremely flexible pricing policies, the so-called 'rack rates' (published rates) often bearing little relationship to actual prices charged, which will vary according to season, day and even time of day, depending upon levels of demand. Even top-class hotels are prepared to bargain at the front desk with prospective guests who appear late in the evening, in order to fill unsold rooms, for which revenue will be lost for ever if no sale is made.

The phenomenon of variable prices informally available in popular tourist centres is well known to frequent travellers, where lowest prices will be quoted to locals, slightly higher prices to those tourists who demonstrate a good working knowledge of the local language, with the highest prices being charged to the mass visitors. This arrangement holds good in many popular tourism centres, especially those in the developing countries, and has in fact even been formalised in some regions: in Italy, Venice has introduced a charge four times higher than locals for tourists using ferries, and twice as high for the use of local toilets, while Florence introduced admission charges for all tourists to the city. Many museums permit free or reduced entry charges for locals. Tour operators have made strenuous efforts to keep basic prices for their programmes low while introducing complex supplementary charges previously included in the basic cost of a holiday. In 2001, to take one example, Airtours introduced a three-tier pricing structure, with Holiday Plus, Economy Holidays and Sundeal Holidays. Prices were variable between these programmes, with supplements charged in certain cases for resort transfers, pre-bookable seating on aircraft, in-flight meals, check-in times, wallet packs and membership in the company's children's clubs. Conditions relating to deposits, changes to dates, accommodation and flights also varied according to price paid.

One unusual example of a change in pricing policy has been that pursued by the cross-channel operator Eurotunnel, on its short sea crossing between Britain and France. The initial appeal of this subterranean rail tunnel operator was enhanced by a 'turn-up-and-go' policy, where prior bookings were not necessary – this, together with highly flexible fares, was seen as offering a strong sales advantage over the ferry operators on the route, who worked to published timetables and less flexible fares. However, ferry companies quickly retaliated by offering a similar 'turn-up-and-go' policy, while Eurotunnel backtracked by first introducing the obligation to book in advance at fixed times, and subsequently incorporated a penalty of between £10 and £30 payable for departures other than the one for which the customer had booked. The objective was to increase yield, but in attempting to do so the company antagonised their customers to little advantage while at the same time increasing the appeal of short sea crossings by ferry.

Internal influences on pricing

In the long run, all commercial organisations will continue to produce a product only if it can realise a profit; but profit can be defined in a number of ways.

Gross profit is the price of the product less the direct costs of its production. For a travel agent, the figure represents the difference between the price paid for travel services and the price charged to the consumer, that is, the commission received on the holidays and other travel services sold. These commissions will usually range between 7 and 10 per cent depending upon the travel services supplied. In some sectors, particularly the tour operating sector, *override commission* of an extra 1–5 per cent or even more may be paid for volume-based performance. Use of this override commission to pass on discounts to the consumer is now a major weapon in the armoury of travel agents. The cost of a package tour to a tour operator is the price that the operator must pay to airlines, hotels and other organisations offering the services which are included in the package – the *raw materials* cost. To these costs must be added the *overheads* which the company must meet – the costs involved in running the company, including administrative costs (office rent and rates, light and heat, telephones, etc.), salaries, and marketing costs such as advertising, distribution, reservations including website or call centre, plus brochure production and any other miscellaneous expenses incurred in running the business. These costs are deducted from the gross profits to ascertain the net profits before tax.

Accounting practice dictates that total costs are divided between *variable costs* (VC), that is, costs that vary with the number of units produced, and *fixed costs* (FC), which are relatively difficult to change in the short term and will accrue regardless of the number of units produced. The cost of renting an office and cleaning it will not vary in the short term regardless of how many, or how few, of its products the company succeeds in selling.

The marketing manager will need to know at what stage of sales revenue *break-even point* is achieved. This is the point where total costs exactly equal the total revenue received from sales; it will then be possible to establish how this break-even point will be affected by charging different prices for the product. This will reveal how many extra holidays (or other units of production) must be sold at a lower price in order to recover costs.

Let us take an example of a theme park or tourist attraction which is considering three different pricing possibilities as its basic entry price: £4.50, £5.50 and £6.50. In Figure 6.3, the lines VC and FC represent respectively the variable costs and the fixed

Figure 6.3
Break-even chart

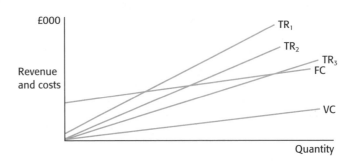

costs associated with running the project. In a venture such as this, fixed costs represent a very high proportion of total costs, since the major expenditure is in the capital
outlay to construct the attraction and to staff it. Variable costs will be a small element,
and will include some staff costs (seasonal part-time labour), catering, and energy costs
(power for amusement rides, etc.), plus some additional maintenance costs associated
with the added wear and tear resulting from larger crowds. Diagrammatically, the
break-even chart tells the marketing staff how many customers they must attract at
each level of price in order to cover their costs.

TR_1, TR_2 and TR_3 represent the total revenue received at entry charges of £6.50,
£5.50 and £4.50 respectively. Presenting the diagram in this form tells us not only
where the break-even points occur, but also what contribution the revenue will make
to the fixed costs at each pricing level, should sales fail to break even. If sales fall below
the break-even point, and as long as the variable costs are covered, the income received
will still make a useful *contribution* to the ongoing costs of the project, which will have
to be paid regardless of the number of visitors.

Recognising the importance of contribution has been a significant development in
pricing policy in the travel industry. Railways, for example, have high fixed costs in
track and signalling equipment and their maintenance, as well as substantial investment in rolling stock. Apart from certain high-demand routes and during periods such
as the rush hour, much of this rolling stock would lie idle, unless markets can be
attracted through low-priced off-peak excursion fares. These fares will easily cover the
small element of variable cost involved in operating the equipment (little more than
the minute cost of extra power to carry more passengers) while making a significant
contribution to the high overheads of running a railway. Where ownership of rolling
stock and track is discrete, as is the case with railways in Britain, contracts between the
track owner and the operating company often call for the latter to pay a fixed fee for
the use of the track over a period of time, regardless of the number of passengers
carried. This reduces the track owner's risk, and has, for example, been of substantial
benefit to Eurotunnel, in that the train operator Eurostar has consistently failed to
achieve the passenger numbers originally envisaged for the cross-channel route.
Another example of a contribution to operating cost is provided by the educational
institutions who make available student accommodation out of term for holiday use.
Students are away from universities and colleges for up to 20 weeks in the year. Many
of these weeks coincide with peak holiday periods. This, coupled with the fact that
many educational institutions are situated in geographically attractive regions of their

country, means that the colleges have found it worthwhile to rent out their accommodation at 'marginal costs' little above variable cost, to avoid closing down during the holidays. They have gone on to promote the use of their public rooms for meetings and conferences, thus increasing demand for bedroom accommodation during the holiday periods.

Costs establish the floor price below which a company would be unprepared to consider selling its products. But simply ascertaining costs and adding a 'mark-up' of some arbitrary percentage to determine the selling price does not represent a marketing approach to pricing, since it ignores the dynamics of the marketplace – what competitors are charging, the elasticity of demand for the product and what the market will bear. It also fails to take into account that price actually influences cost through its effect on the volume of sales. Low prices stimulate demand leading to high turnover, which provides increased negotiating power with suppliers, enabling tour operators, for instance, to drive costs down by promising very large purchases of hotel rooms. If the proposed selling price appears too high against competitors' prices, an appraisal of the costs is needed. Can costs be shaved? Might it be possible, for example, to adopt a new distribution system such as direct sell, to reduce costs and make the product competitive in price? It is just this realisation that has driven the competition between the airlines in recent years, with the introduction of budget operators forcing the established airlines to trim costs. One way in which this has been achieved is to reduce or eliminate the payment of commission to travel agents, either by adopting a policy of direct sell exclusively (with best prices available through cheapest distributive outlets, usually this being the Internet) or requiring their agents to pay full price for tickets, adding a mark-up fee for the service provided to their clients.

One further complication in costing is the allocation of fixed costs to a product. Some acceptable means has to be found to apportion the fixed costs of a company to each product and range of products in a manner which can be judged appropriate. An airline might divide its costs according to the routes served, in relation to the total passenger tonne kilometres flown, or based on the anticipated revenue for a given route. No single system of cost allocation is perfect, however, and it is not uncommon for a lower level of fixed costs to be assigned to any new products launched (such as a new airline route), in order to give them a better chance to achieve rapid profitability.

Pricing and the product mix

It is important that the price set for a product is right not only in itself, but also in relation to the other products marketed by the company. If the product appears cheap by comparison with others in the range, consumers may switch their purchasing patterns, and sales overall will fall; or equally, the market may view the cheaper product with suspicion, unless a satisfactory explanation is given for the price differentials. As most travel products are increasingly viewed as homogeneous, a low-priced holiday in, say, Greece will divert holidaymakers from Spain, unless Spanish holiday benefits are promoted very heavily. However, with many travel products it is common to find that each product in the range faces entirely different market conditions. An airline may experience significant competition both in price and service on one route, while enjoy-ing market leadership on another. Airlines are generally reluctant to allow authorised routes to lapse, which would allow competitors to step in, often preferring to cross-subsidise a loss-making route with the profits from more successful routes provided that a satisfactory overall level of profitability can be achieved in the year.

Let us take a hypothetical example of cross-subsidies, using the services of Britainair, a British carrier with three routes. Let us assume that the marketing plan for the airline calls for targeted profits of not less than 7 per cent overall. This could be achieved by balancing the profit levels on all routes as follows:

Route A is a recently awarded route which faces intense competition from other air-lines who are well established in the market, and who are themselves cutting prices in efforts to increase their market shares. Britainair is anxious to get a toehold in the mar-ket and gain a 10 per cent share of what is thought to be a potentially lucrative route.

Route B is one on which the airline is already well established; it is shared with two other carriers, with roughly equal market shares. While market share is stable, and profits satisfactory, the route is not growing and load factors, while adequate, could be healthier. All three airlines are anxious to discourage any new entrants to this market.

Route C is one on which Britainair is the market leader. There is strong flag loyalty from the major market segment, and the company generally enjoys an excellent reputation.

The marketing plan for the coming year suggests the price structure shown in Table 6.1.

Such cross-subsidies would be considered appropriate only in the comparatively short term, to achieve strictly short-term objectives such as those outlined. In the long term each route, or 'product', will normally be expected to become profitable in its own right (although in the case of certain airline routes which serve the needs of the community, the public sector may provide grants to keep otherwise unprofitable routes in operation). However, it is not uncommon for companies which are horizon-tally or vertically integrated to accept lower than normal profits when 'selling' or trans-ferring their products to other divisions within the company. This practice, known as 'transfer pricing' or 'shadow pricing', could be employed, for example, where a tour

Table 6.1 Pricing based on targeted profits

Sales		Average unit price per seat (£)	Total revenue per route (£)	Target profit % at average prices	Target profit (£)
Route A:	50 000	180	9 000 000	3	270 000
Route B:	250 000	220	55 000 000	5	2 750 000
Route C:	200 000	200	40 000 000	11	4 400 000
Total revenue, all routes:			104 000 000		
Total target profit overall:					7 420 000
Total target profit (weighted average)				7.13	

operator owns its own airline, and the aircraft are 'leased' to the tour operator at an artificially low price to enable the operator to compete at a time when cut-throat competition is restricting profits generally. It should be added that the leading tour operators owning their own airlines have always denied that this practice occurs within their own sphere of operations. However, it is generally accepted that ticket prices on many international ferry routes (now excluding routes within the European Union) have been kept artificially low due to accompanying profits made on the sale of duty-free goods. In effect, ferry companies attract passengers with low prices in order to recoup profits overall through the sale of on-board goods and services. This applies less in the case of airlines because most duty-free purchases are made at airports rather than on-board the aircraft – however, airport landing fees have been contained, to the ultimate benefit of air passengers, as a result of these supplementary profits.

The role of price in the tourism marketing mix

Pricing, as we have already emphasised, is only one tool in the marketing mix, and pricing decisions must be determined in relationship with all the other elements of the mix. Although there is strong evidence that price is the major factor in many travel purchase decisions, it is by no means the sole criterion. While it is true that brand images (with a handful of notable exceptions) have not played a big role in tourism marketing up until the present, this is not to say that symbolic values in travel products are of no importance, and the evidence suggests that as discretionary income rises, there is a simultaneous increase in the symbolic and emotional values attached to branded names in tourism as well.

To a great extent, the larger travel companies have chosen to ignore the creation of added value in their marketing plans, focusing instead on the promotion of price – a glance at the wealth of advertising pages in the travel sections of Britain's (and other countries') weekend press will provide all the evidence one needs to substantiate this statement. The major tour operators in particular have used low price as a means of increasing their market shares, at the expense of profit levels. There can be little doubt that this policy was highly successful during the latter part of the twentieth century, although this may have had as much to do with the publicity that resulted from the price wars between operators, causing consumers to become conscious of price rather than value. Consistently over-optimistic sales projections led to heavy discounts to 'dump' unsold seats through late bookings, encouraging consumers both to shop around for the best bargains and to book later. In retrospect, it now seems likely that increasing disposable income and other favourable factors such as exchange rates would have led to substantial increases in the number of package tours sold, even had discounting not been introduced. Instead, the industry has long struggled to survive with minimal profits, and the era has seen the collapse, or near collapse, of a number of leading names. With the dawning of the twenty-first century, the low-price emphasis shifted to the airline industry, which, already severely affected by terrorism threats and economic depression, became engaged in cut-throat competition between the traditional carriers and the new budget airlines.

Other influences on price

Earlier, we explored some of the factors affecting price decisions over which the company will have very little control. Chief of these are:

1   The economic health of the country (or region). It is notable that not all regions in the UK were equally affected by the recession of the late 1990s and early 2000s, and that Britain as a whole was less severely affected than many mainland European countries like Germany and France.
2   The elasticity of demand for travel and tourism products.
3   The volatility of changing economic circumstances in generating and destination countries, such as relative exchange rates and taxation (e.g. VAT rates, airport or other local taxes).
4   Levels of competition faced by individual companies and substitutability between competing products.
5   The nature of the target market, which will determine what kind of holiday or other travel products they will buy and at what price.

There will also be ethical considerations to be taken into account. A company concerned about its public image will wish to reassure its public that it is not making excess profits, even assuming it is in a position to do so without challenge from the Competition Commission in Britain, or other regulatory bodies in other countries. It would also be short-sighted of companies to attempt to introduce substantial price increases at a time when the political climate favours price restraint, even were the market able to bear such increases.

Legal constraints

Under certain conditions there may even be legal considerations affecting price decisions. In the past, prices in Britain have been politically controlled under price and wage 'freezes' to hold down inflation, while legislation exists to affect pricing tactics in a number of ways. The Office of Fair Trading (OFT) requires clarity in the price panels in tour operators' brochures because some of these chose to exclude air travel taxes, leading to confusion and difficulties in making price comparisons on the part of the public. The OFT prohibits the imposition of resale price maintenance on travel agents, who are at liberty to discount their own commission to reduce the price if they wish to do so. British regulations also spell out the need for clarity in displaying prices in the accommodation sector: for example, the Tourism (Sleeping Accommodation Price Display) Order (1977) requires hotels with four or more letting rooms to display room prices at reception, and the Price Marking (Food and Drink on Premises) Order (1979) enforces similar requirements for the display of food and drink prices where they can be seen by customers before entering. The Price Marking (Bargain Offers) Order (1979) requires any money-off offers to be genuine reductions on original prices.

Codes of Practice

Additionally, there are a number of organisations, quasi-governmental and industrial, which exercise some influence on pricing policies and strategies. Many of these exercise control through Codes of Practice which companies are either obliged, or strongly advised, to follow, if they are to be accepted as professionals. The Independent Broadcasting Authority (IBA) has its own code relating to advertising, to which reference is made in Chapter 10. The Chartered Institute of Marketing, the professional body representing marketing staff in all sectors of industry – which, incidentally, has its own travel and tourism sector, the Chartered Institute of Marketing Travel Industry Group (CIMTIG) – has its own Code of Conduct, and ABTA itself enforces Codes of Conduct for both tour operator and travel agent members. The Tour Operators' Code, for example, includes a section devoted to standards on brochures which requires the brochure to carry 'the total price, or the means of arriving at the total price, together with a precise statement of the services included therein'. Clear directions on surcharges and how these can be imposed must be given, and in the event such surcharges are imposed, a detailed explanation of the reasons for the surcharge must be provided to customers. Airport and seaport taxes must be integrated into the price of all European holidays.

Agents are permitted to charge fees for services they render, but such fees must be determined individually, not 'in collusion' by ABTA, under OFT rules. Bodies such as the Air Transport Users' Committee, who are the watchdogs concerned with the protection of passengers, closely monitor air fares and will react strongly where they find evidence of price anomalies (this could mean concern with low prices, too, if these are seen as evidence of 'predatory pricing' – prices set below cost, designed to drive a competitor out of business). The National Consumers' Council, Consumers' Association and, indeed, the media themselves, all play a role in publicising prices thought to be out of line with the achievement of normal business profits.

Developing a price policy

Policies are plans for the future direction of the business. A company's price policy therefore appears in the marketing plan as an indication of the company's objectives in setting prices. In some cases, price policy may be no more than a reaction to market forces or the result of a failure to plan, but good marketing implies a more positive approach to considerations of price, and the development of an active plan to influence the market through price. These policies will now be examined.

Profit maximisation

This is a commonly stated objective which combines charging what the market will bear with attempts to reduce costs. One difficulty associated with the policy is to know exactly what any market will bear, and the problems inherent in constant price adjustment cause many companies to settle for a policy of 'satisfactory' rather than maximum profits. There is also the danger in maximising profits that the firm will attract unwelcome competition; by keeping profits moderate, and prices low, this may deter opportunist firms from entering the market.

There is another argument against the reduction of costs to their minimum. A hotel, for example, could adopt a strategy of employing casual labour in season and closing down out of season, as a means of maximising profits. This may still be true even after assessing the marginal contribution of staying open throughout the year, which we have discussed earlier. However, there is a social cost in hiring and firing indiscriminately in areas of already high unemployment. Such jobs attract the less committed casual workers, and in a business like the hotel industry, where good service is fundamental to profitability and survival, it will be hard to attract the qualified staff necessary to achieve this. Customers who are disappointed do not rebook, and the long-term effects may actually be to reduce profits.

Target return on investment (ROI)

A common practice is to measure the amount of profits achieved each year as a proportion of the total capital invested in the company. This can be helpful, since comparisons can then be made with the profit potential if the capital were invested in other forms of business. Many small tourism businesses do not achieve the same level of profit which might be possible through other investments (indeed, at times of moderate to high interest, it will probably be more profitable simply to invest one's capital in a building society) and it therefore has to be assumed that profit is not the only, or even most important, motive in setting up a tourism business. Owners of many SMEs are content to achieve low returns on their invested capital for the privilege of working for themselves, or running their own businesses. This has always been the case with proprietors of small hotels and guesthouses, which are frequently family-run concerns, while proprietors of travel agencies and others in the travel industry enjoy the opportunities for cheap travel offered by their jobs. Larger companies tend to measure success purely in economic terms.

It should be recognised that in the case of some sectors of the travel business, capital appreciation on assets can be as important as operating profit. Hotels in London, for instance, have seen the scarcity of building land in the city centre lead to huge rises in the value of their property over the past 20 years, far exceeding any operating profit they have achieved.

Finally, ROI is not a good measure of travel agency success, since the actual cost of setting up an agency is quite small, involving as it does no investment in stock. The cost of purchase of a well-established travel agency will include a large element of 'goodwill', based on the assumption that present customers of the agency will continue to trade there after the change in ownership.

Pricing for market share

Many companies will set their prices at a level designed to ensure that they will achieve a certain share of the market. This, disparagingly known in the industry as 'playing the numbers game', generally calls for price restraint, especially in the early stages of the product life cycle (PLC), where the aim is market *penetration* (as opposed to market *expansion* in later stages of the PLC). However, if it is the intention to deliberately curb profits in the early stages of the PLC in order to achieve a given market share, there must be the underlying objective of achieving a good profit level in the longer term, since there would be little point in becoming locked into a long-term price war without some evidence of ultimate benefit to the company.

Falling profitability in British tour operations resulted from the agreed objectives of the major companies to hold down prices in order to build market share. This had the effect of driving some SMEs out of business, but the substantial growth achieved by the market leaders promised potentially larger turnover and profits. However, this drive for growth has led to expansion internationally, especially between tour operating companies within the European Union, with greater concentration between the lead operators and little evidence that this is leading to greater profits in the uncertain climate of the early twenty-first century.

For a low-price policy to succeed, the product itself must be elastic in demand, and costs per unit must fall as 'production' increases (as they do in the case of tour operations, where lower prices can be negotiated if more customers are guaranteed to the suppliers). Additionally, the product should anticipate a long life cycle (expansion of leisure time and discretionary income encourage a belief that holidays and travel will continue to enjoy a long-term growth curve). Any company embarking on such a policy also needs, of course, to be in a very strong financial position to survive the occasional price war which may result.

Although instances are much rarer, the reader should be aware that on occasion a company may set prices in order to decrease their share of the market. Such a policy would be followed if the company estimates that it will become more profitable by increasing specialisation within the overall market, allowing it to charge a higher price to its selected customers (assuming relatively inelastic demand). This policy also makes sense where the firm in question is concerned that its market share has grown to a point where its dominant position in the market might come under the scrutiny of a disciplinary body like the Competition Commission. By divesting itself of some of its market share before investigation, the company may lessen the threat of such an investigation.

Pricing for market share becomes a key policy where the company is operating in a saturated market, since the best way in which the company can increase sales is to take business away from the competition. Most travel products still offer considerable potential for increases in markets, but a few offer very small prospects for growth. For example, the transport of military personnel and their dependants on leave is a static or declining market without any expansion in the recruitment to the armed services. Special price offers to this market will attract business from competitors, although there may also be some scope to increase the frequency of use; that is, by getting existing consumers to travel more often.

Increasing turnover

It is important to note the distinction between pricing policies which aim to increase turnover, and those aiming to increase market share. Certainly, turnover is easier to measure than market share, but using turnover as a yardstick for success may disguise the fact that a company's actual share of the market is falling. If, for example, demand for overseas flights increases dramatically, an airline could experience a 3 per cent growth in its traffic although its total market share might have fallen by 10 per cent or more, suggesting that management has not maximised its opportunities. By focusing on turnover, there is also the danger that a decline in profitability can be overlooked. Turnover may be increased in one of four ways:

- by getting more people to buy the product
- by getting present purchasers to buy it more frequently
- by finding new uses for the product
- by increasing the price of the product.

Example   The Old Swan

The Old Swan is a large country hotel seeking to attract more visitors. It refurbishes its rooms without a commensurate increase in price, promoting this improvement in those regions where its major markets are generated. Summer guests are encouraged to return for a three-day winter break, with special package prices available only to guests booking during their summer holidays. Later, with an extension providing new meeting rooms and leisure facilities (pool, gymnasium), and a noted professional chef in the kitchen, conference users are attracted, with a moderate increase in price. Public space is used more cost-effectively by subcontracting retail shopping space in the lobbies, either with a straightforward rental contract or an agreement to share a percentage of the shop's revenue. Off-season occupancy is increased by selling some rooms on a timeshare basis.

All these are strategies which will help the hotel achieve its price policy, which is simply to increase operating turnover for the hotel by appropriate pricing strategies.

Price restraint

Sometimes companies will take the decision to maintain or lower prices simply in order to retain existing markets. This could be a response to falling sales generally, or even a goodwill gesture at a time when economy as a whole is performing badly, or the government is actively seeking price restraint to control inflation. This will normally be a short-term policy designed to meet current market conditions.

Meeting competitors' prices

On the face of it, this is an attractive policy for consumers, since it reassures them that they will not find the product more cheaply by shopping around. Although the outstanding example of this is to be found outside the travel industry, in the John Lewis

Partnership's guarantee 'we are never knowingly undersold', the policy has been used by travel companies, including Thomas Cook in their 'price promise' which offered to refund the difference in price on package tours which could be bought more cheaply elsewhere. As travel customers become more price-conscious and shop around between different agents, as well as call centres and the Internet, to get the cheapest prices, so are more agents having to agree to match prices offered by their competitors to close a sale.

If a policy such as this is adopted by several leading suppliers, a price war may break out, with smaller companies adopting 'survival pricing' to remain in business. Without sufficient reserves, they will be driven out of business. If this results in a handful of major companies forming an oligopoly to dominate the market, this may be contrary to the consumer's long-term interests, since new companies will find it difficult to get established in the market, and the larger companies may force up prices and profits. This in turn can lead to the formation of new market gaps for cheaper holidays.

Example   Princess Cruises

Britain's P&O Princess Cruises agreed a merger with leading US cruise operator Royal Caribbean International, but a counter-bid from the world's leading operator Carnival Cruises later overturned the merger, and P&O Princess was absorbed into the Carnival empire. At mid-point in 2002 it was estimated that the P&O Princess/RCI merger would result in the company controlling 40 per cent of the US cruise market, 30 per cent of the UK market and 24 per cent of the German market. The merger with Carnival was then estimated to give Carnival 48 per cent of the US market, 35 per cent of the UK market and 27 per cent of the German market. In spite of these substantial market shares the merger with Carnival was approved by the US Federal Trade Commission, the British Department of Trade and Industry and the European Union's competition directorate.

Short-term profit maximisation

Often known as 'skimming the cream', this policy calls for the setting of high prices at the launch stage, with a progressive lowering of price as the product becomes better established, and progresses through the life cycle. Reducing prices to boost sales is an alternative to innovating the product to rejuvenate it when sales falter, as discussed in Chapter 5. This is illustrated in Figure 6.4. The policy takes advantage of the fact that most products are in high demand in the early stage of the life cycle when they are

Figure 6.4
Skimming the cream

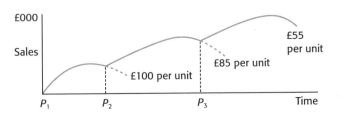

novel or unique, or when supplies are limited. A new museum with exhibits that will attract many tourists such as the Eden Centre in Cornwall, or a theme park with exciting new rides, will both be limited in their ability to expand sales when popularity peaks – in fact, visitors to the Eden Centre, with its modernistic biodomes, so far exceeded anticipated demand during its first summer season that transport access was severely under pressure and a ticket rationing system was introduced. Longer opening hours during the season may be one possibility to spread demand, but a weather-dependent site with much of its attractions outdoors will discourage longer annual opening hours, and within the summer season, long queues will form without some form of rationing. Under such circumstances it makes commercial sense to maximise profits during the peak periods of the year by charging relatively high entrance fees. A small property such as Down House in Kent, the former home of Charles Darwin, requires advance booking to restrict visitors to manageable numbers, while exhibitions like the annual Chelsea Garden Show in London prove so popular that both ticket rationing and high prices are essential to control demand. Demand can also be managed by setting very high prices to cream off those prepared to pay them under certain conditions (first nights, previews, popular days of the week), gradually reducing the price to meet different market segments' price elasticities. Museums will frequently offer a lower entrance price, or even free entry, on one, usually less popular, day of the week, or an hour before an exhibition closes, to attract those unwilling or unable to pay the high prices demanded for their very popular special exhibitions.

If there is no problem with supply, the object will be to obtain the highest level of sales possible in the post-launch period at the highest price. This will call for a large promotional spend at the launch stage to make the market aware of the new product as quickly as possible and influence them to buy it.

The particular value of this policy is that it provides a high inflow of funds to the company when the marketing costs are highest. As high prices in travel will increase the revenue earned by travel agents, this will also encourage the distributors' support. If the product also anticipates a very short life cycle, as is the case with event tourism such as the Olympic Games, where costs of organising and marketing the programme must be recovered quickly, this is a sensible policy to pursue. Care must be taken, however, not to antagonise regular markets for short-term benefits. All too often hotel prices have been increased very substantially during events such as World Fairs, and if accommodation thereby becomes unavailable or overpriced to the regular markets, there may be a consumer reaction: loyal customers may simply go elsewhere, and not return under more normal conditions.

Non-commercial pricing policies

This is a useful point at which to recognise that not all pricing results from commercial considerations. In the business of tourism, many bodies, such as government organisations, have other considerations apart from purely economic ones, in determining the prices which tourists will pay for products. The need to demarket destinations facing over-demand is one consideration which central and local governments have to take into account, particularly in sensitive areas where environmental protection is important. National parks are examples of such sites, where either rationing or road pricing have been used to reduce demand. In Britain, a good example of the use of road pricing is to be found in the Peak District National Park (see below).

Example   Peak District National Park

This national park receives over 22 million visitors each year (the second highest in the world after Mt Fuji in Japan), and many of these are concentrated in the few short high season summer months. In 2003, Derbyshire County Council declared their intention of introducing an experimental road toll for cars entering the national park in the following year. If successful in reducing tourist congestion, the experiment is likely to be repeated in other British national parks.

Premium pricing

In premium pricing, the intention is to price high in the long term, using price as an indication of quality, or symbolic value, as with the case of high-status holidays. Here one is dealing with a highly inelastic market demand, but the product must deliver what it promises. Its scarcity value may be a major part of its appeal, therefore such products in travel are more likely to be developed by small specialist firms. The package tour sold largely to the North American market, comprising a visit to a British stately home, with dinner hosted by its titled owners, is one example of such a product which has both scarcity and prestige value.

While all the above policies involve active decisions to influence markets through price, some companies will adopt passive price policies, of which three can be identified:

- following price leadership
- price agreements
- cost-plus pricing.

Following price leadership

Sometimes referred to as *going rate pricing*, this policy is adopted by those who feel that their products are indistinguishable from those of their leading competitors. Prices are set based on what the competitors charge.

A drawback to the policy is that prices cannot be established or marketed until the competitors' decision on price has been publicised. Small seaside hotels, guesthouses and B&Bs traditionally wait to see what shape prices are taking before determining their own for the coming season, while many tour operators in Britain wait for the launch of the major companies' brochures to see the prices charged before going to print with their own brochures. This policy will obviously inhibit forward sales.

Price agreements

The concept of a *cartel*, a group of companies coming together in order to set uniform prices, is now rare, and indeed in Britain – virtually without exception – it is illegal. The OFT has made it clear that fixed price agreements cannot be imposed on travel agents for package tours, nor is ABTA permitted to agree uniform fees for the services provided by agents. Distributors are therefore required to determine their own pricing policy, which allows them to discount inclusive holidays by some proportion of their commission if they so choose.

Tourism, however, is an international product, and may be subject to other regulations. Until the 1970s, price regulation in the air transport industry represented one of the very few examples of an officially sanctioned cartel, with prices agreed through the International Air Transport Association (IATA). The growth of deregulation of air transport, first in North America and later in Europe, ended the international air fare cartel, although on some (largely Third World) routes price regulation is still in force. In other areas of tourism within the UK, the OFT will investigate any suspected cases of price collusion.

Cost-plus pricing

This is the simplest mechanism of all for pricing decisions. The company establishes its costs for a particular product, allocates some share of overhead costs to production plus a percentage mark-up for profits, and this then becomes the selling price. Clearly, this takes little account of market forces, and while costs do have to be covered in the long run, policies have to respond more to changing market conditions and 'what the market will bear', as we discussed earlier in this chapter.

However, the concept of *marginal costing*, which attempts to identify the cost of one or more additional units of a product, is an important one in cost-plus pricing, since it offers the marketing manager a flexible tool for pricing. We earlier examined the concept of 'contribution' to fixed costs, in which the variable cost of one more unit is ascertained. In the case of, say, an airline ticket to the USA, the additional cost of carrying one more passenger is extremely small: an added meal, a minute addition to fuel and equally minuscule costs for ticket issuance, etc. Therefore, once break-even is achieved it becomes very attractive to price the 'marginal seat' (any remaining seats over the number that have to be sold to break even) at a price which will attract market demand from those unwilling to pay regular fares. Scheduled carriers introduce such fares as 'stand-by' to fill these last remaining seats, and charter services originally introduced 'seat only' sales to achieve the same purpose. Hotels equally look at the contribution to revenue made by selling unsold beds at much reduced prices to late bookers once break-even point is achieved.

It makes good sense for all companies to predetermine their pricing policies, but in fact of those that do, most tend to be the larger corporations, where marketing theory and practice are treated more seriously. The idea that pricing policy is linked through marketing plans to the achievement of organisational objectives is still to receive widespread application in the travel and tourism industry.

Price policies have many important implications for other areas of the marketing mix. The price determined for a product will influence the decision on whether 'push' or 'pull' strategies are more appropriate to use, with promotional tactics developed to support one or the other approach. A decision to price for rapid penetration in a new market will call for the widest possible distribution of the product, while the decision to 'skim the cream' would suggest a more select distribution system to be appropriate.

We shall now turn to the ways in which pricing policies are implemented as part of the overall marketing campaign.

Strategic and tactical pricing

Strategies are concerned with the overall plans for the implementation of policy, while tactics relate to the day-to-day techniques in pricing which can be rapidly altered to suit changing conditions in the marketplace. Thus a *strategy* of discriminatory pricing, involving the setting of different prices to different market groups (e.g. business travellers and holiday travellers) may be introduced, but the actual prices to be charged and the ways in which these will be adjusted will imply *tactical* decisions.

One of the strategic decisions which must be taken will be whether to price differentially to different geographic areas. Should the price set be common to all customers, or should it vary to reflect different market demand in the various regions of a country, or between different countries? It may be more costly to sell one's incoming package tour arrangements in the USA, for instance, than in France, or it may be necessary in one country to boost commission levels to agents to secure their support. Long-haul holidays sold in Britain used to be cheaper on the whole than identical holidays sold in Germany, partly because of higher marketing costs and salaries in mainland Europe, partly because the German market at the time accepted higher prices, but this pattern has reversed in many cases since the turn of the century, with the comparatively poor performance of the German economy and greater competition between the tour operators in a more concentrated industry resulting in a more price-conscious consumer. If differentials between prices charged in two geographically close countries vary substantially, travellers are likely to divert to the cheaper country by flying to join their package holidays there. The introduction of the euro throughout many of the EU countries has made price comparisons more transparent, and this trend to international price comparison is likely to increase with greater use of World Wide Web booking systems. Alternatively, the organisation supplying the product must consider whether to price identically in all markets, with some adjustment to take into account varying conditions – night flights versus day flights, low season versus high season.

When Billy Butlin launched his first holiday camps, his pricing strategy was *all-in pricing*; a single price gave his customers access to every entertainment facility in the camp. This meant that there was always plenty to do even in inclement weather, and the strategy proved highly successful. French operator Club Méditerranée was later to use this pricing strategy to build their holiday resort empire around the world, and in recent years the concept of the all-inclusive holiday, in which everything, even alcoholic drinks, is included in the basic price has proved a great marketing success both within Europe and in the Caribbean. Cruise companies have in some cases introduced all-in pricing at the higher end of the market, to include excursions, drinks and even tips. The decision to charge a low basic price (which in some cases may be below break-even), recouping profits through *add-ons* is a critical one for the tour operators, who choose different approaches. Long-haul package tours to destinations such as the Far East and Latin America may have a relatively high basic tariff, but this can often include excursions, most meals, drinks and the services of an accompanying tour manager, while a similar programme to the USA may be costed on the basis of flight, transfers and room only at the hotel. In the short-haul market, we have earlier recounted how budget pricing is being widely introduced with add-ons for any services, however insignificant. Each pricing decision must be made on its own merits and will reflect market conditions in both the destination and generating countries. The two destinations in the long-haul example given above have totally different tourism industry structures, with little or no tradition in the USA of inclusive meals or transfers on tours, and these would be more expensive and difficult to include than would be the case in other parts of the world.

Strategies must also be designed to respond to the marketing initiatives of competitors. If a market leader realises that their competitors are waiting for them to launch their brochure before determining prices, and then adjusting prices to undercut them, they will need to adopt tactics to unsettle their rivals. This might suggest a relaunch of the brochure with lower prices – a common marketing ploy within the UK in recent years, to the point where relaunches were built into the print run, with a 'second edition' to adjust prices introduced if the market showed signs of flagging at the earlier tariffs, or if the leader's prices appeared no longer competitive. While this significantly added to print costs, it gave the company much greater flexibility for fine tuning on price.

How should a company respond when challenged on price? The immediate decision to slash prices is not necessarily the best one, and only has the effect of reducing profits for everyone. It may be justifiable where there is evidence of extreme price sensitivity, or where it is thought to be difficult to recapture market share once lost. However, if the company has a strong brand image, believes in the quality of its products and has the financial strength to survive a price attack, it may well ride out the threat, or it can counter-attack by improving product quality, or by engaging in heavy promotion. With a sufficiently distinctive product, it may even be possible for the company to increase the price, and hence the psychological 'distance' between its own products and those of the competition. In short, there are a variety of solutions, of which price reduction is only one, and the company under attack needs to consider each option carefully.

Example   The stately home – Beaulieu

Beaulieu, the heritage attraction in Hampshire in the south of England, provides an interesting example of the use of tactical pricing to solve a problem. Its strategy was to charge a high entry price giving access to a wide range of attractions which were perceived as providing poor value by those unfamiliar with the site, who would not have understood the length of time they could expect to spend there. The solution was to make little advance information available about the actual cost of entry, and to site the parking area at some distance from the entry kiosk. Customers, having parked and walked as far as the kiosk, would be reluctant to forgo a visit at that point because of cost alone, and grudgingly paid up, only to find themselves with much more to see and do than they had anticipated. A survey of visitors leaving the site found that they were well satisfied with the visit and voted it good value for money.

A contrasting approach is taken by other attractions, where *offset pricing* (sometimes known as *bait pricing*) will set a very low entry charge, possibly even a 'loss leader' at below cost, in order to attract visitors, who then find themselves facing extra charges for every event (a common tactic for fairground amusement sites such as the Tivoli, Copenhagen). One interesting example of bait pricing is shown by the hotels in Las Vegas, USA, where prices are extremely reasonable for rooms and food because profits are reaped through gambling on the premises. Fruit machines are to be found in every lobby, public rooms, even around the swimming pools. Ferry operator DFDS has also used bait pricing to attract off-season visitors to round voyages on their UK–Denmark route, on the basis that the service will operate anyway (for freight needs) and the additional on-board spend during the 24-hour crossing will enable satisfactory overall profits to be achieved, or will at least provide a substantial contribution to operating costs during the winter.

Discounting tactics

Discounting has become a notable feature of the travel industry over the past 20 years. This is a reflection of the industry's general inability to forecast accurately in a volatile world market, and hence the difficulty in matching supply to demand. In a market situation where 'money-off' incentives have become widespread, where hotel receptionists and front office managers are given almost unlimited freedom to adjust prices for late arrivals, where travel agents commonly split commissions with their business house and leisure clients in order to retain a sale, and where auctions are held through call centres or Internet connections for air tickets or tours, the idea of a set price for travel services is rapidly disappearing. This might be seen as the almost inevitable result of deregulation in the industry coupled with an emphasis on tactical pricing which, for instance, led to some airline fare structures so complex that over 100 fares could be applied to a single route between two points. The rapid development of the cruising industry, with fast growing demand still outstripped by even more substantial new shipbuilding, coupled with the many crises to have hit the travel industry in the early 2000s, led to 'deep discounting', with reductions of 40–50 per cent becoming common in popular cruising locations like the Caribbean.

Travel discounts are obviously here to stay. The question is whether they can be controlled, and how far the practice is contributing to the development, or decay, of the industry. Evidence suggests that in many cases we have moved too far towards making the discount the principal selling tool, and have chosen to ignore the other tools of marketing.

Marketing theory recognises at least six forms of discounting, although not all these are to be found in the travel and tourism industry:

1 *Discounts for cash payment, or early settlement of invoice* Common in business where credit is normally given.

2 *Price reductions for quantity purchases* (bulk discounts) Common in negotiations between tour operators and their suppliers, and available for businesses purchasing large numbers of air seats.

3 *Trade discounts* Discounts offered to people in the travel industry for their personal travel.

4 *Trade-in allowances* Only applicable where tangible products are surrendered as part exchange on the sale of a new product. However, loyalty programmes such as the Air Miles schemes could be embraced within this tactic.

5 *Seasonal and period discounts* It is customary to charge lower prices for tourism products purchased 'out of season', while night flights are generally cheaper than day flights and weekend hotel rooms cheaper than weekdays.

6 *Distressed stock* (and similar discount tactics) Includes examples such as Advance and Late Saver discounts. The former, by encouraging early bookings, offers two benefits to the company; more precise information on its forward booking situation and (assuming full payment is also made early) the use of prepayment for investment. Late Savers are the equivalent in other businesses of sales, that is the clearance of distressed, or unsaleable, stock. This is doubly important in the case of travel, since unsold stock cannot be stored and sold later.

The popularity of Late Savers among travel consumers has played an important part in the market's tendency to book travel later each year, in the hope of securing a bargain. However, apart from advance booking of tickets on airlines, early booking discounts have been rare in the travel industry. In recent years attempts to offer discounts for early bookings have met with some success, as tour operators try to reverse the consumer trend towards booking late. Perhaps the most common discount for early booking is to be found in conference bookings, since the decision to hold or abandon the conference must be made well in advance of the event.

There is an important distinction between 'discounting', which is a regular pricing tactic, and 'money-off' offers which accompany special promotions. The use of the latter tactic will be discussed further in Chapter 12.

Clearly, any discounting schemes should be introduced only where there is evidence of price elasticity, i.e. that lower prices will sell the product. In order for discounting tactics to be successful, the discount must be large enough to be seen as a bargain. Here, the concept of the *just noticeable difference* (JND) needs to be understood. This is the amount by which a product must be reduced in price in order for it to attract the bargain-hunter. Some firms make it a practice successively to reduce prices until stock is cleared, and this too is a practice which has been a feature of tour operators' Late Savers.

Another price tactic which has become common in the industry is the use of the 'psychological discount'. The firm in this case introduces an artificially high price, with the expectation that this will seldom, if ever, be used. Instead, all markets will be offered attractive 'bargains' against the hypothetical price. In the field of consumer durables, references to 'manufacturer's suggested price' provides a base for retailers to fix their own price. While the practice is less widespread in travel and tourism, it is found in areas such as some hotel printed 'rack rates' from which a wide range of discounted prices are offered. Hotels, and cruise ships, have been able to offer apparent bargains by selling accommodation at the basic price and upgrading clients to superior accommodation without additional charge, while airlines have scope to upgrade clients from economy to higher category seats, subject to availability. This provides apparent bargains, but without any cost to the principals. It has now become common for tour operators to include 'artificial' tariffs in their brochure pricing panels, with the expectation that most of these rates will be discountable, either through their direct sell lines or through their agents by negotiation.

The total number of price tactics which can be employed is beyond calculation, and limited only by the initiative of the company introducing them. The pricing tool remains a powerful technique for market manipulation and a means to respond quickly to changing market conditions.

Questions, tasks and issues for discussion

1   One controversial pricing tactic introduced in the above chapter is the extra charge for pre-bookable seats in aircraft when travelling on budget tours. While this ensures that families can travel together, where they may otherwise be split up, the tactic has generated a lot of ill feeling among package tourists. To what extent do you believe the tactic is justified, and what other shortcomings can you identify with the scheme?

2   Pricing is increasingly being used as a mechanism to encourage customers to switch their bookings to the Internet, which offers lower costs for ISPs. Will this trend lead eventually to the collapse of other forms of sales outlet (call centre, phone reservations, travel agents, etc.)? How are each of these likely to be affected, and how might their survival be assured?

3   Under what conditions is 'meeting the competitor's price' an unsuitable policy for a travel company?

4   What are the arguments in favour of reducing prices for advance bookings instead of later bookings? Why have not more travel companies chosen this policy?

5   To what extent is price the critical factor in the competition between Eurostar and the budget airlines on the route between London and the Continental European cities of Paris and Brussels?

6 Restaurant prices represent the sale of a product which combines food and drink, service and ambience. Select three restaurants in your immediate area – one luxury, one medium-priced, and one budget – and explain why you believe each represents good value for money.

Exercise

Working with the travel pages of the national press, consider the extent to which advertisements for travel are today focusing largely on price as the principal factor in attracting customers, whether for transport, package holidays or accommodation. Identify a selection of advertisements in the same pages where other factors appear to take precedence over price, and list these factors in order of frequency.

How effective is price as a motivator in all these advertisements compared with all other factors, in attracting (a) enquiries, and (b) bookings? What criticisms would you make about the price-oriented advertisements as a whole, in terms of sameness in layout and appeal, eye-appeal and impact, failure to communicate other attributes of the product? Which factors, in your view, have the greatest appeal to encourage further enquiries?

Now, taking any of the price-focused advertisements, try to construct an advertisement with a different appeal for the product, using any one of the other factors you identified.

References

1 Quoted in *Leisure Opportunities* 18 February 2003
2 Cawley, M, Park Entry Charges, *Annals of Tourism Research* vol 21, 1994, pp 158–60

Further reading

Greene, M, *Marketing Hotels into the 1990s: a Systematic Approach to Increasing Sales*, Heinemann, 1983, pp 38–43 and 46–67

Herbert, D, Prentice, R and Thomas, C (eds), *Heritage Sites: Strategies for Marketing and Development*, Avebury, 1989, pp 231–71

Kotler, P, Bowen, J and Makens, J, *Marketing for Hospitality and Tourism*, Prentice Hall, 2nd edn 1999, pp 401–47 and 694–5

Middleton, V T C with Clarke, J, *Marketing in Travel and Tourism*, Butterworth Heinemann, 3rd edn 2001, pp 138–52

Morgan, M, *Marketing for Leisure and Tourism*, Prentice Hall, 1996, pp 170–86

Shaw, S, *Airline Marketing and Management*, Pitman, 3rd edn 1990, pp 182–201

Part II Reaching the customer

7 Marketing communications and ICT applications

Learning outcomes

After studying this chapter, you should be able to:

- understand the role of communication in marketing
- list the elements of the promotional mix and assess their qualities for communicating
- evaluate alternative strategies for communications budgeting
- understand what is required to create successful promotional messages
- recognise the importance of personal presentation skills in the travel and tourism industry
- appreciate the growing role of information and communications technology in facilitating communication between marketers, their suppliers and consumers.

Introduction

Once a product has been created and a price determined for it, the marketing focus switches to finding the best means by which to get this information to the customer. However good it is, no product can be expected to sell itself. Knowledge about it has to be *communicated* to the consumers who are the target markets; and while consumers themselves often provide an effective means of supporting sales through their word of mouth recommendation to others, most forms of communication require the application of techniques, and the use of tools, which are at the disposal of the marketing team. Identifying these, and explaining how they work, will be the purpose of the second part of this text.

An organisation must determine not only the best means of bringing its products to the attention of the market in a cost-effective manner, but also (in the case of most goods) how best to deliver these to its customers. The former process is concerned with promotion; the latter, with distribution. Although travel and tourism products are by their nature intangible, distribution is still an important element of marketing in this industry, which has first to create awareness of, interest in and desire for its products, and then explain how, when and where prospective customers can buy them. There are even tangible elements of the product – brochures, itineraries, tickets and vouchers, insurance policies, for example – which have to be physically delivered. Distribution entails the selection and support of suitable channels to reach the customers, and this will be discussed in detail in the following chapter. In this chapter readers will be introduced to the task of promotion, and subsequently we will look in turn at each of the promotional techniques.

The communications process

Figure 7.1 explains the process by which an organisation communicates with its target market. All communication starts with an information *source* – the person, organis-ation or company with a message to deliver. This source must determine what message it wants to deliver to its target, the receiver. An airline, to take just one example, will have many different messages to deliver to the different target markets it serves. Directed to business customers, the purpose of the message might be to communicate details of convenient mid-morning flights to European capitals, or reassuring infor-mation about the airline's outstanding on-time record, while messages to leisure customers might more appropriately focus on offers of free airport parking, or the availability of new low prices to the main holiday resorts served by the airline. The kind of message we want to deliver will determine the form in which the message will appear, that is, how we will *encode* the message to achieve the greatest likelihood of its being received and understood by our target market. If we have a lot of facts to com-municate to our customers, such as a list of cheap fares and their dates of availability, we shall probably need to have the message printed, so that our customers can study it at length, absorb it and even tear it out and keep it for future reference. Encoding means determining not only the best way of getting our message across, but also the most cost-effective way, given the typical constraints under which any company oper-ates. With unlimited money, it is relatively easy to ensure that every potential cus-tomer is made aware of our product, simply by bombarding the public with endless messages; and global companies such as Coca-Cola engage in just this kind of satur-ation publicity. But for most companies, and certainly for SMEs, funds are always lim-ited, and profit targets will restrain our promotions budget. Encoding means putting the *message* into a form in which it will be clearly understood and absorbed by the target market. We could choose, for instance, to place an advertisement in English in a Continental magazine, designed to attract people to visit Britain and take a tour, but this would hardly be an effective way of getting business. Not only would many

Figure 7.1
The communications process

non-English-speaking Europeans fail to understand our message, but also we could anticipate some antagonism from those who do speak the language, on the grounds that we are not making a very serious effort to sell our product if we do not put it into our customers' language. If on the other hand we are advertising for a new member of staff who speaks fluent Japanese, to deal with incoming tour clients, it would be highly appropriate to prepare an advertisement in Japanese, for an English newspaper, to ensure that we will not receive applications that waste our time. We have to design our message for maximum impact.

The next step is to decide which *channel* we shall use to deliver our message. If we have already decided that it must be a printed message, this partly determines the medium to use. We could advertise in magazines or papers read by our target audience (Figure 7.2), or we could place advertisements in the travel trade press, directed to travel agents, to make them aware of our product's attributes, so that they in turn will recommend our product to their clients. We could also send a newsletter through the mail to agents with the same message, or provide our sales staff with a circular to give to agents during their calls. This latter technique would also give us the added advantage of being able to reinforce our message with a personal selling presentation.

Having in this way settled on our strategy for putting our message across, we sit back and wait for the bookings to start rolling in. Unfortunately, though, all our best efforts can be frustrated if the *receiver* does not *decode* our message. *Interference* in the communications process can affect the decoding of messages in a number of ways. A big news story breaking in the morning paper on the day of our advertisement could mean that many of our customers fail to notice our message.

Our mailshot to travel agents may be ignored because the agent that day has unusual pressure of work and does not find time to read 'non-priority' mail. A train derailment could mean that newspapers for one region of the country fail to get through, and nobody in that region gets to see our advertisement. Some of our potential clients may simply not be in the right mood for receiving messages when they see our advertisement, while others may have had a poor experience of our service at some point in the past, and will therefore ignore our messages. About to read the message in the newspaper over morning breakfast, another potential customer will be interrupted by a phone call. There are hundreds of ways in which our message can be hindered by interference, many beyond our control. Even if the message is received and believed, many potential customers will have forgotten it within a few minutes; people are bombarded with messages every day of their lives, and only a tiny percentage are likely to be retained. All we can hope to do is to minimise this loss of communication by designing our messages carefully in the first place.

A well-known and very apposite quotation, attributed to Lord Leverhulme, is 'Half of my advertising is wasted; the problem is, I don't know which half.' No advertisers can be certain that their message will get through. What must be recognised from the outset is that the communications process is not restricted to a single advertisement or promotion, but depends for its success on constant repetition, a never-ending process of drip-feeding messages to the market. It is the cumulative effect over time of perhaps many different types of message and different forms of communication – advertisement, mail, personal contact – that will eventually help to build a consumer's image of an organisation and its products.

Figure 7.2
An unusual communication from the top: the Spanish Minister of Tourism appeals for tourists in advertisements appearing in the British National Press, July 2001

Message from the Spanish Minister for Tourism

Dear friends,

I write this open letter to our British visitors – 12.8 million last year – extending you a warm invitation to spend some time in Spain over the coming weeks.

British customers and the British travel trade have made the holiday market in Spain the phenomenal success it is today. Through very high customer satisfaction ratings (96%)* and repeat holidays (78%)**, it's clear that you are still continuing to enjoy Spanish hospitality combined with holiday facilities that are among the best in the world.

The beautiful islands of Majorca, Menorca and Ibiza have long been special favourites with our British friends and we have ensured the quality and the continuity of tourist services in the Balearic Islands to make them even more attractive to you.

In fact, there's never been a more rewarding time to visit us. There is an unusually high number of great holiday packages to choose from at the moment, all offering exceptional quality and value for money, particularly for holiday-makers looking to book quickly.

I hope you will consider making the most of such a favourable opportunity and that we'll be welcoming you to Spain in the very near future.

Yours sincerely,

Juan Costa
Minister for Tourism

*relates to hospitality: Institute of Tourism Studies, Madrid
**Institute of Tourism Studies, Madrid

(Courtesy: Spanish Tourist Office)

Determining the promotions mix

The marketing manager has four distinct ways of communicating informative and promotional messages to the public:

1   By *advertising* the product through a selected medium such as television or the press.
2   By using staff to engage in *personal selling*, either behind the counter, over the phone, or calling on clients as sales representatives. It can also engage intermediaries, such as retailers, whose staff will undertake this task on behalf of the principal.
3   By engaging in *sales promotion* activities, such as window display or exhibitions.
4   By generating *publicity* about the product through public relations activities, such as inviting travel writers to experience the product, in the hope that they will review it favourably in their papers.

It should also be recognised that much communication about products actually takes place by *word of mouth recommendation*. The benefits of a satisfied customer suggesting your product to another potential customer cannot be overemphasised. This 'hidden sales force' costs a company nothing, yet it is the most highly effective of all communications modes, since the channel has credibility in the eyes of the potential customer, and will be judged as more objective than any other forms of assessment.

The converse is also true, of course; an account of a bad experience relayed by word of mouth has a very strong negative influence on purchase. And human nature being what it is, research shows us that consumers tell 10 times as many people about a bad experience as they do about a good one!

Recognising the importance of influencing those who can in turn influence others to buy new products leads to the concept of the *two-step flow of communication*, in which messages are directed by the company to the opinion leaders in society, rather than to the general public. Opinion leaders include representatives of the mass media as well as those most likely to make initial purchases of new products. A travel company with a limited promotional budget might be best advised to concentrate its expenditure largely on influencing travel writers, by offering them an opportunity to sample products at first hand, since a favourable report in the media will reach many more potential purchasers than an equivalent expenditure on advertisements in the same media. Those responsible for the marketing of destinations have long recognised the impact made by encouraging film producers to use their regions as settings – some 20 films featuring 007 James Bond have led to enormous benefits for the regions in which the films are set, including the Lake Palace at Udaipur in India (where locals still mention the *Octopussy* connection with pride) and Khao Phingkan in Thailand (where the subsequent mass tourism following the popularity of *The Man with the Golden Gun* rapidly led to unrestricted development which destroyed the original peaceful setting). New Zealand was the setting for the first *Lord of the Rings* film, making the country among the most popular of all long-haul destinations in the year after its release – a factor which the New Zealand Tourist Board was not slow to exploit in its press and television advertising (see Figure 7.3, colour plate). Television programmes, too, generate curiosity about the settings for dramas; costume dramas have become a popular feature of British television in recent years, leading to their sales to television stations all over the world. Such curiosity is quickly translated into a flood of visits to the setting.

Factors influencing the choice of the mix

What determines the mix of these four promotional tools in the marketing plan? In some cases, companies will choose to employ only one of these elements in the mix, while other companies will use a combination of all four. There are no right or wrong answers about such choices, although guidelines based on the following criteria can be helpful:

1 *The nature of the product*   Clearly, it will be difficult to sell a complex or technical product without personal sales advice. Many in the holiday trade would argue that, although resorts are often thought of as homogeneous and interchangeable, a customer actually needs quite a sophisticated level of knowledge to make a decision about what resort or hotel to choose. A brochure can spell out in cold print, and a video cassette can demonstrate visually, what kind of beach the resort offers, or the facilities the hotel provides, but more subjective issues are difficult to put across in print or on film. Questions such as the ambience of the resort, the quality of the food served in the hotel, what kind of fellow holidaymakers the client will encounter in the resort can properly be answered only in a direct face-to-face sales situation, where the salesperson should be equipped to help match the customer's needs to the products on offer, thereby ensuring customer satisfaction.

2 *The target at which the communication is aimed*   A decision will be made on the mix of communications directed to the consumer and to the trade. Communications aimed at the trade employ what is known as a 'push' strategy, that is, the aim of the company is to encourage dealers to stock the product, and to push it to their customers. This will often involve direct selling, supported by trade advertising, or sales promotion techniques such as the payment of bonuses for achieved targets.

   A 'pull' strategy, on the other hand, is designed to generate consumer demand for the product, pulling customers into the shops and encouraging retailers to stock the product through the sheer level of demand. Here, the emphasis will be on extensive national advertising, with perhaps some sales promotion support. British retail travel agents cannot afford to ignore the products of the leading tour operators such as TUI, Thomas Cook or First Choice Holidays to concentrate exclusively on selling smaller companies because of the sheer popularity of the big brands. Agents cannot turn bread-and-butter business away.

3 *The stage in the life cycle in which the product is to be found*   The communications task for a new product is to make customers aware of its existence. This means informative messages, usually carried by mass media advertising, with some sales support, to let as many people know what it is you have to sell, and the product's benefits. Later, as competition for the new product increases, the task will switch to

that of persuading the public that your product is the best of those available, calling for greater emphasis on sales promotion. As the product becomes well established and sales have peaked, the task will be to remind clients of the product's existence, and encourage them to think of their brand first when shopping. This is achieved by a mix of 'reminder' advertising (perhaps little more than constant repetition of the brand name) and point of sale display material. These tactics will be discussed more fully in subsequent chapters.

4   *The situation in which the company finds itself in the marketplace*   In a highly competitive environment, a company will be under pressure to employ many of the same promotion techniques as its major competitors, to ensure that its products are seen by the same consumers. This may require regional adjustment of the communications mix, depending upon the relative strengths and weaknesses of the company in different areas. This is particularly the case where a company is also selling its products abroad, where both the message conveyed and the channels used to reach the market may be quite different from those in the home country.

5   *The company's budget for its promotional strategy*   This is the most important factor that any company must determine. This budget can, of course, include a contingency to allow for ad hoc activity that exploits unforeseen opportunities as they arise, as well as ensuring sufficient funds for a planned programme of activity.

Communications and ICT

We live today in a high-tech world which those in the industry could only dream of a generation ago. In 1967, the first hole-in-the-wall cash dispenser arrived in Britain (at Barclays Bank in Enfield), a move which was to transform the banking business. Computer reservations systems, introduced a little earlier, were rapidly developed to a point where the tourism distribution system was similarly transformed within a matter of years. But it is only in the past decade that the development of the Internet and the World Wide Web have made all former modes of distribution if not obsolete, then substantially less significant than formerly. The previous edition of this text carried little more than a fleeting reference to the introduction of new forms of information technology (IT) which were then beginning to be adopted by the industry, but such has been its impact over the past decade that the marketing world has been changed out of all recognition. In Britain, 11.5 million homes had access to the Internet by the beginning of 2003, a figure expected to rise by 17.5 per cent by the end of that year. Two-thirds of all businesses in the UK were already making some use of electronic marketing by 2001, mainly through the use of websites. Nowhere has this impact been more marked than in the travel and tourism business, whose needs for rapid communication and distribution (in the forms of information and reservations) are ideally met electronically.

Information and communications technology, as it is now known, has come to play a key role in all elements of the marketing mix, and the new term recognises the importance of communication in the interface between a business and its customers.

Electronic, or 'online' communications have become affordable and practicable for even the smallest SMEs, and no sector of the travel industry is unaffected by this revolution. The prefix 'e-' is increasingly being applied in all areas of business involving the use of electronic means to improve business efficiency, with *e-commerce* the popular term to describe buying and selling electronically, and *e-marketing* the overarching term embracing all forms of electronic marketing.

Electronic communication offers a business four major benefits. First, it provides the opportunity for principals to *interact* with customers directly. Second, it is hugely *cost-effective*, and in particular this has greatly reduced distribution costs in reservations departments. Third, it provides an *efficient and convenient* means of regular contact between organisations and their customers, and finally, it offers a *speed* of communication unrivalled in any other medium. This last factor has been crucial in enabling travel suppliers to update and change their product offerings at short notice, enabling tour operators to sell last minute bookings and airlines to amend fares in the light of changing patterns of demand.

Example   Thomas Cook

In 1996, Thomas Cook created a website, and soon compiled an initial database of 17 000 e-mail addresses from 'hits' on this site. They e-mailed all on the list with the offer of a prize for those willing to subscribe to future mailings. In this manner, a database of 3000 initial subscribers was achieved. These subscribers were then encouraged to solicit further names for the base, against another free holiday prize offer. This resulted in a total pool of 250 000 names, which soon escalated to over half a million. Names are added when customers visit the retail shops and are asked if they would like to receive e-mail contact from the company. Cook were careful to maintain good relations with their customers by ensuring that permission was first obtained for all mailshots, then finding out what they wanted and how they wanted to hear about it.

For all the benefits that e-marketing has brought to the industry, the potential it offers has scarcely been tapped, and it is safe to forecast that within the next decade huge strides will have been taken to improve this form of communication. Just to cite one example, new developments in optical fibres currently under way have the potential to send 622 megabits of information in both directions along a single fibre using light of many colours. This will vastly expand the amount of information that can be distributed electronically, with every strand of fibre carrying the capacity to supply Internet access to an average sized town in the UK.

In Chapter 8 we will be examining how reservations systems are benefiting from developments in ICT. Apart from information and bookings, online systems can link in advertising, store information about customers on constantly updated databases, deal with payments from agents and, increasingly, from customers themselves, and issue electronic tickets and other documentation. Cost savings are considerable, to a point where several major airlines are now making a charge to passengers for paper tickets on routes where e-tickets are available. Paperless air travel is rapidly becoming the norm, especially in processing business travellers.

This section should end with a word of caution, however. For all its benefits to suppliers, there is still considerable resistance to making bookings over the Internet. In most cases the system lacks reassurance, with customers obliged to start their travels with nothing more in writing than a reference number to guarantee their booking. Computer users remain concerned about possible unauthorised access to their records, as well as the possibility of a virus affecting their software (although viral screening is becoming increasingly effective) and many are reluctant to input credit card details online for fear of misuse. Suppliers, too, can misjudge set-up costs, and new systems are still prone to random failures severely affecting trading. Nevertheless, there can be little doubt that as familiarity with the new technology grows its use will be favoured by an increasing minority of consumers, and with principals keen to keep costs down by using e-commerce efficiently, the Internet will continue to impact on traditional methods of distribution.

The communications budget

How much should a company spend to promote its products? Theoretically, the answer is simple. It should continue to spend money on promotion until the point is reached where the additional cost of producing and promoting the product becomes greater than the sales revenue it produces; that is, you keep spending as long as marginal revenue exceeds marginal cost, in economic terms. In practice, this point is not easily ascertained, and the marketing manager will fall back on one of several traditional approaches to budget setting.

It is still not uncommon in the travel industry to find expenditure on promotion being determined on an ad hoc basis, with little or no attempt to budget for this in advance. The criterion is, 'What can we afford at present?' and an advertisement is inserted into a local paper as the need arises. While this has the advantage that the company is being seen to respond to changing market conditions, the procedure lacks foresight and planning. It may be that at the point where expenditure is needed to take advantage of an opportunity (a tour operator, for instance, offers a retailer a 50/50 deal to jointly advertise its services), no funds are available. It makes more sense to budget at the beginning of the financial year for anticipated promotional expenditure.

At its least sophisticated, this simply means deciding what it is believed the company can afford to spend in the coming year. This could be based on some percentage of the previous year's sales, or the expected sales in the coming year. The exact percentage to be allocated again tends to be arbitrary. Some managers have fixed ideas about the appropriate proportion of sales to be allocated to promotion; in the travel industry, figures ranging between 1 and 6 per cent are commonly quoted, although many travel agents make no advance commitment for promotional spend whatsoever. If the trend in sales is linear, that is, progressing each year at roughly the same rate of increase, some justification might be found for the principle, although it would need some 'fine tuning' to take into account such changing circumstances as inflation rates; obviously any major change in marketing such as the launch of a new product would call for a total reappraisal of the system.

Without specifically matching promotional funds to objectives, there is also a danger that marketing managers will be tempted to overspend in the early months of the financial year, to avoid any possibility of cutbacks occurring later in the year. When travel businesses face a decline in sales, they tend to look at how costs can be readily pruned, and the communications budget is an easy target by which to effect savings.

In a highly volatile industry such as travel and tourism, it is in any case problematical to forecast accurately anticipated sales for future years. But a more serious criticism of this method of budgeting is that it suggests that sales should dictate promotion, rather than being the outcome of promotion. One could even argue that if sales are expected to go up by so much next year, why should one invest money for promotion anyway? Availability of funds is only one criterion for determining the budget, and if it becomes the sole criterion there is a danger that promotional opportunities will be missed.

Other firms set budgets on the strength of what their leading competitors are planning to spend. This is seen as safe, in that it will at least reduce promotional competition if all companies spend the same amount. However, there is no reason to suppose that other companies have better means of judging what is an appropriate budget for promotion, and their circumstances are likely to be different anyway. While the expenditure of major companies can be ascertained (the *Advertising Statistical Review* carries such information within the UK), the information may not be available at the time the company's budget is prepared, and in any case most travel companies are small, and are working with comparatively small budgets, details of which are unlikely to be easily accessible.

It is far better to argue that the promotional budget should be decided on the basis of the sales objectives for the coming year. This technique is known as *objective-task budgeting*. The company predetermines what it would cost in promotional spend, for example, to increase the level of awareness of its products to 60 per cent of the total market, or to increase sales by 10 per cent, and sets aside a budget sufficient to achieve these aims.

There should be a clear relationship between the size of the budget and the overall size and share of the market at which the product is aimed. Market size and share determine profit expectations, and the promotion plan should be geared to achieving a satisfactory level of sales in that market. This can be most effectively quantified when planning an advertising campaign; Chapter 10 will illustrate how budgets are related to objectives.

Determining the message objectives

If communications are to be effective, it is critical that they follow clear objectives, and are designed to maximise the achievement of these objectives. This means that we must start by having a very clear idea both about the market's knowledge of the company and its products, and its attitudes towards these. The sorts of questions the company must ask itself are:

■ 'What proportion of our market is aware of who we are, the products we produce and the benefits they offer?'
■ 'What image of the company do our customers have? Is it specific, that is, does our market share a common view? Is it diffused, that is, do people have different or confused views about what the company is trying to be and to say?'
■ 'What image or beliefs about the company or its products do we need to change?'
■ 'What have our present goals been aiming to achieve?'

Readers who take a short-term view about communications, believing that they have only to do with promoting current opportunities to the market, may feel that this emphasis on image creation is academic, or at best appropriate only to the largest companies. This is not true at all. The image that a company projects is critical in enabling the consumer to differentiate one company and its products from another. While a travel agent should certainly include as part of the promotional activities a list of Late Savers in the shop window, and perhaps advertise such opportunities in the local press, there are also many far-sighted agents who are concerned about their long-term image. This may mean taking a regular column in the local paper with photographs of their staff, drawing the public's attention to the fact that the staff regularly visit resorts abroad to improve their product knowledge. This is part of the process of polishing the image, by building public opinion to see that agent as 'caring', 'expert' and 'personal' in its approach, for example if the first names of individual staff members accompany the photos in the advertisements, new and potential clients will become familiar with the name, location and image of the company, and will tend to think of that agent first when booking a holiday. For personal security reasons it is advisable not to publish surnames with people's photographs.

Consumers should be reached at three different levels by the communications process:

1   At a *cognitive* level, consumers must be made aware of the product and understand what it can do for them.
2   At an *affective* level, consumers must be made to respond emotionally to the message, to believe it and to be in sympathy with it.
3   At a *behavioural* level, the message must make consumers act on what they have learned; in short, consumers must be motivated to buy the product.

These points will remind us of what we learned about the purchasing, or adoption, process in Chapter 4. One model of this is illustrated below:

awareness→interest→evaluation→trial→adoption

Here, awareness represents the cognitive element; interest and evaluation represent the affective; trial and adoption represent the behavioural. The company's aim is not only to get consumers to try the product for the first time, but also to convince them that this particular product serves their needs best so that they will buy again either the same product or another product from the same company; in short, to turn the consumer into a loyal user of the company's products.

At any given point in time, individual consumers in the company's total market will have reached different stages in this process of adoption. Some will already purchase the product regularly, others will have tried it for the first time and are still evaluating it, still others will have only just become aware of it, while a number of potential purchasers will have yet to become familiar with it. Each of these buying stages represents a different challenge for the communications team.

The full range of possible objectives in communicating have been well categorised in the seminal work by Russell Colley, in which he developed his classic DAGMAR (Defining Advertising Goals for Measured Advertising Results) model.[1] The value of Colley's approach is that it forces the communications team to define their objectives in terms which can be measured, so that the effectiveness of the communication can be judged. A communication campaign has to be planned to specify what each individual message is designed to achieve, to which stage of the buying process it is directed, and how much is to be spent in achieving it. This will be made clearer in Chapter 10.

In all, Colley identifies some 50 objectives, but for our purposes it is sufficient to list these under three groups of objectives:

- those intended to *inform* clients about the product
- those designed to *persuade* customers to buy
- those whose purpose is to *remind* customers of the product or the company.

As we revealed earlier, these different objectives are closely linked to the stage in the life cycle of the product, but there are also other criteria which will influence the form of the message.

A package holiday may represent anything from a highly homogeneous programme of sun, sea and sand aimed largely at a mass market, to an escorted cultural tour which may be unique in the market and is aimed at a small but discerning clientele who have money and are prepared to spend it on esoteric travel. In the former case, the holiday is being sold in a highly competitive environment where price has become a critical factor; there is little or no brand loyalty, and little to distinguish the product of one company from another. Assuming that this product is already well established, the task becomes largely one of persuading clients to buy this product rather than those of competitors. In the latter case, we are dealing with a sophisticated market making the choice between a far smaller number of distinctive holidays. Paying perhaps £3000 or more per head, the clients will want a great deal of detail about what they will be getting for their money. Brochure photographs of exotic locations can draw their interest, but alone are unlikely to do the selling job. They must be supported by comprehensive details about the historical and cultural sites to be visited, the background to the accompanying guide-lecturer's expertise, the size and composition of the group they will be joining for the tour. While some of this information can be conveyed by a good brochure, it is likely to be achieved far more effectively with word of mouth selling.

While a knowledgeable travel agent (likely to be an independent specialist) would be indispensable if customers seek advice on such holidays from the retail sector, it would be more likely that selling for this type of holiday would be direct, with experienced tour operating staff answering telephones to discuss the details of the programme with their clients.

Designing the message

Message design has to take four factors into account:

- the source of the message
- the message appeal
- the channel to be used
- the target audience.

The source of the message will be a major factor in establishing its credibility, and it goes without saying that credibility is vital if the communication is to be effective.

A message gains credibility in a number of ways. First, it will be believed if the source is seen as dependable. A recommendation by a close friend or relative, whose judgement we value, will be a strong stimulus to buy, and this is reinforced by person-to-person communication, where the receiver has the opportunity to question the source and elicit more details about the product. If the product information is coming from a stranger, other means must be found to judge its trustworthiness.

If, for example, the person delivering the message is seen as an expert on the subject in question, this will greatly add to credibility. Travel writers who commend a holiday on the BBC *Holiday* programme will be immensely credible both because of their perceived expertise and objectivity and because the message is delivered by the BBC itself. (The *Holiday* programme appears to represent an interesting bending of the rules governing advertising on the BBC!)

Second, trustworthiness can be achieved by using well-known or popular personalities closely associated with the product. The use of celebrities, especially from the world of sport or show business, in advertisements linked with products is now common practice, and is by no means unknown in promoting travel and tourism products and destinations. More commonly, however, this link is to be found today in the travel pages of the national press, and is frequently achieved through public relations activities conducted by the destination's tourism authorities. As just one example of the cult of the personality in this sphere, one British Sunday newspaper cited the following associations within a single article:[2] celebrities Sharon Stone, Geri Halliwell, Michael Barrymore, Sting, and Prince Charles's escort Camilla Parker Bowles stay at le Saint Géran in Mauritius, British Prime Minister Tony Blair has holidayed with his wife at la Digue in the Seychelles, Hollywood stars Brad Pitt and Jennifer Aniston holiday on Frégate Island in the Seychelles, while former Beatle Paul McCartney honeymooned with Heather Mills on Cousine Island nearby; football manager Sven-Göran Eriksson and pop singer Gareth Gates have spent time in the Maldives, the former 'at the über-exclusive Soneva Gili resort'. It is symptomatic of the post-modern world of travel that this form of name-dropping both popularises the destination and attracts those who seek to emulate the travel behaviour of their iconic heroes and heroines.

There is a risk attached to such personality-based advertising, however: if the personality suffers adverse public relations exposure, the credibility of the advertising suffers too. One example is the withdrawal of the Michael Jackson campaign by Pepsi in 1994 – and the scandal surrounding the death of a guest at TV star Michael Barrymore's party in 2002 would not have been welcome publicity for Mauritius.

A third way to offer credibility to a message is to ensure that it is likeable. A message delivered by someone who is natural, straightforward, or able to inject an element of humour into the delivery, will help to aid its credibility. In a non-tourism context, Victor Kiam's wonderful series of advertisements for Remington achieved their objectives because the source proved to be genuine – not an actor playing a role, but a real company president whose business acumen was unquestioned – as well as natural and humorous. The combination of these qualities proved outstandingly successful in creating a memorable series of television ads. One caveat, however: research has shown that there is a danger in making messages too humorous, since the humour can interfere with the learning process. It is the product that the advertiser wants remembered, not the personality! In Figure 7.4 (colour plate), the use of popular TV personality David Dickinson enhances the appeal of a MyTravelLite advertisement.

Messages can be devised to appeal in two ways to an audience. First, the appeal can be rational, using an economic argument to sway the consumer: an airline may feature its low prices on key routes, or its punctuality record. Second, the appeal may be emotional. Singapore Airlines (SIA) featured attractive female cabin staff in its advertisements to lure the (typically male) business passenger. Of course, these appeals are not necessarily mutually exclusive. If SIA's objective is to encourage travellers to believe that its stewardesses provide a level of service not found in other airlines, the appeal combines logic and emotion. There are, however, dangers in using such sexist advertising in Western countries. We can use emotional benefits such as safety, by playing on fear (although care must be taken not to become counterproductive here; there is a danger that by suggesting one's competitors are unsafe, one may instil a fear of flying in general!). A more subtle approach is reflected in British Airways' message, which plays on the theme 'the world's favourite airline'.

In the late 1980s, Thomas Cook produced a controversial series of television ads in which its aim was to encourage consumers to choose Cooks rather than other travel agents because – it was hinted – only Cooks offered complete financial stability. This 'fear appeal' of losing holidays had strong market impact, although the decision to produce what was tantamount to 'knocking copy' produced many complaints from other agents to ABTA, who ruled that Cooks were casting unjustified doubts and damaging the business per se. This form of message can also be counterproductive if the impression gained by consumers is of general instability within the retail travel sector. This could lead merely to an increase in direct bookings.

In considering whether to use rational or emotional arguments in communications, it is worth bearing in mind that rational messages are generally more likely to appeal to the better-educated consumer than are emotional messages, unless carefully tailored.

The three pictures in Figure 7.5 (colour plates) offer good examples, by Thomas Cook, of logical reasons for purchasing their product, based on the care with which the company screens its package holidays, while Figure 7.6 (colour plate) illustrates a very different approach; an advertisement from Emirates Airline with an emotional message targeting the higher end of the market.

Promotional messages are sometimes criticised on the grounds that their arguments are too one-sided. In fairness to the communicator, the aim of commercial messages is to present a company's products in the best possible light. However, in some instances they will achieve more by presenting a more balanced view of the products. This is particularly true when one is dealing with better-educated consumers or where the consumer is potentially hostile to the concept. In the travel world, the hyperbole of the copywriter and past inaccuracies in brochure texts have led to some suspicion about travel brochures in general, although the ABTA Code of Conduct and an increase in control through statutory law have led to marked improvements. However, some travel companies have taken to producing 'objective guides' to resorts and hotels which present a two-sided picture of refreshing honesty, and this has greatly helped to increase the trust in, and loyalty towards, those agents by their clients.

Successful communications

We can summarise this introduction to the communications process by saying that good communications require that a company:

■ determines its communication objectives clearly, and defines these in terms that are measurable

■ assigns sufficient funds to the campaign to ensure that the mission can be accomplished

■ limits the objectives set, so that the receivers clearly understand the message and remember it

■ wherever possible, directs the message to a specific market whose traits and characteristics are known and understood

■ designs a message which is short, attention-getting and credible, and one which reinforces the desired image of the company and its products

■ tests all communications before launching the campaign, to ensure that they will be effective.

Huge sums of money are spent by the larger travel companies on promotion. Major campaigns such as those offered by leading airlines, shipping companies, hotel chains or tour operators will often exceed £1 million – too much to gamble. The companies must make every effort to ensure that the campaign achieves the sales level, or other target, determined. In the following eight chapters, we shall go on to look in detail at each of the communications tools available to marketing organisations, and see how these can be most effectively used.

Questions, tasks and issues for discussion

1 ECPAT (UK), an organisation set up to eradicate child prostitution, pornography and trafficking, recently gained the cooperation of ABTA and UK government bodies to produce a leaflet which was designed to be given to tour operators to pass on to their clients, drawing the latter's attention to new criminal laws prohibiting engaging in sexual activities with children abroad or organising child sex tours. Although the leaflet made it clear that the aim was to encourage responsible travellers to inform the authorities of any infringements of the law they noted while abroad, the reaction from tour operators was negative. In their view it would be insulting to include the leaflet in the package of material sent to their clients, and would appear to be raising questions about their clients' own morals.

   Do you believe this would be the best way of communicating this message to travellers, or do you consider that this approach would be insensitive? How else might the message be effectively 'sold' to tour operators and/or their customers, given the importance attached to stamping out this trade?

2 Two countries which, doubtless unfairly, have gained the reputation around the world of being dull and 'uncool', are Belgium and Canada. Collect promotional material for travel to these two countries, including brochures from their respective national tourist offices, and see to what extent the strategic message either reinforces this image or overcomes it. How could each enhance their image among a younger market in your own country?

3 Collect two advertisements promoting identical sectors of the travel industry (e.g. transport, hotels, destinations), one of which offers a rational appeal and the other an emotional appeal. Explain to what markets each of these are aimed to appeal, and weigh up the relative attractions and effectiveness of each.

Exercise

(a) You are to appraise the effectiveness of travel websites, in terms of:

   ■ ease of use
   ■ ease of understanding
   ■ clarity of presentation

   Select six comparable sites (e.g. hotel chains, hotel intermediaries, cheap flight intermediaries, late holiday offers) available to the public and evaluate each up to the point of booking, based on the above criteria. Write a report on your findings.

(b) Most such websites now carry unsolicited advertising which partly obliterates the screen and must often be eradicated before proceeding. As a viewer, how helpful do you feel these advertisements are? Do they enhance the site, or do they merely antagonise the viewer? Do you believe them to be effective by comparison with other forms of promotional media? Which advertisements do you consider are best, and why? Did one advertisement appear on your screen, or more, at each site? Draw up a checklist covering the pros and cons of each advertisement found during your surfing.

References

1 Colley, I R, *Defining Advertising Goals for Measured Advertising Results*, New York, Association of National Advertisers, 1961
2 I'm a celebrity . . . Get me into here, *Observer Weekend Magazine*, 26 January 2003, p 8

Further reading

Amor, D, *The e-Business (R)evolution: Living and Working in an Interconnected World*, Prentice Hall, 2000

Blythe, J, *Essentials of Marketing*, Prentice Hall, 2nd edn 2001, ch 9

Gold, J and Ward, S (eds), *Place Promotion: the Use of Publicity and Marketing to Sell Towns and Regions*, Wiley, 1994

Horner, S, and Swarbrooke, J, *Marketing Tourism, Hospitality and Leisure in Europe*, International Thomson Business Press, 1996, pp 204–27

Kotler, P, Armstrong, A, Saunders, J and Wong, V, *Principles of Marketing*, Prentice Hall, 3rd European edn 2001, pp 624–60

Theobald, W and Dunsmore, H, *Internet Resources for Leisure and Tourism*, Butterworth Heinemann, 1999

8 Distributing travel and tourism

Learning outcomes

After studying this chapter, you should be able to:

- identify the factors affecting the choice of different distribution systems

- be aware of the growing number of new methods of distribution and the importance of ICT in this development

- appreciate the changing role of the travel agent as traditional retailer of travel services

- distinguish between methods of cooperative distribution and evaluate the respective merits of each

- understand the function of inventory control in travel and tourism reservation systems.

Introduction

It is convenient to think of distribution as part of the overall communications function in marketing, since it relates to the selection and operation of *channels* by which an organisation communicates with its suppliers and markets. Technically speaking, in marketing theory there are two aspects to distribution. One is concerned with the distributive channels, whose function is to handle enquiries and sales on behalf of a supplier or principal; the other with the physical delivery of products to those channels, and ultimately to the consumer. The latter process entails the keeping of inventories of goods to balance supply and demand, the warehousing and storage of goods, and the transportation of goods between suppliers, dealers and customers. However, many of these latter functions relate to the marketing of tangible products, and therefore have less relevance where travel and tourism products are concerned. Customers for tourism's services have to be brought to the product, rather than having a product delivered to them – in this sense, delivery and service take place simultaneously.

One important characteristic which goods and tourism distribution have in common is the requirement that many sectors of the tourism industry establish an inventory system. In travel parlance, this is known as the *reservations system*, and is a key element in marketing the products of several sectors, as we shall see presently, embracing as it does both booking and ticketing functions. The reservations system acts as a sales outlet and a means of inventory control, balancing supply and demand. A reservations system can usefully be thought of as a 'travel distribution system', closely linked to the way in which channels are managed, and this will be central to our examination of the role and function of distribution channels. Furthermore, recent ICT development has opened up opportunities to handle reservations systems in totally new ways, widening the scope of distributive channels and leading to enormous changes in the structure of the industry.

Channel choice

Before considering how channels are chosen, we need to be aware of the options open to any travel and tourism organisation in planning its distribution strategy. Figure 8.1 explains the process by which all goods and services reach customers through a *chain of distribution*, starting at the producer and ending at the point where the customer accepts 'delivery' of the product. The diagram has been simplified to indicate a typical number of links found in the chain, but in the case of some products, additional intermediaries can extend this chain considerably.

A principal, such as an airline, cruise company or hotel, can if it so wishes choose to deal entirely direct with its customers, entirely through intermediaries, or some combination of direct sell and sales through intermediaries. The term *intermediary* is used to describe any dealer who acts as a link in the chain of distribution between an organisation and its customers. Most larger organisations choose to deal through one or more intermediaries. The reason for this is partly cost based: it is generally cheaper for a company to deal through agencies than it is to set up its own network of retail shops. By paying a commission or other agreed form of financial remuneration to intermediaries, organisations buy the use of a distributive network. The system is also designed to act as a convenience to consumers, as they can choose from a range of different products under one roof, instead of having to visit each producer's shop in turn to select their product.

Figure 8.1
The chain of
distribution

Because each sector of the travel industry has distinct distributive needs we will need to examine these sectors individually, but there are some general considerations that will apply to all sectors, and these can be basically summed up under three headings:

- cost
- control and level of service
- efficiency.

Cost

A principal's first consideration is how its products can be sold at the lowest possible cost. Given the intense competition between tourism businesses and the pressure on prices, principals (and airlines in particular) are continuously seeking ways of reducing their distribution costs without losing their competitive edge. Companies selling their products through retailers have one considerable advantage over those concentrating on direct sell, in that a significant proportion of their distribution costs are variable, only arising when a sale is made. Any supplier opening its own shop will have the continuing overheads of running the shop whether or not products are selling, just as a call centre will have ongoing costs of sales staff and telephone equipment regardless of how many clients call. This means that the direct sell business must enjoy a high level of turnover if it is to justify the cost of the shop, or even a call centre. SMEs, however, may have far less choice, as with a limited, and possibly esoteric, product range they will find it difficult to gain support from retail chains. This will make smaller companies largely dependent on a telephone sales team.

Control and level of service

Principals have also to consider the degree of influence they can exercise over their distributive outlets. The use of intermediaries necessarily results in some loss of autonomy, although if the principal owns its own retail shops it can exercise a much higher level of control.

There is the loss of personal contact with clients, if the sales function is in the hands of an independent distributive outlet. It becomes more difficult for the company to understand its market, or identify changing market needs, and it is very dependent on receiving regular feedback from dealers or agents who, without a personal vested interest in one company's products, may not keep their ear so close to the ground. A greater problem still for effective marketing is that the travel agent, dealing with many hundreds of products, will be less committed to any one product than would the staff of one's own company. Bonus commissions can be used to provide some incentive, but other companies may be offering similar financial rewards to increase sales, and travel agents will have their own priorities in pushing products. In a field where there is so little brand loyalty, this lack of control over distribution is of great concern to principals, especially in the case of companies such as airlines which have invested massively in aircraft, but with only limited control over seat sales.

Having one's own distributive outlets offers a further advantage. It becomes far easier to coordinate and control the company's level of service and marketing activities generally. An airline launching a new route can be certain that the route is featured in the retail shop windows, that brochures are in stock and prominently displayed, that special point of sale material is on show, and that the sales staff know the product and bring it to their customers' attention.

Product knowledge among retail agents is a controversial issue among principals. Any company that can convince agents that their staff have intimate and first-hand knowledge of the destinations they feature in their brochures will have a considerable sales advantage over other operators, as the agent will feel more confident in calling that operator's staff to discuss their clients' needs. Similarly, a company retailing its own products can far more effectively mount a promotional campaign to support their sale, and ensure good coordination between all aspects of the promotion. The promotional support that any travel agent can give to one product among all those they represent is necessarily limited. Their staff's product knowledge, too, having to be wide enough to know something about all the hundreds of holidays they sell, must equally be more shallow in dealing with any individual company's products.

Efficiency

The final consideration for a company is whether the distributive arrangement can guarantee delivering the maximum number of sales. By choosing to sell direct, a business has to rely on effective marketing (at high cost) to ensure that all potential customers are aware of the product and how to buy it. Impulse purchasing opportunities may be lost, as will be the opportunity that retailers have to match their customers' needs to your business's products. It is the desire to increase revenue and market share by ensuring that no possible sales are lost that leads principals to continue to work through retailers – and as many other forms of distribution as can be cost-effectively managed – as well as their own outlets.

Direct marketing is of sufficient importance to devote an entire chapter to it, and we will be investigating this process in Chapter 13, while the role of travel agents, at this point still the most important of all methods of travel distribution, will be examined in this, and the coming chapter, which will examine the sales task as a tool of marketing. The balance of this chapter will be devoted to distribution through intermediary channels.

Reservations systems are needed in transport companies and the accommodation and tour operating sectors. Booking and ticketing functions are also needed in businesses such as museums and art galleries, exhibitions and similar tourist attractions, and theatres, although not all of these will require advance booking facilities. Other organisations such as tourist boards must also have some form of distributive outlet through which they can provide information, and in some areas of the world these, too, deal with bookings for services within their territory. Let us consider each of these in turn.

Transport distribution

Airlines dominate the travel industry, although other forms of transport, including cruise ships, ferries, railways, coaches and car hire companies all play their part in meeting the needs of the tourist or traveller. However, the importance of the airline industry is such that the changes they have effected in their distribution systems in recent years have had by far the largest impact on the rest of the industry, not least within the retail sector.

An airline is of course a producer of a transport product, and is therefore at the start of the 'travel chain of distribution', although the reader should be aware that the product chain in this case actually stretches back through the aircraft manufacturer to the supplier of raw materials for the aircraft. While this text will not be focusing on B2B (business to business) marketing between aircraft manufacturers and airlines, since such interactions do not strictly form part of the travel industry, we do need to recognise that these relationships are every bit as important in the distribution chain as those between principals and their customers.

An airline sells its seats in a variety of ways. Individual seats can be sold direct to a customer, through telephone sales, sometimes through the airline's own shops, and increasingly through electronic means; or they can be sold through a retail travel agent. The airline will also sell seats in bulk through tour operators or 'air brokers'. Tour operators in turn use these seats to create package tours (some argue that in so doing, they are creating new products, and should therefore more correctly be termed 'producers' of products rather than wholesalers), which are then sold either direct or through agents. Some types of air brokers enter the chain at a level between the airline and the tour operator, purchasing large blocks of seats at bulk prices and selling these in turn to operators, while other brokers act as 'consolidators' for airline charter flights, helping tour operators with low load factors to integrate their flights with other operators who are similarly placed. Some of these consolidation seats will find their way on to the market, being sold individually through travel agents to the public at 'late booking saver fares'. Tour operators may themselves offload unsold seats at 'saver fares' to the public through intermediaries such as the online .com agencies (see below), through travel agents or direct. The distribution system for air seats thus becomes quite complex, with seats being sold through a variety of different dealers. This can be seen in Figure 8.2.

An airline operating both scheduled and charter flights will typically use all of these distribution methods to maximise its load factors, but must continually re-evaluate the service provided by each of these links in the chain, to ensure that the current system offers the most effective means of reaching customers at the lowest possible cost commensurate with the quality of service required. Some airlines, particularly the new budget carriers like Ryanair, have chosen to deal direct with their passengers exclusively,

Figure 8.2
Distribution
channels for
airline seats

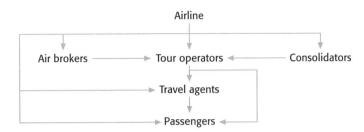

while others are encouraging passengers to deal direct by offering discounts on book-ings made online. In effect, even those airlines ostensibly supporting the traditional agency network are attempting to divert sales to cut distribution costs, and it is by no means unknown for them to undercut quoted fares in response to direct enquiries from the public – much to the chagrin of the retailers.

Airlines were the first to adopt global distribution systems for reservations, as we saw in the preceding chapter, and while these were first designed to meet the needs of the retail sector, it was clearly a case that sooner or later the same systems would become available to the general public, first for business travellers but ultimately for leisure travellers. Seats are now also available through integrated direct sell online systems such as Opodo, an online booking agency set up and operated by a number of leading airlines including British Airways. Further seat bookings are retailed to the public through online intermediaries like travelocity.com or lastminute.com, in a system known as 'e-tailing', or electronic retailing.

Online booking systems widely accessible either by the trade or the general public are becoming a major, fast growing source of airline revenue, displacing the traditional reliance on retail travel agents, although these continue (at the time of writing) to sell the bulk of most airlines' business.

The strength of online reservations systems is that they can be amended at short notice, so that prices can be adjusted according to market demand, and are therefore infinitely flexible. These systems are also proving to become increasingly inexpensive as a means of informing and booking passengers, and now pose a considerable threat to agents. The extension of online booking to include ticketless travel has further reduced carriers' costs and simplified the booking procedure (although not without some concern among the travelling public, some of whom are uncomfortable turning up at an airport with nothing apart from a reference number to guarantee their pas-sage). Variations on the standard online system are developing, most notably the so-called cyber auctions, already popularised in the USA and now spreading to Britain. Infinitely flexible fares have led to online bidding by travellers for airline seats, and auction techniques include examples such as that of priceline.com, in which bids are solicited for an allocation of seats on flights on the given date to a specified desti-nation, while in other cases passengers specify the price they are prepared to bid and the website attempts to find an airline willing to sell a seat at the bid price. Fully flexible fares allow budget airlines to almost give away seats on some promotional routes, with lead-in fares between Britain and the Continent being offered as low as £19 or even £9 – indeed, Ryanair has been one of a number of carriers giving free or almost free seats for limited periods to boost traffic demand.

As far as distribution through the traditional travel agency route is concerned, airlines are constantly reappraising their levels of support for this form of distribution. The scheduled carriers, badly hit in the aftermath of world terrorist strikes, moved away from the traditional system of commission-based fares (with agents usually receiving commission of between 5 and 10 per cent, plus some uplifting for achievement of high sales) in favour of either greatly reduced levels of commission or flat rate payments for route sectors. This has severely damaged agents' revenues, and was initially resisted by attempts to switch-sell to airlines maintaining more traditional commission structures, but the action was defeated when most leading airlines fell into line with the new policy.

Many airlines in the United States also supplement sales through their own retail outlets in the major commercial centres within their country, but this strategy is really only affordable within countries with very high levels of demand for air travel. In Britain demand for air tickets can just support a limited number of British Airways (BA) shops in major cities, but most travellers continue to find it more convenient to book their BA flights through their local travel agents (still handling about 70 per cent of the total volume of air tickets at the time of writing). In spite of the attempts to divert sales from agents mentioned above, airlines are still sensitive to the relationship they have with their retailers, not wishing to antagonise them to a point where agency support would be threatened. Brand loyalty for particular carriers is not strong among the flying public, and agents would have no hesitation in attempting to switch-sell if they thought it in their interest to do so.

Airlines will constantly seek new distribution alternatives, particularly as these develop through advances in ICT, in order to improve convenience, speed of service and cost reductions. While electronic distribution costs are generally falling sharply, there are instances where this is not the case. Global distribution system (GDS) fees through the four major systems, for example, rose between 28 and 45 per cent between 1995 and 2002,[1] encouraging some airlines to consider switching fares to alternative systems. Automatic vending machines at airports already exist, and 'turn up and go' no-reservations ticketless flights are well established on popular routes in some countries. Another innovation undergoing rapid development at the time of writing is interactive television (iTV), which allows travellers to browse travel channels online through their television sets rather than computers, making bookings or calling up information which can include film of the facilities and attractions in destinations served by the airline. The introduction of digital television, due to replace terrestrial TV in the UK by 2010, will further boost direct distribution through iDTV channels, encouraging product searches by consumers who may be presently reluctant to surf the net.

Shipping companies have rather different problems of distribution to consider. Cruising in particular is not an easy product to sell; expertise is needed to sell a product where each cruise line is different, offering an enormous variety of cabins, fare structures, on-board facilities and clientele. One result of this is that the luxury cruise operators have chosen to select a limited number of retailers to represent their services and have concentrated on giving these extra support, especially in the form of staff training. Traditional commissions and bonus payments remain the norm within this sector, although the competitive environment within which cruise companies have been operating since the 11 September 2001 terrorist attack in New York and the subsequent war in Iraq has encouraged deep discounting through alternative distribution outlets as well as agents.

Although computerised reservations systems (CRSs) are necessarily more complex to set up for cruise lines than for airlines, the former have a long history of computer reservations, dating back to the 1960s, and have not been slow to exploit innovation in ICT. Online bookable websites have been established by some companies, although a fully interactive site has yet to be developed at the time of writing. Fred Olsen Line has set up a website which provides virtual tours of their ships – a valuable sales tool to make complex products simpler for consumers to understand.

Short sea ferry operators have a simpler product to sell, and have established online reservations systems. In Britain and France, short sea cross-Channel ferry companies competing with the Channel Tunnel have introduced Turn Up and Go tickets coupled with very frequent sailings to obviate the necessity to make bookings for specific sailings.

Example   The marketing of cross-Channel tunnel services

Eurotunnel operates all cross-Channel services via the Tunnel apart from passenger trains, which are operated by Eurostar. Marketing and distribution strategies of both have been criticised in the trade and by consumers – not least for apparent early failures to support retailers adequately, in the belief that travellers would be willing to book direct. Eurotunnel's initial Turn Up and Go system for car drivers, coupled with frequent departures (up to three an hour at peak periods) – one of the principal marketing advantages over rival shipping lines – was replaced by the obligation to make advance bookings for specific departures. Later, a financial penalty was imposed on drivers who arrived early and wished to take an earlier departure, or those missing the connection and obliged to take the next available departure. Pricing has become so flexible according to market demand that printed material with price bands is no longer available and customers have to request fares for specific departures.

Similarly, Eurostar failed to capitalise on through-rail marketing opportunities from London to Continental Europe. Beyond the terminal points of Paris and Brussels, reservations can be effected to only very limited stations. What is more, in spite of an efficient CRS, the ELGAR system, retail sales outlets have been sharply reduced, and even many mainline stations have no means of selling a Eurostar ticket to Continental destinations.

In the face of retailers' apathy towards the sale of rail tickets in general, which bring in little revenue, rail companies in Britain and elsewhere in Europe have struggled to popularise sales via the website, particularly for special offers and advance sale discounted bookings, but with limited success. It remains true that this sector, coupled with the bus and coach networks, have been among the slowest to innovate, achieving only moderate success with alternative methods of ticket sales.

Tour operators

The desire for control over distribution has led several tour operators, in Britain and elsewhere in Europe, to develop or buy their own retail outlets. Thus TUI, Europe's largest tour operating company and owner of Britain's Thomson Holidays, also owns retailer Lunn Poly, one of the UK's largest retail multiples. MyTravel owns leading tour operator Airtours and the second of Britain's two large retail chains Going Places. JMC, the Thomas Cook Group, now German-owned, has capitalised on its chain of retail agencies to build up its tour operating business in Britain and on the Continent. These are examples of vertically integrated companies, with the travel organisation wholly owning the tour operator, retailer and the charter airline which carries its customers, as well as other components of travel (MyTravel and TUI, for example, also operate cruise ships).

Such vertical integration provides a powerful advantage by protecting sales of the organisation's products. As competition has intensified, this has led to strong *directional selling* by the wholly owned subsidiary retailers: under firm corporate direction, the multiples concerned are becoming progressively more successful at channelling sales towards their own tour operating companies.

While this trend has become well established in the early twenty-first century, it is not without its problems. Alternative strategies adopted by operators without links to major chains have been either to form commercial relationships with the independent retail consortia or to develop closer links with individual retailers. These operators are then not judged as rivals in retailing and achieve greater support from the independent outlets than the large integrated operators.

Much has been made of the belief that so-called 'direct sell' tour operators can sell their product more cheaply to the public by cutting out the intermediaries. In fact, the issue is not clear-cut. Certainly, some holidays sold direct are cheaper than identical holidays sold through more traditional channels, but this is not always so, nor is it necessarily the case that the same level of profit is being achieved on the holiday. The critical factor in reducing price is the reduction in cost, and while cost reduction in distribution may be a factor in cheaper prices, there may be other factors involved such as more astute contract negotiations with airlines and hotels, or simply greater 'muscle' with suppliers due to the greater number of beds or seats under contract.

Companies selling their products through retailers have one great advantage over the direct sell operators. As we have seen with the airlines, most of their distribution costs will be variable, costs arising only when a sale is made. Direct sell operators bear fixed operating costs – in the case of telephone sales, of having a manned reservations system (a call centre in the case of the larger operators) to deal with questions and bookings from the public, or in the (rarer) case of operating a shop, all the set up and operating costs associated with this whether or not members of the public come in to buy their products. Those mass market operators who have chosen to sell direct, such as Portland Direct and Eclipse, are required to invest heavily in promotion at the launch stage, and later in advertising, to bring the product to the public's attention and to persuade them to buy in what is still a comparatively novel way for many travel consumers. There are also heavy direct mail expenses in sending brochures out to prospective customers. Any failures here will drive the customer back to the more familiar travel agent. Great care must therefore be taken to ensure that the information and booking system is capable of supporting the level of demand which it creates. However, once the direct sell company achieves a satisfactory market share, enabling it to reduce marketing costs relative to other costs, its avoidance of intermediaries' commissions and the anticipated steady reduction in online marketing costs will make this form of distribution increasingly competitive.

It must be remembered that reference has largely been to the larger mass market operators here. SMEs in the tour operating sector often have little choice between distributing direct or through retailers, since few agents – and certainly not the multiples – will consider stocking their products. SME operators carry relatively few customers, and would not be in a position to support a national chain of retail outlets, either in terms of promotional support or brochure supplies. However, apart from a handful seeking to emulate the larger operators' offerings, most of these companies are dealing with specialist products, and often have a database of loyal repeat customers, with a flow of new business achieved through word of mouth recommendation. They provide a high level of personal service via telephone reservations systems, offering both expert knowledge of their products and what is today an unusual level of personal business to customer (B2C) contact (enquiries to companies like Bales and Journey Latin America go directly to individual sales staff).

British customers remain fairly conservative in their buying habits. A study in 2002[2] found that some 41 per cent of holidaymaking families still buy their travel arrangements through travel agents (and 52 per cent make their own arrangements). Although websites are making inroads, they remain primarily a means of surfing for information rather than an outlet for bookings at present, and many believe the agent will play a continuing role as the major distributor in the chain for many years to come. Convenience of location is a critical factor in the success of any agent, just as it is for any fast-moving consumer good; with low brand loyalty towards travel products, the convenience and accessibility of the retail outlet become second only to price in importance in distribution, while level of service received is also a highly significant factor. Agents are having to face challenges as never before in their history with the growth of e-tailing alternatives, and only those capable of adding value to the distribution channel can expect to survive.

Distributing accommodation

Finally, we turn to the distribution channels of the accommodation industry. Here, we are largely, but by no means exclusively, dealing with the hotel industry, which, owing to the marketing success of the large chains, has been most effective in organising its worldwide distribution networks. However, guest houses, bed and breakfast accommodation, ryokans, paradores and all the other varied forms of overnight accommodation available around the world must find means of reaching their customers as well.

Hotels distribute their product through a wide variety of sources, including tour operators and travel agents, hotel representative agencies, regional tourist offices, GDSs and websites, Internet intermediaries and third parties such as the motoring organisations. Direct sales are accomplished through call centres and hotel reservations systems, and personal sales contact, particularly with groups (clubs, educational outlets, conference organisers, etc.). Major airports often allow desk space to hotel chains or their representatives where new arrivals can make bookings, and in other cases charge-free telephones are installed for customers to book direct (these are sometimes also to be found in city centre sites). In some areas, again particularly in city centres, impulse purchases form an important component in sales, with customers free to bargain at the front office desk over rates for late bookings. Clearly, this is an important source of business from motoring holidaymakers, especially in countries like the United States, where the motel is ubiquitous.

Hotel representative agencies are mainly appointed to represent and sell facilities to overseas markets, especially in countries where the hotel may find it difficult to reach consumers direct or through travel agents. These hotel representatives, which include such established companies as Utell International, Hotels Abroad and Windotel, receive 'overriding' agency commissions sufficient to allow them to act as intermediaries in accepting bookings from travel agents, to whom they in turn allow the normal agency commission. Sometimes the contract between hotel and representative will include a clause that the latter will not represent any of the hotel's leading competitors.

Smaller hotels and other accommodation such as farmhouses, French *gîtes* and B & Bs find distribution a greater challenge, although again tourist offices in many countries will provide addresses to callers and even make reservations for an agreed fee. Farmhouse accommodation and *gîtes* have become popular with holidaymakers in Europe and many small specialist operators now sell packages including these facilities. Small businesses such as these are also forming themselves into regional consortia to market their services more effectively, allowing the publication of joint brochures which can reach a wider market, disseminated through motorway service centres, tourist information centres and similar outlets. Once again, the growth of the World Wide Web is helping the smaller units to reach international markets through the establishment of individual websites or Internet intermediaries dealing with this form of accommodation.

The desire of hoteliers to clear unsold bedspace has made the accommodation sector an important adjunct of transport sold over the World Wide Web. Late availability of bedspace, especially in major cities around the world, is now widely distributed through online intermediaries such as lastminute.com, or through the websites of automobile associations like the AA.

Intensive versus selective distribution

As we have seen, a medium- to large-sized company has a far easier choice of alternatives open to it when planning its distribution strategy than does the small company. If the larger company sells products appealing to the mass market, and that market is geographically widely dispersed throughout the country, it could be anticipated that the company would normally seek to maximise the number of possible outlets through which its products can be purchased. Such a strategy is termed *intensive distribution*.

Earlier, it was pointed out that sales achieved by way of commission paid to travel agents involve a proportionately small fixed cost element of the total transaction costs. However, this should not disguise the fact that establishing a network of dealers does involve a substantial ongoing cost to a company. There are nearly 7000 branches of ABTA travel agents in Britain. Each must receive at least a minimal level of servicing if it is expected to be productive for the company. In addition to supplying brochures, this will mean regular mailings to keep agents informed of new products or changes to existing products; the offer of merchandising assistance and materials such as window displays; providing agents with educational or other forms of training in product knowledge. Additionally, agents offering strong support will expect to be kept in regular contact with their suppliers, either through websites or through calls or visits from the company's sales representative.

All these support services will have to be committed over and above any commissions paid to the agents for sales achieved. Such support is clearly beyond the means of the smaller company. Few hotels, even the chains, actively promote the sale of their rooms through travel agents – although many will allow commission on sales achieved through this source. A small tour operator expecting to carry, say, 5000–6000 passengers in a year could not begin to contemplate a strategy of intensive distribution, since on average less than one booking from each agency will be received. Instead, the operator will opt either to sell products direct or go for some form of *selective distribution* network. If for instance the market in France is strongly Paris-based, a limited number of agents located in that region may be appointed as retailers for the company; if the market is more evenly distributed throughout the country, a strategy of *exclusive distribution* could be employed, with the appointment of a 'sole agency' in each major conurbation.

Distribution through travel agents

The role of the agent will be examined at length in the following chapter, but here will be a convenient point at which to discuss a principal's decision to select a retailer as one means of distribution.

Since a 1994 European Union ruling on restrictive practices in travel distribution, the former limitations on retailing travel have been abandoned, and in Britain ABTA travel agents no longer have rights as exclusive sales outlets for ABTA tour operators. Price control has also been abandoned, allowing agents to discount travel from their commissions. The result has been a much freer distributive system, with a sharp reduction in ABTA's previous role and authority. Principals have sought new ways of retailing travel, most notably through the online travel agents, which in some cases (such as the Opodo airline e-tailer) is wholly owned by the principal. A new breed of travel agent outside of the ABTA organisation has sprung up, free to sell the products of any supplier (the obligatory financial security of these retailers guaranteed through new bonding arrangements).

ABTA membership is split between the multi-branch retailers owned by the big tour operating companies and the much smaller independents, typically with one or two branches, although there are a handful of medium-sized retailers with up to 60 or so branches. It is impractical, as we have noted earlier, for small-scale businesses to distribute their products through retail agents. As it is, the display area within an agency is unlikely to provide more than some 100–150 brochure facings (spaces) – even the biggest seldom exceed 300. With the limited rack space available, by the time 'preferred operators' have been racked – major companies' brochures (which are virtually guaranteed to sell anyway) and those paying bonus commissions and receiving the approbation of management – there will be very limited space for new products coming on the market, or for products from small companies, however attractive. Where a travel agent is keen to adopt a new product, there must be a good match between consumers in the agent's catchment area and the company's targeted market. To some extent, the image of a company is reflected in the image of its distributor.

Agents can no longer be expected to offer expert product knowledge in the wide variety of holiday products available, especially as low salaries for counter staff tend to restrict recruitment to very young staff with limited experience and training. Consequently, most agents have become essentially convenience outlets for principals rather than consultants, with the independents choosing to stock the products of a limited range of operators and the multiple chains emphasising the sale of products of their own parent companies. A MORI holiday survey carried out in 2002 found that, while in 1990 78 per cent of package holiday consumers bought their holidays from a travel agent, by 2002 only 60 per cent were doing so, and these sales were concentrated in relatively simple, straightforward travel bookings. The drop in sales through agents was attributed largely to the growth of call centres and the Internet.

Competition between agents is increasingly a matter of price, with those offering the highest discounts garnering the larger share of bookings. Multiples, with their high market shares, have been able to negotiate the highest commissions, and have therefore been able to offer the greatest discounts. Independents are fighting back with the promise of a more personal service and better product knowledge, and have attempted (with some success) to introduce fees to replace loss of income from reduced commissions.

Convenience of a local outlet is only one attribute of service: the times at which the outlet is open to the public are no less important. Some agents have experimented with late night openings one or more evenings a week, and increasingly, others are opening on Sundays, since trading laws were relaxed. One company in Britain, Holiday Hypermarkets, introduced 24-hour opening in 2001, siting their branches wherever possible close to the 24-hour supermarkets to gain out-of-hours business. The introduction of more flexible working hours, giving customers the ability to book holidays outside the normal hours of opening, has been popular with the public, and helps to combat the threat posed by the online agencies. In areas such as city centres where a lot of travel bookings are made during office workers' lunchtimes, agents are learning to become more flexible by recruiting part-time staff during the peak lunch periods to cater for extra demand. Such work is attractive for former employees who have left their companies to raise children, for example.

Example   Travel Counsellors

Travel Counsellors became Britain's fourth fastest growing company in the late 1990s, with annual sales increase of 147 per cent between 1994 and 1997. This is a travel agency with a difference. Based on forecasts that more people would be shopping and working from their homes in the near future, the agency recruited staff to work from home, visiting customers in their homes equipped with laptops and mobile phones to complete bookings. They had soon built up a staff of 50 travelling counsellors and 30 online counsellors working from their homes handling teletext enquiries and bookings.

The company were looking for:

■ large volumes of business
■ low overheads
■ no fixed labour costs – staff are paid commission according to sales made.

To reduce feelings of alienation from the workplace suffered by staff working on their own, the company encourages social networking via the Internet, disseminating a 'joke of the day' and other regular communications. Staff are brought together for four meetings a year, for social as well as administrative reasons.

Perhaps agents' greatest concern is the inroads that online agencies are making to their high street sales. The traditional retailers, whether independent or multiple, are seeking to improve the service they themselves can offer their clients through advanced online ICT facilities, where innovations are taking place almost daily. A recent example, launched in 2002, is the self-packaging facility for online agents, known as 'dynamic packaging', which allows customers to select a combination of a flight and a variety of other products to produce a tailor-made tour, with the agent obtaining the ATOL Bond for the package. Initially introduced for the short-break market into the Continent, the package is sold to the customer at an all-inclusive price, like the more traditional inclusive tour, with customers unable to break down individual costs. The website for long-haul operator Kuoni, for example, allows packagers to select the length of holiday, date of departure and flight time, hotel and meal plans. Expedia and the On-Line Travel Corporation (OTC) have introduced their own forms of dynamic packaging, which overcome the problems posed by directional selling, agents being offered the choice of all flights and hotels in the real-time databases. However, dynamic packaging carries with it the threat of consumers themselves creating tailor-made programmes without the assistance of an agent.

However, if agents can combine quality service – good product knowledge, objective advice, with convenient location and opening hours – with similar improvements in ICT which will deliver information and bookings quickly and simply while allowing prices to be held down, the retail sector of the travel industry can continue to flourish.

Cooperative distribution systems

Consortia

One means by which agents, and principals, can market themselves more effectively is by becoming part of a cooperative marketing venture. The consortium is a character-istic development in joint travel and tourism marketing, allowing organisations to unite for marketing purposes while retaining their financial independence. Consortia are prominent in the marketing of tourist attractions, hotels and retail travel agents.

The consortium provides a means by which individual companies with common interests can join together for mutual benefit. Perhaps the marketing consortium is the most common form in the industry, offering the benefit of joint brochure publication. This enables companies to cut costs while reaching a far wider market through better distribution. A group of tourist attractions, such as ABLE (Association of Bath and District Leisure Attractions) or DATA (Devon Area Tourist Association) can in this way afford to produce thousands of brochures to provide bulk supplies to hotels, restaur-ants, tourist information centres, libraries and other outlets where holidaymakers in the area are likely to enquire for information (see Figure 8.3).

With each member sharing the cost according to the brochure coverage they buy, the attractions can gain far wider circulation and publicity than would be the case if each company were to produce and distribute its own brochure. The consortium also gains marketing clout, by persuading their national tourist office to promote their products, or distribute their brochures overseas, something which would be impossible for the single operator. Groups of stately homes, heritage sites and small hotels have similarly banded together to publicise their products nationally and internationally.

While the production of a joint brochure is the most common benefit to be found in consortia, there are many other benefits to be achieved in a marketing consortium. In the case of travel agency consortia, a major benefit is the negotiation of higher rates of commission for group members. The Worldchoice and Advantage chains are examples in the UK, while in the USA agencies have formed similar regional or area consortia, typically comprising between 200 and 600 branches. A number of agents coming together within a region can equal the sales power of a major multiple in the same region, and can therefore gain substantial bonus commissions for targeted sales. One such consortium, Woodside Management Systems (with headquarters in the USA) has built up an international network of business travel agents to negotiate lower prices for hotel accommodation and other travel products for its members.

A consortium can also reduce its members' operating costs by offering opportunities for bulk purchase of supplies such as stationery, computers, and services such as window dressing. A growing advantage is the prospect of establishing a website integrating all the members' products, which will receive far more hits than an individual company could expect. Hoteliers gain from the economies of scale inherent in the bulk purchase of food, drinks and other hotel supplies purchased through a central buying organisation.

Hotel and other accommodation consortia are frequently established with a com-mon theme underlining their marketing policy. Examples include themes of historic interest, common price categories or equivalent standard (e.g. three star, deluxe). The Pride of Britain, a consortium of exclusive upmarket hotels, is one example of the top

Figures 4.3 and 4.4 Two examples of advertising using psychographic segmentation coupled with price appeal, by Tourism Ireland

(Courtesy: Tourism Ireland)

Figure 7.3 New Zealand was not slow to exploit the use of its landscapes in *Lord of the Rings*, which attracted many new visitors
(Courtesy: Tourism New Zealand)

Figure 7.5 (a), (b) and (c) The rational message: Thomas Cook reassures its market about quality control over its hotels, beaches and golf courses
(Courtesy: Thomas Cook/TBWA London)

Figure 7.5 (b)
(Courtesy: Thomas Cook/ TWBA London)

Figure 7.5 (c)
(Courtesy: Thomas Cook/ TWBA London)

Figure 7.6 The emotive message: Emirates Airline uses the charming face of a young child to promote its worldwide routes

(Courtesy: Emirates/HDM)

Figure 10.1   A notably bizarre, but highly effective, campaign to promote Spain:
five advertisements from the Spain Marks campaign organised by the Spanish Tourist Office
(a) Altamira
(Courtesy: Spanish Tourist Office)

Figure 10.1 (b) Meninas (Madrid – culture)
(Courtesy: Spanish Tourist Office)

Figure 10.1   (c) fiesta
(Courtesy: Spanish Tourist Office)

Figure 10.1 (d) Dali – art
(Courtesy: Spanish Tourist Office)

Figure 10.1   (e) feet – sun, sea, sand
(Courtesy: Spanish Tourist Office)

Figure 7.4 The use of popular TV personality David Dickinson enhances the appeal of a MyTravelLite advertisement
(Courtesy: MyTravelLite)

Figure 10.2 A Eurocamp advertisement uses colour (a red background) to gain attention on the predominantly black and white travel pages of the national press
(Courtesy: Eurocamp)

Figure 10.4 A joint advertisement sponsored by the French Government Tourist Office and the Aquitaine region makes good use of colour in the weekend supplements
(Courtesy: Maison de la France/DDB&Co, Paris)

Figure 13.1 Brittany Ferries advertisement carrying a direct response stick-on reply card
(Courtesy: Brittany Ferries/The Walker Agency)

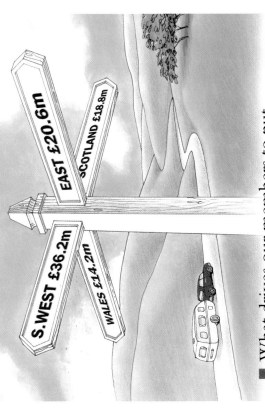

(a)

(b)

Figure 14.3 (a) and (b) Two advertisements from the Caravan Club publicising the benefits of caravanning to the community

(Courtesy: the Caravan Club)

Figure CS7.1 TV celebrity Alan Titchmarsh features in TV and press advertising for YTB
(Courtesy: Senior King)

Figure CS7.2 Popular singing star Mel B featured in the campaign
(Courtesy: Senior King)

Figure 8.3
Cooperative
promotion:
Bath's ABLE
consortium
of tourist
attractions
brings together
36 local
attractions in a
joint brochure

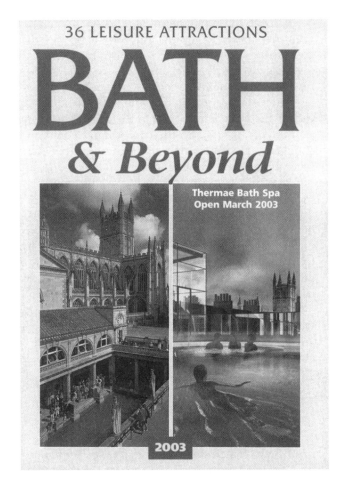

(Courtesy: ABLE)

of the range marketing consortium. Other hotel consortia concentrate on marketing their members' products within a given area. Examples include the Torquay Leisure Hotels group, formed to promote the sale of hotel rooms in the same geographical region of the country. Consortia provide the added benefit of cooperative marketing, enabling each member to act as an agent for the others' products. Where these units are based in a number of different countries, this is an effective means of creating an international distribution network. Consortia also allow smaller hotels and accommodation units to compete with the big chains: while the latter have the benefit of international reservations systems and membership of the airlines' GDSs, websites are now creating a more level playing field. There are many examples of the success of small unit integrated marketing; one is Devon Farms, a consortium of farmhouse accommodation offering bed and breakfast accommodation throughout the county of Devon, which publishes a brochure listing properties, facilities and prices, and is now a key selling tool for members.

One other advantage of the consortium is that it provides the means to recruit management expertise on a scale unthinkable for the small company alone. Travel agents and small units of accommodation can for the first time employ centralised accounting, legal assistance and staff training, as well as marketing expertise for the members.

While the benefits of consortia are self-evident, readers should be aware that the operation of consortia is not without its problems. One results from the autonomy of each individual company within the consortium. Determining the financial contribution of each member to the consortium's common fund can lead to disagreement. Should this be in proportion to the turnover that each achieves? Should the amount of space in the brochure be equal for all members, or variable according to the number of products each company offers, the relative size of the company or how much space each wishes to buy and pay for? Hotel consortia, for instance, generally determine their contribution according to the number of beds in each unit. Then a method of determining which pages will be allocated in the brochure must be agreed. Members prefer to have their products listed in the opening pages, since the consumer is more likely to notice the first pages than those towards the back of a brochure. Should members therefore pay proportionately more for the early pages in a brochure than those occurring later?

Above all, a decision has to be made about how the consortium is to be managed. Often, especially in the early years of a new consortium, members take it in turns to appoint someone from their management to administer the consortium's affairs, although as time progresses, and the success of the consortium becomes more assured, a small secretariat is likely to be formed.

Franchises

A second means by which an organisation can expand its system of distribution rapidly is by franchising. This is an arrangement under which a business (whether principal or distributor), known as the franchiser, grants an organisation (the franchisee) the right to use the company's name and market its products in exchange for a financial consideration – usually some form of 'royalty', or percentage of turnover. In most cases the rights are exclusive within a district, so that the franchisee becomes the sole distributor of the product in the area. The franchisee will also usually pay an initial sum to the franchiser to cover various 'set-up' costs, which can include help with site planning, practical advice in setting up the business, and staff training. The franchisee will also agree to conform with the terms of the contract, such as purchasing raw materials or products exclusively from the franchiser, and maintain clearly defined standards of quality.

While there are a number of different ways in which a franchiser may operate, the most common benefits which the franchisee gains are the rights to sell an established brand name product, and the centralised marketing support provided by the franchiser. In turn, the franchiser gains by the rapid expansion of sites operating under one name, and a fast-accumulating central fund with which a national or international advertising campaign can be launched. This campaign creates brand awareness and a ready demand for the product, which leads to further demand for franchises by those eager to start up in business by themselves at reduced risk. Since franchisees are their own bosses, they can also be relied upon to work harder to ensure the success of the organisation.

The franchise concept is not a new one; indeed, its origins go back over 200 years to the breweries' 'tied house', under which an inn or pub is licensed to sell ales and beers of the brewer only, still a common practice in Britain in the 1990s. However, the modern franchise was introduced on a major scale in the USA in the early 1970s, and became prevalent with the expansion of the fast food business (Kentucky Fried Chicken, McDonalds', Pizza Hut).

The travel and tourism industry has been in the forefront in franchising developments in Britain, as well as elsewhere. Apart from catering institutions, hotels, camping grounds and car hire companies have all launched successful franchise operations. Hotel chains such as Holiday Inns achieved enormous growth in the 1960s and 1970s with their operating franchises around the world; in the 1980s car hire franchising led to the expansion of companies such as Budget Rent-a-Car, as well as Hertz and Avis.

While attempts to franchise travel agencies in Britain can be traced as far back as the 1960s, these were largely unsuccessful, for a number of reasons. To begin with, a successful franchise needs a name with strong drawing power, as well as offering a unique product. The franchising of a travel agency offered neither product nor price advantages, and the possession of a franchise in itself did not guarantee the necessary official appointments by principals. At the same time, exaggerated claims were often made about potential profits that could be expected, while the promised training or other back-up marketing facilities frequently did not materialise. In a business such as travel where the product is highly specialised, lack of adequate training for staff is fatal. Even promises of exclusivity were sometimes broken. All too often, in order to get franchisee support, the ability to pay became the main criterion for the award of a franchise, regardless of any business acumen, with the inevitable result that standards were inconsistent and quality suffered. While most former restrictions on franchising in the UK are no longer in place, the other reasons for failure have not been adequately addressed, and there have been comparatively few attempts (apart from the business travel field) to develop franchise networks in the retail sector.

Building links with the retail agent

We have now discussed two ways in which individual agents can come together to become more effective in their distribution. In this section we will examine how travel principals continue to support the traditional retail travel network in order to maximise their own sales.

Agents traditionally conducted their business by selling products at their principals' agreed price and receiving a commission for each sale, usually varying between 7 and 10 per cent of the gross price. This time-honoured format has been subject to major change in the past few years, not just in the way agents are compensated but also in terms of what and how agents sell. First, a division appeared between agents who dealt with business travel and those focusing on the leisure market. While previously most agents dealt with both sources of business, the additional demands in terms of expertise and service called for in servicing business customers led some agents to specialise in this sector, as a result generally becoming better rewarded. Intense competition among business travel agents led to this sector being the first to move away from the traditional commission structure in favour of discounting their commission earnings to clients and instead charging annual management fees for their services, often based on promises to reduce their clients' travel costs by negotiating lower prices on their behalf. Most other agents were unable to compete on price with the experts in business travel, and concentrated on the leisure market, where sales were generated largely from demand for package holidays, complemented by air tickets.

Earnings from these two sources were undermined in the early part of the new century by two factors. In the tour operating sector, the large operators moved to support their own retail chains and rewarded others on the basis of turnover targets, with bonus commissions which allowed those agents to discount heavily to their customers, to an extent that the independents could not match. This was followed by the airline sector, facing massive losses in the wake of the September 11th (2001) terrorist strike, moving away from a strategy of commission payments to their retailers in favour of flat rate payments, or greatly reduced commissions. The result was a huge drop in earnings for agents, especially against premium price tickets. Only by increasing turnover and efficiency could agents hope to equal their earlier slim profits.

Facing reduced earnings, how would retailers react to their principals' moves? The answer to this is more complex than is at first apparent. Certainly, agents will take account of whatever opportunities remained to increase profits through higher commissions paid by some operators, but this is by no means the sole criterion. Furthermore, a decision taken by the management of an agency to rack a company's brochures is only the first step for the principal, who must also ensure that the staff of that agency actively push the company's products.

Market share is clearly a factor here. All independent leisure agents will still want to sell the products of the half a dozen leading tour operators, since these will continue to generate a substantial proportion of their earnings and not to do so would be tantamount to commercial suicide. Other criteria will also come into play. The determinants in this 'trade-off' can be listed as follows:

1   *The image of the company and its perceived stability*   There must be no danger or rumours that the company is headed for collapse.

2   *The match between the company's products and the client's needs*   Most agents see that it is in their own interests to satisfy their customers.

3   *The reliability of the company in such issues as overbooking, consolidations, delivery of tickets, and communications*   Thus, if agents find it frequently difficult to get through to the reservations department of one particular company's CRS or on the telephone, or have no contact to whom they can complain when problems arise, they may switch to another company which proves easier to reach.

4   *Agency staff product knowledge*   There is no substitute for personal experience gained by sales staff, in encouraging them to sell hotels or destinations, and enabling them to be more convincing in doing so.

5 *Cooperative programmes* Many companies continue actively to support travel agents in their sales efforts by paying 50 per cent of the costs of special promotional events run by agents, or as contributions to specific advertising programmes. These joint promotions enhance the image of both organisations in the other's eyes. To the agents, it shows a willingness to support their efforts to sell, while it reveals to a principal that agents are more than merely order takers, and are actively selling the company's products.

6 *The personal relations generated between a principal's sales representative and the agency counter staff* This factor must never be underestimated. For many agents, the sales rep *is* the company he or she represents, and the rep's personality is a significant factor influencing agency support, both in terms of recollection and recommendation. For a small specialist company, the role becomes even more significant, since the principal's aim will be to get the agent to think first of their company when handling enquiries.

7 *The relative ease with which transactions can be completed* Time is money to an agent. If procedures are too complicated, and especially where the total value of the sale is small, the amount of work in which the agent becomes involved will cost more than the relative commission earned. It is for this reason that few agents will deal with rail or coach tickets or what are seen as 'fringe' travel products which earn little or no revenue for the retailer. Some services, such as hotels, require agents to claim their commission after clients have used the facilities. Not only is this an onerous procedure, but also it slows the agent's cash flow. Agents are still reluctant to deal with hotels which are without booking offices or representative agencies in the agents' home country, although fax and e-mail facilities have greatly aided communications between them and these principals.

8 *The sale of domestic holidays* Many agents have been reluctant to deal with UK domestic package holidays, either believing that commissions are inadequate or that booking procedures are too complex. However, the increase in short-break holidays in Britain, coupled with the aggressive marketing of packages by some UK domestic operators, have encouraged some agents to include domestic holiday packages in their display racks.

9 *The availability of credit terms* Most principals allow a measure of credit to their better supporting agents. The small, less well-established independent agents are therefore doubly disadvantaged, in that they not only find it difficult to negotiate higher commissions but also are required to pay cash for transactions. Managing cash flow is a critical issue for agents, and its successful management can increase profits substantially, while the absence of credit is a major operating drawback.

10 *The 'honesty' of the principal* Many tour operators pay lip-service to the support of agents but privately encourage direct bookings, sometimes promising discounts to customers calling direct, in spite of their being aware of an agency connection. Agents discovering this will clearly be antipathetic towards such companies.

Two other factors should perhaps be mentioned here. First, patriotism is hard to measure, but does play a role in some agency recommendations, where air travel or cruising is concerned. A British travel agent may prefer to recommend a British product, other factors being equal. However, the abrasive manner in which British Airways announced their decision to reduce agents' remissions did not help to endear them to the retail sector, and it will require more than national flag waving to restore good relations between this carrier and their travel agents. The second point is that, on a regional scale, similar support is to be found among travel agents for local companies, which goes beyond mere commercial interest. A local tour operator will be able to establish closer personal relations with travel agents in the area, and as a member of the local community will derive further goodwill from the public. After assessing their organisation's relative strengths and weaknesses in distribution, principals can then develop a strategy within the overall marketing plan which will aim to improve their standing with agents.

It will also be helpful for principals to be aware of their agents' policies regarding the racking of brochures. Each agent or chain of agents determines its own policies as to what products it will sell and what brochures it will display. This will include guidelines on how the brochures of the various companies represented will be displayed. Thomas Cook's approach is not untypical, in their designating four categories of tour operator product:

- *winners' list*: roughly the top 20 operators in size
- *recommended operators*: roughly the next 35 in size
- *authorised operators*: those which the company is also prepared to sell
- *non-authorised operators*.

Those companies on any agent's winners' list will automatically receive full agency support; recommended operators receive more limited support; policy for authorised operators may be to sell but not display brochures, so only a file copy of the company's brochure may be kept in the office.

Clearly, such a policy is demand-led. Some agents may reserve racking for products where local demand is higher than average (for example, car ferry and cruise line companies' brochures will be prominently featured by travel agencies situated near the shipping ports). Companies with which special commission deals have been negotiated, or jointly sponsored promotions have been arranged, should also receive more prominent racking.

This selection and categorisation also operates in reverse, with principals grading their distributors according to the level of sales they achieve. As in all businesses, the 'Pareto Principle' applies, in that a small proportion of agents tend to produce the bulk of the business for any company's total sales. Typical ratios would result in 20 per cent of retail distributors making 80 per cent of the bookings.

It is this feature of distribution which determines a company's policy regarding agency support. Companies could, justifiably, decide to support only those agents providing them with a reasonable level of bookings. This will reduce distribution costs, but it will inhibit the maximisation of sales, and will tend to discourage any potential sales from new, or marginal, agents. Tour operators still chase market share (if not quite to the same extent as a few years earlier), and can ill afford to ignore potential business which might otherwise be lost. Most companies therefore still opt for a distribution strategy which categorises agents into bands based on turnover achieved. This will determine how much support the principal gives the agent.

One operator, a specialist medium-sized company, has used the following grading system for its agents. While the number of bookings will vary according to the total number of passengers carried by the company, the principle is common to most operators and other travel companies:

category	definition
P	preferred multiple, with substantial number of bookings achieved each year
AA	agency with at least 12 bookings
A	agency with minimum of 6 bookings
B	agency with 2 bookings each year
C	agency making at least one booking
D	agency failing to make any bookings
Z	agency without bookings but demonstrating some potential

'Preferred multiples' will generally be supported with bonus commissions for targets achieved, based on some percentage increase over their performance in the previous year. They may also receive offers of 50/50 promotional help, a regular cycle of calls by sales representatives, full merchandising service such as window display material, a regular mailing of information in the company's newsletter, invitations to brochure launches in the region and offers to attend 'educationals', or familiarisation trips, allowing staff to gain first-hand experience of the company's package tours. Those in lower categories will have reduced levels of support, to a point where the lowest category agent may be given only an office copy of the company's brochure and minimal support in other ways. This still enables the agent to 'prove itself' and be offered increased support when the number of bookings justify this.

The principal must also exercise control over brochure supplies distributed to agents. A watch must be maintained on the ratio of bookings to brochures. This ratio can vary widely, with some agents achieving bookings for every three brochures they give out, and others perhaps making only one booking in 20 brochures. A high ratio of brochures to bookings is indicative either of poor sales techniques, with little attempt being made to do more than distribute brochures in response to enquiries, or lack of control over brochure orders given to principals: junior agency staff are sometimes given the task of reordering brochures without any clear idea of actual numbers needed, resulting in a high wastage rate at the end of the year. Fortunately, today databases and computerised management systems have greatly facilitated keeping these records and allowing access quickly, making the control task very much easier.

John MacNeill, former managing director of Thomson Holidays, once pinpointed seven characteristics by which a principal could identify the efficient travel agent. These are listed below as a useful checklist for those considering making agency appointments:

■ the agent will have a Viewdata reservations system in use (today, additional ICT facilities would be expected as a matter of course)

■ staff will have enough product knowledge to satisfy their more demanding clients

- the agency shows evidence of efficiency in reducing its costs
- the agent operates a well-planned policy of selective brochure racking
- its management has the ability to recognise booking patterns and trends over time
- the agency actively sells, using its initiative to tap the local market
- helpful feedback is provided to its principals regarding the local marketplace

Although this list was drawn up some years ago, its relevance today is no less than it was then. The principles of good distribution do not change radically over time.

Inventory control

The marketing manager's task is to manage demand, that is, to achieve a balance between supply and demand, both in the short and long term. This is not easy in the travel business, where demand differs not just seasonally but also from week to week, from day to day and even hour by hour (rail transport being a typical example of the latter). Demand can be difficult to predict, being affected by political as well as economic circumstances; the terrorist attacks in New York in 2001 and in Bali in 2002 (and, at a national level, the foot and mouth crisis in Britain in 2001) are already classic case studies in which the demand for tourism underwent an immediate transformation – such disruptions to tourist flow have become more common in recent years, and are now passing almost for normal in this crisis-ridden industry. Many of the industry's resources are finite; popular destinations like the fishing ports of Clovelly and Polperro in England or Yosemite National Park in the USA, and tourist sites such as Shakespeare's house in Stratford-upon-Avon and the Taj Mahal in Agra, India, cannot possibly accommodate all who are interested in visiting them during the high season. Access to many sensitive sites may have to be limited due to ecological damage caused by excessive demand. Marketing may mean not just controlling the flow of demand, but also de-marketing – actually reducing demand at over-popular sites, and switching this demand to less popular areas or attractions.

In the short term, a marketing manager can employ any of three techniques to control demand without changing supply:

- prices can be raised or lowered to influence demand
- waitlists can be built up
- forward booking systems can be introduced.

Of course, it is also possible to *ban* access to tourists entirely, although this extreme action is rare. It has been advocated by some environmentalists concerned at the growth of tourism to Antarctica, and short-term bans at peak periods are by no means unknown.

However, the most common means of day-to-day control over tourist flows is the use of forward booking systems, usually in the form of a *reservations system*. This is of key importance in the distribution of the travel product.

Reservations systems

Reservations systems are used in most forms of transport and accommodation, and in booking theatre tickets, popular exhibitions and package tours. They are also employed at popular tourist attractions. Some sites, including the Galapagos Islands, the temples at Angkor Wat in Cambodia and the Grand Canyon in Arizona are so much in demand that a rationing system covering access is in force (see Figure 8.4), and travel to these destinations needs to be arranged in advance. Allocations of tickets to sites such as these will be made to tour operators or ground handling agents who build the products into their packages. Products like theatre seats and art or museum exhibitions cannot increase supply, and even transport such as air flights are not easily increased in the short term. Other settings where supply may be constrained include

Figure 8.4
The popularity of Angkor Wat's temples in Cambodia has led to the enforcement of a rationing system for visitors

(Photographed by the author)

upmarket restaurants and campsites during peak season periods. Arguably, reservations systems could also be more widely used to control demand at other tourist facilities such as beaches (which become unattractive if unlimited access is permitted) and ski slopes (where long queues can form during periods of high demand).

Reservations systems also enable organisations whose resources are not finite to forecast future demand more accurately and arrange to expand supply. Thus, inclusive tour companies can negotiate for more airplane seats and hotel rooms during the peak season at those destinations which, while not full, have shown indications of being more popular than was first forecast. Advance reservations have also made possible pricing structures such as the Advance Purchase Excursion (APEX) fares on airlines and train services, which enable the transport operators to predict more accurately their future patterns of demand and load factors. Above all, reservations permit principals to maximise their load factors (or occupancy rates) by repricing or by repackaging, or in some cases by switching customers from products experiencing excess demand to those where demand is light.

The criteria for a reservations system, whether it be manually operated or (now almost invariably) computer operated, are that it is capable of displaying availability, can register bookings as they are made, and can effect cancellations and redisplay the cancelled booking for resale. The cost must be kept low as a proportion of total service charges, whether to travel agents or to the general public (if access is direct). Access should be easy and user friendly, that is, it should be simple to understand and to operate.

Reservations systems can be organised in one of three ways:

1 *A manual system, in which entries are made into diaries or other record books*   A practice common among smaller tour operators used to be to hang huge charts of hotels and airline seats on the walls of the reservations department, with staff entering bookings with erasable marking pens. Bookings were then expunged as cancellations were received. Other operators used a system of colour-coded discs hung on pegs, or cards stored in slots, on the charts, which could be removed if cancellations occur. With this form of reservations system, travel agents telephoned their bookings through to a reservations clerk, who registered options, or made bookings, by removing discs or cards. These systems, while not totally defunct, are now rare, as the cost of computer reservations systems fell to a point where every company, no matter how small, could afford one.

2 *Reservations are held in the principal's computer system*   Agents telephone the reservations clerk, who consults the computer and offers bookings over the phone, again normally subject to receipt of deposits by mail within a period of seven days.

3 *The principal operates an entirely automated computer reservations system*   Agents access the computer live ('online') by means of a visual display unit (VDU) in their offices, and can take options, or make a booking, without the intercession of any member of the principal's staff. Increasingly, many of these systems can also now be accessed by consumers themselves.

Both manual and computerised reservations systems may provide for *overbooking*, whereby more units (plane seats, hotel beds or whatever) can be sold than can be supplied. Although widely condemned (and under certain circumstances illegal), principals argue that overbooking is a necessary distributive technique to allow for the 'no-shows' which are common practice in travel, especially where business travel is concerned. Business people have been in the habit of making several return flight reservations if they are uncertain about when their business dealings will be completed. The alternative would be for companies such as airlines to settle for lower overall load factors, with a commensurate increase in prices to the consumer. Attempts to introduce the payment of deposits or cancellation fees have proved inoperable in the past, and the overbooking system has become a fact of life to which the travelling public have become accustomed, within the bounds of 'acceptable risk'. However, where overbooking becomes too extensive, as has occasionally happened in the case of hotel bookings on package tours, other control mechanisms come into force, such as the intercession of government agencies or threats of action from bodies such as the Federation of Tour Operators (FTO), consisting of leading members of the inclusive tour business in Britain. Tour operators themselves can no longer legally claim exemption from responsibility for overbooking by others, and therefore have to resolve overbooking problems for their clients as they arise.

The cost of using different reservations systems is a major consideration for travel agents, who seek to reduce their overheads. Some reservations for the products of small companies still have to be made over the telephone to reservations clerks. However, for this system to be effective, the agent must be able to obtain a connection quickly with the principal. If an agent finds difficulty in getting through to the reservations department, or if calls are 'queued' at busy times, leading to high telephone bills, there will be a marked reluctance to use the services of that company unless no suitable alternatives exist. Principals can reduce agents' overheads through the use of telephone calls in which the agent is not billed for the cost of the call (e.g. 'Freefone' 0800 calls in Britain) or by using a system in which telephone charges are billed at only the local call cost for long distance calls.

Computerised reservations systems

Reservations systems have advanced immeasurably over the past decade or so, with the advent of ever more sophisticated CRSs at ever-reducing prices. Major airlines, and shipping companies like P&O, were already making use of such systems as long ago as the early 1960s. Originally seen merely as a method of controlling huge inventory speedily and efficiently, it soon became apparent that the way in which information was made available could radically improve the carriers' sales potential.

Global distribution systems followed, primarily for airline bookings, with comprehensive listings of the flights and routes of all or most carriers. Later, key fares were added to the systems, together with access to hotel and car hire booking systems and much other information. These GDSs were ultimately consolidated into the four principal systems in use today, Amadeus, Galileo, Sabre and Worldspan. Although controlled in the first instance by leading competitive airlines, these later came under independent management. The systems were primarily designed for the use of travel agents, using a fairly complex language requiring periods of training for agency staff.

At the same time, the tour operators were also developing their own systems which would allow access by travel agents without recourse to the telephone. A major breakthrough was that of British brand leader Thomson Holidays, who launched their 'TOPS' system in the 1980s. This was a low-cost, user-friendly and extremely reliable CRS that enabled the company to increase sales substantially, establishing a huge lead over competitive operators, who were soon forced to follow suit. It was not long before telephone reservation systems were abandoned entirely by these large operators.

These developments were soon overshadowed, however, by the arrival of the Internet, a global computer network allowing all computers, business or private, to be linked. Although devised in the USA as early as the 1960s, essentially for government work, the Internet was boosted in the 1990s by the development of the World Wide Web, which offers a user-friendly access standard easily understood and applied without formal training. Users can access information, send e-mails, shop for products and exchange documentation in the form of text, images, sound or video. Other developments using the Internet include Intranet, which allows businesses to communicate electronically internally between staff, and the Extranet, permitting closed communication between a business and its suppliers. Retail travel agents can, for example, make bookings by accessing tour operators' reservations systems which are inaccessible to members of the public.

More recent innovations include the introduction of interactive digital television, allowing home TVs to be used in the same manner as home computers, and WAP (wireless application protocol) technology enabling mobile phones to access the Internet, allowing the development of *m-commerce*, or mobile e-commerce. *Broadband* access, allowing computers to be permanently connected to the net without dialling up and without the ongoing cost of telephone calls, has significantly enhanced the attraction of the system. Accessing data 10–50 times faster than through ordinary modems, the system is being widely adopted at the time of writing (broadband was at that point accessible by some two-thirds of all homes, and 70 per cent of Internet users, in the UK). The next stage in technological development will be UMTS (universal mobile telecommunications system), a 3G (third generation) system bringing broadband capacity to mobile phones and palm-held computers and expected to be in place in Europe by 2004. So-called *v-commerce*, or voice commerce, allowing consumers to interact verbally with web servers, also lies in the near future.

Example   5pm.co.uk

5pm.co.uk is a website on which some 900 top restaurant suppliers in the UK offer discounts of up to 30 per cent for early evening bookings. The website contains room descriptions, menus and prices, allowing customers to make bookings and choose meals online. Awareness of the system is publicised in the local press and via poster sites. The company has a call centre in Glasgow for those wishing to take advantage of the scheme after seeing the advertisements and who do not have access to the Internet.

As far as the travel industry is concerned, online ICT has the potential to offer three major advantages to consumers: information about products, the ability to compare products offered by different companies and the ability to make a booking – but at the time of writing, few websites offer all three of these. Agents in particular are still dependent to a considerable extent on Viewdata systems for package tour bookings, which are reliable and simple to use, but limited in scope and dated. The Travel Technology Initiative launched in 2002 enables operators to distribute their inclusive tours to travel agents over the Internet, bypassing both Viewdata and the GDSs, using a common XML language, which may undermine the long-term loyalty of agents to Viewdata. New Internet systems are beginning to emerge which allow multiple operator searches, cutting out the agents' obligation to access each operator's booking system separately. This may be the beginning of an answer to the industry's needs for a trade portal or Extranet which would replace Viewdata and offer a better and more complete set of data than has been currently available to consumers in the home – in particular, to include the ability to compare offerings of different tour operators. Operators themselves, however, fear brand dilution will follow such developments, at a time when they are concentrating on developing greater brand awareness and loyalty.

Airline bookings over the Internet are still mainly point to point, and complex itineraries are not easy to put together. As long as this remains true, the agents will continue to have a role in booking airline seats on behalf of their travel customers. However, the budget airlines have emphasised their online booking systems and have gained financially in doing so.

Example   easyJet

Ninety per cent of all easyJet sales are made via the Internet, with a website maintained by just three people. The company's call centre, which handles the remaining 10 per cent, employs some 200 staff. The cost-effectiveness of the online booking system has encouraged easyJet to offer incentives of £5 to customers who are willing to switch to the Internet to make their bookings. easyJet has also launched the world's first Internet-only car hire service, easyRentacar.

One of the most interesting innovations has been the introduction of virtual representatives, or *V-reps*, to handle calls and reservations from the public. These highly sophisticated robotic voices can engage callers in limited forms of conversation, as well as handling bookings. The American railroad operator AMTRAK has created 'Julie', who handles over 32 million calls every year, and has enabled the company to reduce its labour force by over 100. United Airlines uses a male robotic voice, 'Simon', in a similar capacity. The widespread introduction of robotic answering services of this nature could lead to the replacement of many existing call centres in time.

Future directions

Along with these developments in computer technology, other new factors are beginning to shape the future of distributive systems. The practice of *networking* between travel companies is leading to expansion in potential new distribution systems. Tourist Information Centres (TICs), for example, are increasingly acting as commercial booking agents for travel and tourism products, especially for the sale of overnight accommodation, and CRSs have been created to deal with this form of demand. In Britain, as in other countries, destination marketing staff are rapidly developing sophisticated web-linked destination management systems (DMSs) enabling agents (and ultimately, consumers) to access information of all kinds about resorts, regions and countries.

The trend to *integration* in the travel industry, which allows tourism principals to exercise greater control over the distribution systems through their ownership of retail agencies, has had a major impact on booking patterns through directional selling, as we have seen, but at the time of writing it does appear, at least in Britain, as though the market share of bookings taken by the multiples is stabilising, as independent agents learn to accommodate this form of competition.

Reciprocal referrals between hotels, links between hotels and airlines, and between hotels and car hire companies, all provide alternative routes for the sale of travel products which are being exploited.

Finally, the concept of *net bulk purchasing*, by which travel agents actually purchase in advance travel products and are then responsible for their sale, offers the prospect of a radically different way of retailing, and perhaps a threat to the smaller agent who would be less able to fund this type of investment or stand the risk that it implies. While the concept has been mooted for a number of years, it has not yet taken off in any significant way – but the threat remains.

Questions, tasks and issues for discussion

1   Discuss whether the expansion of directional selling policies by the major travel agency chains is leading consumers to shop around, develop stronger brand loyalties, make greater use of independent agents or go direct to principals for their bookings.

2   Computer technology is a fast-moving subject, and events will have overtaken some of the developments and predictions contained in this chapter. Prepare a paper which updates the latest developments in computers as they affect the distribution of travel products. What conclusions would you draw about the importance of technology in travel distribution, and the survival of travel agents, within the next five years?

3   Is the Internet the best solution for B&Bs, farmhouses and similar SMEs, to promote and distribute their services? And will this reduce their need to belong to consortia?

4   Discuss the pros and cons of the following means of reducing demand during peak periods for popular destinations or attractions:

   ■ rationing by local or central government or quasi-governmental agencies
   ■ variable pricing policies

■ selective distribution techniques

■ laissez-faire, on the principle that eventually equilibrium will be achieved, as visitors, dissuaded by congestion, go elsewhere.

Exercise

Many airlines, faced by cost pressures and decline in demand for air transport in recent years, have chosen either to reduce or withdraw completely the commission formerly paid to travel agents, requiring agents to charge their customers a 'handling fee' for retailing these services. How has this affected the distribution of airline tickets?

Undertake a survey of the population in your area, drawing up a questionnaire to determine:

(a)   the sensitivity to any booking charges in principle
(b)   reactions to different handling fees. Draw up a scale of fees, to include both absolute figures (ranging, say, from £1 to £20) and percentages of the ticket price (ranging, say, from 2 to 10 per cent). How does sensitivity vary towards budget fares and long-haul fares?
(c)   how many of those interviewed have already had to pay handling fees
(d)   how many have switched to booking direct to avoid fees.

Based on your results, make recommendations about the future direction of distribution for airline tickets.

References

1   Reported in *The Times*, 28 June 2002
2   Mintel Report, *Family Holidays, the UK Market*, 2002

Further reading

Buhalis, D and Laws, E, *Tourism Distribution Channels: Practices, Issues and Transformations*, Continuum, 2001

Horner, S and Swarbrooke, J, *Marketing Tourism Hospitality and Leisure in Europe*, International Thomson Business Press, 1996, ch 10

Kotler, P, Bowen, J and Makens, J, *Marketing for Hospitality and Tourism*, Prentice Hall, 2nd edn 1999, ch 13 pp 449–85

9 The sales function

Learning outcomes

After studying this chapter, you should be able to:

- recognise the technical and social skills sales staff need to perform their roles effectively
- distinguish between the sales roles of retail counter staff, resort representatives and sales representatives
- understand the importance of good design and facilities within an agency
- appreciate innovatory solutions now being adopted by agencies to compete with ICT sales techniques.

Introduction

I sat in an agency last week next to a couple who wanted a special holiday. The agent frowned and said, 'I'm afraid that would cost £1500 per person.'

Melvyn Greene, quoted in the *Travel Weekly*, 6 August 2001

Melvyn Greene is a prominent writer on tourism marketing. Writing in the *Travel Weekly* trade newspaper, he was drawing attention to the fact that travel agency staff lack empathy for the high-spend sectors of the market to which they are ostensibly appealing. Young and inexperienced, they cannot conceive what it might be like to spend between £6000 and £8000 for a holiday – yet this spend is in no way unusual today, and some holidaymakers travelling to long-haul destinations may be taking two or three high-spend holidays a year. Some of these sales may be lost to an agency for no better reason than that the salesperson tries to undersell, without recognising that a cheaper holiday may not meet their customers' expectations.

Travel and tourism is a people business; that is to say, the people who attend to the needs of tourists are an essential ingredient in the product itself, and constitute an element of the marketing mix under the four Ps definition outlined in Chapter 2.

Whether referring to sales staff who are responsible for dealing with customers behind the counter, resort representatives who cater to their needs when they arrive at their destination, or any of the hundreds of staff with whom the customer will come in contact – hotel waiters, bar staff, porters, hotel cleaners and chambermaids, coach drivers, airline check-in staff and cabin crew, all play their part in ensuring that the total product satisfies the client.

It may be self-evident, but it has to be stressed, particularly to young people, that service does not mean servility. People must learn to take a greater pride in their skills at serving the needs of others. Above all, this means being outgoing or friendly in dealings with tourists at all times: the phrase 'the customer is always right' applies especially to the business of tourism, and irrespective of the long hours and hard work which travel staff are called upon to perform, the customers will always expect them to be friendly and cheerful on or off duty. In short, *the travel product is indivisible from the staff who deliver it*. If we are buying a television set from a sales assistant who is poorly dressed, unkempt or unfriendly, we may be disappointed, but the reputation of the brand name may still ensure that we go ahead and buy it, if the price is right. With travel, no reduction in price will compensate for an impolite tour guide, a surly coach driver or a slovenly dressed waiter.

Those who intend to work in the travel industry in a role which will in any way bring them into contact with tourists must be willing to present a well-turned-out appearance, to be patient and helpful, and above all to smile and appear friendly. The way employees express themselves on paper when communicating with clients is also an important element in the travel transaction. Good written communications call for tact, especially when dealing with complaints, attention to detail and the use of correct English; poor grammar and spelling reflect badly not just on the employee signing the correspondence but also on the company itself, and the effect is compounded when that employee occupies a more senior position in the company (inadequate grammar does not mysteriously improve when we are promoted!).

Good sales technique is much more than just successfully effecting a transaction. It is part of a process designed to ensure that the single transaction converts that purchaser into a regular customer, and in this sense it is an element of customer relationship management (CRM), which is concerned with building and maintaining long-term relationships with clients. Other ways in which this is effected will be discussed later in sales promotion (Chapter 12), but at this point it is important to recognise that direct interpersonal communication between a principal and client is a vital part of the tourism experience. Salesmanship takes place not just at the transaction stage before consumption, it also forms a part of the consumption of the product itself, and can be further reinforced as part of the after-sales experience – for instance, as when the agent calls a client upon their return from holiday to find out how everything went and whether they had enjoyed themselves. When such communication is well conducted, it helps to overcome the inevitable uncontrollable shortcomings encountered in tourism, such as poor weather or air traffic delays. As such, it is therefore a vital element in any company's marketing strategy, and adequate training must be built into the marketing plan to ensure that personal selling, with all its associated social skills, is effectively communicated to all staff who are likely at any time to come into contact with customers. Evidence suggesting that good interactive communications with clients pays off is not difficult to find. Personal relations between staff and customers build brand loyalty, and there is plenty of evidence that long-term regular customers are actually more profitable to a company than single transaction customers.[1]

It is common in the travel industry to find clients who insist on booking their holidays at destinations where they will remember a particular member or members of staff from previous visits. Cruise companies thrive on repeat bookings from passengers who have travelled so frequently on a particular ship that they know most of the crew, and will only sail if they can be guaranteed to be served in the restaurant by a waiter who served them previously, or they insist on a cabin serviced by familiar cabin staff.

Example Noble Caledonia

Noble Caledonia is a direct sell cruise operator selling high-price cruises, often to exotic destinations. Sailings to certain destinations have particular appeal to birdwatchers, and the company employs a team of lecturers to enhance these cruises. For some years, these have worked under the direction of Tony Soper, a well-known broadcaster with the BBC and expert on birds and mammals. His presence on a cruise is a strong incentive to book for many loyal cruise passengers.

The use of social and personal skills

Two types of skills have to be employed when dealing with clients (and with other colleagues): personal skills and interpersonal, or social, skills. Both involve verbal and non-verbal communications, the more important forms of which we shall deal with here.

Personal skills

In the initial encounter with clients, first impressions are crucial. The way that travel clerks, hotel receptionists or resort representatives appear and present themselves will set the scene for a successful company–client relationship. For this reason many companies impose strict rules on matters of appearance and grooming. Yet people live in an age of freedom that would have been inconceivable even in the 1960s, and do not readily accept restrictions on their right to dress as they please, adopt the hairstyles of their choice, and use their preferred cosmetics. For many people, the world of employment provides the first challenge to these rights, and tourism employees must learn to adjust to the constraints that the conditions of employment will impose.

At a basic level, this will mean conforming to a style of dress and grooming that the employer requires. Airlines, for example, will insist that cabin staff adopt a conservative and manageable hairstyle. Women who have formerly felt that the 'natural' look suits them will be told to use make-up, including perhaps a bright shade of lipstick. They will also encounter restrictions on the amount and type of jewellery they will be permitted to wear. They conform, or they do not stay in the job.

Needless to say, travel staff coming into close contact with customers must be fastidious about personal hygiene. Regular washing and bathing are essential, together with oral and dental care, avoidance of food which may offend clients such as garlic or onions, and the use of antiperspirants being strongly recommended, especially for those engaged in physical work (such as stowing hand baggage in overhead compartments).

Deportment is important, too; we communicate non-verbally as well as verbally, and the way we walk, sit or stand reflects an attitude of mind towards the job. Staff will be expected to look alert and interested in their clients, to avoid slouching when they walk, to sit upright rather than slumped in a chair. Clothes must always be clean and neatly pressed, as well as suitable for their purpose. The objective of most companies is to present a 'uniform' appearance, to convey a corporate image of the company, and increasingly this means actually wearing a uniform. Hotel, airline and car rental staff, couriers, resort representatives and even some travel agents are being asked to adopt uniforms. Representatives serving in warm climates are having to give up the casual leisure wear that has been customary in order to present a more formal image, with skirt, blouse and neckscarf, or slacks, shirt and tie. Of course, in such conditions, it is doubly important that uniforms are washed and pressed regularly. Jewellery in this setting is also generally frowned upon, and must be kept to a minimum.

These are all indirect and non-verbal communication skills which tell the client something about the company and its employees. Next we shall turn our attention to direct communications skills, both verbal and non-verbal, which involve interaction with clients.

Social skills

Reference was made earlier to the importance attached to friendliness in dealing with clients. Employees must approach customers in a friendly and confident manner. This means a welcoming smile, eye contact, attentiveness and a willingness to listen. When shaking hands, a firm handshake will convey a sense of confidence and responsibility – vital for the client seeking reassurance or help, or opening negotiations to buy a product. The use of the client's name enhances the image of interest and attention (hotel porters are trained to read the labels of incoming guests' baggage, so they can use the client's name as early as possible in the host–guest relationship). The tone of voice is also important; voices should be well modulated and soothing, especially when dealing with an irate customer. Fortunately, earlier prejudices against regional accents have largely disappeared, but a strident or whining voice grates, and it requires only a little effort to change this.

When handling complaints, the voice should convey concern. Many clients look for a sounding board to work off their anger when they have a legitimate complaint, and agreement rather than argument will help to modify their anger. A wronged customer is seeking two things, an apology and a reassurance that action will be taken to investigate the complaint. It costs a company nothing to deliver both.

Attentiveness to the client's needs can be demonstrated by volunteering an interest in the client. A resort representative, for instance, can enquire in passing whether clients are enjoying themselves, or a counter clerk can ask a customer browsing through the brochures, 'Is there any particular kind of holiday you have in mind?' to generate a sales sequence.

In general, people working in service industries in Britain have far to go, to perform at the level of service which many of our foreign competitors offer. This is perhaps the greatest weakness of the British travel product, and it is a salutary experience to observe a professional waiter in, say, Italy or Spain, and compare the quality of service they offer with the general level to be found in Britain. There are many excellent and well-trained staff in the UK, however, and the increasing emphasis on training is steadily improving the picture, at least in the larger companies. In the USA, which is not always thought of as a service-orientated country, the level of control exercised over staff in tourism often astonishes the British observer. Training programmes for Disneyworld, for example, dictate the exact form and level of performance of all employees coming into contact with clients, even down to an obligatory smile and saying 'Have a nice day' on parting. Whether it is possible, or even desirable, to emulate this example in Britain is debatable, but our overt concern for our clients must improve in all sectors of the industry. Above all, our attitude of mind towards service must change, to one of pride in one's job and a respect for the client. The use of derisive terms for customers such as 'punters' is symptomatic of a poor attitude to service which is indefensible if the industry is to become professional in its approach.

The sales sequence

We have talked about the vital ingredients – deportment, appearance and facial expression – which are needed to give clients initial confidence when dealing with representatives of a company. In this final section on personal communication, we shall look at the sales sequence itself.

While the most common setting for selling is the retail agency, and the examples below will be particularly appropriate to that setting, the principles of selling skills apply equally in all situations where client and sales staff come face to face, as in the case of resort representatives selling trips or cruise staff selling shore excursions. Although visual contact is not part of telephone sales, the bullet points outlined below will apply equally to this setting, and with the growing importance of call centres, in which staff spend their entire day responding to telephone enquiries, it is vital that sales staff in these centres also follow these key pointers.

The sales sequence requires a salesperson to proceed in five steps, by:

■ establishing rapport with clients
■ investigating client needs
■ presenting the product to clients
■ handling objections
■ closing the sale: getting the clients to commit themselves.

Establishing rapport

The sales sequence has two aims: to sell the company's products, and to match these products to client needs so as to ensure that the client receives satisfaction. In order to meet the latter objective, the initial task for any salesperson is to engage the client in conversation, to gain the client's trust and learn about the client's needs. This process, known as establishing rapport, will reveal how open the client is to ideas, and how willing to be sold. Some customers are suspicious of any attempts to sell them products, preferring a self-selection process. They may see sales staff as ignorant about the products, or 'pushy', but even such clients as these can be put in the right frame of mind to buy from a particular shop if they receive friendly and helpful service.

In order to strike up a conversation with a client, one must avoid the phrase 'Can I help you?', common as it is. The phrase simply invites the reply, 'Thank you, no, I'm just looking.' A more useful opening to generate discussion would be, 'Do you have a particular kind of holiday in mind?', or to a customer who has just picked up a brochure, 'That company has a particularly good choice of holidays this year. Were you thinking of a particular destination?'

The good salesperson must be something of a psychologist, judging from clients' facial expressions their frame of mind and their reactions to questioning. Customers in a hurry, who appear to know exactly what they want, will not thank you for holding them up to engage in a conversation, but a fast, efficient service accompanied by a friendly smile will encourage them to return. Above all, the salesperson should act as naturally as possible. Being yourself will best reassure clients that you are genuine in your desire to help and advise.

Investigating needs

Having gained the client's trust, the next step is to investigate their needs. Once again it is necessary to ask open questions which elicit full answers, rather than closed questions which call for yes/no replies. The sorts of questions the sales staff will need to know include:

- Who is travelling, and how many will be in the group?
- When do they wish to travel, and for how long?
- How do they want to travel?
- Where do they want to go to?
- How much do they expect to pay?

Clients will not necessarily know the answers to all these questions themselves, so one needs to start out asking those that they can reply to easily, and gradually draw out their answers to questions they may not have thought about yet. Some of these answers will be vague to start with ('We had thought about somewhere hot, not too pricey, sometime in the summer') and can be gradually detailed as the conversation proceeds.

Needs must never be assumed. Clients might say that they do not want to go on a package holiday. There could be many different reasons for this, ranging from a bad experience on earlier packages to a desire for complete flexibility or a wish to escape from the holiday masses. The exact reason for the preference should be known so that the salesperson knows what products to offer – there are, for instance, very flexible (independent inclusive tour) packages where the client would not be one of a crowd. It may be that friends have put the client off the idea of a package because of their experiences. In any case, at each stage of the investigation, it is as well to make sure that the needs identified are agreed between the client and the salesperson:

'Let me see, you wanted somewhere quiet and remote, just to lie back and relax, is that right?'
'You did say that you didn't want a large hotel, is that right?'

Presenting the product

Once the salesperson is satisfied that there is enough information about the client's needs, then the next step is that of presentation. This means presenting the right product to meet the client's needs, and presenting it in a way which will convince the client that it is the right product. Here, the key to success is to mention not only the features of the holiday or other product being sold, but also the benefits to the client:

'I would suggest that you stay in Igls rather than Innsbruck itself. It's quieter at that time of the year, less congested, and offers some very attractive woodland walks, just what you were saying you wanted. There's a small hotel, the Ritter, which is owner-managed and has an unusually friendly and personal atmosphere, ideal for someone like yourself staying alone.'

Obviously, product knowledge is crucial to the success of this stage, but personal experience of the resort itself is not always necessary; sound knowledge of the brochure material will generally suffice.

Even if the product you are offering is exactly what the client requires, it is always well to offer one or two alternatives. Clients like to feel they are being offered a choice. Pick out the benefits of each, but stress that the first choice really seems to meet the client's needs best. Too many alternatives, on the other hand, will lead to confusion, and may delay a sale.

Handling objections

One important aspect of the sales sequence which generally arises here is the need to handle objections from the client. Objections may be genuine, based on price, or they may be due to the client being offered insufficient choice. On the other hand, they may be made because the client has an additional need that has not yet been met, and this may require the salesperson returning to the investigation stage to draw out this need. It may also be because the client is not yet ready to buy, and may need more time to consider.

If the product is more expensive than was originally envisaged, the client will need reassurance of the extra benefits included and that the product is offering real value for money. This is best achieved by showing clients a product at the price they were willing to pay, and comparing the two, pointing out the additional benefits of paying a little more.

Whatever the reason for the objections, it must be identified and countered by matching all the client's needs to a product as closely as is possible to achieve.

Closing the sale

The final stage in the sequence is to close the sale. This means getting clients to take action and commit themselves. There can be several outcomes to a sales sequence. Clients may buy the product, either by paying in full or leaving a deposit; they may take an option on it; they may agree to the salesperson calling them later, or agree to call back later; or they may leave the shop without any commitment of any kind. Although ideally the aim of all sales conversations is to close with a sale, this is clearly not possible, and the important thing from the salesperson's point of view is to ensure that the best possible outcome is obtained. Clients may want to go home to talk over the product with their partner, but if they leave satisfied that they have received good service, there is a high likelihood that they will return to make the booking. Of course, if they are merely uncertain, the sale may be clinched by going over the benefits once more, and reminding them that it is better to take an option (which does not commit them) to avoid disappointment if the particular holiday they have in mind has been sold by the time they return.

A good salesperson is continually looking for the buying signals emitted by clients: statements such as 'Yes, that sounds good' clearly indicate a desire to buy. Where the signals are not clear, a comment from the salesperson such as 'Would you like me to try and book that for you?' may prompt the client into action. However, clients should never be pushed into a decision; not only will they not buy, but also they may determine never to return again.

Finally, remember that the selling job does not end when the clients have paid. Hopefully, they will become regular customers. Reassurance of your desire to help them at any time with their travel arrangements, and a closing comment such as, 'I know you will be happy with that particular hotel. Do come and tell me about it when you get back' will reinforce the sale and reassure customers that they have made the best possible choice, not only of the product but also of the retailer through which they purchased it.

Sales training for overseas representatives

An important part of the role of a tour operator's overseas representative is to sell excursions, car hire and merchandise to the clients in the resort. This makes a significant contribution to profits for little extra cost (see Chapter 6). It is fair to say that many clients wish to take advantage of excursions and consider them an important part of their holiday experience. They therefore appreciate a representative who can put over the benefits of different trips in a professional manner. The

▶

local economy and job prospects are also boosted by the extra business generated for taxi and coach firms, restaurants, tourist attractions and shops.

Tour operators are increasingly investing in training for their overseas staff, and sales training represents an important part of this. All First Choice Holidays representatives, for example, attend a two-day course where they learn sales skills and practise them in role plays. Of course, the basic principles of selling and the sales sequence already discussed remain the same whether you are selling the main holiday package or an excursion. Therefore First Choice Holidays representatives are trained to follow the following pattern:

1 *Establishing rapport* The 'Welcome Get-together' is an important vehicle for representatives to establish rapport with their clients. The tour operator provides help and support to ensure that representatives know how to introduce and structure such an event for their clients. The company provides help in terms of 'welcome packs' and support material. However, representatives must also learn how to gather and present the specific, local information unique to their own resort.

2 *Investigating needs* Exactly as with matching a holiday type to an individual, representatives must often spend time on a one-to-one basis with their clients asking open questions in order to find out what they like doing and the sort of trip which matches their needs.

3 *Presenting the product benefits* The art of matching product benefits to needs is emphasised, as this is the heart of selling. There is a difference between a mere itinerary and the specific appeal of certain excursions to individual clients. Thus the representative must learn to tune into the wants of each different client:

> 'The coach is air-conditioned so your kids will enjoy the trip without getting too hot.'
> 'The boat is open decked, so you need not worry that you will miss out on an opportunity to work on your tan!'
> 'The cabaret night is a really sociable and fun evening, so it's a great opportunity for people travelling alone to meet other guests.'

4 *Handling objections and closing the sale* While the principles remain the same, in practice the representative probably has a shorter time span in which to achieve the sale, as the days rush by on a seven-night holiday. Their ability to close the sale and make a firm booking is therefore imperative.

The role of the sales representative

It is the author's belief that a principal's sales representatives continue to play a crucial role in the relationship between the company and its agents. The 'local rep' will be the main – sometimes the only – point of contact between the two, and with the ever-expanding role of ICT in distribution, personal contact is becoming ever rarer between principals and their distributors. In recent years principals have tended to trim their costs by reducing the human sales function as they opt for cheaper means of communication. There is no doubt that keeping a team of sales reps on the road is expensive. However, there is arguably no more effective way of building links with retailers, and many principals do continue to employ a field sales force, whose task is to develop existing business and generate new business by making regular calls on retail agencies, and by calling direct on businesses (in the case of transport and accommodation principals) or other organisations offering the potential for group bookings.

Sales reps keep travel agents regularly informed about product development, and some will be offered merchandising help, or advice on any promotions to support the company's sales. Perhaps the most valuable service they have rendered in the past, in the eyes of many agents, was to have acted as 'troubleshooters' in solving problems. Knowing them personally, agency managers would call them first to resolve a problem, or to try to get seats on a fully booked flight for valued customers. The rep's own personality, and his or her ability to help in these circumstances, has often been crucial in developing the agent's image of the company. Sadly, other channels are increasingly used to communicate with principals today, and these are often less rewarding and less satisfactory. The regular string of complaints in the letters pages of the trade press about poor communications with principals will confirm that new systems, however convenient to the principal, are not necessarily an improvement for their agents.

Although principals' databases now supply up-to-date information about sales achieved by agents in each product category, human contact with a company representative is still valuable. They can best advise the company on agency potential, determine what level of support each agent should receive, and recommend counter staff to be considered for invitations on familiarisation trips.

If representatives are employed, it is their responsibility to get to know each agency manager and their members of staff. They will be expected to be thoroughly familiar not only with their own company and its products, but also with those of their leading competitors and their relative prices. They should have clear objectives to achieve on each visit, to ensure that it is cost-effective.

Attitudes towards these sales visits differ considerably between agents. While most prefer to see a company representative at some point during the year, they may resent 'cold calls' made without prior appointment, and some object to giving up their time to dealing with the many different representatives who call on them. Some retailers have gone as far as to impose a ban on sales calls, a move seen at the time as an attempt to ensure that head office directional selling control was not undermined at the local level. The reps therefore have to ascertain the views of each travel agency manager towards visits, using considerable tact, picking convenient times for visiting and determining whether an agent is interested primarily in learning about the company's products, exchanging social and trade gossip, or keeping the visit as brief as possible and merely noting that the principal is expressing an interest in them.

In the past, reps were frequently used to deliver the principal's brochures, but this is now more cheaply undertaken by professional carriers, usually employed by the printers. The bigger tour operator chains have largely disbanded their teams of sales representatives altogether. In their place they employ teams of *merchandisers*, who are sales personnel employed by an external agency and are used by operators on an ad hoc basis. Typical tasks for these agencies will include:

■ explaining the concept of new brands or products

■ ensuring that brochures are racked correctly

■ motivating retailer staff to sell the brand through sales promotion.

This type of activity depends for its success on a tight and specific focus, together with detailed briefing from the tour operator. Merchandisers in no way replace the role of the sales representative: they often have little knowledge about the company and its products outside their specific brief, but their use is becoming widespread.

Telephone or e-mail contacts are alternative means for keeping in touch with agents. Many of the functions common to sales reps can be conveniently and far more cheaply undertaken by either of these methods. Many travel businesses, including some of the airlines, have switched away entirely from using sales reps, a symptom of the pressure on companies to reduce marketing costs as competition increases. Some principals make use of quieter booking periods to utilise their reservations staff to make contact with their retailers.

Another means of maintaining sales calls while reducing cost is to employ an external sales team. Merchandising agencies provide a team of knowledgeable sales staff to call on the company's agents and generally represent the company's interests. Members of the sales force are frequently staffed by people with prior experience of working in travel, and are therefore already familiar with the industry, so only minimal training is needed to update them on the company's own products. Costs are reduced because these teams may also represent a number of other travel products (generally non-competitive in nature) at the same time, when they call on agents. The cost of each individual agency call is therefore divided between several principals. An example is one company of merchandisers who represent four non-competitive principals; their staff make calls on agents at 12-weekly intervals, covering all four products in a single call. While undoubtedly reducing distribution costs, it can be argued that the system fails to establish either a unique image for the company or a genuine relationship between principal and agent, since these intermediaries are not direct employees of the company. Moreover, the level of control which can be exercised over the sales force is reduced. Nevertheless, for the smaller principal with a limited budget for sales representation, this can offer an acceptable solution to the problem of maintaining contact with distributors at a low outlay.

Managing sales representatives

Whether company policy is to employ its own sales force or to buy in the use of an outside team, the sales manager's role starts with the need to set objectives for the team. This will include establishing the tasks they are to undertake, and setting any targets which they are to achieve. However, many of their tasks will not be directly revenue-generating. As we have seen, sales staff have a servicing function, building good relations with the travel agents and with businesses, grading agency potential, gathering feedback from agents about market trends, providing merchandising assistance, and generally acting as a source of reference for agents. Reps will play a key role in the annual brochure launch presentations (see Chapter 11), helping to organise regional functions and participating in them. However, where an outside sales force is employed, the objectives are likely to be less ambitious. The size of sales force will be determined by the objectives the team will be expected to achieve. These can be determined by taking the following four steps:

1   Totalling the number of customer contacts to be made, whether agencies or other sources of potential business, and dividing these into categories according to the level of service each is to receive.

2   Deciding how often each category is to be visited, and what other forms of support the sales staff are to provide.

3   Totalling the number of sales calls required and assessing time allowances for other activities.

4   Establishing the number of sales staff to be employed in order for these duties to be performed, and dividing their responsibilities into geographic regions.

In the case of a large company such as a large airline or tour operator, this could mean employing an internal sales team of anything up to 20 or 30 people. Obviously, a much smaller company could never afford to offer the same coverage, and would have either to reduce the call frequency or employ an outside sales team. A further drawback for sales staff hoping to work for a small company is that there is little potential career structure. Working for a large company, reps can move up the management ladder to district, regional or area sales managers, with promotion ultimately to controller of sales or sales director. In the small company the sales rep will probably report directly to the general manager, and will almost certainly have less autonomy over the budget than would be the case in a larger organisation.

However, smaller companies do offset some of these disadvantages by providing more flexible employment opportunities for their sales reps. Tour operating staff often work as overseas resort representatives during the summer season, and are brought back to head office during the winter either to call on agents as sales reps or to complement the reservations staff, especially during the busy booking season which traditionally follows the Christmas holidays. This has meant full-time employment for many former seasonal staff, which has improved staff quality and ensures that sales staff have excellent product knowledge through direct personal experience.

Other tasks of the sales manager are to determine scales of remuneration and conditions of work for the sales team, and plan their training. These functions are likely to be undertaken in conjunction with other members of staff in a large company, such as the personnel or human resources manager and the training officer. However, the sales manager alone has direct responsibility to motivate staff, direct them and monitor their performances. We shall examine these latter functions briefly here.

It is wise to give sales reps as much autonomy as possible and minimise direct supervision. Greater individual control over their job leads to greater job satisfaction for the reps, who will give better performance as a result. Sales reps will require a period of induction training, to give them a background on the company and its products, sales methods and record keeping and other procedures specific to the company. They will also require refresher training periodically, as procedures or products change. Although more commonly found in the larger organisations, training manuals can be helpful in initial training, but need to be regularly updated, so a loose-leaf manual is probably best suited for the purpose, or the material could be accessed via the company's Intranet website. Record keeping, again using the Intranet facilities, allows sales reps to communicate with their sales manager, but this should not be at the expense of regular meetings to exchange feedback. Reps in some sectors of industry may be away from their head office for long periods while on the road, and can feel alienated unless opportunities are given to meet up regularly. Increasing ICT facilities, including mobile phones and e-mail, allow reps to keep in frequent contact with head office. Additionally, the rep will be expected to complete report forms, usually on a weekly basis.

The report form provides the basis for the schedule of visits planned by the rep each week. A typical report form will come in triplicate, with the top sheet outlining the weekly plan, which lists the planned schedule of calls for the coming week. This is sent in advance to the sales manager, who will then know where to find the reps should any of them be needed urgently. Sheet 2, the weekly check sheet, includes the information from the top sheet together with comments by the sales rep on the outcome of each visit. Explanations are given for any changes to the programme that had to be made during the week. This information is passed back to head office at the end of the week's cycle of calls. Reps retain the third copy for their own records.

In this way sales managers are kept fully informed of events in the field, while any sales leads received at head office will be passed on quickly to the sales rep in the appropriate territory for prompt action within an agreed timescale. Details of any new agency appointments must be passed quickly to the reps, since a new agent is highly motivated to generate business for principals and will benefit from early encouragement. Leads followed up by the rep are reported back on the weekly report forms, with an assessment of the potential for business. New agents or potential sources of business will be given the rep's name and contact address.

With fully computerised reservations systems, and databases on customers and distributors, sales managers have access to a vast amount of statistical data regarding sales by territory, agency and period. These data alert sales managers to revenue achieved within each rep's territory, enabling comparisons to be made between targeted and actual sales performance, and indicating trends over time. These figures are regularly disseminated to the reps in the field, so that they have access to full information on their own performance and that of the distributors in their territory. At the same time, reps must receive up-to-date information on other promotions under way or planned by the company, and the organisation's overall marketing plans, so that promotion efforts can be effectively coordinated. Sales staff need opportunities to provide structured feedback to others in the marketing department; many excellent marketing initiatives had their roots in pertinent observations on the market made by the sales team. Conversely, lack of communication between head office and the sales force can be the downfall of otherwise sound marketing ideas. Discussions should take place between the sales manager and the reps themselves when agency sales targets are determined each year, particularly if these are to be linked with bonus commissions. Finally, the travel expenses incurred by reps must be monitored by the manager. While these are generally predetermined as part of the overall sales budget, they need to be reviewed from time to time, not only because costs change but also because a company should not inhibit the potential for increased business by too tightly controlling a rep's expenses. A sales rep over budget on expenses should not be criticised if these expenses have resulted in a comparable increase in sales as a result of the rep's efforts.

Selling through travel agents

Personal selling can be conducted in many ways: over the phone, on the doorstep, in the customer's own home to give three common examples. The Internet is now challenging these traditional modes of selling, allowing customers to communicate directly with the reservations systems of travel principals. This has the convenience of home connections, speedy, up-to-date information and, increasingly, bookability. Yet personal face-to-face selling still retains many advantages. Many consumers have yet to adopt the Internet as a favoured means of booking a holiday or other travel arrangement, and one report[2] suggests that consumers are experiencing growing disenchantment with this form of communication as a means of booking. While the slow take-up of the Internet for bookings – as distinct from enquiries – has led to large losses on investment made by the industry to encourage this cost-effective means of selling, it also offers hope for the survival of the traditional travel agent, and it is now becoming accepted that this form of retailing will continue to play an active role in the distribution system. Conservative customers, however familiar with technology they may become, may still prefer to consult an agent when booking their holidays, providing they are convinced that they are receiving objective advice, and, perhaps still more importantly, that the sales staff with whom they are dealing have the necessary knowledge and expertise to handle the sale. On both counts, the evidence is not presently encouraging. In one of the regular 'Mystery Shopper' features in *Travel Weekly* magazine,[3] none of the four English agencies visited (one independent, three chain branches) expressed any knowledge of Bilbao (one agent thought it was in France), nor had any of them heard of the Guggenheim Museum, the major attraction in the city for the past decade and a globally significant destination for cultural tourism. The author experienced similar broadly based ignorance when enquiring about tours to Angkor Wat, a UNESCO World Heritage Site. Yet, worryingly, articles featuring sites such as these appear regularly in both the trade and national press. While training can to a considerable extent develop the skills needed by the travel agent to sell destinations, individual counter staff must also possess a personal curiosity about the world, and about their customers' interests, if they are to develop into well-rounded sales staff able to perform their task adequately.

It has been frequently stated that the travel agent's role in tourism distribution is essentially that of providing a convenient location for the travelling public to make reservations and to buy their tickets; and to do this at a cost which is compatible with other forms of distribution. The information-giving role of an agency, while also significant, has tended to become less so as their customers have become more sophisticated and sought knowledge of their destinations elsewhere. Whether this will suffice in the future remains to be seen, but it is true that proximity of location to the market has always been the principal factor in a travel agent's success. A street-level shop in or close to the high street or main shopping centre is a key criterion, even though such a site will involve the proprietor in increased costs. However, since a travel agent's stock consists entirely of brochures, less space is required than in most other forms of retail outlet, and costs can be held down by sacrificing space. This does mean that the travel agent must measure success in terms of turnover per square foot/metre, and consequently modern shops have been designed for a fast throughput of clients, even where the product might in some cases (e.g. cruising and long-haul holidays) be thought to need the care and attention of a professional counselling service. A characteristic of agency operations in recent years has been the low margins of profitability which most have achieved. This has come about partly as a result of the intense competition between tour operating companies, forcing down package holiday prices, and hence commission payments. This was exacerbated by the introduction of late booking discounts, further reducing the average turnover per booking. Without a commensurate increase in levels of commission to atone for this decline, agents have had to push for higher turnover per branch, and per staff employed, in order to survive. Finally, changes imposed by the airlines to traditional commission structures, in favour of low commissions or even flat fees, dealt a body blow to retailers, and the total number of travel agents in the UK, stable for many years at around 7000 ABTA members, finally began to fall in the early years of the twenty-first century. However, the so-called 'march of the multiples', the rapid expansion in market share held by the leading travel agency chains in the UK, appears to have finally faltered, or at least stabilised, in these years. While power appeared to be moving from the principals to the distributive sector in the travel industry, as chains and consortia negotiated higher commissions for their branches from positions of relative strength, the growth of alternative means of distribution, especially through the Internet, is now weakening the retail channels.

Smaller agents have been forced to rethink their role in order to survive. Since small agents cannot compete on price, they must adopt alternative strategies to compete. Four possible solutions include:

■ more aggressive sales techniques

■ developing 'exclusive distribution' contracts, to represent the smaller, specialist tour operators whom the larger chains are reluctant to support

■ providing a superior professional service with informed recommendations rather than merely retailing whatever the consumer asks for

■ emphasising the value of the independence of the advice given – the agency has no vested tour operator interests to bias its recommendations.

As we have seen earlier, the last two of these are difficult to achieve in practice. The drive towards directional selling on the part of the multiples, and the tendency for independents to sell products paying higher commissions, militate against objectivity, while the low salaries discourage recruitment of well-educated counter staff. In the past, travel agencies were seen largely as 'order takers', but agents must now be more than a convenient point for the purchase of travel arrangements. Charging fees for professional advice may be one solution which will allow higher salaries to be paid and encourage clients to consult *travel counsellors* for their expertise, particularly where independent, tailor-made travel arrangements are involved. This approach is evident in the development of highly specialised agencies (see, for example, the Trips World-wide case study No. 2 at the end of this book).

Innovative improvements in retail practice have been introduced by a number of travel agents, both independent and chain. The example given below of one original approach to retailing may point the way to the future.

Example   Independent Holiday Shop: innovatory travel retailing

One agent has sought to change the methods by which retailers do business. The Independent Holiday Shop, based in Winchester, southern England, was formed in 1993 by two partners who had formerly run a small company chartering classic yachts in Turkey and Greece. The difficulty they found in reaching their potential market was one that they recognised they shared with other specialist holiday companies. Their non-ABTA agency was established with the objective of representing exclusively up to 120 of the smaller, independent specialist operators, and focusing particularly on the tailor-made holiday built around an independent package arrangement.

The company was launched with a novel approach to the contract with their principals: these were charged a fixed fee per calendar month or year for racking their brochure. Premiums were charged for eye-level racking, and for window display of brochures. Commission rates were then negotiated, but at rates lower than the traditional 10 per cent received by agents. This meant that the retailer could cover start-up costs in advance through the charge to principals.

In practice, the agent has found that in the longer run profitability has been improved by eventually reverting to a normal commission structure without a racking fee, but the initial charges proved a highly successful way of launching the agency. Agency commission is payable in retrospect by the principals, with clients paying the principal direct. While this resulted in a poorer cash flow for the agent, it obviated the legal necessity to be bonded.

The company has continued to innovate. They claim to have been the first UK-based travel agent to establish (in 1995) a website on the World Wide Web, which was soon generating over 200 e-mail enquiries a day. The valuable domain name they had purchased, www.holidays.co.uk, was sold to a leading tour operator at a substantial profit, and replaced by a new web address, www.netholidayshop.com, which provides them with a useful extension to their shop front and a means of keeping in touch with their clients. They expanded into franchising, establishing three franchises by 2003 (which pay a percentage of profits to the parent). Their product portfolio has expanded to include some 160 independent tour operators, and they have increased their margins by fully bonding their business through the independent bonding agency the Travel Trust Association.

Travel agency design

It is appropriate to close this chapter with a look at travel agency design, since the effective presentation and design of an agency are critical to its acceptance as a location for the purchase of travel by consumers.

It has often been said that travel agents are fortunate. All they need is a shop, some posters and a telephone, and they can set up in business. Of course, it is not as easy as that, and today's competitive climate makes it certain that design of travel agencies will become ever more important to their success.

While it used to be considered that a travel agent need not take premises in the centre of town because customers would seek it out when they required advice, this too is no longer the case. Most high streets have their own travel agency and the number of customers they attract is directly related to the position they occupy within the town. Good visibility of the shop, such as being on a prominent road junction, may well be a bonus, but the greatest test of any shop site is the number of pedestrians who pass the door. A counting machine and a stopwatch employed at various times during the week will give the best indication of the relative merits of the position when considering new sites. Availability of car-parking facilities is also worth exploring and considering, especially in the small town location.

Any retail concern will normally obtain the best site it can afford for a new business, and will then do its best to maximise the use of that site. Similar considerations can be applied to existing agency locations. Most research into why customers choose one travel agency in preference to another leads one to the conclusion that the most important factor, apart from the convenience of its location, is its ability to draw attention. Outside appearance is therefore of critical importance, including window display, facia and the image of the interior seen through the window. Other traders have led the way with crisp, colourful facias stating their identities, and merchandise to entice the shopper in. A theme is usually apparent, with displays changed frequently to create interest. Travel agents would do well to learn these lessons, especially to forgo their still all too often 'bargain bazaar' approach, characterised by numerous stickers obliterating the view of the interior, and often carrying conflicting messages.

Shop design now favours large, unobscured windows which allow a view of what is beyond the window display. Preference is for a fairly flat shopfront maximising the space available within.

From the outside, and within, two factors dominate first impressions – colour and light.

Colour

Colour plays a key part in establishing an identity. Different colours are credited with individual values:

- red conveys warmth and vitality
- white is clean, cold and clinical
- green is considered natural, caring and wholesome

- blue is seen as crisp and efficient
- yellow is happy and joyful (though sometimes it can be garish)
- burgundy looks sophisticated
- brown and orange are comfortable, relaxing colours.

Above all, the choice of colour will establish a background for whatever is to be displayed. It is important to bear in mind that the interior will look very different when stocked with brochures and posters. Examples of colour usage are the new blue and yellow facias of Thomas Cook, the royal blue facia of Going Places and American Express's burgundy facias.

Lighting

Lights can make or break any scheme. While fluorescent lighting is economical and highly efficient for overall background levels, it is extremely poor for creating impact. Concentrations of light in small areas of relative darkness will highlight any goods much more effectively. The intensity will depend upon the method chosen, with tungsten bulbs, spotlight bulbs and quartz halogen low-voltage units improving in effectiveness by degree. Modern lighting deserves expert advice, once the objectives of the shop design have been decided upon.

Lighting also leads into practicalities, for the overall light levels within a shop will affect the environment for both the customer and the workers. High overall light levels are seldom attractive, and they will also interfere with ease of vision on computer screens. However, the level of light in which staff undertake clerical duties, especially poring over closely packed timetable information, must be good.

Within the travel agency, the first impression should be friendly and welcoming, and designed to put customers at ease. It must be clean (and therefore designed to be easy to clean), up to date in design and practical to operate. Figures 9.1–9.3 provide illustrations of travel agency layout design, lighting and racking considerations.

Practicalities

To convert enquiries into bookings will need not only a desk, but also access to telephones, computer visual display units (VDUs), and reference material. These facilities must be to hand and tidily arranged. Consideration must be given to storage and security of money; it must be decided whether each clerk will have a personal till or whether a central cash desk is to be operated.

Display, demonstration and excitement

Travel is about selling dreams, about people enjoying themselves and taking a break from their drab daily routines. Travel agencies should exude some of this excitement of possibilities, but it is all too easy for an agency to lose this edge, and hence become less effective. The use of display panels with emotive photographs, dramatic and eye-catching posters, video walls and video demonstration players for travel information

Figure 9.1
Shop plan for
Go-Right Travel

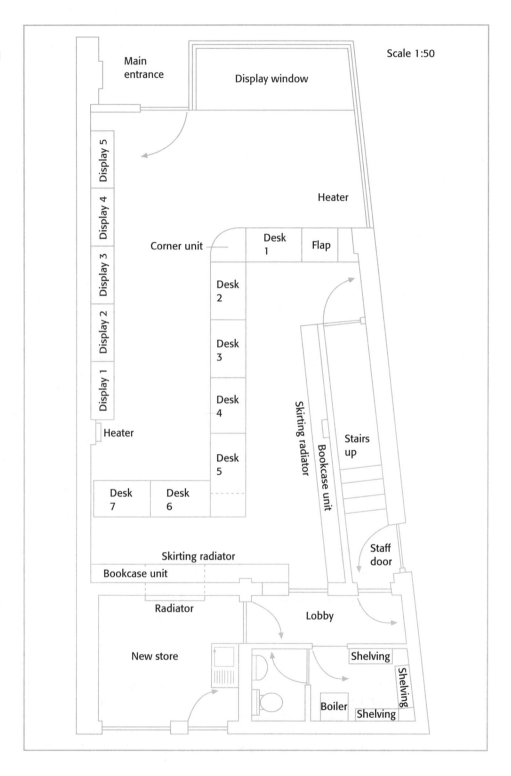

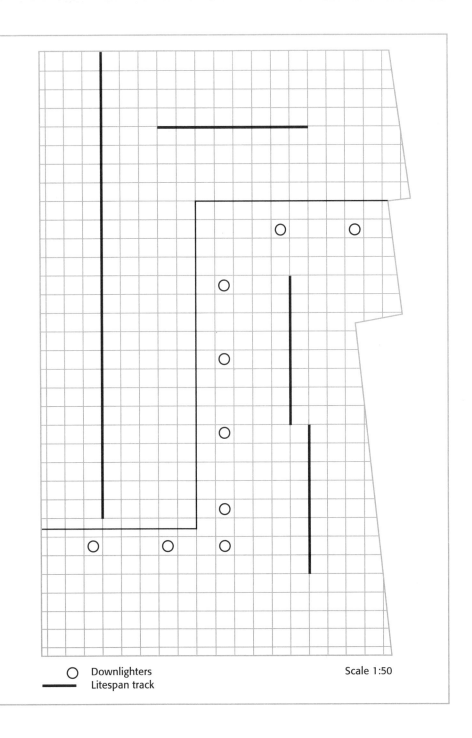

Figure 9.2
Overhead lighting and suspended ceiling for Go-Right Travel shop

○ Downlighters
— Litespan track

Scale 1:50

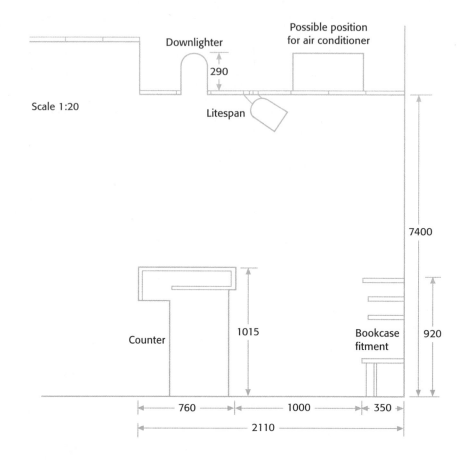

Figure 9.3
Elevation of interior, showing counter, bookshelves and lighting for Go-Right Travel shop

and even the use of modern computer booking systems, all help to add to the atmosphere of growing excitement. Leading chain Lunn Poly was also experimenting, at the time of writing, with the use of aromas in their stores to encourage sales, employing machines that wafted the aroma of eau de coconut through the shop to develop a 'holiday mood' among customers.

Moods are the result of careful planning rather than accident. The relationship between space and distance is important to develop the right atmosphere within the shop. Staff positioned too far away from brochure racks will tend to appear uncaring. The way in which layouts are thought out will help to provide a tidy appearance; for example, one must not leave convenient space where new brochure supplies can be dumped by delivery carriers in full view of customers. The shop will need to be comfortably warm in winter and cool in summer. The layout has to be equally effective for customer comfort and staff convenience – no mean task. What is certain is that to do the job well is both important and expensive.

Desks or counters?

One debate that has continued for many years is whether desks or counters are the best methods for carrying out transactions with the customer. There are divided views, and these can be summed up as follows.

Counters

- do not encourage customers to 'settle in' and stay for longer than necessary
- enable staff (on high stools) to work at the correct height to deal with customers standing up and prevent them feeling dominated by the customer standing above them in a 'superior' position
- provide a security barrier and enable cash to be kept at each position
- provide adequate space below the desk top for either a split-level desk with computer screens, etc., tidily built out of view, or for other storage and reference facilities.

Desks

- are more friendly, encouraging customers to sit and chat
- can be set out informally near brochure racks
- are much less expensive in shopfitting terms as they are able to be deployed without being fixed or specially fitted.

Which policy is chosen is not important, as long as it is implemented well. However, some shops have successfully integrated both approaches, by directing high-spend clients for cruises and long-haul holidays to desks – usually situated at the far end of the shop interior – while cheaper and more quickly transacted business is conducted at counters near the shop's entrance. One agent introduced an even more innovatory approach to handling customers, as detailed below.

Example ■ Let's Go Travel, Exeter

Let's Go, an independent agency, has employed a maître d' to greet customers at the door, taking details of their needs. Customers are then shown to a lounge area, where free refreshments are provided while they wait until a member of the sales staff with the appropriate expertise becomes available.

This novel approach earned the company a *Travel Weekly* Globe award in 2003, as winner in the category NTL Business (Travel Division) Innovation in Travel and Tourism.

The emphasis on corporate design in all areas of business will require the travel agency of the future, if it is to survive as a distribution system, to employ the newest techniques in retailing and above all to provide the welcoming, attractive and comfortable

Figure 9.4
Bright, modern
and efficient
layout for a
multiple agent's
office

(Courtesy: Thomas Cook Group)

trading outlet which customers have come to expect in all shops (see Figures 9.4 and 9.5).

Some retail agencies are going still further. An example of the kind of agency which might become typical in the future is given by the model below.

Example   Travelcaf Milton Keynes

Travelcaf is an agency which, taking a leaf out of modern bookstore practice, teamed up with Esquires Coffee House in 2001 to provide a 'relaxing and fun atmosphere' in which to book a holiday. Visitors to the agency have been encouraged to browse through brochures and on the Internet to obtain destination information while enjoying a cup of coffee. A play area is set aside for children, supplied with colouring books, Lego and computer games. If the scheme is successful, the company planned to roll out up to 70 branches over the next four years.

One can be encouraged by developments such as these to believe that, while the agents' role is constantly evolving, those retailers who survive will offer higher standards of service and facilities than any we could expect in the past.

Figure 9.5
Modern desks
for personal
selling in a
multiple agent's
office

(Courtesy: Thomas Cook Group)

Questions, tasks and issues for discussion

1   What travel products can you think of in which personal selling is likely to be far more effective than any other means?

2   Given that very comprehensive information is now available for virtually any travel product on the World Wide Web, in your considered opinion, will this spell the end of personal selling in a travel agency?

3   To what extent is the information given out in travel agents today objective and unbiased advice? And how can the customers know whether the advice they seek is unbiased?

4   Auctioning is becoming a common means of selling travel products on the Internet. Does this demean the product, or is it a move to be welcomed by the travelling public as offering the lowest prices possible?

Exercise

Analyse the mystery shopper reports from the travel trade press for the past year. List the weaknesses in selling under four criteria:

- ■ ignorance of the product or of companies marketing it
- ■ off-hand service
- ■ lack of knowledge of sources of information
- ■ lack of awareness of the customer's needs.

Put forward your recommendations in the form of a report, suggesting how recruitment and training could help to improve these weaknesses. What other steps would you recommend which would enable an agency to survive against the growth of e-selling?

References

1 See, for example, Reichheld, F and Sasser, S Jr, Zero Defections: Quality Comes to Services, *Harvard Business Review* October 1990
2 Mintel, *British Lifestyles* 2001
3 *Travel Weekly* 14 October 2002

Further reading

Bottomley Renshaw, M, *The Travel Agent*, Business Education Publishers, 1992
Lovelock, C, Vandermerwe, S and Lewis, B, *Services Marketing: a European Perspective*, Prentice Hall, 1999, ch 6
Morgan, M, *Marketing for Leisure and Tourism*, Prentice Hall, 1996, ch 20
Syratt, G with Archer, J, *A Manual of Travel Agency Practice*, Butterworth Heinemann, 3rd edn 2003

10 Tourism advertising

Learning outcomes

After studying this chapter, you should be able to:

- understand the purpose of advertising
- know how to create effective advertisements
- appreciate the role of the advertising agent
- understand the factors behind choice of media
- recognise the need to plan for promotional budgets.

Introduction: ethical issues

Market hyperbole refers to it [the Isle of Bute] as Scotland's Madeira, partly because of the warming influence of the Gulf Stream producing a lush vegetation, and partly thanks to the tortured imagination of the area's promoters.

S Boyne, D Hall and C Gallagher, Tourism Restructuring in Bute, in F Brown and D Hall, *Tourism in Peripheral Areas*, Wiley, 2000, p 104

The following four chapters will be devoted to examining forms of non-personal promotion, as opposed to the *personal sales* function we looked at in the previous chapter. Advertising is just one element in this promotional mix, but an extremely important one in getting a message across to the consumer.

Advertising is also one of the more controversial subjects within the marketing curriculum, attracting a good deal of criticism on ethical grounds. Claims are made that advertising is loaded with hyperbole, that it often distorts the truth and persuades consumers to buy things they do not need, that it is wasteful of resources, that it leads to the creation of a materialistic society, and that it generates false aspirations, by encouraging people to believe that the purchase of certain goods and services will raise their standing in society. While some of these criticisms are no doubt well founded, and the travel industry is certainly not guilt-free in helping to create illusions about its products (witness the frequent hyperbolic 'selling of dreams' in television and other media advertising exotic destinations), we must not lose sight of the underlying aim of advertising. It exists to make consumers aware of products, to inform them about the products and to demonstrate how these products can satisfy their needs and wants. Thereafter it provides a periodic reminder of this relationship between product and need. The commercial world would find it difficult to communicate these aims without the aid of advertising, and some would argue that the world would indeed be a duller place without the colour and imagination which advertisements impart in our daily lives. Where more extreme distortions of the truth are concerned, there are legal and quasi-legal constraints in force to inhibit inappropriate promotion; in the UK, for example, the British IBA Codes of Advertising Practice and Sales Promotion, and the Advertising Standards Authority's (ASA) obligation to ensure that advertisements are 'legal, decent, honest and truthful' help to restrain the more extreme forms of malpractice in communications.

Example   Club 18–30

The tour operator Club 18–30 has been frequently criticised for the sexually explicit nature of its advertising campaigns, including the infamous 'Discover your erogenous zones' campaign of 1994. In spring the following year, the ASA banned a billboard campaign carrying Club 18–30 messages following the appearance of a series of posters in key sites around the UK. The campaign aroused considerable controversy, with a high level of complaints from the public and wide coverage in the press which generated maximum publicity for the company while the ASA undertook its slow process of investigation. Advertising agents Saatchi and Saatchi claimed that there had been no intention to offend the general public, the advertisements being aimed at the target market of Club 18–30 holidaymakers, who were interested in 'sex and booze' holidays. It was also their declared intention to make clearer the nature of these holidays, so turning away many consumers who were inadvertently buying the wrong type of holiday. It was found that the target market was not offended by the ads, but the general public were. The ads were held to infringe the bounds of decency, mainly due to the channels through which they were communicated. Subsequently advertisements were redirected into consumer magazines more likely to be read by the target market only.

Similarly, criticism dogged the BOGOF advertising campaign of major tour operator First Choice in 2001. Although the acronym promoted the opportunity to 'Buy One Get One Free', its association with a term of abuse was viewed as offensive by many members of the public, and after attracting negative publicity in the press, the company's management team agreed that the discount campaign was in bad taste and withdrew it.

In this book we will be considering the three main uses of advertising, namely advertising by the principal addressed to the consumer, advertising by intermediaries addressed to the consumer, and advertising by the principal directed at intermediaries in the chain of distribution.

The decision to conduct an advertising campaign, whether this involves no more than a single insert in a local newspaper or an extended series of national television advertisements, necessitates a number of secondary decisions. A company must first establish what are to be the objectives of the campaign, followed by how much it will cost, and what strategy is to be employed to achieve the objectives. This is also usually accompanied by an evaluation of the campaign to determine whether the objectives have been reached. We will look at these decision-making issues in turn.

Advertising objectives

The first decision involves something of a chicken and egg situation. Does one decide what is to be achieved and then how much to spend to achieve this, or is the promotions budget the first constraint, with objectives based on what is realistically achievable within the confines of a given budget? Marketing theorists would argue that the objectives come first, since the revenue achieved by the advertising campaign should produce profits that will enable any overspend or 'borrowing outside the promotions budget' to be redeemed in full. Realistically, however, most firms will have to work within the confines of an agreed promotions budget determined at an earlier date, and advertising will have to fight for a share of the budget with other elements of the promotions mix, whose objectives may be focused elsewhere.

It must first be determined who is to be the target market for the advertisements – the trade or the consumer? If the consumer, which potential customers are to be attracted? How is the product to be positioned in order to attract them? Is the intention merely to disseminate information about the company and its products, or to produce a sale?

Should consumers be the target, the advertiser must still determine whom it is intended to reach. The purchase of a product such as travel may be the outcome of decisions taken by a number of different individuals. Just to take one example, the business consumer may play only a small role in the decision to travel; the employer may make the decision on the destination, and there may be other influencers as to which carrier will be used and which hotel will be booked for the trip. Influencers will include secretaries, perhaps personnel staff or travel managers within the firm, even the family of the business traveller. There may also be a number of different decision makers or influencers in the purchase of the leisure traveller; families, for example, usually make decisions together about where to go and what to do on their annual holiday. All of these influencers have to be targeted by the advertiser if the product is to be successfully sold.

The tactical aims in advertising tourism products will be no different from those of any other product, in line with the objectives given above of *informing, persuading* and *reminding*. Essentially, the aims will follow the AIDA principle outlined in Chapter 4 of:

- attracting *Attention*
- creating *Interest*

- fostering *Desire*
- inspiring *Action*.

Advertising can, and often does, follow this pattern step by step in the different stages of the campaign, although some campaigns will require a compression of the time frame so that information and action are closely embodied within the same communication. The launch of a new product is often marked by frequently bizarre, attention-getting advertisements which may have little overtly to do with the product itself. Having titillated the public and made them *aware* of the product through such advertisements, the next series of ads will be directed to gaining their *interest*, perhaps with an invitation to receive a package of information specially designed to convert curiosity into readiness to consider a purchase. *Desire* can then be fostered using a combination of other communications tools. *Action* may be promoted by a call centre following up on the enquiry, and suggesting how easy the purchase could be.

Tourism principals' approaches can vary markedly in their advertising aims. Well-established destinations, transport companies and tour operators will often focus on brand awareness and the qualities with which the brand is associated (thus Thomas Cook's series of television advertisements in 2003 emphasising their quality control mechanisms). Others will use the less expensive medium of press advertising to achieve all four of the AIDA aims, with the action element translated into sending for a brochure. The drive to make the most of tight budgets has increased pressure for advertising to feature some kind of 'call to action' which can be measured – thus, the addition of a reply-paid card glued to the advertisement appears in many weekend national newspapers in the peak booking period following the turn of each new year (see Figure 13.1 colour plate, for example). In addition, tour operators will underpin their strategic advertising with a year-round programme encompassing relatively short-term tactical aims.

The call to action to the consumer is often to request a brochure, and the principal then dispatches this direct to the consumer (usually through a distributive agency). The brochure will be accompanied by a sales letter encouraging the consumer to make contact either with a travel agent or direct with the company's sales department.

Tactical advertisements will push late availability, often coupled with special price offers which, whether placed by operator or travel agent, will make a strong case to book the holiday then and there. Telephone hotlines, Internet websites, credit card facilities and 7-day 24-hour service are major features of such advertisements.

Expenditure

Inevitably cost will be a major consideration in drawing up plans for an advertising campaign. National advertising is expensive, and will be affordable only by the largest companies if a television campaign is envisaged. Margins are tight in all sectors of the travel industry, never more so than since the September 11th 2001 debacle and the long period of economic recession which followed. Yet the paradox is that without increasing spend on promotion, recovery is even more difficult to achieve. Some firms prefer to invest marketing budgets in public relations activities because it is believed that a similar impact on the market can often be achieved with a lower spend; as a so-called 'glamour' industry it is relatively easy to gain the interest of the media, and hence free publicity. However, abandoning advertising entirely is never wise, and there are numerous examples of companies which, complacent that their product is so well known that customers no longer need to be reminded of it, have found their turnover and market share slipping as a result.

Advertising spend is notably lower in the travel industry – typically less than 5 per cent of revenue – than is the case in other industries, where spend is often 20 per cent or more. This low spend has been a subject of frequent criticism, and advertising budgets tend to be limited to competitive advertising rather than generic advertising; very little is spent in encouraging people to travel per se, as opposed to travelling to a particular destination in a particular airline and with a particular company. In a post-crisis world market, arguably much more needs to be done to sell the idea of international travel, and to encourage people to fly again, when travellers appear to have lost their nerves.

In Chapter 7 we discussed alternative methods of determining a company's overall promotional spend. When deciding how much to spend on advertising, the same alternatives must be weighed up. Should the budget be allocated based on some nominal figure which the marketing or advertising manager believes is affordable, or based on some arbitrary percentage of sales? Or should the company emulate the spend of its leading competitors? It was argued then that a more sophisticated approach is shown by first determining the objectives of the campaign and then estimating how these could be effectively achieved at the lowest possible cost, the so-called objective–task approach. However, if this means going beyond the nominal funds available within the advertising budget, the marketing staff are taking the risk that if the objectives are not reached, they will have overspent and will be answerable to their board or seniors. It would be sensible to reduce this risk by getting the agreement of the chief executive to justify the additional spend before committing it to the campaign.

Products at the launch stage will invariably require a higher advertising spend than those at a later stage of the product life cycle, as the first need is to get the product known as widely as possible. Attempts to position a product, and differentiate it from others which appear similar will also entail a higher rate of spend. However, few businesses are in a start-up situation and most will have previous practice and expenditure with which to compare when creating an advertising plan for the next season, year or other period. Once a current level of expenditure has been established, each element needs to be examined to ensure that it is justified, using the best information available. Whatever expenditure is then confirmed should be considered an inherent cost in selling that product, for too often advertising is seen merely as something to be taken out of available profit margins. In reality, advertising is as much a component of selling a holiday as is the brochure or airline ticket.

The following example gives an indication of how an SME such as a local travel agent might choose to invest in a campaign:

Overall spend established at 0.75 per cent of a £4.4 million turnover = £33 000

The three main objectives are:

- maximising business from existing customers
  - method: direct mail
  - budget: £10 000

- improving firm's reputation and profile
  - method: by weekly advertisement in local paid-for newspaper
  - budget: $52 \times £200 = £10\ 400$

- reaching all residents of the area
  - method: by monthly tactical advertisements in the local freesheet
  - budget: $12 \times £800 = £9600$

This leaves a figure of £3000 for contingencies to which may be added any funds promised by principals for joint promotions. Once the budget is established, then it is sensible to establish a plan that anticipates which products are to be featured at what times of the year and by which medium. The details of such strategies are outlined below.

In an industry where price-cutting has become the dominant theme for all selling, and where competition for popular holidays is already so intense, it makes sense to invest in advertising as one means of adding value to the product.

Above and below the line

Two phrases in common use in referring to the promotional mix are *above the line* and its corollary *below the line*. The distinction is of less significance today than formerly, although the term is still widely used within advertising circles. The former term is defined as any form of non-personal paid-for communication carried in the mass media, while the latter embraces any other form of paid-for promotion, such as direct mail, inserts or indeed any other form of *non-mass media* advertising such as that carried on matchbooks or parking tickets. In this chapter we will be concerned only with above the line advertising, since the distinction between other techniques of advertising and more general forms of promotion is too blurred to be helpful.

Strategy in advertising

Once a decision has been taken on the budget to be established, the next step in drawing up the advertising campaign is to determine the component elements of the campaign – the message, the medium or media which will carry it (press, radio or television?), each specific form of medium (i.e. if press, local newspaper, national newspaper, magazine?) and such detail as the frequency of the advertisements and their timing.

Devising the message

Designing an effective message is a crucial stage of advertising planning, and in an expensive campaign is a function best left to a creative team of advertising professionals.

The *creative concept* describes the topic of the message and the format, or style, in which it will be conveyed. Messages can be conveyed in text or graphic form, according to the medium used, but the aim of any message is that it should be simultaneously meaningful, believable and distinctive. The message's meaning will be dependent upon the company's objectives, so it is important that what the consumer learns and understands from the advertisement is consistent with the company's communication aims. As we saw earlier, these aims can be based on rational or emotional messages, frequently supported by repetition and reminders through the use of slogans. The 'I Love NY' slogan adopted by New York (with the replacement of the 'Love' by a graphic heart) has become a classic example of an effective campaign, imparting a simple message in a short, catchy phrase that is instantly recognised, easily remembered and subsequently often copied by competitive destinations – the sincerest form of flattery.

The effectiveness of any advertisement will also be enhanced if the message is believable. Believability can be achieved in a number of different ways. The popular technique of giving an actor in a television advertisement a white coat suggesting the expertise of a doctor or scientist is one of the more obvious ploys encouraging belief in a product, but an equally effective ploy is to associate the product with a popular celebrity. Endorsement of a product by a star of the popular music or sports world, or the cinema and television screens (see Figure 7.4 colour plate), boosts believability and sales. The 'likeability' of the star is a further factor enhancing credibility, so football stars like David Beckham and Gary Lineker can command huge fees for the endorsement of a product. Tourism products occasionally make use of these ploys, by associating a celebrity with a particular destination or tour operating company, but again the connection needs to be believable if sales are to be enhanced.

Distinctiveness is no less important. Examine any of the countless pages of advertisements for destinations in the travel pages of the national press, and few stand out from the crowd. The tired use of adjectives such as 'surprising' allied to so many popular tourism destinations, and similar hackneyed phrases, reveal a lack of imagination that does nothing to enhance either the destination's credibility or its uniqueness. One series of press advertisements that has proved effective in recent years is that run by the Spanish tourism authorities, simply for their being refreshingly different. While some critics complained that they were hard to understand, this reinforced the impression that they were being read and remembered – a far better result than that achieved by many national government tourist board advertisements which are simply skipped over by readers. Figure 10.1(a)–(e) (colour plates) illustrates just five of these unusual – and puzzling – advertisements produced by the Spanish Tourist Office, designed to intrigue consumers with appeals to the many attractions of the country. These are clearly directed predominantly at upmarket sectors, emphasising the cultural attractions away from the coast. The tourist office describes the aims of the campaign as an attempt 'to communicate the emotional and physical impact resulting from a visit to Spain through marks on the body [e.g. the tan marks on the feet of a child and its parents] at the same time illustrating the passion felt through witnessing Spanish culture'.

Due to the sheer weight of television advertising, it has become increasingly difficult to hold the viewers' attention, and with such short allocations of time – typically between 7 and 30 seconds – humour is often used to enhance the likeability factor. At its best, a humorous advertisement also bears frequent repetition without the problem of 'repeat fatigue', the outcome of so many irritating advertisements. Travel adverts must above all impart a sense of fun, excitement and adventure if they are to succeed in their aims. The holiday is for many the largest single expenditure in the year, and it must therefore deliver the dreams it promises if it is to satisfy the purchasers. The image of a romantic couple wandering along an empty beach makes good – and popular – copy, but if the reality is a packed beach, polluted water and overdevelopment of the infrastructure, the incongruity between advertisement and reality will disappoint the consumer and the all-important repeat sales or word of mouth recommendations will not follow.

As Chapter 2 made clear, there are three marketing strategies that lead to commercial success, namely:

■ *low-cost leadership*, selling more cheaply than your competitors

■ *differentiation*, creating a high added value, a desire for your product in preference to that of your competitors

■ *focus*, specialisation to a substantial degree that makes your product unique and difficult to copy.

The competitive nature of the travel business makes it essential that any advertising campaign is closely tied to the strategic objectives of the business, and these ideas should be inherent within the messages transmitted.

A *price platform* is fragile, and *low-cost leadership* is always vulnerable. To simply claim 'we're cheapest' is difficult to maintain when a price war results in each firm deliberately undercutting its main competitors. Eventually prices will drop to a level that is impossible to sustain, and it is the nerve, or wealth, of each competitor which will determine who survives, rather than the merits of the product, or the management quality of the company. Cheapness is all too often associated in the minds of the public with poor quality, so claims for quality allied to low price are unlikely to be believed.

Differentiation is the path chosen by most brand leaders in any industry. The fact that cellulose tape became known as 'Sellotape', and that vacuum cleaners are referred to as 'Hoovers' is a great credit to the originators. Kellogg's cornflakes, Nescafé, Heinz baked beans and other top-selling products never promote price, but the reputation that they have built up for product reliability. They exploit this with advertising that builds upon their standing. They become natural *first choice brands* against which all competitors are judged. This inherent quality is referred to as *added value*, and it can be increased by advertising. It is, however, a quality that does not come readily or quickly and which can easily be lost if production standards fall and consumer expectations are not realised.

This technique can be used by a local travel agent who concentrates on the experience of staff and their ability to advise more competently than competitors. On a larger scale, a memorable campaign by Thomson Holidays built their reputation for reliability by depicting their quality controllers as serious businessmen (typified by city suits and bowler hats). In both cases the advertisements are about the quality of service provided rather than about the product itself.

Focus is about specialisation. It might be concentration on a new product, or upon product elements that are unique to a company. It is much more difficult to copy quickly a campaign that is based upon a true marketing advantage that has been planned, such as 'all our villas have private swimming pools', or 'we have trained baby patrollers at each of the hotels marked', or 'every cabin has private shower and toilet'. Assessment of unfulfilled customer needs is an integral part of a marketing plan, and enables selling advantages to be established which are unique to the company concerned.

Example **VisitBritain (then known as the British Tourist Authority)**

In January 2002, BTA launched a £20 million advertising campaign under the slogan 'UKOK'. The primary objective was to counter the combined negative impacts of foot and mouth disease in Britain and the September 11th terrorist attack in New York. There were two secondary aims: to drive enquiries from the BTA website into the offices of the travel firms, while galvanising the UK public into inviting friends and relatives from abroad, thus further boosting the inbound market. Over 1500 tourism businesses participated, and 135 000 UK residents sent away for the UKOK packs used to invite the VFR market.

The campaign received a bad press. Immediately labelled 'YouCock', the slogan, described by BTA as 'an expression of pride in Britain, a statement of fact, and an open invitation to visit' seemed to carry little meaning with the general public, and the campaign was abandoned after two months in favour of a public–private enterprise promotion under the direction of a new advertising agency, which was unwilling to be saddled with the earlier campaign. The new strapline, 'Only in Britain, Only in 2002' played on the theme of the Queen's Golden Jubilee, heritage, culture, the cities and countryside, with the aim of attracting 1 million overseas visitors from seven prime tourism markets. The UKOK campaign was thereafter restricted to the VFR markets.

It is interesting to note that the reaction of the city of New York, when so hard hit by the September 11th disaster, was to launch a successful campaign to attract tourists under the strapline 'Come see New York in its finest hour'.

Media planning

Traditional channels for communicating messages include the press (newspapers, magazines, journals), radio, television, cinema, outdoor and direct mail – the latter so important that a separate chapter is devoted to the subject. Promotional literature including the all-important travel brochures and guides can also be defined as a form of advertising, and is also featured in a later chapter. The newest techniques, so-called e-advertising, are linked to the growth of ICT, especially the use of websites, and these will be addressed later in this chapter. To all these must be added the countless forms of imaginative advertising open to use by the travel industry, including advertisements carried on the exteriors of public service vehicles like buses and taxis, interiors of underground trains and train stations, directories, litter bins, airport trolleys, bus stops, parking tickets and tickets to visitor attractions, matchbooks and electronic message boards, balloons and banner-carrying light aircraft – and not least, the display opportunities provided by travel agency windows. In short, the range of media vehicles to carry the travel message is almost unlimited, and larger campaigns are best left in the hands of a professional media planner.

The decision on which particular medium to use for a campaign will be based on a number of criteria, of which financial constraint is only one. While only the largest travel companies can contemplate a national television campaign, there are still opportunities for spots on local television which are affordable by smaller organisations; for example, Bristol Zoo and other local attractions in the UK's West Country purchase spot advertisements on local television station HTV, and such advertisements reach not only local residents but visitors to the region staying in local accommodation. Other considerations will include:

- Who is the target market? An upmarket attraction such as an art gallery or museum is more likely to reach its market through periodicals and newspapers read by that sector of the population, such as quality magazines or the broadsheet press.

- How broadly based is the market? Local, national and international markets will all call for different media. Mass markets for products such as package holidays will merit different advertising considerations than specialised cruises.

- How important is colour, sound or movement in getting the message across? Is the product one that requires some element of demonstration? Black and white text offers the opportunity to get a great deal of information about a product across to the market, but is a poor medium to attract attention or excite the imagination. A colour photograph of an attractive destination placed in the pages of the magazine section of the weekend national press, may have only limited space for text, but offers a wonderful opportunity to demonstrate the product with an accompanying punchy headline or slogan.

- How quickly must the ad appear? Preparation time for a television commercial is lengthy, and magazine ads often have to be booked many months in advance of the issue. Last minute opportunities for package holidays will be best communicated through the press or even the travel agent's windows. Websites offer excellent prospects for late availability airline seats or holidays, as they can be updated at very short notice and appeal to browsers using web searches for last minute bargains. At the time of the Gulf War in 1991, tour operators were forced to scrap their brand-building campaigns, which depended largely on television, in favour of the more flexible national press, where tactically orientated advertisements can be mounted at short notice, designed to get immediate action to attract bookings.

Assessment of the form of medium to use will also take into account the *reach* of the medium, the *frequency* with which the medium can be used to repeat messages, and the *impact* of each form. Reach refers to the proportion of people targeted who will have access to the advertisement and are likely to see or hear it at least once, while frequency is an indicator of how many times on average each person in the target market will see the ad. The *opportunities to see* an advertisement (often referred to in advertising circles as the OTS) will be an important consideration in determining the medium, but this will be weighed against the strength of impact of each type of medium, with a strong TV ad likely to carry far greater weight than a simple black and white ad placed in a newspaper. TV lends itself to frequent repetition to maximise impact, although this will be tempered by viewer fatigue if exposed to the same advertisement too frequently over a short period of time.

Campaigns are assessed on their *cost per thousand*, or CPT; that is, how much it costs the advertiser to reach every 1000 people within what constitutes the target market. Frequent use of an advertisement allows the desired number of consumers to be reached much more quickly, as well as reinforcing the message to those catching it more than once. Where rapid action is sought – as in the case of the late availability booking market – this will be the overriding factor. Many other types of advertising campaign, however, are designed to build brand awareness and loyalty, and different considerations will apply to these.

Publications

The generic title of 'publications' covers a vast range of different printed material, and the selection of the best vehicles within this category in which to advertise is one requiring substantial research – again, a decision wisely left to the media planner, where an advertising agent is employed. The choice will include daily and weekly newspapers, which fall into the categories of broadsheet (quality) or tabloid (popular). There are also local papers and free newspapers with a local circulation, all of which will be useful vehicles for the local travel agent, or airlines operating out of a regional airport.

Newspapers offer great flexibility coupled with low overall cost, but advertising quality is inferior to many other vehicles and the 'shelf life' of a newspaper advertisement is short. Quality newspapers are associated in readers' minds with prestige and believability, and this carries over into the advertising, enhancing the value of upmarket products. As substantial data are available concerning the readership of each paper, markets can be pinpointed and targeted accurately. However, apart from the weekend colour supplements, the scope for colour advertising is very limited in this medium. In Figure 10.2 (colour plate), holiday operator Eurocamp demonstrates one example of the simple use of a single (red) colour in otherwise black and white surrounding text to create impact, while stressing reputation as the main message in a small, brief but effective advertisement. Condor Ferries have taken a different approach with their advertisement on the same travel supplement pages, capturing attention by printing their Supercat travelling at speed across the full width of the page, cutting into the (background) text, accompanied by a brief but powerful message that communicates both speed and price (Figure 10.3).

Magazines, on the other hand, offer colour as well as a higher quality of reproduction, and due to the huge range of different magazines appealing to every variety of reader, markets can be accurately targeted. Many magazine copies are circulated between readers, so a single insertion may be seen by a considerable number of people. There is the added advantage of relatively long life, as many magazines are collected

Figure 10.3
A Condor Ferries
advertisement
captures
attention by
creating a sense
of motion on
the still page

(Courtesy: Condor Ferries Ltd)

and stored by their readers, or find their way to doctors' waiting rooms, to be consulted again later. Obviously, holiday magazines, and magazines related to travel such as the *National Geographic*, will be popular vehicles for advertising travel products. The principal drawbacks are relatively high cost and in some cases a high degree of wastage. They are also unsuitable for mounting a quick campaign, as space has to be planned and booked a long way ahead. Figure 10.4 (colour plate) provides a good example of emotive advertising carried by the national broadsheet weekend colour supplements. Here, the aim has been to communicate something of the feeling of being in the region – the friendliness, culture, range of activities and sense of freedom – all with a minimum of text and a powerful illustration.

Journals also carry advertising, and some lend themselves to this form of communication. The travel press, particularly the weekly trade papers *Travel Weekly* and *Travel Trade Gazette*, is a popular means of communication with travel agents and other distributors.

The International Publishing Corporation (IPC) has done considerable research into patterns of holiday purchase. It contends that women have more effect than men upon holiday choice, thus it promotes the value of advertising in its weekly and monthly women's magazines as a high priority for sellers of holidays. It also analyses readership profiles for each magazine in the group so that advertisers can choose the one that best fits the profile of targeted consumers.

Television and radio

Because television reaches such a wide national market and appeals to all the senses – sight, sound, motion and colour – it is considered the medium with the highest impact. Because of the large numbers of viewers watching any programme (especially during the evenings), the cost per exposure is small, but this disguises the fact that the absolute cost is high, and television commercials are also expensive to make. Because programmes are less selective in their audiences, it is harder to target specific types of audience. Perhaps the strongest criticism of TV advertising is its fleeting nature; ads are easily missed or ignored, with audiences simply 'turning off' when they appear, and with the growth of video recording, commercial breaks can be skimmed through – even jumped through employing modern technology.

In some countries there are opportunities to sponsor a television programme – in the United States, a company's name can even be incorporated into the title of the programme, carrying additional weight with viewers. An interesting example of sponsorship in Britain has been the link between Going Places, a leading travel agency chain, and the popular *Blind Date* programme. Many viewers are keen to see for themselves the destinations in which the contestants spend their date, and the association of the programme and agency provides an obvious cue to booking.

As a medium for national coverage, television is outside the range of all but the largest travel and tourism businesses, although there are opportunities for small-scale local advertising. A bonus is that travel advertising is heaviest in the aftermath of the Christmas and New Year holidays, when advertisers of most other products reduce their expenditure, so rates fall.

By contrast, commercial radio in many countries offers more local coverage, and requires much less investment in production costs. Imagination is the key to its effectiveness, as listeners are not limited to what they see on a screen. It is a particularly effective medium for tactical messages, as production is rapid. Whereas television is generally limited to large businesses, radio can be used even by small independent travel agencies or visitor attractions, and it is a useful medium for regional promotions. Markets for radio can be targeted more accurately than for television, and this is an excellent medium for reaching car drivers and commuters.

Example   Barbados Tourist Board

The Barbados Tourist Board has made highly effective use of radio to get across their message, by sponsoring the weather forecast on radio stations in the UK. Following a typically depressing winter forecast of cold and rain, the sound of waves lapping on the beach accompanied by the soothing tones of the Barbadian voice-over describing the glorious weather in Barbados is an emotional appeal to immediate action.

Outdoor advertising

Outdoor advertising embraces the use of a variety of unusual techniques which include advertisements appearing on the side of parking meters, litter bins or bus shelters – but, of course, most commonly it takes the shape of poster and hoarding advertisements. Some of these vehicles are ideally suited to travel advertising; any advertisements giving information on destinations will have a natural home within the carrier transporting the tourist to that destination, and baggage trolleys have been employed to carry ads at airports for immediate impact. One example of appropriate advertising is to be found within Eurotunnel's trains between England and France. For some half an hour, drivers trapped in the shuttle carriages travelling through the tunnel have little else to focus on, and welcome the destination ads which appear on the sides of the vehicle, illustrating what can be seen within a short drive of either the English or French coasts. A similar example of captive audience viewing is witnessed in advertisements running alongside the travelators, or passenger conveyor belts, at airports.

Poster advertisements are flexible and can be mounted at relatively little cost. They benefit from high repeat exposure as many travellers pass the same sites every day en route between work and home. On the other hand, audiences cannot be selected, and there are limitations to the creativity of a poster ad – although it has to be said that some key sites and hoardings have adopted very creative displays, including three-dimensional images or even models of the product. At the junction of the entry road to London's Heathrow Airport a large-scale model of Concorde in British Airways colours is seen every year by millions of travellers.

Posters need to be replaced frequently, as weathering does not treat them kindly, and they can sometimes be subject to vandalism. Although theoretically their impact is limited to daylight hours, in many key sites posters are illuminated at night. Other sites have moving screens that allow two or three different advertisements to be shown in turn, thus capitalising on the site.

Perhaps the most popular employment of posters in the travel field is in travel agency windows, designed to promote immediate action for late availability holidays. Although less selective, they catch the passer-by market, can be mounted quickly and cheaply, and just as quickly discarded after the campaign. Their use has become universal in travel agency shops, with high – and easily measured – effectiveness.

e-Advertising

To all these familiar forms of advertising must now be added the growing number of e-advertising channels, notably the Internet search engines and websites which permit the insertion of banner ads to catch the attention of consumers logging on to sites, and pop-up pages which appear as searches are carried out. Recently there has been a move away from traditional Internet banner 'pop-up' advertising – seen by many viewers as irritating – towards more creative applications. British Airways, for instance, bought up the rights to use keywords such as 'airline' on search engines, so that keying in the word resulted in an on-screen advert for BA offering cheap flights. Such online advertising has prospered in travel-related fields.

The cost-effectiveness of these new techniques is still being gauged, as some take time to download, and consumers can become impatient and irritated by any increases in spam (unsolicited commercial e-advertising messages) that occur with the growth of websites. Somewhat surprisingly, however, research in Britain has revealed that half the mobile phone owning population are quite happy to receive e-advertising messages on their mobiles, and half of that number remain willing even without any inducements such as discounted bills. Again, relevance and the degree of irritation may be a factor here – this text's author was standing recently on the top of the Säntis Mountain in Switzerland admiring the view, and the peace and quiet, when his mobile rang. The text message from the telephone company welcomed him to Austria (!) – and subsequently billed him for the privilege! However, there appears little doubt that advertising using these channels will expand. Money-off coupons sent by text have been trialled successfully in the USA, revealing one direction in which e-advertising is moving.

On the Internet, banner ads are increasingly giving way to advertising techniques that are designed to move consumers on to the next stage in the buying process, and competitions are frequently tied into this form of promotion to offer rewards (the Travelocity case study 1 at the end of this book illustrates one example of this technique).

Example lastminute.com

lastminute.com is one of the best-known brands in online booking services, including holidays. Their website is accessible via PCs, telephones, mobiles with WAP and interactive digital TV. One successful viral online campaign was the company's 'Office Flirt Test' which traded on workers' curiosity to browse the web during office hours. Set up chiefly to attract office workers in the 25–45 age range, it linked the test with a special offer of romantic getaways, achieving over 1 million hits immediately preceding St Valentine's Day.

The market for e-advertising is still quite small, and skewed in favour of certain segments of the population, although the Internet does deliver selectivity at low cost. The impact, however, is thought to be quite low, and as the audience controls the presentation, wastage is likely to be high. However, the real promise with this form of advertising is in the scope it offers for growth and for interactive marketing.

When budgets are large, the complexity of choice is much greater, but fortunately a great deal of information and advice based upon research is available. It goes without saying that the higher the impact sought, the higher will be the cost of the campaign, but to ensure good value for money any larger campaign should not be undertaken without the professional advice of an agency.

Piggyback advertising

There are many ways that advertising can be linked to other forms of promotion to enhance the impact of a campaign. Often such promotions are carried out linking a travel product with a product from another field, with travel as a reward for purchase. Examples include joint promotions between Toshiba and Virgin Atlantic, retailer Rumbelows and Iberia Airlines, Sony and Thomas Cook, supermarket chain Sainsburys and British Airways. Electrolux has sponsored holidays in its own white goods promotion, while retail chain Currys has similarly sponsored European flights. Such promotions are a useful means of boosting travel, but they need careful handling and control. The 1993 nightmare in which Hoover offered free transatlantic travel to purchasers of their vacuum cleaners – resulting in the sale of so many Hoovers that the availability of flights could no longer be guaranteed – led to massive negative media coverage which backfired badly on both the manufacturer and associated carrier.

The piggyback approach can be employed using different media to promote the same product; see the following example.

Example   SeeAmerica.Org

SeeAmerica.org produced a 16-page colour supplement distributed with the *Sunday Times*, sponsored by the private partnership Travel Industry Association of America (TIA). The supplement was used to advertise the organisation's website, with access to thousands of US travel products.

Timing the campaign

With an unlimited budget, any company might be happy to advertise throughout the year. Inevitably, this will be impractical for all but the largest companies, and judgement has to be exercised about the timing of major campaigns – although an element of the budget should be held back for tactical advertising to publicise late availability or special offers. Global airlines will experience fewer peaks and troughs than, say, tour operators, which traditionally experienced two distinct booking periods, for summer sun and winter sports holidays. Brochures were published anything up to a year in advance of these periods, and advertising peaked in the post-Christmas and New Year period.

Unfortunately for the industry, booking patterns have changed, and whereas it was traditional for the majority of consumers to think about booking their holidays in January or February, many now wait to do so until very shortly before departure. This pattern has been exacerbated by the series of economic and political crises which have hit the industry, discouraging people from booking before they know what the state of the world will be. It would necessitate massive advertising spend – or savage discounting – to encourage people to return to the earlier booking pattern.

Unsold holidays and transport facilities are a prime example of 'perishable goods', for they have no value whatsoever after their departure date. Anything paid for them must be better than nothing, and tactical advertising to recruit bookings for late availability opportunities has become a major element in the campaigns of most travel companies. Heavy discounting has become the norm in advertising cruising, transatlantic and other long-haul flights, and city-centre hotels in the off-peak periods. Unfortunately, these discounts have become so attractive and so well established in the public mind, that they have affected the willingness of early bookers to pay the full price. The result is that a very substantial part of the travel industry's advertising budget is now spent on this 'tactical advertising', with heavy emphasis on price, as a glance at any of the weekend travel pages of the national press will confirm.

If advertisements are to be one of a series, the decision focuses on whether a 'drip' or 'burst' technique is more appropriate. Advertisements can be concentrated by appearing frequently within a short period of time, a burst technique also known as 'pulsing', or they can be phased less frequently over much longer intervals, the 'continuity' approach. Brand building and reminder type messages are more likely to succeed where the drip approach is employed, while calls for immediate action will have greater success with a burst campaign.

One final point on timing: as with any product, advertisements must be timed to ensure they run in advance of the travel arrangements, but not in advance of their bookability. There is little point in running advertisements about a new airline route, of a new package holiday destination, if there are no opportunities to make bookings or receive information about the products. The marketing and production teams need to coordinate their activities to ensure that reservations systems and information back-up are all available when the enquiries begin to flow in. Similarly, if special offers are to be made available in advertisements, it is important that the sales staff and others who may be receiving enquiries from the public are fully briefed about the advertisements before they are published.

Advertising agencies

Paying the piper

Just as the public are encouraged to use the services of a travel agent and are frequently charged nothing extra for their services, advertisers have the option of using an advertising agent to create, design, prepare and place their campaigns. There are many benefits of so doing, not least the fact that the advertising agency will offer professional expertise and access to statistical information from market research that is not readily or economically available to the advertising company. Traditionally, the basis of employment has been the premise that whereas the customer would pay in full for each £100 of space in the press or on television, the advertising agent will pay only £85. The advertising agent will, however, become the principal in the transaction and be expected to pay the media owner even if the eventual client defaults or becomes unable to pay. This margin actually establishes a 17.65 per cent mark-up on the spend by the advertising agent. It has become common practice for this margin also to be added to any additional work that the agency commissions on behalf of a client, such as related point of sale displays, promotional videos, etc. This can be very arbitrary, however, and there is nothing magical about the figure of 17.65 per cent. Where the actual production costs are low, and/or the media spend is small, the agency may not consider it is adequately remunerated in this way for all the management time involved. Equally, a promotion involving a high production cost, such as a very large print run, might result in an artificially high agency commission. Consequently, in practice agencies are now paid on the basis of a mixture of fee and commission. The principle applies just as much to small as to large advertisers, and even local travel agents may find that in return for placing a regular series of advertisements in the local newspaper through an advertising agent, they will be able to have the layout and designs created professionally.

The worst possible foundation for a client–agency relationship is the client's belief that since the agency is being paid for through media commission, the client has no financial responsibility and is entitled to free and virtually unlimited service. In reality, truly productive business relationships are complex two-way processes. Agencies need the income provided by any particular client's work, and this makes it difficult for them to dictate the course of the relationship alone. Who can blame an agency for not proffering unpalatable advice to a difficult client who does not want to hear it? And yet it is the client who loses out ultimately, and who has everything to gain from the most effective relationship possible.

It is important for clients to establish at the outset exactly what they seek from the use of an agency. The motivation will normally be one of the following, or some combination of them:

1   The agency has the resources available to produce the promotional campaign and the client does not have such resources in-house. It is often much more efficient to call in the services of the agency as and when required, as opposed to employing full-time staff. This is especially so if the requirement for promotion peaks and troughs, or is not large enough to represent a full-time job.

2   The agency has special skills that the client does not possess, e.g. creative and design talents.

3   The agency has specialist knowledge and experience, e.g. media knowledge, an understanding of international advertising, or business and marketing expertise drawn from within the client's own market sector.

4   The agency has, by definition, a more objective view than the client, who is too close to the product. In addition, the agency has a breadth of vision drawn from working with different clients across many different industries.

When choosing an agency it is important to have a clear view of the nature of the service that will be required. The strengths and resources of a prospective agency can vary tremendously in the skills and experience of their personnel, and hence in the service that they can offer.

A client who needs to mount a major strategic press campaign on an international basis within short timescales would ask such questions as:

'Does this agency physically have enough people to manage a campaign of this size quickly?'
'Does the agency have in-depth experience of media buying overseas?'
'Does this agency have experience in my market sector?'
'What proportion of this agency's work is press as opposed to other media?'

Equally, a small tactical advertiser with a low budget would ask such questions as:

'Am I paying for high calibre agency staff with business expertise that I don't need and can't afford?'
'Is this agency's creative team used to producing good campaigns but on low budgets?'
'Would my account be very small relative to the agency's other accounts, with a resulting low priority?'

Once a relationship is entered into, the onus is on both parties to create the correct environment for effective working. There are several vital ingredients:

1 *Mutual and honest information exchange* The client will need to devote time to ensuring the agency understands the business, its products and its markets. The more strategic the campaign, the greater the agency understanding has to be. A long-term relationship is often beneficial to capitalise upon the time and effort both agency and client devote to arrive at a detailed mutual understanding. Also, an agency needs to discuss honestly with the client the progress of a campaign and any problems they may be encountering.

2 *Clear lines of communication* There is a tremendous amount of detail surrounding even a small campaign. A good agency will submit work at set points in the production process for client approval. These milestones must be agreed in advance, and all parties must be clear about who within the client organisation is authorised to approve each stage. Thus the managing director may approve the initial creative idea, while the marketing manager may sign off the final prices that appear within an advertisement.

3 *Mutual respect* A good personal relationship and 'chemistry' between client and agency staff undoubtedly helps, as it does in any service business. Mutual respect is vital. A client who employs an agency, but does not value its advice, may be missing out on the objective view. Equally, an agency that cannot assimilate input and opinion from the client into its creative approach is failing to benefit from the greater in-depth product and market knowledge of the client. An open mind is essential. While most clients complain of an agency's creative work 'going stale' over time, most agencies complain of clients being 'boringly resistant to new ideas'.

4 *Specific and reasonable objectives need to be assigned to every promotion* Whether the advertising is 'good' advertising can be assessed only against tangible measures of effectiveness.

5 *The service required determines the choice of agency* At a day-to-day level, the client should not assume that all agencies are the same (they are not), and should define exactly what is expected from the agency, such as attendance at weekly progress meetings, detailed post-campaign response analysis, all changes in the media schedule to be notified in writing. This not only makes it clear to the agency what is expected, but also allows it to resource and cost the campaign accordingly.

6 *Budget and timescales available* These should be clear at the outset, and realistic in terms of the objectives.

7 *Basis of the agency remuneration* This should be fair and clear at the outset. A client who values a long-term relationship will want the agency to make an honest profit. Larger clients will know that they play a significant role in the business survival of their agency. One of the most contentious areas of costing is which party bears the cost of amendments to advertising ideas and copy, and if possible a policy should be agreed in advance.

Evaluating the impact of advertising

No business would advertise if it was believed that sales could be achieved without this added expense. However, there is sufficient evidence to demonstrate that there is a relationship between promotional spend and sales, although the exact correlation is often difficult to establish, given the sheer number of factors accounting for variations in sales. This is not to say that the effects of advertising should not be measured, and there are many simple tools at the disposal of advertisers and their agents to ensure that the most appropriate media and vehicles have been selected, that their cost is justified and their value measurable.

Monitoring advertising entails checking the effectiveness of advertisements both before and after the campaign. Remembering our AIDA model, we will understand that at any point in time the consumers making up our target markets will be at different stages in the model: some will be unaware of the product, others will be aware of it but have little information about it, still others will prefer it to competitors, want to buy it at some point in the future, will already have bought it or will be regularly buying it. What we need to know is the percentages of consumers at each stage, and how our advertising will have affected these percentages. Let us take an example, in the form of a destination like Jerez de la Frontera, a holiday area in southern Spain which is comparatively little known among British holidaymakers. Survey research may have determined that the potential and actual market for holidays to that region falls into the following categories (the figures are hypothetical):

- 73 per cent of the target market are unaware of the destination

- of the remaining 27 per cent, just over half (14 per cent) would favour it as a holiday destination 'within the next five years'; 6 per cent would not consider ever visiting it

- 3 per cent had already visited the destination, and 0.5 per cent intended to do so again within the next five years.

A campaign could be drawn up with the intention of converting awareness of the destination to 90 per cent of the target market within the next 12 months, with 30 per cent of these favouring a visit and at least 6 per cent actually booking to travel within the next year. Advertising agents can estimate the total cost of a campaign which can be expected to deliver these figures, as well as the best media and techniques to employ. It would be likely that any proposed campaign on this level will incorporate a number of different promotional techniques in addition to advertisements, and these might include public relations activities and sales promotion directed to the travel trade.

Once the campaign has been devised, pre-testing can be undertaken. This could involve copy testing – designing an advertisement which is then tested on a group of typical holiday purchasers to see whether they recall the advertisement and its contents, how much they have understood of the message it conveyed, and whether their attitude to the product advertised had changed as a result of seeing the advertisement.

Monitoring an advertisement is also possible, by mounting different campaigns in different regions of the country. In this way, the effectiveness of each can be judged, and one region may be treated as a control group and omitted from the campaign, to see how awareness (or sales) vary in that region compared to others where the campaign is running.

In practice, measuring the effects of advertisements, in terms of awareness or expressed preference for the product, is easier than determining how sales are affected by advertisements. However, many ads have coupons attached which solicit enquiries from consumers, or even allow bookings to be made. Others have a coded reference (e.g. 'Department ST10' which would identify the tenth advertisement, or the date, placed in the *Sunday Times*) which enquirers are asked to quote. This greatly simplifies the process of monitoring, allowing accurate assessments to be made of the number of enquiries pulled in by each advertisement, and it is relatively easy at a later date to measure the number of conversions to sales by checks on names and addresses.

Every day the public is exposed to many hundreds of advertisements, and advertisers face a major challenge in overcoming forgetfulness. Impact of a good ad is important, but so is constant repetition, and a lot of advertising is simply aimed at reminding the consumer of the company's existence. Regular tests of the public's recognition of advertisements and products will monitor general awareness and attitudes towards a company and its products.

Post-testing is as important as pre-testing. The advertiser will want to judge whether the spend on the campaign has been justified, and the usual tests of recall, awareness, attitudes and intention to buy will be made, as well as actual sales achieved during the campaign, to measure value for money.

Case history: Hoseasons – cost justification in practice

A remarkable example of cost justification in practice is demonstrated by Hoseasons, the UK's leading provider of self-catering holidays. Starting as a Norfolk Broads boat-hire agency over 50 years ago, Hoseasons has grown dramatically and now sells more than 1 million holidays a year – in lodges, cottages, holiday parks and boats – in Britain, Ireland and mainland Europe.

Hoseasons estimate that around one-third of their direct customers each year have booked with them previously or have contacted them as a result of a recommendation. Repeat business from this sector is effectively encouraged by a series of targeted direct mailings. This leaves two-thirds of their million-plus customers whose bookings are derived as a result of advertising, direct marketing, joint and trade promotions, Internet activities and PR.

Traditionally, the core advertising for UK self-catering holidays has been small classified advertisements in the weekend national newspapers, magazines and TV guides. More recently, magazine inserts, digital TV and Internet advertising is commonly added to the mix.

▶

With a multiplicity of media it is very difficult to estimate individual effectiveness, which could lead to the advertising budget getting totally out of control. It is thus critical to their success that they can evaluate the effectiveness of their advertising spend – a campaign with over 3000 insertions each year, ranging from small circulation niche magazines to national publications and television advertising.

Hoseasons has a highly refined system for analysing in detail the effectiveness of every advertisement, direct mail piece or promotion. They do this by asking all enquirers to identify where they saw the advertisement – by quoting the unique key number that appears on every ad. Every brochure request generates a personal reference number, which links each subsequent booking to the original advertisement to which they responded. It is then possible to establish not only what brings in the most enquiries, but also which advertisements result in the best conversions.

Thanks to a sophisticated computer system, they are able to evaluate such aspects as:

■ which publications/media work best

■ the best advertising style

■ the most effective times of year for advertising

■ the cost of the advertising space

■ the volume of replies received
  – by phone
  – by post
  – via travel agents
  – via the Internet or e-mail
  – through other digital sources (i.e. interactive digital TV).

Hoseasons have been able to establish a cost per reply analysis which is extremely accurate, and gives guidance in future policy making. It also enables them instantly to test the success, not only of general advertising messages, but the more specific product-led or tactical messages as well.

Door-to-door distribution

If direct mail is the logical quality route for communication to selected customers and/or potential customers (see Chapter 13), door-to-door distribution is its much less expensive counterpart. Particularly for a local travel agent, or a visitor attraction such as a zoo or museum, it can be extremely effective either to cover all households within a given distance of the premises, or to select those areas which it is believed will be most productive. Unlike direct mail, it is not possible to personalise the message, but it can be a very effective way of seeking out the high proportion of locals who currently do not visit the site. This has been widely used as a method of distributing discount vouchers which can be redeemed only through a given outlet. Some travel agency chains produce their own newspaper, supported by advertising from principals, and this, too, is distributed door to door throughout the catchment area of all branches.

Questions, tasks and issues for discussion

1   Collect a set of advertisements from the national press or magazines which, in your view, aim to move readers to each of the objectives of the AIDA model. Identify which objective – attention, interest, desire, action – each advertisement targets, and critically evaluate its effectiveness in this respect.

2   Discuss the Spain Marks campaign in terms of its effectiveness. Can you find other examples of unusual or bizarre travel advertising? If you were responsible for promoting the travel products they advertise, could you think of a better theme to achieve their aims?

3   Identify and list any poster campaigns for transport (air, rail, coach) within your area. List up to 10 of these, and in discussion with others in your group, compare and contrast their effectiveness. Which do you consider best, and why?
    Which seem to be more effective – those with little text, or those with a lot? Does this depend upon where the posters are situated?

4   Which travel advertisements do you remember having seen within the last six months on television? What was it about them that made these ads memorable? Have they prompted you to use the services they promote, or would you plan on doing so at some point in the future as a result of seeing the ads?

Exercise

Assume you are the advertising manager responsible for the promotion of a major event in your city (carnival, fiesta, classic car rally, house and garden exhibition: the choice is yours). Establishing a realistic budget, draw up an advertising campaign to promote this event within your region, identifying the target audience, and the media you will use in as much detail as you can.

NB: In the UK it will help to have access to a recent copy of BRAD (*British Rate and Data*) for up-to-date advertising costs in the different media.

Further reading

Kotler, P, Bowen, J and Makens, J, *Marketing for Hospitality and Tourism*, Prentice Hall, 2nd edn 1999, ch 15

Morgan, M, *Marketing for Leisure and Tourism*, Prentice Hall, 1996, ch 15

Morgan, N and Pritchard, A, *Advertising in Tourism and Leisure*, Butterworth Heinemann, 2000

11 The travel brochure

Learning outcomes

After studying this chapter, you should be able to:

- understand the importance of the travel brochure as a marketing tool
- recognise the regulatory and other constraints affecting brochure production
- identify design and print needs from the perspective of the consumer, the distributor and the printer
- understand the implications of brochure distribution
- be aware of technology leading to the development of alternatives to the traditional brochure.

The role of the travel brochure

The bigger the boobs, the blonder the barnet, the better the babe.
Quotation extracted by *The Times* from a guidebook produced by the
British Tourist Authority employing model and personality girl Melinda Messenger.
A spokesman for the BTA declares, 'Melinda is the message to lure young tourists'[1]

The *Concise Oxford English Dictionary* defines a brochure as 'a booklet or pamphlet, especially one giving information about a place, etc'. The distinction between the travel brochure and all the other forms of print used to support sales promotion in the travel industry is not easy to make, but this chapter will devote itself largely to examining the commonly accepted form of brochure used in particular by tour operating companies to inform consumers about their products and attract bookings for them. However, this will not exclude other, newly developing forms of brochure such as those created electronically, and the chapter will also take account of promotional print like airline timetables, destination guides and similar printed matter which is not purely point of sale material. The significance of this category of material is that it is given or sent free to consumers on demand, as distinct from commercially sold printed literature, such as many guidebooks and maps. Other forms of sales promotional material not normally distributed to consumers, of which there are many varieties in travel, will be examined in Chapter 12.

In general, when we think of a travel brochure, we conjure up an image of a listing of package holidays, or a descriptive booklet on a destination, and these forms of brochure remain the single most important tool in marketing travel and tourism. But regardless of what travel product is being promoted, it is likely that a brochure of some sort will be used. A hotel will need a prospectus; a museum or tourist attraction, a leaflet or pamphlet; an airline, a timetable booklet describing its flights and routes. These forms of hard print remain as popular as ever, even as alternative promotional tools such as the e-brochure develop. Websites can carry all the information contained in a brochure, but up to the present have shown little indication of replacing it, although their complementary role is now recognised. This reliance on brochures as a principal marketing tool distinguishes tourism from virtually any other form of business, and it is for this reason that a separate chapter is devoted to examining their role.

Each travel brochure fulfils a subtly different role for the organisation which produces it, some being produced essentially to provide the consumer with information (e.g. airline timetables) while for others the brochure must both inform and persuade (package holidays). Much of the information it contains is designed to answer the questions which a consumer would otherwise have to raise either with the principals or their intermediaries, such as a travel agent. In this sense, the brochure cuts down the sales task of travel staff, and reduces costs. However, many brochures also have a symbolic role, acting as a substitute for a product which cannot be physically seen or inspected prior to purchase. The ability of the consumer to see descriptions of the product in advance, to refer to the material during their trip, and to look it over at a later date when recalling the trip, identifies the brochure as what sociologists refer to as a 'signifier' for the signified product, the actual travel experience.

Preparing the brochure

The organisation's marketing team will make the decisions about what brochures are needed, and how many should be produced. Again, the first question is one of budget – how much should be spent in brochure production and distribution? The question takes us back to the discussion in Chapter 7, when alternative methods of determining budgets were examined. While many travel companies tend to approach the budgeting for brochures in a somewhat arbitrary manner, the objective/task approach recommended then is equally applicable to this process, with the team considering first the number and characteristics of the target market and what opportunities exist to distribute print through various media, taking into account the likely wastage rate. The latter figure is something that can best be estimated with the experience of hindsight, although advice can be offered by the distributive outlets on likely demand. Wastage is inevitable, but common sense suggests that this be kept to a minimum. Tour operating brochures displayed on the racks of travel agents may have a conversion rate of only 6–10 brochures handed out for every booking made, with an even higher figure if the agent concerned makes little effort to sell, merely allowing these to be collected by anyone dropping in to browse (including schoolchildren doing geography homework projects!). Middleton[2] has estimated that brochure print and distribution accounts for half the gross operating profit for a typical British tour operator, so any effort to control this wastage is commendable. Wastage for some brochures is clearly enormous in Continental European countries like Germany where the largest tour operators, using a 'shotgun' approach to marketing, make racks available on the street outside travel agencies for their brochures to be picked up by passing pedestrians, rather as estate agents display property brochures in Britain. Small tour operators who deal direct with the public may need to print and send out as many as 20–25 copies for every booking they receive – but at least these results are measurable. Destination brochures displayed in the racks of hotels or tourist information centres are freely available to the public, but little is known of their usage, and their production is often an act of faith, although failure to produce any publicity material would clearly be fatal for a resort or tourist destination.

Other factors in determining production cost will have to take into account the quality of the material being prepared. A brochure featuring a consortium of five-star luxury hotels will opt for a much more glossy presentation than that for a company organising cheap weekend breaks in a capital city.

With these guidelines, we will now go on to consider in more detail the processes for planning and designing a travel brochure. Since the tour operating brochure has perhaps the highest profile, it is this example of print on which we will focus, but where other sectors of industry have different demands, this will be picked up in the analysis.

Style and layout

Every organisation strives for its brochure to be distinctive and attractive. In it, the organisation must communicate its brand image, determine its product positioning and convey enough information to reassure the consumer of the organisation's strength and reliability. If the company or destination is unknown to the consumer, the task of reassurance is still more daunting, yet the publication will often be the only tangible evidence that the consumers will have of the product before it is purchased, and it must communicate all these values in the space of a few seconds while consumers initially peruse its contents. Almost subliminally, consumers weigh up a number of factors to gauge a 'good' brochure, including:

- the appeal of the front cover
- the paper quality and its 'glossiness'
- the use of colours and their appeal
- the number and quality of photographs and other illustrations
- the thickness of brochures

■ the clarity of the text, and prices where appropriate

■ the relevance and appeal of the products on offer.

Travel print follows fashion, and as fashions change it is necessary to change not just the product but also the way it is communicated. This is particularly true of covers, which can appear outdated – or too novel – if too far from the 'standard' design of the day. Logic now dictates a standard approach to writing package holiday brochures, so that most now follow a typical three-section pattern:

■ a set of introductory pages

■ the contents pages, which in the case of large companies can run to some 500 pages

■ 'extro' or exit pages.

The introduction establishes the company's style, makes statements about policies and commercial practices, reassures the consumers of the company's stability, promotes its unique selling points and 'bargain' offers, and preferably (though not invariably) contains an index.

Contents pages tend to be arranged in sections defined by destination country. Most companies lead with their strongest destination, but it is not unknown for the first to be a resort that they wish to emphasise for other reasons (such as when launching a new destination). Typically, most destinations will include a simple map locating hotels, photographs of hotel interiors and exteriors (almost inevitably with a swimming pool), descriptive text, and a price box with details of flights, departure points, durations and dates, either on the same page or in the exit pages.

Simply to accommodate all this information on a page is an act of skill. Attempting to make the result understandable and still visually attractive requires specialist abilities, although the widespread introduction of desktop publishing software for personal computers, capable of handling the entire layout and editing of the package holiday brochure, has greatly facilitated this process.

The final section of the brochure contains details of booking conditions, extraneous information, insurance schemes and all the other 'small print' details required by law and by regulatory bodies such as ABTA. The booking form is frequently to be found on the back cover or on one of the last pages in the brochure, but should not be printed on the back of any booking conditions, since such contractual information should be retained by the customer. The larger tour operators no longer carry booking forms in their brochures, but instead provide retail agents with separate booking form pads.

Print material in other sectors is less constrained. Tour operating brochures are required to carry prices, and these are required to be clear and comprehensive, i.e. inclusive of tax or other levies. With the more fluid pricing policies among tour operators now, this can lead to the need to republish brochures at frequent intervals, adding to cost. A hotel chain has greater freedom, and typically will publish its prices in the form of a loose-leaf insert, which can be changed each year, or more frequently where necessary. Destination brochures seldom include any details of prices, although some will include accommodation guidelines for a commercial consideration, in which case they, too, will need regular updating, at least annually.

Brochure covers

The design of the brochure cover is the key to persuading consumers to consider any product. Tour operators therefore put considerable effort into the design of the front cover. They may, for instance, commission a dedicated photographic shoot just to obtain one special shot. Alternative designs may be researched with panels of consumers before the final cover layout is decided. The choice of design is a difficult one for there are many possibilities, but typically the cover will feature:

■ a spectacularly attractive photograph of one or more destinations

■ an attractive holiday situation, such as a family group enjoying themselves in the water

■ a pictorial amalgam of the contents

■ a statement of what is contained or of sales features.

Each policy has its supporters. Long-haul holiday brochures tend to feature a photograph of some idyllic faraway destination. Most Mediterranean holiday brochures favour a happy or glamorous beach scene. Many comprehensive larger brochures hedge their bets with an amalgam of pictures. Sadly, today no major company appears willing to take risks in its brochure design; like the interiors of brochures, the formats for covers have for the most part become dull and unimaginative, and there is little to make one brochure stand out from its competitors.

Whatever design style is chosen it is wise to ensure that it is relevant to the contents, not merely attractive in itself. Some long-haul companies make their covers so appealing that browsing customers are tempted to take a copy even when they have had no intention of buying anything remotely like the contents.

One aspect of design that should never be forgotten is that most brochures will be displayed in standard racks within travel agencies. This means that their design is to some extent predetermined – company names must appear along the top of the page so that if overlapped by lower racks the name will still appear prominently. As agency racks are now a common size, this means also that all brochures will now conform to the standard A4 to fit.

Design and print

Apart from very small – and often struggling – companies, brochures are no longer designed by amateurs. Increasing professionalism dictates that modern brochures are quality marketing tools, and look like it. Designing a brochure goes beyond merely cobbling together graphics and copy; it incorporates artwork, the ability to recommend and use certain fonts and typefaces in the copy which reflect the company's image, and a flair for what will be both attractive and commercial to the reader. It is a highly skilled art which calls for an understanding of the principal's intentions, and the features and statutory provisions that must be included. This will mean devising straplines (main headings or slogans that will feature on the cover and introductory pages, reflecting the image and product positioning aims of the company) and the subheadings that will be used throughout the copy. While it is now possible for larger companies, with desktop publishing facilities, to produce fine quality designs in-house, many firms prefer to put the work in the hands of a professional design house (often, but not necessarily, associated with the advertising agency used by the company).

The brochure can be printed in *landscape* format (in which the top and bottom sides of the page are longer) or *portrait* format (where the left and right sides of the rectangle are longer, i.e. upright). Because most brochures are designed to fit into standard racks, A4 sized portrait is now the common shape, but companies dealing direct with their customers can choose to be a little different and produce a landscape design. Another consideration is the number of pages that will go to make up the brochure. These will always be in multiples of four, and if incorporating a large number of pages, they will be 'stitched' together, either with staples (rarely with real stitches) or in the case of the very largest operators' offerings, with glue (the word *brochure* derives from the French word for stitching).

The next decision centres on the thickness and type of paper to be used. If there are many pages the company will wish to reduce the weight by using thinner paper. This may need to be compensated for by using a heavier paper for the cover to prevent floppiness. If the brochure contains few pages, then extra weight may be less important and the 'feel' can be improved by using heavier than average paper. Matt finish paper will give a certain style to a well-designed publication, especially if full colour is not to be used. It also offers a more opaque quality – important in avoiding photos or text being seen through the paper. Art finished (shiny) paper is preferable if high quality colour reproduction is critical. Within art paper, the heavier the weight, the better the reproduction and the less the transparency is likely to be. High quality but lightweight art paper tends to be expensive, so there is always a trade-off between weight, price, opacity and quality.

The printing process to be chosen will largely depend upon the number of copies to be printed and the colour requirement. There are almost as many processes as there are paper types, but most modern ones are based upon photographically reproduced images and a lithographic, web offset or gravure machine. Professional advice will determine which form of print is best for the purpose. Much printing is now under-taken abroad, where costs tend to be lower and very high quality is available for long print runs at reasonable prices – although longer lead times must be built in to allow for the dispatch of instructions and the finished brochures which, if transmitted by air, will add to cost substantially.

When it comes to pictures, the base rule is – good quality, to professional standards. Photographs should be high in contrast. Almost without exception, brochures today will incorporate colour, which greatly heightens the appeal of beach scenes, land-scapes and action shots, and this means either buying in suitable photographs from agencies or recruiting professional photographers to take the shots that are needed. Some commercially available scenes have become so synonymous with the destination that almost any shot can start to appear hackneyed – consider the now familiar view of the heavily promoted Guggenheim Museum at Bilbao – and a photo taken from a different angle can give a refreshing new slant on a place.

Text and pricing information can be received on computer disk by the chosen design studio, which produces a *page make-up* for each page. The design elements and photographs are included with the text, though the flexibility exists to leave the correct amount of space for information that will arrive later in the process. At this stage the pages can be checked from black and white computer printouts, which are quick and inexpensive to produce.

After possibly a number of iterations, a page will be approved to proceed to the next stage – the production of printer's films by a repro house. Even more sophisticated equipment is used to arrive at *colour separated film*. The colour printing process is achieved by the use of four basic coloured inks, magenta, yellow, cyan (blue) and black, which can be combined in different quantities to produce all other colours. The four films represent where each coloured ink is to be applied by the plates of the printing press. At this stage, the films may be developed photographically to produce a full colour chromalin proof for checking.

The colour separated films are then used to produce the metal printing plates for the printing press itself. The press is 'made ready', and as initial pages are printed the press is adjusted for final correct colour balance. Only once the press is running true and the colours are approved will the printer proceed to print production copies.

Corrections should be made at initial 'rough' proof stage. Remember that printers correct only their own mistakes free – and, apart from last minute corrections, if the commissioning company decides to change any of the material at this stage it will add to expense and possibly result in delivery delay. Final proofs are usually submitted for approval before the order to print goes ahead. Tight timescales to process all these stages are necessary because long print runs have to be booked on the machines well in advance, and if the booked place is lost through delay, rescheduling can be a problem.

One final point: it is always a good idea to get a quote for the printing of additional copies beyond the number ordered. 'Run-ons' are cheap to produce once a machine is set up for printing, but if extra copies have to be ordered at a later date, the set-up costs for the machine will greatly add to the overall expense.

Accuracy and statutory requirements

For ethical reasons alone – and to avoid later customer dissatisfaction and complaints – it is important that brochures are accurate. But beyond this, there are now very clear statutory requirements that principals ensure the accuracy of their printed material. In Britain a host of legislation, including the Trade Descriptions Act (1968), the Unfair Contract Terms Act (1977), the Consumer Protection Act (1987), the EU Directive on Package Travel (1991) and the consequent Package Travel, Package Holidays and Package Tours Regulations (1992), have all magnified the offence of giving inaccurate information or product descriptions in brochures. Once no more than a misdemeanour (that is, a civil matter which could give rise to claims for compensation), it is now classified as a criminal act which may result in prosecution and punishment. No one would justify knowingly issuing incorrect information, but inattention to detail and careless compilation itself can lead to the creation of a serious offence. Even the justification that one did not have knowledge of a change of circumstances is unacceptable now as a defence. Travel agents and tour operators must demonstrate that they have exercised 'due diligence': in other words, that they have taken all reasonable steps to prevent inaccuracies or other breaches of legislation. In practice, operational procedures must be in place, documented and regularly reviewed in order to convince the courts that due diligence is indeed being exercised.

The implications of the EU legislation are far reaching, as they mean that the tour operator is legally responsible not only for monitoring the accuracy of facts but also for ensuring that 'descriptive matter' should not be misleading. In addition, though the operator has no direct control over suppliers such as hoteliers or car hire companies, the operator is legally responsible should a problem occur with these services if they are part of the package.

The Package Travel, Package Holidays and Package Tours Regulations (1992) mean that the Trading Standards departments within local authorities in Britain now act to enforce these regulations, and consumers may raise complaints through their local Trading Standards Officers.

As well as the duty to provide accurate information, the legislation places a number of other practical demands upon the travel industry, including:

1 Authoritative, reliable and current health formalities and passport and visa requirements must be supplied to the consumer.

2 Information on the travel aspects of the package must be verified and provided in good time to the consumer.

3 Appropriate insurance policies must be brought to the attention of the consumer.

4 A clear statement must be available of the arrangements in the event of insolvency of travel agent or tour operator, the security of prepayments and arrangements for repatriation – and these arrangements must be satisfactory.

Dissatisfied clients who bring a complaint to court under the current regulations can claim substantial damages. All of this makes accuracy a high priority, as the results of mistakes are costly in PR as well as financial terms. British laws now place enormous burdens upon a travel company, resort or promoter of any tourist facility. No longer can they rely upon the previous year's definition or tried and tested photographs in their library without checking that each and every fact is still correct. To take a simple example, the tree that stands in front of a hotel may well have grown until it obscures the promised sea view from some of the bedrooms. An operator could not plead ignorance of this and expect to be excused from responsibility.

The scale of the task for the tour operator is put in perspective by the statistic that each brochure page may contain on average 100–200 facts that must be checked. The three major tour operators between them must therefore verify well over a million individual facts for each summer season. It must also be remembered that much information is supplied from overseas, with the resultant logistics and language problems, and that many details change abruptly over time.

Even after the brochure is printed, the tour operator must continue to monitor that the facts remain true. While the tour operators may use their Viewdata reservations systems and websites to relay corrected information to retailers or consumers, this is not in itself necessarily considered sufficient. Once an error is detected, both operator and agent may have a duty to correct the error by such means as printed erratum slips, brochure stickers, 'shelf talkers' on brochure racks, or even ordering a reprint of the entire brochure. In practice this is rarely the case, as reissues of brochures (reflecting price adjustments) allow regular updating of errors and changes.

One effect of these laws is to make the travel literature less interesting and flamboyant, and more coldly factual – and sadly, less helpful, as operators seek to avoid illustrative prose to describe a facility that may conceivably not be available or where different interpretation is possible. Better to say nothing than be pilloried is the dictum.

Similarly, travel agents are now necessarily wary of keeping and/or handing out resort or country pamphlets, in case they have become obsolete due to a change in circumstances, rendering the agent liable to prosecution for giving wrong information. The acid test must be – is the literature correct, honest and wholly truthful? While the aim of this legislation was clearly to protect the client, it had implications probably not envisaged when the regulations were drawn up.

While all the foregoing legislation is demanding in itself, there is a further level of control exercised over agents and operators. While ABTA's authority as the sole arbiter of conduct for these sectors of the industry has declined in recent years, it continues to play an important role in regulating the sale of its members' travel products in the UK. Members are still obliged to agree to abide by that organisation's guidelines and Codes of Conduct, which offer clear directives, including those relating to information which must be contained in brochures. Sanctions can be imposed on members breaching the code, and in extreme cases membership can be withdrawn.

Segmentation of the market

The most important dilemma which faces large holiday companies is whether to address different parts of the market with separate and distinct brochures and/or brands, or whether to include all products in one massive authoritative publication.

If a company is known for its expertise in providing summer beach holidays, will it be regarded as expert or even competent if it decides to branch out into coach tours, or into city holidays or fly cruises?

There is no doubt that some customers like to deal with those that they feel are able to provide a personal, caring and expert service. Others may believe that financial strength simply brings better value and that buying from a larger concern is preferable.

The larger the brochure is, the more pages are irrelevant to the eventual purchase and the greater is the cost of distribution. By contrast, several smaller brochures each covering merely a segment (perhaps defined by destination, but also possibly by holiday type, price or activity) will not reach so large a group of potential purchasers. Similarly if the company's offerings for a segment are not contained in the brochure picked up, it might be assumed that they do not undertake the type of holiday required, and the booking will be placed with a competitor.

While cost will often dictate policy, it is not the sole criterion. Travel agents typically present some 200–300 racking spaces within their branches. There is an

Table 11.1 The full range of a major tour operator's brochures, 2003:
TUI's Thomson Holidays brand

A la Carte	Portland Winter
All-inclusive	Price Breaks Summer
City Breaks	Price Breaks Winter
Club Freestyle	Skytours Summer Sun
Cruises (Summer)	Skytours Winter Sun
Faraway Shores	Small and Friendly East
Flights	Small and Friendly West
Florida	Sports Resorts
Gold	Summer Sun
Greece	Superfamily
Lakes and Mountains	Thomson Ski
Northern Ireland Summer Sun	Weddings
Northern Ireland Winter Sun	Winter Sun
Platinum	Young at Heart
Portland Summer	

obligation to display the brochures of the most popular (and saleable) operators, and this means that if these operators each produce anything up to 20 different brochures for popular types of holiday – summer sun, winter sports, cruising, lakes and mountains, long-haul, etc. – then four leading operators together can ensure that 80 rack spaces are taken up with their products, squeezing out the competition (see Table 11.1 as an example of the range available from just one operator). Just as with supermarkets, the small to medium-sized operators are finding it more and more difficult to secure rack space in their retailers, partly as a result of the marketing ploys of the leading companies.

Evolution problems

Increasingly, there seems to be a 'sameness' about travel brochures. The brightest creative people pour huge amounts of effort into trying to make a brochure distinctive and especially attractive, yet they know that a new formula will be copied quickly if successful. Statutory requirements have to be satisfied, computer logic has to be obeyed (for the booking form, at least), and cost justifications have to be considered. Consider the case of a small operator who creates an attractive villa and apartment brochure. The company will be proud of the finest properties and will be tempted to give them the most space and best photographic coverage. Initially, this may pay off, and bookings will 'overflow' to the less exceptional properties when the first choice has been sold. Year by year, as the programme becomes more successful, the range of properties will expand. Similarly, and because of the increased number of customers, the number of brochures printed will also grow. Even with economies of scale, the brochure cost per booking will inevitably rise. More importantly, the cost per page in the brochure will need to be related to the goods on sale there. However nice an individual villa may be, there will normally be only one. How much better, it might be thought, for an apartment to be featured, particularly if it is one of many similar apartments, which are less expensive and easier to sell.

One major company with a programme of villas and apartments followed this road until they produced a brochure with a picture of a villa on the front cover, yet featured only apartments inside! Their product lacked distinction and profits slid into oblivion.

Similar problems regularly occur when small allocations of rooms at popular hotels can no longer justify the cost of the brochure space, and they have to be replaced by less interesting, but more substantial, allocations in larger establishments. Owners of the hotels prefer not to be beholden to any one travel company, and soon a variety of competitors are offering much the same holiday. Customers quickly spot price differences, and the company taking the least profit sells out first.

There is also an implication that the company offers better value throughout its brochure. Customers unable to obtain their first choice may prefer to change, in the belief that, if more is to be paid, the 'cheaper company' will offer them greater satisfaction for the small extra charge being demanded, whereas the 'more expensive company' is simply overcharging. In practice, a sophisticated 'switch selling' technique may be taking place with the cheaper company having only a few rooms at the comparative hotel, but many more at hotels that are not being shared.

Whatever pricing policy is followed, the highly competitive nature of the market means that prices are forced down to very low levels of profit. Thus tour operators are faced with a dilemma: either they take on huge commitments to fill hotels that they reserve for themselves and keep as exclusive offers (where they can control margins more easily), or they take small batches of rooms at a selection of hotels shared with others and face keen price competition.

As hotels have grown larger (over 1000 beds is not uncommon) the chance of exclusivity has receded. Unique advantages are more difficult to justify and price has become an ever more important factor in consumer choice. This places even greater emphasis upon the need for the brochure to create an individuality and character for the company and its products – no simple task.

Distributing the brochure

Customers seeking information on travel and tourism have a variety of ways in which to obtain their brochures, many of which have already been discussed. Holiday brochures are still largely collected from travel agencies (although subsequent bookings are not necessarily funnelled through this outlet!) while destination brochures are frequently sent through the mail to customers responding to advertising. All of the following are typical methods of distribution used by the trade to get brochures into the hands of their customers. These methods may be used either to initiate an enquiry for a brochure, or in some cases (*) to distribute the brochure itself:

Method of distribution:	**Appropriate for:**
travel agencies	*tour operators, cruise and ferry companies
door-to-door circulars, newsletters	travel agents, local airport, coaches
tourist information centres	*tourist attractions, destinations, hotels
hotels	*tourist attractions, destinations
websites	all travel principals
magazine inserts, press supplements	all travel principals, especially destinations and tourist attractions
coupons in magazines and newspapers	all travel principals
direct mail	travel agents and principals
exhibitions, trade fairs	*destinations, attractions, operators and transport principals
airports	*airlines, hotels, attractions
travel agents' presentation events	*tour operators and other principals
national or local television/radio	national destinations, large operators, travel agency chains, popular attractions

Travel agencies largely rack only tour operating products in their branches, for reasons of space and commercial interest. In most agencies, the brochure racks will be easily accessible and piled high with the offerings of competing companies. In some, the display may reflect company policy regarding commission agreements, customer satisfaction or simply the manager's personal preference. It is probable that the prime positions, that is at eye level and close to the door, will also reflect the policy adopted (at head office, where chains are concerned).

Ideally, the sales staff will wish to discuss requirements and direct the customer to the most appropriate choice. In practice, this is still the exception rather than the rule, and the customer is likely to be significantly influenced by the attractiveness of the brochure cover itself, or by recognition of the name of the tour operator.

Selection can be extremely subjective. The cover picture may well set the scene for consideration of a brochure. Often, it has little relevance to the contents. Sometimes a specialist company will make their brochure cover so attractive that they run out of brochures early. They may take very few bookings because the contents are not what the customer actually sought, or were relatively expensive, when other more reasonable choices were still available.

Timing distribution

Timing of distribution is also important. The production of a tour operating brochure is a lengthy process, and these must be planned over many months with the assurance that they will be available when the new season of holidays is launched. The leading operators tend to publish their brochures at around the same time of the year (although the exact launch dates have come forward over the past decade), and smaller companies may produce their own brochures after first checking the price leaders' offerings. The tendency in recent years has also been for new editions of leading brochures to be launched quite soon after the initial version, to 'adjust' prices in the light of competition.

Brochure stocks must be in place (and in the hands of the travel agents) before advertising campaigns get under way. Inadequate stock is bad publicity for a company, and consumers are notoriously fickle; having got them into the travel agents to obtain the brochure, they will not leave empty-handed when so many alternatives are available, and many bookings can be lost in this way.

While other principals do not generally have to consider supplying travel agencies, most will need to deliver supplies to intermediaries of some kind, whether TICs, hotels or other customer collection point. The same caveats apply here, and goodwill is lost if the promise of racking cannot be met with the delivery of stocks at the appropriate time.

The brochure at point of sale

Research into the booking process identifies that once a decision to take a package tour has been made, the first call is normally on the travel agent, to collect brochures. Disappointingly, the majority of consumers see little difference between different travel agents, just as they do with tour operators.

Brochure collection is influenced by the factors discussed earlier in this chapter, previous experience, recommendation by friends and by the travel agent. Most frequently it is the impact of the front cover and a very cursory examination to 'get a feel' for the brochure and the types of holidays covered.

The brochures are most often collected by women, who are the chief organisers of holidays. Women also do most of the comprehensive homework when brochures are examined and compared in detail. It is clarity and ease of research that makes a winning brochure in the eyes of most consumers, who can regard the process of drawing up a short list as a time-consuming and onerous task.

The role of the brochure is now reduced as the consumer normally returns to the travel agent to make the booking. The ideal travel agent is seen as a source of extra information above and beyond the brochure (possibly first-hand knowledge), and in particular the agent is expected to be able to advise on the suitability of resorts for the kind of holiday required, such as a family with young children. The travel agent is also there to verify the price, flight details and availability, which are often complex for the consumers to work out for themselves.

The e-brochure

The first task of a travel brochure is to describe a facility being offered. How much better can that be done with movement and greater use of pictures? The development of modern technology is opening up new ways of presenting travel products to the public, and the ability to display moving and still pictures alongside text on a website is beginning to change the long-standing reliance on hard print, in a way that could scarcely be imagined a decade ago. This ability had developed in three stages since the 1990s.

In stage one, the video cassette made it possible for travel companies to commission a variety of video programmes that offered in-depth information about particular holiday areas and types of holiday, with accompanying pictures of hotel interiors and exteriors. This gave consumers a far better impression of a resort and its facilities, and proved a valuable supplement to the brochure. Some travel agencies went as far as to establish libraries of such cassettes that could either be viewed in the shop or taken home on loan so that other members of the household or travel companions could see them.

Valuable as the new medium was, it was an expensive marketing tool for the travel company producing it. In particular, it could not achieve the same economies of scale as the printing process for very large volumes. Production costs were high, and necessitated the shooting of new footage of resorts and hotels where there already existed a vast investment in still photography. Other major flaws in video from the consumer point of view were that it was not interactive, and that the medium made it difficult to skip through a video seeking specific resorts and information, in the way they were accustomed to do with a brochure.

The second stage offered far more versatility. The development of the CD-ROM, which can hold photographic images of every hotel in every ABTA tour operators' programmes for the complete season, resulted in a very powerful promotional tool which could be produced at modest cost. The difficulties inherent in videotape are overcome in using a CD-ROM, which can be viewed by anyone with access to a modern personal computer. The tour operator's investment in existing photography is preserved, as these can be scanned into the computer to be copied onto a CD-ROM disk. Also, the travel agent or consumer accessing information on CD-ROM through the computer is able to find the information instantly, interactively and flexibly.

Example   Tourism Malaysia

The Malaysian Tourist Board cooperated with Malaysian Airlines in a joint campaign in 2003 to promote Malaysia, with the strapline 'A truly unique holiday destination'. A free CD-ROM was attached to copies of the trade paper *Travel Weekly*, distributed to most UK travel agents, as an educational tool and to encourage agents to promote the destination. This was accompanied by selective advertising in the national press, with the additional cooperation of tour operator Travelmood, under the strapline 'Truly luxurious, truly outstanding value' promoting city and beach holidays in the resort and inviting consumers to send away for the same CD-ROM or to seek additional information from Travelmood through their website or by telephone.

A number of operators, including Nouvelles Frontières in France, have introduced CD-ROMs experimentally, and undoubtedly their use will become more widespread over the next few years.

It is equally certain that we shall see the use of DVD recordable disks coming into common use as another tool in the marketing repertoire of brochures in the coming years. However, the CD-ROM has been recently supplemented by the third stage in technological brochure development. This was reached when website providers, prompted by the greatly increased capacity of personal computers, began to add still and moving pictures of their facilities to the sites. This is currently in the process of rapid expansion, and more and more data will become available as the power of PCs expands exponentially. In 2003, Kuoni launched a full-colour e-brochure on its website which allowed agents to download information and pictures of hotels and destinations in which their clients were interested, thus building a personalised brochure. This company is one of several now placing their brochures online, reducing costs and storage for both agents and operators and providing immediate delivery of information to agents and their clients.

Finally, Thomas Cook has experimented with Check-T cards, a system in which clients search for a holiday of their choice on a series of cards generated by computer. Those selected can then be scanned by a bar code reader, and details of the holidays appear on the agent's screen. This also reduces cost and wastage for the agent, who can provide hard copies of the screen data for their customer. This not only cuts the costs of brochure production and wastage, but also opens up the prospect for the sale of holidays and travel through other retail outlets.

Whether these new developments will replace hard print is more difficult to foresee, although most experts believe that they will largely complement rather than replace the hard copy – at least, in the short term. For all their attractiveness, pictures of hotels and destinations, even if printed off and collated into an individual handout, are on the whole less user-friendly than a hard print brochure, which can be easily referred to, searched, and offers a reassuring touch and feel to those taking it home. The reality and symbolic value of the brochure cannot be easily replaced. The real value of electronic marketing is that a search of website pictures can reinforce the decision-making processes of the consumer, making it easier and quicker to sell the end product, thus cutting costs for principals and agents.

However, with the growing tendency towards independence and later bookings, one can see a diminishing role for brochures that attempt to predict customer desires so long in advance. The combination of a database that contains all the flights currently available, and all the accommodation available, accompanied by colour pictures of the facilities, will present the agent with the capability of mixing and matching any options required by a customer. Having achieved the best possible combination of flight, holiday and hotel, the agent can then present the result on a screen for the customer to view, with accompanying pictures. The customer could then be provided with a printout of the information, together with any amendments that have occurred and a photographic print of the hotel.

The implications of these developments are clear. It is but a short step beyond this scenario to recognising that this information could easily be called up on the customer's home television screen, and through interactive booking (already available on satellite television programmes) the customer can book directly with the principal, cutting out the agent entirely. Such a development poses a very real threat to the continued existence of travel retailing, which will survive only if the agent can add value – i.e. expertise and objective advice – to the process of booking direct.

Evaluating the brochure

Attempting to evaluate the likely success of a travel brochure is no easy task – measures do not exist to undertake this as they do with advertising. This is not to say that attempts should be abandoned, and there are some simple checks which will help to ensure that the brochure produced is the best possible for its task. Focus groups can be used in pre-testing, to gather views on the merits of different colours, covers and style, and tests, or later, surveys, can be carried out to check recall of the brochure and its key points. Keeping records of website 'hits' is an easy means of judging how much e-brochures are being viewed, and any distribution of brochures to the public should be coded so that responses, in the form of firm bookings, can be monitored. Larger companies might produce different brochures for different regions of a country or different countries if multinational, and judgements can be made, controlling for other factors, of the relative success of each.

Monitoring of distribution is a vital task. It is all too common to see out-of-date brochures in the racks of hotels – in some cases, these relate to the previous year – and even TICs are not always careful to keep their material updated. It is easy to view one's hard print as no longer the company's responsibility once it has left the office, but once in the public domain, the brochure is the public face of the organisation; out-of-date print reflects badly on the image of the company. Tour operators need to check brochure supplies to their agents, to ensure stock is adequate and that wastage is kept to a minimum. Regular visits by representatives to agency branches will enable the company to know whether their brochures are being prominently displayed and effectively presented. Brochures are increasingly delivered to agencies by 'merchandisers' whose knowledge of the products they are distributing is often limited. This not only misses a sales opportunity, it avoids adequate monitoring of how the brochures are treated once they are in the agent's office. Agents can sometimes be encouraged to offer more prominent display space for brochures if a personal approach is made.

Questions, tasks and issues for discussion

1 Does the advent of the e-brochure spell the end for the traditional brochure? Discuss the case for and against retaining hard print.

2 'A genuinely consumer-orientated brochure would tell the truth about destinations, warts and all.'

Argue in favour of this proposition. Search for a holiday brochure which includes destination(s) with which you are familiar, and judge to what extent the copy is truthful about those destinations. Based on your own experience, what would you add to the text which would render it more truthful and would assist consumers, without dissuading them from booking? How clear is the brochure about the parentage of the brand and retailer? (This is particularly relevant in the case of vertically integrated companies.)

3 Using a selection of current or recent travel brochures, identify which you consider is most effective in:

(a) communicating the brand name, and
(b) standing out against other brochures in an agency rack.

Give reasons for your decision, and offer suggestions as to how the cover could be further improved.

Exercise

Working together in small groups, each member is to select and bring along one current package holiday brochure promoting adventure holidays, and one promoting tailor-made holidays.

Identify which markets the brochures are designed to appeal to, and how successfully they get their messages across, drawing on the points outlined in this chapter.

Which do you consider a winner in its field, based on clarity of layout, accuracy and truthfulness of the text, transparency of pricing (or in the case of tailor-made holidays, of procedures for quoting prices) and overall quality of presentation?

References

1 *The Times*, 23 February 1998
2 Middleton, V T C with Clarke, J, *Marketing in Travel and Tourism*, Butterworth Heinemann, 3rd edn 2001, p 274

Further reading

Middleton, op cit, ch 17

12 Sales promotion for travel and tourism

Learning outcomes

After studying this chapter, you should be able to:

- distinguish between different sales promotion activities
- understand their use in achieving differing objectives
- be aware of the stages in campaign planning for promotions
- understand how to evaluate the effectiveness of campaigns
- appreciate the role of exhibitions, workshops and presentations in the travel industry.

The nature of sales promotion

Sales promotion techniques should be seen first and foremost as aids in building a relationship between organisations and their customers. They should not be viewed merely as a 'quick fix' to unload surplus stock, even where this may be one of the objectives within a promotional campaign. Behind any such campaign there should always be the overall aim of building loyalty and adding value to the product, rather than undermining it.

Sales promotion is a 'below the line activity', as we explained in Chapter 10, while advertising is technically referred to as 'above the line' promotion. However, the division between the two is by no means clear-cut. Window display, for example, is one of the *merchandising techniques* designed to promote products at the point of sale. Although it could be argued that travel agencies' windows are used to advertise products such as current bargain offers for flights and holidays, window display is still generally treated as a form of below the line promotion.

Most members of the travel industry are familiar with advertising and its uses, but are less confident in the use of sales promotion techniques. This is unfortunate, since there are so many forms of sales promotion which can be undertaken, limited only by the imagination of the marketing staff. However, they must be used with caution, since not all sales promotion is suitable for all forms of product.

Sales promotion activities are *attention getters*, since their objective is to achieve immediate sales impact. However, in many instances this is a prelude to building longer-term loyalty, so that objectives may not be focused only on short-term gain. There is also a danger in some promotional techniques that if sales boosts are achieved through money-off or bargain offers, this can have the effect of demeaning the brand and the perceived value of the product, and may suggest that the seller's only interest is to unload surplus stock. Ronnie Corbett's joke that he remembered an event 'because it was the week Allied Carpets were not having a sale' carries an important message for the marketer: that too much emphasis on 'deals' will degrade the product in the consumers' eyes at the same time as it undermines profit levels. This is a lesson which the industry has failed to learn, with discounting remaining the principal promotional tool in all sectors of the business, to a point where 'looking for a bargain' has become for many consumers the first step in making a booking.

When planning promotional strategies, it is best to think of sales promotion as complementary to advertising. In very few instances is it appropriate to use one or the other communications techniques alone in the marketing plan, even though they may serve different objectives. Each has its place in the overall plan. Often, advertising is seen as the main tool to achieve longer-term strategic objectives, such as building the corporate image of the organisation and its products, while sales promotion is principally concerned with tactical objectives such as clearing current stock. In fact, this distinction is too simplistic. A travel agent's window display can help to build a brand identity for the retailer as much as to sell current products. What is important is that the sales promotion and advertising objectives do not conflict, but rather are mutually reinforcing. If, for instance, the advertising objectives aim to create an image of quality and service for the company, this can be undermined by sales promotion objectives focusing on price bargains.

Many sales promotion techniques centre on price deals, designed to appeal particularly to those customers who are price sensitive. Such techniques tend to attract buyers with little brand loyalty. It follows, therefore, that in those areas of travel characterised by brand loyalty, sales promotion will be a useful tool if its aim is to boost sales among the existing clientele, rather than trying to encourage brand switching from competitive companies. In fact, there is little loyalty to brands in most sectors of the industry, but cruise lines and some specialist tour operators are the exception, and can benefit from promotional rewards, such as special offers on board ship (frequent passengers on cruises will be rewarded with seating at the captain's table, to take one example). In fast-moving consumer goods (FMCG) businesses there are powerful sales promotion techniques to encourage brand switching such as free samples to attract trial. With travel there is less opportunity for such techniques (although efforts to sell timeshare apartments in Spain have been accompanied by free trips by air to see the accommodation). We must remember, though, that with less expensive products, in travel as in other businesses, sales promotion using bargain offers can gain many uncommitted consumers. Entrance tickets to theme parks, museums, zoos and similar tourist attractions all make extensive use of discount vouchers to increase their 'gate'.

While part of today's emphasis on sales promotion in the marketing plan arises from overuse of advertising as a communications tool in the past, another factor is the increased competition in the travel industry, which has caused marketing managers to consider more carefully the use of all methods of persuasive communication available to them. Cooperative merchandising between agents and principals, in particular, has been extensively used to increase sales and to generate more agency commission. It also has the attraction of being easily understood and measured in its effectiveness, since it aims for an immediate boost to turnover, while not all advertising is so easily assessed.

Today, given the huge databases accessible to principals and their agents, a substantial amount of information is known about an organisation's customers, including their buying patterns and, in many instances, the likelihood of their responding to particular appeals. This greatly facilitates devising campaigns that will attract different market segments, and help in the underlying aim of sales promotion, that of building customer relationships.

The techniques of sales promotion

Before looking at the various techniques available, it will be helpful to identify all the tools in the sales promotion 'armoury'. These can be categorised as techniques aimed at an organisation's own staff, such as sales representatives or counter sales staff, those directed at intermediaries such as travel agents, and those directed at consumers themselves.

The list that follows is not intended to be exhaustive (there are many hundreds of sales promotion techniques, and not all are pertinent to selling an intangible product) but it will cover those more commonly used within this industry.

Promotions directed at a company's staff:

■ incentives (financial, travel, etc.) including exotic conference locations

■ bonuses for targets achieved or other performance

■ contests and competitions

■ familiarisation trips

■ free gifts.

Promotions directed at dealers or retailers:

■ 'giveaways' (pens, ashtrays, calendars, diaries, etc., usually bearing the principal's name)

■ contests

■ trade shows

■ product/brochure launches (presentations, buffets, etc.)

■ direct mail (letters, circulars, etc.)

■ joint promotion schemes (financial, organisational help)

■ familiarisation trips

- discounted travel
- training packages.

Promotions directed at consumers (either through retailers or direct):

- point of sale (POS*) material (window display, wall display, posters, counter cards, special brochure racks, etc.)
- sales literature and print
- direct mail
- free samples
- 'giveaways' (e.g. flight bags) and 'self-liquidating offers' (products promoting the company's name, and sold at cost price by the company)
- competitions
- low-interest financing
- money-off vouchers
- purchase privilege plans (e.g. 'twofers', whereby two are charged the price of one for entrance)
- joint promotions with non-travel companies (e.g. cheap weekends in a major city through the collection of washing powder vouchers)
- loyalty bonuses (e.g. airline Frequent Flyer programmes, or accumulating 'honoured guest' points for frequent hotel stays).

* also known as point of purchase (POP)

It will be appreciated from a glance at this list that the scope for new ideas in sales promotion is almost unlimited. Travel companies offer a huge range of giveaways to their clients, including flight bags, carrier bags, wallets for tickets and foreign exchange, and passport covers. Hotels offer a steadily increasing range of useful facilities to their guests, including shoeshine cloths, 'first aid' sewing kits, shower caps and shampoo. Additionally, important clients might receive fruit, wine, flowers and/or chocolates in their room. Many hotels deliver a single chocolate on the pillow when making up beds.

Quite apart from these examples, under the single category of print one can add numerous forms of promotional print quite distinct from the brochures discussed in the previous chapter. Most principals produce in-house magazines, some of which solicit advertising: airline magazines found in the seat backs of aircraft are important selling tools as well as dispensers of information about safety features, fleet details and destinations served. Hotels promote their restaurants in their lifts, and the restaurants themselves will have tent cards on the table, perhaps promoting recommended wines or special offers. Hotel rooms have notices drawing attention to the hotel's environmental policies, appealing to the environmentally aware guest. Visitor attractions such as stately homes and national museums will often give out with their entry tickets a short pamphlet describing the attraction and including a plan of the building to help visitors find their way around. Even the letterhead paper and envelopes used by an organisation help reinforce the brand identity.

Figure 12.1
Effective
'reminder'
promotion:
Jersey Tourism's
travel agent gift,
to take a mobile
phone (website
features
strongly)

(Courtesy: Jersey Tourism)

While many of these promotional tools are designed to do no more than create goodwill among clients and provide a sense of *added value* to the product, they will often also have an underlying purpose: that of ensuring the company or its products are remembered. Therefore the more exposure received by the item, the greater the impact. One of the most successful promotions in this respect was a giveaway presented to travel agents which was considered attractive or useful enough to be put on display in the office (see Figure 12.1). Ashtrays, paperweights and calendars also serve this purpose very well. Lists of useful telephone numbers which agents might want to keep in sight next to their desks will ensure that the principal's name is kept prominently displayed throughout the year, and aid recall. Such sales promotion aids serve similar purposes to advertising: they can be used to remind, to inform and to persuade customers to buy and retailers to sell.

Where the product is sold through retailers, the marketing manager can adopt one of two courses of action. One method is to aim the promotion at the consumer directly, in order to build brand awareness and create a demand that will pull people into the shops to buy the product. Readers were introduced to this technique in an earlier chapter as *pull strategy*, with the customer pulled into the shop by the effects of the promotion. In effect, to a considerable extent the client is pre-sold. Retailers will be persuaded to stock or sell the product simply by reason of demand. In the second method, sales promotion is geared to merchandising activities, which are designed to encourage retailers to stock the product and help them to sell it. This is termed *push strategy*, with promotion aimed to attract customer sales at the point of sale.

A new tour operator seeking to develop a market is unlikely to be able to afford the national advertising which a pull strategy would call for, but could successfully develop a push strategy by selecting key retailers and helping them, through 50/50 joint promotional expenditure, to sell to their customers. Another recent example is that of Tourism Malaysia, which has introduced a points system for its specialist agencies. Points are awarded as agents make bookings, for which rewards such as familiarisation trips are offered. Top-selling agents are listed on Tourism Malaysia's website as specialists in the destination.

Cooperative promotions with non-travel companies are also proving a popular way of reaching the travelling public. Travel can be offered as an incentive to purchase other goods or services, or consumer durables can be offered to those booking holidays. Specially priced package tours have been offered as incentives to purchase a variety of FMCGs, and railway companies frequently team up with retailers or manufacturers of household goods to provide free rail travel against in-store purchases. Hoteliers have promoted short-break holidays in this way, too, while other examples of successful joint promotions include cross-Channel ferry companies liaising with manufacturers of alcoholic drinks. Vouchers, redeemable for travel arrangements, have been successfully used as staff incentives in many large companies, particularly as rewards for the achievement of sales targets. Travel has been found to be a greater incentive than straight financial compensation, in motivating staff.

Price is still the most popular form of promotional technique used in travel. Thomas Cook, for instance, ran a promotion which offered three forms of sales promotion based on price, and one more novel technique:

- *price promise*: Cooks agreed to match the price of any holidays they sold which could be purchased more cheaply elsewhere
- *trading charter*: a money-back guarantee to Cooks' clients who purchased the products of any tour operator which failed
- *formal guarantee*: Cooks guaranteed to match their customers' need with an appropriate holiday
- *business travel challenge*: companies were encouraged to submit to Cooks details of their expenditure on staff business travel booked through other agents over a three-month period. Cooks then undertook to estimate what savings could have been achieved had the bookings been made through them.

Planning the sales promotion

As with any marketing activity, the establishment of a promotional campaign requires careful advance planning. The stages by which such planning is undertaken is found in Figure 12.2.

We must be clear what our objectives are before we prepare the programme. It is not sufficient to define these in the broadest terms, such as 'increase our winter sports programme sales by 10 per cent'. We need to identify our target market – indicating whether our objective is to attract new buyers or to increase sales to current buyers, for instance, since different approaches will be called for in each case.

The targets will be either the organisation's own sales force, its retail agents, or the consumers themselves, depending on whether a push or pull strategy is determined upon. It may increase effectiveness if the campaign tackles more than one of these targets simultaneously in the promotional plan.

Before considering what methods to use to influence the target markets, the company should be in possession of as many facts as possible which might affect the decision. The question of the product itself, its nature and quality must be considered. If the image of the product has always been one of quality, what form should the promotion take that will not demean it in the eyes of its audience? A promotion undertaken jointly with a company that markets a well-established premium product (executive car, upmarket alcoholic drink) will enhance the image of the travel company. However, all companies like to believe that theirs is a quality product. It is important that the company first identifies through research what image the firm actually enjoys.

Strategically, it can be useful to take into account the forms of sales promotion which the firm's competitors employ. It may be thought desirable to compete head-on with a competitor by emulating the methods they have used to attract new business, while in other cases it might be better to distance the product from its competitors by deliberately introducing a very different form of promotional strategy.

Figure 12.2
Stages in the organisation of a sales promotion campaign

Strategies will vary according to both the nature of the product and the stage in the product life cycle (PLC). At the launch stage, it will be the intention to build awareness of the new product, and this is best achieved in the case of travel by focusing on advertising and public relations activities, supported by a smaller proportion of the budget spent on sales promotion. This could entail direct mailings to key addresses, or incentives to retailers. A new museum may have different artefacts on display, but to many potential visitors it may be seen as just another museum, and it will be competing for business from local holidaymakers with all other museums and attractions in the area. Local advertising can be used to draw attention to the product, while cooperative voucher schemes may be introduced to provide discounts for entry to two or more attractions.

As markets for products become saturated in later stages of the PLC, promotional stimuli may have to be increased to draw second- or third-time visitors, pending product innovation. The use of 'twofer' tickets to increase sales in theatres towards the end of a show's life cycle is an example of a promotion used to boost sales. With the excellent databases now available to most large firms, it is common to send out brochures and direct mail letters to previous passengers for a period of several years, to encourage further bookings. Cunard Line automatically registers its previous passengers in its World Club, and its mailings include discounted travel opportunities.

As with all forms of communication, decisions on the selection of techniques will be based on which combination of these can be best expected to achieve the desired objectives in the most cost-effective manner. If a money-off deal is being considered for a tourist attraction, marketing staff must decide how many of these discounted tickets are to be offered, and to whom, at what reduction in normal price. Means must be sought of ensuring that those willing to pay full price will not be seduced into paying lower entry prices, and the total cost of the programme and increase in revenue expected must be estimated. The programme cost will be not only the loss in normal entrance price, but also the cost of communicating the offer to the public. Against this, one must weigh the benefits of increased entry numbers, and probable increased spend on facilities at the attraction. The final figure must then be compared with other promotional techniques under consideration, to judge the best package.

Liaising with the operations departments to ensure sufficient stocks to meet demand is another simple precaution when preparing a campaign. One must be able to judge approximately what levels of demand will be generated by the promotion, and ensure that these can be satisfied.

Example   Eurostar

The *Evening Standard* newspaper and Eurostar ran a joint promotion offering cheap rail travel to Paris, Brussels and Lille from London. Big discounts were offered for booking via the website, and the conditions included a very limited booking period. Demand proved so great that lines were swamped and the website collapsed. The associated call centre was overwhelmed. Many potential customers were lost, and regular customers who had not been offered similar opportunities were offended.

Timing is all-important when setting up the programme. A decision must be taken on when to start the campaign, how long it is to last, and exactly how it is to be delivered. There must be sufficient *lead time* (time available) to introduce the programme, which in some forms of promotion (such as cooperative ventures involving on-pack coupons in consumer goods) can take months of planning. If the duration of the campaign is too short, there may not be time for it to become effective, while if it is allowed to run for too long, it not only loses its impact, but also may affect the company's image and annual profitability.

Each promotion is developed within the context of the overall promotional mix, so that the timescale and activities tie in with any other communications activities. A major promotional campaign may include advertising support, sales calls on intermediaries or customers by sales representatives, and publicity (an innovative campaign could, for example, get coverage in the trade press, or even local press).

Legal aspects

An essential part in planning any form of promotion that involves a competition or prize draw is to ensure that the promotion is legal. There are fewer legal constraints in promotional activities in the UK than in many other EU countries, and partly for this reason such activities have blossomed in Britain. However, there are still laws to which organisations must adhere. The Lotteries and Amusements Act (1976) spells out many of these conditions. One key condition is that entry to a lottery or prize draw cannot be restricted only to those consumers who order goods. This does not apply, however, to a competition.

The Advertising Standards Authority publishes a Code of Practice to guide marketers in the preparation of a sales promotion and the advertising material that supports it. This covers such aspects as the rules which should always be printed on prize draw and competition entries, and the terms and conditions which should be printed on vouchers. The size and design of money-off or discount vouchers are also covered by the guidelines.

Administration

Meticulous planning will take into account the administration and resources involved in the sales promotion. What is often forgotten is that even relatively simple promotions may generate a significant administration workload. A sales promotion may involve any or all of the following overheads:

- the cost of staff time, e.g. spending several days at an exhibition
- the need to have systems to cope with the logistics of the promotion itself, e.g. checking hundreds of competition entries or issuing vouchers to those qualifying
- the need to provide sufficiently rigorous checks to prevent fraud and financial errors, e.g. invalid use of vouchers
- the need to monitor redemption rates or other measures of take-up.

As with other forms of communication, there are agencies with specialist knowledge and resources who can be employed to help a company mount a sales promotion.

Evaluating the impact of promotion

Evaluation is the final stage in preparing the promotional campaign. Particularly if the campaign is to operate on a large scale and involve substantial investment, it is wise to test its effectiveness in advance, wherever that is possible. Market research can be used to question a cross-section of a potential market on the sensitivity towards different prices for a product, or the degree of preference between money-off offers and other forms of promotion. The following could represent the line of questioning to be employed:

1 *How willing would you be to purchase a ticket to this attraction at a price of £5.50?*

   very willing   ☐
   quite willing   ☐
   uncertain   ☐
   quite unwilling   ☐
   very unwilling   ☐

2 *If this ticket were to be made available at a discount, how likely would you be to buy it at a price of . . .*

	£5.00	£4.50	£4.00
very likely	☐	☐	☐
quite likely	☐	☐	☐
uncertain	☐	☐	☐
quite unlikely	☐	☐	☐
very unlikely	☐	☐	☐

3 *If you were planning to visit this attraction, with a regular entrance price of £5.50, would you rather have the offer of:*

   (a) *a discount of £2.50, or*
   (b) *a second ticket free, to use either for yourself for a return visit, or for a friend or relative to accompany you?*

   discount   ☐
   second ticket free   ☐
   both equally suitable ☐
   don't know   ☐

An alternative to this form of research is to conduct an experiment with different forms of sales promotion for a limited time, to judge which is the most effective. A direct mailing, circulation of brochures to local hotels with money-off vouchers, and an advertisement in a local paper carrying a money-off coupon could each be judged for effectiveness over a given period of time, prior to a full-scale launch. One must take care, however, that other factors do not account for any change experienced in turnover. Where possible, these activities in 'experimental areas' are compared with the results in 'control areas', regions where no campaigns have been mounted, since sales increases may be the result of factors other than the promotion itself. If the increase in turnover is proportionate in all regions, the effect of the campaign itself is likely to have been minimal.

Once the campaign is concluded, monitoring the degree of success or otherwise is the final step. There are a number of ways in which the effectiveness of an organisation's sales promotion efforts can be judged. It is, of course, relatively simple to measure the effectiveness of money-off offers where these are given against vouchers or coupons clipped from advertisements, returned from direct mailshots or redeemed following any other form of distribution. Equally, competitions for consumers or for retailers can be judged from the numbers of entries they attract. Most sales promotions of this kind are designed to generate immediate sales and are judged in those terms. A comparison is then made between the level of sales achieved before the promotion and after it. However, the objective may have been to 'clear current stock' (i.e. to sell off unsold holidays) which may not increase the overall level of sales. Reduced price offers may simply encourage early booking by clients who would have been prepared to pay normal prices later in the year, rather than attracting new customers who would not otherwise have booked a holiday. If the intention was to clear unsold stock in this way, all well and good; but if this unwittingly leads to a slump in later sales and overall reduction in turnover, the campaign can hardly be deemed to have been successful. This is illustrated in Figure 12.3. A return to sales at level 2 following the promotion will be satisfactory, since the promotion will have had the effect of increasing sales during the period of the campaign without subsequent losses. But the company may have aimed to attract a larger market through increased awareness, with resulting sales at level 3. If the actual result is a fall to level 1 for the balance of the season, the campaign's objectives will not have been realised.

However, sales promotion should not be judged only in terms of its success at generating sales in the short term, and its success in achieving other objectives should be likewise measured. Let us take the example of a travel agency window display – an area of unrealised potential for many agents. If it is designed to bring people into the shop to purchase a holiday, a simple count of enquiries and bookings resulting from the products on display is easy to keep. But a window is also designed to attract passers-by to notice and remember the agency and what it sells. It is rarely tested for its effectiveness in achieving this, however. An hour spent observing passers-by and their

Figure 12.3
Sales resulting from a sales promotion campaign at a tourist attraction

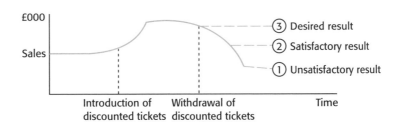

behaviour in front of the window can be illuminating. How many of those passing glance at the window? How many actually stop to take in the contents? What are they actually looking at in the window: bargain offers or special displays for long-haul travel?

Surveys can be carried out locally, before and after campaigns, to measure increases in awareness of the agency, or changes in the company's perceived image. In the same way, visitors to a tourist attraction can be questioned on leaving, so that patterns of purchase behaviour can be compared between those who took advantage of a promotional offer and those who did not.

Unfortunately, not all promotions lend themselves to easy means of measurement. Dealer or consumer 'giveaways' are designed to build long-term goodwill and recognition, and their impact is much harder to assess. Finally, it should be borne in mind that the best way to evaluate any tactic is to see how it compares with other sales promotions in its effects. A business must experiment over time with different forms of promotions and learn to judge which seems to work most effectively. Any one technique employed continuously, however, will pall, and a variation in the tactics employed is likely to have greatest impact.

At this point, we shall look at some of the more common methods of sales promotion in use in the travel industry.

Exhibitions and trade fairs

Exhibitions and trade fairs play an important role in the travel industry, providing opportunities for buyers and sellers of travel products to meet and do business. Some, like the World Travel Market (WTM) in London, and the International Tourism Exchange in Berlin, have become of international significance.

Three types of exhibitions can be identified:

■ those aimed at the public
■ those aimed at the trade
■ those which are private, and to which entrance is gained by invitation only.

Some trade shows are also open to the public only on certain days, so that serious trade buyers can visit the fair on days closed to the public, to conduct their business. Events such as the WTM, which is open only to the trade, feature prominently in the travel trade calendar, and their function is as much social as commercial, giving members of the industry an opportunity to see and be seen. Few major companies can afford not to be represented at the show, which covers all sectors of the trade: incoming, domestic and outbound tourism. Retail agents have the chance to enhance their product knowledge, while it provides national and local tourist offices with a rare opportunity to demonstrate publicly their product, the country or region they represent, through the medium of film, wine tasting, national costume, ethnic dancing and other forms of entertainment. The importance of the show will also ensure that it receives a good press coverage. However, it is undoubtedly the opportunities for personal contact that the trade welcomes most. Often, trade symposia or meetings will be organised to discuss current topics of interest, running concurrently with the exhibition, to take advantage of the presence of so many key figures in the industry.

Against these benefits, however, it has to be said that exhibitions are costly to stage, and to participate in. In addition to rental costs based on the floor area occupied by stands, there are stand design and construction costs, set-up costs for equipment, hospitality and literature costs, and other incidentals to be considered. The competition for status among larger companies means renting larger stands than are strictly needed, often in the most prominent sites, for which premium prices can be commanded by the organisers. Sales staff are tied up while participating in the show, and other marketing staff must be employed in planning and organising the event (a major show can involve year-round planning). In spite of all the planning, attendance figures can disappoint at many unproven travel exhibitions, while even with a good attendance it is not always easy to measure benefits against costs. For this reason, participants may well treat the event as a public relations exercise rather than a sales promotion.

The marketing objective is to make any such ventures as cost-effective as possible. Every attempt should be made to weigh up the cost of reaching and influencing consumers through the medium of the exhibition compared with other means. Participants should obtain in advance an analysis of attendance figures for previous years or audience survey data if published. New exhibitions may be able to provide only calculated guesswork about attendance expectation, which is often wildly optimistic. Some estimate should also be made about the proportion of the audience likely to be interested in visiting a particular stand (something approaching 40 per cent is the audience interest factor for national exhibitions) and an estimate can be made of the cost of reaching that market compared with attempts to communicate with them through other marketing techniques.

An average salesperson can deal with 12–15 enquiries in an hour, and each salesperson will need about 50 sq ft (approx. 5 sq metres) to accommodate visitors. An estimate of the size of the stand can then be made, based on the number of sales staff required to answer enquiries and the space required for display material. This does provide a rule of thumb for the space to be rented, although taking no account of the demands for 'space status' for individual companies. A small cubicle for dealing privately with important visitors to the stand is also recommended.

Some preliminary planning can help to ensure a successful exhibition stand. It is not sufficient merely to staff the stand. Those working on the stand should be well versed in the firm's products, well trained in sales techniques and equally at home dealing with clients and with trade enquiries. Good clients of the company could be sent advance tickets and a map of the exhibition and stand. Adequate supplies of literature should be available, but some control should be exercised over their distribution to ensure brochures are taken by people with a genuine interest in the product rather than children with an avid interest in collecting anything on display! All visitors to the stand should be welcomed, and an attempt made to explore their interests. Potential sales leads should be recorded on stand cards or in a visitors' book for subsequent follow-up. One must never lose sight of the principal purpose of the exhibition, which is to sell travel.

The travel workshop

The travel workshop deserves a separate mention here, due to its importance in this particular industry. Strictly speaking, this is not a trade 'fair', but purely a forum for trade buyers and sellers of travel products to come together and negotiate business. British travel workshops are often organised under the sponsorship of the National Tourist Boards, with venues in the UK and overseas, in centres wherever there are sufficient numbers of prospective tourists to Britain. Typical sites for BTA workshops would include New York, Chicago, Los Angeles, Sydney and Frankfurt. Some workshops have particular themes such as coaching holidays, or a regional emphasis, such as tourism in south-west England. Suppliers with an interest in incoming tourists, such as hoteliers, coach companies and ground handling agents, arrange to rent desk space in the workshop, which normally runs for between one and three days. Tour operators and others from the tourist-generating countries can in this way conveniently meet their suppliers of tourism services under one roof (often without having to travel far from their own home territory) and can negotiate with them for the following season's tour programme requirements – beds, transfer services, excursion programmes, etc. This is one of the most cost-effective means of organising the production of package tours.

Making trade presentations

A presentation may be defined as an 'act of introducing or bringing to notice'. The presentation is widely used in the travel industry to introduce a company's programme to retail travel agents, although these in turn can run their own presentations for clients, to bring a particular range of holidays to the public's notice. The major tour operators generally organise presentations to agents throughout the country when launching their new programme of holidays for the year.

This will typically take the form of a reception, perhaps a buffet meal, and a formal talk about the new programme or product, given by senior members of the sales force. The approach is typically low key, since it is aimed at young agency counter staff, and the emphasis is on personal contact and a 'fun evening', although it also provides an excellent opportunity for sales staff of the principal to meet agency counter staff at first hand and obtain feedback about the market.

Effective presentations call for good visual promotion: flip charts, overhead projectors or other forms of instructional aids should be used to accompany the formal talk, and it is customary to demonstrate the product with videos, a tape-slide presentation or film. The largest principals mount highly impressive shows, usually in half a dozen or more different centres around the UK, using a tape-slice dissolve unit (or multi-dissolve unit), stereo sound, stroboscopic lights or even laser beams. This can at times mean a promotional budget running into thousands of pounds.

Planning and organising consumer presentations

If a presentation is being made to potential consumers, the aim will be both to generate direct bookings and to build goodwill among the clientele, or potential clientele, of the company. It is therefore well worth taking a little effort with the planning and organisation of the event, to maximise the prospects of its success.

First, the venue and date for presentation must be carefully chosen. Even with the best intentions and with good decorative effects, the local hall can be a depressing venue for such an event, and this can reflect on the image of the company. Better a conference room at a good quality hotel or at a purpose-built conference centre, which will be comfortable, well decorated and geared to meet the company's requirements. Arrangements for booking these facilities have to be made well in advance to ensure their availability. The company should also make sure there are adequate parking facilities and good public transport to the venue.

An evening meeting will attract more people than a daytime event, especially if the aim is to attract working people to a public presentation. Couples usually consult each other in the arrangement of holiday bookings, so the sale must be made to both partners. Wherever possible, dates should avoid any clashes with local or national events. For example, a presentation designed to attract the public would be unlikely to succeed if it is scheduled to occur at the time of the World Cup Final or the Grand Finale of a television drama series.

Entry should always be by ticket invitation, to control numbers (this is vital where food and drink have been laid on) and tickets should be checked at the door. Announcements of the event can be made through a direct mailing to clients, and an invitation in the local paper to others to apply for tickets (with the possible chance of arranging some editorial coverage in the paper alongside your advertisement).

It is advisable to ask people to reply or to book their place so that the company can anticipate numbers attending. One should always expect a 'drop-out' rate of people who say they will attend and then do not turn up. The drop-out rate can be reduced by a courtesy phone call a week before the event, confirming that they still intend to come. People will feel more committed if they feel that they are personally expected.

The formal presentation should be prepared and rehearsed in advance. Not only will this allow speakers to be more relaxed and to speak more fluently, it also gives them an opportunity to time the speech and judge whether it is the right length.

A presentation should follow the general guidelines for other forms of communication:

- gain attention
- generate interest
- build desire
- end with emphasis on the action the company wishes its audience to take.

An event and personal presentation gives the speaker the opportunity to express the values associated with the company's service: specialist, caring, quality, family oriented, or whatever.

If drinks are to be served, it is sensible to provide not more than one glass before the formal proceedings of the event, if an attentive and receptive audience is desired.

Where a film or video is also to be shown, it is advisable to run not more than two films, with a total running time not exceeding about 20 minutes; the span of attention of presentation audiences is limited, however good the film. Whoever is responsible for giving the presentation should ensure that they have seen the film in advance, and that the right one has been delivered. All mechanical and electrical equipment should be in good working order, but it still makes good sense to carry spare parts that might be useful – adaptor plugs, new bulbs for overhead projectors (OHPs) and slide carousels, etc. – especially if there is any doubt about the reliability of the venue itself to cater for such emergencies. Arrangements must be agreed in advance for lighting controls, with someone present to help dim the lights as needed.

Presenter and staff should be at the venue well in advance of the start, to allow ample time to check on, or arrange for, directional signs, and to ensure that the room is decorated with appropriate travel material. A 'publicity pack' of travel material should be placed on each seat in the auditorium. Adequate cloakroom and toilet facilities must be available near to the auditorium, and clearly signposted.

All members of staff present should have name badges, with first name *and* surname (a customer may want to write to you one day). However, some people may prefer not to display their surname, because of the potential personal security risks. When guests arrive, they should be greeted by a member of staff and given a drink to help 'break the ice'; background music can be useful as an ice-breaker or mood-setter when people arrive and mingle, especially in a large gathering. Sufficient staff should be on hand to cope with the expected number of attendees. This is not just to smooth administration; organising promotional presentations takes skill, an eye to detail, and the ability to keep calm when under pressure. The team will have worked hard to get people to come, and must now exploit the promotional opportunity to the full. It is important to establish personal contact with as many attendees as possible.

Where the objective is to encourage sales, the company should make it as easy as possible to complete a booking. Sales desks can be available and staffed after the presentation to deal with further enquiries. Prepaid reply cards can be inserted in the publicity packs for more information. It is also a good idea to follow up on some or all attendees with a personal phone call, e-mail communication or letter afterwards.

Above all, one should exploit whatever opportunities arise for publicity associated with the event. Photographs can be taken during the evening, and sent to the local or trade press with a covering press release, which may gain a few valuable column inches in the local press (especially if local personalities are invited to the event).

The cost of events of this kind can be reduced for smaller companies such as travel agents by linking together with other SMEs to make a joint presentation. Many tour operators are willing to pay 50 per cent of the costs of mounting an agency presentation to the public, if they are convinced that it will be productive, and they may also contribute staff to talk at the event. However, they may wish to ensure that only their company is represented at the event, so the agent will be wiser to focus on a single principal's products, if seeking support. On the other hand, where a destination is to be promoted, the national tourist board of the country, or a carrier operating to the country, may be willing to support an agent in a joint promotion. Such sharing of costs will ensure that the promotional budget is stretched to gain maximum cost-effectiveness.

Questions, tasks and issues for discussion

1 T-shirts are often used as a medium to promote a message for travel companies. Identify two or three T-shirt campaigns which have caught your imagination, and explain why you think they are good at getting their message across.

Students of tourism and hospitality are often invited by their tutors to conjure up imaginative slogans for T-shirts to promote their courses/departments/institutions. Perhaps two of the most imaginative – and suitably ambiguous – slogans to catch the eye of this author were those produced by a group of hotel management students in the USA:

'One day you'll pay to sleep with me'
'XXXXX University students do it on all floors'

You will doubtless agree that these are the equal of anything produced professionally!

Now create and design a T-shirt slogan yourself, either for the course which you are following or for the company/organisation for whom you work. Clearly identify your objectives, spelling out why you think it will be successful.

2 The range of accessories available from one supplier which can be personalised to carry the name of the principal includes: address books, attaché cases, bottle openers, business card files, calculators, calendars, clocks, cocktail trays, conference folders, cutlery, desk diaries, flight bags, leatherware (purses, wallets, etc.), lighters, magnifiers, paperweights, pens, pencils, pen watches, rulers, silver trays, tankards, tape measures, ties and umbrellas.

Discuss the merits of these different 'giveaways', and suggest which you would adopt if you were responsible for promotions in a tour operating company.

3 Study different brochure racks in local travel agencies (there are many different designs in use). Describe how they differ in function and in customer appeal. Which do you think is best, and why?

4 Which is it better to spend a limited promotional budget on: sales promotion activities or advertising? Justify your decision.

5 'Domestic marketing by the public sector does not add value to UK plc. Local government and regional tourist board promotional spending on their own narrow tourism product is wasteful and, at best, merely moves tourism spending from one area of Britain to another.' Andrew Grieve, Managing Director, Discover Britain.

Is he right? And if he is, can such promotional spend still be justified?

Exercise

In summer 2001, the British Tourism Authority sponsored a 'Britfest' event in Hamburg, promoting Britain through an exhibition which took over the historic town hall marketplace for five days. Among the exhibitors were to be found stands promoting:

- an Indian restaurant
- Moroccan mocca coffee
- Tchibo (German) coffee
- Gröninger Pils beer
- Mediterranean olives
- a German Bierstube selling fruit wines
- sauerkraut and frankfurters
- Chinese musicians

The one truly British stand – a fish and chips stall – was inadequately staffed, resulting at one time in a queue running the entire length of the marketplace – perhaps an attempt to recreate a true image of life in Britain? Also to be found within the grounds was a plentiful supply of fake Beefeaters, plastic galleons occupied by pirates in medieval clothing, 'celtic' silver – and the inevitable morris dancers. Yet, arguably, Hamburg represents one of the most sophisticated markets for tourism to Britain.

What do you believe should be the aim of a 'Britfest'?

- to portray Britain as it is, or as the British believe it should be?
- to portray Britain as the British *think* the Germans see it?
- to portray Britain as the British *wish* the Germans to perceive it?
- to portray anything vaguely related to Britain as long as someone is willing to sponsor a stand?

Determine your own aims, as an organiser of a Britfest, and suggest what you would wish to be included and whom you would invite to participate.

Further reading

Gold, J and Ward, S (eds), *Place Promotion: the Use of Publicity and Marketing to Sell Towns and Regions*, Wiley, 1994, pp 39–52

Lovelock, C, Vandermerwe, S and Lewis, B, *Services Marketing: a European Perspective*, Prentice Hall, Harlow, 1999, ch 6 pp 188–90

13 Direct marketing: theory and practice

Learning outcomes

After studying this chapter, you should be able to:

- identify and distinguish between the various forms of direct marketing
- be aware of the growing importance of, and opportunities for, direct marketing generated by ICT
- recognise the benefits to customers and principals which direct marketing offers over other forms of marketing communication
- understand, through the application of basic principles, and drawing on examples of successful techniques used in the industry, how each form of direct marketing can be successfully applied
- be capable of mounting a successful direct mail campaign.

What is direct marketing?

All marketing activity by a principal is ultimately designed to influence the consumer. This can be achieved in two ways: indirectly, through an intermediary, such as a travel agent in the case of travel products; or directly, through direct communication between principals and their customers. Whatever the product being marketed, the better known brands depend heavily on traditional retailing channels for product purchase. Kellogg create a demand for their cornflakes through television advertising, but they do not feel it necessary to tell you where you can purchase your next packet.

Direct marketing is defined as 'direct communication with carefully targeted individual customers to obtain an immediate response and cultivate lasting customer relationships'.[1] In this sense, it is distinguished from other forms of marketing which, apart from personal selling, depend upon mass communications to reach customers. The key here is the ability, using these techniques, to target individuals so that their needs can be matched with products available, enhancing customer satisfaction.

The concept is scarcely new; direct mail activities have been undertaken for many years, as has selling from catalogues, where customers can choose products in the privacy of their own home and order items direct from the company. Mailing lists were bought and sold, or composed from electoral registers, so that letters could be sent to carefully chosen targets, with offers that could be expected to appeal to recipients. Even selling by telephone has been a well-established technique in direct marketing for some time, although the methods employed today are infinitely more sophisticated than one could have anticipated a few years ago. All these techniques continue in use: but what has radically transformed direct marketing has been the growth of ICT, and in particular the Internet, which offers customers and organisations benefits unimagined by earlier generations of marketers. Above all, this new medium has aided the creation of sophisticated databases to manage customer relations to an extent never previously possible.

Example   Thomas Cook

Thomas Cook Direct has claimed savings of 23 per cent after refocusing its activities on 'best prospects' – those identified after analysing their behaviour and lifestyles as most likely to rebook. These represented 6 per cent of their customer database, and by targeting these, the company's revenue was increased by 18 per cent. The balance of the organisation's customers now receive only limited and low-cost direct mailings.

Direct marketing means interactive marketing, two-way communication between the organisation and its clients, allowing immediate and direct responses to promotion.

It is convenient to divide direct marketing techniques into two distinct categories, the now traditional, and the more recently developed. We will examine the former first, and identify ways in which these have been updated in recent practice.

The most common techniques in use are:

■ mail order catalogues or lists
■ direct response advertising
■ direct mail
■ telephone selling.

Mail order

Mail order marketing generally makes use of catalogues from which consumers can order products direct, either through the mail or in some cases through direct outlets of the company. An extension of this form of marketing is *party selling*, for example Tupperware kitchenware was originally sold in the USA through a social gathering in the representative's or a friend's home, using catalogues and/or direct demonstration of the product. Ann Summers' 'intimate' products are now sold in the same way in Britain.

The holiday brochure of the direct sell tour operator is, in essence, little different from any other mail order catalogue. As such its design tends to share the characteristics of all such catalogues. The technique has been updated with the development of the web-based catalogue, although this is still in the early stages of development at the time of writing. However, this already offers many advantages not shared with the more traditional hard print catalogue. In particular, it offers the opportunity for immediate response from the customer, and for immediate updating as product availability changes. Inevitably, this form of catalogue can be expected to displace the hard print version to a large extent in coming years.

Direct response advertising

Direct response advertising involves placing advertisements in the media which encourage consumers to reply direct to the supplier, often using a suitable coupon clipped from a newspaper or magazine advertisement. As these coupons can be coded according to the publication in which the advertisement appears, it is easy for the company to measure the success of each advertisement. A travel advertisement which makes use of this technique, actually providing an attached miniature leaflet (known as a *tip-on coupon*) which can be returned to the company without postage charges ('Freepost') is illustrated in Figure 13.1 (colour plate). The technique of direct response advertising can be an effective one, providing the product is well established and its benefits are clearly understood.

The technique is also used tactically for late sales. With the worldwide downturn in sales in leading hotel chains in the early part of the new millennium, this became an important tool in helping to shift unsold rooms through bargain rates advertised in the press. Tour operators also move unsold stock through last-minute deals, and encourage brochure requests. Direct sell tour operators make extensive use of press advertising to attract demand for brochures, followed up by direct mailing of brochures, with a hard-sell covering letter, to solicit bookings.

Direct mail

Direct mail is the technique whereby a company communicates directly with its potential customers through the post, in order to put across a sales message. This will hinge on having a good mailing list – rather more than simply a list of names and addresses. More than 5 billion items of direct mail are posted each year in Britain, and although it is claimed that two-thirds of recipients object to receiving it (with one-third throwing the offending item directly into the waste bin) some 10 per cent respond to it, and research has shown that more than a quarter of the population has bought something as a result of receiving direct mail. The technique has the considerable advantage that letters can be personalised, and target markets can be clearly identified, so that customers should be expected to be reasonably interested in the product, providing the mailing list is sufficiently comprehensive. Wastage is in this way minimised. The process has been greatly aided by the introduction of computer databases which can pinpoint specific target markets with far more comprehensive details of clients and their interests. 'Lifestyle' databases allow for very accurate selection of potential customers, based on information about age, income, type of occupation, hobbies, residential area including type of property occupied, and previous holidays.

Travel companies are increasingly aware that direct mail can play an important part in their own communications mix, and evidence suggests that travel-related mailings are far more successful than others. One piece of research[2] revealed that over 90 per cent of recipients of travel-related direct mail opened and read the material, with one-third responding to it.

Direct mail can be used in:

■ *generating brochure requests* for tour operators, especially where holidays are aimed at very well-defined groups (e.g. golfers), although bookings may still primarily be via the travel agent

■ *generating late sales*, especially when aimed at previous customers who booked late the previous year

■ *channel support*, whereby the travel company communicates sales benefits to the travel agent

■ *customer care*, where the communication is to strengthen the brand image and customer loyalty for next season, for example a client returns from holiday to receive a personal letter from the principal of the travel agency where the holiday was booked.

Direct mail is now being supplemented by the use of direct fax, e-mail and voice mail. These can all prove useful tools, particularly in the speed with which information about products can be delivered, but like any form of promotion they can be abused. There is real concern about the use of junk mail and 'spam' (unsolicited junk mail sent via e-mail or over the Internet) which may simply annoy recipients and defeat the purpose of the mailing. Some 40 per cent of e-mails dispatched in Britain are spam, and legislation to control this is constantly being tightened.

Finally, direct mail shots can take the form of a personal magazine, with accompanying letter. For a local travel agent, there is actually very limited opportunity to reach customers through local advertising, given that only about one-third of the homes in a given area regularly purchase a local paper; many do so only for specific items such as the classified advertisements and the births and deaths announcements. An alternative then is to create one's own medium for reaching the customer. Saga, the older people's specialist operator, has its own highly regarded (subscription) magazine dealing with matters that are of interest to that age group; this also acts as a regular sales brochure for the company, and separate travel brochures are also sent in regular mailshots to subscribers.

At least one travel agency maintained contact with its local market by the use of a 'freesheet', making use of full colour (few local tabloids yet offer this facility) and accurately targeting the defined catchment area, so that wastage was minimised. Editorial content included travel opportunities and descriptions of travel agency staff and their travel experience, to ensure that potential customers would be aware of the depth and range of personal experience the staff could offer. Advertisements by travel companies were solicited to help offset agency production costs. The success of this direct mail effort was such that eventually a 16-page freesheet was being distributed to over 100 000 homes in the catchment area, and it became a recognised vehicle for information on new travel products for the coming season, for details of special trips from the area, and for travel-orientated competitions for readers. The agency group concerned outpaced all local retail competition and achieved blanket coverage in the region – an example of exceptionally effective direct mail activity.

Telemarketing

Telemarketing (or telesales) represents a growing form of direct marketing, built on the use of the telephone, either to initiate sales or to respond to enquiries generated through advertising. As a sales medium, sales staff will generate sales by using local telephone directories to 'cold call', or calling pre-screened lists of prospective customers. Such lists can be bought in from mail houses, but they are increasingly composed in-house through computer databases, which allow more sophisticated targeting of potential customers. Telemarketing is widely used both in B2C (business to consumer) and B2B (business to business) promotion, although in the latter case the cold call is rarer. Cold calling directed at consumers can suffer a similar fate to other unsolicited promotion, with the additional disadvantages that it is seen by many as an invasion of privacy and a disturbance, especially around mealtimes in the private home. Public aggravation is not what a travel company wants to foster, and the use of this technique should be limited.

While well established in selling travel products to the public, the technique has thrived in recent years with the development of the *call centre*, now a major feature of travel marketing. Call centres may have upwards of 100 or more sales staff taking bookings and answering queries from travel consumers, often based on freephone numbers for responses to advertisements. It has become a popular medium for the sale of sector products like budget airline seats and car hire. Call centres are increasingly based abroad, often in India, since global communication is now instantaneous and labour costs are greatly reduced by farming out these responsibilities.

There are constant refinements to telemarketing. One is the increasing emphasis on personal service, for which the telephone offers considerable scope. Training given to call centre staff has moved away from insistence on the use of somewhat mechanistic stock phrases with which to reply to enquiries, towards encouraging a more personal and individual style of conversation to develop. While the original emphasis had been to minimise time spent on each call, the new customer-friendly approach takes better into account good customer relations management practice, and is designed to enhance the relationship between the organisation's sales personnel and their customers, thus raising overall levels of customer satisfaction. The equal importance of answering phones quickly led to the introduction of automatic call distribution (ACD) systems to ensure that callers are not kept waiting, and that each incoming call is handled in strict rotation. Many companies now guarantee that calls will be answered within a given period of time, recognising that expensive advertising is wasted if, unable to get through to the business quickly, prospective customers hang up in frustration.

Future developments encompassing computer integrated telephoning (CIT) will further refine telemarketing. Calling line identification, for instance, allows the recipient of a call to identify who is on the line before answering, giving scope for redirecting the selection of replies, although this has not yet been approved for business practice.

While all these techniques continue in use, and their lifespan is by no means drawing to a close, the new opportunities created by ICT are rapidly supplementing, and in some cases overtaking, traditional direct marketing. There are two key techniques:

■ online marketing
■ DRTV, or direct response television.

We will examine each of these in turn.

Online marketing

Online direct marketing is conducted in two ways: directing commercial messages using the medium of an Internet service provider (ISP), and through the transmission of e-mails.

E-mail databases offer one of the cheapest and most effective means of reaching the consumer. Kotler[3] claims that between 5 and 10 per cent of all recipients respond to this medium. It has another great advantage, that of timing. E-mails containing holiday information can be sent out on weekends, when travel customers are in the right mood, and have the time, to consider planning for their holidays. Restaurateurs have successfully e-mailed their customers' offices between 4.30 and 5.30 pm, with dinner menus and tempting offers to attract the latter's patronage just at the point where they are thinking about an evening meal.

The interactive nature of online communications helps to build good customer relations. A two-way flow of communication allows the principal to adjust products in light of consumer comment, and this is particularly valuable in designing tailor-made tours, which are rapidly coming to usurp the traditional pattern of standardised, mass market holidays.

This is also true of Internet communications, which as we have seen in earlier chapters, are effective means both of advertising and making reservations, building databases and enhancing customer relations. Developments in the fields of digital TV (with web TV boxes) and mobile telephones using WAP technology reveal further opportunities for consumers to gain product knowledge by replacing their computer screens by TV and phone screens to surf the net.

Marketing in these ways brings huge advantages to the consumer. Low cost to the principals means lower prices to consumers, and many travel products, especially air and rail tickets, car hire and hotel accommodation, are offered at substantial discounts when booked over the Internet. The system is easy to use and immediate, with a vast choice of products and up-to-date information about them. It guarantees greater privacy and the convenience of not having to visit a shop or other outlet. Products can be customised to meet individual needs. What is more, its scope is truly global – holidays can be bought, hotels booked, in any country in the world at a moment's notice. The organisation using these promotional techniques benefits from building more complete and accurate databases, establishing stronger relations and brand loyalty with customers, and increasing profits through cost reductions.

Example   TUI

The world's leading tour operator, TUI, has moved some of its specialist services into direct sell Internet-only format, launching Budget Holidays in 2003, aimed at couples and young families. The website makes no reference to its connections to either TUI (or Thomson, its British brand) which continues to operate its direct sell operator Portland Holidays, aimed at more traditional markets.

This development is not without its downsides. It is true to say that websites are currently used far more for browsing than for booking (although the exact links between the two have not been clearly established, and building interest on the website is also likely to encourage bookings through traditional channels). There are limitations on the travel products that lend themselves to sales in this way – buying a complex product like a cruise or tailor-made long-haul holiday may require more expert sales assistance. Dependency on the customer's own keyboard skills means that making a booking can be a much slower process than simply telephoning, and many older generation customers unused to the computer revolution are never likely to come to terms with what they see as a complex medium. Although some (but by no means all) companies offer booking references, this is not as reassuring to a customer as a ticket in the hand, and the uncertainty of proof of purchase, coupled with the constant danger of inaccurate entries by the customer onto the booking screen, and the fear of misuse and fraud despite company reassurances, would suggest that the traditional retailing methods will continue to appeal to a sizeable percentage of the population for many years to come.

DRTV

Direct response television, which is rapidly expanding through satellite/cable and digital television in many countries, provides yet another opportunity for high-tech marketing. The technique offers two distinct forms of promotion. Commercial programmes contain advertisements which are accompanied by a freephone number encouraging viewers to order by telephone, and some channels offer opportunities for so-called 'infomercials', lengthy commercials – sometimes as long as half an hour – to provide information about products through discussion, focus group meetings, street surveys and similar means by which consumers are drawn into participating in the sales pitch. The second form of DRTV is the Home Shopping Channel, in which television programmes or entire channels are devoted to selling various types of product. Travel channels are already well established both in North America and Europe, and in the UK at the time of writing four of these exist: TV Travel Shop, Travel Deals Direct,

Thomas Cook TV and Going Places TV. The latter, the most recent entry (in 2003) to the field, planned to establish public auctions for late availability products, with holidays offered from as little as £1.

Evaluating the impact of direct marketing

We have now looked at a number of different ways in which organisations market their products direct to consumers, and the many benefits that accrue. The fact that most objectives of direct marketing are tactically oriented makes measurement a great deal easier, although immediate enquiries and sales are never the sole end result of any campaign, and one must be aware that many of the techniques discussed also reinforce brand names and develop long-term customer satisfaction for products. Apart from these tactical benefits, we can summarise some other principal benefits as:

1 *Precise targeting*   The list selection can be very precise, reducing waste and allowing very focused copy and offers that reflect the prospect's likely requirements.

2 *Personalised messages*   The mailing can be personalised not only by name, but also by being accurately based on behaviour and lifestyle of each individual customer, for example 'as a valued customer who has booked with us three times before, we would like to extend you a special invitation . . .' Messages that demonstrate a knowledge of and feeling for the needs of the customer will inevitably be better received.

3 *Response orientation*   By its very nature, the medium generates high levels of response through coupons, reply cards and telephone. Internet and telephone communication encourages response through low price and instantaneous appeal. Direct marketing can be very 'sales orientated' and directed.

4 *Detail*   The written word and flexibility of format where necessary allow a great deal of detail to be imparted. Product descriptions, including complete information and terms and conditions of purchase, can be transmitted via print, while the Internet allows the added benefit of full colour graphics to depict products – giving customers added confidence in buying. The downside of the detail is that preparation time for campaigns is extended.

5 *Discreet*   Television and press advertising will be immediately obvious to a company's competitors. With a little care, such as avoiding such obvious faux pas as including competitors on the mailing list, direct marketing campaigns will take longer to be noticed, and may even escape the competition's notice until well beyond their termination.

6 *Measurable*   The medium generates response which can be tracked accurately, whether it is enquiries for more information or actual sales. Therefore the return on the costs of the promotion can be directly measured.

As with other marketing campaigns, evaluation should always start with a clear expression of objectives. To whom is the campaign designed to appeal? What proportion of the market is it hoped to reach, in terms of (a) awareness, (b) enquiries generated, and (c) bookings achieved? The importance of timing for these tactical campaigns has already been stressed, so the plan must embrace exact dates for launch and the insertion of messages in the various media, or mailing dates for letters and e-mails.

Once these tasks are completed, evaluation strategies can be drawn up. All responses to messages need to be logged, and the overall results itemised and reviewed. Estimates can then be made of the costs per enquiry, and the cost of converting these into sales. Pre- and post-tests on copy or graphics are still appropriate, as is the selection of different messages aimed at different regions to judge effectiveness before major national or international campaigns. Post-campaign tests of awareness and attitudes towards the company and its products can also be beneficial, in terms of recognising the longer-term impact of what are in essence tactical tools.

Direct sell holidays

All sectors of the travel industry engage in some forms of direct marketing, and in some cases this is now deliberately skewed to encourage consumers to book direct, avoiding payment of the traditional commission to intermediaries. Some sectors (including destinations and tourist attractions) have no intermediaries through whom they can sell, and are dependent on one or more of the techniques we have described here. Others (e.g. some budget airlines) have deliberately chosen direct sell only as their distribution policy, in some cases even limiting sales to the Internet. The tour operating sector, however, is unique in that some elements of that sector have chosen to sell direct even where a strong retailing sector exists to serve their needs.

Initially, this undoubtedly arose because of a genuine belief that holidays could be sold in this way at cheaper cost than through traditional channels. In the event, it soon became clear that while sales could be achieved without the assistance of agents, the savings on commission were whittled down by the added expenses of direct marketing. Greatly increased advertising spend, the need for increased phone lines and more time taken to answer queries when selling over the phone all added to the marketing budget, while late availability offers proved more difficult to sell without an agent's support. The threat to traditional channels at first envisaged when the mass market direct sell operators appeared on the scene did not materialise, and eventually the market share they enjoyed stabilised at around 20 per cent. ICT tools have greatly aided these companies in facilitating access to their markets while cutting costs, but these benefits are equally impacting on all tour operators who are now seeking to build up the proportion of direct sales they achieve, using the same techniques.

Of course, it is possible to sell any product by a different method from that adopted by the majority of the suppliers in a given market. The reason for the existence of any distribution channel, however, is because the consumers want it; because they like to purchase their products in a particular way. Clothing is sold in many different ways: though direct catalogue companies exist, selling either to the customer (for example, those of Next) or through an agent (Marshall Ward, for instance), many buyers still prefer to visit shops. So it is with travel – apart from one very important distinction;

travel is an intangible, and cannot be inspected. Hence if any new forms of direct marketing can improve on the traditional demonstration in a travel agency of a series of photographs in a brochure, while simultaneously keeping prices low and reassuring customers of the organisation's integrity and security of booking, then direct selling can be expected increasingly to supplement, but not replace, the agency role.

Many tourism SMEs, whether small bed and breakfast establishments, visitor attractions or specialist tour operators, have few options. A glance at the weekend press advertisements for holidays will show that many travel companies rely almost entirely upon direct responses from their customers. The reason for this is simple: if a market is scattered nationally, yet the company is dealing in comparatively small numbers, the cost of using a retailer to distribute one's products is too great. At the same time, fewer agents are willing to stock such products because individually their sales will be too small to provide rack space, and they do not have the specialist knowledge needed to make a sale.

Example   Noble Caledonia

Noble Caledonia is a good example of a small company which has grown by offering a highly specialised holiday product, so that it has little direct competition. The company is one of a handful of specialist, largely long-haul, operators which are constantly searching for new and unusual destinations, appealing to the frequent traveller who has 'been everywhere' and is seeking something original. The company has prospered by seeking out hard-to-reach destinations but keeping costs under control by chartering foreign-owned (particularly Russian) vessels to provide a cruise programme for comparatively small numbers of like-minded individuals. Themed cruises are also evident, and the company has found an effective niche in catering to those interested in exotic flora and fauna. Ornithologists are attracted by guest lecturer personalities such as Tony Soper, well known for his BBC television programmes on birds. Destinations include the Arctic, Antarctic and mid-Atlantic Islands. The company reaches its customers through relatively expensive full-page advertisements in the quality weekend press, making particular use of the magazine sections. Customers, once attracted to these products, are added to the company's database and are regularly mailed with brochures and news of new products on offer. This approach has led to a high level of brand loyalty and repeat business.

Using databases

There are two possible sources of mailing databases: information held within the company and mailing lists obtained from third parties. A company's own customer list is likely to be the most fruitful in terms of sales; however, any company will lose a number of customers over the course of time. New names should be brought into the process through logging responders to advertising and other promotions, and possibly through the use of third-party lists.

Customer lists will perform well only if the data are accurate and well maintained. The administrative burden should not be underestimated. Pitfalls to avoid are such things as duplicates, out-of-date information and names and addresses incorrectly entered. If the information is incomplete, steps should be taken to fill in the gaps. For instance, if the only information held is 'Hilary Morgan', how is a personal letter to be addressed? 'Dear Hilary Morgan', although increasingly finding its way into direct mail communications, is not a correct mode of address, while 'Dear Mr Morgan' takes a risk on both gender and title (the addressee might be a doctor, for example). These facts should be established before sending out material. At all times, as much information as possible should be gathered and stored in the database to help in future mailings.

Any well-run business can today maintain a wealth of relevant data on their customers inexpensively by building up its computer database, as we discussed earlier in this chapter. Database use has become increasingly sophisticated, and wastage vastly reduced by a 'rifle' approach as distinct from the former 'shotgun' approach in directing messages. So-called *closed loop* marketing ensures constant adjustments are made to messages and appeals in the light of feedback received from consumers whose responses are tracked on software promotion.

Computer databases now permit the collection and collation of information on customers and potential customers which will include geographic, demographic, psychographic and buyer behaviour patterns on a scale which would be unimaginable just a few years ago. Invaluable as such a list as this is, its use must be constrained. The Data Protection Act (1984) demands that if a database of personal information is held then this must be registered with the Data Protection Authority. Even names and addresses alone constitute personal information. Though a firm may write to its own customers freely, it may not pass this information on to another company without the permission of the individual. In practice, this is often obtained by 'default', with tick boxes on reply cards that say 'if you do not wish to receive information and offers from other companies at a later date, please tick this box'.

Such in-house databanks are far removed from third-party mailing lists, although these, too, are becoming more sophisticated. Normally available on a 'rental' basis, such lists are made available for one-time use only. The company may not be allowed to actually see the list: the owner of the list may designate a mailing house to carry out the mailing, and will receive the promotional material for onward dispatch. This is because of the value of the information to the list owner, who makes money from the list; if it is sold outright, then the owner loses control over the asset, and would therefore also lose income from it. Some lists are, however, available for sale.

In selecting a third-party list, the marketer should exercise caution, and ask some searching questions of the list owner:

1 Is the list owner registered under the Data Protection Act?
2 Has the list been recently matched against the Mailing Preference File? (This is a list set up under the Data Protection Act where individuals can register that they do not wish to receive direct mail. All lists should in theory be matched against this, and such individuals removed prior to a mailing being dispatched.)
3 What selections can be made on the data to refine the list to more accurately reflect the desired profile?

4   How old are the data?

5   How and why were the data compiled?

6   How are data maintained and kept up to date?

The marketer may wish to mail only a small test quantity of a large list before committing the whole promotion to a particular source.

The more personal any communication becomes, the more effective it is likely to be. At one end of the scale it is easy simply to place an advertisement in a publication produced by others, but at the other end, the single individually compiled sales letter, personally addressed and describing why a specific proposition is appropriate to the addressee, will have a strong sales appeal. Between these two extremes are a myriad of other possibilities, and the initiative of the direct marketer will be tested by the way the customer responds.

Direct marketing for destinations

Destinations will invariably rely to a greater extent on direct marketing than other sectors of the industry, since there are no convenient intermediaries to promote their products. Many destinations use great imagination to get their message across: one particularly effective direct marketing campaign was that carried out by the Tunisian National Tourist Office which, because of its imagination and success, remains a model to this day.

Tunisian National Tourist Office Marketing Campaign

At the end of the 1980s, the newly appointed director of the Tunisian National Tourist Office in London was faced with disappointing sales for his country in the coming season. His budget was limited, and though a small consumer advertising campaign had been planned around Easter to arouse the public's interest in holidays to Tunisia, he was also aware that too few of the 30 000 or so travel agency staff employed by the 7000 UK travel agencies were really conscious of the opportunities that his country's resorts presented. This was hardly surprising, given that the whole of North Africa accounted at the time for only 0.73 per cent of annual air holidays taken by British tourists. It follows naturally that if less than one in 100 customers is likely to choose Tunisia, staff of the travel agencies are hardly likely to devote too much time and effort to improving their own knowledge of the travel destination.

The director saw that a major objective must be that of creating awareness of his destination among travel agency staff. At his disposal he had a small but enthusiastic staff in the office to answer enquiries and to give promotional assistance; he had a newly published colour brochure giving information on the main holiday features of the country, and he had a new video cassette which also described the resorts.

With the help of an outside consultant, a scheme was devised to undertake a series of mailings to every travel agency in the UK, in an attempt to capture their attention. In the first instance, humour and local colour were to be established by a pun on the theme. A package was sent out which contained a box of best quality dates from Tunisia, for the travel agency staff to share. The date palm had been used in previous advertising, and it was here used as a visual anchor to promote the theme 'You have a date with Tunisia.'

A letter followed (see Figure 13.2), produced simply on an office word processor and personally addressed by the director 'Dear Travel Agent', and signed by him. This set out the five main sales features of Tunisian holidays, then:

- gave details of the video that was available on request
- described a competition for travel agency staff to go on a 'dream trip' to Tunisia themselves
- offered low-price holiday opportunities to travel staff in the early season (to get better product knowledge)
- gave prior notice of study tours for staff in the autumn
- offered promotional help upon request.

Enclosed with the mailing were simple-to-complete postcard entry forms so that each member of the travel agency could enter the 'dream trip' competition after reading the relevant brochures (see Figure 13.3); a request postcard for a copy of the video; and a list of the names and addresses of all holiday companies publishing brochures to Tunisia, from which the travel agent could sell. The items were enclosed in a specially constructed box carrying an attractive label bearing the date palm symbol and an instruction to 'open immediately', to distinguish it from packets of brochures that might languish in the agency before being opened.

The response of competition entries and video requests confirmed that the contents had been well received and that Tunisia had obtained the high profile attention it sought for the valuable Easter booking period.

The creative quality of this campaign was in marked contrast with competitor countries, and helped Tunisia to return good results in what would otherwise have proved to be a difficult season.

Some guidelines for good direct mail letters

The previous section has emphasised the importance of letters being directed personally, by name and by appropriate business title, if relevant. This will ensure that the letter gets to the right person, and makes it more likely to be read. Many people believe that using the name again in the text reinforces the message, but although this can be

TUNISIA
THE MEDITERRANEAN HOLIDAY THAT'S NEVER OUT OF SEASON

COMPETITION FOR A DREAM TRIP

1. Where is one of Tunisia's golf courses situated?

2. What was the name of the visitor to Djerba, the Island of the Lotus Eaters, 3,000 years ago?

3. Which of the following companies feature Tunisia in their Summer 1989 brochures?   Please tick as appropriate.

   □ Airtours   □ Select
   □ Cosmos   □ Sky Tours
   □ Enterprise   □ Sol Holidays
   □ Holiday Club International   □ Sovereign
   □ Intasun   □ Thomson
   □ Panorama's Tunisia Experience

NAME

I confirm that the above named is a full time member of our sales staff at this travel agency

Signed _____ (Manager)

AGENT'S STAMP

Note: Only one entry per person is allowed.

□ Finally I'd like to be considered for a study tour of Tunisia and my manager says please send details

Figure 13.3 Competition entry for travel agents accompanying the mailshot in Figure 13.2

(Courtesy: Tunisian National Tourist Office)

TUNISIA
THE MEDITERRANEAN HOLIDAY THAT'S NEVER OUT OF SEASON

March 1989

Dear Travel Agent,

YOU HAVE A DATE WITH TUNISIA

Dates are just one of the many things of which Tunisia is proud and we hope you will enjoy our gift whilst you think about Tunisia for a few moments.

For the holidaymaker we offer a variety of plus points.

- sophisticated hotels and resorts
- superb food
- sports galore from golf to windsurfing and horseriding
- the best beaches in the Mediterranean, and
- the magic of the Sahara desert and its oases

It is no wonder that our advertising has featured the theme:

"WHY JUST HAVE ONE HOLIDAY WHEN YOU CAN GO TO TUNISIA ?'

We know that 1989 is a difficult year and we are doing our best to help you sell our holidays. We are now running a national and regional press campaign which is intended to highlight the remarkably low prices at which your customers can purchase a dream holiday in our varied country.

In order that you can see for yourself just what we have to offer we are also undertaking a number of initiatives aimed at supporting you, our valued travel agent partner.

YOUR DATE WITH OUR NEW VIDEO

Those travel agents who we know have video facilities, are being sent a copy of the new unbiased video 'Tunisia - Dream Holiday Destination' produced by Travid. This will help you and all of your colleagues in the office to appreciate the range of facilities we have to offer.

The Tunisian National Tourist Office, 7a Stafford Street, London, W1X 4EQ
Travel Enquiries 01-499 2234, Administration 01-629 0858, Fax 01 495 3321
Prestel Tunisia Information 344 220
Director Kader Chelbi

Figure 13.2 Front page of direct mailshot to travel agents from the Tunisian National Tourist Office

(Courtesy: Tunisian National Tourist Office)

achieved with most mail-merge software programs, the technique can make the letter appear contrived.

There is inevitably a trade-off between cost and quality, but generally cost savings are counterproductive if the mail is well directed. Printing should be of the highest standard. Brown envelopes are cheaper than white, but they imply penny-pinching economies. Window envelopes may seem less desirable than plain ones, but a personally addressed letter in a window looks better than an envelope with a label, and typing individual envelopes requires more sophisticated equipment.

The content of the letter itself is of crucial importance. The aim of the text will be to:

- capture attention with a headline that intrigues
- start by stating how the recipient will benefit
- describe what is offered and demonstrate the product's benefits
- fully detail the offer being made
- explain what the recipient needs to do next, i.e. how to purchase the product.

A direct mail letter is one type of promotion where brevity is not necessarily the best technique. To be effective, the text must capture the reader's attention and interest. The text should be written in good, simple (and correct!) English, preferably in relatively short, punchy sentences. Many of the leaders in this field use devices such as indented paragraphs, emboldened or underlined words for emphasis or clarity, and add apparent afterthoughts in postscripts. If inviting a response by mail, then it is essential to encourage action by making it easy to reply. An order form or reply card should serve this purpose. A simple printed, addressed envelope will help to increase replies, but still better is a reply-paid envelope or 'freepost' facility where the cost is met by the promoter (at a small premium on the number of replies received). Most effective of all is actually to put a stamp on the envelope: many people seem to feel guilty about the waste if they do not send it back.

The Wales Tourist Board represents one organisation that regularly makes good use of direct mail letters to potential visitors. Two recent examples are reproduced in Figures 13.4 and 13.5. The board has a good record of responses to these mailings, which are personally addressed and signed by the Director of Marketing, with a brief but punchy text accompanied by colourful images within an appealing layout.

Questions, tasks and issues for discussion

1 Over the space of two weeks, and along with all members of your group, collect all the unsolicited direct mail you receive in your household (include stuffers within any magazines delivered to your household). Take a count of the number of pieces received, and break these down by the type of product or service being marketed (e.g. financial, information technology, house and garden, etc.) How relevant are they to your household's needs? Do any show evidence of pinpoint targeting (e.g. Acorn classification outlined in Chapter 4) and in which would you be potentially interested? Are any addressed by name? Do any include travel offers? Which do you feel is the best (a) of those sent to you, and (b) of those sent to the entire group?

Figure 13.4 (Left letter)

WALES CYMRU
THE BIG COUNTRY

WALES TOURIST BOARD
PO BOX 1, CARDIFF
CF24 2XN.

Mr A Sample
55 any house
any street,
near any where
Postcode

Hold on to your hat, your journey's about to begin.

Dear Mr Sample

This year take your family to Wales – The Big Country for a holiday packed with adventure and fun. You're all guaranteed to return home brimming with stories and smiles.

FAMILY FUN.

Our beautiful coastline and wide-open countryside will let you and your kids have a real adventure. Explore the rock pools or fly a kite on one of our 18 Blue Flag beaches. Take a boat trip in search of dolphins and seals. Or explore the mysterious hidden world at one of Wales' many underground attractions. Then continue your journey aboard an old steam train spiralling round the mountains. All this and more makes Wales the perfect place to have fun together as a family.

GO WILD!

For the really daring enjoy getting wet on a white water ride at a theme park, race each other at go-karting, visit an indoor rope centre or just splash about in the surf. The children will love the wildlife attractions where they can see exotic animals close up or meet creatures from the deep.

WIN!

If you can't decide what to do first, choose 3 of our brochures from the leaflet. They'll help you pick the best places to visit and ensure you spend less time travelling, and more time enjoying The Big Country. WHAT'S MORE if you send back the coupon with your choice of brochures, we'll automatically enter you into our prize draw. You could win a superb Alfa 147. Perfect for zipping the family around The Big Country!

We look forward to welcoming you to Wales – The Big Country soon.

Yours sincerely

Roger Pride
Director of Marketing – Wales Tourist Board

Win Send off for a brochure and you could **WIN** an ALFA 147. See leaflet for details.

Figure 13.4 'Hold on to your hat', a direct mail letter from the Wales Tourist Board
(Courtesy: Wales Tourist Board)

Figure 13.5 (Right letter)

WALES CYMRU
THE BIG COUNTRY

WALES TOURIST BOARD
PO BOX 1, CARDIFF
CF24 2XN.

Mr A Sample
55 any house
any street,
near any where
Postcode

Discover a new way of life.

Dear Mr Sample

BROADER...

Now that we are into a new year, let's make it one to remember! Rediscover a favourite pastime, or try something you have always dreamed of doing but never seemed to find the time.

HORIZONS

Visit Wales and discover a whole new world. Try a new activity, from leisurely bike rides to capturing Wales' beautiful landscape on canvas or film. Or maybe discover a new hideaway – there is good reason why Wales is described as Britain's best-kept secret. Try a new dish to eat, with superb local ingredients cooked in a fusion of traditional and modern styles, which are sure to whet the appetite.

Even if you've been to Wales before, there's still plenty to discover. Have you seen our spring hedgerows bursting with wild flowers or the long golden beaches and blue skies in summer? There are food and music festivals, art exhibitions, cultural celebrations and plenty more at special events throughout the year.

WIN!

Do something different, pick three brochures, and start planning your holiday. Maybe even consider an area of Wales that you've never visited before. Send your choices back on the coupon and we'll enter you into our competition. You could be driving away in a fantastic car – the Alfa 147. Just the thing for discovering Wales.

We look forward to welcoming you to Wales – The Big Country soon.

Yours sincerely

Roger Pride
Director of Marketing
Wales Tourist Board

Win Send off for a brochure and you could **WIN** an ALFA 147. See leaflet for details.

Figure 13.5 'Discover a new way of life', a direct mail letter from the Wales Tourist Board
(Courtesy: Wales Tourist Board)

2   With all the unsolicited mail that pours through the nation's letterboxes, there are many missed opportunities for effective marketing. To cite one good example (seldom replicated), a window cleaner setting up in business toured the streets within his business area, taking note of all the windows which did not appear to have been cleaned recently. He delivered a letter to each of these houses, introducing his services, and a contact number – and achieved enough business to make his employment profitable without any further investment in sales.

New housing estates are springing up everywhere – yet how often do local trades deliver direct mail to each new household introducing their services and inviting business?

Discuss whether any in your group have received such mail. Have any received a letter from a local travel agent soliciting your business? Why not?!

3   If you were drawing up a mailing list in order to send out a direct mail letter to residents within your immediate neighbourhood, how would you describe the 'market profile' of the area? What kinds of travel products might the residents be interested in?

Exercise

The example of the Tunisian National Tourist Office in this chapter is an unusually successful one, but is not unique in effective promotion – other successful campaigns involved delivering free dates to agents to remind them of the destination.

Given the success of Tunisia as a destination featuring in a host of popular films in recent years (*Star Wars, Raiders of the Lost Ark* and *The English Patient* were all filmed there), assume you have been commissioned by the TNTO to produce a direct mail letter to be sent to a selected list of targeted potential tourists to the country.

Devise an appropriate letter, identifying the target market(s), the objective of the letter, the product to be marketed (country/resorts/adventure tourism, etc.) and the theme of the letter, and any enclosures you are recommending to be sent out with the letter. Ensure that the letter closes with an invitation to the reader to take some form of action (send for a particular brochure, make further enquiries, make a booking).

Accompany your letter with a short brief to the Marketing Director of the TNTO explaining your mission and the reasons for your decisions.

References

1 Kotler, P, Armstrong, G, Saunders, J and Wong, V, *Principles of Marketing*, Prentice Hall, Harlow, 3rd edn 2001, p 784
2 Direct Mail Information Service Intelligence Report, reported in *Travel Weekly*, 26 April 1999
3 Kotler, P *et al*, op cit, p 806

Further reading

Kotler, P *et al*, op cit, ch 22
Kotler, P, Bowen, J and Makens, J, *Marketing for Hospitality and Tourism*, Prentice Hall, 2nd edn 1999, ch 15

14 Public relations and its uses in the tourism industry

Learning outcomes

After studying this chapter, you should be able to:

- compare the benefits of a public relations (PR) campaign with other forms of communication
- list the functions of PR and understand the role of the public relations officer (PRO)
- understand how PR campaigns are mounted
- evaluate alternative approaches to gaining positive publicity and stemming negative publicity
- appreciate the importance of measuring the success of all forms of promotional technique
- understand the importance of corporate social responsibility to an organisation and its image.

Why PR?

Transylvanian pop duo The Cheeky Girls have announced a summer tour of Britain's airports to promote new single *Hooray, Hooray (It's a Cheeky Holiday)*. The plan is to cheer up holiday-makers whose flights have been delayed, with renditions of their 'greatest hits'. Dates are still to be confirmed, but airports to avoid include Heathrow, Manchester, Gatwick, Edinburgh, Glasgow and Newcastle.

Travel Weekly Diary 16 June 2003

David Ogilvy, former head of the advertising agency Ogilvy & Mather and one of Britain's greatest exponents of advertising, once declared to an audience in New York composed of senior travel industry staff that he would choose to spend $250 000 on PR before he spent a penny on travel advertising. His aims were to highlight the import-ance of an area of communications often overlooked by many of those working in the industry, and to make clear that expenditure on PR generally produces better value for money than other more traditional promotional techniques.

One reason why PR has tended to play a minor role in the communications mix is that it is the most difficult of all marketing techniques to measure results against expenditure. PR generally takes longer to achieve results, and these are by definition dependent upon the attitudes and actions of third parties outside the direct control of the organisation. It also calls for levels of skill and business contacts that are beyond the reach of many small businesses. This adds up to a challenge which many marketers prefer to sidestep, not least because PR is not well understood by many in the travel industry. There are some notable examples of entrepreneurs who have recognised its power in promoting personal charisma to generate public awareness of the company and its products, and have used it very successfully: Sir Richard Branson of airways and railways fame springs immediately to mind, as does Stelios Haji-Ioannou at easyJet. There are dangers associated with over-reliance on this manifestation of the medium, and too high a public profile can attract unwelcome publicity, especially when things start to go wrong, as Branson would be the first to admit. However, there are many other forms of PR which any organisation can employ, and we will examine these in the forthcoming chapter.

Example   VisitBritain

VisitBritain, formerly the British Tourist Authority, is also an organisation which believes in spending on PR before any other promotional investment. Its emphasis in 2002 was on two approaches to build awareness:

1   Two thousand journalists and broadcasters from around the world were invited to the UK to inspect and experience the product at first hand.
2   The organisation invests in high-quality information services, with offices in key strategic cities around the globe to field direct enquiries, while the website (visitbritain.com) is designed to deliver comprehensive information and acts as a portal to all regional, sub-regional and resort webs. In 2002, the BTA website received over 30 million hits.

PR: its definition, characteristics and role

PR is best defined as a set of communications techniques which are designed to create and maintain favourable relations between an organisation and its publics. The last word is deliberately used in the plural, since an organisation actually has to deal with several different publics, of which its consumers are only one. Companies will want to build good relations with their shareholders, with suppliers, distribution channels, and, where pertinent, with trade unions. External bodies such as trade and professional associations and local chambers of commerce are other organisations that a company might wish to influence, while opinion leaders such as Members of Parliament, travel writers, hotel and restaurant guide publishers are yet more groups with which the organisation must maintain good relations. Finally, companies will wish to be on good terms with their neighbours, and will want to be seen as part of the local community and to support local activities.

This relationship with publics other than consumers goes beyond the marketing role, but the PR activities associated with good marketing play an active part in communicating a sense of goodwill towards the company among locals and the wider world. Corporate social responsibility is now recognised as an important element in the management of any organisation, and in the case of tourism this also embraces the concept of sustainable tourism. We will return to this subject a little later in the chapter.

Characteristics

The need for PR arose as a result of the growth in size of organisations. The resultant lessening of personal contact between a firm and its customers led to criticisms of impersonality, a belief that big corporations had become 'faceless' and 'uncaring'. Some observers such as Robert Townsend[1] believed that the answer was to scrap the PR departments and get back to personal relations again, but it is questionable how far this is practicable once any organisation grows beyond a certain point. Until the 1970s, most tour operators handled their reservations systems manually, and specific staff were assigned to handle bookings from agents over the telephone. Retailers were on first-name terms with individual staff members, and knew who to call when they had a problem. This close relationship eased any failures of the company in other directions – not least because sufficient trust existed between the individuals in the organisation and its retailers that the failures would be looked into and corrected. The movement to online computer reservations systems, coupled with a reduction in agency calls by sales representatives, depersonalised these businesses, and agents became less willing to condone the occasional organisational weaknesses. Customers, too, grew alienated from the businesses with which they dealt, and organisations were set up to safeguard consumer interests and to lobby for better consumer protection. The Air Transport Users' Committee (AUC) is one such body in the travel industry which has been established to safeguard the interests of the travelling public – yet its sanctions are restricted to publicising bad practice, and this can only be effective if the company concerned is sensitive to public criticism.

Role

Travel and tourism is a service industry, consequently the reputation of a travel company's products is indivisible from that of its staff, based on the relations established between staff and customers. Even when a company is carrying in excess of a million passengers abroad each year, it must still make great efforts to present a friendly and personal image – in fact, this becomes even more important as its customer base grows. PR plays a role in supporting and publicising that image, but its creation lies with those in the organisation with responsibilities for staff recruitment and training, and for maintenance of quality control.

As with other communications techniques, PR plays a part in informing and reminding customers about the company and its products, and in generating an attitude favouring the purchase of its products. In its information-giving role, however, the task is to ensure that messages are both accurate and unbiased, while still reflecting the needs and interests of the company – a considerable challenge for the PRO! Objectivity is essential if PR is to be seen to do its job effectively, as the media determine what appears in public, and will publicise only what they believe to be truthful.

Given credibility, PR messages, with their perceived objectivity, are more convincing than advertising and in the long run are likely to have a greater impact on sales. This, however, underlines the fact that PR is essentially a weapon for long-term strategic impact in the marketing plan. Travel consumers are becoming ever more sophisticated, and hence immune to messages carried by advertising, so PR's role within marketing takes on added importance.

Lest readers feel that PR is the concern only of the largest companies, it should be emphasised that it has a part to play in any organisation, regardless of size. SMEs, too, need the goodwill of their local community and a sound reputation, which can be helped with the application of simple techniques.

In addition to creating favourable publicity for the company, PR has an equally important role in diminishing the impact of unfavourable publicity. The travel industry has more than its fair share of this, and there are some in the industry who feel that the media are concerned only to report the negative events, focusing on disasters such as overbooking, air traffic controllers' strikes, aircraft near misses, ferry disasters, coach crashes and the collapse of tour operating companies. Many of these events are beyond the control of individual companies, but the impact of negative publicity will affect them anyway and must be tackled. Tackling such crises will be discussed towards the end of this chapter.

There is a misconception in some circles that PR's role is to 'paper over the cracks' which result from poor management or product faults. No amount of publicity will help a company which does not seek to correct underlying problems. PR must be used as an adjunct to good marketing practice, not as a substitute for it.

Five distinct activities are associated with the role of PR:

1 *Press relations* This requires the company to maintain a close working relationship with press journalists and others associated with the media, with the aim of generating favourable publicity at every available opportunity.

2 *Product publicity* This involves the implementation of tactics designed to bring products to the attention of the public, whether through the use of the media, or in some other manner.

3 *Corporate publicity* This concerns efforts to publicise the firm itself, either internally or externally, in order to create a favourable image.

4 *Lobbying* This involves activities designed to promote a cause. A firm may, for instance, support plans for legislation or regulation, such as airlines' attempts to gain legislation for more night flights out of London airports; or a lobby may be mounted to defeat a proposal for legislation, such as draft European Union plans for certification of travel agents. While lobbying is commonly concerned with

governmental or local authority issues, it can also be employed to influence trade regulation, such as the move to defeat ABTA's proposals to increase bonding requirements.

5 *Counselling* The PRO has the task of counselling management about public issues, identifying developments internally and external to the firm which could influence a company's image. The PRO will then recommend a plan of action to counter any unfavourable developments. Thus the PR department has a monitoring and research function also.

The organisation of PR

It will be appreciated that while some of the above activities are directly associated with the marketing function, others are only peripheral to it, in the sense that overall objectives are always designed to enhance a company's sales opportunities. For this reason, in large organisations some PR activities may be carried out within the marketing department, while others are conducted autonomously at a senior level. One air carrier, for instance, has employed a PRO as assistant to the managing director, with all corporate publicity conducted under the direct supervision of the managing director. In such a situation, the PRO becomes a highly influential figure within the organisation, while technically still a member of 'staff' rather than 'line' management.

A difficulty in large companies, where marketing and PR functions are separated, is that the priorities of the two become distinct, although both are concerned with external relations. Where a PR function is not the responsibility of the marketing staff, suspicion of its activities is aroused, since marketing's interest is limited to product enhancement, and the wider responsibilities to the organisation's publics are of less concern. PR staff, for their part, tend to take the view that marketing staff, by focusing only on the customer, may overlook the organisation's corporate social responsibilities to the community at large. They will therefore believe that PR considerations should be taken into account in all decisions governing the company and its products.

By way of example, let us take the case of a major tour operator seeking new destinations for its market. The marketing staff will be principally interested in the attraction of the resort to the company's clients, that the new resort has the right facilities and will be accessible at a price which the company is willing to pay, and that the tourist authorities in the area are supportive. They will be concerned with the impact on the local community of the new development only to the extent that it influences sales one way or another – but given an increase in awareness of sustainable issues among the travelling public, this could well influence their thinking. Of still less concern would be the political consequences of any intention to file for an increase in flights from regional airports, which might be resisted by local communities and would need careful handling. Marketing staff might feel that the use of so-called 'personality girls' to merchandise the launch of a new programme will gain them plenty of press coverage, but PR might urge caution in the portrayal of women in this role, predicting a backlash against what might be seen by the public as sexist publicity.

In the USA, PR staff tend to play a greater role in marketing decisions, in areas of product policy, pricing, packaging and promotions, as US corporations become more sensitive to their social responsibilities. PR is now more prominent in influencing British marketing, as companies seek to understand and respond to the changing attitudes and needs of the buying public.

The PRO

In the very smallest companies PR may be directly carried out by the managing director or principal. Medium-sized and larger companies are more likely to use the services of an external PR consultancy. The largest companies will appoint their own PRO, and may also employ one or more PR agencies with specialist talents to support some or all of the following:

- special events and launches
- day-to-day tactical product PR (if this is not carried out by the marketing staff)
- corporate image PR.

PROs usually have a media/communications, rather than marketing, background. In fact, they often tend to be former journalists or broadcasters, with good media contacts and an intimate knowledge of their modus operandi. This means they will also have good communications skills. It is their contacts which are valued most highly, though, since they will help to gain increased media coverage for the company.

Where PR activities are intermittent and ad hoc, it will be much cheaper for a company to employ a firm of PR consultants to handle campaigns. External PR companies provide an excellent service, having broad-ranging experience of many businesses and good contacts to exploit. Their sole weakness is separation from their client's day-to-day activities; they must rely on being well briefed by the client if they are to do an effective job.

Mounting a PR campaign

Favourable publicity does not just happen; it has to be planned and programmed. Those responsible for PR must create news, as well as exploiting opportunities that arise to make news. A publicity campaign should form an integral part of any marketing plan for the year, as one element in the communications mix.

As a starting-point for the campaign, PR staff must know the publics with whom they will be dealing, and present attitudes towards the organisation and its products, so that there is some understanding of what needs to be done. While market research should already have a picture of the firm's consumers or potential consumers, additional research will probably be needed to establish the attitudes of other publics, such as staff and shareholders. This will provide an overall picture of the strengths and weaknesses of the company in its public affairs, which will allow a set of objectives to be drawn up for the PR campaign. As with all plans, objectives should be stated in a form which is measurable; for example, to raise awareness among the local community of the company's commitment to sustainability from its present 20 per cent to 40 per cent within one year.

The next step is to determine the strategies and tactics which are best suited to achieve these aims, and to decide what budget will be required to undertake the campaign. In the case of PR, the implementation of a campaign may last much longer than the usual one-year marketing plan before targets are achieved. Changing attitudes and opinions through PR is a slow process, and a corporate campaign could easily last as long as five years. Finally, the success or otherwise of the campaign must be monitored. In a campaign lasting several years, this monitoring should take place during the campaign as well as after it, to evaluate its growing effectiveness; some fine-tuning to the campaign, such as tactical adjustments, may be needed in the intervening period.

Gaining publicity

Let us assume that the objective is to generate publicity to develop a favourable attitude towards a local travel agency. How is this best achieved? The first task of an agent is to ensure that the local catchment area is aware of the agency's existence, and of the products it provides. PR can support the advertising and sales promotion activities of the company by, for example, publicising the opening of the offices. New shops and offices open all the time, so in itself, this is hardly newsworthy for the local press. It will be the task of the PRO to make the event newsworthy, in order to attract visitors and gain media coverage. Offering free drinks will bring people through the door, but using a well-known personality (perhaps local, and with some connection to the world of travel and tourism, such as a travel writer) is more likely to gain coverage. It must always be borne in mind that what is newsworthy for the company is not necessarily of interest to the press, and an agency opening will have to contend with many other local events for coverage. Something really attention-getting is needed; perhaps a window display with live models paid to sit in deckchairs for the first few days? This will draw the public's attention, and that of the media too. The important thing about publicity, though, is that it feeds on new ideas all the time, and the agent must continually be thinking up new gimmicks to gain attention.

After the opening, the agent must find ways of keeping the name in front of the public. Some agents have been able to establish themselves with the local press or radio station as 'gurus' of travel, who are then called upon to be interviewed whenever something newsworthy occurs in the industry. This is particularly valuable for long-term image building (it helps if the proprietor's name is the same as the company's, since the company name may not receive a mention!). Senior staff who are skilled speakers soon become known and invited as after-dinner speakers at local events, or deliver guest lectures at their local educational establishments. Participation at local fairs, providing raffle prizes at fund-raising events or charities, sponsoring an entrant for a local hot-air balloon race (one well-known agent in Britain even sponsors the balloon itself) – all offer chances for building community awareness and generating local goodwill.

A firm can build on the particular strengths of its own staff to gain additional press coverage. One agent employed a counter clerk with excellent skiing skills. This not only enabled the agent to build up a specialist expertise in winter sports holidays, but also gained some useful column inches in the local press. Another well-established agency proprietor was known in the trade and the local community for his enthusiasm for golf, losing no opportunity to publicise his links with golfing personalities, and participating in golf tournaments at home and abroad which received good press coverage. Key names in the retail world, in their role as spokespersons for ABTA, have become well-known faces to hundreds of thousands of television viewers through their appearances on interview programmes or travel programmes. There is a 'caveat' in guesting on television, however. Television is still largely a medium for entertainment, and the role calls for a special kind of talent in presenting oneself effectively on camera.

Press relations

Developing and maintaining links with the press and other media is a critical task for the PRO, who will also need to be on first-name terms with prominent travel writers if representing a major principal. It is to the PRO as spokesperson for the organisation that the media will turn to get information about the company, and the PRO's skills must include the ability to be both tactful and frank when dealing with journalists and broadcasters.

If a major organisation plans to announce some prominent event, such as a takeover, or the establishment of a new trading division, this may be sufficiently newsworthy to merit calling a press conference. This will entail invitations to travel journalists and other representatives from the trade, national and local media to attend a meeting at which senior executives will announce details of the new plans. A press reception will include provision of food and drink (some form of hospitality is normal for all press conferences). The conference itself is usually preceded by a press release, or news release, which is the principal method of communicating to the media any information about the company thought newsworthy.

The press release is an organisation's principal means of communication with the media, so it is important that it exemplifies the quality and efficiency of the organisation. News releases should always be attractively presented on special letterhead paper which gives the name and address of the company, a contact name (usually that of the PRO) and both home and work phone numbers, as a PRO must be contactable 24 hours a day if the media want more information. Companies devise their own titles for letterheads, usually a phrase such as 'NEWS FROM . . .' Pursuing a policy of integrated communications, the letterhead may carry strong product branding, as well as the company details.

The news release should be composed of no more than a brief summary of the news which the company wishes to publicise, generally occupying one side, or at most two, of A4 stationery. The text needs as much care as any advertising copy, since the material

Eurocamp

Hartford Manor, Greenbank Lane,
Northwich, Cheshire CW8 1HW, England
Telephone: **01606 787000**
Facsimile: **0870 3667 631**
email: **enquiries@eurocamp.co.uk**
www.eurocamp.co.uk

Background Information

EUROCAMP CUSTOMER SATISFACTION RESEARCH STUDY BY TARP

Eurocamp took part in the TARP study as a commitment to ensuring customer satisfaction and loyalty.

The findings on behalf of Eurocamp were presented against benchmarks calculated by drawing on comparable data sets from 19 leisure accommodation and airline businesses from the UK.

THE 'VITAL STATISTICS'

- **90% of customers would definitely or probably recommend a Eurocamp holiday to someone else.** 66% would definitely recommend a Eurocamp holiday to someone else, again placing Eurocamp at the top of the industry minimum–maximum benchmark scale of 20-70%.

- **91% of customers were very satisfied or somewhat satisfied with Eurocamp.** 57% were very satisfied, placing Eurocamp at the top of the industry minimum–maximum benchmark scale of 10-60 %.

- **79% of customers would definitely or probably book again with Eurocamp in the next 5 years.** 41% would definitely book again in the next 5 years placing Eurocamp in the middle of the industry minimum–maximum benchmark scale of 25-60%, relating to an 'intention to continue using in the future'.

- **84% of customers identified Eurocamp as the best holiday company, compared to other leading holiday operators, including Airtours, JMC, Thomson and First Choice.** The top 5 competitive advantages attributed to Eurocamp in comparison to industry competition were as follows :-

1. **Helpful and professional staff.** Eurocamp scored 75% in comparison to the competition's 34%.
2. **Range of locations.** Eurocamp scored 74% in comparison to the competition's 52%.
3. **Quality of accommodation.** Eurocamp scored 66% in comparison to the competition's 59%.
4. **Flexibility of holiday options.** Eurocamp scored 65% in comparison to the competition's 32%.
5. **Information in the brochure and on the website.** Eurocamp scored 65% in comparison to the competition's 34%.

-Ends-

For executive comment on the TARP research study and further press information, please contact Nicky Fairweather or Heloise d'Souza at DFPR on 01422 345 827.

Note to editors. TARP (Technical Assistance Research Programmes), is an independent research-based consultancy – a market leader in satisfaction and loyalty measurement since 1971.

Eurocamp is a trading name of Greenbank Holidays Ltd.
Registered Office: As above   Registered in England 1160442

(b)

Eurocamp

Hartford Manor, Greenbank Lane,
Northwich, Cheshire CW8 1HW, England
Telephone: **01606 787000**
Facsimile: **0870 3667 631**
email: **enquiries@eurocamp.co.uk**
www.eurocamp.co.uk

**Good Service not Gimmicks puts Eurocamp
Ahead in the Loyalty Stakes**

When more than 8 out of 10 of your customers say you're the best, you must be doing something right.

In an independent customer satisfaction study conducted by TARP on behalf of Eurocamp Travel, an impressive 84% of customers identified Eurocamp as the best holiday company, leaving big holiday brands in the shade, including Airtours, JMC, First Choice and Thomson.

The study brings the snapshot of happy holidaymakers into clearer focus with 90% of customers confident to recommend Eurocamp to others, 91% very satisfied or at least satisfied with Eurocamp and 79% emerging as potential repeat bookers within 5 years. The Eurocamp findings were presented against industry benchmarks calculated by drawing on comparable data sets from 19 leisure accommodation and airline businesses from the UK.

Significantly for marketers, the study demonstrates that customer satisfaction and loyalty is still rooted in getting the basics right and not simply established through tempting BOGOF offers or even a tasty new club card. On average, Eurocamp scored 30-40% higher than comparative industry competitors in key aspects of product and service including helpfulness and professionalism of staff, quality of accommodation, range and flexibility of holidays.

On behalf of Eurocamp Travel, Sales and Marketing Director, Morwenna Angove comments, "Over almost 30 years Eurocamp has firmly established its leading position in the family holiday market, fundamentally through delivering consistently high standards of customer service and quality holidays. When it comes to buying holidays consumers need peace of mind, more than anything else, that what they are going to get is all that they expect and ideally even more. We work hard to deliver peace of mind through our team of knowledgeable, efficient staff and through providing reliably good holidays. This study by TARP demonstrates that these key selling propositions are at the very heart of Eurocamp customer satisfaction and our greatest advantage over other holiday operators".

-Ends-

Note to editors. TARP (Technical Assistance Research Programmes), is an independent research-based consultancy – a market leader in satisfaction and loyalty measurement since 1971.

For executive comment on the TARP research study and further press information, please contact Nicky Fairweather or Heloise d'Souza at DFPR on 01422 345 827.

Eurocamp is a trading name of Greenbank Holidays Ltd.
Registered Office: As above   Registered in England 1160442

(a)

Figure 14.1(a) and (b) Two press releases from Eurocamp expounding the company's successes
(Courtesy: Eurocamp)

may well be used verbatim by a newspaper's busy editing staff, who employ 'cut and paste' methods to fill their columns. If succinct and well written, the copy has a much greater chance of being used. Copy should be double spaced, with wide margins. As with direct mail letters, the opening sentence needs to be an attention getter, conveying the main theme of the message. Information must be accurate and newsworthy, not a company 'plug' which editors will immediately see for what it is and discard. If it is essential to continue on to a second side, the word 'MORE . . .' should appear at the foot of the page. The text should be carefully proofread for grammatical or spelling errors before posting.

Figures 14.1(a) and (b) provide two examples of recent press releases from tour operator Eurocamp. The information each contains would appeal particularly to the travel trade press, and paragraphs can be easily cut and pasted into media editorial matter.

The Wigan Pier press release in Figure 14.2, by contrast, offers the media more general information about the product (a popular visitor attraction in the North Country in England) which might be picked up by media interests such as the local press, as well as trade journals.

Once a press release has been issued, the company must be geared up to respond very quickly and efficiently to any press enquiries. Journalists usually work to very short deadlines, and rapidly lose interest if they do not get instant answers. As well as easy access to the PRO, the press office may pass a journalist on to other senior staff. These must be specially briefed to talk to the press in order to answer specific questions or provide an interview. Journalists may also need to support their story with photographs of staff, etc., so it is a good idea to retain a small photographic library of high-quality prints for this purpose. Information about the photos should not be written on the back, but a title and brief description of what the photo portrays should be typed on a separate sheet of paper, fastened with adhesive tape to the bottom of the photo, and folded behind it.

Feature articles

Sometimes an opportunity arises to prepare a 'feature article' on travel and tourism. An example is the Guest Writer's column in the trade papers *Travel Weekly* and *Travel Trade Gazette*, and often local newspapers invite contributions on a travel theme. Feature articles are easier to arrange with local papers when accompanied by a commitment to advertise in the same edition. Some 'advertising features' such as this almost cross the borders between publicity and promotion, becoming a thinly veiled plug for the company's products. None the less, the material must be newsworthy – a topical issue of interest to readers, for instance – if it is to be used.

When advertising is tied in with potential coverage in this way, care should be taken not to upset the sensibilities of the editorial staff of the publication concerned. They often at least try to take a stance of 'editorial independence'. It may not always be possible overtly to 'buy' coverage by placing advertising.

Figure 14.2
'Explore a
century in a day':
a media release
from the Wigan
Pier attraction

4th June 2003

The Wigan Pier Experience
Trencherfield Mill
Wigan
WN3 4EF

Tel: 01942 323666
Fax: 01942 701927

MEDIA INFORMATION

"Explore a Century in a day"

At The Wigan Pier Experience, you can "Explore a Century in a day" … from the hardships and home-made fun of Victorian times in "The Way We Were", or the jazz age of the last century and the excitement of the swinging sixties in "The Museum of Memories" and visit the world's largest original mill steam engine … it's an interactive experience you'll never forget.

Have a trip on our waterbus and don't forget to visit our super gift shop and take home a memory of your visit or pop into our café at any time of the day for a selection of meals, snacks and drinks.

A day of fun and revelation for all the family on the banks of the Leeds and Liverpool Canal.

Additional Text

At "The Way We Were" Heritage Centre you can take a trip into our *Victorian Schoolroom* … misbehave and you'll be sent to the back of the class with your hands on your head – so sit up straight and keep your slate clean. Walk through our recreated *Coal Mine* and you'll appreciate the horrors that faced men and witness the local *Maypole Colliery Disaster*.

Take a trip across the canal to visit Wigan Pier's restored Trencherfield Mill for another amazing experience at "The Museum of Memories" – a unique interactive tour through 100 years of domestic life in Britain, all linked with national and international events of the day.

PR/WP0088
Explore a Century in a day
17/11/03

Here, you'll see, feel and hear life as no-one will ever know it again. Memories will be jogged for all but the very youngest of visitors and there'll be amusement round every corner at the way our parents, grandparents and great-grandparents used to live.

You'll meet some of the characters that bring the different decades to life … perhaps Alf the Spiv in the WWII Anderson Shelter; Pam the friendly shop assistant in the 60's boutique or Grocer Jack in our 1970's mini-mart.

A highlight of your visit will be performances by The Wigan Pier Theatre Company. You'll find them bringing the past to life throughout The Wigan Pier Experience including the Victorian Schoolroom, The Museum of Memories and Palace of Varieties.

Don't forget to visit our super gift shop and take home a memory of your visit or pop into our café at any time of the day for a selection of meals, snacks and drinks.

A day of fun and revelation for all the family on the banks of the Leeds and Liverpool Canal.

Ends

Contact: Melanie Hamer, Marketing Manager   01942 700402

Notes for the Editor

The Wigan Pier Experience is open every day apart from Friday's, Christmas Day, Boxing Day and New Years Day. Monday – Thursday 10am-5pm and Saturday – Sunday 11am-5pm.

Adult Site Ticket	£7.95
Concessionary Site Ticket	£6.25
Site Saver Ticket	£22.75 (admits 2 adults & 2 concessions)

PR/WP0088
Explore a Century in a day
17/11/03

(Courtesy: The Wigan Pier Experience)

Press facility visits

One other function falls within the domain of the PR department. This is the press facility visit. Organised in a similar fashion to the agents' familiarisation trip, which will be discussed a little later in the chapter, its purpose is to invite the media representatives – travel writers, journalists or correspondents from television and radio – to visit a particular attraction or destination, or to use the services of a particular travel company, in the hope that the trip will receive a favourable commentary in the media.

This can be a two-edged sword, since it invites opportunity for critical comment as well. An example of a press trip backfiring in spectacular fashion was the inaugural trip on the Eurostar train service through the Channel Tunnel. In the autumn of 1994 Eurostar invited a trainload of journalists to travel from London through to Paris on a special trip in advance of normal passenger services. The train broke down at Waterloo Station without travelling an inch and no back-up train was available. The group finally arrived in Paris too late for lunch. The resulting press comment was extremely negative and damaging for a service that hoped to lure business travellers away from the airlines – a target market where punctuality is paramount.

The strategy is widely used, however, by national or regional tourist offices, air and sea carriers, and tour operators, since a favourable press will have a huge impact on bookings. Principals may also invite correspondents from TV travel programmes to film their product. If favourable, the resulting show can generate substantial business for the region or company concerned.

Product placement

Product placement has become a well-established means of gaining publicity for branded products on films or television, and has to some extent usurped advertising spend in generating awareness (a move encouraged by the tendency of viewers to fast forward recorded ads on their TVs). There are some notorious examples of excessive use of this technique in recent years, notably Steven Spielberg's film *Minority Report*, which involved commercial expenditure on product placement of $25 million, fully one-quarter of the film's budget. The most recent James Bond films have also become notable for the use of this technique, using so-called 'halo marketing', or lingering camera shots of the product. In particular, the publicity received for the cars driven by Bond delivered a valuable boost to sales of BMW, Aston Martin and Lotus models.

In the case of travel and tourism, product placement is defined as encouraging plays or films to be made on location in areas or sites that will attract tourists. There are many examples of the link between popular films shot on location in exotic destinations and discrete support or sponsorship. Tunisia, as revealed in Chapter 13, gained considerable tourism growth following its support for films shot in that country, which included *Star Wars*, *Raiders of the Lost Ark* and *The English Patient*. In the case of the latter film, the Tunisian Tourist Office spent £20 000 sponsoring the UK premiere, later helping to develop an 'English Patient route' through the locations appearing in the film. Popular books can also boost tourism, an outstanding example being Peter Mayle's extraordinarily successful *A Year in Provence*. There are, of course, dangers in such publicity, not least that of spoiling remote destinations by encouraging over-demand, and some tourism authorities have lived to regret their support for locations as film sites.

Sponsorship

Sponsorship is a further means of achieving publicity for the name of a company. An organisation might sponsor the publication of a book or film about the history of the company or the industry, which could not be a commercial success without subsidy. Many long-established companies in the travel industry, such as shipping companies, have used this means of sponsorship. Other companies might choose to sponsor an academic text on travel and tourism, as did Barclays Merchant Services in the case of Alan Beaver's textbook *Mind Your Own Travel Business* (1993). Here, the aim was to generate interest in the company's credit card facilities, which are now used extensively in travel purchases. Alternatively, a documentary film might be produced on some subject concerning tourism.

Within the local community, sponsorship is also sought for floral displays, and in some cities in Britain, for the landscaping of roundabouts or other key features. Given the volume of traffic entering roundabouts each day, the small signs identifying the sponsor help to keep the name of the company in front of a large number of local residents, and this represents an ideal publicity medium for SMEs such as travel agents.

Other altruistic forms of sponsorship include financial support for the arts – theatre, fine art, concerts, festivals – and sporting events. The attraction of this form of publicity is that it generates goodwill, while costs can be set against taxes, and suitable activities for sponsorship can be found to fit any organisation's purse. Travel companies have sponsored educational study trips for young people, and in some cases have even sponsored staff for full- and part-time educational courses, as a gesture to generate goodwill among employees.

Example   Holiday Inn

The Holiday Inn chain invested over £1 million in a three-year sponsorship deal with England's Rugby Football Union in 2003. The aims of the deal were to increase the company's customer base and to maintain its current market position. The investment paid for high-profile outdoor advertising at key international matches held at the Twickenham ground, as well as other collaborative activities.

Local goodwill

Cultivating local goodwill is part and parcel of a firm's social responsibility. Apart from sponsoring events in the local community, there are many other ways in which a company can generate local goodwill. A retail agent in particular is highly dependent upon good relations with locals, since the catchment area exclusively provides the clients, so it is important to keep the name in front of the public. Events such as anniversaries of the company's founding can be used as a theme for generating news, organising contests and competitions, or mounting exhibitions. One agent saw an opportunity to build goodwill with the local school by offering to provide out-of-date brochures for geography assignments. This simultaneously solved the problem of getting rid of unwanted brochures and preventing the racks being depleted of current brochures.

Contact with shareholders of large companies is usually maintained through the annual report, except where crises emerge such as takeover bids, at which time a hastily mounted corporate advertising campaign aimed at shareholders may have to be mounted to counter the bid. Such campaigns are organised in consultation with management and the advertising agency.

Annual reports have become much more than simply a means of reporting performance to shareholders or would-be shareholders. Reports are now glossy and attractive, designed to create a sense of pride; travel companies, such as Singapore Airlines, have received international acclaim for the quality of their annual reports, which have a readership extending well beyond the shareholders themselves.

Lobbying

Sometimes the 'public' to be influenced are the law-makers. If legislation is planned which is thought to be contrary to interests of the company, a campaign may be launched to persuade Members of Parliament (MPs) to abandon the plans for legislation, or to sway public opinion against it. Such a campaign could be mounted by an individual company, but it is more likely to be taken up by the trade body, or a group of bodies. The usual vehicle for 'lobbying' is the direct mail letter, or an advertisement may encourage the travelling public to write to their MPs to protest. Figure 14.3 (a) and (b) (colour plate) provides two examples of lobbying the public, in the form of advertisements placed by the Caravan Club, designed to offset a negative view of the impact of caravanning on the countryside by emphasising its benefits in the form of economic contributions to the regions.

In 2002, the heads of the England, Wales and Scotland tourist boards came together to form Tourism UK, a body designed to lobby government for more support for domestic tourism. Concerted and determined efforts of this kind get listened to by governments, as the following example will reveal.

Example   The air passenger duty lobby

In 1999, the EU advised the British government that charging air passenger duty (APD) on a single leg only of a return journey was contrary to the EU single market legislation, and therefore illegal. Several of Britain's major aviation and tourism organisations, including the British Incoming Tour Operators' Association, formed an alliance under the banner 'F-Air Passenger Duty for All'. Supported by the trade paper *Travel Weekly*, the alliance lobbied the Treasury to hand back the additional duty to the industry in the form of lower APD for both legs of the journey. Individual MPs were lobbied during the annual Labour conference. The lobby was successful in persuading the Chancellor of the Exchequer that the added tax burden risked disaster for the airline industry, a decision hailed as a 'victory for common sense' by the industry.

Corporate identity

The PR department should also take responsibility for the introduction or modification of the company's corporate livery. The development of a 'house style' is an important element in an organisation's communications strategy, designed to support a particular image of the organisation. The development of an image for a company and its products, with associated logo, was outlined in Chapter 5, and the interrelationship between a product, its image and its brand is indivisible; but the creation of a logo, and the image which an organisation intends to project to its publics, should rest firmly with PR.

The logotype or logo is a symbol, name or combination of these forming a design which will instantly communicate the company and its image to the public. In the travel industry, this 'instant communication' takes on added significance, since the logo will appear on vehicles such as coaches, aircraft, ships and trains, as well as on stationery and shopfronts. It must therefore be instantly recognisable on the sides of fast-moving vehicles as well as under adverse conditions such as poor weather or failing light. Above all, once adopted, the logo should be standardised and appear identically on every form of communication used by the company. If the company wishes to project a modern, dynamic image, the design should be modern, too. Care must be taken, though, not to produce a design which will date quickly. Design fads, for all their contemporary appeal, soon date and will need frequent updating, an expensive undertaking and one where the benefits of a recognisable logo may be lost. A notable example of too frequent design change has been that of British Airways, which attempted to inject a more international image of their services through the introduction of artistically designed tail fins on their aircraft, drawing on global ethnicity for inspiration. The loss of national identity which this incurred infuriated many in the UK, including the prime minister of the day, Margaret Thatcher, and confused consumers from other countries. Within a fairly short timescale the tail fin designs were replaced by a more traditional image, reinforcing the national identity once again.

Thomas Cook is another travel company where frequent design change has puzzled its publics. The company reappraised its livery in the 1970s as it had neither a recognisable logo nor a standardised company name. The company appeared under various guises around the world, including Thomas Cook and Son, Thos Cook and Wagons Lits/Cook. The decision was taken to standardise the name and incorporate this into a new logo. For the travel division, a bright pillar-box red was chosen for maximum impact, while a more sedate silver grey was selected for the financial services. The result of the redesign was a new, exciting and immediately recognisable insignia on vehicles, stationery and travel shops. However, later Cooks passed into foreign ownership, and the parent company decided on a rebranding, introducing a yellow and blue motif to replace the now well-established lettering and red flashing. Colour changes such as this undermine recognition and take a long time to be assimilated by the public.

Example   TUI

> The formation of TUI, the world's leading travel company, brought together many brands in Europe including, at a slightly later date, Britain's Thomson Holidays, Britannia Airlines and travel chain Lunn Poly. International agency Interbrand was retained in 1991 to create the TUI 'smile' logo for the organisation, and this was used in the rebranding of all shops, other operations and stationery. With the incorporation of the Thomson travel empire, a complete redesign of Thomson's UK operations was called for. Cruise ships, aircraft, buses, airport sites, all had to be redesigned, together with brochures, stationery and point of sale material. Britannia's name was (at least temporarily) retained, but the traditional dark blue name banner disappeared, to be replaced by the World of TUI brand alongside the TUI smile logo on a light blue background. In-flight videos were used to explain the new brand to passengers. While the Thomson name was retained for the tour operations, the TUI smile was added to the company's logo. However, the retail chain posed a different problem; it was felt that the existing facia image of Lunn Poly (white on a red ground) was too strong to discard, so the TUI smile in white was simply added to the existing brand name/logo.

B2B PR

PR techniques are also used to help develop and maintain the organisation's reputation with suppliers, distributors and colleagues in the industry. Membership of both trade and professional bodies offers means by which individuals can exert influence through building up a circle of contacts. Travel companies are generally pleased to support staff who volunteer to serve on ABTA committees, and may pay subscriptions for staff who qualify for membership in the Institute of Travel and Tourism (ITT), or the Tourism Society, the Hotel and Catering International Management Association (HCIMA) or the Chartered Institute of Transport (CIT). Even membership in Skål, the association of travel executives, ostensibly a social club, provides a forum for contacts and the strengthening of influence among colleagues in the trade on a local basis, and for this reason some companies are willing to underwrite members' subscriptions.

Some larger corporations go beyond this by agreeing to donate funds or other forms of direct support towards the maintenance of the organisations. When the ITT found itself in trouble financially in 2003, several companies stepped in to offer their support, including TUI UK, MyTravel and Stena Line.

The familiarisation visit

A travel agent who personally knows a destination is more likely to sell it with enthusiasm. There is no stronger force in a selling conversation with a customer than personal experience.

Although agents cannot hope to have knowledge of every area of the world, most can reasonably be expected to have personal knowledge of the nearer and more frequently demanded destinations. The accumulation of such knowledge is aided by the *familiarisation visits*, sometimes referred to as *educationals*, arranged by principals for retail travel personnel. Often tour operators organise such trips, but it is equally common for national tourist offices, in cooperation with airlines serving the destination, to help in the organisation or to undertake their own programmes of study visits. Hotels at the destination will make their own contributions by offering free or heavily subsidised accommodation. Malta offers an example of one such destination committed to providing agents with personal experience of a destination.

Example   Malta's familiarisation visits for travel agency staff

Following independence in 1964, Malta had a long period of estrangement from Britain, with whom close ties had previously existed. Tourism from the UK had halved during a period of growth for Mediterranean holidays. The only way to rebuild numbers was to be seen to be offering low prices that were directly competitive with nearer destinations. Whereas many Spanish destinations are only two hours' flying time from British airports, Malta is three. This obviously affected costs, and to remain competitive meant effectively discounting the local costs substantially, by offering a lower 'tour operators' exchange rate. In the longer term, however, it was clear that Malta would have to justify higher prices by offering something different. Higher prices also meant that higher quality would be demanded, and government policies moved towards encouragement of the best in hotels and other facilities.

One problem to be overcome was that Malta's perceived quality in the eyes of past visitors was not always good. It was therefore decided to embark upon a policy of facilitating as many travel agents' visits as possible in order that they could see the improvements for themselves. Careful planning was needed to determine the best time for such visits, when there would be unsold seats on aircraft undertaking regular services, yet when the weather would be kind as well. All major tour operators with programmes to the island were invited to participate in hosting the visitors and showing off their wares, but within strictly controlled criteria. Visitors were to be generously hosted, given little free time (these were working trips, not substitute holidays) and shown a range of the facilities that Malta offered to emphasise how different it was from other rivals for clients' attention. As well as seeing hotels, visits were included to historic sites and churches, as well as to the ubiquitous high tech disco.

This pattern was repeated many times, with well over 1000 travel agency staff benefiting. All had to make applications to go, to ensure that they actually wanted to visit Malta rather than being pressed by their managers to do so. All paid to go, to ensure commitment, even though the sum was nominal and employers were asked to fund the cost. Returning agents expressed their delight about what they had experienced, and promised to recommend Malta in the future. The formula proved successful in the most important way possible, a visible growth in the size and quality of Malta's tourism against falling levels elsewhere.

Small group agency visits

Though this pattern of major visits (involving more than 200 agents at a time) has been used by other destinations, more common are small group visits organised by individual tour operators responding to identified gaps in their future sales charts.

Sadly, these are often less objective, sometimes being little more than excuses for sales executives to entertain favoured agents. Even this, though, will have a beneficial rub-off in cementing relations between suppliers and retailers.

Progressive agency managements try to plan the attendance of staff on visits that will result in a commercial benefit in the future, but it is also recognised that the provision of fully paid educational opportunities is one of the perks of a fairly low-paid job and, as such, a means of promoting staff loyalty. However, efforts by tax inspectors to treat this as a taxable perk undermines the value of this essential training, agents rightly arguing that gaining product knowledge in this way is a vital element in their distribution role.

Preparation for an educational visit

It is important that preparation, organisation of the event itself, and any follow-up, should be faultless, and this does not happen by chance. The organiser needs to establish exactly who is eligible, considering the following points:

- which agencies are eligible for an invitation
- at what level and status of staff the programme is to be aimed, usually those actively working as salespeople
- whether those who have been before to the destination will be eligible
- what age range is preferred
- whether more than one person can come from the same agency
- how long those invited should have worked for the agency
- whether, if named invitations are to be issued, substitutes will be accepted.

In addition, it will be sensible to arrange to have adequate information on file such as:

- home emergency contacts
- whether a smoker or non-smoker (for rooming purposes)
- whether the agency requires specific information or specially arranged visits to a particular property or facility, such as a golf course for golf promoters
- details of the agency's local paper for any publicity shots taken during the trip and copy about the visit.

Before setting out it can be useful to obtain the participants' views on what they think they will see, in order to be able later to compare these with a similar questionnaire completed after their return. It is fairly certain that whatever the views expressed may be, they will represent a microcosm of the opinions of potential clients and may give suitable information for use in later promotional campaigns. These 'before/after' views are now commonly reported in the trade press for the benefit of other agencies.

It is also worthwhile inviting journalists from the trade press to accompany the group, to maximise trade publicity.

It is now common for participants' employers to ask for a report on the visit, in the employee's own words, that can be circulated to other members of staff. This helps to establish pools of expertise within the agency, as well as giving sales pointers to other staff. Organisers will also benefit by issuing participants with a certificate to display within the agency, to publicise that he or she has 'successfully undertaken a study tour' of the destination concerned.

Opinion leaders' familiarisation

Travel agents represent only one form of public which organisations seek to influence. Of equal importance are the persuaders, or opinion leaders – journalists, broadcasters and others who might in one way or another exert influence over the buying decisions of the consuming public. Familiarisation visits for these usually fall to the responsibility of the national tourist offices, but maximum cooperation is sought from hoteliers, tourist attractions and others to keep costs down and ensure a positive experience by the participants. This means bringing on the big guns – the proprietors of hotels, museum curators, directors of local attractions – to make formal addresses to the visitors, as well as granting them high-quality hospitality. Even the best programmes cannot guarantee that positive publicity will ensue, but potential coverage in the press can make a huge difference to demand, as readers are heavily influenced by the travel pages of the national press, or short TV articles about destinations or cruises.

Internal goodwill

Internally, too, there are publics to be wooed. The concept of the 'internal market' has now been widely recognised, and employers are aware that poor staff morale will undermine the efficiency of an organisation as well as its appeal to other publics, such as its customers, shareholders and members of the local community. PR plays an important part in showing employers how they can help to improve staff morale, or improve relations between staff and management, and in so doing reduce staff turnover or increase productivity.

In a large company, this will mean establishing a campaign just as is done with external publics. A common means of communication in the large travel firm is the house journal, an internal magazine of news and views about the company and its staff. While some of these journals are excellent, many are seen by staff as no more than a thinly disguised management tool to incite them to greater sales efforts, or boost the egos of senior management.

Good staff relations are vital for the health and success of a company. Unfortunately, it is widely recognised that many managers in travel and tourism businesses have neither the skills to manage staff properly nor the financial means to reward them to an appropriate standard. If financial rewards are impossible, other means have to be found of creating job satisfaction. There is ample evidence that good management can achieve this.

Example   The Flight Centre

The Flight Centre is an Australian owned global chain of travel agents, with 80 shops in the UK alone. In 2003, the *Sunday Times* identified the company as the third-best employer in the country, in their competition to find the 100 best companies to work for. The criteria on which companies were judged included best leadership (for which the Travel Centre came top), job satisfaction, open management, caring colleagues, laughter at work, fair pay. Employees were judged not to be taken advantage of, they were glad to work for the company and they treated their customers well. In all these categories, the company came within the first 10 in the country.

Other travel firms also coming within the top 100 were Fred Olsen and Travel Inns.

Reports such as these are invaluable in boosting the reputation of a business, and the publicity attached to wide press coverage of the results (enhanced by good press relations) can gain maximum publicity for the company.

Given that staff represent an important element within the traditional four Ps of the marketing mix, their recruitment and training must inevitably be seen as the responsibility of good marketing, and good PR, as well as of personnel management. Training for retail agency work remains weak, and recruitment is still difficult because of the demands of the job; but retail agents must know more than consumers can find out for themselves on the Internet, otherwise their future cannot be guaranteed. Staff must be skilled, informed, motivated and well led if the company itself is to have a future – yet the difficult trading conditions of the early 2000s led employers to tighten up on pay and conditions instead of focusing on improving the work environment. Even at the time of writing, new conditions of employment are being drawn up by leading companies which makes employment less attractive, including in one case conditions governing behaviour outside of office hours, sick pay entitlement at management discretion, obligatory weekend working without supplementary pay and requirements for staff to give up to 13 weeks' notice of resignation – all conditions not conducive to building staff morale. Good relations with the 'internal public' are as important as those with the consuming public, and it is the job of the PRO to convince management of this.

Pay and conditions, while inadequate in the retail sector, are even poorer in other sectors of the travel industry. The hotel sector is notorious both for its long antisocial hours, low salaries and poor conditions of work at the lower levels, but the passenger shipping business is perhaps the most outstanding example of bad pay and conditions for staff, expected to provide a friendly and polished service to wealthy customers who are often enjoying very luxurious holidays representing many years' salary for most of the crew. One report[1] reveals how conditions might typically include a 14–16-hour day seven days a week, a cabin shared with five others as the sole personal space on board, and inadequate showers or toilets. Overseeing officers are frequently abusive, and staff have only limited rights with little or no worker representation to negotiate with employers or deal with their aggravations. Such conditions are demotivating and demoralising for workers who, unsurprisingly, are largely recruited from poorer Third World countries. In this respect the travel industry lags some way behind the conditions of work deemed normally acceptable in the developed world.

Handling unfavourable publicity

Having earlier discussed ways in which favourable publicity can be generated, we must now turn our attention to dealing with the inevitable unfavourable publicity that will arise from time to time. Negative publicity can develop at both the macro and micro levels. At a *macro level*, the impact of strikes or 'go-slows' by air traffic controllers or customs officers can create enormous disruptions to travellers, which the media are not slow to exploit. As far as Britain is concerned, there has been almost constant bad news in the foreign press in relation to foot and mouth disease, mad cow disease, transport chaos and the state of the National Health Service, while even before the September 11th tragedy high prices for hotels and food, coupled with a strong pound, made the task of selling Britain difficult for the national tourist boards. At a *micro level* an individual company can be affected by such diverse problems as fires in hotels with locked emergency exits, dangerous hotel lifts, and faulty gas heaters causing asphyxiation in self-catering facilities – all calamities which have befallen British travel businesses in recent years – to say nothing of disasters such as food poisoning on board cruise ships or aircraft crashes. Quite apart from disasters of this magnitude, many minor problems arise with which PR must deal. Rumours of redundancy or takeovers can affect staff morale, resulting in the loss of key members of the company through resignation at a crucial time, while a CAA refusal to grant an air travel organiser's licence (ATOL), or a request from ABTA for a company's bond to be increased, may sow seeds of doubt in the minds of the travelling public or within the trade, which can undermine the company's reputation and lead to its collapse.

It may be thought that PROs have a thankless task in having to help 'pick up the pieces' after such events; but their close relationship with the media makes their role invaluable when crises such as these occur. In a situation where a major crisis has occurred, successful PR will depend upon three things:

1 The PRO must be well briefed and in full possession of the facts. A good working relationship with a frank and trusting management is essential if this is to be achieved.

2 PROs must in turn be as frank as is possible with the media. An obvious attempt to cover up will be seized upon by journalists, which will threaten the whole future relationship between the two parties.

3 PROs must act fast, taking the initiative in calling the press and other media to a press conference to announce details of the event, rather than waiting to respond to media pressure. Fast action helps to dispel rumours which may paint a worse picture of the crisis than reality.

Larger companies need to be prepared in advance to handle disasters, by forming disaster committees – with staff who are reachable 24 hours a day, seven days a week – to include a PRO where these are employed. Decisions should be taken in advance as to who within the committee will draft press releases, and represent the company at press conferences. The individuals chosen must be senior enough to carry weight, and have suitable presentation and on-camera skills. Staff must also be briefed immediately where emergencies occur, and should not have to hear about disasters affecting their company by watching television news stories. All key staff need training in handling disasters, and these need to be informed of what key individuals – legal, insurance, expert investigators – are to be contacted when emergencies occur.

There are too many examples of inadequate training and poor handling of crises. One of the most notable is now a historical case study, and helped in bringing about the collapse of one of the world's best known airlines, as detailed below.

Example   Pan American Airways

PAA, as one of the oldest airlines in the world, used the strapline 'The World's Most Experienced Airline' but by the 1980s the company was listed by *Fortune* magazine as one of the 10 least admired corporations in the USA. The company also did not employ an external PRO.

Just before Christmas in 1988, PAA flight 103 was blown up by terrorists over Lockerbie in Scotland, and 270 people died in consequence. The initial disaster was badly handled – unable to control the information filtering to the media, the company demonstrated reluctance to display any compassion or to accept responsibility, through fears of legal action. The Chief Executive Officer made no public appearance until eight days after the disaster. Although the company contacted an external PR consultancy immediately after the crash, there was insufficient time to develop an appropriate action programme.

Among other mistakes,

■ coffins were seen the day following the crash, unloaded in New York wrapped in cardboard
■ names of students aboard were released to their universities before relatives had been informed
■ the company's phone number, already jammed by media enquiries, was released to the public to make enquiries into the crash
■ relatives were not protected from the media scrum when they eventually visited the crash site.

By 1991 the airline had filed for Chapter 11 bankruptcy protection, but was not seen as an attractive prospect for a takeover, and was eventually dissolved.

The failure of the company to act quickly and appropriately can be contrasted with the disaster that hit Thomas Cook in 1999, which became a model of good PR work, described in the following example.

Example   Thomas Cook

In 1999 a coach chartered by Thomas Cook crashed in South Africa, killing a total of 29 people, of whom 26 were UK tourists. Cooks had a crisis management policy which was implemented within 10 minutes of hearing the news. Staff were mobilised in teams to deal with the various aspects of the crisis. The media were briefed within four hours of the crash, and the first team flown out four hours later including legal representatives and an expert on coach operations. A director and general manager also flew out to oversee operations in South Africa. The company recruited a professional counselling service to counsel next of kin and the staff directly affected. One person in a team was given sole responsibility to deal with all enquiries from relatives, while a hot-line task force of 16 was established to take calls from the public in the UK.

The company liaised with SAA to fly relatives out the following day, and to bring back the survivors. Another team dealt with hospital admissions for the injured and the return of the deceased by air.

All passengers booked for long-haul coach holidays were given the opportunity to cancel and receive a full refund. Only 6 out of a total of 150 due to take a holiday in South Africa took up the offer.

Well-handled crises draw much smaller press coverage than badly managed ones. Cunard Line suffered for many months from the bad publicity generated when in 1994 its flagship *QE2* was put into service on the North Atlantic too quickly following a refit, resulting in a calamitous voyage which received maximum publicity on television, including amateur videotapes of burst pipes, soggy carpets and inadequate help from staff on board. A complacent CEO did nothing to resolve the calamity when faced by the media in the UK (later leading to his departure from the company). Contrast this with a well-handled, if relatively minor, crisis experienced by the cruise line P&O.

Example   P&O Cruises

P&O's *Aurora* had a troubled maiden voyage in 2000, which was eventually cancelled in mid-cruise when a bearing in the propeller shaft overheated. Passengers on board were offered generous compensation terms – full refund of their money, plus a free cruise after the problem had been fixed. They were given liberal free drinks on board, and kept fully informed of developments as they occurred. Press reports which followed were uniformly favourable.

Evaluating campaign results

At the beginning of this chapter it was pointed out that evaluating PR campaigns is often more difficult than evaluating the success of other forms of communication, since PR has long-term objectives and these are often qualitative in nature. However, many PR exercises are measurable, providing targets are established initially determining what the campaign is to achieve. One means of measuring PR success is through the measurement of media exposure. An analysis of press cuttings, for instance, will enable the company to measure the number of column inches of publicity received during the period of the PR campaign. Press clipping services are provided by PR agencies, if the company does not have the resources to undertake this itself. Depending upon the media carrying the coverage, an estimate can be made of the audience reached through these reports, and some comparison made of the comparative costs if this coverage had had to be purchased commercially for advertising. While such tools of measurement are helpful, they provide no measure of the impact of the exposure, or whether goodwill, or recall of the company, would have been more effectively achieved through paid advertisements. Nevertheless, publicity achieved through PR campaigns can often be gained at very small cost to the company, and offers a valuable contribution to the overall communications process.

It will also be helpful to attempt some measure of the coverage achieved by the company's leading competitors, since this will give an indication of the relative success of the organisations' PR departments.

A more accurate means of measuring PR effectiveness, if more expensive, is through the implementation of a programme of research to check changes in awareness, understanding or attitude. This will require surveys to be carried out before, after and sometimes during campaigns, which can be conducted among a sample of national consumers, among members of the local community, or among the firm's distributors. However, national surveys, involving sampling opinion of 1500–2000 randomly selected respondents, are beyond the resources of all but the largest travel companies, or the public sector.

Within the company, figures on staff turnover can offer pointers on levels of job satisfaction, but must be supported by staff interviews to ascertain reasons for departure.

Finally, the impact of any campaign can be measured in terms of increased sales and profits. It may be difficult to be certain that increases are the result of any PR activities, or what proportion of the increases can be ascribed to PR compared with other communications campaigns of the company. Allowances must be made for external influences on market growth, and increases must be compared with comparative figures achieved by the company's competitors. At best, measurement will be inaccurate, but it will give some indication of the effectiveness of the PR department's activities, and help to justify the budget allocated to this function.

Corporate social responsibility

It might be helpful to close this chapter by bringing us full circle. In Chapter 1 the importance of developing an ethical stance in developing and marketing tourism programmes was stressed, while in Chapter 5 stress was laid on developing sustainable products for the survival of destinations, and indeed, the planet. In this chapter we have looked at the role of PR in helping an organisation to benefit and make its products more saleable by generating good relations between the organisation and its publics. However, it is increasingly recognised that simply making an organisation look good is insufficient; it must not only be *seen* to be good, but must *be* good, respected for itself and without any hidden agenda. The concept of corporate social responsibility (CSR) makes clear that organisations by their existence take on responsibilities towards others in society, not merely to their shareholders and customers.

Closely allied to the concept of CSR in the travel and tourism industry is the issue of sustainability. As one senior executive in the industry claims, CSR can be defined as 'the part that social and environmental performance play in corporate well-being alongside financial performance'.[2] Sustainable tourism cannot merely be seen as a PR exercise designed to win over the hearts and minds of the public, but should be a genuine attempt to improve and protect the planet for future generations. This view reflects a radical change in business attitudes which would have been unthinkable a decade ago. Indeed, recent research by Britain's Institute of Public Policy revealed that only 4 out of 10 businesses (of any description) discuss social or environmental issues at board level, either routinely or occasionally. Tourism businesses lag behind even this record, but at the time of writing, ABTA was working with members of the industry in Britain to develop CSR strategies and means of implementing them; and a number of organisations, both large and small, were making the first tentative efforts to incorporate CSR into their management strategies. The hotel industry in particular has introduced many innovations designed to encourage sustainability, including the International Hotel Environment Initiative (IHEI), in which over 8000 hotels worldwide participate. One interesting example of CSR in the European sphere is demonstrated by Spanish airline Iberia.

Example   Iberia Airlines

Iberia has expressed its determination to meet society's needs and to make altruistic contributions to non-profit-making schemes. In 2003 the company planned to publish its first Social Responsibility Report alongside the annual Financial Report, detailing the social and environmental projects in which it and its employees had become involved. These include the APMIB, an association of Iberia employees with handicapped offspring, which had grown since its inception to become a body running job centres, occupational workshops and health centres, no longer restricted to the families of Iberia staff. Much of the equipment and food supplied on board Iberia airlines is now packed by handicapped employees at the association's work centre.

The NGO Mano a Mano (hand to hand) organisation has also been formed by employees who volunteer to help resource humanitarian projects in Spain, Latin America and Africa, supported by the company itself. Each day more than a ton of humanitarian aid is carried free on aircraft, while human organs for transplant are also freely transported across Spain. Passengers are encouraged to foster sport among the handicapped by donating spare foreign currency to the Special Olympics. The company also made available 50 000 free seats to the Spanish government and the Galicia Aid Commission for volunteers to help clean up the beaches after the *Prestige* oil disaster.

In Britain, British Airways has also led the way with its Tourism for Tomorrow annual awards for sustainable tourism ventures. Winners of these awards receive widespread publicity via BA's media communications, national media coverage, the awards ceremony itself which takes place in London, and an opportunity to feature in a UK travel programme on television. While cynics might view these perks as a good opportunity for self-promotion as much as any genuine reflection of concern for the environment, the beneficial end results of programmes gaining awards cannot be doubted, in terms of the social and/or environmental sustainability they have brought to the regions concerned.

Britain's tourism interests took a giant step forward in 2003 with the creation of the Travel Foundation, a charity supported by the big four tour operators (TUI/Thomson, Thomas Cook, First Choice and MyTravel) and specialist operator Sunvil, backed by the Foreign Office and in cooperation with ABTA, AITO and the FTO. This organisation was founded as a charity following pressure from the British government, which in the previous year had announced its own Sustainable Tourism Initiative. Its aim is to encourage the development of environmentally friendly tourism programmes by travel companies. Where previously only lip-service had been paid to sustainable considerations in many travel companies' planning, this departure seems to represent the first genuinely altruistic move by the industry as a whole to ensure the environment is protected for future tourists and indigenous populations.

As far as marketing is concerned, these issues go well beyond the question of PR. Tour operators and transport companies have marketing power to influence consumer decisions on where to go and when, what kind of holidays to buy, even how their customers should comport themselves when in a foreign country. Multinational operators can exercise great influence over the economic and social direction of destinations thousands of miles away from their head offices, whether by promoting a destination or withdrawing from it. They have a responsibility towards the local communities, as much as to their customers. Product design must take into account the sensitivity of the environment they are exploiting just as much as the interests of the companies themselves and their shareholders. Tourism organisations around the world are finally awakening to these needs.

Questions, tasks and issues for discussion

1   This task will involve a role play between two people, one of whom will take the role of spokesperson for a coach company which has just suffered the loss of a vehicle en route from the south of France, killing 3 and injuring 11 passengers. The second person will take the role of a television reporter interviewing the spokesperson about the crash (if this can be conducted on closed circuit TV for later playback, so much the better). The media have heard rumours that the coach driver fell asleep at the wheel, after having had to curtail his rest hours in France, due to late arrival at the site on the outbound journey.

2   Write a press release designed to publicise the forthcoming launch of a new series of package tours to the Maldives, Mauritius and Madagascar which combine beach and activity (snorkeling, etc.) holidays.

3   Identify the key issues which go to make a successful educational visit for travel agents. Now carry out a small-scale survey among agency counter staff who have been on an educational visit, in order to judge how well organised their visits were. Write a brief summary of your conclusions, and recommendations to principals and agency managers for the conduct of future educationals.

4   London Heathrow Airport is shortly to expand with the development of a fifth terminal, and a very lengthy process of consultation spread over many years. A decision is also to be reached about the siting of a new runway, or development of a new airport for London. BAA is keen to see the continuing expansion of Heathrow, in spite of powerful lobbying by environmental groups. Outline a plan of action to lobby for the expansion at Heathrow on behalf of BAA, identifying the publics to be influenced and key opinion leaders to be approached. Suggest which tools and media would be appropriate for getting the message across.

Exercise

Taking any notable crisis which has affected one travel business during the past two years, assume the role of the PRO for the company concerned. Identify your priorities and set out a plan for a PR campaign to handle the problem. Write this up in the form of a brief for your managing director/chief executive.

References

1 Mather, C, *What it's Really Like to Work on Board Cruise Ships*. War on Want/International Transport Workers' Federation 2002
2 Hugh Somerville, Head of Sustainable Business Unit, British Airways, quoted in Kalisch, A (see below)

Further reading

Eber, S, *Beyond the Green Horizon: Principles for Sustainable Tourism*, Tourism Concern/WWF, 1992

Kalisch, A, *Corporate Futures: Social Responsibility in the Tourism Industry*, Tourism Concern, 2002

Kotler, P, Armstrong, G, Saunders, J and Wong, V, *Principles of Marketing*, Prentice Hall, 3rd European edn 2001, ch 2 pp 43–69

Kotler, P, Bowen, J and Makens, J, *Marketing for Hospitality and Tourism*, Prentice Hall, 2nd edn 1999, ch 16

Morgan, M, *Marketing Leisure and Tourism*, Prentice Hall, 1996, ch 18

Some sustainable tourism websites

www.ihei.org	International Hotel Environmental Initiative
www.sustainabletourism.net	research into sustainable tourism
www.toinitiative.org	UN responsible tourism programme
www.tourismconcern.org.uk	UK-based organisation concerned with sustainability in tourism
www.world-tourism.org	WTO website including policy on sustainable tourism

15 Marketing control

Learning outcomes

After studying this chapter, you should be able to:

- recognise the importance of control mechanisms in the marketing plan
- distinguish between different techniques of control
- implement simple control procedures in marketing.

Control in the marketing process

In preceding chapters we have explained how each element of the marketing mix, including communication in all its forms, must be continuously reviewed to ensure that it is functioning adequately, with corrective action taken if actual performance is failing to meet expectations. This process of ongoing separate monitoring and evaluation of each element of the mix is an important task for marketing management, which we might term micro-control. However, the marketing function within an organisation is just one element in the overall *business system*. That is to say that certain *inputs* into the business, namely labour, capital and enterprise, are brought together in a *process* designed to create one or more end-products for consumers. These end-products are the organisation's *output*. Any system consists of these three components, an input, a process and an output, and management must monitor the overall performance of the organisation's inputs and processes at a macro level, to measure and evaluate not only the organisation's operational performance, but also its strategic performance. Good marketing practice is classically defined as ensuring that the output is the right product, at the right price, in the right place at the right time, to ensure that the sales and profit targets laid down in the marketing plan are met; but monitoring is also needed to ensure that opportunities are maximised, and that the strengths of the organisation are being employed and developed. These are matters of strategy, and extend beyond the monitoring responsibilities of the marketing department alone.

Figure 15.1
The monitoring
and control
system

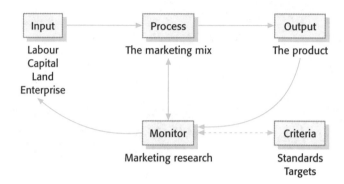

The keyword here is *monitoring*; the process which is designed to provide feedback on the effectiveness and efficiency of the system as a whole, to compare actual and expected performance, to control it, and where necessary either to change it or to adjust the original objectives in the light of changing circumstances. This is illustrated in Figure 15.1.

In this chapter we shall look at the role of the monitoring procedures which are designed to control the marketing system. All along we have stressed that planning is an essential part of the marketing process, but the plan will only be as good as the control to which it is subject. Plans are not carved on tablets of stone; they have to be adjusted constantly in the light of changing circumstances, as the company reacts to new opportunities and market forces.

Marketing is carried out in an organisation in three stages:

1   *Pre-action*   At this stage, activities associated with planning for action have to be undertaken. This includes the development of an information system, and a programme of planned market research. Marketing objectives are established, including sales volume and profit targets, and strategies are devised to achieve the objectives. Forecasts are drawn up based on the strategies to be implemented.

2   *Action*   At this stage, the marketing plan is implemented. This brings into play the coordinating role of the marketing manager, who must ensure that the channels of communication are integrated within the department, so that promotional activities serve a common aim. The coordinator must also make certain that where other departments are contributing to the marketing plan, these commitments are met, and in time. Typically, this will include the need to ensure that supply is in line with demand. Day-to-day activities undertaken as part of the plan will be regularly reviewed and adjusted as necessary.

3   *Post-action*   At this final stage, organisational plans are reviewed as a whole, with the marketing manager evaluating the marketing plan in its entirety, looking at actual against anticipated performance and exploring opportunities further to improve the performance of the department. In this final chapter, we shall be examining aspects of both macro- and micro-control, and the monitoring processes involved in exercising this control.

Although control is a key management function, it should not become a responsibility which exercises too much of a marketing manager's time. The objective of good management is to build a marketing control system which is self-correcting as far as possible. This is achieved by good information systems, the use of management by objectives and the delegation of authority to take corrective action in day-to-day operational activities. Staff within the department need to be aware of what is expected of them as individuals, how they are performing, and to whom they are accountable. It is by no means unusual in a large travel company (as in any other large company) to find staff unclear about their accountability, or staff who are accountable to more than one member of management, each setting different priorities and having different expectations of their staff.

It is equally important that staff not only know their responsibilities but also are given power to regulate their activities, even at the most junior level. A member of a travel agent's counter staff given responsibility for racking brochures must know, for example, what the agency's policy is for racking brochures, procedures for ordering and reordering brochures, what action to take when brochures are refused by a principal or out of stock at the principal's. The clerk must be given full responsibility for maintenance of adequate stock, and control over the stockroom so that brochures are placed in an orderly system so they can be found quickly when needed. With such a system, the manager should seldom have to intervene, and occasional spot checks or an end-of-season survey to ensure that old stock is being cleared is all that is needed to maintain effective control.

Five different forms of control can be identified in a control system:

- performance control
- quality control
- financial control
- efficiency control
- strategic control.

Each of these will be examined in the light of travel and tourism practice.

Performance control

This is designed to make sure the organisation meets its set targets. Typical targets identified in the marketing plan will include:

- turnover
- profitability
- market share
- return on investment
- quality
- consumer attitudes.

The extent to which these targets are being met can be monitored on a daily or weekly basis, and control depends upon a regular flow of information which identifies performance variance and is transmitted quickly to those responsible for taking corrective action. These members of staff must ascertain why the deviance is occurring and whether action can be taken to bring it back into line with forecasts.

Actual identification of variance is a largely mechanical process, but correcting it calls for management skills, both in interpreting data and in the suitable deployment of resources. Here the manager must distinguish between controllable factors, and those outside the control of the business which will require readjustment of the forecast or the marketing plan's goals. Let us say that the sale of tours to Britain from the United States has declined, and is failing to reach the targets set. This may be accounted for entirely by changing economic or political circumstances, such as the drop in US visitors to Europe resulting from a combination of the September 11th terrorist attack, the after-effects of the wars in Afghanistan and Iraq, an economic recession at home, or fluctuating exchange rates between the two countries.

Nevertheless, it is important that the decline in the company's bookings is compared with those of other businesses handling US traffic to Britain, since it may be that internal factors account for part of the deviance. Assuming the organisation's performance is broadly in line with that of the total market, the marketing plan will require adjustment, so that targets are less dependent on US traffic in the coming year. The marketing manager will also want to look at the original objectives, and determine whether they were realistic. A close look will be taken of the controllable elements in the marketing plan; is the structure of the department designed to get the results sought in the marketing plan, for example? What factors in the marketing mix require to be changed to achieve the targets set?

Remedial action to bring performance back on target needs to be taken quickly, but not so quickly as to reflect a panic response to a temporary aberration, which may be self-correcting. In the lead-up to conflict with Iraq in early 2003, tour operators started discounting massively to counter a sharp drop in forward sales, even though experience in the Gulf War 12 years earlier suggested that a short war would lead to rapid escalation of demand for holidays abroad.

In looking at profitability control, businesses will be concerned not just with overall profitability, but equally with the profitability of each 'profit centre', or product range. A tour operator will be observing profitability on each programme operated, just as a travel agent should examine profitability for each form of travel service sold. In fact, tour operators will want to know their profitability not only at the programme level, but also by brand, season, resort and hotel. This allows for continual adjustment throughout the season to attempt to maintain profit levels. Resort and hotel performance will also influence decisions taken in the following season, in terms of the room rates the operator is willing to pay hoteliers, and the supply balance between destinations served. Airlines, suffering badly in the aftermath of September 11th and the Iraqi crisis, were ruthless in adjusting flights and destinations served in order to reduce losses.

As we have seen, the tour operator's business is extremely competitive and all operators are very conscious of their overall market share as well as individual sales levels. It is relatively easy for an operator to assess its own sales. Those of the competition pose a rather more difficult problem. Yet even if sales are up, an operator will wish to know that this increase is not in fact less than it ought to be, relative to the whole market and the competition.

Recognition of the need for timely (often weekly) performance information within the travel industry has led several research companies to provide a statistics service to travel organisations. Basically, third-party research companies pull together information that individual companies would find difficult or costly to prepare. This consolidated information is then sold to a number of companies who use it for performance monitoring. Typically, purchasers are provided with detailed weekly statistics on sales made through ABTA travel agents, broken down by destination, party size, holiday type, operator and booking month.

Interestingly, even though the tour operators are fiercely competitive, the hunger for performance measures means that the industry is rich in syndicated research. This is research where operators join together to share the costs of a particular research programme. They may also provide information knowing that the only way they will know what their competitors are doing is by revealing their own position.

One of the most significant factors affecting profitability of a tour operator is *load factor*, or the extent to which individual flights are filled. In Chapter 6 we discussed fixed and marginal costs; an aeroplane represents a very high fixed cost, and with the low individual margins of the tour operating business, if aircraft are less than around 90 per cent full they are unlikely to be generating any profit contribution at all. Thus, for instance, an operator may 'consolidate' two undersold flights into one in order to reduce costs. This of course is unpopular with consumers who have their travel arrangements altered, perhaps at short notice; there may be a hidden cost to the savings overtly made in terms of compensation and lost future business. However, the operator may simply have no option if it is to remain in business and make a profit.

Tour operators will track the performance of individual retailers closely in order to identify the most productive outlets. While the multiple agency chains and independent consortia have buying power and in the past have frequently negotiated better rates of commission for all their branches or agencies, there is evidence that operators are now looking more closely at whether standard rewards for all offices are appropriate, where some may actually generate only a limited number of bookings. Performance needs to be judged in a wider context: will the overall increased commission rates actually result in increasing or reducing the operator's profits?

Quality control

Measuring quality and ensuring that quality is maintained is a relatively simple matter in the production of durable goods; these can be inspected, rejected if below standard, and some tolerance agreed for the proportion falling below standard. Maintaining quality control over a product such as tourism is far less straightforward. Uncontrollable factors such as weather exert a considerable influence over the perceived quality of a tourism service.

Tour operators pay close attention to the requirement that their products live up to their description in their brochure, because this is required under law. Increasingly, they are establishing acceptable tolerances for levels of complaints, as this is a simple means of measuring quality control. Complaints can be measured by recording letters of complaint received by the company, or complaints made verbally to the resort representatives, which should always be recorded. The correct operation of a monitoring system means that complaints are fed back in the form of corrective actions that help to avoid complaints arising in the future. Thus, as well as counting overall numbers of complaints, even just one complaint could mean, for instance, a change implemented in copy for the next edition of the brochure. The use of questionnaires is less effective in monitoring complaints, as most questionnaires used require only that clients list their levels of satisfaction or dissatisfaction with the product; and there may be insufficient information to take action to correct a situation even where a high level of complaints is registered. One needs to know *exactly* what is wrong with the service, and what *action* is needed to correct the situation. Suggestion boxes can provide a good picture of consumer dissatisfaction, as can debriefing of staff such as resort representatives at the end of a season.

All the major tour operators have for many years monitored performance through customer satisfaction questionnaires. Some companies also empower their resort representatives to pay compensation to clients on the spot in order to satisfy complaints at the earliest opportunity. Research has shown that prompt and appropriate action of this kind not only saves future costly customer service, but also makes the client more likely to repeat book.

It is all too easy to believe that if levels of complaint are low, all is well with the company. In fact, there may be a high level of 'disguised dissatisfaction' with the company. Many British holidaymakers make vociferous complaints to resort representatives on the first day of their holidays. A good rep is able to placate clients who might otherwise return home with a simmering dissatisfaction, leading them to book with another company in the following year. Consequently the level of repeat bookings must be taken into account in measuring quality control. For this reason again the major operators subscribe to syndicated 'attitude' surveys which sample both consumers and the retail trade to ascertain their true opinions of the different operators.

Financial control

It is not only the financial controller who will be concerned that departments keep within their budgets. While the budget itself is designed to exercise an automatic control over the operations of the business, the marketing department must constantly check that sales, promotion and other expenses remain within the agreed limits. However, too tight control can lead to missed marketing opportunities. The marketing plan must not become a straitjacket.

The use of ratios to determine marketing mix expenditure is a common means of judging performance, but can be misleading if it is based on what 'the average company in the industry' is achieving. While it is common to determine that a fixed proportion of turnover be allocated to promotion, the earlier discussion on communications budgets will have made it clear that spend will need to vary according to the established objectives of the marketing plan. In a time of falling sales, too often the control mechanisms go into operation to cut promotional spend where it might be more appropriate to increase it to generate more sales.

Changing circumstances can also result in a particular product carrying too high a proportion of the company's overheads. Let us say that fuel prices have been increased. This could lead to a disproportionately large fall in long-haul tour bookings, which will require some readjustment to the allocation of overheads to those programmes.

Efficiency control

If performance control has indicated a weakness in some aspect of the organisation's marketing, analysis will be needed to determine whether the marketing activities or the structure of the department need to be changed in some way to make the marketing more efficient. Even if marketing targets are being met, sheer pressures of competition between principals or between retailers require that ways be constantly sought to reduce costs without impairing efficiency. This means constant re-evaluation of the marketing mix. All means of measuring success must be taken into account, not merely levels of turnover.

Reviewing the organisational structure of the department might mean considering whether sales should be separated from marketing and given its own head; or whether the department has grown to a point where it is worth introducing a marketing controller to coordinate activities in the department. Should the marketing functions become increasingly centralised, as has happened in some large hotel chains, or should they be more decentralised, as other chains have done? Does the administrative structure facilitate the marketing function, or does it hinder it? Above all, is the quality of the staff up to the standard required?

This last question is a crucial one for the travel and tourism industry. In most sectors of the industry, the belief remains that profit levels do not allow better salaries to be paid, and therefore better staff cannot be recruited. However, performance standards do vary between companies, and different management styles are a major contribution to these variations. Are staff being properly trained in marketing techniques? Are they being promoted beyond their capabilities? Are they adequately motivated? What does the manager know about levels of satisfaction among the staff? How is the staff managed – by sanctions, rewards, or, simplest of all but surprisingly rare, by thanking them for a job well done? Frequent examples can be shown of small companies in travel (employing between 20 and 50 members of staff) where the manager seldom meets or greets the staff, but nevertheless expects them to give of their best for the company. Measures of staff turnover and levels of staff satisfaction are important methods of judging the efficiency of the organisation with respect to staff. It is not sufficient simply to count the proportion of staff leaving the company; managers must know for what *reasons* the staff are leaving. Even where turnover is low, this is not necessarily an indicator of job satisfaction; at times of economic depression, few staff will take the chance of moving – but may well be lining up the intention of doing so as soon as circumstances improve, so monitoring staff satisfaction levels is as important in difficult times as in times of high employment.

Even with a good workforce and organisation, the communications mix should be monitored constantly to compare the relative performance of different promotional tactics and to seek ways of making these more cost-effective. Such procedures are an integral part of the control system.

Since the travel brochure itself is such a critical element in the promotional mix, a company should regularly monitor its brochures by soliciting consumer and retailer views about its brochures compared with those of the competition. Wastage rates need to be checked and kept under control. Tests of awareness and recall for different brochures can be carried out, and sales representatives calling on travel agents should be required to report which brochures are racked and where.

The ratio of sales to cost of sales should be regularly monitored, taking into account both the cost of servicing distributors such as travel agents and the cost of maintaining the sales force. With advances in technology, and with new cost-efficient techniques coming on stream all the time, costs for processing reservations should be compared regularly. Similarly, new technology is being introduced for processing tickets and documentation, as carriers check the comparative costs to improve efficiency.

Identification of more productive distribution outlets will determine future levels of support and should permit analysis of the relative performance of national multiples versus independent agents and small chains. Results of joint promotional schemes will have to be assessed, as will the effect of different incentives provided to retailers.

Example   The Eden Project

The Eden Project (see Figure 15.2) provides us with a neat example of an organisation which, through lack of foresight and control, actually failed to maximise the advantage of huge consumer demand in the opening year of its operation. A finely landscaped horticultural tourist attraction near St Austell in Cornwall, its appeal was based on the construction of three vast geodesic domes known as biomes containing micro-climates, in which many exotic plants, including fully grown tropical trees, were installed.

Demand was stimulated by massive publicity in the national press prior to launch, so that the original marketing plan anticipating 750 000 visitors in the opening year became rapidly outpaced. Over 200 000 visited in the first six weeks, and over 2 million in the first year of operation. Access roads proved inadequate to handle this volume of traffic, and long queues into the site itself built up over the first bank holiday weekend, during Easter 2001.

The organisation reacted rapidly in the opening year by installing two more entry tills, increasing the total to 12, employing 20 more staff (including street entertainers for the queues), building new catering facilities and limiting entry to the biomes to 2200 at one time. Promotion concentrated on attracting visitors on weekdays outside of the holiday seasons.

Figure 15.2
Site of the Eden
Project, Cornwall

(Photographed by the author)

Strategic control

Apart from these many operational monitoring procedures, organisations should regularly review their strategic goals and plans. This process is known as the marketing audit, and it aims to identify unclear or inappropriate objectives or strategies, to encourage improvements in expenditure, planning, execution and control, and to determine whether the organisation is taking advantage of new marketing opportunities as they arise.

Some audits are undertaken using senior staff from outside the department to consider the effectiveness and efficiency of the marketing staff as part of the assessment of the organisation's abilities as a whole; how effectively it has spotted opportunities when they occurred and exploited them, how well the marketing team has built on its strengths and overcome its weaknesses, how effectively it has overcome threats (hugely important given the instability of the global economy and the need to be flexible in planning for change).

Example British Airways

British Airways is an example of a travel company which, after achieving great success in the 1990s, began to lose its way in the early part of the new millennium. Reacting to global economic downturns, it took the decision to pursue the premium customer, offloading its small budget operation Go in favour of building up its high-price, high-quality market. The subsequent growth of the budget airlines, even for business travel, as businesses cut back on travel costs in the aftermath of poor financial trading years, caught the company off balance and led to losses in share value to a point where the company was dropped from the FTSE 100 index of top companies.

No travel business today can afford to rest on its laurels; markets change too rapidly, and complacency over present occupancy levels, load factors or bookings can quickly change to concern as new challenges emerge to face the company.

Ideally, marketing audits are best undertaken by external consultants, who will operate more objectively and independently, bringing a fresh perspective to their evaluation of the company and its strategies. While few organisations would consider the expense of employing external teams annually for this purpose, at very least consultants should be recruited periodically on an ad hoc basis to carry out in-depth investigations of the company's fortunes.

Consultants can also play a useful role in reviewing the effectiveness of the business's internal, as well as its external, communications. Do the staff share common aims, and are these in sympathy with the company's expressed aims? Do they have a positive attitude towards the company and its products? How closely do other departments cooperate with the marketing staff in satisfying their needs? These are important questions which relate to the operating efficiency and effectiveness of the company as a whole. Where there are divisions of the company on separate sites, or staff are employed far from head office, communications can easily suffer. One of the most common management problems in tour operating is the failure to communicate, and above all the failure to establish common aims between the head office staff and staff in the field such as area managers and resort representatives. It is not hard to find examples of companies whose head office staff making field visits to resorts overseas fail to take the trouble to meet their own resort representatives; yet it is these 'chalk face' workers who are closest to the company's clients, know their problems and can best offer suggestions for the improvement of services.

Where responsibility is delegated, as is the case in large organisations, control is easier to exercise in one sense because a system of checks and balances is introduced by assigning individual responsibility and accountability. A very small company, where management is vested in a single individual who takes on total responsibility for marketing, as well as general management of the company's day-to-day affairs, will be less likely, and less willing, to build in a system of control. It is this aspect of marketing management which poses the greatest threat to the many SMEs which still make up the bulk of companies operating in the travel and tourism industry, and which are today struggling to survive in the face of increasing uncertainty and the threat from larger companies with a more professional approach to marketing.

Questions, tasks and issues for discussion

1 Entry to visitor attractions is commonly controlled either by rationing (in the form of reservations and limiting ticket supplies), or pricing. Discuss the merits of these two approaches, drawing on your knowledge of specific sites employing one or other of these methods. To what extent can marketing contribute to the control of demand (for example, by redirecting advertising away from these sites in favour of others)?

2 To what extent can the crises at Network Rail (and former Railtrack) in the UK be ascribed to lack of control?

3 One of the weakest sectors within travel and tourism is the accommodation business (some typical examples were given in Chapter 1). There are serious issues of inadequate quality control in the operation of many hotel chains as well as independents. Is this only the result of poor salaries and conditions, or are there other underlying explanations? How might control be improved?

4 The early years of the twenty-first century have been dogged by disaster for the travel industry – wars, terrorism, global diseases, financial and economic crises, all have undermined the profitability of the industry to a point where survival is uppermost in most managers' minds. Based on this experience, can we say that external factors have now become so important that good marketing – and control – are no longer enough?

Exercise

Based on any visitor attraction to which you have access and knowledge, outline a plan of quality control for the organisation, identifying those elements of the product which can be internally controlled, the means of exercising control, plans for measuring performance and the standards against which quality is to be judged. Write a report for the director of the site, with a timescale for introducing the plan of action.

Further reading

Kotler, P, Bowen, J and Makens, J, *Marketing for Hospitality and Tourism*, Prentice Hall, 2nd edn 1999, ch 19

Wöber, K, *Benchmarking in Tourism and Hospitality Industries: the Selection of Benchmarking Partners*, CABI, 2002

Part III Case studies

Case study 1
An integrated marketing campaign to expand Travelocity's member base

(Prepared by Karen Mullins, CRM Manager, Travelocity Europe and with the help of Jamie Cole, Vice President, Partner Marketing Europe)

Introduction: Travelocity – a global business

Figure CS1.1
Travelocity logo

Travelocity pioneered online travel and has become a market leader in travel services on the Web, giving consumers the tools and information to plan, save and make their travel better. With more than 35 million members and more than $3 billion in gross sales, by 2001 Travelocity had become the sixth largest travel agency in the United States. Travelocity was named the World's Leading Travel Internet Site for six consecutive years at the World Travel Awards (most recent award at the time of writing 20 January 2003), and it operates or powers websites in seven languages across four continents. Travelocity Europe, its European offshoot, has also grown rapidly through acquisition and joint venture deals, and currently employs around 500 staff in 5 countries.

Background: Travelocity.co.uk

Travelocity.co.uk was launched in 1998, offering its members access to reservations and information for more than 700 airlines, 55 000 hotels and 50 car rental companies, plus cruise, ski and holiday packages. In September 2001, it acquired Stansted-based Air Tickets Direct, and has changed from a solely online company into a multi-channelled organisation.

Travelocity effectively acts as a travel agent, earning commission from the sale of travel products and services, and is increasingly acting as the merchant of record in the sale of travel products. The company brings together components of travel, including inclusive tour airfares and wholesale hotel rates to provide great package deals for consumers. Travelocity also acts as a distribution marketing company and earns revenues from the development of integrated marketing campaigns for key supplier partners.

In the UK its main competitors are Expedia, Ebookers, Opodo and Lastminute, from which it is fast gaining market share, in this 'catch-up phase'. In September 2002 Travelocity.co.uk won Best Travel Website, in the *Travel Trade Gazette* Awards.

Objectives of the Fare Watcher campaign

The main objective for the Fare Watcher campaign was to drive registration to the Travelocity.co.uk site. The campaign was targeted to acquire 20 000 new site members.

Timing

Taking into account the typical seasonal trends in the industry, an active booking period was chosen to launch the campaign. The timings for the campaign were advised by Travelocity's advertising agency, St Lukes.

What is Fare Watcher?

Travelocity Fare Watcher is a free, personalised subscription service on the website that tracks the best round-trip fares offered for up to five city pairs. The subscriber decides which cities to track, for how long and whether they want to be notified of changes to those fares via e-mail.

A person must first become a site member, before subscribing to Fare Watcher. Therefore there are two levels of membership:

1   Non-Fare Watcher members (people who have joined as site members).
2   Fare Watcher members (people who have joined the site as a member and have also subscribed to Fare Watcher).

The Fare Watcher product was chosen as a vehicle for the campaign, as research has shown that Fare Watcher members are more likely to book than non-Fare Watcher members.

Marketing activity

A three-pronged strategy, along with a promotion, was adopted with the principal aim of acquiring the targeted 20 000 new site members. This strategy was provided by Klondike, Travelocity's media planning agency. Within the strategy, a primary focus was based on attracting sectors of the target audience who would benefit from, and recognise, the values encompassed in the Fare Watcher product.

The strategy was based on online activity, and telephone numbers were not included in any of the chosen media. This was due to the fact that the Fare Watcher product does not lend itself to offline channels.

Target audience

The target audience was consumers aged 25–54, well educated, living in large cities, and happy to book online but expecting a high-quality service.

Media activity calendar

Figure CS1.2
Fare Watcher media activity calendar

	May				June				July					August			
	6	13	20	27	3	10	17	24	1	8	15	22	29	5	12	19	26
Radio (London only)																	
95.8 Capital FM																	
Virgin London (AM/FM)																	
Heart 106.2 FM																	
ITN News Direct 97.3 FM																	
Press (National Saturday)																	
Guardian – 4clr classified																	
Independent – 4clr classified																	
Times – Mono display																	
Press (National Sunday)																	
Observer – 4clr classified																	
Independent on Sunday – 4clr classified																	
Sunday Times – Front Page Solus – 4clr																	
Sandwich bags (London only)																	
Promotion																	
Win Fare Watcher flights featured on Home Page																	
Email 'Win free flights with Fare Watcher'																	
Email 'Reduced air fares that find you!'																	

Media: three-pronged strategy (advised by Klondike, Travelocity's media agency)

Three-pronged strategy – the model

Figure CS1.3
Fare Watcher
three-pronged
strategy

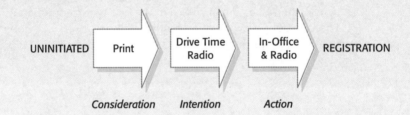

1 The role of print

Figure CS1.4
Your weekend

The weekend travel sections of the broadsheet national press are a focal point for upmarket travellers seeking inspiration or practical help for travel arrangements. It is within the dense mêlée of the classified pages that people seek to find the best price corresponding to their planned itinerary. It was the ideal environment in which to talk about a product benefit that could save them the confusion of sourcing real prices from misleading classified advertising. Furthermore, the fact that the travel sections are focused around the weekend was beneficial to the company, which knew that Travelocity users are most likely to visit on Monday and Tuesday mornings after a weekend period of consideration. The proximity of exposure to the message and the recipients' most likely time of action would be expected to maximise results.

2 The role of radio

Radio can reach people on the way to work and is listened to in the work environment. It is therefore uniquely placed as a medium to help galvanise people's intention to use Fare Watcher during working hours. Its flexibility offers the possibility of up-weighting important times of the week such as Monday and Tuesday morning drive time. Creatively, it offered more scope for explaining the Fare Watcher concept, as posters would be too restrictive.

Therefore, radio performed three functions: a general stimulus to consideration during non-specific airing hours (to build cover), a prompt to intention during the gap between weekend travel consideration and arriving in the office (morning drive time) and a direct call to action (weekday airtime during office hours).

3 The role of office media

Traditional media are not generally consumed heavily within the office environment yet this is ultimately where the company needed to be prompting people to action. It therefore set about distributing 1 million sandwich bags (see Figure CS1.5) to 280 independent outlets in west London and the City of London. Eating sandwiches at the desk

Figure CS1.5
The sandwich
bag

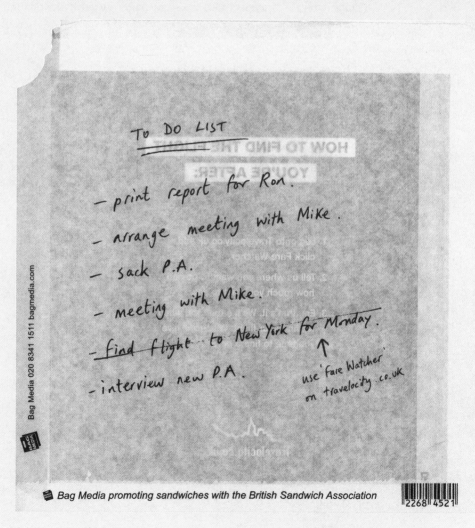

Bag Media promoting sandwiches with the British Sandwich Association

(Courtesy: Travelocity)

during lunchtime has become another symptom of the rigorous working hours afflicting the modern office worker. To prompt them into making travel plans while they are sitting in front of a computer, and at a time when, nominally, they are on a 'guiltless' break, is about as highly targeted a message as could be channelled through media.

The promotion

The Fare Watcher promotion gave both new and existing Fare Watcher subscribers the chance to win all the destinations they were tracking on Fare Watcher on the final day of the promotion. This translated into the opportunity to win five flights, from any airport and to any airport in the world.

The promotion launched on 18 May and ended on 31 July 2002. It was advertised via a graphic on the Travelocity.co.uk home page, and in two viral e-mails (see Figures CS1.6 and CS1.7).

Results

As in any marketing activity, the success of any campaign can only be measured against the results it produces. ECRM (electronic customer relationship management) technology allowed Travelocity to delve into almost every aspect of member generation, whether it was attributed to looking, joining or booking. This section covers the aspects of these analytical discoveries that are felt to be of most significance to the original objectives and targets.

Total results

Total results were measured in terms of new site members, new Fare Watcher subscribers and page views on the website (see Table CS1.1).

Table CS1.1 Fare Watcher results

	New Fare Watcher subscribers	New members	Page views
Total results			
Campaign	8913	24 682	4 632 949
Control group	1801	16 569	3 194 603
Daily averages			
Campaign	119	329	61 773
Control group	24	221	42 595
% Increase	**395**	**49**	**45**

Figure CS1.6
'Win free flights
with Fare
Watcher' viral
e-mail

 Travelocity.co.uk

Use Travelocity's Fare Watcher

Fare Watcher will monitor 95 per cent of the world's air fares for you. Simply tell it where you're thinking of going and when. It will instantly tell you today's best price. But if you're not travelling for a while, it will watch fares for you and notify you the day they change. You can even nominate a best price you are willing to pay.

Win free flights to all your Fare Watcher destinations when you register.*

No one can afford to waste their day searching for flights. Can they...?

* **Fare Watcher competition** - subscribe to Fare Watcher for the chance to win flights to all the destinations you are watching. Terms and conditions apply. Please see Travelocity.co.uk for further details.

Forgotten your password - Travelocity's online Customer Service can help you remember it. Click Here to enter your User ID and your e-mail address, and if it matches our files, we will e-mail your password to you.

Unsubscribe - When you registered at Travelocity.co.uk, you agreed to receive email.
If you no longer wish to receive email from Travelocity.co.uk, please Click Here.

How?

1. Give Fare Watcher a list of the places you'd like to fly to.
2. Fare Watcher scans 95 per cent of the world's air fares and tells you today's best prices.
3. Too expensive?
   Say what you'd be prepared to pay and how long you can wait for the price
4. Fare Watcher emails you when a flight for that fare is available.

Simple.

It takes about as long to activate Fare Watcher as it does to read this email.
So why not try it now?

Win free flights to all your Fare Watcher destinations when you register.*

* **Fare Watcher competition** - subscribe to Fare Watcher for the chance to win flights to all the destinations you are watching. Terms and conditions apply. Please see Travelocity.co.uk for further details.

Forgotten your password - Travelocity's online Customer Service can help you remember it. Click Here to enter your User ID and your e-mail address, and if it matches our files, we will e-mail your password to you.

Unsubscribe - When you registered at Travelocity.co.uk, you agreed to receive email.
If you no longer wish to receive email from Travelocity.co.uk, please Click Here.

Figure CS1.8
Marketing
activity and
results (1),
April–July 2002

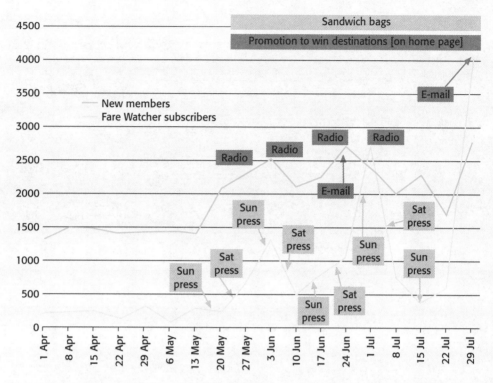

Media graph and new members

The graph in Figure CS1.8 shows the direct correlation between new members and Fare Watcher acquisition, and the marketing activity used to motivate those results.

The trend, throughout the period leading up to the campaign, was for a fairly even, or static, acquisition of both Fare Watcher members and site members. With the arrival of the first phase of marketing activity – the national press – there was an instant surge in membership levels. New membership sign-up steadily increased throughout, peaking when the radio advertisements were on air, trailing off after radio coverage and peaking at the end of the campaign when the second viral e-mail was sent.

Growth in Fare Watcher members was much more sporadic than new site members. The levels rose dramatically during the second phase of radio adverts, dropped during the middle of the campaign, and had an enormous surge on the dates of both viral e-mails.

Media graph and page views

The graph in Figure CS1.9 shows the rise of page views, alongside marketing activity. Unlike the growth in Fare Watcher members and new members, the graph for page views was more of a consistent gradient, with the exception of the two viral e-mails, where a spurt in site activity was experienced.

Figure CS1.9
Marketing
activity and
results (2),
April–July 2002

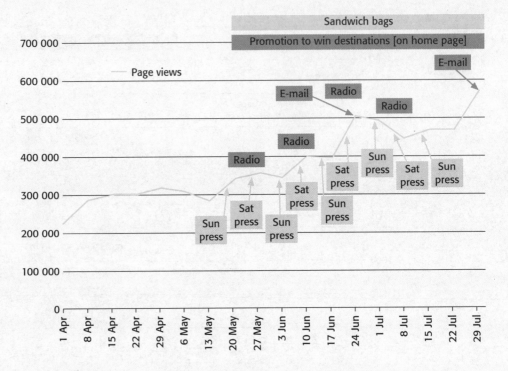

Incremental results

Incremental results (see Table CS1.2) show the 'additional' results that the campaign generated. In order to discover this we have a 'control group'. The control group is a comparative group of members, which can also be referred to as the 'norm'. In other words, what levels of activity did the campaign generate, when compared to the activity that we would *normally* expect to see. This campaign ran for 75 days, therefore in this case the control group represents the activity in the 75-day period prior to the campaign (4 March to 17 May 2002).

Table CS1.2   Incremental member acquisition (minus control group)

	New Fare Watcher members	New members	Page views (UK site)
Total results	7112	8113	1 438 346
Daily average	95	108	19 178
% Increase	395	49	45

During the campaign there was a 395 per cent increase in Fare Watcher members, a 49 per cent rise in new members and a 45 per cent growth in page views. These were *incremental* increases, over and above what we would normally expect to see.

Table CS1.3 shows member acquisition in terms of bookers, i.e. number of new Fare Watcher members multiplied by the percentage likelihood of booking, and likewise with non-Fare Watcher members. For example, the incremental increase in new Fare Watcher Members was 7112. Therefore, the incremental increase in potential new Fare Watcher 'bookers' is 7112 multiplied by 28.5 per cent (the probability of a Fare Watcher member booking).

Table CS1.3 Incremental members as potential bookers

	New Fare Watcher members	New members	Total
Campaign	2537	3916	6452
Control group	513	2629	3141
Incremental increase	2024	1287	3311
% Increase	**395**	**49**	**105**

The combined *incremental increase* in new members and new Fare Watcher members was 85 per cent. However, a Fare Watcher member is 55 per cent more likely to book than a non-Fare Watcher member. The growth in Fare Watcher members during the campaign was approximately eight times that of the growth in new members. When the incremental member acquisition is calculated in terms of the number of members who will book, then the actual growth equates to 105 per cent. Growth can therefore be measured in two dimensions: (a) a 105 per cent increase in qualified members, or (b) an 85 per cent increase in valuable bookers.

Throughout the campaign, a total of 5.83 per cent of all new Fare Watcher members booked, and a total of 10.9 per cent of new members booked (on top of the 'norm') (see Table CS1.4).

Table CS1.4 Incremental booking conversion

	New Fare Watcher members	New members	Total members
No. members that have booked since joining	415	885	1455
% Members that have booked since joining	5.83	10.90	9.56
Revenue generated	£162 878	£442 085	£604 963
Average revenue per booker	£393	£500	£416
Estimated no. of future bookers	2024	1287	3311
Estimated revenue generation (based on average spend)	£794 590	£643 258	£1 376 564

On average, each Fare Watcher booker spent £393 and each non-Fare Watcher booker spent £500, on a combination of flights, hotels and car hire. Thus, the *incremental increase* in revenue generation was £604 963, over and above the revenue generated by the control group. Based on the fact that a Fare Watcher member has a 28.5 per cent chance of booking, and a non-Fare Watcher member a 15.9 per cent chance of booking, it is estimated that in the future, 3311 members will have booked. If each of these bookers spends the average £416, Travelocity can expect to generate a further £771 600.

Costs vs targets

As previously discussed in the objectives, the campaign was targeted to acquire 20 000 (total) new site members. In actual fact, 24 682 members were obtained, exceeding the target by 23 per cent (see Table CS1.5).

Table CS1.5   Costs and targets

Cost of campaign	£292 000
Target (new members)	20 000
No. of target fulfilled	24 682
% of target fulfilled	123
Revenue generation	£604 963
Estimated future revenue generation	£1 376 564

Although the campaign can be perceived to be a success in terms of meeting the target for new members, there are other, more comprehensive, measurements that can be utilised. Firstly, as above, the new members can be viewed in terms of booking probability, which shows a 105 per cent incremental increase, as opposed to an 85 per cent increase when viewed in terms of 'quality' members. Secondly, and most importantly, when viewed in terms of incremental revenue generation, the campaign paid for itself twice over, and will continually generate profit throughout the membership lifespan of each new member.

Customer behaviour

Although the booking conversion gives us an idea of how many members are booking, it is extremely useful, with regards to segmentation and targeting, to understand the specific behaviour of the members.

Table CS1.6 shows the top 10 results for air destinations, both watched and booked.

Table CS1.6   Top results of the campaign

Watched fares (new Fare Watcher subscribers)		Booked air destinations (new Fare Watcher subscribers)	
1 Amsterdam	3.92	1 Amsterdam	6.86
2 New York City	3.68	2 Edinburgh	3.77
3 New York JFK	2.83	3 Paris	3.50
4 Barcelona	2.41	4 New York JFK	3.10
5 Toronto	2.23	5 Frankfurt	2.42
6 Alicante	2.17	6 Dublin	2.29
7 Orlando	2.11	7 Nice	2.15
8 Malaga	2.05	8 London Heathrow	1.88
9 Sydney	1.81	9 Budapest	1.88
10 San Francisco	1.81	10 Madrid	1.88
Other	74.98%	Other	70.26%
(as at 31 July 2002)			

Note: New York City represents all New York Airports.

Only two destinations appear in both the watched and booked tables. This may be attributed to the fact that the majority of booked destinations are short haul, and may therefore be purchases that require less planning. Travelocity is aware that most members spend 2–3 days on their travels, and these trips are often business trips, making them fairly habitual purchases. The destinations that members choose to 'watch' through Fare Watcher tend to be long-haul destinations, which require more planning. While planning these trips members seek as much information as possible, and the Fare Watcher tool lends itself to this exact need.

A second explanation for this may be a direct result of the promotion. As the promotion stated that a member would win all of their chosen Fare Watcher destinations, more subscribers entered long-haul destinations as part of their five cities, as a long-haul flight has more value than a short-haul flight.

Fare Watcher vs non-Fare Watcher members

Table CS1.7 demonstrates the comparative value between Fare Watcher members and non-Fare Watcher members. A Fare Watcher member is more valuable, in terms of

Table CS1.7   Fare Watcher and non-Fare Watcher value

	Fare Watcher members	Non-Fare Watcher members	Total members
Total no. of members	30 968	381 096	**412 064**
No. members that have booked since joining	8814	60 457	**69 271**
% Members that have booked since joining	28.5	15.9	**16.8**

booking status, than a non-Fare Watcher member. The most important, and perhaps influential, fact to come out of the analysis involved in monitoring the campaign, is that a Fare Watcher member is 55 per cent more likely to book than a non-Fare Watcher member.

The future

The Fare Watcher campaign has enabled Travelocity to gain experience on various fronts, including media strategy, customer retention and customer behavioural activity.

With regards to media strategy, the marketing team have had a beneficial insight into the way the UK target audience consume media, in relation to Travelocity as a brand. The team has also gained knowledge of the effect of an integrated marketing communications strategy and the way different media impact upon each other.

The differential significance in the familiarity a member feels towards the brand, for example, is the difference between an active member who feels the need to be 'touched' (by e-mail communication) by Travelocity on a frequent basis, and hence joins Fare Watcher, and a slightly more inactive member, who wishes to have a more distanced relationship with the brand. Travelocity will be using this knowledge as it moves forward with ECRM technologies.

Since the success of the campaign, the company has gone on to build on these results. A newlook website was launched in September 2002, which won *Travel Trade Gazette*'s award for best travel website. Another major campaign was initiated between September and December 2002, which focused on radio and national press advertising, Z cards in London Underground wallets, business cards in large London offices and an e-mail promotion. This was followed by a further campaign in early 2003, building on the success of radio advertising and centred on the theme of the 700 airlines competing for consumers' business on the Travelocity website.

By mid-2003, the company had added cruise lines to their website, as well as the Lonely Planet collection of guidebooks. Finally, the first move into dynamic packaging has taken place, with the introduction to the site of a city breaks programme.

Editor's conclusions

This extensive case study provides us with a highly detailed account of an integrated marketing communications strategy carried out by one of the world's leading e-tailers. US-owned Travelocity has expanded its activities massively since its inception, and remains actively involved in taking over travel companies even as this book goes to print. The campaign, carried out with the aid of a professional advertising agency, is a textbook exercise in strategic marketing in which clear objectives, focus on a specified market, good timing and well-chosen media result in a level of success far exceeding the company's own expectations. Creative promotion is demonstrated by the use of sandwich bags as advertising media to create awareness among a target market that would otherwise prove hard to reach. The case gives the best possible example of what can be achieved by a large global travel corporation backed by substantial marketing funds.

Questions

1   Price is obviously a key factor in the success of a website retailer, but other factors are important, such as ease of access to the site and clarity of layout. However, the level of service, even if excellent, must by its nature remain impersonal in comparison with that provided by a travel agent. If agents, through their own websites, can match prices offered by companies like Travelocity, can they effectively compete, or do other considerations come into play? And how might demand vary between different market segments?

2   The case tends to suggest that brand recognition and loyalty play an important role in gaining business for the e-tailer, as in any other sector of the travel industry. Travelocity's leading competitors, named in this study, are also becoming more widely known. What, in your view, is the interplay between brand image and price in this sector?

3   Given the successful outcome of this campaign, it would apparently be difficult to suggest ways in which it could be improved. But could you propose the use of other forms of media, or other innovative promotional ploys, which might also find favour with the targeted market?

Case study 2
Small business survival in the wake of September 11th: the case of Trips Worldwide

(Prepared with the help of Jo Clarkson, Trips Worldwide)

Background

Trips was launched in 1991 as a travel company specialising in tailor-made holidays to Mexico and Central America. Initially, the company operated from the home of its founder.

In 1993 Trips relocated to offices with a shopfront in a more commercially prominent location. With a change of title to Trips Worldwide, it functioned as a retail agency for other specialist travel companies, as well as organising its own tailor-made holidays.

In 1999 Trips launched a South America programme to run alongside the established Mexico and Central America product. By 2000, their product range had further increased with the launch of an Alternative Caribbean programme.

With a much wider product range, Trips then planned for expansion in 2001. In the early part of the year the staff levels were increased from 9 to 12 in order to have a well-trained sales staff for the busy period starting in September. A new role of Aviation Manager was created to deal with airline contracts, reservations, etc. The first six months of the year operated at a loss as expected, with staffing levels high due to preparation for the busier second half of the year where the profit would be made.

The problem

The terrorist attacks of September 11th stopped the phones dead. No one was booking holidays in what the company would normally anticipate to be the busiest time of the year. Substantial investment made in the earlier part of the year on IT and personnel now threatened to turn anticipated growth and profits into serious losses. No one could forecast what shape business would take in the coming months, but it was

Figure CS2.1
Original Trips newsletter

Figure CS2.2
New newsletter

TRIPS TRAVEL NEWS

Panama

Torres Del Paine

Buenos Aires

www.tripsworldwide.co.uk   Issue 2

Jamaica - The Exclusive Alternative

The Caves

Look beyond the confines of the large package resorts and you will discover that the Caribbean's third largest island has some extraordinary scenery, incredible natural interest, extremely rich culture and, contrary to certain recent press reports, one of the warmest welcomes in the Caribbean. Jamaica also has the most exquisite range of small luxury hotels and villas so if you're looking for a little pampering or to cleanse body and soul at a spa retreat then Jamaica is an ideal choice. Each of these properties takes pride in having their own distinctive character, individually furnishing rooms with local materials and Jamaican artwork.

The Caves feature a series of sea-facing grottos in which you can dine or take your own private jacuzzi with a view of the sunset. There are also a series of 'jumping platforms' (from 5 feet to 25 feet high). Jakes at Treasure Beach (described as the "chicest shack in the Caribbean) enjoys a fantastically orchestrated mix of colours and architectural styles. Seafront cottages are your best choice with their uninterrupted sea-views and outside showers combining privacy with the chance to spot passing pelicans. The 12 Georgian style cottages of Strawberry Hill teeter on a hill top with a 360 degree view of the countryside and down to Kingston. This is also the place to treat your body in the Caribbean's only full-service Aveda Concept Spa. 'Goldeneye', on Jamaica's north coast has to be one of the Caribbean's most exclusive addresses. Bond author Ian Fleming's former home has been beautifully developed as a handful of very distinctive, imaginatively designed villas.

Bird watchers take note! Of the 250 bird species that occupy Jamaican air space, most are migratory while 25 species are indigenous and 21 varieties are found nowhere else in the world which means that Jamaica has more endemic birds than any other Caribbean island.

Treasure Beach on the quiet and rural south is a great bolt-hole and an excellent base from which you can explore the region.

There are some terrific hiking trails in the Blue Mountains and you really should try to visit one of the local coffee plantations to find out how Jamaicans manage to make Blue Mountain coffee taste so good.

One of Jamaica's undiscovered gems is the Port Antonio area, where Errol Flynn popularised bamboo rafting as a past-time. The small town is very friendly and the coast is a series of picturesque hidden coves and deep blue lagoons but for me biggest thrill here is trekking along the Rio Grande Valley. This is one of Jamaica's wettest and therefore greenest areas with a hinterland of tropical rainforests, rivers and waterfalls.

One of the great thrills (apart from sheer unadulterated luxury) of staying at Goldeneye is to sit at the very desk where Fleming penned his Bond novels and ponder the big question: how on earth did the whimsical adventures of a flying car flow from the same pen that gave birth to the coolest secret agent in literary history? Oracabessa was quite a magnet for authors and artists. Noel Coward was Fleming's neighbour and his home is now a museum just a short drive up the hill from Goldeneye.

Driving back to Montego Bay along the north coast you pass the beautiful old Great Houses of Greenwood and Rose Hall, the spectacular waterfalls of Dunn's River, the lush green grotto of Fern Gully, extensive botanical gardens and spectacular bays. My guide however, was more concerned with pointing out where James Bond's speedboat jumped the road, the location of UB40s Jamaican home, where Bond hopped across

crocodile heads to safety and where Ursula Andress emerged from the sea sporting that bikini!

This is a country that revels in poular culture and I am more than happy to help our clients experience the mixture of cultural, historical, scenic, natural and popular elements that make up the 'real' Jamaica.

FACT BOX

Trips Experts: John Faithfull
Best time to go: Year round although possibility of hurricanes in Sep/Oct/Nov. Dryest time is December - April.
Prices per person (based on two sharing) start from £1629.00
Contact details:
Tel: 0117 311 4402
john@tripsworldwide.co.uk
Fax: 0117 311 4401

Outside Bath - Golden...

TO ORDER A COPY
OF OUR JAMAICA SUPPLEMENT AND ALTERNATIVE CARIBBEAN TRIP PLANNER

Telephone - 0117 311 4400   Fax - 0117 311 4401   E-mail us - info@tripsworldwide.co.uk
Or fill in the coupon below

☐ Please remove my details from your mailing list.

☐ Please send me a copy of the Jamaica Supplement and Alternative Caribbean Trip planner.

Name

Address

Send to Trips Worldwide, Freepost (SWB 370), Bristol BS8 1BR

**Trips Worldwide
14 Frederick Place
Clifton
Bristol
BS8 1AS**

TRIPS
worldwide

**Tel: 0117 311 4400
Fax: 0117 311 4401**

**E-mail: info@tripsworldwide.co.uk
www.tripsworldwide.co.uk**

obvious that there could be no alternative to cutting back on overheads. Action had to be taken fast, to cut costs with immediate effect, and avoid the company's bankruptcy.

The solution

Appropriate cuts were identified. The focus was on reducing expenditure and increasing profit. The company re-examined its marketing mix and its use of the traditional four Ps.

Products

The first step was to consider the product range. Direct enquiries and sales of tailor-made products taken over the phone and via e-mail were quiet but the good news was that a few people were still booking, and no cancellations were received. On the agency side, however, sales over the counter had completely stopped, and cancellations were also coming in.

Although the retail side of the business had made up 27 per cent of turnover in the previous 12 months, the profit margins on these sales were much lower than was the case for the tailor-made products. It was also evident that during the previous year a lot of staff time had been wasted, dealing with walk-in browsers who failed to make a booking and phone call enquiries requesting quotes for flight-only fares which never converted into bookings. The company was not interested in the cut-price, high-discount marketplace, and in consequence was losing business to competitors.

It was decided to radically streamline the agency side of the business. Flight-only sales would be abandoned, and tour operator suppliers would be reduced from over 50 to just 12 of the most profitable, easy-to-sell companies.

In the case of the tailor-made product, the company determined to streamline sales and focus on the higher, more profitable end of the tailor-made market. Tailor-made holidays are a very labour-intensive product and staff need to be well travelled and well trained before they can sell them. The company had invested heavily in this product, which was the core of the business. It was decided that the company would simply stop selling certain tailor-made budget itineraries and hotels, which were as time consuming to create as the more luxurious itineraries, yet yielded lower profits. It had also not gone unnoticed that the only complaints received in the previous year had been from those on budget itineraries.

It was also recognised that the staffing level, the single highest-cost item in the business, would have to be reduced, but this decision was much harder to take. One of the major strengths of the company was its small and friendly team. However, the more streamlined product mix made it inevitable that some staff positions had become redundant, and staffing was reduced by 30 per cent.

The company was fortunate in that its heavy investment in technology paid off, and it was able to utilise the new reservation and back office software (tailored to the company's exact needs) to run a much more efficient organisation. The system also provided improved management and marketing reports and information, helping the management team to make better, more informed decisions.

Place

With the substantial reduction of the company's retail operations and the termination of its air fare quotations, it rapidly became apparent that the company no longer needed to occupy offices with a prestigious shopfront. Unprofitable walk-in trade was a hindrance to productive work, and the reduced workforce now spread out over three floors was not conducive to a good working atmosphere. The decision was taken, therefore, to move to a modern, airy, open plan office in a serviced office building in an adjacent street. This immediately reduced overheads, as well as dramatically improving staff morale, giving the team a fresh start. While it was recognised that some agency business would be lost by the move (the new site had fewer passers-by), the company took the view that the reduction in time-wasters and improved productivity from the new work environment would deliver benefits.

Promotion

The next step was to look at the company's product image in its brochures and newsletters. Reproducing these brochures in the short term was not financially viable, but it was felt that there was a need to improve the corporate image if the company was to attract the more discerning upmarket traveller who would appreciate high-quality, individually tailored trips. It would be important to emphasise the extremely high levels of personal service and product knowledge which were the company's unique selling points.

The company had in the past produced a newsletter entitled *World Comic* to promote the travel agency side of the business, and this had quite a young, fun 'backpacker' type of feel to it. While it had been totally appropriate for the market then served, the new image needed something more upmarket. The publication was relaunched and rebranded *Trips Travel News*. This entailed a redesign of layout and typeface, adding colour for the first time to produce a look more representative of a broadsheet travel supplement, and a long way from the original comic style of the earlier newsletter.

Sales activity was not ignored, either. To expand on the personal approach on which the company prided itself it was decided that all staff returning from a destination research trip should send personalised letters to selected clients from the database, telling them of the wonderful experiences they had encountered and personally promoting the destination.

Finally, the company's promotional plan was reviewed. In the past, the dominant strategy had been to increase public awareness of Trips which had meant that every opportunity would be taken to gain a mention in the press. Trips employs a London PR agency to promote brand and corporate awareness, and also take every opportunity to develop close relationships with the press themselves. The PR agency analysed these results and compared enquiry to booking ratios. From the data gathered, it was decided that in the following year a much more focused approach should be taken to PR through press releases, screening to ensure that only high-quality products received a mention – no references were to be made to special offers, discounts or budget holidays. This would help to ensure that products would match the clients' requirements. It was expected that the company would receive a lower level of responses, but management hoped for a higher conversion rate.

Price

The mainstream travel industry still tends to concentrate on chasing market share, but profit margins are the crucial factor for the smaller, specialist section of the travel industry. The reorganised company set about to ensure that profits were in line with its marketing objectives.

First, the streamlined retail agency selected only suppliers that offered commissions at or above a minimum level deemed acceptable. Next, a strategy was introduced to increase gross profit percentage. Tailor-made products were compared with those of the company's competitors; ground handling and airline costs were reviewed. Wherever possible profit margins were increased, while costs were streamlined and improvements introduced to products at each destination. Finally, a small handling fee was introduced for all tailor-made bookings (but not on simple packages) – a move that has become increasingly common among specialist agencies in response to commission reductions and lower profits. It has become evident that these fees are not resented by customers who can perceive that the agency is offering value for money and an appropriate level of expertise.

Conclusion

Trips Worldwide made a turnaround in 2002, and weathered the storm.

Redundancies in a company can seriously destroy staff morale. However, the remaining team stuck together and worked brilliantly as a team. The move to the new offices in June rejuvenated motivation, and sales targets were beaten every month until the terrorist attack in Bali in October, when the sales again dropped dramatically. However, the impact of this second attack was more limited; business picked up the following month, and the company went on to have their busiest December on record.

Streamlining the products and improving promotion proved to be very successful. Sales turnover for 2002 was almost identical to that for 2001, but was delivered with 30 per cent less staff. The best news of all was the gross profit, which rose by 5 per cent, with an even greater increase in net profit. The new look *Trips Travel News* was also very well received, resulting in a sharp rise in enquiries.

Early 2003 was dominated by further crises affecting the travel industry: first the Iraq war, then the SARS scare, affecting bookings to the Far East in particular. The adjustment to new market conditions which Trips had made after the Twin Towers catastrophe stood them in good stead to weather further storms, and bookings had recovered well by midsummer.

The company received an added boost by being voted Best Website of the Year in the annual *Guardian/Observer* travel awards for 2003, being praised for its 'distinct, appealing character . . . which gave great introductions to its destinations and made you want to travel with them'.

The steps taken by the company to retrench and develop a more selective approach to the products sold have clearly paid off handsomely.

Editor's conclusions

Many small businesses in the travel and tourism industry have struggled in the face of the major calamities affecting global travel in the period 2000–3. This case provides a classic example of the circumstances facing one small company, forcing it to re-evaluate its entire approach to business in order to survive. The approach taken is classic: the re-examination of where its business is coming from and the identification of high-profit areas, leading the company to concentrate on particular products and to target specific markets through more focused promotional and PR activities. The introduction of handling fees, especially for tailor-made services, is becoming widespread in the UK, with retailers claiming that such fees are not resented by consumers where an adequate level of professional advice and service is provided. This seems to be borne out in Trips' experience.

The success of the company is borne out by the decision of the owner at the end of 2003 to accept an attractive offer for the business from leading operator First Choice, which announced its intention to integrate the company into its range of specialist 'soft adventure' operators.

Questions

1 A change of image can be rewarding, as this case reveals, but it carries with it the danger of alienating existing markets. Can, and should, a company attempt to retain its loyal (but lower-profit-producing) markets while shifting its emphasis, and if so, how?

2 Given that the quality of personal service and product knowledge were identified as the company's USPs, and that good staff are difficult to find in the retailing sector, what alternatives could be proposed to staffing reductions and the inevitable (even if temporary) effect on staff morale that this would have had?

3 Cost-cutting for retail agents means controlling salaries of counter staff, a major element in overall cost – yet adequate salaries to recruit quality staff are seen by many as the only means of retaining business in the face of moves by suppliers to direct sell via the Internet. How do you see this conflict being resolved over the next few years?

Case study 3
Marketing a specialist product: the holiday homes rental market in Norway

(Prepared with the help of Axel Eikner, International Development Manager for the Merkantilt Instituut Colleges in Norway)

This case examines the increasing development of small, independent, single-proprietor businesses renting out holiday homes, a feature of the Norwegian tourism industry, and the challenges facing these businesses as they seek to develop satisfactory holiday experiences for international visitors while remaining profitable in a highly competitive international market.

Introduction

Tourism is of major importance to the Norwegian economy. It is the fourth largest industry in terms of contribution to GNP and total employment in Norway, surpassed only by the petroleum industry (30 per cent), the traditional fishing industry (still important along the 2500 km coast) and hydroelectric power. By comparison with these other industries, tourism is still growing rapidly.

Nevertheless, Norway is a high-cost country, with similarities to Switzerland and Iceland, making it very hard to compete for tourists in the European marketplace against countries such as Spain, Italy and France. Similarly, it is at a disadvantage climatically against these same southern European countries and Greece, Portugal and Turkey. However, due to the Gulf Stream running along the Norwegian coast, temperatures are surprisingly mild, considering its geographical position so close to the North Pole, summer temperatures often exceed 30 °C, and even in winter the temperature seldom falls below −10 °C in most places.

The general high cost of living, and a strong currency (in 2002) compared to international visitors' home countries, have encouraged the development of low-cost products especially in the areas of accommodation and food. Norway is also generally perceived as a relatively unsophisticated destination compared to Switzerland and France, or even its neighbours Sweden and Denmark; another good reason for the development of inexpensive alternatives to international hotel groups and exclusive restaurants.

Norway in total has about 4.5 million people scattered around the country, with small hubs such as Oslo (the capital) with half a million inhabitants, and Bergen, Stavanger and Trondheim each with less than half of the capital's population.

The history of Norwegian tourism reveals that natural beauty and natural resources were the main attractions bringing the first international visitors to the country a mere 150 years ago. This same motivation remains true today. The first tourists to arrive in the 1850s were said to be the British 'salmon lords' coming to exercise their angling skills and enjoy the tranquillity of fishing in beautiful and fertile rivers. Today lords are rare, and heavily outnumbered by independent middle-class travellers from Germany, the Netherlands and Belgium, often renting a place for a week or two just to be at one with nature and to experience the fresh air and cleanliness of unspoiled nature, as a contrast with their own often polluted home environments.

Holiday Home Rental as a product

Statistics reveal that in recent years Germany is the major international generating market for Norway, with some 35 per cent of all international tourist arrivals. This is followed by Sweden, the Netherlands, Denmark, USA and Great Britain. These six countries accounted for 75 per cent of total overnight bookings (9.5 million nights sold) during the summer season in 2000.[1]

In Norway today there are 32 000 cabins for rent and 65 per cent of all bookings are made by foreigners, especially visitors from Germany, the Netherlands and Belgium.[2]

The most common forms of accommodation among international tourists are camping, cabin rentals and holiday home rentals (58 per cent). By contrast, hotels account for just 24 per cent of bookings, and the VFR market staying with family/ friends represents a further 13 per cent. Some 4 per cent make alternative arrangements.[3] The strongest trend today in the international market is choosing alternative accommodation such as cabins or holiday home rentals; this is particularly true of individual travellers.[4]

In general, holiday home rental is a modest form of holiday, conforming to the accommodation trend identified earlier as well as to the overall image of Norway. In September 2000 the Norwegian Tourist Board (NTR) undertook major research on Norway's image as a holiday destination.[5] More than 1200 respondents from Denmark, Germany, Italy, UK, USA and Japan were asked about the attraction of their next potential holiday destination.

An impressive 94 per cent of the respondents put nature-based activities as one of the most important features of a holiday – a factor that should favour a country like Norway. However, out of 10 countries listed in the survey, Norway was found to be only the seventh most attractive destination by respondents, the top three being New Zealand, Canada and Scotland.

Coinciding with this marketing research, other surveys over the last couple of years made by both NTR and SNIDE (the Norwegian Industrial and Regional Development Fund) reveal that the product segments most obvious for Norway are all nature based:

- nature-based active holidays
- experiences linked to nature and culture
- nature-based relaxation and revitalisation.

Holiday home rental as a tourism product is all about nature and culture, and could well be defined in the following terms:

> Holiday home rental (HHR) is a form of holiday whose duration normally exceeds a week-end, comprising an individual and discrete unit of accommodation located in a peripheral, unspoiled and scenic area, within a region or country that travellers express a wish to visit while accommodating to locals and their lifestyles. The design of the unit complements the setting, reinforcing the image of the product as a base for natural and culture-based activities.

This definition distinguishes HHR from short-term cabins in camping grounds (including mobile homes, etc.) whose rental is incidental to the holiday, purpose-built holiday villages found in islands such as the Balearics and Canary Islands, timeshare accommodation and even property purchased abroad as a holiday home (popular with Norwegians, particularly in Spain). This tightly defined concept is important in targeting a clearly defined market niche, to ensure the product is appropriately tailored to the market. Furthermore, the definition emphasises the fact that HHR visitors are anxious to use local transport and mingle with locals in exploring the region or country, as opposed to the mass market tourist who chooses to travel in tourist coaches, thus failing to experience contact either with locals or their culture. However, not all HHR travellers are viewed by locals as successful in achieving these aims. The definition clearly distinguishes HHR from other sorts of holiday and makes clear that the product is not merely accommodation but an integral and encompassing holiday. Tourism statistics seldom make clear the distinctions between HHR, camping and cabin rentals in their summarised reports, but by limiting the definition to that given above, this case study will allow the focus to fall on HHR as a specific international product, catering to an international market.

Norwegians themselves tend to travel to Denmark, Sweden, England/Scotland/Ireland (cottages, farmhouses, farm homes) or France (*gîtes*) for HHR holidays, very often giving culture, heritage, mountaineering/cycling, or sun and sea (summer)/ski (winter) as the most attractive features. Holidays are often chosen by people with prior knowledge of, or particular interest in, the region they have selected. This may also be true among those choosing this form of holiday coming to Norway.

A large percentage of the market – some 65 per cent – making up the demand for cabin rental holidays in Norway are international guests. This compares with a mere 32 per cent in the case of demand for hotel accommodation (SND statistics).

In general, HHR and cabin rent can be categorised according to the markets and products shown in Figure CS3.1. It is scarcely surprising that the longer the travel involved, the longer visitors wish to stay at their destination, but it is still important that owners recognise this fact. Figure CS3.1 shows that only one product segment is relevant for the long-haul visitor: holidays of one or more weeks' stay, which involve

Figure CS3.1
Product/market
mix for holiday
home rentals in
Norway

	Product	One night accommodation	Weekend accommodation and activities	Holidays of one or more week(s) stay with both nature-based and cultural activities
Market				
Local		✓	✓	
Domestic			✓	✓
International				✓

both nature-based and cultural activities. This is significant when choosing target markets, promotional mix and distribution channels, for instance.

In a report on cabin rental/HHR in Norway in 2000 from the SND[6] it was found that most operators within this market in Norway are single owners or one-person businesses, employing seasonal staff, but appealing above all to self-catering guests. Most principals rely on other activities and hold down regular jobs, frequently in the agricultural sector, to ensure an adequate income. Principals typically rent out an average of five houses (units), each unit normally contributing an average of some 55 000 NOK (£4500) a year, with some variation according to the standard of units and the services provided.

The following is an illustration of one (semi-professional) operator in the Norwegian market, the Kvalheim Holiday Centre. This centre is based on the west coast of Norway, some 50 minutes by car or boat from Bergen, the regional capital (or 'the Fjord Capital of Norway' as the tourist industry proclaim it).

Marketing and distribution of an HHR product

As most principals are small businesses and major chains of operators do not exist in Norway, promotion and distribution are a considerable challenge. This text follows one operator through the eight Ps of hospitality and travel marketing, introduced by the Canadian author Alastair M. Morrison as early as 1989[7] and still relevant today.

The eight Ps are obvious spin-offs from Kotler's better known four Ps in general marketing theory, price, product, place, promotion to which a fifth P was added, embracing people, especially important for the tourism industry. Morrison's additional three Ps, packaging, programming and partnership, are also tailor-made for tourism, since the industry depends on all these factors as elements of a holiday, not merely the accommodation or the mode of transportation. We will look at each in turn.

Product

This embraces the actual product and the perceived product.

Actual product

Kvalheim Holiday Centre (Kvalheim Fritid in Norwegian) is a new operator with four individual houses as well as a block of four apartments on the sea front.[8] It is located in a rural area which is dependent upon traditional enterprises such as farming and fishing.

Kvalheim is within easy reach of the second largest city and airport in Norway, Bergen (former capital and port of the Hanseatic traders, the city still of significant importance as a resource centre both in terms of business and culture). In today's international tourism market the city of Bergen is important as a gateway to the famous fjord region, possibly the best known features of Norway and certainly the most promoted (second only maybe to the midnight sun)! The proximity to a tourism hub is of course beneficial when trying to attract international guests or even domestic travellers from other parts of Norway.

The immediate environment around Kvalheim is both scenic and unspoilt, but not something one might consider breathtaking by comparison with the dramatic fjord region; somewhat dull, but calm, friendly and relaxing.

Each unit at Kvalheim has all essential facilities such as fully equipped kitchens, bathrooms (including jacuzzi) and washrooms. The living room has TV with satellite receiver, radio and CD player.

Perceived product

The product is seen as an active holiday offering revitalisation through communion with nature and local culture, very often including activities such as fishing, mountaineering, cycling, etc.

People

Kvalheim Holiday Centre is a self-catering unit but offers several services as needed, such as supplying fishing gear/boats, transportation to cultural events and activities, golf, maps and guides, etc.

The market being targeted is, however, those wanting time for themselves rather than contact with others, whether locals or other guests. People, as part of Kvalheim's eight Ps, should be invisible until needed by the visitor.

Packaging and programming

In many ways both packaging and programming epitomise a marketing orientation. They are both a result of finding what visitors really need and want and then assembling various services and facilities to match these needs.

Kvalheim Holiday Centre is a new operator, but one already introducing activities and facilities believed to be attractive to visitors, whether it be the jacuzzi, fishing gear or walking trails. Many operators would naturally include activities or packages, working together with the local tourism board or other attractions in the area.

Tour operators in general provide customers with a package, programmed with activities and attractions, as well as transportation, accommodation and service personnel. As inclusive packages, the products of tour operators are less relevant to HHR operators.

However, in Norway one finds that ferry companies are major contributors in terms of semi-inclusive tours, i.e. packages including travel planning, onshore accommodation and transportation for the customers. This makes sense as a large percentage of ferry passengers arrive at their destinations using their own vehicles. While not normally approaching tour operators for their holiday plans, they nonetheless require basic services such as food, beverages and accommodation.

Ferry companies such as Color Line, DFDS and Stena Line offering a package with onshore accommodation in addition to sea transportation are seen as an attractive proposition for a lot of the HHR customers. Independent niche operators in areas such as fishing, gaming and sport are contributors as well. The group Top Destinations, for instance, is programming activities for foreign tour operators and domestic incoming operators. www.dintur.no ('Your trip.no') is another example of a company focusing solely on organising fishing and game adventure tours.

Place

The distribution channels are of vital importance to be able to reach target markets. Direct distribution occurs when the operator assumes total responsibility for promoting, reserving and providing services to customers.[9] This is the case for Kvalheim Holiday Centre today, utilising their own website as well as personal contacts. This means Kvalheim is very dependent on the effectiveness of its own promotional mix.

Indirect distribution or indeed a channel of distribution makes use of several intermediaries such as tour operators, booking agents, tourism boards, travel agents, etc. Kvalheim distributes leaflets and information on a small scale through the local and regional tourist offices.

As most HHR operators are small and without professional marketing skills (as is the case with Kvalheim), it would probably be wise to let intermediaries play a major role in developing the product.

In Norway the following groups have been found to be significant intermediaries for HHR operators:[10]

(a) Tourism offices (national/regional/local), mostly involved in the customer information process. The national organisation in Norway, Norges Turistraad, typically promotes Norway as a whole at home and abroad, prior to the visitors' arrival. The regional organisation (e.g. Fjord Norway and Hordaland & Bergen Reiselivsraad) and the local (e.g. Norhordland Reiselivslag) provide information to arriving tourists/visitors.

(b) Partnerships between different HHR operators, normally with the aim of cost-effectiveness and promotional benefits. See a further description under the Partnership section.

(c) Distribution and booking agencies, of which several can be found in the Norwegian market, a few operating at the national level while most are regionally based. PlussCamp and Norway Apartments are examples of national booking chains, where the first concentrates on camping sites (and is thus irrelevant to Kvalheim), while the latter is a marketing organisation for fully equipped apartments.

Most national booking agencies in Norway are regionally based, focusing on a limited geographical area of operation or a single destination, e.g. Trysil Booking (reachable through www.skiinfo.no), or Fjordbooking and Norbooking (both reachable through www.visitnorway.com). These are all agencies normally less expensive to use as distribution channels compared to the major international chains such as Novasol, DanCenter, DanSommer, Wolters and Inter Chalêt.

The Internet has notably changed the way most agencies operate, and has certainly diminished the importance of geography and international, national or regional based operations. Referring to NSD, most agencies now report that anything from 50 to 100 per cent of their bookings are made over the Internet.

In fact the Internet could very well have been listed as a separate intermediary as many HHR operators for instance are trying to reach markets through this channel alone. However, very few will succeed without the help of Internet hubs and links to major sites more easily found by the sought-after target groups.

(d) Tour operators and travel agencies, providing customers with a set package including a defined programme/content, something already discussed under the Packaging and Programming section. Travel agencies are part of the distribution system utilised by major international agencies such as DanCenter.

Promotion

Kvalheim Holiday Centre, being an independent provider of HHR, is as already mentioned very dependent on its own skilful use of the promotional mix. Morrison[11] includes the following elements: advertising, personal selling, sales promotion, merchandising, PR and publicity. Kvalheim Holiday Centre is only using personal selling effectively.

Partnership

The Norwegian HHR product is in certain respects different from other countries where several major chains of operators are commonly found. In Norway, most operators are solo organisations. However, partnerships normally achieve cost reduction benefits, enhance marketing effort, increase marketplace visibility and finally work as a resource base for all partners. Kvalheim is in no partnership today.

Pricing

Pricing can be very hard both to determine and to set. When the operator is solo and independent, prices can in theory be set at whatever the owner decides. However, customers are price sensitive and will only be willing to pay a price which they consider reasonable.

What constitutes a reasonable price depends on a number of factors including the market segment itself, the quality of the product (in tourism, this even includes the attractiveness of the country/destination in question) and content (in the case of HHR this includes size, facilities and activities).

When included in a major distribution chain such as DanCenter prices are established based on certain criteria; for instance season, location, size, facilities, number of guests and length of stay. If Kvalheim Holiday Centre were in fact to join DanCenter they would have to surrender 40 per cent of their gross income to the DanCenter organisation, as well as losing the flexibility of setting prices themselves. This would be offset, of course, by the benefits of centralised marketing and distribution of their product.

Marketing and distribution through DanCenter[12] includes entry in the annual catalogue printed in two languages (German and Norwegian) with a print run of over 1 million copies, and direct distribution of the same catalogue to families in Germany, Belgium, the Netherlands, Denmark, Sweden and Norway. It would also include reservations facilities and promotion through sales offices in Norway, Germany and Denmark – 10 000 travel agencies with access to online booking, the Larsen sales office in Copenhagen, 1265 Westlotto shops in Germany, and all Jysk shops in Norway, Sweden, Denmark and Germany. There would be the further possibility of advertising support in relevant newspapers and magazines via DanCenter. Finally, of course, there is the benefit of access through the Internet using www.dancenter.no.

If a customer were to pay £1000 for a two-week stay at Kvalheim Holiday Centre, the split would look something like as shown in Figure CS3.2.

In Norway, Kvalheim would only pay income tax on amounts exceeding 10 000 NOK, at a rate of 35 per cent on 90 per cent of the gross income. Given the chance of better distribution and market segment reach, joining DanCenter may not be the worst scenario for a tourism product like Kvalheim Holiday Centre.

Figure CS3.2
Breakdown of expenditure for a Kvalheim HHR

Gross Income £1000 (two weeks stay)			
	✓ **£600** Kvalheim Holiday Centre		
✓ **£100** Travel agency commission	✓ **£100** Customer and operator service	✓ **£60** Catalogue costs	✓ **£50** Administration costs
✓ **£40** Sales costs	✓ **£10** Depreciation	✓ **£10** Taxes	✓ **£30** DanCenter profit

Figure CS3.3
The western fjords of Norway, within easy reach of the Kvalheim Holiday Centre

Figure CS3.4
Outdoor activities at the Kvalheim Holiday Centre at Radoey, near Bergen

(Courtesy: Fjord Norge/Joop Folkers)

Conclusions and suggestions

The idea behind this text was to explore the increasing development of small, independent, sole-proprietor businesses producing sensible holiday experiences in Norway while still competing on the international tourism market. Kvalheim Holiday Centre on the west coast of Norway provides a good example on which to draw.

Remembering the definition of HHR given earlier in this text, Norway is indeed a country suitable for HHR, based on its layout, geography, general living costs and nature-based activities.

Furthermore the main markets for Norway, Germany and Belgium among them, all focus on natural beauty and closeness to nature when choosing Norway as their holiday destination. This is despite the fact that a general lack of knowledge about Norway in potential markets is the tourism industry's greatest challenge, with 64 per cent of the respondents in a tourism survey knowing little or nothing about Norway.

A description of marketing and distribution activities available for HHR in the international arena has been given. The Internet now offers everyone the chance to distribute their product, but with very little chance of being found in the 'jungle' without professional intermediaries or Internet sites to assist them.

Consequently most HHR operators of a certain size and quality probably would benefit from being included in the major distribution channels such as those of DanCenter, or less commercial organisations such as Fjordbooking.

It is hoped that this case study has been able to pinpoint tools that are important and valuable in marketing SMEs in the accommodation sector, as well as revealing how these can be best employed by small operators within the tourism industry.

Editor's conclusions

This case offers a good insight into the marketing problems facing an SME within the hospitality sector of a country not immediately associated with mass tourism. As a destination, Norway faces many classic challenges – as a high-cost country with unfavourable rates of exchange against generating countries, relatively unsophisticated facilities, with a limited tourist season and weather that is inclement (although less so than its perception abroad). As a result, the country appeals only to limited tourist markets, yet tourism continues to make a critical contribution to its economy. The difficulty for an SME of reaching small, globally dispersed markets is made clear. Nevertheless, the country itself offers a product which has widening appeal: rural tourism, with its promise of accompanying peace, relaxation, cleanliness and an unspoilt environment, while simultaneously attracting those seeking activity holidays such as hiking, cycling, boating and angling. Coupled with some of Europe's most majestic landscapes and attractive coastal towns, the destination clearly offers more than it is credited with, but faces a problem in getting its message across. The challenge for any SME is to overcome initial ignorance about the country abroad, as well as to promote its attractions in competition with better-known destinations where prices are seen as keenly competitive.

Questions

1 What are the features of the Kvalheim product best presented in advertising to the public, and given a necessarily limited budget, which media might be selected if advertisements were to be carried in your country?

2 Does the description of this product define a more sustainable holiday than those of the traditional mass market operators? If so, how should this sustainability be expressed (and ensured) through marketing?

3 The case identifies several intermediaries capable of carrying the message for the Kvalheim package, including tourist offices, partnerships, distribution and booking agencies, tour operators, travel agencies and the Internet. Attention is also drawn to the potential role of the ferry operators in promoting this product. Consider which of these outlets would offer the most potential for distribution of a similar product in your own country. What are the pros and cons of each, and which would you recommend Kvalheim to adopt?

References

1 http://www.ssb.no (SSB=National Statistics Norway)
2 As note 1
3 http://www.snd.no (SND=the Norwegian Industrial and Regional Development Fund) *Report on Cabin Rental in Norway 2000*, Statens Nærings- og Distriktsutviklingsfond: Hytteutleie i Norge 2000, Horwarth Consulting AS, 2001
4 http://www.ntr.no (NTR=the Norwegian Tourist Board)
5 As note 4
6 As note 3
7 Morrison, Alastair M, *Hospitality and Travel Marketing*, Delmar Publisher, 1989
8 http://www.kvalheim-fritid.no (Kvalheim Holiday Centre, 2003; HHR operator on the west coast of Norway)
9 Morrison, op cit, p 274
10 As note 3
11 Morrison, op cit, p 310
12 DanCenter Catalogue, Rules and Regulations, 2003 (international HHR booking agency)

Other sources

OMH Business School, Bergen: Student research project for an HHR operator in Rogaland, 2002

Kotler, P, *Marketing Management/Markedsføringsledelse*, Universitetsforlaget, 4th edn 1999

Kamfjord, Georg, *The Tourism Product/Reiselivsproduktet*, Reiselivskompetanse AS, 3rd edn 2001

Case study 4
Restructuring an airline:
the fall and rise of Adria Airways

(Prepared at the Business Case Centre of the Faculty of Economics, University of Ljubljana, by Prof. Dr Tanja Mihalič, Viktorija Herodež and Nena Dokuzov of Adria Airways)

(All photographs courtesy Adria Airways archives, photos by Igor Lapajne 2003)

Figure CS4.1
Former Adria
Airways logo

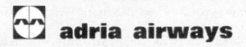

Introduction

Adria Airways is a Slovenian air carrier which celebrated 40 years of service in 2001. Founded in 1961 as Adria Aviopromet, it commenced operations with two DC6B aircraft and a crew from the Dutch carrier KLM. As one of the republics of the Yugoslav federation, Slovenia sustained its own airline, with largely international routes, taking on additional traffic as demand grew to an extent which the Yugoslav operator JAT was unable to meet. Initially the company specialised in catering to the needs of tour operators organising package holidays from the developed European countries to Adriatic resorts, maintaining contracts with companies such as TUI, Thomson Holidays and Neckermann und Reisen. Charters operated from Britain, France, Germany and the Scandinavian countries to popular destinations in the Adriatic including Dubrovnik, Split and Pula. These flights were mainly seasonal, with domestic services within Yugoslavia operating outside the tourist season.

Following a difficult period in the late 1960s, when the airline merged with Interexport (resulting in a temporary change in name), the company prospered in the 1970s and 1980s as both charter and scheduled demand grew, and the fleet was extended with the purchase of, first, five MD80s, and later, three Airbus A320s (Figure CS4.2). Resuming its old name in the mid-1980s, the company formed a joint-venture project with Air France on the Paris–Ljubljana route, and became members of IATA and the ICAO. Its operations were included for the first time on European and world global distribution systems (GDSs).

Figure CS4.2
Airbus A320

However, by the end of the 1980s tourism along the Adriatic was stagnating – and in some cases even declining. Attempts to reverse this trend included cutting prices on some flights, reducing flight operations, and directing marketing energy towards distinct market niches, especially those connected with the Yugoslav guest workers in Germany and Switzerland. This last move was to become an important element in the later restructuring of the airline's marketing campaign.

Political disruption

With Slovenia's declaration of independence from the former Yugoslavia in 1991, the carrier was forced to undertake a radical reappraisal of its activities. During the 10-day war of independence, four of the carrier's aircraft were damaged, and with the ending of hostilities the Yugoslav authorities, which continued to exercise jurisdiction over Slovenian airspace, grounded the airline for three months in retaliation. Slovenia suffered from the fact that, as a newly independent country, it was not a member of the international bodies responsible for aircraft safety, and consequently Adria lost its European contracts, and with them the outgoing tourist markets. The war severely disrupted tourism to the Adriatic, while many former destinations the airline had previously served had become part of other countries, therefore no longer accessible to the airline. Adria had become the national carrier of a country too small to provide for viable domestic flights.

The aircraft fleet was reduced from its original 13 planes to 7, while staff were cut from 931 to 538. Traffic continued to fall drastically in 1991–2, eventually reaching only 10 per cent of that achieved before independence.

A new market orientation

The drastic curtailment of services resulting from the war of independence led to a total reappraisal of the airline's marketing after 1991. Key elements of the campaign were:

- continued switch from domestic to international scheduled and charter movements
- greater emphasis on scheduled services attracting business and individual passengers
- emphasising improved standards of quality for these passengers
- cost cutting by shrinking the fleet and operations
- adapting timetables to ensure better flight connections at other European destinations, increasing the attraction of the services for the domestic market
- development of a frequent flyer programme for loyal customers
- search for partnership opportunities among European carriers, to include code-sharing agreements and GDSs
- Emphasis on marketing via the new GDSs to grow the global market.

Restructuring the product

The three new A320s, ordered before the outbreak of hostilities, had arrived in 1990. In 1996, the Bank Rehabilitation Agency took over the company; in 1998 the ownership structure changed again, with the Development Corporation of Slovenia taking a 91 per cent share of the company, with the remaining 9 per cent in the hands of the NLB Bank. The takeover increased the resources of the airline, allowing the purchase in 1998 of four of the most modern aircraft designed for regional services – the Canadair Regional Jet (CRJ) 200 LR (Figure CS4.3). These offered the advantage of lower fuel consumption, were less noisy than previous regional models while still offering a high level of speed and comfort, and were capable of upgrading to permit instrument landing during reduced visibility. This ensured that by the beginning of the twenty-first century Adria were operating one of the most modern and youngest fleets in Europe, putting them into a very competitive position among European carriers.

Figure CS4.3
Canadair CRJ
200 LR

The market for Adria's services

Adria serves the needs of both business and economy passengers. Clearly, business passengers offer prospects of higher prices and profits, hence the airline focuses on serving these needs. The CRJ 200 LR is the aircraft most commonly used on business routes, providing as it does a high degree of comfort, and extra space for the hand baggage frequently carried by these passengers, while boasting a good record for reliability, safety and punctuality. Economy class is geared to meet the needs of three markets, including tourists travelling in groups or individually, travellers from the former Yugoslav republics returning from seasonal work abroad (and benefiting from frequent flyer discounts) and other individuals travelling on business or leisure.

In company with most air carriers, Adria offers a frequent flyer programme, the Adria Privilege Club, with a minimum of 500 points accumulating for each economy flight and 1000 for business tickets. The Privilege Club offers other benefits, including the possibility of upgrading economy bookings, higher luggage allowances, priority in checking-in and special prices in certain hotels at destinations served by the airline. The Club grants passengers its Blue, Silver or Golden cards according to the mileages flown, with additional benefits for those with higher-level cards.

In 1996, Adria formed a partnership with Lufthansa German airlines, thus opening the door to greater cooperation with Star Alliance members. Since then, code-sharing agreements have been reached with Air France, Austrian Airlines, Croatia Airlines and El Al Israel Airlines. In 2001, Adria opened a route within the European Union, between Frankfurt and Vienna. At the time of writing (mid-2003), Adria is planning to open another EU route between Vienna and Munich, as well as starting regular flights to Dubrovnik (Croatia) and Belgrade (under a code-sharing agreement with JAT) (see Table CS4.1).

Table CS4.1 Adria Airways' destinations in 2002 and plans for 2003

Destination	Agreement
Ljubljana – Amsterdam – Ljubljana	
Ljubljana – Brussels – Ljubljana	
Ljubljana – Copenhagen – Ljubljana	
Ljubljana – Dublin – Ljubljana	
Ljubljana – Frankfurt – Ljubljana	Code-share agreement with Lufthansa
Ljubljana – Kristianstad – Ljubljana	
Ljubljana – London – Ljubljana	
Ljubljana – Manchester – Ljubljana	
Ljubljana – Moscow – Ljubljana	
Ljubljana – Munich – Ljubljana	
Ljubljana – Ohrid – Ljubljana	
Ljubljana – Paris – Ljubljana	Code-share agreement with Air France
Ljubljana – Podgorica – Ljubljana	
Ljubljana – Pristina- Ljubljana	
Ljubljana – Sarajevo – Ljubljana	
Ljubljana – Skopje – Ljubljana	
Ljubljana – Split – Ljubljana	
Ljubljana – Tel Aviv – Ljubljana	
Ljubljana – Tirana – Ljubljana	
Ljubljana – Vienna – Ljubljana	Code-share agreement with Austrian Airlines
Ljubljana – Zurich – Ljubljana	
Vienna – Frankfurt – Vienna	Departure and arrival in third country
Vienna – Munich – Vienna*	Departure and arrival in third country
Ljubljana – Dubrovnik – Ljubljana*	
Ljubljana – Beograd – Ljubljana*	Code-share agreement with JAT

* Flights will start in 2003

Brand identification

The airline has introduced a new logotype in blue and green, in recognition of its improved services and repositioning (Figure CS4.4). This logo is displayed not only on the outside of the aircraft itself but also prominently on air tickets, baggage tags, tableware used on-board and all aircraft seats. The logo colours also feature in the uniforms of ground and air staff. The logo is designed to communicate quality, reliability, competence, service, safety, credibility and effective communication.

Restructuring the distribution channels

With the recent development of the airline and its routes, the marketing focus shifted to distribution channels. Currently, 59 per cent of sales are generated through travel agents, with the balance sold through Adria's own outlets or those of its strategic partners as general sales agents (GSAs).

Scheduled flights are sold through:

▪ contracted sales agents (Adria has 5 sales offices in Slovenia, 15 information offices around the world and sales contracts with 48 IATA and 140 non-IATA agents)

▪ Lufthansa's global distribution system and the central reservations systems of the Star Alliance partners

▪ Participation in the AMADEUS GDS, and cooperation with other CRSs including GALILEO, SABRE, System One and ABACUS

▪ Adria is a member of the Slovenian NMC (National Marketing Company), covering 50 agencies with 75 terminals in Slovenia, 30 agencies with 35 terminals in Macedonia and 20 agencies with a similar number of terminals in Albania

▪ Adria has an SPA (Special Prorata Agreement) with 35 other carriers, allowing the sales of each other's air tickets and pro rata commission earnings on sales

▪ since 1998, reservations can also be effected through the Internet pages of the airline (www.adria.si).

Charter flights are of course also sold through tour operators, travel agencies and other organisations abroad.

Successful marketing of the airline

Adria Airline has developed dramatically since its early days as predominantly a charter operator. By 2001, 80 per cent of its services were scheduled flights. It links the Slovenian capital Ljubljana to 40 destinations, and operates 140 flights every week. Its fleet is one of the youngest in Europe and adapted to current market conditions. Adria has formed alliances with many key players on the international airline scene and expanded into flights between EU countries. The airline became profitable by 1997. In common with airlines throughout the world, Adria has faced changed conditions since the September 11th disaster in the United States, but careful cost control enabled the airline to survive, albeit with minimal profits, and it is ready to prosper with the anticipated growth in air travel within its regions.

Editor's conclusions

This case study allows us to focus on a transport principal which over many years has had to operate first under state control, and later within a climate of political instability and turmoil discouraging promotion to visitors from the leading generating countries, who had the choice of many similar but perceptibly safer destinations. There can be no greater challenge for marketing than to be obliged to operate under such constraints – a fall-off of 90 per cent in one's passengers must be one of the most extreme in recent history – yet the airline has met the challenge with intelligent strategies and forward vision. The operation of any global airline today calls for flexibility and the ability to adapt quickly in the face of rapidly changing circumstances, and it says much for the ability of this organisation's management that they have emerged from a period of great difficulty stronger and better prepared to compete than has been the case with many larger airlines.

The example constitutes one of the strongest arguments in favour of rebranding, and the airline has successfully accomplished this to divorce itself from its previous image as a state-run carrier from an impoverished country. Careful selection of the right products for its routes and markets, the establishment of global distribution systems and sensible niche marketing all contribute to the formation of a leaner, more efficient airline to meet the challenges of the future.

Questions

1 The case highlights the wide variety of factors necessary to consider when investing in an airline fleet. How many factors can you associate with the choice of buying (or leasing) a fleet of aircraft, based on the choices made by Adria and any other possible choices not identified in the case study? To what extent might some of these factors be in conflict with one another? (Possible example: noise versus fuel efficiency.)

2 The case would apparently underline some of the advantages of operating an airline under conditions of the free market. Contrast these with operations under state control. It would also be

possible to identify some advantages for operating under state control. What might these be, and how might state control limit or otherwise affect the role of marketing within the organisation?

3   The case gives some examples of the concept of added value through extra benefits offered to passengers. Identify these, and suggest other benefits which might strengthen the product still further.

Case study 5
Leeds Castle: reappraising marketing strategy to maximise opportunities

(Prepared with the help of Sandra Matthews-Marsh, Customer Services Director, Leeds Castle, Kent)

(All illustrations courtesy Leeds Castle)

Background

Leeds Castle (Figure CS5.1) is a magnificent heritage site located in the south-east of England in the county of Kent (Figure CS5.2). One of the oldest stately homes, and listed in the Domesday Book, this castle has been a Norman stronghold, a royal residence for six of England's medieval queens, a palace of Henry VIII and a retreat for the powerful and influential. Raised in stone on an island by a Norman baron in the reign of William the Conqueror's son nearly 900 years ago, the castle passed into royal ownership for three centuries starting with Edward the First, the founder of Parliament, and ending with Henry VIII. Thereafter, it passed into the hands of some of England's influential private families as a country home. Bought in 1926 by a young Anglo-American heiress, the Hon. Olive Lady Baillie, the castle was her lifelong love; and with

Figure CS5.1
Leeds Castle

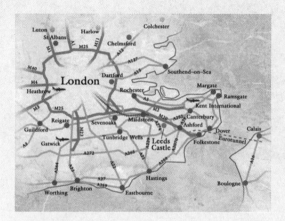

great vision and considerable generosity she lovingly restored it. Towards the end of her life, she planned to ensure that after her death the castle would be enjoyed by visitors from all over the world. Today Leeds Castle is a private charitable foundation, run by a board of trustees and a team of professional paid staff who operate the business. Leeds Castle, with its attractions, offers a high-quality visitor experience focusing on the historic castle at its heart, but now embracing formal and informal gardens, a vineyard and greenhouses, aviary and maze, shops and restaurants and a comprehensive calendar of daytime and evening special events ranging from a food and wine festival, to classical open air concerts, fireworks and falconry displays.

Visitors to Leeds Castle

Since opening to the public as a destination in 1976, Leeds Castle has welcomed 10 million visitors from all corners of the world.

The visitor profile is composed of:

- more adults than children
- more couples – over 35–55 = 24 per cent, over 55s = 23 per cent
- more small adult groups (4) – families without children = 24 per cent
- predominantly social groups ABC1
- 62 per cent on first time visits, and 12 per cent having not visited for at least two years.

The profile of adults and families has remained broadly similar since 1994 (Figure CS5.3).

In line with the national trend for domestic and overseas tourism, visitor numbers to Leeds Castle largely grew through the 1980s and 1990s (Figure CS5.4). A good location with access to large domestic and continental markets and a clear marketing and development strategy aided this growth.

Figure CS5.3
Origin of visitors

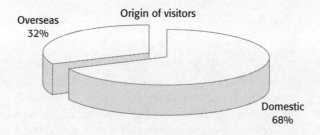

Figure CS5.4
Day visitor
numbers

At the end of the 1990s and the start of the new century, like other attractions Leeds Castle faced several unforeseen challenges which placed traditional markets under pressure and created the need to review business and marketing strategy.

Along with many other tourism destinations throughout the country, 'the loveliest castle in the world' faced pressure from external factors, including foot and mouth disease, flooding, petrol shortages and terrorism, and most recently the Iraqi War. The abolition of entry charges to the country's top museums and the significant investment through lottery funds into other attractions and museums changed the competitive landscape and the market conditions in which the castle operated. Obviously, the castle was not in a position to control these factors; all it could do was to manage their effects.

The shifting sands of market conditions, dilution and customer expectations

Leeds Castle did more than respond to such overwhelming odds; it took the opportunity to examine the whole of its business, commissioning research to fully understand the needs of its changing customer base. As a result, new strategies were implemented and, at the time of writing, continue to be developed to arrest the decline in visitor numbers.

Marketing strategy

Brand awareness

The commissioned research highlighted potential growth areas for 2003 with the London and near Continent markets seen as possible targets. The need to be tactical in reliance on traditional markets, for example long-haul visitors who in the past contributed significantly to visitor numbers, was very evident, with National Tourist Board forecasts looking gloomy – particularly from Leeds Castle's traditional long-haul 'Anglophile', primarily English-speaking, markets. Without losing sight of these key markets, it was evident that the attraction would have to be committed to widening audiences and increasing access to the site from under-represented groups.

With a high proportion of first-time visitors, the need to retain high-profile presence in core accessible markets was the key. This is costly and hard to measure, but, to take as one example, the high recognition factor in visitor research into the London outdoor campaign (through the rail and tube networks above and below ground, giving presence in both the London resident, commuter and visitor markets) offered clear pointers to future strategy. The 2002/3 campaign was deliberately designed to appeal both to visitors, residents and commuters and focused around the natural beauty, space and greenness of 'the loveliest castle in the world' as a contrast to the hustle and bustle of the city (Figures CS5.5(a) and (b)). The fortune of Leeds Castle is

Figure CS5.5 (a) and (b) Two leaflets promoting the attraction

(a)

(b)

directly affected by that of visitor levels to London, but such is the volume of visitors to London, that even at the much lower level than through the 1990s, a strong presence was seen as key. The weight of this campaign was increased to gain greater share of voice, particularly as other attractions followed Leeds Castle's early example and were soon offering advertisements in these outdoor media as well.

Local markets and strategic alliances

Added to the London campaign, substantial efforts to increase the domestic markets saw 'locals' rediscovering or discovering their heritage. Strategic alliances with regional media owners enabled extended reach at low cost, in particular by linking local newspapers with TV and radio to events. Equally, finding brand partners with similar target markets enabled the extension of distribution channels, for example local employers, and lifestyle magazines with closed user groups.

Equally, the market on the doorstep – almost 1 million people live in Kent – was largely untapped, and repeat visits from local markets grew significantly through the development of an annual season ticket. Between 1998, when the Privilege Pass replaced the modestly successful Castle Card, and 2002, such visits grew from 5400 to over 52 500 (Figure CS5.6).

Part of the key to the success of the pass (Figure CS5.7) was the good value for money it represented, with passes starting at £23 – but considering that it was a single

Figure CS5.6
Privilege Pass visits, 1998/9 to 2003/4

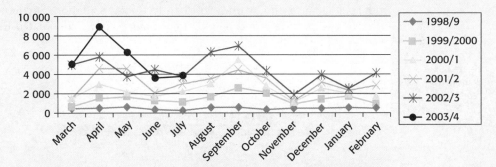

Figure CS5.7
Example of the Privilege Pass

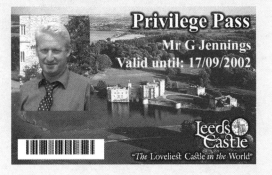

venue pass (in contrast to others in a similar price bracket for the National Trust or English Heritage) the organisation was delighted with its success. Other key factors were that Privilege Pass holders brought other full-paying friends and they visited more consistently throughout the year, boosting all-important off-peak visits. The scheme was marketed at low cost on site only, supported by a dedicated sales leaflet and a full-time seven days a week sales administrator located in the shop at the main entrance. All staff on site were trained, had a high awareness of the scheme and as such were part of the informal 'sales force' at the customer interface.

E-commerce and website

A key priority in 2002 (under continuing development in 2003) was Leeds Castle's website and e-commerce activities. At that point 40 per cent of ticket sales for special events were being sold via the website, through a 24/7 e-box office. Traditionally the box office opened seasonally, and tickets were released at the convenience of the business rather than the customers; the online box office, on the other hand, enabled tickets to be available all year round. It was the management's intention to extend this customer service to day visitor tickets in the near future. This would allow the organisation to fast track those who pre-purchase and aid cash flow with advance sales. The website (Figure CS5.8) also enabled management to expand its customer relationship management strategies. In 2002, the business achieved its goal of registering some 4000 of its regular contacts online. The declared future aim was to work more tactically in the marketplace, and by using low-cost technology solutions to communicate more effectively with current and potential customers. Efforts culminated in growing this

Figure CS5.8
Website for
Leeds Castle

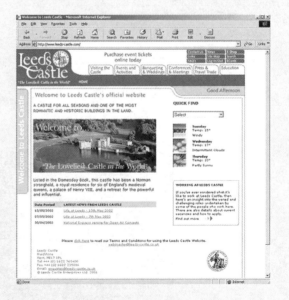

area of the business substantially, thereby keeping pace with the changing needs of customers to communicate conveniently with the attraction – a degree of success which led to the business gaining the Silver award in the National Excellence in England Awards sponsored by the National Tourist Office. Thus, a castle steeped in history is demonstrably capable of leading the way with twenty-first-century technology.

Innovating and winning awards

Leeds Castle went on to win the Tourist Attraction of the Year category at the keenly contested Kent Tourism Awards for Excellence, a unanimous decision on a public vote. At the SEETB awards, the castle was Tourist Attraction of the Year runner-up. At the Kent Business Awards, the castle was given the Welcome to Kent Accolade with judges praising the professionalism and excellence in its contribution to the tourism industry.

Boosted by these accolades, the organisation remains confident to face the future. Research has helped to deepen understanding of customers' needs, underpinning product development and marketing strategy for the coming years.

Working with partners

Another initiative undertaken in 2002 was to work alongside other major tourism businesses in the county to form the Kent Tourism Alliance (KTA), a £1.5 million private/public sector initiative which aimed to raise the region's profile nationally and internationally. At a time when the BTA and South East England Tourist Board were facing their own reorganisation, the business community of Kent saw it as important for the county to establish its own direction with this ground-breaking venture. Early 2003 saw the KTA's first major marketing campaign to attract domestic and overseas visitors, in a bid to make 'the Garden of England' one of the top tourist destinations in the country.

On a national basis, the alliance with eight other privately owned historic houses in the Treasure Houses of England group allowed for cost-effective marketing under the umbrella of *the* most important and unique properties in England. In the company of Beaulieu, Blenheim Palace, Castle Howard, Chatsworth, Harewood House, Woburn Abbey, Warwick Castle and Wilton House, Leeds Castle is jointly marketed in print and at exhibitions.

An alliance with quality food retailer Waitrose in 2003 in association with open air concerts also proved highly successful. Ticket sales have grown strongly as a result of the alliance, and significantly enhanced customer service experiences have added value to the event, including a food court at the concerts at supermarket prices, large broadcast to audience screens, improved marketing and advertising and additional resources to implement a signage strategy for the concert site which enables the 16 000 concert-goers to make their way around the site more easily.

Improving the product

The research also gave important clues to where improvements in products should be focused, and a start on these was made in 2003 with the reorganisation of one of the shops and the complete restyling of the main visitor restaurant – with a new menu, service style, furniture and presentation. The organisation has learnt that these ancillary facilities are becoming more and more key to delivering enjoyment and satisfaction. The next task will be to look at the more fundamental matter of historical presentation and visitor experience in the castle. Improvements here, coupled with the aim of making their customer care the finest in the world, are in line with the belief that attractions like Leeds Castle have recognised the importance of quality experience and excellent customer service if they are to survive in the leisure market.

Conclusion

Certainly, 2002 taught the organisation how powerless it was to predict external factors that would impact on its business. It also learnt how important it was to rise above such factors and to turn threats into opportunities.

In mid-2003 there was talk within the tourism industry of resurgence in the domestic market, as people reconsider their leisure options in light of security and safety. While this may prove to be the case, Leeds Castle has learnt that gambling on what may happen is not necessarily the answer. They see the way forward as being based on greater understanding of visitors and their needs, tailoring offers to meet the rising expectations of sophisticated guests, and innovating service delivery and marketing in order to continue as one of Britain's top visitor attractions.

Editor's conclusions

This case underlines the value of commissioned primary research, rather than an evaluation of existing raw data, as a prelude to the development of new marketing strategies. It also highlights the significance of competition arising from unanticipated directions, inasmuch as the attraction found itself suddenly in competition with museums whose entry charges had been discontinued after some years of paid admissions, while other attractions were also benefiting from subsidies in the form of lottery funding. The case also provides an example of an SME heavily dependent upon one-time visits which, through the introduction of season tickets for locals and other innovations, changed the nature of the attraction and expanded its benefits. Techniques such as these and advance ticket sales have provided opportunities for improving customer relationships, while partnership agreements on both a local and national scale improve distribution and widen access to the marketplace.

Questions

1   Due to relatively easy accessibility, two obvious markets for Leeds Castle are visitors to London seeking days out, and short-break visitors to Kent from the Continent. How would campaigns targeting these two markets differ?

2   From the data supplied in this case study and the obvious attractions of a classic medieval castle with an enviable history, it is clear that Leeds Castle has wide appeal to different markets, including the family market, couples and older visitors as well as educational groups and, no doubt, numerous visitors with only limited English language ability. What are the resulting implications for interpretation within the site, and for activities and events laid on at the attraction?

3   We are not given the full details of the commissioned research undertaken for this attraction. Suggest a programme of research that might be commissioned to produce the data you would need to overhaul existing marketing practice, bearing in mind that this is a relatively small-scale attraction with limited funds. Consider the relative importance of both qualitative and quantitative approaches in the research programme.

Case study 6
Marketing the concept of a destination: the launch of Destination Wessex

(Prepared with the help of John Seekings, Director, Aviation and Tourism International)

Figure CS6.1
The Destination
Wessex logo

(Courtesy: Wessex Tourism Association)

The boundary problem

Implicit in the concept of a tourism destination is the *genius loci*, or sense of place to which travellers are destined. In the mind of the traveller, the 'place' can vary from an entire continent to an isolated hut. To attract the traveller, those responsible for marketing must project an image that is consistent with the image in the mind of particular travellers. Most countries, recognising the highly fragmented nature of the tourism product, have placed the main thrust of destination promotion in the hands of government agencies. The problem this presents is that governments are inevitably under political pressure to fit their definition of 'place' to existing administrative boundaries rather than to those boundaries that make most sense from a marketing viewpoint.

At a national level, administrative boundaries can occasionally be a problem where travellers' perception of a 'place' straddles national boundaries. Localised examples are the Niagara, Iguacu and Victoria Falls, all of which straddle national boundaries. Less localised examples are the Pyrenees and the Alps in Europe. An unusual example is the island of Borneo, divided as it is among three nations. Similarly, Lake Constance (or the Bodensee as it is known locally) is bordered by three separate countries: Germany, Austria and Switzerland. There is little doubt that, at each of these destinations, tourism is less effectively managed and promoted than would be the case were the 'place' within the boundaries of a single country, or were the neighbouring countries to cooperate effectively as partners (in the case of Lake Constance, some attempts have been made to do so, but financial constraints have limited successful marketing). A more successful approach has been taken in the case of Ireland, where recognition of the problem, and of the need to solve it, has resulted in the two national governments jointly establishing a single tourism agency to promote the entire island overseas as one destination.

In contrast to the relatively few boundary problems evident at a national level, at a subnational level the problems caused by administrative boundaries are legion. Many destinations that are seen in the marketplace as distinct 'places' are arbitrarily spread among several uncooperative neighbouring local authorities. Many local authorities bear official names that they wish for political reasons to publicise but which fail to resonate with travellers, while other subnational authorities lack the resources to promote their local destination effectively. Britain's regions provide a notable example.

Britain's boundary problem

Since the eleventh-century Norman invasion, Britain has been divided into a large number of relatively small administrative areas. This was deliberately manipulated by the Normans, who had a political motive: the creation of a strongly centralised state based on rule from a dominant capital, London. This centralised character has persisted to the present day. Despite political pressure for devolution, and notwithstanding the limited measures of independence now granted to Scotland and, to a lesser extent, Wales, the four small nations that together form Britain – England, Scotland, Wales and Northern Ireland – are still effectively ruled from London. Local government at its various levels – from county to parish – remains dependent on central government for both deciding and funding its functions.

Since the mid-twentieth century, central government in Britain has accepted responsibility for the overseas promotion of tourism, essentially through its agency, the former British Tourist Authority (BTA), although from time to time government recognition of the need to support the agency has faltered, especially in terms of finance. Over the past two decades financial constraints obliged the BTA to reduce its services. However, despite persistent cutbacks, the agency remained as one of the world's most effective national tourism authorities, a reputation on which its successor, VisitBritain, created in 2003, will undoubtedly build.

The BTA has consistently promoted 'Great Britain' as a distinct 'place' to visit. It has also succeeded, at the same time, in promoting England, Scotland, Wales and

Northern Ireland as distinct 'places'. It has been less successful – except in the rather special case of London – in promoting those subnational 'places' which might otherwise be expected to qualify as worthy destinations in their own right.

In contrast, central government has never managed to create a coherent tourism role for local government. From the dawn of the railway age in the mid-nineteenth century, local government at all levels gave enthusiastic but limited promotional support to tourism. This role was expanded during the 1920s and 1930s to attract a new generation of motorists. In the period following the Second World War the then socialist central government decided to actively promote domestic tourism within Britain and set up so-called 'national' tourist boards in England, Scotland, Northern Ireland and Wales. Except in the case of England, these 'national' agencies have slowly evolved and have recently been strengthened as a result of growing political interest in devolution. In the case of England, central government intervention vacillated erratically from strong support for a powerful English Tourist Board (ETB) through nominal support for its successor, the English Tourism Council (ETC), and more recently to still uncertain support for an ill-defined body manifested as VisitEngland. As a result of this vacillation, in recent years 'England' has ceased to be effectively promoted as a 'place' to visit.

England's boundary problem

Under the original umbrella of the ETB, England was divided into 12 regions, each with its own regional tourist board (RTB). These depended on the ETB for their main funding. With the demise of the ETB, and its replacement by an ETC with no marketing budget, the role of the RTBs was inevitably much reduced. But even in their early days the then well-resourced RTBs suffered from boundary problems, resulting from the arbitrary political boundaries around which they had originally been formed.

The Peak District, the Cotswolds and the historic kingdom of Wessex were three examples of 'places' which were never effectively marketed because they happened to straddle the boundaries of several competing RTBs. The only RTB whose boundaries could be said to coincide with a real 'place' was that for East Anglia.

Central government vacillation also presented local government with an acute problem. Given the absence of promotional support from central government for local tourism, there is considerable local political support for involvement by local government. However, central government has persistently denied local government the resources to become effectively involved. As a result, local government intervention in tourism has generally been reduced to the operation of tourist information centres (TICs) and the provision of local accommodation brochures (for distribution mainly through TICs). Local authorities have often attempted to overcome this lack of resources by putting together elaborate schemes to extract funds from the European Commission. These schemes have frequently been successful in attracting money from Brussels; but whether they can be said to have been successful in a wider sense is open to doubt. Many local authorities have devoted a disproportionate share of their limited resources to bidding for EC funds for projects which all too frequently were of questionable worth. Project control was often deficient, and few projects were either sustained or monitored.

Fortunately for local authorities, the need to devote scarce resources to the extraction of funds from the EC diminished as a result of the decision by central government to reduce the number of regions to nine, each with its own regional development agency (RDA). Responsibility for economic development, including tourism, is at the time of writing gradually being transferred from central government to these RDAs, together with appropriate funding. Although in its infancy, the new structure is likely to transform the funding of tourism in England on a regional and local basis. Not only will it allow the direction of substantial funding into tourism, it will also clear the way for funding to be freed from the boundary constraints which have bedevilled British tourism. Nowhere will this be more welcome than in the place known as Wessex.

The *genius loci* of Wessex

Thanks to its unique historic quality, Wessex is widely perceived as having a 'sense of place', despite uncertainty today over its present boundaries. It originated in the seventh century as the kingdom of the West Saxons. By the time of the Norman invasion, the West Saxons had acquired control from their neighbours of the entire territory up to the borders of Scotland and Wales, thus creating the infant state of England which they ruled from their capital, Winchester. Although Wessex was to lose its political identity it never lost its identity as a 'place'. This is still evident in the widespread use of Wessex as a business name by several thousand separate business enterprises in the four counties which formed the core of ancient Wessex – Dorset, Wiltshire, Somerset and Hampshire. It is also evident in the abundant commercially produced travel literature – including most of the best respected travel handbooks – which describe this area as Wessex. An important factor in its sustained identity is the writing of the nineteenth-century author Thomas Hardy, who used Wessex as the focus for his popular historical novels.

As an identifiable destination, Wessex has become an extreme example of England's regional boundary problems. The region is divided territorially between three RTBs, in each of which it was given low priority. It also spreads across four counties, three of which were seriously under-resourced as far as tourism was concerned. Even with the formation of RDAs, it remained arbitrarily divided between the two bodies representing respectively the South-West and the South-East. Few of the district councils in the region – numbering over 30 – were in a position to promote tourism other than on a purely local basis.

The marketing of Wessex

The idea of promoting Wessex as a distinct destination originated at a workshop in Bradford-on-Avon organised by the London-based Tourism Society in the mid-1990s. The object of this seminar was to consider why so few foreign visitors came to such an interesting historic town. Among the meeting's recommendations was the idea that Bradford-on-Avon would benefit from the development of Wessex as an internationally branded destination. This was soon followed by a new master plan for the local district council of West Wiltshire which gave support to the idea of Wessex being adopted as a brand. This in turn encouraged a group of local tourism enterprises – mostly small accommodation providers – to set up the Wessex Tourism Forum with the object of promoting the idea throughout the wider Wessex area.

Among those to be attracted by this idea was the county council of neighbouring Somerset which decided to submit a bid to the European Commission, for funding under the EC's InterReg programme, to support an interregional marketing programme 'in the field of heritage tourism' involving Wessex in Britain and the Pays de la Loire in France. By this time the Wessex Tourism Forum had advanced to the point of deciding to convert into a more formal organisation known as the Wessex Tourism Association with the specific object of promoting Wessex as a quality heritage destination. At the most recent meeting of the forum it was agreed that the first task of the new association should be to carry out a convincing research study on the feasibility of promoting Wessex as a destination brand.

The Somerset County Council realised that a Wessex research study would be of immediate relevance to other destinations in Europe with similar boundary problems. They agreed to incorporate the research study within their InterReg project on condition that the study was undertaken by a professional team of experts from the ranks of the Tourism Society. Entitled *Wessex: Building a Heritage Destination*, the team's report was published early in 2001. Among its main conclusions were:

- in terms of volume, Wessex constitutes a viable destination, already attracting 18 million staying visitors in 1999, plus perhaps 50 million day visitors
- in terms of landscape and heritage attraction, Wessex is acknowledged as a world-class destination
- although the region has substantial accommodation capacity – equivalent to around a quarter of a million bed places – this is not well matched to the market requirements of a predominantly heritage destination, there being an abundance of budget 'beach holiday' properties but a severe shortage of the quality accommodation sought by travellers attracted by heritage; this mismatch was a major factor in the small number of overseas visitors (only 2 million in 1999)
- while the region enjoyed good road access, the absence of adequate direct air service from abroad was another factor constraining foreign visitors
- although the region and its attraction were well known within Britain, it was little known abroad, a major factor being the very limited and fragmented promotional support being given to the private sector by the public sector
- this weak public sector support reflected the unusual problem faced by a region such as Wessex which failed to conform to politically defined boundaries
- across Europe there were many examples of similar 'heritage' destinations which suffered from this boundary problem
- given Europe's falling share of global tourism, including the 'heritage' segment of the market, this boundary problem deserved further attention by the EC.

Figure CS6.2
Promotional leaflet for Destination Wessex identifying the geographical region

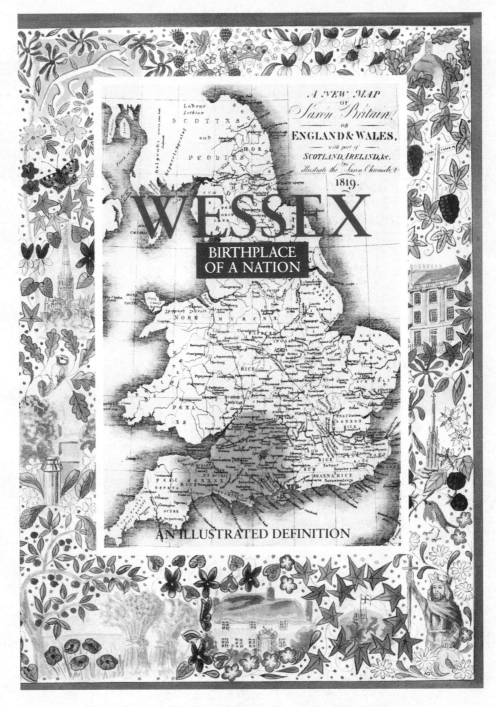

(Courtesy: Wessex Tourism Association)

Evaluating the project

While appeals to the EC have yet to bear fruit, within Britain the research study has been actively followed up. Acting on the findings of the survey, the Wessex Tourism Association decided to concentrate on promoting travel from abroad. Early in 2003 its 'Destination Wessex' programme was successfully launched, with the enthusiastic support of the BTA (see Figure CS6.2). The next task for the association was to enlist the region's major private sector players to participate in the programme, and to prepare a bid for funding aid from the RDA for the South-West. A series of promotions with selected overseas tour operators has already been put into operation. Parallelling this, extensive consultation was initiated with representatives of local government throughout the region, the aim being to provide assurance that the association's aim is concentrated on attracting foreign visitors.

At the time of writing, it is still too early to judge whether or not the experience of Wessex will prove successful. There are several other regions of Britain which will be following the experiment with interest – and as the research study revealed, there are regions elsewhere in Europe which could also benefit from the efforts of Wessex to surmount inappropriate political boundaries to reinforce their touristic *genii loci.*

Editor's conclusions

The case highlights two issues which have serious implications for marketing destinations. First, it identifies the difficulties faced by a geographically ill-defined region in gaining market awareness, especially abroad, as a necessary prerequisite to visitor demand. Second, it draws attention to the need for public–private collaboration in marketing such regions. Current geopolitical boundaries, and the absence of established public bodies with overall responsibility for promoting these regions, are severe constraints, although the development of RDAs in Britain may be a step towards helping to overcome these – but similar regions in other countries may be less fortunate, unless those regions already benefit from a strong international image. The case study also endorses the recognition that tourism initiatives often derive from the experiences of members from the private sector of the industry, while the scale of marketing called for in launching the appeal of a new destination requires financial and other support from the public sector, if it is to succeed.

Questions

1 This case raises the issue of 'brand' as a concept applied to a destination. Consider the issue in the context of the discussion contained in Chapter 5.

2 Wessex is only one example of an ill-defined tourist region in the UK – mention is also made of the Cotswolds, the Peak District, and, outside of the UK, the Loire region, the Pyrenees and Alps. Some of the Mediterranean coastal regions provide further examples. Are the problems faced by

all of these identical, or are there other issues arising from their geographical and political differences? What other ill-defined regions can you identify, in the UK or elsewhere? How well are these promoted currently, or how could they be better marketed?

3   Many towns attempt to promote themselves as 'gateways' to regions, as means of generating income for their accommodation and shopping facilities. Such towns are often promoted in competition with one another: examples include Cheltenham and Cirencester, two of several 'Gateways to the Cotswolds'. What criteria would you use to define a 'gateway', and how would you promote it in competition with other cities with similar credibility? How important is it that the town in question is in itself seen as an attractive place to visit?

Case study 7
The use of personalities to support a campaign for recovery: Yorkshire Tourist Board

(Prepared with the help of Jeremy Aspinall and Martyn Lewis, Senior King Communications Group)

Introduction

For UK domestic tourism, 2001 was a year to forget. The rampage of foot and mouth disease (FMD) across the country was the most visible sign of an industry suffering as footpaths were closed, tourist attractions emptied and vacancy signs hung in hotel windows.

To make matters worse, and overshadowed by the FMD crisis, the high value of the pound sterling and the boom in discount airlines meant that the British already had enough reasons to holiday elsewhere. The events of September 11th also had a significant impact, although by this point the campaign was already under way.

Although Yorkshire is familiar to many in Britain – often through its larger than life television characters and celebrities – it is a region that is not readily associated with holidays and short breaks. The stereotypic view of Yorkshire is that of warm beer, whippet dogs, wrinkled stockings and cricketer Geoff Boycott. The destination was clearly in need of a bold makeover.

The advertising brief presented by Yorkshire Forward (the Regional Development Agency) and Yorkshire Tourist Board (YTB) to agents Senior King contained a considerable challenge: to present Yorkshire as an attractive and modern destination for holidays and short breaks. Success would be judged by the response generated: occupancy rates in the county's hotels and B&Bs and if possible a change in the UK public's perception of the county's personality. The brief was to devise a multimedia campaign reaching a wide UK audience, but with a bias towards residents in the Midlands and South. A secondary aim was to stimulate the day trip market among the local population during the autumn of that year so that tourism could begin to get back on its feet.

The business case

Yorkshire, a county famous for its rural landscapes of the Dales and Moors and its eastern sea coast, suffered more than most during the FMD crisis. At the time, some 135 000 employees worked in tourism within the county, generating £3337 million in revenue, half of which was contributed by rural tourism. It was estimated that the loss of business due to FMD amounted to some 60 per cent of this total – between £60 and £75 million a month.

Yorkshire Forward responded to the crisis by committing £6 million towards a recovery programme; £1.5 million of this amount was earmarked specifically for the advertising campaign to be run from September until the end of April 2002.

The marketing background

Although each British region works together to attract overseas visitors through the auspices of the British Tourist Authority (BTA), marketing the product domestically is less coordinated. In that sense, the county sees each other region as directly competitive. In effect, targeting the South and Midlands means competing with those regions – Scotland, Wales, Ireland and the West Country – with the strongest appeal to key concentrations of the UK population. Each of these locations uses the classic destination marketing messages emphasising their region's idyllic countryside, friendly people and healthy living. Those regions with the largest budgets regularly employ television commercials as the main creative plank of their campaigns, with direct marketing, press and Internet advertising to back up the main thrust of the campaign.

Senior King recognised that one of their biggest challenges would be to compete with high-profile destinations that have traditionally gained the greatest impact through high media spend. While £1.5 million was the largest single budget ever committed by Yorkshire to one campaign, it paled beside the sums invested by its leading competitors. The answer was seen to lie in the careful use of media rather than any attempt at saturation press and media advertising or direct mail activities.

The aim of the campaign strategy was twofold. Initially, because of the dire state of the regional tourism industry, the campaign needed to drive late season visitors. A Two-4-One card, presented inside a folded A4 leaflet and featuring 60 museums, eateries and attractions in Yorkshire was developed and used as a call to action to stimulate this market.

The second aim of the campaign was to ensure that Yorkshire had a high profile during the traditional peak holiday booking season of January to March. With this intention in mind, a large slice of the budget had been set aside to buy space on Carlton and Central TV stations, primarily around peak-time slots. The 10-second format of the five commercials allowed flexibility to book space around some of the most suitable programmes, which included Yorkshire series *Emmerdale* and *Heartbeat*.

The budget for all promotion was apportioned as follows:

TV (production and media)	50%
national press	21%
roadshow promotions	5%
local radio	4%
direct mail	3%
regional press	2%
trade advertising	2%
Internet	1%
PR	1%
research	1%
fulfilment	6%
miscellaneous costs	4%

The timing of the promotion and channels used were:

September 2001

Roadshow promotions: Ten railway stations in Yorkshire, the Midlands and London were used to launch the campaign. Bags containing the latest brochures, a Two-4-One attractions discount card and leaflet and samples of famous Yorkshire brands of tea and biscuits were distributed to commuters throughout the two weeks of the promotion.

Direct mail: 105 000 households on the YTB database received a mailer including the Two-4-One card, leaflet and personalised letter inviting them to get out and enjoy Yorkshire.

Internet: Banner advertising targeted surfers searching for holiday ideas. Keywords were bought on popular search engines and specialist holiday sites such as Telegraph Travel. Different creatives were used on each site to test the effectiveness of a brand message over a promotional message. A splash page was added to the YTB website to provide visitors with the opportunity to order a guide or discount card online.

Local radio: Radio advertising provided a high-impact channel for reaching a large regional population. Two executions encouraged the local population to visit Yorkshire's tourist attractions, and to order the Two-4-One card by phone or via the website.

January 2002

Television: Five 10-second commercials, featuring Yorkshire celebrities, were used to demonstrate the scale of the county's tourism attractions. Mel B's glamour emphasised the city life of Leeds and Harrogate: Darren Gough fronted an ad highlighting some of the region's activities. Brian Blessed was seen outside the Woolpack (of *Emmerdale* fame), while Brian Turner tucked into Scarborough's fish and chips. Meanwhile, Alan Titchmarsh enjoyed one of Yorkshire's many country houses and gardens.

National and local press: A mix of colour and mono advertising across key national and regional titles provided a high reach across the campaign's target audience. At the centre point of the schedule were a series of advertorials run in the *Sunday Mirror Personal*, *Daily Mail Weekend*, *Daily Express* and *Radio Times* magazines.

Tip-on postcards were added to the latter three and included an incentive to order the YTB 2002 Guide.

Specialist press: Brochure panels are a staple part of any marketing campaign. These small ads appeared in a cross-section of titles, from *TV Times* to *Smart Shopper* magazine. Reader competitions were also featured in *Essentials* and *Good Housekeeping* magazines.

The creative strategy for this media strategy is detailed in 'Creative implications' below.

Consumer insight

The first phase of the campaign was targeted primarily at audiences who were familiar with the region – either because they were previous visitors or enquirers, or because they were local. The media used, regional radio and roadshows, allowed the campaigns to reach a large number of people very quickly. The Two-4-One card was a mechanism that appealed across the demographic profile (who does not like a discount?), but especially to families looking for a good value day out. ABC1 couples, a key market for short breaks, were also targeted via the mailshot and the Internet.

The campaign's second phase sought to appeal to the markets that traditionally respond strongly to holiday advertising: female, either with a family or as a couple. Yorkshire, partly because of its historic sites and open countryside, also had a bias towards more affluent, professional target markets.

Domestic tourism is made up of VFR day trips, short breaks and those taking their main annual holiday. It was vital that the campaign touched on the different motivations of these audiences and provided reasons to travel. Therefore, the discount card was aimed primarily at day-trippers and short-break takers, whereas the television and press advertising showcased the variety of attractions around the county.

The choice of celebrities to front the campaign was carefully arranged to hit a broad market. Mel B provided a focus for the younger end of the scale, whereas the housewives' favourite, Alan Titchmarsh (Figures CS7.1 and 7.2, colour plates), and TV chef Brian Turner, appeal especially to mid-aged females and their 'hands-on' husbands. Darren Gough, many people's idea of a modern-day Yorkshireman, is especially well known among men, whereas Brian Blessed's familiar voice is instantly recognisable across the audience profile. Sean Bean, the commercial's voice-over, provided grit or sex appeal, depending on your preference.

Creative implications

The campaign theme, 'Yorkshire – Britain's Biggest Break', evolved from the fact that Yorkshire is the largest county in England. In a marketplace where differentiation can be difficult and 'something for everyone' is often used as a destination unique selling point (USP), it was important to present Yorkshire's proposition as something easily understandable and sustainable. Therefore, the creative concept revolved around illustrating Yorkshire's potential as a holiday and short break destination through the sheer number of historic houses, racecourses and miles of parkland – all of which Yorkshire lays claim to having the biggest, most or, to take the concept to its extreme, grandest the UK has to offer.

The television commercials started life as a 'big' concept – one very long commercial run as many times as the budget would allow (very few in all probability): but from here, the concept gravitated, somewhat paradoxically, to the production of a series of 10-second commercials, each of which would showcase a theme. The celebrities were approached to feature in each execution (for a nominal fee) in order to provide each with a talking point and a stamp of credibility.

In order to satisfy the variety of stakeholders that are invariably involved with a tourist board, it was important to feature an even geographic spread of locations and attractions. This requirement placed a high demand on the commercial's creative team, not least because of the short time available for shooting due to the limited budget and shortening days (the commercials were shot in October). Ultimately it was possible to produce five executions, each of which focused on a key element of Yorkshire's appeal and exploited target market motivations: shopping, landscapes, heritage, houses and gardens, sports and activities.

'Yorkshire – Britain's Biggest Break' was the common thread that bound all the communications activities together. The campaign's advertising and advertorials (or long-copy ads) worked around the same themes as the TV commercials and prompted readers to log onto the dedicated web page set up by YTB, or call to order a guide. Advertorials were tailored either to the time of their publication (a Valentine's competition ran in the *Daily Mail*) or the nature of the magazines (the *Radio Times* advertorial was based on Yorkshire's screen heritage).

Finally, at the outset of the campaign the roadshow promotion appealed to commuters by offering a tea break courtesy of two of Yorkshire's best known brands, Foxes Biscuits and Taylor of Harrogate's Yorkshire Tea. This tactic provided the campaign with an unmissable opportunity to demonstrate the appropriateness of a break in Yorkshire to the people who most needed one.

The proof of effectiveness

The initial success of the campaign came from the excellent response received from commuters at the railway promotions. Over 75 000 Yorkshire Break bags containing the Two-4-One card, samples and YTB Guide were distributed – the majority of which were snapped up within hours of each roadshow beginning.

From September onwards the traffic to the YTB website began to grow dramatically. By the end of March the site had received 50 per cent more traffic than for the same period the previous year. Furthermore, many of these people were return visitors to the site, demonstrating that they were interested in what Yorkshire had to offer as a holiday destination.

The direct mail campaign provided a response rate of over 8.5 per cent, a significant return, especially for a campaign run during the tail end of the holiday season.

The TV campaign was not designed to provoke direct response calls although the website and phone number were provided. The commercials were created to challenge stereotypes and to show all that Yorkshire has to offer as a holiday destination. With these broadcasts coinciding with a significant national and regional press presence, it was hoped that the increases in Yorkshire's share of voice would have a knock-on effect.

Senior King commissioned Capibus Research (a national quantitative survey) which revealed that in the two regions where the TV commercials were broadcast, awareness figures increased significantly. Among the Greater London respondents, the rating increased by 4 per cent, whilst in the West Midlands it grew by 8 per cent and in the East Midlands the figure jumped by over 20 per cent.

By the end of April over 180 000 requests for Guides had been received, more than three times the estimated response rate. Advertorials in the national newspapers and *Radio Times* produced tens of thousands of replies each, and YTB was forced to undertake a second print run of its Guide to cope with the demand. The costs per response for the January and February advertorials were all approximately £1.00 – an almost unprecedented cost efficiency for this media channel.

The campaign's success can be set against the underachievement of some of the media used at the campaign's launch in September. At first it was anticipated that a terrorist act abroad might prove to be a stimulus to the late domestic market. In fact, it seemed to have the opposite effect for the first few weeks of the campaign. Banner advertising, usually very productive, provided disappointing results and features in the *Daily Telegraph* and *Evening Standard* came in short of expectations. It seems that during September and October few people were in the mood to think about a holiday. The turn of the year, however, saw a huge uplift, well beyond expectations. The 50 000 responses hoped for were soon achieved and the figure continued to grow with each passing week.

Yorkshire Forward estimated, based on conservative conversion rates (the number of people ordering a guide who eventually visit the region), that an additional 57 000 people would take a break or holiday in Yorkshire during 2002. It was estimated that the campaign would generate an additional £18 million for the regional economy, of which £12 million would go direct to the hotel and catering sector and £6 million into other industries, creating or safeguarding up to 800 direct or indirect jobs. The English Tourism Council also released figures indicating that among the regions Yorkshire had the second highest room occupancy rate after London, at 61 per cent by the end of 2001. The campaign resulted in an IPA Effectiveness Award for Senior King in 2002.

Editor's conclusions

This case study outlines in some detail a public sector advertising campaign with clearly defined objectives and target markets, which became a notable success. It represents an early example of a campaign in which a regional tourist board and a regional development agency collaborated, with the latter providing direct financial aid. The multimedia campaign reveals how careful analysis and selection of advertising media can achieve maximum impact with limited funding, when in the hands of professional advertising agents.

Nationally popular personalities having close associations with the destination helped to reinforce the message through advertisements (compare with Chapter 7, and in particular the advertisement used by MyTravel in Figure 7.4). The mention of a 'nominal' fee charged by these personalities would suggest that where they have a personal interest in, or association with, the subject being promoted, they will not necessarily seek to maximise their commercial earnings, making tie-ins with celebrities a reasonable proposition even for lower-budget campaigns. Similarly, partnership promotion with products such as food and drink associated with the region stretch marketing budgets to maximise effectiveness.

Questions

1   Personalities have sell-by dates! Given that fame, particularly in the pop world, is ephemeral, should the use of celebrities be limited to advertising campaigns having short-term objectives only? What internationally known figures would you select for representing the UK, France, USA or Australia in promotional campaigns over a longer term, assuming a budget unconstrained by financial considerations?

2   The briefing for this campaign makes it clear that, where public sector destination advertising for a region is concerned, equal publicity has to be given to all attractions and sites. In what ways might this deplete the effectiveness of the campaign? Is it a serious constraint in marketing a region which has only a limited number of highly popular destinations?

3   The campaign includes an imaginative tie-in with food products associated with Yorkshire. What products associated with the town or region where you live or work would lend themselves to a similar promotion, and what would be the best strategy, in your view, to undertake a joint promotion?

Case study 8
Piran: establishing a sustainable 'gem city'

(Prepared by David Bruce, Principal Lecturer, Bristol Business School, University of the West of England)

Location and background

Piran (Pirano) is a historic walled town on the Istrian coast of Slovenia. Down below its dominating cathedral with its Venice-like campanile, lies the oval inner harbour, which was replaced in the nineteenth century with an elegant town square, focused on a statue of Tartini – an eighteenth-century composer, violinist and native of Pirano (Figure CS8.1). The town had its urban development constricted by its peninsular site and town walls and then by the twentieth century's border and social upheavals. Luckily the town escaped significant war damage and with the exception of one 1960s hotel extension, was saved from inappropriate 'modernisation'. It has been described by successive guidebooks as 'an attractive medieval-looking town', as 'one of the most beautiful small towns on the whole Adriatic coastline', as preserving 'tangible remnants of atmosphere', as 'a large outdoor museum', as 'an exquisite cultural pearl' and most recently and independently as 'a gem of Venetian Gothic'. Gradually the town is acquiring or is being set up for 'gem city' status.[1]

Since 1991, Piran has been the icon of Mediterranean Slovenia. But where is Slovenia? Slovenia (Slovenija) is the small country of 1.5 million people that was a republic of former Yugoslavia (Figure CS8.2). It is often confused with Slovakia (called Slovensko in that country's language), which is the inland country that separated from the Czech Republic in 1993. For tourism, Piran the town is associated with the resort of Portoroz (Portorose). Together they have a long but disrupted history of tourism and are located on the short coast between Trieste (Italy) and Croatia, which has most of the Istrian peninsula. The area is formally bilingual (Slovene/Italian) and the Italian minority (now fewer than 10 per cent) has entrenched democratic and cultural rights.

The municipal area comprises Piran, Portoroz, Lucija and a couple of neighbouring bays including extensive salt pans. The shoreline is stony rather than sandy and the bathing places are therefore more like a lakeside than the traditional image of the sea-side. The climate is northern Adriatic with Mediterranean summers, but winters from

Figure CS8.1
Tartini Square,
Piran

(Courtesy: David Bruce)

Figure CS8.2
Map of Slovenia
locating Piran

(Courtesy: Walled Towns Friendship Circle)

time to time tormented by the *borja*. This sharp north-east wind is moderated by the sheltering hills above Portoroz and the inner town of Piran but lashes the sea and creates interesting windsurfing conditions. The hillsides of the South Primorska region around the three coastal towns of Piran, Koper and Izola produce large quantities of wine; the sea provides local fish and mussels.

Küstenland, Trieste and Yugoslavia

Before 1918, Pirano and Portorose were part of a province of the Austro-Hungarian Empire, centred on Trieste, called Küstenland[2] ('Coastland') in German, or 'Litorale' in Italian. The area was seen as the coast for central Europe. There were direct rail connections to Vienna, Munich and even Berlin. Pirano and Portorose were accessible by sea and by rail from Trieste. Travelling by sea, Baedeker in 1911 reported favourably on Pirano but had not in fact landed as evidenced by a rare mistake – he describes the town walls as if they were a fortress on the hill above. Portorose at that time had a narrow gauge railway, which linked it on the one hand to Trieste and on the other to Parenza/Porec (now in Croatian Istria). A tramway linked Pirano to Portorose. After 1918 until the Second World War all the coast and Istria were part of Italy. Eventually the United Nations redefined the border and in 1956, Trieste was confirmed as part of Italy and this stretch of the coast as part of Yugoslavia in the Republic of Slovenia. In 2004 Slovenia joins the EU, reducing the significance of the border with Italy but emphasising that with Croatia.

During the Yugoslav period (until 1991) Portoroz (and Piran) were successfully marketed with other resorts on the Istrian and Dalmatian coast and developed a strong German-speaking and also Western European traditional family tourism. The saltwater spa (thalassotherapy) in Portoroz was distinctive but in general tourism competed with other similar places. The grand Palace Hotel had fallen out of use after the Second World War and its gardens, which ran down to the sea, were cut through by the main road. A casino, founded in 1913, prospered by exploiting gambling laws that were relatively liberal compared to Italy or Austria. The casino and all the hotels were owned cooperatively, under the Yugoslav version of communism. Substantial surpluses were reinvested locally, providing funds for a massive 1350-boat marina, a small airport and an open air conference centre/arena as well as an enormous 1970s conference hotel taking over the headland between the resort of Portoroz and the historic walled town of Piran.

Wars and even rumours of wars can, and in this case did, ruin tourism. What might be called the 'Wars of the Yugoslav Succession' had virtually no physical effect on this, or indeed any, part of Slovenia. Slovenia's war of independence lasted just 10 days. Even Croatian Istria was unaffected. Nevertheless, tourism collapsed after 1991 when the whole of the Balkans was perceived as 'bandit country'. For 10 years tour operators from Western Europe diverted their custom to the western Mediterranean. For Portoroz and Piran the result was a period of no investment in tourism infrastructure. The hotels from the 1960s became outdated and the physical appearance of the town of Piran and the resort of Portoroz became rundown.

Figure CS8.3
View over the
town of Piran
Figure CS8.4
Piran harbour

(Courtesy: David Bruce)   (Courtesy: David Bruce)

Very quickly hotel standards became unacceptable for conventional tour operators. As an impression of peace returns, less conventional tourists are the first to return and a gradual process of reinvestment – both upgrading existing and creating new facilities – may take place. Both require cash and Portoroz has benefited from the money generated by the casino, even though the central government in Ljubljana now takes a larger slice than did the old Yugoslavia. After 1991, all the hotels in Portoroz were privatised and have been well renovated, often with the financial involvement of the casino.

Piran town had meanwhile declined massively in population terms (from an over-crowded 15 000 in 1911 to less than 5000 today). Its old dependence on providing winter and family accommodation for the workers of the salt pans, a fishing fleet and trading ships had meant tight-packed housing with narrow streets, surrounding fine municipal and patrician buildings. These include fine Venetian and (heavier) Austrian architecture, laid out theatrically around the harbour and beneath the dominating cathedral and the hilltop town walls (see Figures CS8.3 and CS8.4). A feature is the well-preserved, though still threatened, Jewish ghetto hidden deep in the oldest part of town.

As much of the original population moved out to purpose-built flats beyond Portoroz, many houses in the town were converted to holiday homes of varying quality, and the business of the town became monopolised by restaurants, serving the neighbouring resort. The population of the municipal area has grown strongly since 1961 when it was 11 000 to over 17 000 in the year 2000.

The old town of Piran shows signs of its depopulation. Only the most visible streets and squares have been restored to something like their former style. Some land has been reclaimed from the sea to allow restaurants, a hotel and a nineteenth-century theatre to extend beyond the old town-wall-defined shoreline. This area and the town square (Trg Tartini) are liable to flooding in the same way as Venice suffers from the 'Alto'. The high water is driven north by a combination of south-westerly winds and spring tides. With global warming, this is becoming more frequent. There were only two hotels and a hostel in the old town but one has been cleverly expanded to 45 rooms behind the old façade on the Trg Tartini (see Figures CS8.5 and CS8.6).

Figure CS8.5
Tartini Hotel
façade
Figure CS8.6
Extended
development
of Tartini Hotel

(Courtesy: David Bruce)

(Courtesy: David Bruce)

Portoroz, always remembering its name as 'the port of roses', never allowed the standards of its municipal horticulture to drop, although there is some recent evidence to suggest that plants requiring less high maintenance than roses have been favoured. It is estimated that about a third of the economy of the municipal area of Piran is directly attributable to tourism, that figure rising to above 60 per cent, when the local multiplier effect is included.

The market

The tourists who have returned to Portoroz have come with increasing frequency by car for short breaks. This has meant more and more traffic and greater demand for parking. Even by 2001, total numbers of tourist nights were still less than in the last years of Yugoslavia. In 1986, 305 000 tourists stayed for an average of nearly six nights. By 1999, while numbers had recovered from the 1991 low of 158 000, the average length of stay had declined to less than four nights. The total volume of tourism was therefore still substantially (about a third) down. Hotel occupancy on an annual basis is just over 50 per cent but that reflects use close to capacity during the summer season and very little except some conference business and some weekend breaks during the October to May off-season. There are also day visitors but because of the road and rail access to the area – neither motorway nor railway come within 20 kilometres – their numbers in summer are restricted by congestion.

Since before the crisis, the proportion of domestic (Slovene) visitors had risen from a third to a half. Among the visitors from abroad, the largest numbers (in the 1998/9 survey) were German (18 per cent), followed by Italian (13 per cent), Austrians (10 per cent) and smaller numbers of Russians, Belgians, Hungarians, Swiss and Croats. The pattern of the originating markets is clearly still, or rather again, dominated by the central European hinterland and neighbouring Italy. The Western European market, significant in the 1980s, has not yet returned.

In terms of age and life cycle, young families and the elderly are the main particip-ants. The average spend per day at 59 euros is high in comparison with the national income of Slovenes (10 500 euros a year or about 28 euros a day) and reflects the importance of the casino. Over 50 per cent of the tourists say they are seeking the sun and the sea, while 20 per cent are seeking entertainment – the casino and associated nightlife – 15 per cent are conference delegates and 10 per cent are described as 'explorers' – those seeking new experiences.[3]

Players and stakeholders

Slovenia as a whole, and Piran in particular, are examples of a tourist economy in transition from the public sector dominated and undemocratic but stable central European communist society. Since 1991, that has been replaced by increasing free enterprise, through privatisation and private, including foreign, investment and also by democratic central and local government. The casino, now privatised, and the Portoroz hoteliers, many linked financially to the casino, are the main commercial stakeholders in the economy of the municipal area of Piran. There are, however, other significant players.

The Slovenian central government in Ljubljana has both a strategic interest in Piran/Portoroz as a critical part of its Mediterranean coast and as the contributor of about 20 per cent of all Slovenia's tourist revenues. It also takes significant taxation revenue from the casino. Slovenia is currently a centralised state with relatively few powers delegated to local authorities and only weak regional structures. It is at national level that strategic transport decisions are made and also about the development of higher education.

Such regional structures as do exist in the South Primorska region, tend to be dominated by the port city of Koper (Capodistria) where the authorities do not necessarily see the value of Piran in terms of its cultural quality and tourism potential. This governmental level sets the priorities for planning decisions and public investment, for instance for the supply of water, which has become of critical importance because traditional sources are now in Croatian Istria.

The municipality itself is still a commercial player, owning the marina, the small airport, a large conference centre and parts of the historical housing stock. It has recently put together a consortium to take on the shell of the grand Palace Hotel in Portoroz. The intention is to restore it as a five-star centrepiece to the resort.

So-called civil society – the network of non-governmental organisations (NGOs) – such as environmental associations and heritage protection societies tend to be weak in former communist Europe but are of growing influence and are reinforced by the presence of relevant higher education research institutes such as the Ljubljana University Marine Biology Institute. Higher education is itself important as a stakeholder, with different colleges, including one for tourism and another for business, now merging to form a University of the Primorska with facilities using restored buildings in Piran as well as other campus areas.

There are various constituencies in the local community with differing overlapping interests. They include the residents of the old town itself, the former old-town residents now living in Lucija near Portoroz, the Italian-speaking minority (represented in both the previous groups), those employed in each part of the tourism industry and those employed in other economic activities. Fishermen and farmers with others in outlying villages that depend on Piran's market and who supply wine and fish to the restaurants and hotels are further elements.

The municipality of Piran, with its directly elected mayor, seeks within its limited powers to reconcile these interests and to promote the area as a *tourist municipality*.

The services

Of the Piran municipal area's hotels, over 80 per cent (by beds) are in Portoroz, about 6 per cent in Piran itself and the remainder in smaller bays along the coast. Significant accommodation (but mainly summer seasonal) is also provided by guesthouses, apartments and a large caravan camping site for 1000 people. The enormous marina with 1350 berths also provides accommodation on board many of its boats. There are some 80 restaurants, bars and clubs in the area, with many of the most successful within the old town of Piran.

The larger hotels have conference facilities and there is in addition the municipality-owned conference centre/arena, which until recently was open air but has now been modernised and covered. With its ownership also of the marina and the small airport, the local public sector is actively engaged in and financially committed to the success of tourism. The municipality also has museums in the old town and has inherited substantial landlord interests not only in twentieth-century public housing – mainly in Lucija – but also in the old town.

A sensitive environment

The built heritage of Piran town, the seascape and the surrounding landscape all make important contributions to the tourism value of Piran/Portoroz but they also create critical constraints on its exploitation. Along the coast are national nature reserves and the salt pans are important for wading birds, for the quality of the air and sea as well as for traditional employment.

The sea is the area's fundamental natural resource. Carefully monitored by the Marine Biology Institute, its water quality is affected locally by the marina – the threat of oil and other boat waste – and other local waste. At a wider level, threats exist from industrial waste from ports around the northern Adriatic in Slovenia, Croatia and Italy. In the late spring and early summer it can even be severely affected by pollution brought down by the great river Po from as far away as Milan. Slovenia's membership of the EU in 2004 makes this a potentially manageable problem.

The whole of the old walled town of Piran is a conservation area and the major buildings are individually subject to protection. Many of them became almost derelict before 1991 due either to the withdrawal of their Italian owners or the severe attitude of the Yugoslav state towards religion or simply through the population decline. A backlog of essential renovation and repair built up. Since 1991, the churches and cathedral have received a lot of attention and both the interior and exterior of the cathedral are approaching their traditional splendour. The front façade and public rooms of the town hall have equally been brought to a high standard. The fine municipal theatre has been restored, with the lobby turned into an attractive bar. More problematic have been the large warehouses/town mansions of the merchants, but expanding higher education, combined with ground-floor bars, offers one solution.

Transport

The large day visitor movements are within the immediate area, particularly between the old town of Piran and Portoroz, which is 4 kilometres distant. The road winds up over a steep hill, while pedestrians and cyclists can make their way along by the sea. The old electric trams were stopped in 1956 and dreadful traffic congestion has been the result. Already in the 1980s a short distance Park and Ride was introduced from a large and recently further expanded car park on land reclaimed from the sea just outside Piran. The whole of the town itself was designated as a single car park and a barrier installed which has reduced excessive visitor access and made even locals pay (a discounted amount) to enter the town. It was therefore an implicit, early and largely unreported example of road pricing for residents and tourists. The management of the system has become rather rigid and it operates with the same fixed prices: summer and winter, weekend and weekday, day and night. There is a frequent but often overloaded and congestion-affected bus service between old town and resort, made up partly of a shuttle bus that goes as far as the main Tartini Square and regional services that reach only to the bus station on the edge of the historic area.

The ancient narrow-gauge railway from Trieste has not survived the frontier changes. Parts of it are used as a cycle track with a long tunnel, allowing walkers and cyclists to escape from Portoroz directly into the countryside. It is on the designated Euro-Velo route down the Adriatic coast.

Over 75 per cent of tourists to Portoroz come by car, the remainder mainly by coach with a few by public bus and by boat to the marina. Salt from the local salt pans is trans-shipped from a wharf near Portoroz, and excursion boats to Venice and Trieste, operating in the summer, tend to take people only out of the area. Few tourists currently arrive by air at the local airport, which is seen as capable of expansion.

Marketing for the sustainable development of Piran as a tourist gem city

As early as 1995, Piran proclaimed itself a *Green Municipality* in line with the United Nations Rio Declaration and Local Agenda 21. Successive mayors and councils have renewed this commitment with the prime objective of leaving to their children 'their heritage in a better state than it was in when we received it'. From this statement flow a number of tasks and policies. For tourism, the councillors say they will 'support development of high quality tourism, improve accommodation facilities, create more jobs for fewer tourists who will be spending their holidays here also outside the high tourist season and promote development of soft, sustainable tourism'. Such wording is not uncommon and taken with similar paragraphs on other activities, provides a mission statement compatible with strategies which may or may not prove genuinely sustainable. However, it would be difficult to see national government plans to extend the motorway network right up to the edge of the resort area and the major growth strategy put forward by the Portoroz hoteliers as consistent with it.

The municipality is outward-looking, with the mayor acting as a Slovenian Representative on the Council of Europe in Strasbourg, and the town is also an active member of the European Walled Towns Friendship Circle,[4] giving access to useful information about comparable towns, even competitors. As Slovenia including Piran prepares for full membership of the EU in 2004, a broad view of marketing that acknowledges both the needs of the tourists and the constraints imposed by conditions at this destination is needed. The challenge will be to polish the precious built and natural environment to a quality worthy of even World Heritage status, while developing tourism for and with the local community and its future needs. Only effective sustainable development can reconcile the conflicting pressures and reveal Piran as a true gem city.

Editor's conclusions

This case study is unique among those presented here, in that it seeks to outline the problems facing the destination rather than offering planned solutions. It fully recognises the marketing challenges facing the destination, and identifies its potential, not least in terms of sustainable development, given that it is starting with what is virtually a blank canvas. The development of an appropriate infrastructure to meet the needs of the twenty-first century Western tourist is merely a first step, and the study makes clear the difficulties facing local authorities in seeking to establish an adequate transport system which will reduce reliance upon the private car. The case can be usefully read alongside that of Case Study 4 (Adria Airways) where the product is based in the same region, with its similarities in political and historical background.

Central government control over tourism still remains strong within this part of Europe, with local authorities having only limited autonomy and suffering severe shortages of funds with which to aid regeneration of the potentially exciting attractions of the region. Gambling appears to offer one way forward, while a revived interest in thalassotherapy in Europe holds out the promise of further marketing opportunities. With the arrival of Slovenia into the EU in 2004, hopes of development and marketing assistance from that body must be very much in the minds of the tourism authorities of the region.

Acknowledgements

I would like to thank Vojka Stular, Mayor, and Nada Zajc, International Officer, the Municipality of Piran, and also the students and staff of Turistica College, Portoroz, and the students of the University of the West of England, Bristol.

All responsibility for the content and the views implied or expressed remains with the author.

Questions

1 Compare the control over tourism exercised respectively by the Slovenian central and regional authorities with that in Britain (or your home country). To what extent does greater diversification of control assist or impede the marketing of a destination (a) within the country and (b) abroad?

2 Thalassotherapy (salt water spas) has long enjoyed popularity on the European Continent, and is a useful adjunct to attractions in many resorts – and not only those in the Balkan countries (e.g. le Touquet on the French coast). Spa treatments generally are gaining support in Britain as well, but awareness of thalassotherapy is still limited. Suggest ways in which the marketing of this amenity might be enhanced, by the public or private sectors, or by a partnership between them.

3 Gambling clearly constitutes an encouraging underpinning for the future growth and funding of tourism in Piran, as it has done in the past in many other key resorts (e.g. Monte Carlo, Macao, Atlantic City NJ and Las Vegas). Proposals are now well advanced for an expansion of gambling in the seaside resort of Blackpool in England, as a means of regenerating tourism to this formerly popular mass-tourist destination. To what extent would such a development be viable or desirable? How should the local authorities market the new image of the town, and to what markets?

References

1 The 'gem city' is a concept originally defined by Ashworth and Tunbridge in the *Tourist-Historic City*, 2nd edn (2000) and refers to single-function, tourist-dominated historic towns. These are characterised by an architectural completeness, achieved by development being arrested at some stage in the past.

2 The name was ominously revived as Adriatisches Küstenland for the two years of Hitler's German occupation (1943–5).

3 The source for these figures is a 2002 tourism strategy, supported by the municipality of Piran but commissioned by the local hotel association, most of whose hotels are in Portoroz ('Portoroz 2005/2025').

4 http://www.walledtowns.com

Case study 9
Repositioning a hospitality product: The Cross at Kingussie, Scotland

(Prepared with the help of David Young, proprietor of The Cross at Kingussie)

Figure CS9.1
The Cross at Kingusssie

Background to the region

Kingussie is a small town in the Highlands of Scotland with a population of some 1600 inhabitants. The nearest important commercial centre is Inverness, which lies within commuting distance.

Kingussie is the capital of the Badenoch region, with council offices, schools and a small leisure and community centre. The economy is dependent largely upon tourism, agriculture, forestry and the production of whisky. While the town itself has only limited attractions to offer – a folk museum and wildlife park being the most notable – it lies within the Cairngorm National Park (designated a national park as recently as September 2003), a major tourist destination and base for activity holidays, including climbing, walking and sailing in summer, and skiing in winter, and these activities all lie within a few minutes of the town. The region's popularity has been enhanced in recent years as the setting for the popular BBC television series, *Monarch of the Glen*.

The Cross

Until February 2003 the property enjoyed 20 years under the same ownership. The business started out as a small restaurant in the main street of the town, before the owners decided to expand into accommodation, adding two bedrooms. After 10 years of trading, the business moved to a converted tweed mill around 300 metres from the main street, combining the restaurant with eight/nine en-suite bedrooms.

In the following 10 years The Cross enjoyed critical acclaim, including consistently favourable reviews in the *Good Food Guide* and *Which? Hotel Guide*, Red Stars and 3 Rosettes in the AA guides. It won Taste of Scotland, Egon Ronay, Ackerman and other major awards as recently as 2001.

The restaurant format was a five- or six-course set menu at the fixed price of £39.50, but offering virtually no choice. This was coupled with an extensive (400 bin) wine list (but curiously excluding any French wines).

The previous owners had planned their retirement and the sale of the property for some time, and as a result had deliberately allowed trade to fall off over the preceding 2–3 years. In consequence, by late summer 2002 The Cross was trading mainly at weekends, local restaurant business was negligible, and in fact the establishment was frequently closed to allow the owners to attend to the needs of ailing relatives.

Marketing to the end of 2002

The business was always driven by its reputation for good food and fine wines, a reputation which placed it within the top 10 or so restaurants in the north of Scotland, drawing customers from across the UK and abroad. However, in spite of the fine quality of the food, it was showing signs of becoming outdated. The somewhat unconventional style of hospitality and service was enjoyed or disparaged in almost equal measure.

Accommodation was sold as an adjunct to the restaurant, at premium prices to attract a niche customer base, and consistent with rates charged by rival establishments such as other AA Red Star properties. Room occupancy levels rarely ventured above 50 per cent, but the combined restaurant and room revenues provided the owners with a healthy level of profitability on a low turnover. Meanwhile, the local eating out market was left deliberately untapped, the previous owners believing that the quality of their food was unappreciated by this sector.

The marketing budget was spent on a combination of direct mailing to the existing customer database of around 2000 addresses (off-season weekend deals, wine weekends, etc.) and subscriptions to a number of guidebooks, including the AA, Taste of Scotland, Signpost, and Alastair Sawday. Virtually nothing was budgeted for advertising, and other exposure (such as independent newspaper reviews) was seldom proactive.

A new marketing plan: The Cross in 2003

Early in 2003 the business came under new ownership. The new proprietor, David Young, a former chief inspector for the AA, and his wife Katie, set about drawing up a new campaign to win business. They set themselves two key objectives:

■ to increase turnover from £170 000 to £250 000 by their third year of operation, and

■ to maintain the previous level of profitability (approximately 30 per cent) from the second year onwards.

They recognised that to achieve this, they needed to:

(a) enhance the reputation for good food and wine

(b) enhance the reputation for service and hospitality

(c) clarify the product, as a 'restaurant with rooms'

(d) redesign and relaunch the website (www.thecross.co.uk)

(e) redesign all printed materials

(f) improve the appearance of the property, inside and out, and embark upon a three-year programme of quality enhancement to bedrooms and bathrooms

(g) improve the perception of value for money (for both food and accommodation)

(h) change the profile of the 'typical' Cross customer from retired non-drinkers (*Scottish Field* readers) to younger professionals with more disposable income (Edinburgh and Glasgow weekenders) – but without alienating the existing customer base, which accounted for significant repeat business

(i) increase local use of The Cross as a neighbourhood restaurant.

They did not believe that in order to reposition themselves and increase turnover they needed necessarily to spend a fortune on conventional advertising. Figures to mid-point 2003 suggested that around 70 per cent of their guests were repeat business, with a further 5 per cent resulting from independent reviews in newspapers, 10 per cent from fee-based guidebooks (split almost equally between AA, Signpost and Alastair Sawday), and 10 per cent from independent guidebooks (Fodor, Dummies, *Scotland the Best*, *Good Food Guide*, etc.) Their aim was to spend the majority of their budget on niche guidebook advertising and direct mailing, coupled with a major drive to secure free column inches in local and national newspaper and magazine publications.

At the time of writing, in mid-2003, their campaign plan had been translated into the following actions:

■ some £5000 had been spent on improving the grounds and gardens

■ all bedlinen had been renewed

■ more contemporary toiletries and mineral waters had been introduced to bedrooms and bathrooms

■ bedrooms had been equipped with CD/radio/alarm cubes with contemporary Scottish CDs, all reading materials were replaced, with low-key Scottish themes

■ increased expenditure was directed to providing flowers throughout the public rooms.

The final step was to adjust rack rates. These were trimmed by just 5 per cent, as it was felt that more drastic price changes should not be attempted too quickly. Once they had had the benefit of a full year's trading experience, they felt they would have become more competent in judging what tariffs to set in the longer term, but their early thinking was moving towards a clearer differentiation between standard and premium rooms, and the offer of interesting special deals all year round – heavily promoted on the website – with standby rates to be considered after midday.

Meanwhile, for the all-important restaurant trade several changes were initiated. First, opening dates were changed to Tuesday to Saturday instead of Wednesday to Monday. This seemed better to fit existing business patterns, while at the same time allowing the proprietors more quality time with their family.

Dinner menus were changed to a more flexible menu offering three choices of each course, priced for two-, three- or four-course, and ranging from £28.50 to £38.50. The decision was taken to understate menu descriptions, focusing instead on good quality ingredients simply cooked, and with some interesting twists. The breakfast quality was improved, and a hot dish introduced where previously only Continental breakfasts had been served.

The wine stock was reduced to 200 bins (but still ensuring stock was never exhausted!), and French wines were reintroduced.

The new proprietors introduced a deliberate policy of offering a more natural style of hospitality, with relaxed, informal service, including an attempt to take the fuss out of wine service.

Plans were put in hand to exploit the local restaurant market by creating a separate mailing list, with opportunities to stimulate local interest.

Marketing spend to date has been limited to the following budget:

1   £200 on local newspaper advertorial, plus a further £100 support advertising for local events, and £400 unallocated.

2   £500 was spent on a direct mail campaign, with an introductory offer in February/ March and a further £500 campaign aimed at the autumn breaks market in September/October.

3   The major proportion of the budget was directed at guidebook entries, including the following:

AA	£1000
RAC	£500
VisitScotland (including board membership)	£1000
Signpost	£600
Sawday	£500
Stevenson	£500

A further £1500 was set aside for website and printing design. The overall promotional spend will have amounted to something like 3–4 per cent of turnover in the first year of operation.

Conclusion

This case study represents a very typical picture of a small business in the hospitality trade, seeking to establish a niche in what is usually a highly competitive market, by clearly repositioning the product. The Scottish Highlands, in fact, have rather fewer high-standard restaurants cum hotels than do equivalent areas elsewhere in the UK, and if sufficient awareness of the product is achieved, within a limited spend, the prospects of success are seen as good. It is too early to judge to what extent the objectives the management has set itself are being achieved, or whether the spend outlined in the budget represents the ideal allocation of funds to achieve these aims, but the direction appears to be right, management provides the appropriate level of expertise to accomplish the makeover, and prospects look encouraging.

Editor's conclusions

This is the sole case devoted to an examination of the hospitality sector of the industry and as such it provides a valuable insight into the operation of the kind of small, proprietor-run hotel which is typically to be found in many regions of the world to which tourists are attracted. Such owner-managed facilities are frequently run in a haphazard manner, with little evidence of professional planning or marketing, but considerable dependence upon the idiosyncratic charms and whims of their owners, to retain their loyal market. This was evidently the case (witness the 'unconventional style of hospitality and service') before the takeover by the hotel's current, and very professional, owner who has recognised what needs to be done, established clear objectives and introduced soundly based practices and a sensible time frame in which to accomplish them.

Questions

Scotland's rural tourism regions are highly seasonal in their appeal, attracting visitors in the high summer and a rather different market for winter sports activities (when snowfall allows) in the generally shorter winter season. The challenge for any hotel proprietor is how to fill the shoulder seasons, and whether to remain open year-round to retain staff – or in this case as an adjunct to the restaurant. What further suggestions to accomplish these aims can be added to those already undertaken by the proprietor?

2   The local eating-out market is scarcely big enough or sophisticated enough to ensure high occupancy for this top-quality restaurant, and the proprietor is targeting the Glasgow and Edinburgh weekend markets in particular, as well as special events aimed at the local markets. The owner is also keen to expand demand without losing his present loyal regulars. What further advice could you give him to boost sales?

3   The new owner has taken the decision to play down menu descriptions in favour of concentrating on the quality of the food itself. This is contrary to the approach of many restaurants, which revel in somewhat flowery language to appeal to their customers' taste buds. Which approach do you favour, and to what extent should this depend upon the markets targeted? Do you support the use of the French language in marketing top-flight restaurant menus?

Case study 10
Branding a tourist attraction: Middleton, the National Botanic Garden of Wales

(Prepared by Brian Griffiths, Senior Lecturer, School of Leisure, Tourism and Sport, Swansea Institute of Higher Education)

Introduction

Middleton, the National Botanic Garden of Wales, is set in the eighteenth-century gardens and parkland of the former Middleton Hall in Carmarthenshire. An estate of 568 acres, it lies on the edge of the Towy Valley, with spectacular views across one of the most beautiful landscapes of unspoilt Wales, an area rich in culture (Figure CS10.1).

Figure CS10.1
Middleton, the National Botanic Garden of Wales

(Courtesy: NBGW)

The idea of a National Botanic Garden of Wales at Middleton Hall originated with William Wilkins, a local botanist who is also heavily involved with a project to restore a historic garden at Aberglasney, a few miles from Middleton. The original concept for the development of Middleton was as a facility of local interest and importance, but Wilkins and his fellow trustees recognised the lack of knowledge of Wales's rich garden heritage, and the Middleton concept was raised to national level.

It is a registered charity, and to a large extent relies on the help and support it receives from government agencies, the Welsh Assembly government and voluntary sources. It is the first new major botanic garden in the UK this century, and is regarded as a national institution for Wales. It is hoped that the Garden will develop into a facility of international significance, dedicated to conservation, horticulture, science, education, leisure and the arts.

The centrepiece is the largest single span glasshouse in the world, designed by Sir Norman Foster and Partners, which houses a living collection of threatened Mediterranean plants. Also within the glasshouse is 'Bioverse', a 'hands-on' educational experience aimed at educating the visitor about the mysteries of plant life. The 'Great Glasshouse' took almost three years to complete, and is a high-tech, computer-controlled facility featuring, for example, glass panes opening and closing automatically in line with temperature and weather conditions, and recycling systems to provide water for irrigation.

Other features within the Garden:

▪ the Gatehouse – the point of entry for visitors to the Garden, clad with Canadian red cedar and with a water feature as a focal point

▪ the Broadwalk – a 220-metre long walkway, including the 'Circle of Decision' fountain (Figure CS10.2)

▪ the Science Centre – dedicated to plant and fungi conservation, research and environmental education

▪ the Hyder Water Discovery Centre – sponsored by Hyder (originally Welsh Water) and designed for educational purposes. It includes a large teaching area fitted out as a laboratory and a resource/quiet working area. It is the venue for various educational programmes and has nearby dipping pools providing safe access to the study of pond life.

▪ the Wallace Garden – a showcase for plant genetics and genetic engineering

▪ the Physicians of Myddfai Exhibition Centre – exhibiting herbal medicines

▪ the Theatre – presenting a film show of the importance of plants to life and in various environmental conditions

▪ Principality House – the Lifelong Learning Centre, a building which also hosts meetings and small conferences

▪ the Nursery Glasshouses – the main horticultural facility in the Garden for propagation purposes

▪ the Biomass Energy Centre – using recycling and 'green' technology to service the Garden's needs

Figure CS10.2
The Broadwalk,
National Botanic
Garden of Wales

(Courtesy: NBGW)

- Stables Court – a courtyard area containing a visitor centre, restaurant, café and souvenir shop
- Millennium Square – a central point for hosting events
- the Double Walled Garden – a reconstructed area historically used for fruit and vegetables, including more exotic varieties
- the Lakes – seven in total, linked by pathways and encircling the Gardens
- the Japanese Garden – brought to the Gardens after winning a gold medal and the prestigious 'Best of Show Award' at the Chelsea Flower Show.

Attendance figures (opened May 2000)

2000	192 642*
2001	187 026
2002	175 000

*Attendance in the first year of opening (2000) has also been reported in another official document to be 202 000 over the first 10-month period, while a report in a local newspaper states the first-year attendance to be as high as 220 000.

Attendance targets have not officially been made available, but the author has been led to believe on previous discussions with Garden officials that targets for the initial feasibility study were anticipated to be in the region of 240 000 per annum.

Admission fees (2003)

	Individuals	Groups (10+)
Adults	£6.95	£5.75
Children (5–15)	£3.50	£2.50
Under 5s	Free	Free
Seniors (60+)	£5.00	£4.00
Students	£5.00	£4.00
Family (2 adults + 2 children)	£17.50	

The site is open every day except Christmas Day, with shorter opening hours between October and Easter.

Financing

Initial design and build costs were reported to be in the region of £43 million, made possible by a £21.7 million grant from the National Lottery Fund.

However, for reasons that will be considered later in this case study, managers have needed to approach the Welsh Assembly government for additional financial support. The level of such aid is somewhat unclear and elements of double-counting are possible, but research based on local newspaper reports suggests that additional financial support needed since opening amounted to:

£360 000 in July 2002
£1 million in February 2003
£600 000 in July 2003

Branding and rebranding

The Garden is now working under its *third* title in just three years:

1 On opening in May 2000, the site bore the title 'The National Botanic Garden of Wales'. This title was apparently felt to suggest too scientific an approach, rather than a visitor attraction of interest to the general public.

2 In spring 2002, the site was rebranded 'The Garden of Wales', but this name was in turn felt to be too vague, lacking identity and focus on the location.

3 Consequently, in February 2003 the term 'Middleton, the National Botanic Garden of Wales' was introduced in an attempt to refocus the public perception on an identifiable product and location.

Issues

Purpose and priorities

There appears to be potential for confusion and therefore conflict of purpose, identity and priorities according to which documents are read, how they are interpreted and how spending is allocated.

The key question, which influences many of the issues contained within this case study, is *what exactly is this facility*? Is this a visitor attraction that seeks to educate visitors on environmental issues, or is it a science/conservation facility that allows those interested to visit if they so wish?

An examination of some of the various documents published by the Garden is worthy of further thought in this respect:

■ The Garden 'Fact File' of 2001 quotes the Garden as being 'dedicated to horticulture, conservation, science, education, *leisure*, and the arts . . .'

■ A Wales Tourist Board publication in 2000 states that it is 'dedicated to *leisure*, science and education . . .'

■ The Garden 'Visitor Guide' for 2001 states that the Garden '. . . works to conserve threatened plant species, research plant diversity *and create an experience leaving visitors with a wealth of memories . . .*'

■ The Garden's website in 2003 states the aim to be '. . . *heightening visitor awareness and understanding . . .*' (suggesting an educational approach) but elsewhere in the site portrays a '. . . *spectacular attraction, also internationally renowned centre for botanical science . . .*'

The terminologies, and particularly the order in which the aims are stated, are very interesting. Elsewhere in this case study the issue of marketing and target audiences is addressed, as is an evaluation of visitor numbers. This potential for mixed messages may well be having an effect on visitor perception and expectations, and should perhaps be revisited as other issues are considered.

Marketing

Although access to strategic marketing documents has not been possible, anecdotal evidence suggests that the rationale and possibly the original justification for the establishment and siting of the Garden indicated a target catchment area ranging as far as Bristol to the east and the Midlands to the north. This large area contains an appropriate population base from which to draw the 250 000 visitors or so which it is understood are required to sustain the Garden and ensure a viable business.

During the author's regular visits and discussions with various officials, the target market has, since inception, been variably cited as 'gardeners and garden clubs from the Midlands', to 'avid gardeners', and immediately after the fall in visitor numbers was identified as a major problem, 'anyone'.

While it is not within the remit of this case study to undertake a detailed evaluation of the Garden's marketing strategy, it is necessary to critically evaluate these apparent uncertainties about the identity of the target market. If this target market is vague, changing and unclear, how may this be reflected in the product on offer, the pricing policies adopted and the public's perception of the facility? Indeed, if it is accepted that there is no such thing as a 'general public', and that there are in fact 'many publics', then this issue becomes even more complex.

Branding/rebranding

The fact that the Garden has adopted three names in the first three years of its existence in itself reflects lack of clarity and purpose. The primary reasons for the changes are summarised previously in this document, but a more in-depth examination poses similar questions to those raised previously.

As the 'National Botanic Garden of Wales' the word 'botanic' was apparently seen to be somewhat too scientific and specialised, and the change to the 'Garden of Wales' attempted to soften this image and appeal to more general garden lovers, a trait for which the UK is renowned. This title, however, was felt to lack a geographical identity, thus the change to 'Middleton', though interestingly the Middleton area is only identified as such on detailed and small-scale maps, whereas the nearest town (Carmarthen) is much more widely known and identifiable geographically.

An additional factor was the desire to create a similar identity and image as found at the key major garden-type attractions at, for example, Kew and Wisley. The long-term aim is for Middleton to achieve comparative status as those facilities, and it thus needed a single, key and recognisable word by which it should be known.

Financing

The high initial building and development costs have been justified largely by the argument that the area needed a major focal point around which to build a tourism identity. The Garden has been quoted as having a major impact on incoming tourism, economic development and employment creation in the area. It is very interesting to note that the county of Carmarthenshire now markets itself in tourism terms as 'The Garden of Wales', and increased its tourism staff considerably as a result.

When evaluating issues such as economic impact, however, there is a need to consider in more detail the source and type of visitors, the length of stay in the Garden, and more particularly the area, the number of jobs created and whether they are full or part-time, seasonal, etc.

The *source and type of visitor* is a matter that is also debated elsewhere in this study. It is understood that the vast majority of visitors come from the South Wales area, are aged 50+ and are garden enthusiasts. It is felt to be unlikely that many are visiting the area specifically to view the Garden, so the Garden is possibly more accurately viewed as an additional resource for the area, rather than the primary reason for visiting. However, this view may be amended slightly when visited together with Aberglasney Garden, a neighbouring sister facility. These two jointly provide a full day's visit and therefore a legitimate attraction for garden enthusiasts from further afield.

Jobs created have been somewhat susceptible to the reduction in visitor numbers, and are discussed later in this case study.

The *local infrastructure* has been quite slow to react in terms of the provision of facilities near the Garden, yet such businesses may be expected to have obtained the best advantage of the 'honeypot' effect.

In more positive terms, however, the *local tourist association* (*Tourlink*) has developed enormously in recent times. While much of this development may be due to a proactive and funded organisation, the creation of the Garden as a focal point for marketing, etc. would certainly have been influential in this development.

The Garden's need to apply to the National Assembly Government for Wales for additional financial support has provided its critics with ample opportunity to publicise their concerns. Its management deny that falling visitor numbers are the reason for the applications, suggesting that the drop in numbers is a cash flow issue, whereas the additional funding is to enable the completion of major capital works. In typical media fashion, however, critics link the two issues and suggest that if visitor numbers were up to expected levels then money would naturally be available for capital projects via internal, rather than external, finances. Such headlines naturally draw attention to the drop in numbers, which in turn may well lead to public perception of a 'failing' facility, thus potentially reducing visitor numbers still further.

Attention has also been drawn in the press to the fact that the Garden continues to receive public subsidy, whereas the private sector attractions in the area feel that they are being 'short-changed' by not being able to receive such financial aid themselves. In this respect many feel that the private attractions have a justifiable complaint, as the area relies on its private as well as publicly funded attractions, and needs all of them to be financially secure and of high quality in order for the region as a whole to provide a good visitor experience.

Attendances

These continue to fall at a very disappointing rate. It is possibly reasonable to assume that the figures achieved in the first year are somewhat artificial, in that they are inflated by the free publicity created by the opening of a new and high-profile facility, the 'curiosity' factor for visitors, etc. It is suggested that the possible reasons for this decline, and the opportunities for reversing the trend and moving towards anticipating growth, should be evaluated and debated against the case study as a whole, rather than viewed in isolation.

The product and product development

Early in this case study the rationale and 'reason for being' was identified as a possible issue affecting operations, strategy and attendances. The question of 'who or what is the market' has also been raised. After all, if the market and visitor expectations are uncertain, how can you provide what the visitor requires and achieve customer satisfaction?

The Garden has made great efforts to continue with the building and development work across an array of product areas. It has needed to fund and complete, for example, the new science facility, the theatre, the visitor centre, a new art and exhibition area, the walled garden, etc., while at the same time being open to the public. In recognition of the lack of facilities for children, a new themed play area has also been established. New projects include the redesigning and rebuilding of the Gatehouse to provide improved visitor facilities and additional catering outlets. These admirable and costly achievements are to be applauded, and are seen by management as essential to the product development and provision of appropriate visitor facilities. The fundamental question remains, however – is it realistic to provide as many facilities as possible for as wide a market as possible, or would it be better to identify a target market and strive to meet the requirements of that market?

It is important to recognise that Gardens such as Middleton arguably have two key advantages over some other tourist attractions:

■ The current 'fad' of gardening which proliferates on British television screens has created wide-scale awareness of the leisure benefits of gardening. Programmes such as *Ground Force* are also repeated on satellite as well as terrestrial television, and attract huge audiences.

■ The garden 'product' has four changes in a year, provided by nature. While other attractions need to invest heavily to ensure a new product for repeat visitors, gardens are naturally refreshed and present a different view of the product as the seasons change. Indeed, this seasonal change provides marketing opportunities in its own right.

Staffing

The staffing structure has undergone major changes since the original team commenced work some time before opening. Departments have been redesigned, merged and demerged, and personnel at all levels have changed. It is understood that redundancies have also been necessary.

Change in organisations may be unsettling, and generally could be viewed as healthy if new ideas are needed, etc., or unhealthy if the loyalty, commitment and detailed knowledge of staff are lost. In the author's opinion the Garden has gained enormously from its previous and current employees, whose friendliness and openness have done a great deal to secure the loyalty and appreciation of the visitors and the local community. This factor is paramount in the study of attraction management. While the quality of the facilities is obviously important, so too is the quality provided by a good staff, prepared to 'go that extra yard' when it is needed.

Key questions faced by management of the Garden are, for example, the primary elements and focus of job descriptions and person specifications, what should be the balance between employed and voluntary staff, and so on. To take one instance, in an attraction such as this should you employ someone for their expert skills, or should you seek someone with excellent public presentation skills whose expertise may not be as good? Similarly, is it fair and reasonable to expect voluntary staff to regularly undertake duties that perhaps a full employee should be doing?

Pricing and value for money (VFM)

Pricing is a complex calculation. Should you price, for example, at a level which your visitor can afford, how 'valuable' you think the product is, what neighbouring facilities are priced at, their level and quality of facilities as compared with yours, etc.?

Admission prices for 2003 have been quoted earlier in this case study, and again need to be considered against the market and its expectations. The 'new' target market for 2003 was defined as the 'local' area (within 1.5 hours' driving distance). This area contains a mixed economy but includes areas of relatively high unemployment due to industrial decline. There is a strong tourism market in the surrounding areas, providing in the main family/beach holidays. The average duration of stay on site is approximately 2.5–3 hours. The major 'competition' for the family market, of national renown, is Oakwood, a white-knuckle type theme park which attracted 384 000 visitors in 2002 (up 9 per cent on 2001) but where entry prices are much higher.

Against such a scenario, the current admission prices to the Garden may be viewed as reasonable. Until its facilities are fully completed, the issue of admission prices, and particularly VFM, need to be paramount in the thoughts of management. The temptation to increase fees must be argued against the potential for poor customer reaction if they feel that VFM is poor. The counter-argument, that a low admission price may reflect a poor quality facility, is also important.

Middleton presents a good quality image, with design and build completed to very high specifications, and the pricing must reflect the expectations of the visitor and their ability/willingness to pay for a facility which is presented to a good level of quality but which is still evolving.

Editor's conclusions

The interest in this case is heightened by the fact that, as this book goes to press, the long-term survival of the attraction is under threat. The site is one of several in England and Wales benefiting from governmental or quasi-governmental funding, a number being launched as an adjunct to the Millennium celebrations, which have failed to achieve their minimum number of targeted visitors and have either closed or face an uncertain future. These include the Walsall Art Gallery, the Baltic Centre in Gateshead, the National Centre for Popular Music in Sheffield and the Centre for Visual Arts in Cardiff. The interesting question this poses is whether these have failed as a result of the basic concept, over-optimistic visitor estimates or just inadequate marketing. Certainly, the frequent name changes have confused the public, as have changes in the markets which are the declared targets of the attraction. The site bears useful comparison with other garden attractions which have been successful, including the Eden Project in Cornwall, and the long-established Westonbirt Arboretum which attracts many repeat visitors through its special events, including designer gardens, exhibitions of sculpture carving in wood and illumination of the trees over the Christmas and early New Year period to draw in winter crowds.

While personality clashes have undoubtedly played a part in undermining the operation of this attraction, a contributory cause has been the failure to appoint a marketing manager or, indeed, to place adequate emphasis on the marketing role. While the Welsh Assembly subsequently refused to provide further subsidies to the attraction, a breathing space was granted, as this went to press, by the arrival of an anonymous benefactor on the scene, enabling the attraction to avoid going into receivership.

(For further contemporary accounts, read *The Times* 7 October 2003 'Welsh Garden Cuts 70 Jobs in Last-ditch Attempt to Remain Open', and subsequent readers' letters on October 2, 6, 15 and 23.)

Questions

1 What arguments are there for and against public subsidy funding for tourism projects such as this? And should they be expected to be self-sustaining in the long run?

2 How far is the attempt to be 'all things to all people' responsible for the failure of this attraction? Are there lessons to be learned from the changing approaches by zoos in Britain and elsewhere to move away from entertainment in favour of conservation of species and breeding, as zoos fell out of favour with the public?

3 'The area needed a focal point around which to build an identity.' Most sites have developed their tourism industries around an existing attraction, but some purpose-built attractions (notably the Disney sites in Florida, California and near Paris) have been built on greenfield sites to attract visitors to the region for the first time. On what does the success of this approach depend: on the scale of the venture and financial investment, on the appeal of the attraction, on successful marketing, or some combination of all three? It is said that a tourist destination needs the synergy of several sites to appeal more widely than to a strictly local market; the case gives the example of another garden in the vicinity which, together with Middleton, constitutes sufficient for a day's outing for gardening enthusiasts. Is this enough?

Case study 11
Marketing little-known destinations: the island of Saaremaa, Estonia

(Prepared with the help of Neil Taylor, Director, Regent Holidays)

Travel to the countries of the Soviet Union will be remembered for its restrictions rather than for its possibilities. Only a few towns were open to foreigners and visas were only granted on the basis of an agreed itinerary which could not be changed. Most tourists had to travel in groups with fixed tours, fixed meals and certainly fixed hotels. With the unexpected collapse of this regime in the summer of 1991, and the return to independence of the Baltic states of Estonia, Latvia and Lithuania, an area the size of England and Wales was suddenly completely open to anyone who wanted to come. Yet hardly any foreigners had been there for 50 years.

Tourism prior to 1991

The Estonian island of Saaremaa shows how a totally unknown product can be marketed while at the same time maintaining its environmental integrity. Until 1940, first under the Tsarist Empire and then as part of independent Estonia, the island enjoyed a development similar to that of many other islands in the Baltic Sea and resorts along the mainland coast. While rich tourists from Sweden, Finland and Russia continued to travel south to the Mediterranean, the new middle classes bought summer cottages, or took seaside holidays, nearer home. Spas along the coast enjoyed year-round business, while small hotels and guest houses had to make do with a short summer season of around four months.

In Scandinavia, the Second World War merely interrupted this business for about 10 years. However, when the Soviet Union seized the three Baltic republics from the retreating German armies in 1944, those countries' tourism was doomed for 45 years. The island of Saaremaa suffered particularly badly in this respect, as the Russians converted it into a military base and banned all non-essential travel there, including that by Estonians themselves. Other areas of Estonia were less affected; the capital, Tallinn, benefited from a ferry service twice a week from Finland during the 1970s and 1980s. In 1980 some of the Olympic Games were held there, so some knowledge circulated abroad about this medieval town, and it was accustomed to handling (mostly unofficial) tourist business. Once independence was gained, Tallinn could therefore market itself in conventional ways and build on an existing image. Saaremaa, on the other hand, had to start from scratch.

Building tourism from scratch

In 1991, when the Soviet Union suddenly collapsed and Estonia returned to independence, the national and local authorities were suddenly faced with the problem of promoting an island that few local people, let alone foreigners, had ever seen. The difficulty was compounded by the fact that no one on the island had any experience of running a business; under the Soviet system, there had been no scope for private initiative, whether running a hotel, opening a restaurant or setting up a visitor attraction. It was therefore necessary to bring in outside assistance, mainly from abroad, to assess the potential, to offer financial guidance on long-term tourism development and to prepare local people for the wide-ranging needs of outsiders used to choice, who expected to be able to communicate in their own language and to enjoy a level of comfort far exceeding anything the islanders could provide.

Yet within three years a product had been developed which could safely be promoted to the international travel market. Western branded consumer goods were widely available on the island, and facilities introduced which included mobile phones, air-conditioned coaches and multilingual guides. Credit cards were widely accepted. Hotel telephones were linked to international lines, and all rooms offered satellite television. Perhaps even more surprisingly, hotel staff spoke English, and many spoke other languages as well.

Saaremaa divorced itself from the rest of Estonia by looking positively at many aspects of its past which could be maintained as attractions for discerning tourists; and it took the sensible decision to keep the product largely as it had remained since 1939, with the intention of promoting 'nostalgia' tourism. Some 5 per cent of the island had been marred by Soviet military installations such as barracks and an airport, but the rest of the island had been virtually ignored. By leaving the other 95 per cent intact, the authorities saved vast expense and the gamble of what sort of facilities to build for which markets.

At this point they took stock of the island's strengths and opportunities. One fortunate legacy from the Soviet regime was the infrastructure of wide roads that existed, constructed to allow aircraft to take off if an emergency dictated. These now made driving a pleasure; and with a ban on private motoring under the Soviets, the island benefited from the development of an excellent public transport network. With private building similarly banned, nothing had been built since the 1930s in the towns and villages. Saaremaa has wooden and stone churches covering a period of 700 years, undisturbed countryside where flora and fauna have flourished, excellent cliff-side walks, a bird sanctuary, manor houses and windmills. In few other places in Europe had nature been allowed such a free rein; even along the Baltic coast, there are many examples of tower-block hotels, new coastal roads and harbours being carved out of river mouths. Saaremaa had been spared all this. Furthermore, the island had an attractive capital, Kuressaare, with a population of 16 000 and the only intact mediaeval castle in the Baltics (see Figures CS11.1 and CS11.2). All of these attractions are within

**Figures CS11.1
and CS11.2**
Views of
Kuressaare
Castle,
Saaremaa

(Courtesy: Kuressaare Tourism, Saaremaa)

easy reach on a two- or three-day coach tour or by individuals hiring cars, while cyclists and walkers can explore the island at a more leisurely pace.

Private action, public inaction

If Saaremaa has failed in any respect, it is perhaps in over-modesty. No serious guidebook has yet been produced by the local authorities, and those that cover the whole of Estonia inevitably have to restrict their coverage. A church full of stained glass, a leaning lighthouse, a cliff-side walk and the first collective farm set up in the USSR are among the many attractions that as yet hardly see foreigners as they are not mentioned either in tourist literature or on websites. There has been little serious effort to increase the ferry or air services from the mainland. Only lip-service is paid to this need, perhaps because the complications and expense involved in reaching the island contribute to its exclusivity. Twelve years on, some voices are pushing for less restrictive planning regulations to allow an increase in discotheques, the development of leisure centres and construction of larger hotels, but most feel that the right decision has been taken: the young, lively market is a fickle one, and may easily desert one resort for another, while the elderly and adventurous markets tend to be more loyal and to return to places that satisfy them.

The private sector has been much more active than the public one in generating tourism from the Estonian mainland and abroad. There are still lapses in the public sector, which has so far failed to plan ahead or to generate formal discussions on tourism development – although regular talks are held on ferry scheduling, the possibility of building a bridge to the mainland and proposed new buildings. Much effort is still geared to satisfying local needs, rather than income-generating markets. Ferry and air schedules are only announced a few weeks before they are implemented, and while information leaflets have been translated from Estonian, they have not been adapted to meet the needs of foreigners – outsiders have little interest in visiting the houses of local artists and poets unknown to them, but would be interested in visiting the tombs of British or Germans in the cemetery which date from various nineteenth- and twentieth-century invasions and disasters. While publishers abroad in several countries have included sections on Saaremaa in their guidebooks, this has not been matched by local authority interest or commitment in this field. No newsletters are sent to foreign tour operators, and no attempts have been made to contact potential new operators who are active in neighbouring areas. No statistics are collated which distinguish foreigners from Estonians or day visitors from longer-stay tourists. No brochure subsidies are offered, nor are educational visits to the trade, a situation which operators have continued to accept, despite the increasing affluence of the island. Only travel writers have occasionally received invitations, and their subsequent articles have certainly helped to increase awareness abroad.

What international marketing efforts have been made have been initiated by the national rather than local tourism authorities, and these have concentrated on liaison with tour operators abroad. This of course costs much less than attempting to reach a very dispersed range of possible consumers. Saaremaa has therefore been present at the

Figure CS11.3
Veski restaurant,
Kuressaare,
Saaremaa

(Courtesy: Kuressaare Tourism, Saaremaa)

large travel trade fairs such as the World Travel Market in London and ITB in Berlin and is now an integral part of most Baltic states' brochures. Operators find the product a useful one to continue promoting since competition from the Web is less of a problem than is the case for large cities. Consumers are still nervous of booking the unknown from the Web. They need a brochure, a knowledgeable agent and financial guarantees before parting with their money, which they might do less reluctantly for a short city-break.

The island is particularly lucky that foreign investors have placed so much faith in it. The spa hotels have been renovated with foreign investment, as have many shops and farms. While the public sector has not been hostile to this, neither has it been supportive. However, the investment has encouraged Scandinavian tour operators to promote health packages to the spas, and more conventional coach excursions for passengers arriving by cruise ship, or staying in the limited supply of accommodation currently available.

Saaremaa offers many lessons to islands wishing to offer themselves as a niche market. People will come for what there is and what there has been. They will not want a pale imitation of something bigger and brasher. They want predictability, not constant change. 'Small' sells but 'big' does not. Any large city offers cathedrals, casinos, restaurants and formal gardens. Islands can be much more exclusive, with their quaint wooden churches, teahouses and untouched forests (compare the success of Denmark's Bornholm island, which trades on a very similar image). Saaremaa changed what it had to between 1991 and 1994, and most of what was left will remain an attraction for many years to come.

The future, and lessons to be learned

It is hard to see disaster striking Saaremaa again. For many years it will be seen as a cheaper Finland or Sweden, and nationals from those countries are likely to be drawn in large numbers by this prospect, as are the British to French regions like the Dordogne. With the uncertainty surrounding many tourist destinations around the world in 2003, the safety of the Baltics drew many tourists to Saaremaa who might have gone elsewhere.

The lessons of Saaremaa should have been that public and private cooperation can always pay dividends. What it has in fact proved is that the private sector can operate on its own, if unimpeded by the public sector, and the island can count itself fortunate that this freedom has not yet been abused. However, should a causeway to the mainland finally be built, the public sector will have to intervene firmly to avoid the destruction of what has been the island's principal appeal – its peace and traditional way of life – in favour of a rebranding to boost its appeal for mass tourism.

Editor's conclusions

The case bears further comparison with Case Study 8 (Piran), not least in the problem of marketing a relatively unknown (and in the current case, virtually unknown) destination to a wider global market. It is to be hoped that after reviewing both these cases, no reader will any longer confuse the Baltics with the Balkans! There are significant differences, however, in the approach towards developing these two destinations, with Saaremaa intent on preserving its product to an exceptional degree in order to attract the nostalgia market and remain a resort from which to escape the twenty-first century. While there is far less public investment in Saaremaa compared with Piran, its transport infrastructure is in many respects superior, with good, and uncongested, access roads and an excellent public transport network (although still lacking adequate ferry and air services). It also benefits from being little more than 150 km from the capital, Tallinn, now one of the world's major tourist destinations.

What distinguishes the case is the evident weakness of the public sector's marketing, and even the will to market, as the area emerges from a long period of central government control and its accompanying restrictions on the use of local initiative and application of free world management principles. However, this has not been true of development in the private sector, which is keen to see the island expand its tourism base and has initiated a number of moves to promote and enhance its image. The case also makes the interesting point that website marketing is less suitable for a destination of this kind, which is little known to surfers of travel products, and the medium is not viewed as ideal as a means of imparting reassurance or credibility.

Questions

1 Given what is known from this case, would you recommend to the authorities on the island that they prioritise their marketing to attract the Nordic and Russian markets, which already constitute a firm base, or attempt to build new markets in more distant European countries?

2 Should Saaremaa improve access by ferry, or plan on the construction of a bridge to the mainland, as a means of expanding tourism? Or should its authorities aim to limit the appeal of the island in its existing isolation, by boosting income from a smaller base of visitors?

3 The case briefly touches on the appeal of the island as a port of call on Baltic cruises. At present, this is very limited. Could it be made to appeal to more cruise companies, and how would the appeal be phrased? What development and support would a cruise company require if it were to consider introducing a port of call here?

Case study 12
The small museum and its struggle to survive: the Museum of Bath at Work

(Prepared with the help of Stuart Burroughs, Curator, the Museum of Bath at Work)

Note: Museum of Bath at Work is operated by the Bath Industrial Heritage Trust Ltd

Figure CS12.1
Façade of the Museum of Bath at Work

(Courtesy: Museum of Bath at Work)

Note: This case study formed the basis of an earlier case study in the second edition of this text, under the title 'Mr Bowler's Business'. The intervening years have been eventful for this small attraction, and have included a further change of name. The challenge of surviving as a small tourist attraction, slightly off the beaten track, with

Figure CS12.2
Promotional leaflet for the museum

(Courtesy: Museum of Bath at Work)

severely limited finance and throughout a period when economic and political disasters have threatened much larger companies in the industry, is not untypical of SMEs in tourism, and deserves an update. Consequently, the marketing background to this attraction is repeated here, along with more recent developments.

Background

The Museum of Bath at Work is an industrial heritage museum situated in Bath. The origins of the museum go back to 1978, when it was established to conserve and display the work and contents of the firm of J B Bowler. This firm manufactured aerated waters, as well as operating a brass foundry, engineering works, locksmiths and other sundry business interests.

The firm was founded in 1872 and closed in 1969, at which point the premises were demolished. However, during the 100 years of its operation the firm never threw anything away, amassing a huge collection of tools, machines, bottles and papers that together provide a unique insight into a century of business operations.

In all, the collection comprises around 100 000 objects and 250 000 documents. All these were purchased in 1969, with the intention of finding a suitable building in which they could be presented to the public.

The establishment of the museum

In 1978, with conservation as the principal motive, a group of enthusiasts formed the Bath Industrial Heritage Trust, which was registered as a charity. With the aid of significant grants from private trusts and the public sector (including Bath City Council and the Science Museum, London), the Trust was able to lease and convert the Camden Works building, a city-owned property built in 1777 as a real tennis court. This site had later become in turn a school, a malthouse, a soap works and a packing case factory.

The building was rented from the city at a subsidised rent, and the Council also advanced a small annual grant. The site, however, had drawbacks, in that it is some minutes' walk north of the city centre, and away from the heart of the city and its attractions.

Bath is a city in which a number of attractions compete for the tourists' attention, and with so many visitors coming only for the day, fringe attractions have always found it difficult to compete for an audience, especially when the visitor is faced with a choice between such attractions as the Roman Baths and the Assembly Rooms, the Museum of Costume and the many fine Georgian buildings that dominate the city.

Bath is also a notoriously difficult city in which to find parking space, for those coming by private car. The Museum of Bath at Work has no visitor parking space, either for cars or coaches. Although there is a bus bay nearby for coaches to drop off passengers, parking is not permitted on adjacent roads, so the casual visitor coming by car has a very real problem in reaching the site. However, one recent improvement for pedestrians is that signposting from the centre is now available at modest cost from a contractor working for the Bath and North East Somerset Council.

In 1988, the Trust became a company limited by guarantee, giving the organisation the scope to attract shareholders with the financial motivation and expertise to boost the museum.

Since then, the museum has continued to develop, and now comprises a whole floor devoted to a scale reconstruction of J B Bowler's engineering and mineral water business, correct in every detail, a reconstructed cabinetmaking workshop, Bath stone mine and a new permanent gallery completed in 2003, 'Bath at Work: 2000 Years of Earning a Living', funded through the Heritage Lottery Fund.

Marketing the original museum

The museum is administered through a Council of Management, consisting of 10 members who meet twice a year. From this body, a smaller committee, the Management Group, meets each month to oversee the operation. The Curator is a member of both bodies. It was the original intention to, at the very least, break even and achieve an estimated throughput of around 30 000 visitors a year – a figure which in retrospect appears unduly optimistic. Budget limitations made promotion on any significant scale difficult, and the museum has never achieved even half its targeted number. Attendance for the years 1990 to 2002 were:

1990	11 205
1991	13 016
1992	12 206
1993	12 009
1994	11 181
1995	9 610
1996	9 381
1997	8 285
1998	6 506
1999	7 426
2000	6 633
2001	6 942
2002	7 566

(The figures include free admission during one week in October each year, when local residents are permitted free entry.)

Surveys have been held at intervals over the years, which reveal that the museum is increasingly used by local visitors from Bath and north-east Somerset. Foreign visitors account for over 20 per cent of visitors, while the remainder travel principally from other parts of the south of England.

The consultant's report

In 1988, following a steady decline in admissions from inception, it was recognised that a radical overhaul would be necessary if the museum were to survive. The museum was overly dependent upon donations, which far exceeded revenue from admission charges each year, and apart from a long-term interest-free loan, there were no other sources of finance on which to draw. In 1989, the Council of Management called in a consultant to prepare an independent evaluation of the attraction's prospects and to determine the way forward.

The report agreed that attendance figures should be tripled, and that there was a need to raise awareness of the attraction among the local population, particularly in education circles, where it was felt there was considerable scope to boost attendance.

The report further recommended repositioning the museum, with a name change to support this. The attractions of the museum were clearly aimed at two distinct audiences: the serious industrial archeologist, for whom the 'museum' concept was important, and the visitor seeking a more entertaining experience, for whom the 'heritage centre/tourist attraction' concept was paramount. The original title of the attraction, 'Camden Works: the Museum of Bath at Work' had failed to generate much enthusiasm among the mass tourist market, and the adoption of a later title, the Bath Industrial Heritage Centre, had similarly failed to motivate the mass visitor. A number of alternative titles were considered, but eventually the name 'Mr Bowler's Business' was selected, with the Bath Industrial Heritage Centre retained as a subtitle. The new title was seen as catchy and intriguing, while still retaining connotations of the firm's social and industrial history within the city.

The 1990 relaunch involved considerable extra expenditure on targeted marketing, which increased from £2219 to £10 708 and this did result in an increase in visitors in 1990 and 1991. Unfortunately, extra expenditure on salaries absorbed the increased ticket income and the decision to open throughout the winter was, in retrospect, a mistake.

In the original consultant's plan no changes were made to the museum itself other than improvements to the shop and café facilities. Since 1990 a number of additional permanent display spaces have been opened and temporary exhibitions have also been organised.

Staffing

The original complement of staff comprised three full-time members and up to seven part-time employees (often students employed during the peak summer months). Additionally, volunteer guides conducted tours of the museum for visitors.

By 1991, and after the consultancy report had been submitted, this staffing was revealed as clearly unsustainable, and as a result staff were pared to the bone. All part-time staff were laid off, and two of the three full-time staff were made redundant. A new Curator was appointed, who became, and remains, the only full-time paid staff member, but a pool of volunteers was formed, who could be called upon to deputise and staff the museum as necessary. This left the museum vulnerable to shortages of volunteers, and subject to other demands on volunteer time.

A shortcoming of the original rebranding policy was that insufficient consultation took place with staff about the proposed changes. In particular, the volunteers, on whom the museum relied, were unconvinced by the proposed changes and out of sympathy with them.

The new marketing plan

In 2000 the museum changed its name for the last time and became the Museum of Bath at Work. Mr Bowler's Business was felt by then to place too great an emphasis on part of the museum's displays to the detriment of the other stories the museum had to tell. In addition, the serious nature of the organisation in providing an educational service was felt to be best placed by returning the word 'museum' to the title.

The calculation of attracting 30 000 visitors had proved hopelessly optimistic, with the highest attendance at only 13 016 in 1991. The earlier assumption that the higher figure could be derived from the visitors attending the nearby Assembly Rooms took it for granted that short-stay visitors to that attraction would be equally interested in Mr Bowler's Business – by no means a logical conclusion.

The local awareness of the museum has improved through good contacts with the local newspaper, good links with local schools and community-based exhibitions, and projects. Success in getting grant assistance from organisations such as the Heritage Lottery Fund has also helped, while the concessionary admission charge of £1.50 (see below) has also generated good publicity.

Pricing policy

In line with other attractions offering a similar service, the museum charges £3.50 for adults, £2.50 for children/OAP/UB40/students/disabled and £1.50 for B&NES residents. This compares with an adult entry charge to the Roman Baths of £7.60. Group rates for educational groups vary according to which of a range of activities are booked. For a general tour of the museum for groups over 10 in number the charge is £2.00 per visitor and group leaders or teachers are admitted without charge.

A number of concessions are offered with local council admission schemes and commercial publications' offers (e.g. one child admitted free with one paying adult). A scheme of issuing tickets allowing accompanying adults free admission have been distributed to visiting schools since 1993.

Communications

Leaflets are produced for general publicity purposes and also for educational use. The original and brightly coloured 'Mr Bowler's Business' leaflet of an A4 sheet folded three times has been replaced. Not only was the original leaflet unpopular with staff, but visitors were surprised to find that although soft drinks were available, other museum provisions had been ignored in the publicity. As other displays appeared, the concentration on Mr Bowler seemed inadequate.

The present leaflet is two-thirds of an A4 sheet which makes the leaflet more easily handled and more economical when posted in quantity. The general publicity leaflet is distributed to all guest houses and hotels in the B&NES area by post or by paid distributor. In addition, all shops willing to accommodate the leaflet, libraries, galleries, museums and tourist information centres are also contacted regularly. Given the restricted budget it has not proved economic to distribute the leaflets further afield. Very little press advertising has been undertaken since 1991, but regular press releases to the local press and radio have generated local publicity. A newsletter (Figure CS12.3) is produced, and the museum remains a member of the ABLE Consortium (see Chapter 8).

Facing the future

The trust has managed to survive the period since 1991 with reduced staff and reduced ticket income, largely through business sponsorship. The museum continues to face an uncertain future, and will undoubtedly continue to depend upon sponsorship to cover core costs. However, lower running costs due to the reliance on volunteer staff and general savings elsewhere have enabled the museum, if not to flourish, at least to survive and to continue to provide a wide range of services, limited only by the demands on staff time.

Market research is conducted regularly from the museum counter on home town, country, etc. by the volunteers. Each year, this information helps to determine the budget to be allocated to promotion.

That this small museum has survived in the face of all the economic difficulties suffered by the tourism industry in recent years, and given the slim resources on which it has been dependent, is remarkable in itself. In 2003, the museum reached its twenty-fifth year, and with a new permanent exhibition now open, and a complete reassessment of marketing policy set against realistic targets, the trustees have faith that, with some additional expenditure on marketing, they will be successful in restoring admission figures to 10 000 by 2005.

Figure CS12.3
Newsletter

Museum *of* Bath at Work Newsletter 25

1978 2003

Julian Road BATH BA1 2RH *Telephone & Facsimile* 01225 318348   *www.bath-at-work.org.uk*

| *Industrial Archaeology in The National Trust – see page 3* | Summer 2003 |

THE MUSEUM OF BATH AT WORK

Serving the Community

Enclosures:

Michael Cross Lecture ticket application form

A Poster for the New Exhibition
Please ask your local Post Office or shop to display it in the Window
Thank you

Inside this issue:

Duke of Gloucester Opens New Exhibition

His Royal Highness the Duke of Gloucester re-visited the Museum on 10 July this year, 25 years after he opened it in 1978, to view the new permanent exhibition 'Bath at Work– 2000 Years of Earning a Living'. Among those present at the ceremony were some of those who were part of the opening celebrations a quarter of a century ago, including Dr Marianna Clark and Russell Frears, founder trustees, and Lady Craufurd (nee Georgina Russell), the first curator. Volunteers who were in at the start included Peter Rouse and Roy Goddard who continue to help at the Museum.

The extensive Bowler Archive and a trawl through the thousands of items held in trust by the Museum was the basis of the new exhibition. Generous help was given by other museums, local companies and private individuals.

In the afternoon, donors to the various Newsletter appeals, volunteers and those who contributed through their generous loan or gifts of historical items were entertained to afternoon tea.

The Museum is open from 10am until 5pm every day until the end of October. From then until Easter 2004 the Museum will be open on Saturdays and Sundays only – same times.

How Did We Do It?

The idea for the new exhibition came into Stuart Burroughs' head nearly three years ago when we were in the early stages of planning the celebrations for our 25th anniversary.

Over that time the Museum had collected a wealth of material, from companies (many of whom have ceased trading) and all kept out of sight in the basement.

Why not use part of the mezzanine to bring these items into the daylight for everyone to see? A careful plan was devised and was submitted to the Heritage Lottery Fund's *Your Heritage* scheme just before Christmas 2002 and the news of our successful application broke at the beginning of the New Year.

Our thanks go to everyone who helped with their time , money, advice, items, and in so many other ways.

Bath Industrial Heritage Trust Limited
A company limited by guarantee (2269894) and registered as a charity (800297)

(Courtesy: Museum of Bath at Work)

Editor's conclusions

That this museum has survived for a full 25 years is little short of a miracle, and by all accounts it might have been expected to have failed many years ago. That it has not done so owes much to the dedication of its small staff and its ability to make its very limited promotional budget go a long way. In this, it exemplifies the myriad small, locally based museums scattered around Britain, many of which have opened within the last three decades on the basis of no more than an over-optimistic estimate of visitor numbers and a cash handout.

Additionally, the museum suffers from many natural disadvantages, and the classic quotation 'location, location, location' has never been more appropriate than in this instance. Its site, on the edge of the city centre, is well away from rail and bus termini, and parking in the area is next to impossible, even for visiting coaches. Established with the principal motive of conserving a wonderful collection of industrial memorabilia, and with a budget only to fund its establishment, the museum is now suffering because its founders failed to take into consideration the need for an adequate ongoing cash flow to meet any shortfalls in admission income. Realistic reappraisal inevitably had to be undertaken in due course, but this was not initially accompanied by adequate consultation with its small but dedicated staff, leading to further problems. The museum is now operating on a 'bare bones' basis, with minimal staff, largely voluntary labour and the support of sponsors for additional funding. Consequently, promotion is also limited, largely to brochure production and distribution, publicity through partnership in the local visiting attractions consortium and whatever PR activities can be manipulated. While on a better footing than in the past, the future for the attraction remains precarious.

Questions

1 Given the difficulty of attracting visitors on day visits from outside the region, could the museum attract more repeat visits from the immediate locality? What events or changes would it need to implement to do so?

2 The museum appears to offer good value for money, albeit with a rather complex price structure. It is reluctant to push prices higher, as this is seen to discourage visitors. How might average spend from existing visitors be boosted at this small site?

3 Find out how local museums in your area are funded, and whether they operate under similar financial constraints. Are there any promotional initiatives they have introduced which could be helpful for the curator of the Bath museum?

Case study 13
The past, present and future of a popular tourist destination: the Costa del Sol

(Prepared with the help of Sociedad de Planificación y Desarrollo, SOPDE, para el Patronato de Turismo de la Costa del Sol, and Gabriel Schmilovich Isgut, Madrid)

Introduction

Sociedad de Planificación y Desarrollo, SOPDE, para el Patronato de Turismo de la Costa del Sol is the body responsible for marketing and planning in the Costa del Sol region of Spain. This organisation, mindful of the changes occurring in tourist markets to the region and the need to consider the development of new markets and retention of existing ones, recently undertook a new marketing and development plan for the region. An earlier 'Observatorio Turistico' study covered the period 1991–4, estimating the demand for 1995 at around 4 million visitors annually, but this study now required substantial updating. In particular, it was recognised that there was a lack of current information about the main sources of income and the distribution of visitors to the province. While a leader in the sun and beach type of holiday, the region was facing increased competition. The tourism product within the region had undergone considerable change within the intervening years, with infrastructure improvements (formerly a weakness), and liberalisation of air transport policies within the European Community (leading to changes in the packages offered by tour operators and consequent growth from the affected areas). The market itself was also changing radically, with new patterns of motivation for visits, new market segments from existing generating countries, and demand from new generating countries which was expected to show substantial growth over the next few years. A new marketing plan was viewed as necessary to reduce the uncertainty about the direction and development of tourism in the region.

The geography of the region

The Costa del Sol ('Sun Coast') is one of Europe's most popular tourist playgrounds, situated along Spain's south-eastern coast and lying between the cities of Motril (Granada) and Estepona (Málaga). The area benefits from a number of well-known centres, including Torremolinos, Marbella, Benidorm and Fuengirola. The coast's capital city is Málaga, in Vélez–Málaga municipality, situated in the fertile valley of the Velez River, in the middle of the 'Axarquía'.

Good roads, including a new route opened recently, provide access from Casabermeja, with air and rail services into Málaga. This is a region with contrasting climates, offering snow-capped mountains 2000 m high close to relaxing beaches, and small mountain villages which still retain their Moorish flavour, side by side with tourist complexes offering all the advanced infrastructure one has come to expect of leading Mediterranean resorts. The Axarquía is a privileged region in terms of its climate and geography; all the northern and eastern zones are formed by high mountain ranges, topped by the summits of Chamizo (1637 m), the Rope (2065 m) and Navachica (1832 m). With mountain ranges extending almost to the coast, there are few plains apart from that surrounding the regions of Velez–Málaga. Weather in the region of Axarquía is typically Mediterranean, with warm summers, and little precipitation. The temperate climate, low rainfall and sea breezes have led to a semi-tropical vegetation in which palms and cypresses abound, and bougainvillea, oleander and hibiscus flourish. This semi-tropical landscape of mountains, valleys, orchards and sea has proved to be an immense draw for tourists from all over the world.

The historical origins of tourism to the regions

The city of Málaga was founded by the Phoenicians, who constructed a town near the hill where the fortress stands today. Under the Romans, Málaga enjoyed the privilege of confederation with Rome. The city later came under the influence of the Arabs and flourished, but underwent a period of decline after reconquest by the Catholic kings in 1478. Economic prosperity returned at the end of the eighteenth and beginning of the nineteenth centuries, with the growth of two prominent families in the region, the Larios and the Heredia, who turned the city into the second most important industrial centre in the country. However, the Spanish Civil War (1936–9) impoverished the city, with typhus taking a further toll between 1941 and 1943. The Franco regime imposed strong controls over economic development, while the region gradually developed along parallel lines, with tourism and agriculture the principal economies. By the 1950s the region was enjoying a measure of prosperity.

The economy returned to instability under Franco between 1960 and 1975, with bankruptcy and petrol crises hindering the economy, but with the death of Franco in 1975 the region opened up to a democratic transition. In Málaga, the economic recession of the 1960s gave way to a period of rapid population growth along the coastal region, fuelled by the explosion in tourism and the attraction of foreign capital.

Sun and beach tourism

The Costa del Sol includes some 300 km of Mediterranean coast between Málaga and Cadiz. Protected from northern winds by the mountain chains, the landscape lends itself to the development of sporting activities, including deep-sea angling and most notably, golf. The Coast of the Sun often is referred to as the Golf Coast, hardly surprising if we take into account the concentration of golf courses to be found along this stretch of coast. The popularity of golf has been enhanced by Valderrama and the many European golf enthusiasts that have congregated here over the years. Demand for golfing is now so great that new courses are being created along the coast, with bookings months ahead. Foreign tourists generate more demand for the sport than do domestic Spaniards, with a recent study estimating that some 80 per cent of all golf tourists had visited the area to play. One result has been that most clubs have English-speaking members.

Tourism demand for the Costa del Sol

The steady growth of tourism to the Costa del Sol since the mid-1970s is particularly noteworthy in terms of British visitors. These represent 33 per cent of all foreign visitors, and 16 per cent of the total demand for the region. French demand has risen strongly, representing 10 per cent of total demand, while demand from German tourists has fallen off sharply, with reduced demand also apparent in the Italian and North American markets – these being of relative insignificance, at 2.4 and 1.5 per cent respectively. To help offset this fall, Eastern European demand is rising sharply.

As most foreign tourists arriving in the region do so through Málaga Airport, an examination of the statistics for that airport will be useful (Table CS13.1). In 2002, over five million passengers transited the airport; of these, some two-thirds travelled on scheduled flights. From the data on these tourists, research will identify more information about consumers of the tourist product and their preferences, analysing their lifestyles and behaviour, and distinguishing between leisure and business travellers (the latter representing a smaller proportion of the total in the high season months).

The marketing plan and objectives

A new marketing plan for the region has been drawn up to ensure the retention of existing visitors and to explore the potential for drawing in new market segments. The new plan is open-ended, recognising the need to adapt continually in the face of economic and social changes. The new marketing plan is justified on the basis of present inadequate knowledge of revenue sources and touristic activities while in the province. The aim will be to increase the competitiveness of the destination, emphasising the appeal of the Costa del Sol brand even while extending the plan to embrace the whole province of Málaga.

Table CS13.1 Total passenger arrivals at Málaga Airport, 2002

Countries	Arrivals
United Kingdom	2 094 557
Spain	1 098 102
Germany	529 243
Netherlands	237 868
Ireland	196 151
France	175 044
Belgium	165 872
Italy	96 891
Denmark	91 686
Switzerland	83 108
Norway	67 528
Finland	61 019
Russian Federation	24 064
Austria	22 999
Morocco	17 880
Luxembourg	14 372
Israel	14 233
Portugal	13 343
United States	10 317

Within the marketing plan, the following 14 areas are defined by SOPDE (Provincial Patronage of Tourism and Society of Planning and Development) as of high priority:

1 *Greater municipal awareness of touristic activity as a contributor to the local economy* The principal priority for those in the tourism sector is to achieve greater recognition by public bodies for the importance of tourism's contribution to the economy. Through such recognition, the tourist will achieve greater satisfaction and the tourist products and services of the province improved.

2 *Improvement of local amenities* Tourists' perception of local amenities must be raised, in particular through a cleaner environment to improve visitor satisfaction.

3 *Modernisation of hotel superstructure* Improvements are necessary in the quality of accommodation facilities throughout the region. The continuous modernisation and renovation of hotels, especially within the three-star category, are essential.

4 *Raise standards of the industry through professional training* Greater professionalisation in the industry is essential. This should be achieved by special short courses, including emphasis on new technology, business operations, quality control and marketing.

5 *Improve transport links through connection by rail with the Mediterranean Arc* Rail connections with the Mediterranean Arc will improve existing accessibility and harness existing markets to the eastern zone of the province, encouraging future development of the principal resorts in the region.

6 *Improve infrastructure through better supply and quality of water in the region* South-ern Spain has suffered from severe restrictions in the supply of water in the last few years. The declining image of the region is linked to the problems in supply-ing sufficient water of good quality (i.e. potable). The administrative authorities must work together to provide better supplies, canalisation and purification of water for tourist use.

7 *Improvement in security for tourists* During peak periods, the huge influx of tourists leads to increased opportunities for crime. This is of great concern to incoming visitors, contributing to a negative view of the region. Central and local adminis-trations will need to work together to ensure resources are available for the invest-ment needed for heightened security.

8 *Improved research into tourist markets* Knowledge of tourist demand is fundamental to be able to adapt the product to the needs of the tourists, their tastes and prefer-ences, their motivation in selecting the province as a holiday destination, better knowledge of what tourists find satisfactory and unsatisfactory, etc.

   The body responsible for tourism research in the region (SOPDE) must embark on such research and make known the results of their research to those in the industry, to ensure the product is suitably adapted to meet those consumers' needs and expectations.

9 *Improvement of public sector amenities for tourism* Far-reaching improvements are necessary to the urban nuclei to improve tourist satisfaction. The various tourist municipalities need to work together to improve the decoration of streets and street furniture, and to encourage restoration and renovation of buildings in sensit-ive sites.

10 *Elimination of uncontrolled rubbish and garbage dumps* The organisations respons-ible at the outset for rubbish collection will be the authorised administrations (essentially the provincial one), and these must act not only to eliminate un-sightly garbage dumps but also establish sanctions to ensure new 'blackspots' are not created.

11 *Further research into levels of satisfaction and dissatisfaction among tourists* Aware-ness of demand and patterns of satisfaction will enable municipalities and others to effect the necessary improvements to increase the consumer experience.

12 *Attracting international events to the region* Increased coverage in the media and the heightened image of the Costa del Sol will lead to growth in international events based in the region. These will receive support from both public and pri-vate sectors in the form of collaboration or sponsorship. Support for events such as championships in tennis, golf, volleyball, athletics, etc. will widen knowledge of the region and enhance demand over the coming years.

13 *Promotion aimed at public and trade* Promotion should be aimed directly at the consumer with the objective of increasing visits by specific sectors, and at a small number of tourism intermediaries focusing on tourism to the region. The enter-prise bodies and the local tourism boards should increase their emphasis on niche marketing to key markets, with distinct promotional campaigns relevant to the sectors targeted, instead of more general campaigns. Public relations activities

such as familiarisation visits for the travel trade, presentations and workshops for targeted intermediaries should be the principal emphasis of the campaign.

14 *Improving the skills and expertise of those in the industry* It is important that the professionalism of the tourism sector is constantly reviewed and improved, to increase the overall levels of qualification and service. Skills such as public management, customer relations, foreign languages and new technology should be priority areas to improve competitiveness.

Conclusion

Nature has provided many beautiful places and areas of interest to tourists, but these can be easily damaged if insufficiently resourced. It is the local municipalities' responsibility to ensure that tourists do not destroy what they have come to see, or that complacency does not allow these valuable attributes to wither. Administrative authorities have the responsibility to create programmes of sustainable development and improvement, local inhabitants and visiting tourists must respect and care for the amenities and attractions by which they are surrounded, and the private sector must also play its part in ensuring the sustainability of the product.

The importance of improved infrastructure and transport accessibility must be recognised, but these must be developed with sensitivity. The Costa del Sol is blessed with a wide range of products attractive to the tourist, from landscapes to cultural and heritage attractions, good beaches and outstanding golf courses. Because of their popularity, these stand in danger of being swamped unless care is exercised in their development and expansion.

Editor's conclusions

This final case reveals intentions rather than results, based on public sector responsibilities for the organisation and development of one of Europe's premier tourist destinations. Given the long-term popularity of the region in which Málaga is situated, there has been a surprising lack of research and planning attached to its future development, but the 14-point plan outlined in this study gives an indication of local authority thinking and intention. While the conclusion takes into account the need for sustainability, there is little reference given to it in the areas of priority cited by SOPDE, and a timescale for the extensive improvements listed is not given. It will be interesting to see how, and to what extent, the proposals outlined will have been initiated over the next decade.

Questions

1 Suggest programmes of research which would meet the needs of SOPDE's objectives 8 and 11 above. Could the two objectives be combined within a single research programme, or are they best carried out discretely?

2 Sustainability does not apparently receive a specific mention in any of the priorities outlined in SOPDE's proposals (although possibly implied in objective 2). Reference is made to golf courses, which are notorious consumers of water in areas often afflicted by water shortage. What other sustainable issues or concerns might you envisage in reading the list of priorities here?

3 There are stated aims to raise the professionalisation of the industry in two of the objectives cited, numbers 4 and 14 (there is some overlap between the two objectives, but they recognise the need to improve both standards and skills). Calls are made for additional training to improve perceived weaknesses: yet the travel industry's salaries are notoriously low, and the industry finds it difficult in many instances to recruit people of the right calibre. Can good training overcome the problem, or are there other possible solutions?

Bibliography

The following list comprises most of the recently published texts dealing with marketing applied to the travel, tourism and hospitality fields, together with a number of important texts on general marketing which provide useful background reading and/or have been referred to in this text.

Adcock, D, Halborg, A and Ross, C, *Marketing Principles and Practice*, Prentice Hall, 4th edn 2001

Amor, D, *The e-Business (R)evolution: Living and Working in an Interconnected World*, Prentice Hall, 2000

Ashworth, G J and Goodall, B, *Marketing Tourism Places*, Routledge, 1990

Ashworth, G and Tunbridge, J, *The Tourist-Historic City*, Belhaven Press, 1990

Ashworth, G and Voogd, H, *Selling the City*, Belhaven Press, 1991

Bishop, J, *Travel Marketing*, Bailey Bros and Swinfen, 1981

Blythe, J, *Essentials of Marketing*, Prentice Hall, 2nd edn 2001

Brassington, F and Pettitt, S, *Principles of Marketing*, Prentice Hall, 2nd edn 2000, 3rd edn 2003

Briggs, S, *Successful Tourism Marketing: a Practical Handbook*, Kogan Page, 1997

British Tourist Authority, *Gaining Your Share of an £8 Billion Market* (including market guides to 27 countries), BTA, 1990

Brunt, C, *Market Research in Travel and Tourism*, Butterworth Heinemann, 1997

Buhalis, D and Laws, E, *Tourism Distribution Channels: Practices, Issues and Transformations*, Continuum, 2001

Buttle, F, *Hotel and Food Service Marketing*, Holt Rinehart, 1986

Churchill, G and Iacobucci, D, *Marketing Research: Methodological Foundations*, South Western, 8th edn 2002

Coltman, M, *Tourism Marketing*, Van Nostrand Reinhold, 1989

Crouch, G I, Mazaner, J A, Ritchie, Brent and Woodside, A G (eds), *Consumer Psychology of Tourism, Hospitality and Leisure*, CABI, 2001

Davidoff, D M, *Contact: Customer Service in the Hospitality and Tourism Industry*, Prentice Hall, 1994

Engel, J, Blackwell, R and Miniard, P, *Consumer Behaviour*, Dryden Press, 8th edn 1995

English Tourist Board, *The Arts and Tourism Marketing Handbook*, ETB, 1993

English Tourist Board, *The Future for England's Smaller Seaside Resorts*, ETB, 1991

English Tourist Board, *Report of the Working Party to Review Tourist Information Centre Services and Support Policies*, ETB, 1981

English Tourism Council, *Sea Changes: Creating World-class Resorts in England*, ETC, 2001

Enis, B and Cox, K, *Marketing Classics: a Selection of Influential Articles*, Allyn and Bacon, 8th edn 1991

Fewell, A and Wiles, N, *Marketing*, Butterworth Heinemann (Hospitality Managers Pocket Books), 1992

Foster, D, *Sales and Marketing for the Travel Professional*, McGraw-Hill, 1991

Frechtling, D, *Forecasting Tourist Demand: Methods and Strategies*, Butterworth Heinemann, 2001

French, Y, *The Handbook of Public Relations for Museums, Galleries, Historic Houses, the Visual Arts and Heritage Attractions*, Museum Development Co, 1991

Gartrell, R, *Destination Marketing for Convention and Visitors' Bureaus*, Kendall Hunt, 1989

Gayle, D and Goodrich, J (eds) *Tourism Marketing and Management in the Caribbean*, Routledge, 1993

Getz, D, *Festivals, Special Events and Tourism*, Van Nostrand Reinhold, 1990

Glaesser, D, *Crisis Management in the Tourist Industry,* Butterworth Heinemann, 2003

Gold, J and Ward, S (eds), *Place Promotion: the Use of Publicity and Marketing to Sell Towns and Regions*, Wiley, 1994

Goldblatt, J J, *Special Events, the Art and Science of Celebration*, Van Nostrand Reinhold, 1990

Goodall, B and Ashworth, G, *Marketing in the Tourism Industry: the Promotion of Destination Regions*, Croom Helm, 1988

Goodson, L and Phillimore, J (eds), *Qualitative Research in Tourism*, Routledge, 2004

Greene, M, *Marketing Hotels into the 90s: a Systematic Approach to Increasing Sales*, Heinemann, 2nd edn 1987

Gunn, C and Var, T, *Tourism Planning: Basics, Concepts, Cases*, Routledge, 4th edn 2002

Harris, G and Katz, K, *Promoting International Tourism to the Year 2000 and Beyond*, The Americas Group, 1996

Harris, R, *Sustainable Tourism*, Butterworth Heinemann, 2002

Hart, C W L and Troy, D A, *Strategic Hotel/Motel Marketing*, Educational Institute, American Hotel and Motel Association, 1995

Hawkins, D E, Shafer, E L and Rovelstad, J M (eds), *Tourism Marketing and Management Issues*, George Washington University, 1980

Heath, E and Wall, G, *Marketing Tourism Destinations: a Strategic Planning Approach*, John Wiley, 1992

Herbert, D, Prentice, R and Thomas, C (eds), *Heritage Sites: Strategies for Marketing and Development*, Avebury, 1989

Honey, M, *Ecotourism and Sustainable Development: Who Owns Paradise?* Island Press, 1999

Horner, S, *Consumer Behaviour in Tourism*, Butterworth Heinemann, 1999

Horner, S and Swarbrooke, J, *Marketing Tourism Hospitality and Leisure in Europe*, Thomson Business Press, 1996

Jefferson, A and Lickorish, L, *Marketing Tourism: a Practical Guide*, Longman, 1988

King, B and Hyde, G, *Tourism Marketing in Australia*, Melbourne, Hospitality Press, 1989

Kotler, N and Kotler, P, *Museum Strategy and Marketing*, Jossey-Bass, 1998

Kotler, P, *Marketing Management*, Prentice Hall International, 11th edn 2003

Kotler, P, Armstrong, G, Saunders, J and Wong, V, *Principles of Marketing*, Prentice Hall, 3rd European edn 2001

Kotler, P, Bowen, J and Makens, J, *Marketing for Hospitality and Tourism*, Prentice Hall, 2nd edn 1999

Krippendorf, J, *The Holidaymakers*, Butterworth Heinemann, 1999

Laws, E, *Tourism Destination Management: Issues, Analysis and Policies*, Routledge, 1995

Laws, E, *Tourism Marketing: Service and Quality Management Perspectives*, Stanley Thornes, 1991

Lickorish, L, Bodlender, J, Jefferson, A and Jenkins, C L, *Developing Tourism Destinations: Policies and Perspectives*, Longman, 1991

Lovelock, C, *Services Marketing*, Prentice Hall, 3rd edn 1996

Lovelock, C, Vandermerwe, S and Lewis, B, *Services Marketing: a European Perspective*, Prentice Hall, 3rd edn 1999

Lumsdon, L, *Marketing for Tourism: Case Study Assignments*, Macmillan, 1992

McDonald, M, *Marketing Plans: How to Prepare Them, How to Use Them*, Butterworth Heinemann, 5th edn 2002

Mawson, S, *The Fundamentals of Hospitality Marketing*, Continuum, 2000

Mayo, E J and Jarvis, L P, *The Psychology of Leisure Travel: Effective Marketing and Selling of Travel Services*, CBI, 1981

Middleton, V with Clarke, J, *Marketing in Travel and Tourism*, Butterworth Heinemann, 3nd edn 2001

Middleton, V with Hawkins, R, *Sustainable Tourism: a Marketing Perspective*, Butterworth Heinemann, 1998

Morgan, M, *Marketing for Leisure and Tourism*, Prentice Hall, 1996

Morgan, N and Pritchard, A, *Advertising in Tourism and Leisure*, Butterworth Heinemann, 2001

Morgan, N, Pritchard, A and Pride, R (eds), *Destination Branding: Creating the Unique Destination Proposition*, Butterworth Heinemann, 2001

Morison, A, *Hospitality and Travel Marketing*, Delmar, 2nd edn 1996

Moutinho, L, *Consumer Behaviour in Tourism, Management Bibliographies and Reviews*, vol 12 no 3, MCB University Press, 1986

Moutinho, L, Rita, P and Curry, B, *Expert Systems in Tourism Marketing*, Routledge, 1996

O'Sullivan, C, Hill, E and O'Sullivan, T, *Creative Arts Marketing*, Butterworth Heinemann, 1995

Parker, T, *Marketing Forces for the Small Business*, Eyelevel Books, 1999

Pearce, D G and Butler, R W (eds), *Tourism Research: Critiques and Challenges*, Routledge, 1993

Peck, H, Payne, A, Christopher M and Clark, M, *Relationship Marketing: Strategy and Implementation*, Butterworth Heinemann, 1999

Pender, L, *Marketing Management for Travel and Tourism*, Stanley Thornes, 1999

Powers, T, *Marketing Hospitality*, Wiley, 2nd edn 1997

Poynter, J M, *Tourism Design, Marketing and Management*, Regents/Prentice Hall, 1993

Reich, A, *Marketing Management for the Hospitality Industry*, Wiley, 1997

Renshaw, M Bottomley, *The Travel Agent*, Business Education Publishers, 1992

Richards, B, *How to Market Tourist Attractions, Festivals and Special Events*, Longman, 1992

Richards, G (ed), *Developing and Marketing Crafts Tourism*, ATLAS, 1999

Ritchie, J and Goeldner, C (eds), *Travel, Tourism and Hospitality Research: a Handbook for Managers*, John Wiley, 1987

Seaton, A V and Bennett, M, *The Marketing of Tourism Products: Concepts, Issues and Cases*, Chapman and Hall, 1996

Shaw, S, *Airline Marketing and Management*, Pitman, 3rd edn 1990

Solomon, M, Bamossy, G and Askegaard, S, *Consumer Behaviour: a European Perspective*, Prentice Hall, 2nd edn 2002

Strauss, J and Frost, R, *e-Marketing*, Prentice Hall, 2nd edn 2001

Sumner, J R, *Improve your Marketing Techniques: a Guide for Hotel Managers and Caterers*, Northwood, 1982

Syratt, G with Archer, J, *A Manual of Travel Agency Practice*, Butterworth Heinemann, 3rd edn 2003

Taneja, N K, *Airline Planning: Corporate, Financial and Marketing*, Lexington Books, 1982

Taylor, D, *Hospitality Sales and Promotion*, Butterworth Heinemann, 2001

Teare, R, Mazanek, J, Crawford-Welch, S, Calver, S and Costa, J, *Marketing in Hospitality and Tourism: a Consumer Focus*, Cassell, 1994

Theobald, W and Dunsmore, H, *Internet Resources for Leisure and Tourism*, Butterworth Heinemann, 1999

Veal, A J, *Research Methods for Leisure and Tourism*, Longman, 2nd edn 1997

Vellas, F and Bécherel, L (eds), *The International Marketing of Travel and Tourism: a Strategic Approach*, Macmillan, 1999

Vladimir, A, *The Complete Travel Marketing Handbook*, NTC Business Books, 1988

Wahab, S, Crampon, L and Rothfield, L, *Tourism Marketing*, Tourism International Press, 1976

Ward, S, *Selling Places: the Marketing and Promotion of Towns and Cities 1850–2000*, E & F N Spon, 1998

Wearne, N and Morrison, A, *Hospitality Marketing*, Butterworth Heinemann, 1996

Witt, S and Moutinho, L, *Tourism Marketing and Management Handbook*, Prentice Hall, 2nd edn 1994

Wöber, K, *Benchmarking in Tourism and Hospitality Industries: the Selection of Benchmarking Partners*, CABI, 2002

Wood, M (ed), *Tourism Marketing for the Small Business*, English Tourist Board, 1980

Zuboff, S and Maxmin, J, *The Support Economy: Why Corporations are Failing Individuals and the Next Episode of Capitalism,* Allen Lane Penguin Press, 2003

Leisure, Recreation and Tourism Abstracts on the Net, CABI Publishing. http://www.cabi.org/catalog/journals

Index